AMY VANDERBILT'S COMPLETE BOOK OF ETIQUETTE

DRAWINGS BY FRED MCCARROLL, MARY SUZUKI
AND ANDREW WARHOL

DOUBLEDAY & COMPANY, INC., GARDEN CITY, N.Y.

AMY VANDERBILT'S COMPLETE BOOK OF ETIQUETTE

A Guide to Gracious Living

To Dr. Edwin George Langrock, wise counselor and kind friend

As this is an etiquette book for all Americans, I
have for the sake of interest used a wide variety
of names. If any of these happen to belong to
real people, living or dead, it is sheer coincidence.

A. V.

DRAWINGS ON HOW TO MAKE A BED COURTESY AMERICAN NATIONAL RED CROSS
TABLE SETTING INFORMATION FROM MEMBERS BOOK COURTESY OF
ROYAL CREST STERLING
DRAWINGS ON HOW TO EAT A MAINE LOBSTER COURTESY OF
THE MAINE DEVELOPMENT COMMISSION

LIBRARY OF CONGRESS CATALOG CARD NUMBER 52–10369

INTRODUCTION

Who needs a book of etiquette? Everyone does. The simplest family, if it hopes to move just a little into a wider world, needs to know at least the elementary rules. Even the most sophisticated man or woman used to a great variety of social demands cannot hope to remember every single aspect of etiquette applying to even one possible social contingency. The human mind is so constructed that even if a person were to read through a book such as this from cover to cover he could retain only that information that had interest for him at the time of reading. Consciously, at least, the rest would be discarded as irrelevant to his way of life. But let some new way of living open up for him—a move from city to country, a trip to a new part of the world—and his etiquette book becomes his *reference* book, ready to piece out his own store of information.

You might imagine that the writer of an etiquette book would certainly know everything in it and therefore have no need for it as reference or guide. But even this is not the case. After ten years as an etiquette adviser, four years of writing this book—four years of interviewing dozens of authorities in their own fields for material to be incorporated here—I, too, can remember only those details that have or have had relevance to my own way of living. If you asked me, for example, some detail of a wedding in a faith other than my own, I might have to refer to my own book. The information is here—the result of my research—but in the writing of such sections I made no attempt to memorize all these details. However, in this book, I, like you, have such information in simple, complete form all in one place, and it can be readily found if needed.

The word "etiquette" for all the things I have tried to discuss is really inadequate, yet no other will do. It covers much more than "manners," the way in which we *do* things. It is considerably more than a treatise on a code of social behavior, although all the traditional information still of value has, I feel, been included in a way that is simple and concise, shorn of mumbo-jumbo and clearly learnable. For we must all learn the socially acceptable ways of living with others in no matter what society we move. Even in primitive societies there are such rules, some of them as complex and inexplicable as many of our own. Their original *raison d'être* or purpose is lost, but their acceptance is still unquestioned.

Change in etiquette usually comes slowly, just as changes come slowly in the dictionary. The analogy applies, too, in that it is not necessarily social leaders who bring about such changes, but rather the people themselves who, through slighting certain forms for a long enough period, finally bring about their abolishment or at least their modification.

Inventions, wars, political upheavals, legislation, all, of course, have repercussions, sometimes immediate, in the field of etiquette. In certain Moslem countries *purdah*, the centuries-old veiling of women in public, was abolished by law overnight. Think of the social adjustment that was required! What had been rigorous social custom now became *illegal*.

Etiquette, too, is obviously geographically influenced. In cities thousands of families live under one roof, yet most never speak to one another on meeting. In the country not to speak to one's neighbor on encountering him would be very rude. In some parts of the South girls are quite accustomed to young men asking for late dates, a date—usually with an old beau—following one that may end at about eleven. Elsewhere such behavior might be considered questionable.

In young countries—and ours is certainly one when you think in terms of Paris's two thousand years—etiquette books have an important place. The physical and economic changes the country undergoes inevitably bring about fairly rapid social changes. The people who first come to virgin country usually arrive as workers, for every hand is needed, living facilities are at a premium, and there is little if any of the leisure or money necessary for the immediate development of an aristocracy. That is why all old American families such as mine have strong and simple roots here. Some of them may have brought with them the drawing-room manners of older civilizations, but they found that many of the niceties of living required adaptation—or else had to be discarded—in this vigorous, busy young land.

My great-great-grandfather, who "read law," was one of the founders of the Bank of Manhattan Company and a man of parts, as they used to say in those days. But in the tradition of his father and grandfather, Hollanders both, he was manually proficient and he had a proper respect for whatever work he did. He seems to have owned a number of "shoe manufactories," and I do not doubt that he could apply a sole with the same expertness that he used in some of the fine mahogany furniture he made for his family and which I still use. On the facing page is his advertisement in the *Diary; or Evening Register* of Wednesday, April 9, 1794.

My own line of descent from the first Vanderbilt to settle in America—Jan Aoertsen van der Bilt, who had a farm near Flatbush, Long Island—has been strongly Dutch, but I have a good admixture of Irish, English, and French blood. That and my partly European education, my fairly extensive traveling here and abroad, my years as a writer, as an etiquette adviser, and in business have given me a flexible attitude toward etiquette which is reflected, I am sure, in everything I have written on the subject.

I have a respect for people who do things with their brains and with their hands, who are not afraid of hard physical and mental work. I respect, too,

OLIVER VANDERBILT,

At his Boot and Shoe Manufactory No. 7, the corner of Smith and Princess-Streets,

TAKES this method, to return his thanks to his customers, for their generous encouragement in the line of his business, and hopes by his steady attention and abilities to serve, to merit the same. He has lately discovered a method, which effectually prevents the prevailing evils so common in the present mode of making boots which are these, the folding or running down behind and breaking above the counter and in the tongue, which frequently causes almost new boots not only to look bad, by causing pieces to be put in them, but by running down wears very uncomfortably   He continues to make, and has for sale, the following articles, wholesale and retail. viz.

	£.	s.	d.
Finished boots of English stuff - -	3	0	0
Do. tanned, brain and oil dressed buck skin legs - - - - - -	3	0	0
Do. American calf skin, or cordiwan legs	2	16	0
Second quality do. do. do.	2	10	0
Stout strong boots · - -	2	4	0
Bootees of English legs - -	2	5	0
Do. of American do - -	1	18	0

people who are unpretentious yet mannerly, considerate and honest, forthright yet kind and tactful. I dislike display and foolish expenditure in the sense of what Veblen called "conspicuous waste," that is, spending to impress those who have less, as well as to impress associates. I dislike *chi-chi*.

I believe that knowledge of the rules of living in our society makes us more comfortable even though our particular circumstances may permit us to elide them somewhat. Some of the rudest and most objectionable people I have ever known have been technically the most "correct." Some of the warmest, most lovable, have had little more than an innate feeling of what is right toward others. But, at the same time, they have had the intelligence to inform themselves, as necessary, on the rules of social intercourse as related to their own experiences. Only a great fool or a great genius is likely to flout all social grace with impunity, and neither one, doing so, makes the most comfortable companion.

It is my hope that this book answers as fully and simply as possible all the major questions of etiquette and most of the minor ones too. It is the largest and most complete book of etiquette ever written. Like a dictionary, it will have few cover-to-cover readers aside from my meticulous editor, Marion Patton, the copy editors, and the proofreaders. But this undoubted fact does not in the least disturb me, for a reference book such as this has a long and much-thumbed existence. It can become a reliable friend to whom one may turn many a questioning glance over the years and get a helpful answer. It can put down roots and become an integral part of the family, even be an objective counselor to the children as they enter their teens.

It is axiomatic that as we mature and grow in years and experience we must be able to meet more demanding social situations with confidence and ease. This book contains, I believe, explicit information on every possible social problem one is likely to encounter in modern social living.

Amy Vanderbilt

WESTPORT, CONNECTICUT
1952

ACKNOWLEDGMENTS

Over a period of four years, during the writing of this book, many personal friends have assisted me in my research. Parts of the manuscript traveled back and forth across the ocean several times. Experts of various kinds advised me and in numerous cases edited my material. I have sought every possible authoritative source in an effort to make this a truly complete and accurate book of etiquette, useful in every phase of contemporary life.

Among those individuals, organizations, institutions, and governments whose assistance I have had to a greater or lesser extent are: Eleanor Roosevelt; the United States Department of State; the United States Military Academy, West Point; the United States Naval Academy, Annapolis; Captain J. F. Donovan, Jr., U.S.N. Ret.; Headquarters First Army; Captain Joseph W. Golinkin, U.S.N.R.; Colonel Henry T. Blair, U.S.A.R.; the British Information Services; the French Embassy; the Netherlands Embassy; the Hon. E. C. Zimmerman, former Netherlands Minister to the Netherlands Indies; Mr. Onno Leebaert of the Netherlands National Tourist Office; the Mexican Embassy; Dr. Carlos Dávila, former President of and Ambassador from Chile, member of the Social and Economic Council of the United Nations, and author of *We of the Americas;* Mr. Harold P. Borer, General Manager in the United States for Cunard Steamship Company, Limited; the Pan American World Airways; M. Maurice Dekobra, Paris; Mr. Ulrich Calvosa, Spanish State Tourist Bureau; the Metropolitan Opera Association; the University of the State of New York; Professor Gilbert H. Doane, Director of Libraries, University of Wisconsin, and author of the book on genealogy, *Searching for Your Ancestors;* Mr. Donald C. Vaughan, who while an executive of Brooks Brothers furnished me with much of the material on men's clothes and later, after his retirement, edited the chapter for me; various members of the Overseas Press Club, including Mr. Frank Handy, Mr. Thomas B. Morgan, Mr. Edward P. Morgan, Mr. J. P. McEvoy, and Mr. Eugene Lyons; Senhor Vasco Pinto Basto of Lisbon, Portugal; Mr. I. P. Van Dyke of the Hotel Astor; Mr. Edward F. McSweeney; Sidonie M. Gruenberg, Special Consultant for the Child Study Association of America; Mr. T. Spencer Knight, President, Empire Crafts Corporation, Newark, New York; Mr. Homer N. Calver, President, Paper Cup & Container Corp., New York; the late Mr. Alexander Efron, founder of Checkmaster System, Inc., New

York; Mr. Roger Main, President and Treasurer, West Side Savings Bank, New York; Mr. Charles Northrup, Treasurer, Westport Bank & Trust Co., Westport, Conn.; B. Harris and Sons, New York, jewelers; Cartier, Inc., New York; Tiffany & Co., New York; Abercrombie & Fitch Co., New York; Steuben Glass, New York; Dempsey & Carroll, Inc., New York; Max Schling, Inc., New York; John M. Weyer, President, Van Loan & Co., New York; Bellows' Gourmet's Bazaar, New York; Countess Gösta Morner; the Maine Development Commission; and the following attorneys for their help with material touching on or concerning legal matters: Norman Schur, Gustave Simons, Philip Wittenberg, and Edna Neumann Whittle.

I am indebted to Dr. Richard L. Frank, Clinical Professor of Psychiatry and Psychoanalytic Medicine at State University College of Medicine at New York, for his help, advice, and editorial suggestions especially concerning the chapters on children and family life; also to Dr. Herbert F. Newman, Associate Professor of Clinical Surgery, New York University School of Medicine; Vincent M. Keber, D.D.S., New York, and the American Nurses Association.

Mr. Lawton Mackall, expert on wines, assisted me to a great extent in the preparation of the chapter on wines.

The Reverend W. Ovid Kinsolving, Priest-in-Charge, St. Andrew's and St. Michael's Episcopal churches, Bridgeport, Conn., was of immeasurable aid in the preparation of the material on weddings, christenings, funerals, religious beliefs and the proper address of the clergy. The Reverend Edward N. West, D.D., Canon Sacrist of the Cathedral of St. John the Divine, New York, prepared the material on the correct forms of address of the Protestant Episcopal clergy, and the Reverend George Papadeas of the Hellenic Cathedral, Holy Trinity, New York, assisted me with information on the Greek Catholics. Princess Serge Troubetzkoy and Mrs. David H. Low were of help in giving me information on Eastern Orthodox religious customs. Rabbi Samuel Schwartz of Congregation Beth El, Norwalk, Conn., Rabbi Martin Ryback, Temple Israel of Fairfield County, Conn., and Rabbi Philip Alstat of the Jewish Theological Seminary, New York, assisted me in the matter of Jewish customs and clerical forms of address. The Presiding Bishop, Le Grand Richards, of the Church of Jesus Christ of Latter Day Saints, Salt Lake City, Utah, supplied information on the Mormons. P. J. Kenedy Sons, publishers of the official Catholic Directory, supplied all the material on the proper forms of address for the Catholic clergy, and I had the assistance of Catholic friends and two Catholic priests on Catholic marriage, christening, and funeral customs. I am indebted to the Society of Friends for information on Quaker ceremonies and customs. The Christian Science Committee on Publication for Connecticut checked the references to Christian Science. Mr. F. D. Connell, Sexton of St. Thomas Church, New York, gave me information on Protestant Episcopal church ceremonies. The Reverend Harold Edgar Martin of the First Congregational Church, Norwalk, Conn., the Reverend E. C. Wenzel, of St. Peter's Evangelical Lutheran Church, South Norwalk, the Reverend W. Wesley Williams of Norwalk Methodist Church, Norwalk, the Reverend J.

P. Ball of Grace Baptist Church, Norwalk, and the Reverend Dr. Floyd Leach, retired Episcopal minister of Rowayton, Conn., were among those clergymen who assisted me with information on their own and other denominations.

Miss Alice Maslin (Nancy Craig) of the American Broadcasting Company and Mr. Ben Grauer of the National Broadcasting Company furnished much of the material I have used on radio and television. Elizabeth Verner of Charleston, S.C., Miss Dorothy Valentine Smith of Staten Island, Mr. A. Rush Watkins of Chicago, Mrs. George Washington Kavanaugh of New York, Mr. Paul T. Truitt of Washington, D.C., Mrs. Maurice Metcalf of New Orleans, La., Mr. Robert Taylor of the Pittsburgh *Press*, Miss Peter Carter of the Washington *Times-Herald*, Mr. and Mrs. Max Blitzer, Mr. and Mrs. Basil Lermont, Louisa Béchaut Blumenau, and Helen Pemberton Jones of New York; Miss Dorothy Garrard of Los Angeles; Mr. and Mrs. R. L. Moonan, Mr. D. Leonard Cohen, Mrs. John Kobler, and Mr. Howard Whitman of Westport, Conn., are among the friends who have given me information on local or foreign customs, Washington diplomatic, social, and legislative procedures, and other matters pertaining to the content of the book. I wish to acknowledge, too, the co-operation of the editors of *This Week* and *Better Homes and Gardens* on material relating to the book.

My husband, Hans Knopf, and my friend, Virginia Fortiner, were of inestimable help in reading the manuscript and making suggestions for its improvement.

Special thanks go to my secretary, Miss Marie Ritti, for expert typing of more than a quarter of a million words and to Miss Helen Walsh for her help, too, especially in the handling of my considerable correspondence.

INTRODUCTION

ACKNOWLEDGMENTS

1 THE CEREMONIES OF LIFE

INTRODUCTION 26

CHAPTER ONE WEDDING INVITATIONS AND ANNOUNCEMENTS 27
Making Up the Invitation List · When to Send Invitations and Announce-
ments · Choosing the Time of the Wedding · Stationery and Engraving
How to Address Envelopes · Wording of Formal Invitations and Announce-
ments · Variations of the Usual Wording · Invitation to the House
Wedding · Invitations Combining Invitation to Church Ceremony and
Reception · Pew Cards and Train Cards · Church Cards · The Reception
Card · The Separate Reception Invitation · Wedding Announcements
Variation of the Usual Wording · At Home Cards · Invitation to Informal
Weddings · Invitations to Those in Mourning

Military and Naval Forms for Wedding Invitations and Announcements:
Regular Officer of the U. S. Army, Reserve Officer on Active Duty, Retired
Regular Army and Navy Officer, Retired or Inactive Reserve Officer

Recalling Wedding Invitations · Postponing Weddings · Replying to
Wedding Invitations · Recalling a Formal Acceptance

CHAPTER TWO ARRANGING THE WEDDING 48
The Visit to the Minister · Church Decorations · Wedding Music · The
Bride's Formal Wedding Pictures · When the Groom Has Been Married
Before · Selection of Maid, Matron of Honor, and Bridesmaids · Selection
of Ushers and Best Man · The Groom's Father as Best Man · Duties of
the Best Man · Duties of Ushers · Transportation to and from Church

Gifts for the Bride's Attendants, Ushers, and Best Man · The Couple's Gifts to Each Other · The Bachelor Dinner

Dress for the Wedding: The Bride's Clothes (Superstitions), The Groom's Clothes, Dress for the Ushers, Bridesmaids, Maid and Matron of Honor, Flower Girls and Page Boys, and Guests

Flowers for the Wedding Party · Expenses of the Bride's Parents Groom's Expenses

CHAPTER THREE   THE WEDDING CEREMONY   63

The Rehearsal · The Processional and Recessional · When There Are Two Main Aisles · Procedure during the Ceremony · The Double Ring Ceremony · When the Bride's Mother Gives Her Away · The Double Wedding · Children at Second Marriages · The Thirtyish Bride

Differences in Religious Ceremonies: The Catholic Ceremony, Jewish Ceremonies, The Christian Science Ceremony, Eastern Orthodox Weddings, The Quaker Ceremony, The Mormon Ceremony

CHAPTER FOUR   THE RECEPTION   78

The Receiving Line · Who Receives in Place of the Bride's Mother · Conversation and the Receiving Line · Music and Dancing at the Reception The Bride's Table · The Table for the Parents · When There Is No Bride's Table · The Wedding Breakfast · The Wedding Cake · Problems of the Divided House · Conduct of the Wedding Guests

CHAPTER FIVE   THE HOME WEDDING   88

CHAPTER SIX   THE RECTORY WEDDING   89

CHAPTER SEVEN   THE CLERGYMAN'S WEDDING   90

CHAPTER EIGHT   ELOPEMENTS, CIVIL CEREMONIES   91

CHAPTER NINE   THE TROUSSEAU, BRIDAL SHOWERS   93

Basic Lists of Linens, China, Glassware for the Bride · Silver for the Bride Monogramming ·· Who Gives Bridal Shower · Duties of Shower Guest

CHAPTER TEN   WEDDING GIFTS   102

Must One Send a Gift? · Suitable Gifts · Gifts to the Groom · Gifts

Sent after the Wedding · Display of Wedding Gifts · The Bride's Thank-You Letter

CHAPTER ELEVEN THE HONEYMOON, POST-WEDDING CALLS 105

CHAPTER TWELVE WEDDING ANNIVERSARIES 107
Gift Suggestions and Invitations to Wedding Anniversaries

CHAPTER THIRTEEN CHRISTENINGS 109
When the Baby Is Christened · Invitations to the Christening · Dressing the Baby for the Occasion · What Others Wear · Godparents and Their Responsibilities · Church Christenings · The Clergyman's Fee · The Christening at Home · Refreshments after the Ceremony

CHAPTER FOURTEEN DEBUTS 113
The Kinds of Debuts

The Debutante Tea: The Dress of the Debutante and Her Mother, The Receiving Line, The Guests at a Debutante Tea

CHAPTER FIFTEEN COURTSHIP AND ENGAGEMENTS 115
Meeting a Man's Family and Friends · Gifts before the Engagement · Refusing a Gift · The Proposal · The Conference with Father · How Long Should an Engagement Last? · Is an Engagement Irrevocable? · The Engagement and Wedding Rings · The Man's Wedding Ring

Announcing the Engagement: Your Relations with the Press, How Much Information the Announcement Should Have, Release Date, Sending Pictures, Complicated Relationsips, Calling Editors

If the Engagement Is Broken · Behavior during Engagements

CHAPTER SIXTEEN FUNERALS 127
Immediate Procedures when Death Occurs · Arranging the Funeral Clothing for Burial · Hanging the Bell · Where the Funeral Takes Place Death Notices · Attending a Funeral · Sending Flowers · Mass Cards Funeral Calls · The Funeral Service · Pallbearers · Ushers · Seating Arrangements · Interment and Grave Marking · Fees to the Clergyman, Sexton, and Organist, Acknowledgments of Flowers, Mass Cards, and Charity Contributions · Letters of Condolence and Replies · Mourning · Dress during Mourning · The Traditional Idea of Mourning · Restriction of Activities

2 DRESS AND MANNERS

INTRODUCTION 140

CHAPTER SEVENTEEN MEN'S CLOTHES 140
The Business Suit · The Morning Coat and Accessories · The Dinner Jacket and Accessories · The Tail Coat and Accessories · The Frock Coat The House Suit · Overcoats · Formal and Informal Riding Clothes Ties, Handkerchiefs, and Jewelry · Monogramming Clothes · Bad Weather Wear · What Every Man Should Know about Vests, Socks, and Shoes The Hatless and Gloveless Man · When *Not* to Wear Evening Clothes Wearing Decorations

CHAPTER EIGHTEEN WHAT'S WHAT IN VARIOUS SPORTS 161
Dress and Rules of Behavior for: Golf, Tennis, Badminton, Yachting, Swimming, Hunting, Shooting, Fishing, Skiing, and Skating

CHAPTER NINETEEN THE WELL-GROOMED MAN 171
Hints and Forthright Information for the Man Who Wants to Look His Best at All Times · The Bachelor's Social Problems

CHAPTER TWENTY MAN'S MANNERS IN BUSINESS WORLD 176
When Does a Man Rise? · Who Precedes Whom? · Smoking in the Office Lunching and Dining with One's Secretary

Traveling with a Secretary: Making Reservations, How Should They Register? Does a Secretary Need a Chaperone?

The Executive on the Telephone · When Relatives Visit the Office · Is It Necessary to Meet Socially with One's Employees? · Letters of Resignation

CHAPTER TWENTY-ONE THE MASCULINE GRACES 183
Sending Flowers · Lateness · Lighting Women's Cigarettes · Shaking Hands · Hand Kissing · Conduct in Public · Conveyances · Summoning and Sharing Taxis · A Man's Bow · Manners on the Street · Kissing in Public · Making Apologies · Opening Conversations · A Few Brief Reminders

CHAPTER TWENTY-TWO THE WELL-DRESSED WOMAN 190
Planning the Basic Wardrobe: Colors, Coats, Hats, Suits, Underthings, Dresses, Evening Clothes

Clothes for Active Sports: Tennis, Skiing, Golfing, Skating, Swimming, Yachting, Riding, Shooting

CHAPTER TWENTY-THREE FASTIDIOUS, WELL-MANNERED WOMAN 200

The Art of Being Well Groomed: A Practical Beauty Routine · Changing for Dinner, Make-Up · Cosmetic Defects and Plastic Surgery · How to Sit Comfortably and Gracefully · When a Woman May Remove Her Hat

A Woman's Manners in the Business World: Her Attitude toward Her Job, Her Appearance, The Importance of Promptness, Taking Orders, Smoking and Eating in the Office, Telephone Calls, Personal Letter Writing and Callers

The Woman Executive: Her Attitude toward Other Women, When the Woman Pays the Bill, The Single Woman

CHAPTER TWENTY-FOUR THE SOCIAL PLEASANTRIES 212

A Guide to Tactful Conversation: Replies to Greetings, When to Use a First Name, If You Cannot Remember Names, What Are Personal Questions? Dangerous Topics of Conversation, How to Parry Direct Questions, That Word "Lady," How about "Miss"? Introductions, Duty Dances

CHAPTER TWENTY-FIVE THE SMOKING PROBLEM 219

CHAPTER TWENTY-SIX CLUBS 222

Men's Clubs: Joining a Club, Tipping in Clubs, Proposing and Seconding Suggestions for New Members, Letters of Proposal and Seconding, The Letter of Objection, Putting up a Guest, Resigning from a Club, The Guest of a Private Club

Women's Clubs: How to Obtain Membership, The Elective Clubs, Club Teas

Country Clubs, Yacht Clubs, and Beach Clubs: Club Guests

CHAPTER TWENTY-SEVEN MANNERS AT TABLE 228

Who Is Served First? · When to Begin Eating · Use of the Knife and Fork · Drinking Beverages at the Table · The Napkin · Tipping of Dishes · The Handled Bouillon Cup · Testing Liquids · "Stirring" Food Conserves and Jellies · When Food Is Too Hot · "Spoiled" Food Coughing at the Table · "Foreign Matter" in Food · When You Need Silverware · Tasting Another's Food · Using Bread as a "Pusher" Reaching at the Table · Conversation · Posture · Taking Portions from a Serving Dish · Additional Butter · How to Hold Glasses · Saying Grace

How to Eat Various Foods: Artichokes, Asparagus, Bacon, Cake, Celery and Olives, Chicken, Corn on the Cob, Fish, Fruit—Apples, Pears, Apricots, Cherries, Kumquats, Plums, Halved Avocados, Bananas, Berries, Grapes, Oranges, Mangoes, Peaches, Persimmons, Pineapple, Stewed or Preserved Fruit, Tangerines, Watermelon, Pickles, Potatoes, Salad, Salt, Sandwiches, Seafood, Spaghetti, Tortillas

CHAPTER TWENTY-EIGHT OUR COMMUNITY RELATIONS 243

Interfaith Courtesy and Understanding: Learning about and Respecting Other Religions, Should a Christian Send a Christmas Card to a Jewish Friend? Dietary Laws of Jews, Roman and Greek Catholics, Episcopalians, and Moslems, Religious Holidays, Ceremonies of Many Faiths, Particular Courtesies, Clerical Dress

CHAPTER TWENTY-NINE NEW CITIZEN, HIS PARTICULAR PROBLEMS 250

Our Attitude toward Newcomers to the United States and What They Think of Us

Differences in Manners: Tucking in the Dinner Napkin, The American and Continental Use of the Knife and Fork, The Use of the Toothpick, Acknowledging a Compliment, Introductions and Salutations, Using the Phone, The Use of "Lady" and "Gentleman," Changing Your Name

The New Citizen and the English Language: Is it Necessary to Eliminate All Trace of a Foreign Accent? Foreign Words in English, Writing Letters

3 HOME ENTERTAINING

INTRODUCTION 260

CHAPTER THIRTY INFORMAL ENTERTAINING 261

The Company or Semiformal Dinner Party: Greeting the Arriving Guests, Entering the Dining Room, Suggested Menu for Dinner, Arranging the Table, Dinner Service with One Maid, After-Dinner Coffee or Demitasse

The Informal Lunch: Dress, Suggested Menu, The Service

The Informal Tea: Dress, Arrangement of the Tea Tray

Cocktail Parties: Equipment Necessary, Arranging the Room, How to Handle the Guests Who Linger

Informal Dancing at Home: Preparations for Simple Home Dancing, Refreshments, Duties of Host and Guest

CHAPTER THIRTY-ONE   FORMAL ENTERTAINING   271
The Formal Dinner: The Staff and Equipment Necessary for Giving a Formal Dinner, Arrival and Introduction of Guests, Entering the Dining Room, Seating, Place Cards, Menus and Menu Cards, Service, Turning the Table, Leaving the Dining Room, Departing after the Formal Dinner

The Formal Luncheon: Dress, Greeting Guests, Place Cards and Menus, Arranging the Table, Suggested Menu

The Formal Tea: The Table and Lighting, Service, Food, Bidding Farewell

Formal Dances at Home: Decorations, Introductions at a Formal Dance, Specific Duties of the Male Guest, Supper

CHAPTER THIRTY-TWO   THE GUEST AT FORMAL MEALS   283
Watching the Service, Second Portions, Do Guests Assist with Service? Greeting Servants at Table, The Token Portion, Placement of Used Silver, What to Do about Crumbs and Spilled Food, Presentation of the Finger Bowl, The Signal to Rise

CHAPTER THIRTY-THREE   THE RITUAL OF DRINKING   286
What Kinds of Drinks for Guests? · The Various Cocktails and Highballs— Their Suitability and Preparation · White and Red Wines · Sweet and Dry Wines · Filtered Domestic Wines · Storage of Wines · Glassware Decanting · Pouring of Wines · Toasts

CHAPTER THIRTY-FOUR   ENTERTAINING INDOORS   293
Conversation Is Fun · Ice Breakers · Music in the Evening · Television
Playing Bridge: Setting up Tables, Behavior during the Game
Playing Cards for Money: Paying Off Gambling Debts

CHAPTER THIRTY-FIVE   ENTERTAINING OUT-OF-DOORS   298
Picnics on Your Own Grounds: Necessary Outdoor Cooking Equipment, Arranging the Table, Food Suggestions

Picnics away from Home: Equipment for the "Traveling" Picnic, The Art of Packing the Picnic Hamper

Al Fresco Meals: Selecting the Right Spot, Service and Food Suggestions

CHAPTER THIRTY-SIX   HOSTS AND GUESTS   300
Arrivals and Departures · The Self-Invited Guest   Inviting a Guest to

Another's Party · The Guests Who Won't Go · Problem Drinkers · The Obnoxious Guest

Making Your Overnight Guest Feel at Home: The Extra Touches that Count, The Well-Appointed Guest Room—Beds, Shades, Draperies, and Curtains

Guest Houses: Solving the Heating Problems, What to Do If You Live in the Real Country, Instructions in Case of Emergency

The Week-End Guest: Invitation and Reply, Arrival and Departure, Gift to the Hostess, What Clothes to Take, Rules of Behavior, Greeting Servants, How to Infuriate Your Hostess, How to Help with the Household Routine, Duties of the Overnight Guest in the City

 HOUSEHOLD MANAGEMENT

INTRODUCTION 326

CHAPTER THIRTY-SEVEN FURNISHINGS IN THE ESTABLISHED HOUSEHOLD 326
How to Form Your Own Tastes in Selecting Furniture · Effective Grouping of Furniture · Choosing Furniture to Fit the Individual · Selecting the Right Colors

Linens: Monogramming, Marking Linens for the Laundry, Linens for the Nursery, Formal and Informal Table Linens

China: Blending the Various Kinds of China, China for Formal and Informal Use

Glassware: Special Handling of Fine Glassware, Replacing Broken Glassware, The Right Glass for the Right Occasion

CHAPTER THIRTY-EIGHT SETTING THE TABLE 336
Breakfast at the Table · Breakfast on Trays · Decorations for the Breakfast Table and Breakfast Tray

The Place Setting for the Informal Lunch: Suggested Dishes for the Informal Lunch and Table Decorations

The Informal or Semiformal Dinner: Silver, Table Linen, Glassware, China, Table Decorations

The Formal Luncheon: Silver, Table Linen, Glassware, China, Table Decorations

The Formal Dinner: Silver, Table Linen, Glassware, China, Table Decorations

Arranging the Buffet Table

CHAPTER THIRTY-NINE   SPECIAL PROBLEMS OF SERVICE   351
The Placing of Teaspoons · The Iced-Tea Spoon · Serving Water at Meals
The Service of Tea, Coffee, Demitasse, and Candy · The Service of Food
on Trays · Setting the Table for Card Table Service · The Fine Damask
Cloth · Garnishes · When Are Place Cards Needed?

CHAPTER FORTY   EMPLOYER-SERVANT RELATIONS   358
The Hiring of Servants · The Domestic Employment Agency · Wages
Your Requirements · Interviewing a Prospective Maid · What Recommends You as an Employer? · How Good Are References? · The Part-
Time Worker · Introducing the New Servant to the Household · Introducing Servants and Guests · How to Furnish a Maid's Room · The
General Houseworker · If You Are Your Own Managing Housekeeper
How to Write Notes to Servants and Tradespeople · The Question of Time
Off and Special Privileges · Workman's Compensation · Dismissing a
Servant · The Letter of Reference · Giving References over the Phone

CHAPTER FORTY-ONE   DRESS AND DUTIES OF THE HOUSEHOLD
STAFF   370
The Formal and Informal Attire of the Butler and His Duties · The Valet
The Chauffeur · Duties and Dress of the Housekeeper, the Companion, the
Social Secretary, the Cook and Kitchen Maid, the Lady's Maid, the Chambermaid

CHAPTER FORTY-TWO   GRACIOUS LIVING WITHOUT SERVANTS   377
A Routine for Managing the Servantless Household

Maidless Entertaining: The Buffet Dinner, How to Serve a Sit-Down Dinner
without a Maid, After-Dinner Coffee, After-Dinner Tea, How to Make Tea,
Suggested Menus for Maidless Dinners, Extra Guests at the Dessert Course

CHAPTER FORTY-THREE   HOUSEHOLD FINANCES   387
Financing the Family: Children's Bank Accounts, Letting the Children in
on Finances, Joint Checking Accounts, Who Should Manage the Family
Income, Deficit Financing, Establishing Credit, Poor Credit Risks, Living
within Your Means

Checking Accounts: How to Open a Checking Account, How to Avoid
Errors, Blank Checks, Printing and Dating Checks, Who Accepts Checks,
Stopping Payments on Checks, Drawing against Uncleared Checks, If You
Lose Your Checkbook, Post-Dated Checks

5 CORRESPONDENCE

INTRODUCTION 400

CHAPTER FORTY-FOUR STATIONERY AND LETTERS 401
A Woman's Social Stationery · A Man's Social Stationery · "Personal" Business Stationery · Business Firms' Stationery · Signatures on Checks, Legal Papers, and Letters · Illegible Signatures · Sequence of Pages in a Letter · Addressing Social Envelopes · The Use of "Personal" and "Please Forward" · The Use of "Messrs." · Letters That Must Be Handwritten

Social Letter Writing: The Correct Form for Social Letters, How to Get Started, Bread-and-Butter Letters, Thank-You Notes, "Angry" Letters, A Letter of Complaint to a Neighbor, Letters of Apology, Love Letters, Letters of Social Reference, Writing to a Celebrity, Writing to the White House, Writing to a Public Official, Christmas Cards

Women's Business Letters: Writing the Business Letter, Ordering from a Department Store, Letters of Complaint to a Business Organization, Making Hotel Reservations

CHAPTER FORTY-FIVE INVITATIONS, ACCEPTANCES, AND REGRETS 425

CHAPTER FORTY-SIX CORRECT FORMS OF ADDRESS 437
How to Address in Writing and Speaking—Members of the United States Government, Foreign Representatives, Members of the Clergy, British Officials and Individuals · The British Use of Esquire · Military Forms of Address

CHAPTER FORTY-SEVEN HERALDIC DEVICES 464
What Is a Coat of Arms? · The Lozenge · How Heraldic Devices Are Used

CHAPTER FORTY-EIGHT WRITING AND CONVERSATION CAN BE COLORFUL 467
A Bowing Acquaintance with Other Languages · Familiar Words and Phrases from French, Latin, German, and Other Languages · Common Expressions from English Literature · Words and Phrases Often Incorrectly Used and Pronounced · Musical Terms · Culinary Terms · Regional Accents · The Well-Modulated Voice

6 THE FAMILY AND SOCIAL EDUCATION OF THE CHILDREN

INTRODUCTION 488

CHAPTER FORTY-NINE MANNERS IN MARRIAGE 489
Understanding the Woman in the House · The Agreeable Husband
How a Husband Can Lend a Hand · Business Entertaining · The Agreeable Wife · Meeting Commuter Trains · Special Adjustments · What to Do about Annoying Habits · Overweight and Underweight · Speaking of Diets · The In-Law Problem · Your Mother-in-Law · When Your Spouse's Parents Live with You · What to Do about Real Trouble-Makers When a Parent Requires Financial Support

CHAPTER FIFTY CHILDREN, THE FORMATION OF CHARACTER 499
Choosing the Baby's Name · Does Your Child Need a Middle Name?
Boys' Names for Girls, and Vice Versa

Children's Clothes: Dressing the Baby, Clothes for the Pre-School and the Older Child, Hand-me-downs and Made-overs, When Does a Child Choose His Own Clothes?

About Allowances: How Much Allowance Should a Child Have? · Withholding Allowances

Children's Table Manners: Playing with Food, Must a Child Finish His Food? Should a Child Choose His Own Food? Small Children at Table, Should Children Be Seen and Not Heard? Older Children at Table, Awkwardness in Children

The Social Behavior of Children: Twenty-two Guides for Good Conduct, Calling Parents by Their First Names, "Making" Children Mind Their Manners, Must a Little Girl Curtsy? The Boy's Bow, Extending Invitations, Children's Introductions, Birthday Parties for Children, The Child's Manners at His Party

Special Problems: Taking a Child to the Doctor's Office · The Child in the Hospital, Children in the Dark, Handling the Shy Child

The Baby Sitter: You and Your Sitter, How Old Should a Sitter Be? Should the Sitter Be Allowed to Entertain? Sharing Sitters, Neighbors Sit for Each Other, Mother Needs a Night Out Too

CHAPTER FIFTY-ONE THE RELIGIOUS EDUCATION OF CHILDREN 523

CHAPTER FIFTY-TWO THE ADULT-CHILD RELATIONSHIP 524

Your Manners with Children · Your Tone of Voice · Conversation with Children · Teaching Children to Behave · Why We Must Have Rules Are Threats Effective? · Interference from Friends or Relatives · Is It a Child's World? · The Treatment of Servants by Children

CHAPTER FIFTY-THREE ADOPTING A CHILD 530

CHAPTER FIFTY-FOUR TRAVELING WITH CHILDREN 532

The Advantages of an Early Start · Travel Sickness · The Supplies You'll Need · Travel Clothes · Thoughtfulness of Others · Descending on Friends

CHAPTER FIFTY-FIVE THE TEEN-AGER 535

Is Strictness the Answer? · Teen Drinking · Smoking · Make-Up and Permanents · About Chaperones · Can the Group Chaperone Itself? Teen Dates · How Does a Boy Ask for a Date? · Dates and Money Refusing a Date · Subscription Dances, School Dances, and Proms

CHAPTER FIFTY-SIX DIVORCE AND SEPARATION 541

Procedures and Agencies That Are of Help in Marital Difficulties · Your Relations with Other People and the Press during a Trial Separation Change of Name and Address after a Woman Is Divorced · Our Attitude toward Divorce and the Divorcee

7 YOUR PUBLIC LIFE

INTRODUCTION 548

CHAPTER FIFTY-SEVEN DINING IN RESTAURANTS 549

Entering a Restaurant · Seating and Ordering · Omitting Courses · Ordering Wine · Presentation of Dishes · If There Are Complaints · Buffet Service in Restaurants · Presentation of the Check · Tipping at Private Dinners · Tipping at Public Dinners · The Guest at a Public Dinner Dress at Public Dinners · Leaving Restaurants

CHAPTER FIFTY-EIGHT CARDS AND CALLS 557

When Cards Are Left · The Size and Style of Cards · Children's Cards
Addresses on Cards · Engraving · A Man's Social Card · The Use of
Professional Titles on Cards · Husband and Wife Cards · A Woman's
Social Card · Women's Titles on Cards · Is a Girl Ever a Jr.? · When
You May Send Your Card · Using Your Card for Invitations · How to Mail
Cards · When No R.S.V.P. Is Required · The P.P.C. Card · How Many
Cards Are Left at One Call · To Insure Your Card's Delivery · When
Not to Use Your Card · Men's Business Cards · Women's Business Cards
Social Cards vs. Business Cards · If You Have No Cards

Making and Receiving Calls: The Call Itself, Conversation during Calls,
Bringing Flowers, Calling on the Eligible Man, The Bachelor Host and
Calls, Calls of Condolence, Calling on a Public Official

CHAPTER FIFTY-NINE HOSPITALS AND DOCTORS 577

Visiting the New Mother · Flowers · If You Are the Patient · How to
Share a Hospital Room · You and Your Nurse

Visiting Your Doctor: Professional Ethics, Medical Examinations, Personal
Relationships

CHAPTER SIXTY SPEAKING BEFORE AN AUDIENCE 581

Introducing Your Speech · Using the Voice Correctly · If You Have to
Cough · Reading a Speech · The Use of Jokes, Illustrations, and Anec-
dotes · Closing a Speech · Making Your Departure · Dress of the Man
Speaker · What to Wear If You're a Woman · Your Radio Appearance
If You Appear on Television

CHAPTER SIXTY-ONE SIMPLE PARLIAMENTARY PROCEDURE 588

CHAPTER SIXTY-TWO APPEARANCE AT PUBLIC FUNCTIONS 590

Dressing for the Opera · Seating in Opera Boxes · Applauding at the
Opera and at Concerts · Behavior at the Theater

Attending Auctions: Inspecting before You Buy, Asking for Specific Items,
How to Bid, Must the Auctioneer Accept Your Bid? Dealers as Your Competitors, Imperfect Merchandise, Checking for Authenticity, Buying Antiques, Paying by Check, The Country Auction

CHAPTER SIXTY-THREE YOUR PRESS RELATIONS 598

The Gossip Columnist and the Society Writer · What about Pictures?
You and the Law · Endorsements · Special Press Problems

CHAPTER SIXTY-FOUR   YOU AND CELEBRITIES   602
Asking for Autographs · Entertaining a Celebrity · Pity the Poor Author

8 OFFICIAL ETIQUETTE FOR CIVILIANS

INTRODUCTION   606

CHAPTER SIXTY-FIVE   ATTENDING ANNAPOLIS HOPS   607
What to Do and What Not to Do · Necessary Clothes · The Hop Itself
Entertainment of Midshipmen · The Souvenir Hunter · Annapolis Slang

CHAPTER SIXTY-SIX   VISITING WEST POINT   612
Expenses for the Week End · Necessary Clothes · Entertainment at the
Point · West Point Slanguage

CHAPTER SIXTY-SEVEN   ETIQUETTE FOR BRIDE OF MILITARY
MAN   616
General Protocol on the Military Post or Navy Yard · Post Calls · How
to Tell Military Rank

CHAPTER SIXTY-EIGHT   SHIP LAUNCHINGS, VISITING A NAVAL
VESSEL   619
General Procedure and Correct Dress for a Ship Launching · Boarding a
Naval Vessel and Making a Call · Saluting the Quarter Deck · Prohibi-
tions Concerning Naval Vessels · Officers' Staterooms · Maritime Terms
Formal Naval Invitations and Replies

CHAPTER SIXTY-NINE   THE NEWEST RESIDENT IN WASHINGTON   625
Accepting or Declining a White House Invitation · Being Received at the
White House · Business Calls on the President

CHAPTER SEVENTY   THE FLAG, OUR NATIONAL ANTHEM   628
When and How to Display the Flag · The Singing of Our National Anthem
The Star-Spangled Banner · Anthems of Other Nations · Playing the
Anthem at Home

9 TRAVEL ETIQUETTE AT HOME AND ABROAD

INTRODUCTION 636

CHAPTER SEVENTY-ONE TRAVELING BY SHIP 637

Dress and Behavior aboard Ship · Seating in the Dining Room · Dress aboard Transatlantic Ships · Behavior at Table · Tipping aboard Ship Dressing for Cruises

Plane Travel: Luggage, Behavior aboard the Plane, Duties of the Plane Personnel, Tipping

Train Travel: Baggage, Seating, When Occupying a Section, Dressing and Undressing, Use of the Ladder, The Roomette and the Compartment, The Diner, Tipping, Train Manners

Hotel Tipping · Talking to Strangers while Traveling

CHAPTER SEVENTY-TWO TIPS TO THE STAY-AT-HOME 646

Suitable Bon Voyage Gifts · Going aboard Ship to Say Good-by · Train and Plane Farewells

CHAPTER SEVENTY-THREE HOW CUSTOMS DIFFER ABROAD 647

The American Custom of Taking Baths · The W.C. · The "Pourboire" The "Boots" · Tips on Traveling within a Country and from Country to Country in Europe · Eating Customs · Smoking at Table · Is the Woman Always Placed to the Right of the Man? · Are We Boorish Abroad? · American Women in Latin Countries · American Men in Latin Countries · Dancing · The Paid Dancing Partner · Taking Pictures

CHAPTER SEVENTY-FOUR AN AUDIENCE WITH THE POPE 656

Requesting an Audience · What Clothes to Wear · Taking Religious Objects to Be Blessed · Procedure during the Audience · Taking Leave

CHAPTER SEVENTY-FIVE TRAVELING BY CAR 659

Taking Taxis: Behavior in Taxis, Conversation with the Driver, Losing Articles in Taxis, Tipping

Good Manners and Your Car: Hand Signals, Thoughtless Acts, The Good Driver, The Welcome Passenger, Double Parking, Is the Slow Driver the Best Driver? You and the Law, Hitch-Hikers

Selecting an Automobile: Colors in Cars, Can You Live up to Your Car? The Station Wagon, Marking the Station Wagon

1 THE CEREMONIES OF LIFE

Wedding Invitations and Announcements   27

Arranging the Wedding   48

The Wedding Ceremony   63

The Wedding Reception   78

The Home Wedding   88

The Rectory Wedding   89

The Clergyman's Wedding   90

Elopements and Civil Ceremonies   91

The Trousseau and Bridal Showers   93

Wedding Gifts   102

The Honeymoon and Post-Wedding Calls   105

Wedding Anniversaries   107

Christenings   109

Debuts   113

Courtship and Engagements   115

Funerals   127

THE CEREMONIES OF LIFE

Every life, even that in a primitive society, has its ceremonies great and small, religious and non-religious. We observe small ceremonies when we say "good morning" and "good night," when we celebrate a birthday or attend a graduation. But the important ceremonies of life have to do with its beginning—the ritual of circumcision of the Jews and the Mohammedans, the Christian baptism or dedication of the child, the youthful years of courtship and marriage, and life's finale. People are born, are married, and, at length after a more or less ceremonious life, die. And everywhere friends, neighbors, and relatives take cognizance of at least the major ceremonies affecting each of us.

Of all life's ceremonies that of marriage is the most touching and beautiful. This is the long anticipated climax of girlhood—and boyhood, too—the doorway to true maturity, the farewell to parents as protectors, the acceptance of responsibility. Madame de Staël wrote, "Without marriage there is no happiness in love." Love seeks completion and the protection of marriage and the family.

All people everywhere rightly make a ceremony of marriage. They proclaim it publicly with a variety of rituals devised to impress its enormous importance on the hearts and minds of the participants and witnesses. All marriages should be solemn and well-proclaimed, with the vows exchanged in a dignified, suitable setting.

Whether the bride wears a lovely bridal gown or a simple cotton frock makes, of course, no difference in the dignity and impressiveness of the ceremony. I believe it is good and valuable if parents and friends gather together to witness the marriage in the traditional way and that it take place —preferably under some religious auspices—in the bride's place of worship or in her home. The elaborateness or simplicity of the wedding is of no real consequence. It is the spirit in which we marry that is truly meaningful.

Ceremony is really a protection, too, in times of emotional involvement, particularly at death. If we have a social formula to guide us and do not have to extemporize, we feel better able to handle life.

I know a writer who says he likes Sunday noon dinner because it helps to set the day apart. He makes a ceremony of it. All ceremony, large and small, sets apart certain times of the year, week, and day for special marked atten-

tion. If we ignore ceremony entirely, we are not normal, warm human beings. Conversely, if we never relax it, if we "stand on ceremony" in all things, we are rigid. We must learn which ceremonies may be breached occasionally at our convenience and which ones may never be if we are to live pleasantly with our fellow man.

CHAPTER ONE

WEDDING INVITATIONS AND ANNOUNCEMENTS

It is the bride's family that sets the size and style of the wedding. If a large wedding is decided upon, the necessary invitation lists must be started almost as soon as the engagement is announced or this vital clerical chore will still be hanging fire during the complicated arrangements for such a wedding. The groom and his family must co-operate by furnishing their invitation and announcement lists as early as possible, so the bride may combine them with her own usually larger lists, remove duplications, and, if necessary, shorten the lists with the help of both families.

For a large formal wedding many more people receive invitations than can possibly accept. Even friends at a great distance are informed by means of the invitation that the wedding is taking place. The list should include all relatives of the bride and groom, all close friends of both families, neighbors, old family retainers, business associates of the two fathers and of the groom and, of course, of the bride, if she's a career girl and will continue her work.

The full list is then broken down into (1) those who receive invitations to the wedding, (2) those who will receive a reception card in addition, (3) those who will receive announcements and "At Home" cards, if any.

Ordinary three-inch by five-inch file cards with two sets of alphabetical indexes and two convenient boxes provide the best method of compiling a working list. Cards of different colors may be used on the finished list to indicate quickly into which category each name falls, but the usual method is to write in colored pencil an initial on the top right- or left-hand corner of each card—"C" for ceremony, "R" for reception, as well as ceremony, "A" for announcement.

In filing the cards follow the alphabetical procedure, don't just put all the A's or B's together or duplications will be hard to locate. Using such an easily expansible—or contractible—file is better than just typing up lists on sheets of paper or entering names in a notebook under alphabetical head-ings where they may end up a thicket of crossed-out names that will make addressing confusing.

The second file box should hold "Acceptances" and "Regrets" so that when the reception preparations are made a fairly accurate count may be had, with some allowance made for last-minute changes. Both acceptances and regrets should be filed alphabetically, too.

WHEN SHOULD INVITATIONS AND ANNOUNCEMENTS BE SENT?

Wedding invitations, unlike ordinary social invitations, are sent approximately four weeks in advance of the wedding. Engraved invitations take time and should be ordered at least six weeks before they are to be sent out, with consideration given the time it will take to address outer and inner envelopes. Announcements, ordered at the same time, are not, of course, sent out until after the marriage has taken place, but, if possible, they should be ready for mailing all at once a day or so after the ceremony, so that news of the marriage in the papers does not too much predate friends' receipt of the announcements.

CHOOSING THE TIME OF THE WEDDING

The time of day considered fashionable for weddings differs in different parts of the country. In New York many fashionable Protestant weddings take place at four, four-thirty, or five in the afternoon. Evening weddings are relatively rare in New York but fashionable in many other parts of the country. Their own Sabbath, Christian or Jewish, is usually not chosen for a wedding day by brides of these faiths (Religious Jews may not be married on the Sabbath—Friday sundown through Saturday sundown—or on certain high holy days) nor is Lent by Christians, at least not for religious ceremonies. It is not considered good taste for Christians to have even large home weddings during Lent, though, of course, simple marriages with or without a clergyman do take place during these forty days of penitence.

Formal and fashionable Catholic weddings in church take place with Mass at noon. Simple ceremonies at which the bride may wear her wedding gown and the groom may wear a cutaway or a blue suit (see "The Groom's Clothes") are often performed very early with Low Mass or at ten, followed by a wedding breakfast. No Catholic wedding takes place after seven at night, except in the case of great emergency—grave illness, perhaps, or possibly the sudden arrival of military orders for the groom-to-be.

Protestant morning weddings are usually simple and informal with the bride wearing a dress or suit, not a wedding gown. Wedding breakfasts—really lunch—may follow. In some parts of the country Protestant weddings sometimes do take place at noon, that is, fully formal weddings with a bride in full bridal array and the groom and his attendants in cutaways.

ENGRAVING AND STATIONERY FOR WEDDING INVITATIONS AND ANNOUNCEMENTS

It is far better to write personal letters or inform your friends of your marriage by phone than to have your invitations and announcements printed, rather than properly engraved. Of the various types of lettering available, the least expensive, and the most used, is graceful script. It costs no more to go to a really good, fashionable stationer for your announcements or invitations. There you will see styles of engraving such as the shaded, or shaded antique, Roman currently in vogue. There are slight variations from time to time, but essentially the engraving procedure is rigidly conventional. Do it right, or don't do it at all.

PAPER AND ENVELOPES   Use the best paper you can afford for announcements or invitations. People do look at the quality of paper, and many inspect the envelopes to see the name of the stationer from whom you ordered. The name of a good stationer embossed under the flap of the envelope lends a certain cachet and costs nothing extra.

The most distinguished wedding paper is the traditional ivory or ecru, but pure white is much used, too. Plate-marked papers appear quite frequently, and sometimes you see a fine white paper with a warm, almost imperceptible flesh tint. But the icy blue and pale pink papers sometimes offered—and by good stationers, too—do get away too radically, I feel, from the traditional bridal white or ivory. However, I never could understand, either, why a bride would want to wear a bridal gown in one of these pastel colors, as is sometimes done.

Needless to say, the engraving is always in black and on the first page of the double sheet. If the bride's family has a coat of arms, a small crest, shield, and motto may be embossed—not die-stamped—in color as on ordinary stationery at the top of the first page. However, this is not done if a woman, *alone,* makes the announcement or issues the invitation. If the bride's family has no coat of arms, she may not use the crest of her husband-to-be until they are actually married, but, even then, if her family issues announcements, the husband's device may not be used on them, although the bride's family's may be (see "Heraldry"). If the couple themselves make the announcement, the husband's full coat of arms may be embossed.

Two envelopes are usually used for wedding invitations and announcements, although only one may be. Where two envelopes are used, the inside one is unsealed (and must not be gummed), and is placed in the outer envelope so that it faces the flap. The tissue over the engraving of the invitation is left in place to prevent smudging.

As with calling cards, the length of the names, the style of lettering, and, in this case, whether or not plate-marked paper will be used has much to do with the size of the paper you choose. There are many acceptable variations, but a fairly standard size is seven and one-half inches by five and one-half inches for a folded invitation or announcement. Smaller announcements or invitations which may be inserted into the envelopes unfolded are also correctly used, but if reception or "At Home" cards are to be enclosed, it is possible they may never be seen if the unfolded style is used.

HOW TO ADDRESS THE ENVELOPES   The addressing of wedding invitations and announcements is rigidly prescribed. Abbreviations are not permitted except in "Dr.," "Mr.," "Mrs.," and "Jr." (or "Lt." when combined with "Colonel," etc.), or in an initial of a name if you don't know it in full. The names of cities and states are written out. When an invitation or announcement is being mailed in the same city as that in which the wedding is taking or has taken place, the name of the state does not appear. For instance:

Mr. and Mrs. Cedric Moore McIntosh
1886 Shore Road
Chicago

Where there are several members of a family to be invited, avoid the phrase "and family." On the inside envelope is written:

Mr. and Mrs. McIntosh
(NO CHRISTIAN NAME)
Belinda and Gordon
(IF THE CHILDREN ARE UNDER AGE)

But if there is an adult daughter or other woman in the household you wish to invite, she must receive a separate invitation:

Miss Margaret McIntosh
1886 Shore Road
Chicago

The inside envelope reads:

Miss McIntosh

If there are two sisters write:
The Misses Agnes and Ann McIntosh (or Misses Agnes and Ann McIntosh) and on the inside envelope The Misses McIntosh (or Misses McIntosh) with no address, of course, on the inner one.

Two grown sons (over twenty-one) receive one invitation if they live at the same address. They are addressed as:
The Messrs. Keith and Ian McIntosh (or Messrs. Keith and Ian McIntosh) with simply The Messrs. McIntosh (or Messrs. McIntosh) inside.

RETURN ADDRESSES   It is certainly convenient to have a return address on a wedding announcement or invitation, but this should not be engraved or printed on the flap, though it may be embossed or, if essential in some cases, neatly written on the flap.

STAMPS   The dignity of a wedding invitation or announcement, it almost goes without saying, requires first-class postage. Stamps should be placed carefully, not stuck on any way at all. The necessarily careful addressing and stamping of the envelopes requires that the work be started before the bride or her family is worn out by bridal preparations.

PENMANSHIP It is also traditional for the handwriting (in black ink) on the envelopes of wedding invitations and announcements to be obviously feminine and, if possible, of the rounded, clear, English style affected by social secretaries. The address, of course, may never be typed. If no social secretary is used for a large wedding, friends or relatives may be called on to help, but if more than one person does the addressing, the handwritings should be as similar as possible.

WORDING OF FORMAL INVITATIONS AND ANNOUNCEMENTS

INVITATION TO CHURCH CEREMONY

Dr. and Mrs. Grant Kingsley
request the honour of your presence
at the marriage of their daughter
Penelope
to
Mr. George Frank Carpenter
on Friday, the ninth of June
one thousand nine hundred and fifty
at twelve o'clock
Saint Mary's Church
San Francisco

Mention of the year is optional on an invitation but obligatory on the announcement of the marriage. The word "honour" is always spelled in the old way. The phrase "honour of your presence" is always used for invitations to the church. No R. S. V. P. (optional abbreviation R.s.v.p.) is used where the invitation is for the church ceremony alone. The Reception Cards, if any, carry the R. S. V. P., even for a wedding tea if desired, although invitations to tea do not normally require a reply.

In a large city where there are many churches and the one where the marriage is taking place is not in the category of a landmark, the church address is engraved under the name of the church in this way:

Emmanuel Church
1122 South Moore Street
Denver

If the street number in the invitation or announcement is short, it should be written out—"Five" or "Sixteen."

The time of the ceremony, traditionally on the hour or on the half hour, is usually written out. If it is to be on the half hour the wording reads "at half after four" or sometimes "at half past four." If the ceremony must be on the quarter hour, the wording is "at quarter before four" or "at quarter past four."

The word "junior" is written without a capital, but it now is abbreviated more often than not, just as "Doctor" is. But then it is "Jr." with a capital "J." With certain engraving—London script—it is usually abbreviated as "Jun." and numerals are used for the date and time of the ceremony.

Sometimes the "On" is omitted so that an invitation may read "Friday, the ninth of June," but modern simplification of the form reduces its dignity.

THE GIRL WITH THE SAME NAME AS HER MOTHER If a girl has the same name as her mother and has for convenience's sake been known as Helen Preston, second, she does not use this appellation in her wedding invitations or announcements, since her mother's name, as it must be used in the form, could not possibly be confused with her daughter's.

THE DIVORCED MOTHER'S INVITATION Even if her mother is divorced such an announcement would read:

Mrs. Fenwick Kingsley
(THE MOTHER'S MAIDEN NAME PLUS THAT OF HER DIVORCED HUSBAND)
requests the honour of your presence
at the marriage of her daughter
Penelope
etc.

THE REMARRIED MOTHER'S INVITATION If the bride's mother, widowed or divorced, has remarried, the invitation may read:

Mr. and Mrs. Roderick Merrill
request the honour of your presence
at the marriage of her daughter
Penelope Kingsley

(Sometimes this reads "at the marriage of Mrs. Merrill's daughter.")

It is considered less awkward by some if a remarried woman issues the invitation to her daughter's wedding in her name alone, as:

Mrs. Roderick Merrill
requests the honour of your presence
at the marriage of her daughter
etc.

WHEN THE FATHER OR OTHERS ISSUE THE INVITATION If the daughter after her parents' divorce has made her permanent home with her father, her grandmother, her aunt, brother, or other relative or guardian, the person whose home it is makes the announcement jointly with his or her spouse. For example:

Commander and Mrs. Charles Simonson
request the honour of your presence
at the marriage of her grand-daughter
etc.

or:

The Reverend and Mrs. Myron Cyrus Kingsley
request the honour of your presence
at the marriage of their sister
Penelope Kingsley

In this form the bride's last name is used to show she is Mr., not Mrs., Kingsley's sister.

If the bride's brother is unmarried and he issues the invitation, it reads:

The Reverend Myron Cyrus Kingsley
requests the honour of your presence
at the marriage of his sister
etc.

If the bride's father is a widower he issues the invitation. Also if he is a divorcé and his daughter has lived with him, he issues the invitation, although he may choose to do the more graceful thing and permit the bride's mother to do so for the sake of convention, even if she and her daughter rarely see each other. An invitation from a father alone reads:

Dr. Grant Kingsley   (OR DOCTOR)
requests the honour of your presence
at the marriage of his daughter
etc.

If the bride's sister is issuing the invitations they read:

Miss Cordelia Kingsley
requests the honour of your presence
at the marriage of her sister
Penelope Kingsley

Only if the wedding is being given by a close relative is the relationship shown in the invitation. If cousins, friends, or a guardian issue the invitation, the connection is not shown.

DOUBLE WEDDING OF SISTERS   In a double wedding if the brides are sisters, the elder sister is mentioned first and the invitation reads:

34

Dr. and Mrs. Grant Kingsley
request the honour of your presence
at the marriage of their daughters
Penelope
to
Mr. George Frank Carpenter
and
Felicia
to
Mr. Amos Reynolds
etc.

DOUBLE WEDDING OF COUSINS OR FRIENDS If the brides are cousins or just
friends, the invitation could read:

Dr. and Mrs. Grant Kingsley
and
Mr. and Mrs. Claude Roen
request the honour of your presence
at the marriage of their daughters
Penelope Kingsley
to
Mr. George Frank Carpenter
and
Marie Rose Roen
to
Mr. Gregory Pardee

Here the older bride is mentioned first, with her parents, but when the
brides are more or less the same age the order is alphabetical. However,
when there is a great difference in age between the two groups of parents
or if, for example, one bride's invitations are issued by her grandparents, it
is the older sponsors who take the precedence. Titled parents, too, take precedence over non-titled ones in an invitation to a double wedding. While
such an announcement as this is possible, it is more probable that each
bride would prefer to have her own invitation, even for a double wedding.
Separate invitations also make reception acceptances simple to handle. It is
possible to indicate a double wedding by engraving the two separate invitations, vis-à-vis on the inside of the double sheet.

WEDDING GIVEN BY THE GROOM'S FAMILY

Mr. and Mrs. Perry Coates
request the honour of your presence
at the marriage of
Miss Laura Lee Mercer°
to their son
Mr. Trimble Coates
etc.

°The "Miss" is used when the givers of the wedding are not relatives.

The circumstances would have to be very special indeed for the wedding to be given by the groom's family—and those circumstances very well understood by intimate friends of both the bride and the groom. To give remote examples, if the families were old friends or distantly related or if the bride's home were far from the city in which the wedding is to take place and her own parents could not be with her, then she might properly accept her future mother-in-law's invitation that the wedding be given at the groom's home. But she should never flout convention and suggest such a thing. And unless she is very sure of her welcome in the family she would be better off with a quiet church or registry ceremony and no attempt at a formal reception. Instead, she might ask the witnesses, if any, to the home of a close friend, if she has one nearby, who might act as hostess for anything from sherry and biscuits to breakfast, tea, or champagne, depending on the hour of the ceremony. Or, if she has an apartment of her own, she can have any unpretentious breakfast, tea, or reception she can manage herself, acting as her own hostess—just as she may, if she wishes, under modern convention, issue her own engraved invitations.

THE BRIDE ON HER OWN   Occasionally a young bride has no close relatives or friends to issue her invitation for her or make her wedding announcement. In this case, as with the older bride who wishes to make her own announcement or issue her own wedding invitation, the form reads:

> The honour of your presence
> is requested at the marriage of
> (OR "WEDDING RECEPTION OF")
> Miss Cordelia Kingsley
> (NOTE "MISS")
> to
> (OR "AND")
> Mr. Winthrop Cass Bowers
> etc.

THE DIVORCÉE   The older woman who has been divorced does not send engraved wedding invitations, although she may invite a few close friends and relatives to a small ceremony. She or her family may or may not send announcements.

THE VERY YOUNG WIDOW   A very young widow may have engraved wedding invitations issued by her family or by herself. If her family issues them, they read:

> Mr. and Mrs. Sydney Myers
> request the honour of your presence
> at the marriage of their daughter
> Sylvia Ann Kiser
> to
> etc.

Here her late husband's last name is used with her given names, although some prefer to use the clearer form "Sylvia *Myers* Kiser." Note that she is *not* "Mrs. *Sylvia*," always an ugly appellation and which looks worst of all on a wedding invitation.

If a young widow is issuing her own wedding invitation, it reads:

> The honour of your presence
> is requested at the marriage of
> Mrs. Maximillian Georg Kiser
> to
> etc.

THE OLDER WIDOW   We sometimes see an invitation from an older widow in which she is referred to as "Mrs. Catherine" so and so, the idea being that there may be some lack of propriety in the use of her dead husband's name in her wedding invitation to his successor. Throughout her widowhood there has been no impropriety in continuing the use of her late husband's name. No matter how long she remains a widow, she is, properly, Mrs. John Jones, not Mrs. Catherine Jones. So why, then, when she does remarry should she subject herself to the indignity of being "Mrs. Catherine Jones" and on an engraved invitation, at that! No—let such an invitation from an older widow to her own wedding read:

> The pleasure of your company
> is requested at the marriage of
> Mrs. Grant Kingsley
> to
> etc.

Of course, if the ceremony is to be in church the first line reads, "The honour of your presence . . ."

INVITATION TO THE HOUSE WEDDING

An invitation to a house wedding carries the R.s.v.p. (or R.S.V.P.), as some sort of collation will be served afterward and therefore the number of guests needs to be known. Otherwise the house wedding invitation reads the same as the one to the church except that the second line is changed to "the pleasure of your company." The house address is used in place of the name of the church this way:

> at
> 1339 Belmont Terrace
> Montclair, New Jersey

Or, if the wedding will take place in a home in a large city the address reads:

at

1125 Park Avenue

New York   (WITHOUT THE STATE)

If the wedding, with its reception, takes place in a club or hotel, it is indicated in this way that the R.s.v.p. is sent to the bride's home:

at

The Ritz Carlton

New York

R.s.v.p.

1125 Park Avenue

WEDDING AT FRIEND'S HOME

When the wedding itself is held, for some reason, in the home of friends, the invitation is in the name of the bride's parents, even though they cannot be present. If the parents are not living the bride may either issue the invitation herself (see "The Bride on Her Own") or have her friends as sponsors do so. In the latter case the form is:

Mr. and Mrs. Angus Work

request the pleasure of your company

at the marriage of

Miss Penelope Kingsley   (NOTE MISS)

to

Mr. George Frank Carpenter

on Friday, the ninth of June

one thousand nine hundred and fifty-two

at four o'clock

600 Rose Lane

Waco, Texas

R. S. V. P.

COMBINING INVITATION TO CHURCH CEREMONY AND RECEPTION

If all those at the ceremony are to be invited to the reception the wedding invitation may read as follows and no reception card is necessary:

Dr. and Mrs. Grant Kingsley
request the honour of your presence
at the marriage of their daughter
Penelope
to
Mr. George Frank Carpenter
on Friday, the ninth of June
one thousand nine hundred and fifty
at twelve o'clock
Saint Mary's Church
San Francisco
and afterward at
"The Gulls"
Belvedere

R.s.v.p.   (OR, LESS USUALLY, "THE FAVOUR [NOTE SPELLING] OF A REPLY IS REQUESTED.")

PEW CARDS AND TRAIN CARDS

Today it is fairly rare for an invitation to include either a train card or a pew card. If pews are to be allocated it is preferable that pew numbers not appear on the invitation but for purposes of efficiency be given out after acceptances are received. It is much more usual for the bride's mother and the groom's mother to send their visiting cards along with the wedding invitation to those special friends and relatives they wish to seat in reserved sections "Within the Ribbons"—bride's section (one or two pews) to the *left,* groom's to the *right.* Such a card would read:

Groom's Reserved Section (HANDWRITING—BLACK INK)
Mrs. Norman Snowden Carpenter

A train card makes sense if a private car has been reserved to take guests from a main point to and from the wedding. Then the card is enclosed in those invitations going to guests likely to go by train, and they, in turn, present it to the conductor in lieu of a ticket. Otherwise, it is expedient merely to enclose a regular train schedule for such guests and let them make their own arrangements. A train card, if used, may read:

A SPECIAL CAR WILL BE ATTACHED TO TRAIN LEAVING GRAND CENTRAL STATION AT 3:01 P.M. FOR STAMFORD. TRAIN RETURNS FROM STAMFORD AT 6:35 P.M.
PLEASE PRESENT THIS CARD TO THE CONDUCTOR

For a country or suburban home wedding the kind of rustic map often printed for the assistance of guests coming by car may be reproduced on a card of the same stock used in the invitation and be enclosed with it.

CHURCH CARDS

Only at very large and fashionable weddings in big churches ordinarily filled with sight-seers is it sometimes necessary to have church cards. They should be without the crest, shield, or motto, if the device is used on the invitation, and should be engraved in the same manner as the invitation and on the same stock. They mean that the church has been closed to the public for the period of the ceremony and only bearers of the cards will be admitted. Such cards read:

Please present this card
at St. Patrick's Cathedral
Wednesday, the first of March

Note that here it is usual to abbreviate "Saint."

THE RECEPTION CARD

When not all those attending the wedding are to be invited to the reception a reception card of the same stock as the invitation and about half the size is included with its tissue. It should not bear a crest, shield, or motto and may read:

Dr. and Mrs. Grant Kingsley
request the pleasure of your company
at the wedding breakfast
following the ceremony
at
"The Gulls"
Belvedere

R.s.v.p.
Note "pleasure of your company," as this is now a social occasion.

When the reception is to be held in the home of friends the card reads:

Dr. and Mrs. Grant Kingsley
request the pleasure of your company
at the wedding breakfast
following the ceremony
at the home of
Mr. and Mrs. Curtis Platt
Turkey Hill Road
Belvedere

The favour of a reply is requested to
"The Gulls," Belvedere   (THE BRIDE'S HOME)

If a mother or father, alone, issues the wedding invitation, the reception card must include the name of the spouse, if the divorced or widowed parent has remarried. A reception card bears the name of host *and* hostess.

THE SEPARATE RECEPTION INVITATION

Sometimes an invitation to the wedding reception is engraved on the same kind of double sheet usually used for the wedding invitation. This is useful where there may be only an intimate wedding ceremony, for which no engraved invitations may be issued, followed by a large reception. Such an invitation reads:

Dr. and Mrs. Grant Kingsley
request the pleasure of your company
at the wedding breakfast of their daughter
Penelope
and   (NOTE THE "AND")
Mr. George Frank Carpenter
on Friday, the ninth of June
at one o'clock
"The Gulls"
Belvedere

R.s.v.p.

WEDDING ANNOUNCEMENTS

Wedding announcements, as previously noted, are sent only to those not invited to the wedding. They read:

Dr. and Mrs. Grant Kingsley
have the honour of announcing
(OR HAVE THE HONOUR TO ANNOUNCE)
the marriage of their daughter
Penelope
to
Mr. George Frank Carpenter
on Friday, the ninth of June
one thousand nine hundred and fifty
(MUST GIVE YEAR)
Saint Mary's Church
(OPTIONAL TO MENTION)
San Francisco

THE DIVORCEE'S ANNOUNCEMENT   If a divorcée is young, her parents issue the announcement of her wedding:

> Mr. and Mrs. Sidney Myers
> have the honour of announcing
> the marriage of their daughter
> Sylvia Ann Kiser
> to
> etc.

If she is mature, the divorcée may issue her own announcement, in conjunction with her husband:

> Mrs. Myers Kiser
> and
> Mr. Kurt Samuels
> etc.

AT HOME CARDS

"At Home" cards are often in wedding announcements, less often in invitations to weddings and receptions. They give the new address of the couple. Smaller than the reception card, they are, however, of the same style as it, with abbreviations and without a coat of arms or a lozenge (see "Heraldry"). They carry the correct postal address in detail:

> At Home   (OR THIS MAY BE OMITTED)
> after the first of August
> (CAPITAL "A" FOR "AFTER" IF FIRST LINE IS OMITTED)
> 10 Washington Square, South
> New York, 11, New York

INVITATIONS TO INFORMAL WEDDINGS

A small wedding does not require engraved invitations—in fact, they may seem pretentious. Instead, the mother of the bride may write short notes of invitation, telegraph or phone the relatives and friends who are to be invited to the ceremony or the reception or both.

If the bride's mother is dead her father or some close relative, preferably an aunt or grandmother, issues the invitations. Or she may even issue them herself if she has no close relatives. Often, after such informal weddings, engraved announcements are sent to friends and relatives at a distance, but never to those who have been invited to the ceremony or the reception. An informal invitation to a wedding may be phoned—or it may be written on the household's conservative notepaper, in blue or black ink, this way:

> "The Beaches"
> Meriden, Connecticut
> April 6, 1952

Dear Marion,
Faith is being married here at home to Ronald Ward, Saturday, April 22,

at four-thirty. We do hope you will be with us and will be able to stay for tea, afterwards.

As ever,
Helen

For such an invitation, just such a short note, giving the time and place of the ceremony or, if the invitation is being issued only for the reception, the time and place of the reception is all that is necessary, and it is taken for granted that the invitation will be promptly answered. Informal invitations may be sent on very short notice, if necessary, but the usual two weeks in advance, as for ordinary social invitations, is customary.

REPLY TO AN INFORMAL WEDDING INVITATION A reply to an informal wedding invitation is sent immediately, usually in the form in which it was received. If it was a telegram and the time before the ceremony is short a wire goes in reply. If the invitation came by phone or note a reply by either means is correct. In phoning an acceptance the recipient asks to speak to the sender of the invitation or, if someone responsible answers the phone, leaves the message, "Mr. and Mrs. Wainwright accept Mrs. Samuel's invitation to Miss Consuela's wedding on the fifteenth." A note in reply would read:

Tuesday

Dear Lenore,

We are so happy about Consuela's forthcoming marriage and are delighted to be included. We'll drive over and will stay at the Inn where I have already made reservations. Until Saturday week.

Love,
Maud

INVITATIONS TO THOSE IN MOURNING

People in mourning are included in the wedding invitation list, and even if they are in deep mourning, may accept just as they would attend church services or continue to sing in the choir. If their bereavement had been very recent, they might attend the wedding but not the reception, always a gay social function. It is even possible for one in mourning to be in the bridal party. If she's a bridesmaid she dresses exactly as the rest, and a mourning usher or best man never wears a band on his sleeve. All the attendants are considered to be in wedding uniform, their own problems and personalities subjugated for the day they are in the service of the bride and groom. This is understood by everyone, and only if bereavement has been very recent and very close is it sometimes necessary for an attendant to ask to be excused, not because of possible criticism, but because his own obvious sorrow might cast a shadow on the happy day.

MILITARY AND NAVAL FORMS FOR WEDDING INVITATIONS AND ANNOUNCEMENTS

If officers are of the Army and Navy Reserve it is only when they are *on active duty* that they use their titles on wedding invitations and announcements. Otherwise, they are "Mr." It is modern to abbreviate the titles, just as "Dr." is more often than not abbreviated. If the following form is used, the title is usually written out:

Dr. and Mrs. Grant Kingsley
request the honour of your presence
at the marriage of their daughter
Cordelia Kingsley
to
Winthrop Cass Bowers
Lieutenant United States Army   (NO COMMA)

REGULAR OFFICER U. S. ARMY   Or, where the officer's rank is Captain or above in the Army (or senior lieutenant or better in the Navy) the title appears first:

Capt. (OR CAPTAIN) Winthrop Cass Bowers
United States Army

In either case it is optional to mention the branch of service, though the regiment is omitted. It may read:

Captain Winthrop Cass Bowers
Artillery, United States Army
(OR, UNITED STATES ARMY AIR FORCES)

RESERVE OFFICER ACTIVE DUTY   For a Reserve Officer on active duty the phrase "United States Army" changes to "Army of the United States."

Non-commissioned officers and enlisted men often prefer to use only their names, with the branch of service immediately below:

Wilson Ford   (NOTE, NOT "MR.")
United States Marine Corps

but

Wilson Ford
Staff Sergeant United States Marine Corps

is correct, too.

RETIRED REGULAR ARMY AND NAVY OFFICERS   High-ranking Army and Navy officers retired from regular service keep their titles in civilian life. Their names on wedding invitations, announcements and other engraved forms read:

Commodore Vincent Ludlow Bird
United States Navy, Retired   (NOTE COMMA)

or

Lt. General Packard Deems
United States Marine Corps, Retired

RETIRED OR INACTIVE RESERVE OFFICERS   Retired or inactive Reserve Officers do not use their former titles, socially or otherwise.

RECALLING WEDDING INVITATIONS

If after wedding invitations have been sent out the wedding is called off, guests must be informed as soon as possible. They may be sent notes, telegrams, printed or engraved cards (when there is time for the engraving).

Dr. and Mrs. Grant Kingsley
announce that the marriage of their daughter
Penelope
to
Mr. George Knapp Carpenter
will not take place

A telegram is signed by the person or persons who issued the invitation. In this case it would read, "The marriage of our daughter Penelope to Mr. George Knapp Carpenter will not take place. Dr. and Mrs. Grant Kingsley." Such a telegram to a close relative would be less formally worded and would carry the familiar form of signature.

When an engagement is broken or a wedding does not take place the gifts must be returned to all senders with tactful notes of explanation. Only when the prospective groom has died is it proper for the girl to keep wedding gifts—and then only if she is strongly urged to do so, in some cases, by a donor whose gift may have a sentimental rather than monetary value. She certainly would not keep gifts intended for a joint household that will never be.

If a wedding has been postponed for any reason gifts are not returned, unless after reasonable length of time the marriage still does not take place.

POSTPONING WEDDINGS

If a wedding is postponed and a new date has been set guests may be informed by telegram or sent a new *printed* invitation done in the style of the original engraved one. Such an invitation reads:

Dr. and Mrs. Grant Kingsley
announce that the marriage of their daughter
Penelope
to
Mr. George Frank Carpenter
has been postponed from
Friday, the ninth of June
until
Friday, the eighth of September
at noon
St. Mary's Church
San Francisco

REPLYING TO WEDDING INVITATIONS

Formal, engraved invitations to a church wedding do not require answering. But if a reception card is included or if a separate invitation to the reception is received, then one answers in the traditional form in response to the R.s.v.p. on the lower left of the card or invitation. The reply is written in longhand on one's best conservative notepaper in blue or black ink with the wording and its spacing taking the form of engraving. An acceptance reads (as it does for any engraved invitation):

Mr. and Mrs. Morrow Truitt
accept with pleasure
Dr. and Mrs. Kingsley's
kind invitation for
Friday, the ninth of June
at noon

A regret follows the same form (but see acceptable alternative below). It reads:

Mr. and Mrs. Morrow Truitt
regret that they are unable to accept
Dr. and Mrs. Kingsley's
kind invitation for
Friday, the ninth of June

A more detailed regret states "why" in this way:

Mr. and Mrs. Morrow Truitt
regret (OR REGRET EXCEEDINGLY) that
their absence from the city
(OR A PREVIOUS ENGAGEMENT)
prevents their accepting
Dr. and Mrs. Kingsley's
etc.

In each case, of course, the envelope is addressed, for the reply, to Dr. and Mrs. Grant Kingsley, using the names exactly as they appear in the invitation.

The wedding may be that of your most intimate friend or of your closest relative, but if you have received an engraved invitation you answer it in formal style.

In an acceptance it is well to repeat the hour but optional to repeat the full details of the invitation. But the simple form given is acceptable in all cases except that of a "regret" to the White House (see "White House Etiquette"). If the full form is used in an acceptance most of the wording in the invitation is repeated:

Mr. and Mrs. Morrow Truitt
accept with pleasure
Dr. and Mrs. Kingsley's
(OR DR. AND MRS. GRANT KINGSLEY'S)
kind invitation to
the wedding breakfast of their daughter
Penelope
and
Mr. George Frank Carpenter
at one o'clock
"The Gulls," Belvedere

A fully written out regret does not repeat the place or the hour, merely the date.

It is always a great compliment to receive a wedding invitation. As I have said, it never requires an answer unless it includes an invitation to the reception, but it is a gracious thing for the recipient to write the person to whom he feels indebted for the invitation—the bride's mother, father, the bride herself, or the groom or his family—about his happiness at the forthcoming event. Such a letter, as it is not in direct reply to the invitation, which needs none, is couched in the usual social form, not in the third person. It might read:

Honolulu
April 8

Dear Jack, (to the groom)

It was wonderful to get the impressive news of the wedding. I'd give a lot to be there, as you and Alice know, but I shall drink a toast to your happiness on that day and hope for a quick trip to the States soon, so I may enjoy the sight of you at home together at last.

With warmest regards to you both,
Burt

Of course, engraved wedding invitations are expensive, and, if they must be limited for economy's sake, some who should receive them, such as brother George in Cincinnati or the members of the bridal party, who would certainly like to keep them in their memory books, may have to be satisfied with their oral or written invitations. It is safer to omit the younger than the older generations, since the latter are more likely to feel slighted if they are not treated to all the formality connected with the event, relatives or no.

RECALLING A FORMAL ACCEPTANCE

If you have accepted an engraved wedding invitation and then something occurs that makes it impossible for you to attend, you may write a formal regret, send a telegram, or telephone your excuses, but a valid excuse must be given. You certainly may not back out of an accepted invitation because a more attractive one has arrived. Illness, death in the family, or a sudden business trip are acceptable excuses. If you receive an invitation to the White House for the same date as that of a formal wedding invitation you have already accepted the White House invitation takes precedence over a social one. A regret, following a previous acceptance, may take this form:

> Mr. and Mrs. Morrow Truitt
> regret that the sudden illness
> of Mrs. Truitt
> prevents their attending
> the wedding on
> Friday, the ninth of June

If the regret is occasioned by a summons to the White House, the second and third lines read:

> regret that an invitation to
> The White House
> etc.

DEATH IN THE FAMILY

When a death occurs in a family that has issued formal invitations is it necessary to recall the invitations? It certainly used to be, but our ideas have changed very radically on the subject of mourning. Certainly no bride would want to go through an elaborate wedding ceremony followed by the festivity of a large reception within a few days of her mother's or father's death or of the sudden death of the groom's mother, father, sister, or brother. The death of a very old person, a grandmother or grandfather, rarely calls for the postponement of a wedding these days, but it all very much depends on the feelings of all involved.

If after a family conference it is decided to recall a wedding invitation because of a death, the guests are notified by wire, by phone, or, if there is time, by printed cards in the same style as the invitation. They may read:

Mrs. Grant Kingsley
regrets that the death of
Dr. Kingsley
obliges her to recall the invitations
to the wedding of her daughter
(THE NAMES ARE OPTIONAL)
Friday, the ninth of June

Such notification does not mean, of course, that the marriage won't take place. It may, instead, be a quiet family ceremony on the original day planned. The bride may even wear her bridal gown and have one attendant, but without a crowded church the full panoply of bridesmaids and ushers would be senseless.

CHAPTER TWO

ARRANGING THE WEDDING

No bride, no matter how much her heart is set on it, should go ahead with plans for a formal wedding without the groom's complete acceptance of all it entails. An elaborate wedding should have professional management, if possible, so the wedding day doesn't arrive with the bride harassed and tearful and the groom wondering why he ever consented to such a thing.

A formal wedding is a beautiful and impressive ceremony if everything has been done on schedule—the gowns delivered on time, every last detail of catering attended to, and the bride with the last two weeks to rest as much as she can, although during this time there will be a rehearsal and a dinner for the bridesmaids and ushers. And she may have a tea at which she will show her presents to close friends, if the gifts are not to be exhibited at the reception.

THE VISIT TO THE MINISTER

Where arrangements must be made for a religious ceremony, with or without the use of a church for the wedding, the bride and groom together visit the minister and discuss the hour of the ceremony, the music, the kind of gown the bride will wear (very short sleeves are sometimes not permitted), and any church regulations that must be fulfilled or local customs to be considered.

If the couple are Catholics and the priest they have chosen does not know them they must present baptismal certificates and written indication from their own parishes that they are free to marry. If both are Catholics banns are proclaimed three successive Sundays or holy days before the wedding in their own parish churches. Mixed marriages between Catholics and non-Catholics require special dispensation and a period of preparation for the non-Catholic.

Protestants who have been divorced may have some difficulty marrying in church, especially if they have been divorced more than once. Some ministers make the distinction that they will remarry only the "injured party" in a divorce. They require that divorced persons present the credentials permitting their remarriage. In most states there are blood tests and a necessary "waiting period" (see the *World Almanac*) between the issuance of the license and the marriage. Ministers are not permitted to waive this period. If it must be waived because of some emergency a civil procedure must be followed before the marriage can take place.

Most ministers prefer to see the bride and groom before the ceremony to be sure there is no impediment to the union about to take place. But sometimes for a small non-church wedding, where the principals are well known to the clergyman, the mother of the bride makes arrangements with the family's own clergyman to perform the marriage on the day chosen.

CHURCH DECORATIONS

Decorations in the church may be limited to suitable altar flowers—where decorating of the altar is permitted—for a small wedding or may be extensive and expensive, despite the desired simplicity of effect. Sometimes only the aisle posts on the *reserved* pews are decorated, even for very formal weddings. But a clever florist can do impressive things with boxwood, palms, ferns, and various available greenery, with or without flowers—which, if used, need not be white.

CANOPY AND CARPET   The canopy from the curb to the church door for formal weddings is not used much today, but the church aisle is often carpeted by the florist when he decorates the church. Or immediately before the procession starts and after the bride's mother is seated (and no one should be admitted after she starts down the aisle), two ushers starting in either direction roll a canvas covering down the aisle. This serves as a protection to the bride's train and is left down until all the guests have left. The florist, or whoever furnished it, removes it.

WEDDING MUSIC

It is necessary to discuss the wedding music with the officiating clergyman and the church's music director, as various rules apply. In some churches soloists are not permitted, in others only rigidly prescribed music may be played by the organists. The *Lohengrin* Wedding March is traditional in the processional—the thrilling "Here Comes the Bride!"—with the Mendelssohn March from *Midsummer Night's Dream* for the recessional. During the entrance of guests most churches permit a wide range of music, but it is best to keep to the accepted classics and to avoid sentimental, popular music that might take away from the great dignity of the occasion. Be sure to discuss each selection with the organist, however—don't just "leave it up to him" or you may find that some of the permitted secular music is not up to your own musical taste at all.

There is a fee anywhere from ten to thirty dollars for organ music in church, with additional ones to be fixed for soloists or choir if they are used, too. Even if someone other than the regular organist plays, the organist receives the usual fee.

THE BRIDE'S FORMAL WEDDING PICTURES

The formal photographs of the bride in her bridal costume are rarely taken the day of the wedding but, instead, immediately after the final fitting of her gown. If they are needed for newspaper reproduction it is preferable that they be done and furnished well in advance of the actual wedding day.

Trousseau shops often can arrange for bridal photographs to be taken there before the gown is delivered. Or the bride may have her picture taken at home a few days before the wedding and after most of the preparations for the event have been completed and she has had time to rest. If the wedding is in a church and it is desired to photograph the ceremony, it is absolutely necessary to get permission to do this from the clergyman who will officiate at the ceremony.

A bride should look young, lovely, and innocent, so she should avoid heavy make-up and, for her photographs especially, omit eye shadow, mascara, and dark lipstick. Almost no make-up at all produces the loveliest bridal pictures.

PREVIOUS MARRIAGE OF THE GROOM

The fact that the groom has been married more than once does not affect the marriage plans of his bride if this is her first marriage. If she is young enough she may still wear a bridal veil, if she wishes, even, of course, if the groom is much older than she.

MAIDS AND MATRONS OF HONOR AND BRIDESMAIDS

The bride usually chooses a sister as maid or matron of honor, or, if she has none, a close friend. As she may, if she wishes, have both maid and matron of honor, one could be her sister, the other a friend. The matron of honor may be a widow, but it is preferable that she not be a divorcée or considerably older than the bride—at least not in a large formal wedding.

If the bride chooses to have both maid and matron of honor, she assigns one of them to hold her bouquet during the ceremony and to adjust her veil as she goes down the aisle in the recessional. The one so designated may precede the bride, with the other honored one following the brides-maids in the processional, or maid and matron may walk together directly preceding the bride. In the recessional, of course, the bride and groom lead. If there are both matron and maid of honor, they follow, walking together or with the elder preceding the younger attendant, unless ushers and bridal attendants are paired in the recessional—possible only if there is an equal number.

Bridesmaids, who may be young matrons, are chosen from among the bride's close friends and should not be older than she.

USHERS AND BEST MAN

The groom chooses his ushers and best man. His best man is usually a brother, if he has one and if there isn't too great a difference in age. If a brother does not serve, the groom's closest friend does. His ushers should be chosen from among his most intimate friends, as once asked, a man cannot refuse such an honor except for some serious reason. Although at a small wedding the groom may do without ushers and the bride without bridesmaids, each must have one attendant to serve as a witness, so the best man and maid or matron of honor are quite indispensable. If the best man is to be chosen from among several very close friends of the groom let him be a good executive, if it is to be a large formal wedding, for his duties are legion and he had better take them seriously if things are to run well.

In a big church it is necessary to have enough ushers—more, usually, than bridesmaids—to seat the expected guests. However, even if a big church is chosen, it is not necessary to invite enough guests to fill it, as part of the body of the church near the altar may be enclosed with boxwood or other greens to make a charming small chapel for the ceremony. And, too, in a big church there are always passers-by who enjoy viewing the ceremony from the rear pews if any are available. Ushers seat only invited guests, however, and do not permit anyone of the general public to be seated until all expected guests are in place.

Like the bridesmaids, ushers may be married or single, but it is unusual, though not incorrect, for a husband and wife to serve together, except at a double wedding where the first couple married may act as best man and matron of honor for the second.

When married men act as ushers or matrons act as bridesmaids their husbands and wives must be invited to the wedding, but they need not be asked to sit at the bridal table, which is, officially, only for the bridal party and even excludes the parents of the couple.

The ushers and best man provide all their own clothes for the wedding with the exception of their ties and gloves, which are furnished them by the groom. He, or the best man, has ascertained sizes and has these items delivered well in advance of the wedding. At the bachelor dinner the groom's gifts to his ushers and his best man are at each table place—but never the clothing accessories.

THE GROOM'S FATHER AS BEST MAN Very occasionally, especially if he has no brother, the groom asks his father to be his best man. If the father is very young-looking this does not seem too incongruous, but it is best to keep the wedding party at the same age level as that of the bride and groom.

DUTIES OF THE BEST MAN The best man has always had an important role in all weddings. In ancient times, when marriage was by seizure of some girl outside the tribe, the best man was chosen for his brawn and bravery, as he was needed to fend off the bride's male relatives and, later, to prevent the bride's escape from the groom. Today, while his duties are less vigorous, they are nevertheless extensive at any formal wedding.

The best man is adviser, messenger, valet, secretary, and general factotum to the groom. He takes him firmly in hand from the very start of preparations for the wedding, seeing to it that he is fitted for his wedding clothes, if new ones are to be made for him—or if they are to be rented—that he has the ties and gloves for the ushers, that he confers with the bride on the needed flowers for ushers and for her bouquet and his boutonniere, all of which the groom usually pays for, though she orders (see "Flowers").

He rounds up the ushers for the rehearsal and sees that it goes off according to schedule. He remains with the groom all day before the ceremony, traditionally even rousing him in the morning. He helps the groom dress, making sure there are extra collar buttons ready in case of emergency, laying out all the items of his wardrobe, seeing that his boutonniere is in his buttonhole.

The best man sees that the marriage license is in the groom's pocket and the wedding ring safely on his own little finger or in his vest pocket. He makes sure that he, himself, has the clergyman's fee (anything from ten dollars up, depending on the elaborateness of the wedding) in a sealed envelope to be tendered, quietly, before the ceremony, so it won't be overlooked.

The best man has the ushers at the church at the appointed time—an hour before the church ceremony, or three quarters of an hour before at a home ceremony—and the groom in the vesting room a good half hour before. No bride should ever be kept "waiting at the church."

After the ceremony the best man joins in the recessional, escorting the maid or matron of honor, then hurries to the place of the reception to take up his duties concerning the couple's luggage. This must be placed in the going-away car or assembled in a spot safe from pranksters. Car and baggage keys and baggage checks, sometimes the hotel key, if any, are given to the groom after he has changed into his sack suit.

At the wedding reception the best man hovers in the neighborhood of the groom, acting as his secretary, reminding him to say something special to the bride's Aunt Mathilde, who is about to come down the line. He proposes the first toast to the bride and groom at the bridal table and reads congratulatory telegrams.

When the bride and groom are ready to dress for their departure the best man again valets the groom and sees that nothing has been forgotten. He fetches both sets of parents and any other close relatives for the farewell upstairs. Then he clears the way through the guests for the bride and groom, who, all goodbyes to their families said, race through a rain of confetti or rose petals (rather than rice, let's hope) to the waiting car or cab (also scheduled to be there at the exact moment by the best man). Then, and then only, does the hard-working aide relax and join in the fun. You can see why the best man does not stand on the receiving line.

DUTIES OF USHERS The duties of ushers at a church wedding are quite definite, but ushers at a home wedding serve in a more or less honorary capacity as there is little, if any, formal seating to do. Usually, standards, flower decorated or not, are placed so they will mark off with white ribbon the areas where guests are to stand. Immediately after the ceremony it is the ushers' work to remove the ribbons and standards, so guests may leave.

Ushers should arrive at the church an hour before the ceremony, leaving their hats and outer coats, if any, in the vestry but retaining their gloves. In the vestry they receive their boutonnieres—furnished by the groom— which are their badge of office and should be in place before the ushers enter the church.

Ushers group themselves to the left of the door inside the church, preferably in the vestibule if it is large enough. Each of them should be armed with a list of guests to be seated in reserved pews, but as guests rarely forget they have been honored by being assigned seats, these lists are rarely referred to unless, if pew cards were issued, a guest forgets to bring his. Unrecognized guests are asked their names and should themselves say "friend of the bride" or "friend of the groom," or the usher may ask the question so that they may be correctly seated—on the left of the church for the bride, on the right for the groom. If as the church fills up it seems likely that the seating will not be balanced, the ushers seat later-arriving guests on the side that has fewer filled seats, regardless of the guest's status.

An usher does not allow a lady to find her seat unescorted. If several guests arrive in a group, he offers his right arm to the eldest lady, and the others in the group follow singly, women first, and are seated together by the usher. If two women arrive at the same time, the younger steps back and permits the elder to take the usher's arm while she waits his return or accepts the services of the next available usher.

Ushers should be gracious and seem unhurried even when, at a big wedding, they must seat a great many people. Bustle and self-importance are most inappropriate in church, so the groom should choose his attendants from among his most dignified friends, whose social presence can be counted upon. For, while an usher actually receives each guest and speaks a few gracious words as he goes up the aisle, he must not be too exuberant or, himself, more than part of the background of the principals—the bride and groom.

The "head usher," usually a brother or other relative designated by the groom, escorts the bride's mother to her seat, and her entrance, always carefully timed, is the signal that the processional is about to start. It is after she is seated that the church doors are closed and the canvas, if any, is laid. After the bride's mother is in place no one else may be seated by ushers. Any late-comers must wait outside until after the ceremony is over or quickly seat themselves on aisle seats in the back of the church if the doors have not been closed.

A male guest entering alone is seated by the usher, who naturally does not offer his arm unless the man is very aged and might have trouble negotiating the aisle alone. If two men arrive at the same time the usher walks down the aisle with the elder and the younger man follows so that he may be seated at the same time.

Children—that is, girls and boys under fifteen or sixteen—follow along as their parents are ushered up the aisle. If there is time for such extra courtesy, an usher may escort a girl slightly under this age—to her obvious delight.

After the bride's mother is seated and the canvas, if there is one, is down two designated ushers, starting with their left feet first, walk together up the aisle to the last reserved pews where white satin ribbons have been carefully folded and laid alongside of the decorated aisle posts. They pick up the entire bundle and, again in step, walk the length of the pews, as rehearsed, drawing the ribbons behind the aisle posts in a straight line, placing the loop at the end of each ribbon over the last aisle post.

The ushers are then ready to take their places at the beginning of the procession. Ushers always go up the aisle in pairs, but in the recessional it is optional for them to pair with the bridesmaids, if there is an equal number. The procedure is decided by the bride and the clergyman in the rehearsal. (See "The Rehearsal.")

In a service wedding where the groom is a commissioned officer—and only if he is—brother officers in uniform acting as ushers make the arch of swords for the bride and groom either at the foot of the chancel steps at the end of the ceremony or, if the couple prefers, outside if the weather is good. In the first case, as soon as the ceremony is over the ushers line up and at the command "Draw Swords!" from the head usher unsheathe their swords and make the ceremonial arch for the bride and groom—and for them only—to pass through, then sheath their swords at the command "Return Swords!" and escort the bridesmaids down the aisle. If the arch is to be outside the church the bridesmaids go down the aisle alone and the ushers leave by the side door with the best man and go quickly around to the front of the church to form the arch as the bride and groom appear.

Civilian and military personnel are sometimes together in a bridal party, but where some ushers and perhaps the groom are required to be in uniform others conform to the proper formal dress for the time of day and season.

If the arch of swords is used, civilian ushers line up, too, but merely stand at attention.

Military ushers, because their swords are worn on the left side, offer their right arms to the bridesmaids at all times, and the bride stands to the right of the bridegroom when he is in full dress uniform. All ushers, civilian and military, in the recessional must then be on the right if they are paired with bridesmaids.

(Military personnel never wear boutonnieres, even at weddings.)

After the recessional the ribbons are left in place until the mothers of the bride and groom and at least some of the reserved pew guests have been escorted out. After the first few have gone down the aisle ushers often take out groups in order to clear the church more quickly. It is an extremely ill-mannered guest who, despite the ribbons restraining him on the aisle side, leaves from the far side of the church before the reserved pew guests have been escorted out and the ribbons removed.

Ushers' duties are not over once they have completed their schedules at the church. They must see to it that the bridal party is transported to the reception, if there is one, well in advance of the first guests' arrival, and they should arrange transportation for any reception guests who may not have it. They have limited time to attend to these details, because, although they do not stand in the receiving line, they should be on hand as soon as possible for the wedding group pictures, which should be taken while everyone is still relatively fresh and can be accounted for. And as no guest should arrive and have to wait to be received, you can see that there is split-second timing even here.

At the reception the ushers, at last, may relax and enjoy themselves. At a large formal reception caterers take charge of refreshments, but at a small one the ushers may help serve guests. They aid and abet the couple in a smooth getaway as the reception draws to a close, after the bride has thrown her bouquet to the waiting bridesmaids when she goes to change to her street clothes.

Ushers, as members of the wedding party, always give gifts to the bride, individually, before the wedding or together give the couple some major gift from them all, with contributions to the fund tactfully geared to the circumstances of the least affluent usher. A silver tea tray, a chair, or coffee table—things the new household needs—are appropriate and better than separate gifts from each usher, as men are usually greatly befuddled as to what constitutes a suitable wedding gift. They are often visibly relieved if the bride, when asked, has a concrete suggestion along these lines.

TRANSPORTATION TO AND FROM THE CHURCH

Bridesmaids always meet at the home of the bride before going to the church. They may dress there, if that seems advisable, or arrive dressed. If they are from out of town it is the duty of the bride's mother to find them accommodations either in her own home or with friends or, failing that, at a hotel, chaperoned.

At the bride's home the attendants receive their bouquets. They should all be assembled a full hour before the ceremony and able, if necessary, to aid the bride in her dressing and her mother with the last-minute preparations for the reception.

The mother of the bride, riding alone or with one or two bridesmaids, leaves the house first, followed by the bridesmaids and maid or matron of honor in hired limousines or their own cars. The bride, with her father, always rides in a special car, whose driver, or chauffeur, wears a white boutonniere. The car's tires, if not white-walled, are freshly whitewashed. The bride is very careful not to sit on her wedding gown or crease her veil.

Arrangements are made beforehand with local police or uniformed attendants to keep traffic in order at a large wedding. As each car arrives it moves on to a designated parking space. The bride's car, however, remains in front of the church just where it dispatched her and her father, until she re-enters it with the groom.

GIFTS FOR BRIDE'S ATTENDANTS, USHERS, AND BEST MAN

Both bride and groom give their attendants some lasting memento of the occasion—the groom at his bachelor dinner, the bride at any convenient time before the wedding when all her attendants are together. The gifts are usually silver or gold—something that can be engraved with the date and the initials of the recipients. Desk accessories—silver inkwells, paper weights, or letter openers—or the more usual cigarette boxes are suitable for both maids and ushers. Brides often give charms for bracelets or tiny gold or silver pencils or silver snuff boxes (now used for pills). Gifts for ushers should be all alike, as are those for the bridesmaids. The chief attendants receive the same kind of gift varied a little in design or size—a giant cigarette box or cocktail shaker for the best man, say, and a bracelet for the maid or matron of honor instead of a charm.

THE COUPLE'S GIFTS TO EACH OTHER

On or just before her wedding day the bride receives some personal gift from the groom—usually something to wear. Loveliest is a string of pearls, but the modern bride—if her husband can afford it—may think in terms of a mink coat or her own roadster. A piece of heirloom jewelry, a fitted traveling case, or a watch are all possibilities—very expensive or fairly inexpensive ones, as the groom's circumstances permit.

The bride, in turn, makes some gift to the groom, too—a silver dresser set, cuff links, her wedding picture in a silver frame, or anything of somewhat lasting quality for which he will have personal use.

THE BACHELOR DINNER

Two or three nights before the wedding—certainly not the night before— it is still customary for the groom to give a bachelor dinner to his best man and ushers and perhaps many or few other men friends, usually in a private dining room of a restaurant or club or in the groom's bachelor quarters if he has them.

We usually forget that the groom, too, probably enters marriage with some trepidation, and therefore the bachelor dinner, no doubt, serves to bolster his courage. It was in past generations supposed to allow him a final fling, and it produced a certain "morning after" in everyone attending.

Today, with pre-marriage relationships on a more relaxed plane, the groom has less need, perhaps, to blow off steam at his bachelor dinner and, if he has one at all, it is likely to be a quiet stag affair, distinguished, of course, at the end by the expected toast to the bride. For the toast the groom rises and with him all the men at the table. He raises his glass, traditionally filled with champagne, and says, simply, "To the bride." Each man drains (normally, champagne is sipped, of course) his glass and replaces it on the table, instead of snapping its fragile stem as was formerly customary. Many restaurants, well understanding the bachelor-dinner urge to break the glasses to honor the bride, are still willing to provide the cheapest possible glasses, billing the host for the breakage if it does occur. But any modern bride will feel just as honored if the glasses remain intact, I am sure.

Today's bride is, especially in smaller communities, very likely to make her own farewell to the single life by dining with her bridal attendants or alone with her best friend. Customarily she always spends the night before her wedding with her immediate family. If she does give a "maiden dinner" it usually takes place the evening of the bachelor dinner in some restaurant or club or in the bride's home. At this time, if she wishes, she can give her attendants their gifts and propose a toast to the groom.

BRIDE'S DRESS FOR THE WEDDING

For a formal winter wedding in church or at home the bride wears a full-length bridal gown in a variety of possible materials—satin, velvet, taffeta, chiffon, tulle, and lace. All of them—except the velvet—can be worn for a summer wedding, plus a wide variety of summer cottons, from organdy to dimity.

The formal wedding gown is usually white or ivory (though delicate blue or pink are sometimes seen) with or without a full-length veil of tulle, lace, or other sheer material. A finger-tip veil is often used on even the most formal gown, but a veil may be dispensed with entirely, so long as a bride wears a flower circlet on her head. In a simple country church, however, I saw a charming bride go to the altar bareheaded, because she never wore a hat of any kind. The kindly and liberal minister said he saw no reason why God should be displeased if she did what was for her the natural thing.

A wedding gown should follow a certain decorum—neckline conservative and sleeves preferably long. If the sleeves are fairly short, this necessitates the wearing of long gloves, which may not be removed during the ceremony. Instead, the under seam of the ring finger is ripped, so the bride can bare her finger to receive the ring. The bride who chooses a long-sleeved gown doesn't wear gloves.

The bride's shoes are white silk or satin, her orange blossoms preferably artificial and wiltless, and any jewelry she wears is real and more or less functional. She might wear a strand of pearls or a simple pin or clip, but she wouldn't wear even a tiny diamond-studded watch or bracelet. She might wear simple pearl earrings or small gold ones, but she would avoid chi-chi.

In place of a bridal bouquet (furnished by the groom) the bride may carry a white prayer book, with or without a flower and ribbon marker.

If she wears her engagement ring to the altar it is on her right hand, as the wedding band, once put on, is, at least traditionally, never removed.

At an informal church or home wedding the bride wears a simple dress or suit (not black) through noon, a dressmaker suit or afternoon dress, later.

SHOULD THE BRIDE WEAR A FAMILY GOWN? It is traditional in some families that each generation's brides wear a family gown that has served this romantic purpose before. But no one should assume that a bride will prefer to carry on such a tradition or even wear her mother's own gown rather than have her very own. It is the bride who should decide, and any suggestions that she wear other than her own gown should be very tentative indeed. No family pressure should be permitted, for a bride certainly has the right to make such an important decision herself. And if she decides in favor of a modern gown, it is the obligation of her mother to protect her from criticism by unthinking Aunt Nellies.

HOW PRACTICAL SHOULD A WEDDING GOWN BE? Most brides abandon any thought of practicality when choosing a wedding gown. If a great deal of money goes into it, they like to think that it may become a family heirloom their daughters and granddaughters will wear. However, modern living has created its own storage problems, and it is better, no doubt, to choose the kind of gown that can be remade by a clever seamstress into a dinner or evening dress. If a white dress the first year or so of marriage seems a little obvious, it can very well be dyed. If it is to be dyed, the dyeing should take place before the remodeling, as the fabric will probably shrink. It is more practical to save the veil for future generations than the dress, as wedding veils change very little while dresses change considerably. Think of the bride of the twenties with her knee-length gown she thought her granddaughter would be able to wear!

SUPERSTITIONS   Most brides like to follow the age-old superstition that they must wear "something old, something new, something borrowed, and something blue." And some walk down the aisle with a shiny dime in place of the traditional sixpence in their shoe.

Modern brides, however, scoff at the idea that bad luck will befall them if they rehearse their own weddings, and they seldom have "stand-ins" for the purpose.

The rice, sometimes painful when thrown too enthusiastically at weddings, is usually replaced today by confetti or rose petals furnished by the bride's family. Anything of the sort should be thrown only outside the church.

THE GROOM'S CLOTHES

For a formal wedding in which the bride wears a bridal gown the groom must wear formal clothes—daytime or evening clothes—depending on the hour of the ceremony. If the wedding is in the morning or afternoon—up to 7 P.M.—the groom wears a cutaway with gray striped trousers, gray vest (in summer natural or white linen with spats and gloves to match), a wing collar with ascot or cravat in black and white. He also wears black shoes with black soles (soles are blackened by the shoemaker so they will not be noticeable when the groom kneels), black socks, gray gloves (or, in summer, a color to match vest), and a high silk hat. His boutonniere is distinctive from that of the other men in the bridal party—lilies of the valley or a gardenia preferably. This is, traditionally, a spray from the bridal bouquet.

In the summer for country weddings only, white flannels and navy coats may replace the cutaways for formal wear when the bride is in full regalia. The tie is blue, the shoes pure white, the collar stiff, turned over. No gloves. For an outdoor wedding a white linen or Palm Beach suit may be worn with a white or light tie.

For an informal morning or afternoon wedding, when the bride wears a veil the groom wears a single- or double-breasted Oxford gray coat, striped trousers, a white shirt with stiff collar, a gray tie, black shoes and socks, a black or gray felt, and a distinctive white boutonniere.

For an informal wedding in the morning or afternoon, when the bride does not wear a veil the groom wears a dark business suit in blue or gray, a white shirt with a white fold collar, a conservative tie, a derby or Homburg, gray gloves, and his own special boutonniere. In the summer for such a wedding he wears a light-weight wool suit in gray or blue with white shirt and black shoes, or a Palm Beach suit, conservative tie, white shirt, light socks, and white shoes.

For formal evening weddings—after 7 P.M.—the groom wears a tail coat, as do all the male members of the wedding party. He wears his own boutonniere to distinguish him from the others and an opera or high silk hat. For a smaller, less formal wedding in the evening, a dinner jacket is permissible and the groom's boutonniere essential. If the bride wears street clothes for an evening wedding the groom wears a dark business suit, black shoes. If the bride wears a dinner dress the groom wears a tuxedo.

THE WALKING STICK   The crook-handled Malacca walking stick is customarily carried by the groom, best man, and ushers when they are in cutaways, but it is no longer considered essential.

DIFFERENCES OF DRESS IN WEDDING PARTY

Ushers at a wedding dress alike and for formal afternoon weddings wear identical ties and gloves that the groom gives them. The ties for the ushers may be gray four-in-hands instead of ascots and worn either with a wing or fold collar. Groom and best man always wear either brocaded gray or black and silver-gray striped grosgrain ascots for formal daytime weddings, but their cravats need not match. As sack coats with striped trousers are slightly less formal than the cutaway, groom and best man usually wear the cutaway, even when the ushers wear the more modern type of formal daytime dress. (See "The Morning Coat or Cutaway.")

The maid or matron of honor is usually dressed in a slightly different fashion from the bridesmaids, with a dress that is either of the same design but a different color or of the same color but of a little different design. But all attendants' dresses may be exactly alike, with different flowers or head-dresses distinguishing the maid or matron of honor. The bridesmaids and maid or matron of honor wear dresses the same length as the bride's and, as nearly always required, some appropriate head covering—either hats, Juliet caps, or flower headdresses. The slippers of all the attendants are alike in fabric and style, but the maid or matron of honor may have slippers of a different color to match her dress if it is another color. In the formal wedding party only the bride may be gloveless, as usually her veil or sleeves partially cover her hands. The long sweeping train has virtually disappeared and with it the train bearers.

Flower girls, dressed in picture-book style, are more often seen in formal weddings than page boys, possibly because little girls are more amenable to "dressing up." Little boys tend to think their manhood impugned by frilly blouses and satin knee breeches or long tight velvet trousers of the Dickens era. If either or both small attendants are used, they should not be so young as to create still more problems. A flower girl has no function except that of looking picturesque, but a page boy is supposed to bear the ring—for safety's sake not the real one—on a little white satin pillow. The real ring, of course, is snug in the best man's pocket.

Flower girls and page boys may be all in white, like the bride, or be dressed in pastel shades that match or complement those of the bridesmaids. While period costumes are usually used, a page boy could wear a dark blue Eton suit and a flower girl could wear a party dress and white or colored slippers to match or, with a colored dress, possibly to contrast. Her bouquet should be diminutive—usually a tiny round one with a paper frill—or she may carry a basket of rose petals. And even she must have some little head covering in most churches.

If there is a ring bearer, see that the ring is fastened to the cushion with light silken stitches, especially if precaution has been thrown to the winds and the real ring is borne by the child.

If the actual ring is on the cushion the ring bearer carries, then he will, necessarily, have to remain throughout the ceremony. If he has been used merely for effect, however, it is quite simple for him to leave the procession as it reaches the mother's pew. As children in the processional are usually under seven, they should not stand with the other attendants during the ceremony but should join the bride's mother in her pew and not be in the recessional.

For an informal wedding attendants, if any, wear the same kind of clothes as the principals, geared to the season, the place of the ceremony, and the time of day. Guests wear conservative Sunday best, the women in hats and gloves.

WHAT GUESTS WEAR

When the groom wears formal day or evening wear the fathers of the bride and groom dress as he does, as do all the male members of the wedding party. Men guests at a formal daytime wedding may or may not wear cutaways or sack coats with striped trousers, as they choose. Younger men usually wear dark blue or Oxford gray suits.

At a formal daytime wedding the mothers of the bride and groom may wear soft suits or ensembles in pale or pastel faille, taffeta, satin, or silk, or any delicately colored taffeta, satin, or silk afternoon dress in the current mode. The flowing chiffons that were once thought *de rigueur* for the occasion now seem unyouthful.

For a formal evening wedding women members of the wedding party wear evening-length dresses and the mothers of the bride and groom wear long- or three-quarter-sleeved dinner or evening dresses in any color but black, red, or possibly green, which by some is considered unlucky at weddings. Accessories should not be black, and some headdress should be worn—perhaps an evening hat, a mantilla, or a twist of tulle. Women guests may wear dinner dresses or afternoon wear.

At a formal evening wedding men related to the family wear white tie, as do many older men, but it is usual for young men to wear dinner jackets if they are not actually in the wedding party.

At informal weddings guests wear conservative church-going clothes suitable to the season. The women wear hats and gloves.

FLOWERS FOR THE WEDDING PARTY

The groom's boutonniere is, as I have mentioned before, traditionally a spray from the bridal bouquet and is usually lily of the valley, if in season. But his boutonniere differs from that of the best man and the ushers.

The bridal bouquet is usually white, although, especially with pastel bridal gowns, sometimes other pale-colored flowers are included. It may encircle a going-away corsage if the flowers come from a florist skilled at making these corsages-within-bouquets so they merely untie when the bride wishes to toss away the rest of her bouquet. The corsage included in the bridal bouquet saves the groom the expense of a separate corsage and "fills out" the bouquet at no extra cost.

The attendants' bouquets—carried only with long gowns—are usually Colonial or wrist bouquets, more graceful to manage in a procession than the old-fashioned arm bouquets. If attendants and bride are in street-length gowns corsages take the place of bouquets.

Attendants' bouquets may be anything seasonal that complements their gowns. At a beautiful Christmas season wedding all the attendants were in white velvet and carried wrist bouquets of poinsettias. A country garden wedding might find the bridesmaids carrying Colonial bouquets of purple or blue iris or blue cornflowers—or even field daisies.

EXPENSES OF THE BRIDE'S PARENTS

Engraved invitations and announcements

The bridal outfit and, though it is no longer expected, the costumes of the bride's attendants if money is no object

Bridal photographs

The bridal consultant and social secretary, if needed

The bride's trousseau

The household trousseau

All the cost of the reception

Flowers for the reception

Flowers for the bride and her attendants (but see "Groom's Expenses")

Music at the church and at the reception

Sexton's and organist's fee. Choir fee

Carpets, ribbons, awnings, tents—anything of the kind often rented for large weddings and receptions

A limousine for the bride, at least, and other cars for the transportation of the bridal party to and from church

A wedding gift of substance, usually silver

GROOM'S EXPENSES

The wedding ring

The marriage license

The bride's flowers (the bridal bouquet if she wears a bridal gown, or a corsage. Going-away corsage may be the heart of the bridal bouquet, or supplied separately)

His own and the ushers' boutonnieres
Corsage for his mother
The ushers' gloves
The ushers' ties
Gifts for the ushers
The minister's fee
A wedding gift for his bride—something for her to treasure, usually jewelry
His bachelor dinner
The entire cost of the wedding trip
His own wedding and wedding trip clothes
The home into which they will move, and the equipping of it with its major
   furnishings

NOTE: In large formal weddings the bride's flowers and those of the bridesmaids are considered part of the entire wedding expense and thus borne by
the bride's parents. It is becoming customary however for the groom to send
the bride's bouquet, though she selects it, and to provide, of course, his own
and the best man's and the ushers' boutonnieres. In some communities the
groom pays for the entire bridal party flowers as well as for corsages for both
mothers.

CHAPTER THREE

THE WEDDING CEREMONY

THE REHEARSAL

All weddings with more than two attendants must be rehearsed two or
three days before the event and at the convenience of the clergyman, or in
large churches the sexton, who must be present with the organist and any
other participants.

Often the rehearsal is held in the evening, preceded by a dinner for the
bridal party at the home of the bride.

WHICH ARM DOES THE BRIDE TAKE?   This is always settled at the rehearsal
and depends on the preference of the minister. It is more convenient at a
formal wedding for the bride to go up the aisle on her father's right arm, so that
when his role is completed and he must return to the left front pew to stand
with her mother he does not have to cross over the bride's train but will be
already on the convenient side. However, some ministers prefer the other
procedure in which the bride comes down the aisle on her father's left arm.
(In all recessionals the bride takes the groom's arm and ushers offer their
arms to bridesmaids.) The clergyman's ruling is the deciding one.

ALTAR

PROCESSIONAL, *Christian Ceremony*

Reading from top down: Bride and her father. Sometimes father is on bride's right (*see text*).

Flower girl or page boy, if any, or flower girl and page, page on same side as father.

Maid or matron of honor. If there are both, they may walk together or the younger may precede the elder.

Bridesmaids. Shorter ones precede taller and are paired according to height.

Ushers. Shorter ones precede taller and are paired according to height.

At the chancel steps: best man, groom, clergyman.

THE PROCESSIONAL

Ushers are paired, as are bridesmaids, so that the shorter ones precede the taller. They learn that they do not actually "march" but walk in time, slowly, left foot first down the aisle, keeping four pews apart, and after a little coaching they manage to deliver the bride to the chancel steps at the moment the music stops playing. The bride, no longer afraid to rehearse at her own wedding, counts eight beats of the music before she follows the attendants on her father's right arm.

RECESSIONAL, *Christian Ceremony, Optional Arrangement*

RIGHT PANEL, *Reading from top down:* Groom and bride. In a service wedding men are on bride's right. In other weddings this is sometimes done too (*see text*).

Flower girl or page, if any, or second honor attendant, if any.

Best man and maid or matron of honor. Ushers and bridesmaids paired, only if they are equal in number.

FAR RIGHT PANEL, *Reading from top down:* Groom and bride.

Flower girl or second honor attendant, if any. (Very small children do not appear in recessional necessarily.)

Maid of honor.

Bridesmaids alone *always* when there is not an equal number of ushers.

Ushers alone.

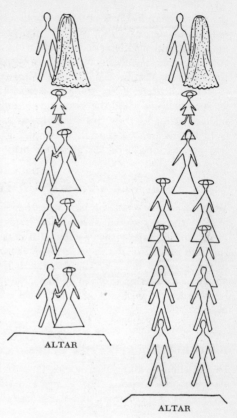

No words of the ceremony are spoken during the rehearsal, although the minister (or the sexton) indicates at what point each member of the party plays his role. The best man learns just when he must produce the ring from his vest pocket or, better, his little finger. The maid or matron of honor notes at what point she takes the bride's bouquet or prayer book. The bride's father—or in some cases her mother—learns when the bride is to be "given away."

THE RECESSIONAL

Most rehearsed of all will be the ushers, who, if it is to be a large wedding, will have real work to do. Two ushers, chosen for the honor, will be shown how to handle the ribbons and, if there is to be one, how to lay the canvas at the right moment. It is at the rehearsal that bride and clergyman, or sexton, decide how the recessional is to go. Bride and groom always lead in the recessional, but it is optional whether or not the ushers and bridesmaids pair up or return as they were in the processional, but this time with the bride's attendants immediately following the couple, in the proper order, then the ushers walking together. If there is an uneven number of ushers the extra man walks alone and the second variation of the recessional is preferred. I prefer to see the attendants paired in the recessional, if possible, as such pairing after the ceremony seems symbolic of other possible romances springing from this wedding—as so often happens.

In the recessional the father is missing—he has joined the mother in the first pew as soon as he has given the bride away.

WHEN THERE ARE TWO MAIN AISLES

When a church has two main aisles one may be used for the processional, one for the recessional. When each is given the same importance the pew posts are decorated exactly alike. If it is decided that one aisle is to be used for both processional and recessional, the other aisle is used only for seating of guests and is not specially decorated. If one aisle is chosen, the grouping at the chancel is on the side of that aisle. When both aisles are given equal importance the grouping at the chancel is as it is for a church with a center aisle.

PROCEDURE DURING THE CEREMONY

In Christian wedding ceremonies the left side is the bride's, as one enters, the right, the groom's. The family and friends of the bride are, therefore, on the left of the church, and the groom's are on the right.

GROUPING AT THE ALTAR, *Protestant Ceremony:* 1. Groom, 2. bride, 3. bride's father, 4. maid or matron of honor, 5. best man, 6. clergyman. Figures far left and right, ushers, maids of honor. NOTE: In the Roman Catholic ceremony the bride's father joins her mother in the first pew as he reaches it. He does not give the bride away. Otherwise the grouping at the chancel is the same, with the addition of an acolyte (*see text*).

As the bride approaches the chancel the clergyman stands at the entrance to the altar and the groom, facing slightly into the nave, is on the right, ready to step forward to assist the bride up the chancel step or steps. Below and behind him a little to the right is the best man. On the left of the chancel as the bride approaches stands her maid or matron of honor in the same position as the best man. Ushers, if any, are lined up below the choir stalls on each side of the chancel with the maids of honor usually in front of them and on a slanting line. In a small church it may be necessary to place only two ushers on the chancel steps, one left, one right, the rest on the floor of the church, flanking the chancel, but many variations of these groupings are used.

In some ceremonies—namely the Catholic and the Episcopal—the bride and groom follow the clergyman to the altar and may kneel at an indicated point in the ceremony. They are followed by the maid and matron of honor, if there are both in attendance, with the maid on the immediate left of the bride and the matron on the far left of the bride, so that it is the maid who assists with the bouquet and veil. The best man on the immediate right of the groom is followed by the ring bearer, if any, at far right, a few feet behind. When the clergyman asks for the ring, the best man produces it from his vest pocket or, better, his little finger. In the Catholic service he proffers it to the groom, who hands it to the acolyte, who in turn gives it to the priest, who blesses it. In the Protestant ceremony—and the Episcopal service or some variation of it is often used in Presbyterian and Congregational churches, too—he hands the ring to the groom, who gives it to the minister for the blessing.

During the blessing of the ring—or, if preferred, as soon as maid and matron of honor (or just the one attendant) are in place—the bride hands her

AT THE ALTAR RAIL, *Roman Catholic and Episcopal Ceremony, Optional Arrangements:* 1. Priest, 2. acolyte (*Roman Catholic service*), 3. bride, 4. groom, 5. best man, 6. matron of honor. NOTE: In elaborate Roman Catholic ceremonies the entire wedding party sometimes enters the sanctuary in a large church. In some churches this is not permitted and only the bride, groom, priest, and acolyte enter the sanctuary.

ALTAR

bouquet or prayer book to the attendant chosen for the honor, so that her left hand will be free to receive the wedding ring.

As soon as the marriage service is completed the bride turns first to the maid or matron of honor for her bouquet and to have her face veil, if she has one, lifted. She then turns, and, although this is not part of the ceremony, receives the groom's kiss if they have decided to kiss at the altar (see "When Does the Groom Kiss the Bride?"), and the good wishes of the clergyman, who usually shakes hands with both bride and groom.

The bride then turns and takes the groom's right arm, and—after the maid of honor has adjusted her train—together they lead off in the recessional.

WHEN DOES THE BRIDE TAKE THE GROOM'S ARM? In the wedding ceremony, although the groom takes a step or two forward to meet the bride and may take her arm to assist her to kneel, if that is part of the ceremony, the bride does not take the groom's arm or place her hand in his until the moment in the ceremony at which this is indicated. In some ceremonies the clergyman places the bride's hand in the groom's, in others the father—or sometimes the mother—makes this symbolic gesture. At other times the bride needs her hands free to arrange her gown for kneeling, to hand her prayer book or bouquet to her attendant. The groom may assist her to rise from a kneeling position, but she must not touch him until the proper moment.

WHEN DOES THE GROOM KISS THE BRIDE? At large formal church weddings it is not usual for the groom to kiss the bride at the altar after the clergyman has congratulated the couple at the end of the ceremony. But if the couple is to receive in the church vestibule or if the marriage takes place at home, the groom always kisses the bride immediately following the ceremony, as no one may kiss the bride before he does. The clergyman, if he has long been an intimate of the family, may be the next to have the privilege, but on the receiving line the bride is kissed only by those who really have the right to offer this intimate form of salutation. Gay blades and old codgers, impelled to kiss the bride merely because they think custom sanctions it, should check their exuberance and wait for the suggestion, if any, to come from the bride—or the groom. The latter might be heard to say, "Darling, this is Alfred, my old roommate—remember—and he's dying to kiss you, of course. So I'll permit it—this once!"

IF AN ATTENDANT DROPS OUT

No attendant asks to be excused from the bridal party except for some very good reason—illness or such a recent death in his or her immediate family that burial does not take place before the wedding day. In any case, the bride or groom is faced with a difficult problem in trying to replace the missing attendant. It may be easier for them to leave the bridal party as it is and let the uneven usher walk alone, if it's a man who's missing, or the extra bridesmaid precede the maid or matron of honor alone in the processional. The friend who is asked at the very last minute to fill in at anything so formal as a bridal procession may well be accepting at considerable inconvenience, while wondering why he was not asked to be a member of the party from the beginning.

THE DOUBLE RING CEREMONY

When both bride and groom give each other rings the question often arises as to who holds the groom's ring until the proper moment. It is the maid or matron of honor who is in charge of the groom's ring just as the best man is always responsible for the bride's until the moment the groom slips it on her finger. The bride's attendant wears the groom's ring for safekeeping. If it won't stay on any finger it should be tied with a small white satin ribbon to her sash or belt, her bouquet or her left wrist, so she can get it off easily.

A man's wedding ring was customarily worn on the right hand, but in recent years, when the double ring ceremony became very popular during wartime, the ring was placed on the man's left hand. So now it is worn on the third finger of either the right or left hand, whichever the bride and bridegroom prefer. The groom's ring is always a gift from the bride. As it is gold and perfectly plain, it may not necessarily match hers, as it used to.

WHEN THE BRIDE'S MOTHER GIVES HER AWAY

If the bride's father is dead the bride's mother may give her away—if a brother, an uncle, or some other male relative hasn't been selected for the honor. There are several ways this may be done. Either the bride's mother may walk down the aisle with her daughter—but not, of course, with the bride on her arm—or the bride may walk in the processional with her brother or other male relative and her mother will join her as the bride reaches the left front pew. Sometimes the bride walks alone in the processional and her mother joins her as she reaches her mother's pew. Still again, a male relative will escort the bride to the chancel steps and when the clergyman asks who is to give the bride away the mother nods from her traditional place or, just before the words are to be spoken, is escorted to the chancel by the best man, who steps down for the gesture. This is necessary only in those ceremonies—the Episcopalian, for example—where the one who "gives the bride away" actually places her hand in the minister's.

GIVING AWAY THE MATURE BRIDE

In the weddings of mature brides—widows or divorcées—it is not necessary that they be "given away," and this portion of the ceremony is often omitted, just as it is in civil ceremonies when there are no designated attendants, merely legal witnesses.

But the older woman who has a church wedding usually chooses to be escorted to the church by some male relative or close family friend, also male, although she may arrive with the best man, the groom, and her own attendant. She does not walk up the church aisle but waits with the groom, best man, and maid of honor in the vestry until the clergyman is ready, then is escorted to her place at the chancel by the best man, while the groom escorts the maid or matron of honor.

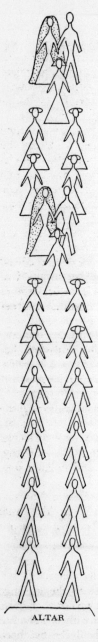

PROCESSIONAL AT DOUBLE WEDDING, *Christian Ceremony, Optional Arrangement*
Reading from top down: Younger bride with father or substitute (*see text*) if brides are sisters.

Maid or matron of honor of younger bride.

Bridesmaids of younger bride.

Senior bride and father.

Maid or matron of honor of senior bride.

Bridesmaids of elder bride.

Ushers paired according to height.

RECESSIONAL AT DOUBLE WEDDING, *Christian Ceremony, Optional Arrangement*
Reading from top down: Elder bride and groom.

Younger bride and groom.

Maids and matrons of honor of both brides, paired.

Ushers of elder bride paired with bridesmaids of elder brides.

Ushers of younger bride paired with bridesmaids of younger bride, or they may go out as they came in.

ALTAR

ALTAR

THE DOUBLE WEDDING

Double weddings with the brides in formal wedding gowns are most impressive. Sometimes the brides are sisters who wish to marry at the same time, occasionally cousins, or just close friends, although in some denominations the brides must be related. The double wedding does not, of course, have to be formal, and the brides, whether in formal attire or in simple traveling suits or street dresses, need not be dressed alike.

In a formal double wedding if each bride and groom have separate attendants it is necessary that they have the same number and that the costumes of the brides' attendants at least harmonize with each other. Sometimes sisters have the same attendants. The brides may act as maid and matron of honor for each other, or each may have separate honor attendants. The grooms, too, may act as best men for each other, or each have his own best man.

In a double wedding all the ushers are paired according to height in the processional. They are followed by the elder's bridesmaids, then her maid or matron of honor, then comes the senior bride on her father's arm, followed by the bridesmaids of the younger bride. After them comes the maid or matron of honor of the younger bride, then the bride herself on her father's arm, unless she is a sister of the elder bride. In that case a brother or other male relative escorts her.

In the recessional the elder bride, who was married first, leads down the chancel steps with her groom and is followed by the younger bride with her groom. The attendants follow in the proper order—those of the first bride, first, or paired with those of the second bride if an equal number makes it possible. Otherwise, they leave as they arrived.

If a church has two aisles, each bridal party may have its own, timing the entrance and exit together.

All the ushers of both groups must be identically dressed, even when the bridesmaids' costumes differ for each bride. The only time, by the way, ushers may ever be dressed differently is when civilians and military men serve together.

The mothers of the brides are escorted up the aisle by ushers in the usual way just before the ceremony begins, with the mother of the elder bride coming first. In entering the first pew they leave room between them for the fathers.

CHILDREN AT SECOND MARRIAGES

It is poor taste for children of a first marriage to even attend the marriage of either parent the second time, if a divorce has taken place. It is quite incorrect for children to attend their mother in a second marriage if she has been divorced. They may be present, or attend her, only if she has been widowed. Where there is remarriage after divorce and there are children of a previous marriage old enough to understand and perhaps resent all the implications of the new marriage, it is certainly more tactful to be married without any but the necessary legal witnesses than to have a small wedding from which the children must be excluded. Etiquette has been devised over the centuries to cushion our sensibilities. In cases such as this we should never forget that children have the most acute sensibilities of all.

THE THIRTY-ISH BRIDE

If a woman has reached her late thirties, then marries for the first time, should she wear a wedding veil and have a formal wedding? Many women of nearly forty today look very much younger. If such a bride feels she can still wear the bridal gown on which she's planned so long and still look her very best, let her wear it. She may find ivory, champagne, or pale blue more becoming than pure white. But if she plans to have bridesmaids and must consider that her close friends, presumably of the same age, may not look *their* best in the traditional costumes of bridesmaids, she may decide to wear the prettiest afternoon gown she can find, or the most becoming traveling suit, and forgo the luxury of a wedding gown and formal wedding.

DIFFERENCES IN RELIGIOUS CEREMONIES

It is interesting to see how essentially alike are the marriage services of different religions. Most Christian ceremonies are similar with but minor differences. As the Christian ceremony developed from that of the ancient Jews, there is between Jewish and Christian ceremonies a definite similarity.

THE ROMAN CATHOLIC CEREMONY   In the Roman Catholic ceremony the father does not give the bride away, although he does accompany her up the church aisle. As he reaches his own pew he steps into it, leaving the bride to make the few steps to the altar with the bridegroom, who comes forward to assist her. The ring is blessed first by the priest before it is given to the groom. Sometimes the entire wedding party enters the sanctuary for the service, with the bride on the left arm of the groom. Some priests prefer that only the couple enter the sanctuary for the blessing of the ring (with an acolyte managing the bridal train), then return to the chancel steps for the balance of the ceremony.

Only if both bride and groom are Catholics may the marriage be celebrated before the church altar. Otherwise, by special dispensation, a Catholic and non-Catholic marry in the church rectory, sacristy, or even in the church, but the marriage must be performed by a Catholic priest. Marriages of Catholics and non-Catholics are also performed at home or elsewhere by special permission, again with a priest officiating.

Civil marriage involving a Catholic is not recognized by the Catholic Church. In mixed marriages performed by a Catholic priest, in which one is a Catholic and one a non-Catholic, the non-Catholic must agree to raise children in the Catholic faith. It is not usual for a Catholic priest to perform the marriage ceremony unless at least one of the two participants is Catholic.

ORTHODOX JEWISH CEREMONY AT ALTAR, *Optional Arrangement:* 1. Rabbi, 2. groom, 3. bride, 4. best man, 5. maid or matron of honor, 6. groom's father and mother, 7. bride's father and mother, 8. bridesmaids, in aisle, 9. ushers. NOTE: The arrangement of the wedding party is not a matter of rabbinical law but of social custom, hence it varies. For example, parents may be under the canopy if there is room. Sometimes only the fathers take part, and their placement is optional.

JEWISH CEREMONIES The Jewish religion has three denominations—the Orthodox, or traditional, whose rituals go back five thousand years; the Conservative, which is less strict; and the Reform, which is the most lenient of all and has among other things no interdictions concerning food.

A friend once told me that in her opinion the very beauty and impressiveness of the Jewish wedding ceremony must be a vital factor in holding Jewish couples together—for the Jewish divorce rate is the lowest of any religious group, even though divorce is not forbidden (as it is among Catholics).

A rabbi of an Orthodox or Reform synagogue will not marry divorced persons who have received only civil decrees. A religious divorce decree is also necessary.

Before the ceremony the bride usually receives the wedding guests in an anteroom of the place where she is to be married. Seated with her attendants, she sees all but the groom before the ceremony. In liberal temples, however, she may even see him.

ORTHODOX JEWISH PROCESSIONAL AND RECESSIONAL, *Optional Arrangements*

PROCESSIONAL *Reading from top down far left:* Bride's mother, bride, bride's father.

Flower girl or page, if any.

Maid or matron of honor.

Groom's mother (*left*) groom, groom's father.

Best man.

Rabbi, not in processional or recessional if ceremony takes place in a temple or synagogue.

RECESSIONAL *left:* Bride and groom.

Bride's parents.

Groom's parents.

(Flower girl or page not in recessional, necessarily.)

Maid or matron of honor and best man.

Rabbi. NOTE: In Jewish ceremony the *left* side is the bride's. Attendants, if any, come up the aisle, paired, before the rabbi and *may* form a guard of honor through which the procession walks.

The Orthodox wedding ceremony is short—just the few minutes, perhaps nine, it takes the rabbi to recite the "Seven Blessings," but in some ceremonies musical participants, the cantor and the choir, may chant the responses and sing special nuptial songs.

When the Orthodox ceremony is held in a synagogue the bride stands to the groom's right before the Ark of the Covenant, which corresponds to the altar, with its cross or crucifix, of most Christian faiths. The bride wears the traditional wedding gown and veil in a formal ceremony—exactly like that of the Christian bride. She has the same attendants, too—maid or matron of honor and bridesmaids if she wishes. Sometimes both fathers and both mothers take part in the ceremony and in the processional accompany the bride and groom. In the recessional both mothers and fathers may walk together side by side. (See illustration.)

In the Jewish ceremony it is the right side of the synagogue or temple, as one enters, which is the bride's, the left, the groom's. Whether or not the ceremony takes place in a synagogue, the couple is wed beneath a canopy supported on standards and symbolizing home. Under the canopy with them stand the rabbi and, usually, their two principal attendants. If the canopy or *chupah* is large enough, the four parents stand beneath it too, otherwise they stand outside the fringe. Next to the rabbi, who faces the bride and groom, is a small covered table containing two cups of ritual wine and two thin wine glasses wrapped in a snowy napkin. The service begins with the blessing of the wine. The service is in Hebrew and Aramaic and, by law in some states, in English, with the rabbi's address to the couple either in Hebrew or in the language of the congregation, for, as not all Catholics understand all the Latin of their own services, so Jews do not necessarily understand Hebrew and Aramaic.

After the wine is blessed the rabbi passes one glass of wine to the groom, who takes a sip and gives it to the bride. The Second Blessing is the blessing of the ring, which must always be plain gold. The best man hands it to the rabbi, who, in those states which require it, says in English, "Dost thou take this woman to be thy wedded wife?" receiving the usual responses in English. The ring is then placed on the bride's right index finger directly by the groom, though any time after the ceremony she may remove it and place it on what our Western society considers the proper wedding ring finger.

The ring ceremony is followed by the rabbi's short address in English (or the language of the congregation) to the couple on the sanctity of marriage and his own personal interest in their future welfare.

Then comes the Threefold Blessing of the High Priest and the ceremonial drinking of the second glass of wine by both bride and groom. The Seventh Blessing, culminating with the crushing of the second wine glass beneath the foot of the bridegroom, symbolizes the sacking of the Temple of Jerusalem and is an admonition to the congregation that despite the happiness of the occasion all should remember and work for the rebuilding of Zion.

The reception-with-collation that follows Jewish weddings is exactly like other receptions except that a special nuptial grace is always offered before food.

As in the Catholic ceremony, the Jewish does not require the father to give his daughter in marriage. He accompanies his daughter up the aisle, always offering his right arm and either steps to his own pew as she stands under the canopy or *chupah* or, in some instances, stands with the attendants and the groom's father (who often accompanies his son) during the ceremony, or with his wife when she is part of it, as in the Orthodox ceremony.

In Orthodox and Conservative Jewish weddings all males in the assemblage must cover their heads. They wear the traditional skull caps or their own hats. Synagogues have skull caps available in the vestibule for men who arrive without their hats. In Orthodox synagogues men and women do not sit together. In both Reform temples and Conservative synagogues men and women sit together and in the Reformed temples men do not wear hats —and women need not.

In the Reformed service the wedding canopy is not required, the second wine glass is not broken, and the rabbi does not read the marriage certificate in Aramaic.

In mixed marriages between Jews and non-Jews a rabbi may perform the ceremony or, as sometimes happens, may assist in a Christian ceremony, acting with the minister and adapting part of his ritual—usually that of the Seventh Blessing—to the occasion. It is only in the most liberal Christian denominations, however, that such a combined ceremony is possible.

THE CHRISTIAN SCIENCE CEREMONY As Christian Science readers are not ordained ministers of the church, merely elected officers, they may not perform the marriage ceremony. When members of the Christian Science faith are married, the ceremony is performed by an ordained minister of the gospel, legally authorized to perform such a duty, or by the proper legal authority.

EASTERN ORTHODOX WEDDINGS The Eastern Orthodox Church, the Holy Eastern Orthodox Catholic Apostolic Church, has numerous followers among White Russians, Greeks, Rumanians, and various Mediterranean groups in this country. It has many ceremonial forms similar to those of the Roman Catholic Church but does not acknowledge the Pope as its spiritual leader.

It requires the publishing of banns on three successive Sundays, and sometimes a brief betrothal service with the exchange of rings is held in the church.

As in the Roman Catholic Church, the bride and groom must fast, make their confessions, and take Communion. The ceremony is celebrated without Mass and always takes place in either the afternoon or evening.

In the Eastern Orthodox Church the ceremony does not take place at the altar but before a table placed in front of the sanctuary toward the center of the church. Relatively few of these churches have pews, a modern development, and guests must stand or kneel before and throughout the hour-long service. None but vocal music is permitted, and the bride enters to the special wedding hymns sung by the choir. The procession is like that in other Christian services. The father of the bride gives the bride away, then returns to the pew with her mother.

In the Eastern Orthodox service the mystical number three, representing the Trinity, has great significance. The double ring ceremony is used—with the rings placed on the right hands of the bride and groom. The priest blesses the rings three times at the altar, then places each ring first on the bride's finger, then on the groom's, Then the best man exchanges the rings three times on the fingers of the bride and groom. Just before the final vows are taken the priest binds the hands of the bride and groom together and leads them three times around the table, which holds the Bible, or Scripture, a cross, a chalice of wine, candles, and flowers. After the final blessing the choir chants "Many Years" three times, then the recessional starts.

Throughout the ceremony the bride and groom hold lighted candles symbolizing the light of the Lord. During the ceremony the priest places gold crowns on their heads.

These are only the highlights of this richly impressive ceremony, usual in all Eastern Orthodox unions. Only during emergencies is the ritual ever shortened.

The Church makes divorce difficult and insists on a religious decree. Remarriage of divorced persons is permitted.

THE QUAKER CEREMONY   Today a Quaker marriage ceremony may see the bride gowned traditionally and veiled, but these simple, unpretentious people believe in the renunciation of worldly display. Their ceremony is as plain as their meeting houses and impressive in its quiet sincerity.

A Quaker wedding may take place in the meeting house or in a private home but notice of intention to wed is made by the couple at least one monthly meeting in advance of the date they have set. It is necessary for at least one of them to be a member of the Society of Friends. It is usual for the parents' permission to be appended to the letter of request, even when the couple is of age. After the letter has been read at the meeting a committee of two women and two men is appointed to discuss with the bride and groom, respectively, the "clearness to proceed with marriage." The committee may discuss marriage and its obligations with the couple just as a minister would, for originally the Quakers had no appointed ministers but instead gathered together in Quaker silence, speaking up in meeting as the inner spirit moved them to express themselves. (In some meetings there now is a regularly appointed minister, especially in the West.)

The committee submits a report on its conferences with the couple to the monthly meeting. Overseers are then appointed to attend the wedding and to advise the couple on the marriage procedure.

On the wedding day bride and groom come down the aisle together—or there may be the usual wedding procession—and take the "facing seats," the benches that face the meeting. After the Quaker silence the couple rises and takes hands. The groom says words to the effect that "in the presence of God I take thee . . . to be my wedded wife promising with divine assistance to be unto thee a loving and faithful husband as long as we both shall live." The bride repeats the answering vow. The couple is then seated again, and the ushers bring forward a table containing the Quaker marriage certificate. This is then read aloud, signed by the bride, groom, and overseers, and later officially registered. The regular Quaker meeting follows.

At the next monthly meeting the overseers report that the marriage "was carried out to the good order of friends." Divorce among Quakers is rare.

THE MORMON CEREMONY   There are two kinds of marriage among the Mormons (members of the Church of Jesus Christ of Latter Day Saints). The first is that of the faithful who are deemed fit to be married in the temples of the church by those holding the Holy Priesthood. In pronouncing the couple man and wife, the priest declares them wed "for time and for all eternity" instead of "until death do you part." Children born to parents so married are believed by the Mormons to belong to them in the eternal world by virtue of such marriages.

Where members of the Church are not considered worthy to be married in the temple for time and for all eternity, they may be married civilly by Bishops of the church or by any properly accredited person. Later, if they comply with the requirements of the church in their daily living they may enter the temples of the church and be married for time and for all eternity despite previous civil marriage.

Mixed marriage, although not encouraged, is permitted. Civil divorce is recognized but divorce is rare among those married in the temples.

IF THERE IS NO RECEPTION

At a small church wedding not followed by a reception the bride often receives with the groom, her mother, and the bridesmaids in the vestibule of the church or on the porch—if there is one in a country church. The groom's mother, if she is unknown in the community, may stand next to the bride's mother, who is always first in line, and have guests introduced to her before they pass on to bride and groom. Or, if she is known, her place is a little beyond the bridesmaids. The father of the bride may or may not stand in line, but he usually circulates in the neighborhood of the receiving line to share in the glory of the great occasion. The father of the groom does not receive with the others when there is no formal reception.

CHAPTER FOUR

THE WEDDING RECEPTION

At a formal reception the mother of the bride is always first in line, as hostess, usually just inside the door. Next to her stands the father of the groom, then the groom's mother, and, last, the bride's father. Then, a little apart, begins the line of the bridal party—the bride to the groom's right, the groom, the maid or matron of honor, and the bridesmaids. Or the bridesmaids may be divided so that half are on one side of the bride with the maid or matron of honor and the other half alongside of the groom. If there is a flower girl old enough to stand in line without getting too restless (pretty unthinkable, I should say) she stands next to the groom. The line remains intact until all guests have been greeted, then the mother, as hostess, leads the group to the bride's table and the parents' table.

MUST FATHERS STAND IN LINE?

At very formal receptions it is usual for the fathers of the bride and groom to stand in line, but not obligatory, especially if the father of the groom is a member of the community. But the fathers stay in the neighborhood of the receiving line, if not actually on it, to make introductions and see that guests are directed to the refreshment tables.

If the father of the groom is quite unknown to the bride's friends it is better for him to be in the line with the bride's father, so he will feel a real part of the important proceedings.

WHO RECEIVES IN PLACE OF THE BRIDE'S MOTHER?

If the bride has no mother to receive for her at her reception her father may receive just inside the door as the host, or he may request a female relative, an aunt, cousin, or grandmother, to receive with him. If this relative is not actually a member of the household the father may be first in line, introducing the guests to the honorary hostess as they file past, "This is Dorothy's Aunt May. May, Mr. Jordan, one of our neighbors."

CONVERSATION AND THE RECEIVING LINE

No one really listens to what you say on the receiving line, as a friend of mine once dramatically proved by muttering something utterly incongruous

RECEIVING LINE AT WEDDING,
Optional Arrangement: Bridal party before fireplace banked with flowers, or possibly in front of picture window.
1. Mother of bride, 2. father of groom (*optional, see text*), 3. mother of groom (*optional, see text*), 4. father of bride (*optional, see text*), 5, 6. bridesmaids, 7. maid or matron of honor, 8. bride, 9. groom, 10. bridesmaid, 11. bridesmaid. NOTE: Whatever arrangement, the bride is on the groom's right except when he's in uniform. The best man is *never* on the line.

as he made his way. You must seem cordial and happy to be where you are. The bride's mother, who—if she doesn't know you—has received your name from an announcer, passes you on to the groom's father, or mother, or whoever is next in line, mentioning your name and if you are someone of particular importance, such as a great-aunt, mentioning the relationship. To each you say, during the brief handclasp, "How do you do," or "Lovely wedding," or "So happy to meet you." To the bride you offer "best wishes" and to the groom "congratulations." (You don't *congratulate* the bride, but you may offer your felicitations.) Your pause before the bridal couple may be perceptibly longer, but you must never hold up the receiving line with long-drawn-out dissertations. You may be able to get the couple's ear sometime during the reception—but even then remember that you are only one of many who deem it their privilege to have a word with the bride or groom.

If there is no one to announce you as you approach the line you announce yourself. Don't assume that the bride's mother, who has perhaps seen you only a few times, is going to remember your name at a difficult time like this. Help her out by saying, "Peter Gossett, Mrs. Kingsley. Such a beautiful wedding!"

HOW TO ADDRESS THE BRIDE If you are on first-name terms with the groom and you are an older relative or family friend, it is expected that you call the bride by her first name. If you are a contemporary of the groom's and on a first-name basis, it does not necessarily follow that he wishes you to be on the same basis with his wife unless she suggests it, especially if you and he merely work together. He may be "Bob" to you, but, especially if your social contact with her is to be very slight, he may be well pleased that you address his wife as "Mrs. Jones" unless you are really urged to do otherwise.

WHAT DOES THE BRIDE SAY? The bride tries to make each acknowledgement of a guest's meeting sound warm and personal. She repeats the name, if possible, "Mrs. Osborn—so very nice of you to come so far for our wedding," or "Cousin Hattie, the coffee table is exactly what I needed!" Unless she is unusually poised and calm, she is safer not trying to remember who gave her what or where strangers to her have come from. She will have to write her thank-you notes anyhow, but the clever bride will, nevertheless, contrive to make everyone imagine that she remembers each gift, in detail, and that she has been waiting impatiently to receive this particular felicitation and present the guest to her new husband or vice versa, if he or she is unknown to him.

WHAT DOES THE GROOM SAY? The groom, usually, less happy than the bride over the necessity of the receiving line, is often less than verbose in his responses. He says an automatic "Thank you so much" or "Lovely, isn't she?" or "So glad you could come" before he introduces the guest to his wife, if introduction is needed—otherwise he passes him along with a "Here is Tom, Angela," or, "Darling, you know Mrs. Osborn."

But the groom, no matter how uncomfortable he may feel at this last necessary formality of his wedding, must look happy at having to greet even a seemingly endless line of guests, when what he needs after all he's been through is a tall drink and his bride to himself, or so he thinks. This is his first public appearance as the head of the house, and he is at this moment as much on display as the bride—in some ways more so, as the guests had a better chance to see the bride during the ceremony than they did him.

MUSIC AND DANCING AT THE RECEPTION

It is not essential to have music at a wedding reception, especially if quarters are small and guests numerous. The choice, if there is music, is a trio—a man who plays both piano and accordion, a violinist, and a guitarist might make a happy combination. If the pianist also is an accordionist the trio is able to move through the rooms or over the lawn, as the case may be, serenading bride, groom, and guests.

For very large weddings, where space permits, a full orchestra with a leader is sometimes seen—but this is doing things in a very pretentious manner, even when the orchestra can convert into a dance band after the receiving line has broken up.

During the actual receiving of the guests the music is restricted to light classical selections. After the line has received all the guests and dispersed, dance music and popular songs are played and sung by the musicians.

THROWING THE BRIDE'S BOUQUET

The bride's bouquet is traditionally thrown to the assembled bridesmaids just before the bride goes to dress for going away. The bride often retains a flower or two for pressing. The girl who catches the bouquet is, as we know, the next to marry.

Occasionally, if some dear relative, such as a grandmother, can't attend the wedding, the bride does not throw her bouquet but sends it to the person who has had to stay at home—with everyone understanding and sympathizing with her action.

THE GROOM GETS THE FIRST DANCE WITH THE BRIDE

As no one but the groom must kiss the bride first, so no one may dance with her before he does. Dancing does not start until the couple has had a little rest and refreshment, and then, at the signal, the groom bows his bride onto the floor and she, gathering up her train, if any, and veil, if long, on her right arm, has the first dance—usually a waltz (and not "The Merry Widow"!), just the two together once around the floor as onlookers applaud. Then the bride's father leads out the mother of the groom and the groom's father dances with the mother of the bride. Attendants join in, candid camera pictures are shot, and finally the guests enter the dance floor, as they desire.

The bride never forgets to dance with her father, or the groom with his mother. After her initial dance with the groom the bride is usually claimed by her father-in-law, and the groom dances with his mother-in-law before asking the pretty bridesmaids. The bride, after dancing with her father, dances next with the best man and then with each of the ushers. Guests may dance with the bride after all her "obligatory" dances are over, but they should not insist, unless she seems still daisy-fresh and really interested in remaining on the dance floor.

After the bride has thrown her bouquet dancing may continue, but usually it begins to come to a close and guests start leaving. It is only the hardy late-stayers who remain to see the bride off.

THE BRIDE'S TABLE

At large formal receptions there is a bride's table, especially decorated with white flowers and with the tiered and iced wedding cake in front of the bride and groom—the groom to the left of the bride. Only members of the wedding party—the maid or matron of honor to the right of the groom, the best man to the right of the bride—are expected to sit at the bride's table, but if some of the attendants are married it is courteous of the bride to include their mates, unless it is certain that they know enough people present to enjoy themselves anyhow. But it is preferable for the unity of the bridal party to be kept even at the bridal table.

Even when the guests are served buffet, the bridal table is waited upon. As soon as the champagne appears the best man proposes the first toast to the bride, with other toasts following as the guests are inspired to offer them—not forgetting, I hope, one to the groom.

At the end of the repast the bride rises—and with her all the gentlemen at the table—to cut the cake. Usually the guests are told that the propitious moment has arrived and gather round.

If the groom is in uniform the cake is cut with his dress sword. At a civilian wedding a silver cake knife is used, and it may have its handle decorated with a streamer of white satin ribbons knotted with bridal flowers. The bride cuts only the first slice, with the groom's help, and she and the groom share it.

THE BRIDE'S TABLE, *seating optional, see text. Reading from left to right:* Usher, bridesmaid, best man, bride, groom, maid or matron of honor, bridesmaid, usher.

THE TABLE FOR THE PARENTS

At a wedding buffet, breakfast, or supper there may be a table for the bride's parents if there is a special bride's table, but not otherwise. It is larger than the guest tables and is the same except for place cards. Placement of guests is as follows: father of groom to right of bride's mother, who is the table's hostess. Opposite the bride's mother sits the bride's father with the groom's mother to his right. The other guests at the table may include the clergyman and his wife. If a high-ranking church official performed the ceremony, or a judge or mayor, he is always placed to the left of the hostess and his wife, if present, sits on the left of the host. Very distinguished guests are seated at this table, but essentially it is for the parents and a few of their close friends.

WHEN THERE IS NO BRIDE'S TABLE

When food served at a reception includes no more than two courses—say chicken salad and ice cream—the dishes may be served in part, at least, from a buffet table whose major decoration is the wedding cake. When there is room, guests, either serving themselves or being served by the caterer's men or waitresses, may be seated at small tables—bridge tables are usual at a home reception. But often they eat standing, with the only service the clearing away of the plates and the passing of the punch or champagne.

When there is no formal bridal table at which all the wedding party—except the parents—are to be served together it is pleasant for the bride and groom alone to be provided with a small table to which they may retire for refreshments after receiving. Although the guests may have been to the buffet table for food and have had several rounds of champagne before the weary bride and groom have a chance to get off their feet for a few minutes before going on with their duties, guests must wait until the bride has finished eating before the cake can be cut and dancing can begin.

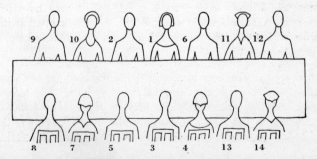

SEATING AT PARENTS' TABLE, *table optional.* 1. Bride's mother, 2. father of groom, 3. father of bride, 4. mother of groom, 5. important officiating clergyman's wife, 6. officiating clergyman (*or see text*), 7, 8, 9, 10, 11, 12, 13, 14, friends of parents.

It is better to serve guests with champagne or punch just as each leaves the line and to make refreshments immediately available than to wait until the bride is through receiving hundreds of guests—at a large reception—before there is any sign of food. Many wise people prefer a little food with champagne or punch as a stabilizer, and there are always guests who must leave early or who have dinner engagements. For them, too, it is preferable to have refreshments early rather than late, as the food at a wedding reception is rarely geared to substitute for a regular meal—with the exception of that at a wedding breakfast.

THE WEDDING BREAKFAST

The wedding breakfast is actually lunch—three courses. When guests are seated it includes a soup course, such as hot clam broth with whipped cream, a main dish, such as sweetbreads *en broche* with green peas and potato balls, plus small biscuits and lettuce salad, and for dessert ice cream in fancy molds, petits fours or tiny petits fours glacés, demitasses, and, of course, the bridal champagne or at least a fine white wine to be served with the luncheon, sometimes both.

When the wedding breakfast is served buffet and there is no way of seating guests, even at small tables, the soup course is usually omitted and the collation limited to two courses. There may be something like whole salmon mayonnaise with wilted cucumbers and dill, green salad, ice cream, not necessarily in forms, little cakes, demitasses, and a good white wine or champagne, or both.

THE WEDDING CAKE

The tiered wedding cake may be a caterer's dream or it may be made in the kitchen of the bride and be as simple or as elaborate as the cook can manage. It need not be topped with the miniature of the bride and groom, as is so often seen, but may be covered with charming sugar flowers in pastel colors with pale green leaves. Or it may be decorated with a pastry tube in white and pastel icing or plain white. The most popular cakes are the silver cake, which is made with the egg whites alone and is light and airy, the gold cake, a yellow pound cake which is richer, and the dark, rich fruit cake, most expensive of all. It should have nothing "written" upon it with icing, however. This sort of decoration is reserved for birthday cakes. The occasional exception is the "ring cake"—a wedding cake baked in the shape of the wedding ring and which may have the bride's initials, first, then the groom's to the right, in icing on the "band." Often little bridal favors are baked in the cake to tell fortunes.

BOXED WEDDING CAKES   Real black fruit cakes, wrapped in foil and boxed in tiny, white, satin-tied boxes, are a luxury these days because of the hand labor they entail. But they are a charming gift to her guests for the bride who can afford this extra but no-longer-necessary expense.

If boxed wedding cake is to be given, it is essential that one is at each place at the bridal table and that some one person, friend or retainer, be designated to give them out to departing guests.

As everyone knows, wedding cake placed under the pillow of a guest brings prophetic dreams. And a bride who looks serenely into a long and happy future with her husband puts aside boxes of her wedding cake to open on her major wedding anniversaries. She may even be able to nibble a piece with her husband when she reaches her Golden Wedding, and enjoy it, too, for good fruit cake grows mellower with age.

PROBLEMS OF THE DIVIDED HOUSE

If the parents of the bride are separated but not divorced they issue a joint invitation to their daughter's wedding and take their accustomed part in the ceremony as if there were no difference. For her sake, too, both officiate at the reception.

Sometimes when divorce has taken place the mother gives the wedding and the father the reception. If he has not married again, he stands first in the line to receive the guests. If he has remarried, his wife acts as hostess. If the bride's mother should attend the reception under the latter circumstances, as might well happen in some instances, she comes as a guest, as she cannot stand at the side of her former husband in his new home and share the duties of hostess with his wife. If, however, her former husband has not remarried she could stand with him on the receiving line in his home, acting as hostess for the occasion, whether or not she has remarried. In this case, as it is his home and not hers, he precedes his former wife on the line.

If the mother, divorced, gives both wedding and reception the father usually gives the bride away, calling for her at her mother's house in the bridal car. If relations are very strained some other male relative may give the bride away, or her mother might if her father is not to attend the wedding. Whether or not he is remarried, he sits in the second or third pew on the left side of the church and, if remarried, may be accompanied by his new wife. She, in turn, may go to the reception if relations are friendly, but neither she nor the bride's father receives.

If the bride's mother has remarried, her husband sits with her in the first pew on the left and the bride's father sits behind them with or without *his* wife in the second or third pew. If the remarried mother gives the reception her husband stands with her on the line and the bride's father, if present, attends only as an important guest.

It is far better to err on the side of too-friendly relations between divorced people on their child's wedding day than to have them remind all present by their stiff attitudes of their own failure in marriage. It must be the bride's great day, and even if her parents have been long divorced and long remarried they are to her forever a unit—the unit that produced her. She needs to feel, if possible, that on this day they are brought together if only briefly by this great common interest, the wedding of their child, and confident that the readjustment they have all had to make has been the kind that will provide future serenity in her own marriage.

CONDUCT OF THE WEDDING GUESTS

As we have seen, formal weddings are complicated affairs and the person receiving an invitation to the reception must reply immediately, although one to the wedding alone, of course, requires no reply. It is important for the bride's family to know as soon as possible how many guests are to attend the reception, so the caterer may receive the necessary instructions.

The guest dresses according to the time of day and the formality of the wedding. (See "What Others Wear.") Unless he or she is actually a member of the wedding party, flowers are not worn.

It is quite incorrect for men to wear any form of evening dress—tuxedos or tails—during the daylight hours, even for a wedding. Evening dress is never worn before six o'clock, although sometimes it is necessary for a man to be seen in formal dress somewhat before this hour but only if he's in transit.

At a church wedding the guest aids the work of the ushers by arriving fifteen to twenty minutes before the ceremony or, at a large wedding, even earlier if pew cards are not issued. It is disappointing to arrive so late that all seats permitting a full view of the altar are taken.

Each guest, man or woman, is met in the church vestibule by an usher who seats each in turn or in groups where all are to sit together (see "Duties of Ushers"). As each guest joins an usher he says, "Friend of the bride" or "Friend of the groom," as the case may be, so that he may be seated on the left or the right side of the church. If he has a reserved seat, he presents the card that has been sent to him to the usher, or tells him his name if he is not recognized. At a formal wedding with ushers on duty no invited guest seats himself.

A guest invited to attend the reception makes his own arrangements to get there, either in his own car or by taxi, or he asks friends he may encounter at the wedding to let him ride with them. The bride's family is not responsible for guests' transportation to or from the reception, although ushers do try to find transportation at least for honored guests who may not have their own.

Before the ceremony begins guests are seated in the pews to which they have been escorted and may talk briefly in low tones suitable to church. They should not move about among their friends, wave, or turn around to talk to friends in rear pews. After the bride's mother is escorted to the front left pew no other guests are seated and the church doors are closed. As the wedding march begins, all guests rise and, turning slightly toward the bride's aisle, await her appearance on her father's arm. In most services all remain standing throughout, bowing their heads if bride and groom kneel or kneeling with them if that is customary. A stranger to the ritual goes as far in following it as his own religious customs permit. If it is not the custom of his own church to kneel, he can at least bow his head over the back of the pew in front of him and stand and sit when others do the same. A Protestant at a Catholic wedding is not expected to make the Sign of the Cross, but a Christian man at an Orthodox or Conservative Jewish wedding would be considered irreverent if he did not wear a hat. For the same reason Protestant women whose own churches do not require head covering in church do cover their heads, if only with a pocket handkerchief or kerchief, when entering a Catholic or Episcopal church or an Orthodox synagogue, so as not to offend.

After the ribbons are in place no one may leave his pew, even if there is possible egress to a side aisle. Ushers escort the bride's mother and honored guests immediately following the recessional, before the ribbons are removed. Other guests leave unhurriedly by themselves only after the ribbons are removed, either by the center or side aisles.

In proceeding to the reception guests give time enough for the bride and her party to assemble for the wedding pictures and have a few minutes to collect themselves before the tiring ordeal of the receiving line begins. As guests arrive they join the waiting line, staying together in family groups, if possible, and never seeking refreshments until they have been officially received, in order, first by the bride's mother.

At large weddings there are always many people from out of town who do not know each other. And, as the parents of the couple are busy on the receiving line and introductions cannot be made in a general way by members of the family in so large a group, it is up to strangers to make themselves known to those in whose immediate neighborhood they find themselves standing or sitting. The host's roof is sufficient introduction.

It is always more tactful for a young girl to approach either an older woman or a girl her own age than for her to speak first to a young man. And a young man shows his breeding by speaking first to an older man or woman, in the hope that he will be taken in hand and introduced to attractive girls. All that is necessary is for an outsider in the group to join others in a casual manner and, when conversation permits, introduces himself or herself with a brief, identifying phrase. "How do you do? I am Nancy Penny (not "Miss Nancy Penny") from Cleveland. Helen (the bride) and I went to school together." Or, "May I introduce myself? I am Joe Choate from Don's (the groom's) office. I'm afraid I don't know a soul here." Any agreeable guest approached in this way will stay and talk and perform introductions or, if he's in the same boat, at least be grateful for company.

Guests may stay until after the bride and groom's departure, if they wish, but if they do stay to see the throwing of the bride's bouquet no woman guest—and never a man—should make any attempt to catch it if there are bridesmaids. It is traditionally thrown to the unmarried girls in the bride's retinue.

As on any other occasion when he has been entertained, the wedding guest seeks out the host or hostess before his departure. He need not write a "bread and butter" letter, call, or send flowers to the hostess after the event, but if he is a close friend he may feel that so festive and joyous an occasion calls for a brief little note of appreciation or a phone call to the bride's mother— or to the person to whom he is indebted for his invitation.

THE EVENING WEDDING

As I have said before, evening weddings take place mainly in the South and West. They may be formal or informal and may take place in church or at home. The preparations and procedures follow those of the daytime wedding. (For dress, see Bride's Dress, Groom's Clothes, etc.)

CHAPTER FIVE

THE HOME WEDDING

Nicest of all weddings, if space permits, is the home wedding. The largest room, usually the living room, is selected, cleared for the ceremony, and an altar improvised before a fireplace or at some other focal point in the room, preferably at the greatest distance from the entrance or entrances. Seats are usually not provided.

If the room is large and the company numerous, "ribbons" are put in place just before the entrance of the bride's mother and the groom's mother to preserve an aisle. At large weddings a small section for the parents and immediate relatives is roped off on either side of the altar, bride's family to the left, groom's to the right.

Where there is a staircase the bride descends it at the first strains of the wedding march; otherwise she and the bridal party congregate outside the entrance to the main room before the music begins. This is only, of course, if the guests are numerous enough, the house large enough to permit a formal wedding if she wants it. Otherwise the bride wears a simple dress (never black) or suit with a hat at noon, an afternoon dress with a hat, or a dressmaker suit, possibly satin. Her attendants dress similarly.

At a very small wedding there may be no music at all and the bride may be in a street dress or suit or afternoon dress. She need not make the usual dramatic entrance but after the clergyman has taken his place merely step before him for the ceremony.

A collation is always served at a home wedding. It may be in the same room as that in which the wedding took place or in the garden or on a porch. A large table is usually moved against a wall and set with the wedding cake as a central theme.

A wedding, of course, may take place out of doors if the climate is sufficiently dependable or if alternative arrangements have been made. Sometimes the witnesses to the ceremony are limited and the reception is large, and often in summer, out of doors.

RECEIVING AT A HOME WEDDING   At a home wedding there is no recessional unless a formal receiving line is to form elsewhere in the house or in the garden. Where there are many guests and space is limited, the receiving line, if there is to be one, is best located in a small room such as a hall or dining room with both exit and entrance to facilitate the flow of traffic. Guests should be able to pass on in to a larger area where they may congregate and have refreshments. In simple home weddings it is usual for the bride and groom merely to turn around at the altar, *after* the groom has kissed the bride, and receive informally with the bridal attendants.

CHAPTER SIX

THE RECTORY WEDDING

Sometimes a couple will choose to be married in the rectory of their church. The simple ceremony takes place in the clergyman's study or in his living room, often before a fireplace. The bride makes no entrance as she would in a formal home wedding, and she wears a suit or a street dress and hat. The groom wears a dark suit or in the country in summer white flannels and a blue coat or a light tropical suit—never slacks and sports jacket.

A few guests may be present, but usually the party is limited to witnesses and parents. Sometimes members of the clergyman's household act as witnesses, and the couple has no attendants. The bride does not have flowers sent for the decoration of the rectory.

After brief preliminary instructions, the bride and groom stand before the clergyman, the bride to the groom's left. Unless the bride's father or a substitute for him is present the "giving away" part of the ceremony, where it is usually used, is done by the bride herself. Bride and groom stand hands at sides until the clergyman asks the question, then she places her hand in that of the groom preliminary to their being joined as man and wife. Afterward the couple receive the congratulations of the minister, then kiss, if they wish. Before leaving the rectory the groom, if unattended, remembers to leave an envelope for the minister containing an appropriate fee—appropriate, that is, to the circumstances of the couple.

Sometimes a couple wishing the privacy of a small rectory wedding do have a reception at a hotel or at the bride's home. In either case, it is never formal, and the bride and groom stand side by side and receive their guests. Later they do not separate as they probably would at a party but remain together to function as host and hostess on this great day.

CHAPTER SEVEN

THE CLERGYMAN'S WEDDING

The wedding of a clergyman presents certain problems not covered in discussions of usual weddings. If he has his own church, synagogue, or temple the bride may wonder if his entire congregation must be invited to the wedding and, if so, how the invitation is tendered. And where does the marriage take place, in his own place of worship or hers? Then there is the question of the clergyman's son's wedding and that of his daughter. Where and when do such weddings take place and who officiates? Who gives a clergyman's daughter away if her father performs the ceremony? What, too, does a clergyman wear to his own wedding? These questions have come up sufficiently often in my correspondence for me to cover them briefly here.

First, a clergyman, like any other groom, is married in the church, temple, or synagogue of his bride by her own clergyman. If her place of worship happens to be his own, then they may be married there by some other clergyman of his faith, his superior, a friend, or a clergyman from a neighboring parish or congregation. Sometimes, if he has an assistant, he is married by him, but someone of his own rank or higher usually would perform the ceremony.

A clergyman usually chooses the morning hours up until noon for his own wedding, avoiding (as a matter of convenience among Protestants) his particular Sabbath. He wears his clericals, if they are customary in his faith, not his vestments. If the hour chosen should happen to be late afternoon, four-thirty, he may wear morning dress or, depending on the season, other suitable clothing (see "The Groom's Clothes"), with or without the clerical collar and rabat depending on his denominational custom.

A clergyman-father performing the marriage for his daughter cannot give her away, where this procedure is called for in the ceremony. Instead, she is escorted at a formal wedding by an older brother, a brother-in-law, a godfather, an uncle, or a family friend. After delivering her to the groom her escort may step back and into the first pew on the bride's side or remain to give her away. When the clergyman asks the question concerning the giving in marriage the bride's mother steps forward and places the hand of the bride in that of the clergyman or in that of the groom, depending on the denominational custom.

In a very small community and in a church, synagogue, or temple that is unusually well-attended, a clergyman might announce his forthcoming marriage from the pulpit and invite the congregation to attend if the marriage is to take place in his own house of worship. But so informal a procedure, though it seems to be followed occasionally, risks the exclusion of some members who might not have attended services on the day the announcement was made. More correct is the sending of individual invitations of some kind (see "Wedding Invitations") to the entire mailing list. The reception, of course, could be and is really expected to be limited to close friends, associates, and relatives of bride and groom. In a small community where a bride, for extenuating reasons (no relatives of her own, for example), might come from a distance to be married in her husband's own church, synagogue, or temple, the people of the congregation might give the reception, especially if the couple's joint circumstances were modest.

A clergyman who has not been assigned his church, temple, or synagogue may be married anywhere by a religious ceremony, even in a quiet one in his bride's home or at a friend's home.

A clergyman whose son is marrying is usually given the honor of conducting the ceremony in the bride's place of worship with the bride's clergyman assisting. If the bride's home is at considerable distance from his own the father's congregation does not usually expect to be invited en masse, though various active members of the congregation might well be included in the invitation list.

CHAPTER EIGHT

ELOPEMENTS AND CIVIL CEREMONIES

THE ELOPEMENT

A friend of mine with three lovely daughters gave the first a traditional big wedding with no expense spared—including that of a dance band for the reception for more than three hundred. His other daughters, of course, were attendants, and he told them that they'd better make the most of their day of glory as one big wedding was all he could stand—and we can sympathize with him. "My other daughters can expect just a good strong ladder on a nice moonlight night," he warned.

There are elopements and elopements, of course. The kind we don't like to see is the one where parents have not become reconciled to the marriage and the couple runs off in defiance of parental displeasure. The young people should both work very hard, if necessary, to win all four parents over to the match. A runaway marriage where there has been bitter objection can start a couple off very defensively.

Then there is the elopement that is frequently a great relief to all concerned, when, because of social position, an elaborate wedding is expected. Sometimes a girl—or her groom—cannot bear the idea of all the complexities and pressures of a big wedding, and, once they have announced their intentions and received the blessings of their friends and parents, they go off and are married—in a religious ceremony, I hope, for civil ones can be very dreary—with two friends as witnesses, perhaps, or even two strangers provided by the officiating person. They then phone or wire their families and friends to whom only the day of the elopement, not the fact of it, will come as a surprise.

The bride and groom with a wide, expectant circle of friends do better to elope in this way than to try to have a small wedding from which they would find it difficult to exclude so many people close to them—friends whom they might greatly prefer to the relatives who must be asked, for example.

GIFTS FOR ELOPERS?

Sometimes formal announcements of the wedding are omitted after elopements, but more usually they are sent, with the place of the marriage always stated and the date and year. If a civil ceremony has been performed, only the name of the city or town appears. If the couple was married in church, it is optional whether the church is mentioned.

Strictly speaking, any couple for whom wedding invitations were not issued should not expect wedding gifts, even if they send formal announcements of the marriage. But of course close friends and relatives will send gifts, as will many friends who receive the announcements. If an elopement is a second—or third—marriage for bride or groom, no gifts at all should be expected, although again there will be friends—usually of the less married or not previously married partner—who may wish to send gifts. But once you have given a wedding gift, even to your dearest friend, you cannot be expected to give one for a second marriage, too.

CIVIL MARRIAGE

For a civil marriage in a registrar's office or in a judge's chambers the groom wears a dark business suit and the bride wears a simple street length suit or dress, never a wedding gown. She wears a corsage, instead of carrying a bouquet, and before the brief ceremony begins she removes her gloves and places them with her handbag. Where there is no best man and witnesses are garnered from the office staff, the groom quietly hands the officiating person a sealed envelope containing the fee before the ceremony—anywhere from ten to twenty-five dollars, depending on the circumstances. Where a high-ranking official—a mayor, governor, or Supreme Court judge—has performed the rite as a special favor to the families involved, no fee is offered but a gift is sent after the ceremony—again depending on the circumstances. Anything from a case of Scotch to a bottle or so of fine champagne or perhaps a fine pipe or a humidor of good cigars might be appropriate.

CHAPTER NINE

THE TROUSSEAU AND BRIDAL SHOWERS

Many of us wish that fashion did not change so often, but the fact that it does has made the matter of her trousseau much easier for the modern bride. Her grandmother was expected to bring with her enough clothes to last at least a year, along with all the linen, bedding, pots and pans—enough to set up housekeeping from scratch. Today's bride, even when her personal allowance permits a lavish wardrobe, seldom buys more than enough clothes for the first few months of her married life—with the exception, of course, of her lingerie. Fashions change too fast. In fact, they change even in the matter of household linens, and Americans move so often, especially in cities. That's why few of us have hope chests kept from our early teens any more. Instead of collecting a lifetime's supply of embroidered linens, we buy what we need and what we have room to store, replacing as needed with linens that suit the taste of the moment.

In fact, the very word "linens" is now a misnomer. Linen sheets which used to be *de rigueur* for the bride's household trousseau are seldom seen now, and a good thing, too, as they needed daily changing to look fresh and inviting, whereas good quality percale keeps its finish and stands up better in commercial laundering.

MUST EVERYTHING BE WHITE?

It is a sound idea to choose white sheets for the trousseau linen. Colored sheets are dramatic but they must be planned for each room and can't be used interchangeably as can basic white sheets. Unless she knows exactly what her decorative scheme is going to be, the bride should introduce colored sheets and pillow cases, if she wants them, only after she is settled in her new home. She may find her new husband has decided opinions concerning sleeping between pink or yellow sheets, with or without rosebud borders. He may be strictly a white-sheet man.

Good white percale or fine cotton top sheets may, of course, be attractively monogrammed in color with one or more initials. There should be some reason for the color—it should match the blankets or pick up a decorative note in the room. But in my opinion the most luxurious monogram of all is done in white, on white, doubly impressive by its subtlety.

While white sheets are always basic, the modern tendency is to treat bathroom linen as part of the decorating scheme. All-white bath linen, therefore, seems a little dull, although white linen guest towels can never be in too great abundance even when bath towels, face towels, and washcloths in terry may combine two or more colors to suit the particular bathroom.

The thing to remember when deciding on colored bath linen is, again, that the towels, like colored sheets, cannot be used interchangeably. They must all match when hung together in a bathroom. Fingertip guest towels are best in white or may match the bath towels or their initialing. Gray bath towels with maroon monograms might be attractively accompanied by maroon fingertip towels with matching monogram in gray. But an ill-assorted collection of towels, no matter how fresh, in any bathroom makes for a "busy" decorative scheme.

WHAT DOES THE BRIDE PROVIDE?

Today's bride still comes to her husband with a dowry, too—the clothes for her honeymoon, as many nice underthings as she can afford or as are given her by her family and friends, and as much in the way of household linens and kitchen equipment as she can manage. If she has a bank account, too, so much the better. But many a bride, married without fanfare or much advance preparation, comes to her husband with little more than the clothes on her back. And the couple acquires what is needed for housekeeping as the home is furnished, with the husband footing all the bills, if necessary.

But the bride who can afford it still brings with her a lavish dowry of household linens—enough to last through their first few years of marriage, at least, and geared of course to the way she and her husband will be living. Here is a basic list for a household trousseau, expansible or contractible, of course, according to the size of home the couple will have and the scale on which they will be living—and, too, depending on the bride's resources.

BASIC LIST

LINENS   4 sheets for each bed (two top and two bottom, if they are to be hemstitched or monogrammed)

2 pairs of blankets for each bed
1 quilt (preferably eiderdown) for each bed
4 pillowcases for each bed
1 bedspread for each bed
6 bath towels for each bathroom
6 matching face towels for each bathroom
6 matching face cloths for each bathroom
1 shower curtain for each bath room (nylon or plastic are best)
6 guest towels for each bathroom
1 doz. kitchen towels
1 doz. glass towels
1 bathmat to match each set of bathroom towels
1 dinner-size damask or linen tablecloth in white or pale colors, to overlap table not less than 12″, not more than 18″, with 1 doz. matching napkins, dinner-size
3 luncheon sets for daily use with matching napkins
2 tray cloths
2 tray sets with 2 napkins each (one napkin for the tray, one for the toast)
1 doz. cocktail napkins
2 or more sets of practical table mats in straw, cotton, woven matting or any of the modern, tasteful materials used for the purpose with matching or contrasting napkins (white luncheon napkins, simply hemmed, go with everything)
1 quilted mattress cover for each bed
1 blanket cover for each bed

KITCHEN EQUIPMENT   (Often provided by showers)

4 paring knives
1 kitchen carving knife and fork
1 canister set
set of mixing bowls
measuring spoons
measuring glasses
kitchen scales
1 bed tray
1 serving tray
4 pot holders
6 kitchen aprons (if the bride will officiate)
vegetable bin (if not
bread box   )built in
1 dishmop
broom and dustpan
1 dry mop

flour sifter
rolling pin
ladle
funnel
meat grinder
cooking spoons
jelly molds
vegetable parer
kitchen teapot
dish drainer
folding steps
1 doz. dish cloths
2 sets covered icebox dishes
bread knife
apple corer
colander
casserole

1 wet mop
carpet sweeper (vacuum can be a
    wedding present or bought
    after marriage)
step-on garbage can
kitchen stool
sieve
frying pans (large and small)
griddle
covered kettle
teakettle
custard cups
electric mixer
waffle iron

muffin tins
cake tins
egg beater
electric blender
toaster
cookie sheet
large and small pitchers
bread board
can and bottle openers
chopping bowls (large and small)
spice sets
grater
coffee maker
paper towel holder with towels

GLASSWARE AND CHINA (These are usually gifts and the bride should state her needs, when asked. Breakage is very heavy and good glass expensive to replace.)

1 dozen or more water glasses
2 dozen ice-tea glasses
1 dozen sherry glasses
1 dozen cordial glasses
1 dozen or more wine glasses
1 dozen champagne glasses, solid
    stems
2 dozen "old-fashioned" glasses

2 dozen cocktail glasses
2 dozen highball glasses
1 dozen sherbet glasses
1 dozen punch glasses
6 "shot" glasses
12 juice glasses
8 fingerbowls, matching plates (op-
    tional)

CHINA FOR A SIMPLE HOUSEHOLD

1 basic set utility china (optional)—may be pottery or some one of the "unbreakable" wares
1 set fine china (optional)
If no matching sets are to be used:
8 breakfast plates
12 breakfast coffee cups (allowing for breakage) not necessarily matching, but if plates are patterned, cups should be solid color, in blending tone (for coffee lovers there are jumbo cups)
8 breakfast butter plates
8 egg cups or small dishes for eggs (milk glass reproductions of setting hens are amusing for the purpose)
8 cereal dishes
1 covered dish for toast (may be in any color that looks well with breakfast plates, or may be silver or silver plate)
1 small platter for bacon, pancakes, etc. to match or blend
1 small creamer

1 sugar bowl

1 large creamer for cereal

12 dinner plates (if matching set is not used)

12 butter plates in plain china, such as white or bordered Wedgwood, or in ruby, amber, green, amethyst or clear glass to blend, if matching set is not used

3 vegetable dishes, may be silver or silver plate or match set

1 small platter, may be silver

1 large well and tree platter, silver or silver plate

1 sauce boat with saucer, or bowl for gravy, may be silver, match set, or in blending china.

1 ladle for gravy, may be china, silver, or glass

1 bread plate, or tray, may be silver, china, or wood. Basket should be wicker. Bread board is pleasant for informal meals. (Queen Victoria used one on her table as an example of thrift—bread was cut only as needed)

Condiment dishes, may be china, fine china, pottery, silver or glass; antique or modern. Cut glass is back in favor

1 water pitcher, may be silver, modern or antique glass, antique china or pottery, such as Majolica or any of the glazed wares for informal use

2 sets of salts and peppers, may be silver but may also be china or glass, antique or modern. Gourmets like wooden pepper and salt grinders

8 cream soups (optional)

8 soup cups (optional)

8 individual covered casseroles (very useful and may be used, informally, for soups)

8 thin teacups for afternoon tea

8 tea plates, need not match and can be in any fine, blending china or in glass

8 demitasses preferably in fine china but may be glass or, for a completely informal household, pottery

1 teapot

1 coffee pot or coffee maker

1 round serving platter for molded desserts, cakes, and pies, may be china, glass, sometimes silver

8 dessert plates, may match set or be in any fine china, glass, or, informally, pottery

8 "English" dessert dishes, deep enough for baked apples, sauced puddings, etc., though these are often successfully served on a flat plate, as is ice cream

1 serving bowl for desserts, fruits, occasionally for salads

1 salad bowl with serving fork and spoon—the choicest, seasoned wood is best

6 individual table ash trays. May be silver, pewter, antique or modern china, glass, pottery (for informal tables along with shells)

SILVER

The bride's family usually gives her her flat silver, and the groom's family gives the silver tea service as a wedding gift.

If having a silver tea service will create a storage problem in small quarters where it can't be on display, the groom's family might better give a china service or, perhaps, broadloom if that is a paramount need of a young couple on a slender budget. It is nicer, of course, for both families to give enduring things such as silver or fine china, but many young couples would prefer checks to use only in part to start purchases of silver or fine china on a budget basis, adding to their stock as their living quarters and their social activities grow.

Whether or not she is to receive her flat silver all at once or purchase it a setting at a time, the bride should choose her pattern and monogram as soon as her invitations are out, so friends who wish to give her silver may match their gifts. She may register her silver pattern and that of her china and glass at shops from which it will probably come. This will be of much help to her friends. Silver serving dishes and platters don't necessarily match the flat silver but should be in a harmonizing style. Loveliest are the old Sheffield platters and serving dishes, plated of course on copper, but there are many modern pieces in sterling or, more usual, plate, in a variety of classic patterns that complement flatware.

If it is out of the question for a bride to have even a starter set of sterling, a fine quality of plate in a simple pattern will do. But, given a choice between a complete set of even the best plate and a four-place setting of sterling, the wise bride will chose the sterling, adding to it on anniversaries and other gift-giving times. Sterling is a permanent investment requiring no upkeep or replacement. It always has a company complexion and will be just as acceptable and beautiful twenty or thirty years after the wedding.

Styles in silver are fairly stable. Heavy embossed or repoussé silver, which is hard to clean, is better avoided for the simpler, more modern, patterns. But if you have inherited heavy, heavily-decorated silver, it is heartening to know that you can still add to your set, as the great silversmiths still produce for these familiar open-stock patterns. And often you can pick up extra forks, spoons, and knives at auctions or old silver shops. In fact, a friend of mine, with no family to give her silver and a slim budget on which to start, deliberately chose one of the lovely, decorative old patterns, buying it secondhand, and from time to time picks up six spoons or a dozen salad forks in antique shops and elsewhere at half the price they would be new from the silversmiths that have been making them for a century. And, as with all fine sterling, their beauty increases with use and the years.

A dozen of everything in all-sterling flatware is ideal, but a young bride can do very well with four- or six-place settings consisting of dinner knife, dinner fork, salad fork, butter knife, teaspoon, and dessert spoon. The teaspoon will be used for consommé and cream soup, for desserts in small containers, for grapefruit or fruit cup, as well as for tea or coffee. The dessert spoon will do for soups in soup plates and for desserts served on flat plates. She will need two tablespoons and two extra dinner forks to serve with, a carving set, a cake knife and, of course, after-dinner coffee spoons.

If her budget is limited she should avoid purchasing flat silver that is used only occasionally—fruit knives and forks, oyster forks, ice-tea spoons, fish forks and knives, cheese scoops, and the like. If ancestral silver is to be used, it is probable that some of these things will be missing anyhow and substitutes will have to be found.

A word of warning to the bride who rejects offers of sterling silver when she marries in favor of household furnishings she feels she needs more. *If you don't get your sterling now, you may never get it.* Once a family starts growing, its constant needs too often absorb funds we thought would be available for something so basic as sterling. So we "make-do" over the years with ill-assorted cutlery, deceptively inexpensive because it wears out. Then come the important little dinners, as a young husband gets up in the world. We push a chair over a hole in the living room rug, put a cushion under the pillow of the sofa with a sagging spring, and distract the guests' attention from the pictureless walls by charming flower arrangements. But there is nothing that can be done about the shabby flatware, which, somehow, is still with us, even though it was bought just to tide us through the first year in the tiny apartment. But then, of course, the baby came.

Never again in her lifetime will a girl find her family and friends in such a giving and sentimental mood as they are at the time of her wedding. At no other time will it occur, very probably, to any of them to give her so much as a silver ash tray. But at the propitious moment they think of sterling silver as *the* gift for the bride as part of her dowry—as it should be. So, though she starts married life without as much as a roasting pan, she should be able to lay her table—if it's only a bridge table—with the kind of silver she'll be proud to see on whatever table the future has in store for her.

Right from the start, it is the wife's task to set the tone of the family's living. And one's everyday living should differ very little from that presented to guests. We are all strongly influenced by things around us. What family doesn't deserve the sight of an attractively set dinner table, even when guests aren't present?

SHOULD GIFTS OF SILVER BE MONOGRAMMED?   The bride should decide how she wishes her silver marked, then, if it is given her in a complete set, it arrives already monogrammed. If friends give her flat silver from a chosen pattern, it is better to send it unmonogrammed, in case she receives many duplicates. Hollow ware and trays should be sent unmonogrammed to make them exchangeable.

HOW SHOULD SILVER BE MARKED?   In hope chest days a girl began collecting her silver piece by piece, long before a knight even appeared over the horizon. It was monogrammed with her maiden initials or the single letter of her last name—or with her family's crest, and it always remained her personal property. After she was married, or if her husband's family presented silver, that silver was marked with her married initials or the single initial of the new family—or with her husband's crest. This meant naturally, differently marked silver used on the same table. And while this is very usual, indeed, especially when we have inherited silver, many brides prefer unity in monogramming. And so the bride often has her silver marked with her new initials, or the single initial of her new name or with her husband's crest, if they both wish (but this is more expensive than simple monogramming).

Ornate initialing or monogramming has given way to very simple markings, usually suggested by the jeweler as being in harmony with the design of the silver. Sometimes triangles or inverted triangles are used, with the bride's initials or her first initial and the groom's combined with his last initial. This may be N (his last name)

    J P (their two first initials)

    or

    J F

    G (her maiden initials in an inverted triangle or with her first two initials at the base if she prefers).

BRIDAL SHOWERS

WHO GIVES SHOWERS   Showers are popular in small communities and a practical and attractive way to help a bride set up housekeeping—but senseless if she comes from a family that "has everything." For the basic idea of a shower *is* practicality—the bride's closest friends give her quite utilitarian things—kitchen supplies, linens, cooking equipment, staple groceries, stockings, all to form a little dowry or nest egg of needed articles with which to start off her new life.

Showers may be given by any close friend, usually a member of the bridal party, if there is to be one. Often they are given by the maid or matron of honor, if she isn't a sister or other relative and if she lives in the community and has the facilities for entertaining. They are not given by members of the bride's or groom's families. Showers are always supposed to be a "surprise" to the bride, who supposedly has no idea that an invitation to tea might mean that she is to be showered with gifts. Actually, she is usually quietly consulted as to her needs.

Shower gifts are mostly quite inexpensive, as the bride's intimate friends usually give her wedding gifts as well—though in some cases it is perfectly possible that the shower gift and wedding gift will be combined, as in the gift of an electric toaster or waffle iron at a kitchen shower. Guests at a shower always take a gift. As only the closest friends of the bride are asked, it seems a slight if someone asked neglects to send a little gift, if she can't take it in person. Of course, if the hostess has erred in asking a mere acquaintance of the bride to attend a shower for her, then the recipient of the invitation is under no obligation either to attend or send a gift. She must, though, in all courtesy, reply to the invitation and give some believable excuse for not attending.

A groom is not supposed to be present at the various daytime showers his bride may be given—and there may be several of them. But in some communities the custom of giving joint evening showers is growing. And the men—among them the ushers and best man—give little special gifts to the groom, usually a poor, neglected soul in the wedding setup. He might receive handkerchiefs or ties or garden tools if the couple is to have a house. It would be poor taste, however, to give a joint shower in which the bride received anything so intimate as lingerie. Here is a list of possible gifts for *joint* showers:

BRIDE	GROOM
stockings	ties
linens	socks
canned goods	shirts
cosmetics	handkerchiefs
soap	barbecue supplies
kitchen utensils	ash trays (who ever has enough?)
cook books	tools
closet accessories	garden equipment
bathroom equipment	books
gloves	wines and liquor
sewing materials	liqueurs (a very nice idea)
plastic container for paper cups for bathroom or kitchen	garden seeds

It is necessary, of course, for shower-givers and guests to get together on themes, colors, and the bride's needs. If she is to have a kitchen with red accessories, a kitchen shower should have all gifts geared to the theme—even to a red step-on garbage can or folding stepladder. If either bride or groom is to receive things to wear, exact sizes should be ascertained.

The kind of shower should be chosen that permits even the most short-of-money bridesmaid, who is involved with her own expenses of the wedding, to make her own gay contribution, if only a dime-store pot-holder.

Gifts should all be assembled, wrapped, and perhaps screened off, before the bride arrives. Any later-arriving guests present theirs personally. The bride opens all gifts at the designated time—usually before the refreshments, which are simple.

The verbal thank-you's of the bride at the time she opens her gifts are sufficient, though she should write brief notes or phone to anyone who sent a gift but could not come herself.

DUTIES OF THE SHOWER GUEST   The girl initiating the shower sends or phones the invitations, stating whether it is a general or a specific shower. Guests are expected to discuss with the hostess what the bride needs or what her color schemes will be.

Shower guests, whenever possible, should all be assembled before the bride arrives, so the "surprise" will be complete.

CHAPTER TEN

WEDDING GIFTS

MUST ONE SEND A GIFT?   People who receive invitations to wedding receptions send a gift if they accept, but need not, necessarily, send one if they regret. If they are close enough to either family to be invited to the reception, though, they usually will want to send a gift whether or not they will be present.

SUITABLE GIFTS   Never feel you must "match your gift to the circumstances." If you are the bride's former teacher, living on a small salary, don't feel you must give a gift well out of proportion to the amount you should spend, just because the bride will have a big wedding and perhaps live on a lavish scale. Lovely gifts need not be expensive. A friend with taste who knows old glass or silver can give a present that will really be treasured and spend anywhere from a dollar to five dollars for it. A gardener with the knack for it might make a dream of an indoor rock garden and take it to the young couple himself. With shears, old maps, or floral wallpaper and some glue, clever fingers can transform a metal waste basket into a most useful and decorative receptacle for the new living room. And how about a charming scrapbook ready for the clippings about the engagement and the wedding— or perhaps already containing them as you have gathered them yourself? Such gifts have real sentimental value and show you have given affectionate thought. They have something money can't buy. One of my own wedding gifts was a single, lovely covered dish of old Meissen removed from her own china shelves for me by an old girlhood friend of my mother. It was the nucleus of my collection of old Meissen, and I never forget who gave it to me, whereas I sometimes come upon one of many silver dishes and serving forks and wonder who sent it, although I did keep the proper record at least until all gifts were acknowledged.

IF THE GIFT IS AFTER THE WEDDING   While wedding gifts should arrive, if possible, well before the wedding to allow for their display should the bride so desire, in actuality many arrive after the wedding has taken place—sometimes months later. Such gifts, if they are monogrammed or initialed, bear the married initials of the bride or the husband's crest and are addressed to the bride and groom, not to the bride alone, as are gifts arriving before her marriage actually takes place.

GIFTS TO THE GROOM   Gifts are always addressed to the bride before the marriage, even when close friends of the groom send them. If no "at home" card is in the invitation they are sent to the home of the bride, if it is certain that they will arrive after the wedding or if they are sent in response to an announcement. Of course, if one knows exactly where the couple's future home is to be the gift can be sent there, if it is certain someone will be present to receive it should it arrive while the bride and groom are still on their wedding trip.

YOUR CARD WITH GIFTS   When you send your wedding gift enclose your card with a brief line of felicitation at the top, in ink. You address your gift to the bride in her maiden name if it is certain to reach her before the wedding. Gifts sent after the wedding—if sent in response to an announcement—are addressed to "Mr. and Mrs." If the gift will arrive after a wedding to which you were invited, send it with a short note of explanation in a sealed envelope if it is sent from a shop. You might write:

Thursday

Dear Betty,
Sorry this is so very late.
We have been traveling. I wanted you to have this from our favorite wedding-gift shop, so I waited until we returned and I could choose it myself.

Love,
Thelma

DISPLAY OF WEDDING GIFTS

A formal display of wedding gifts is less often seen now, although it is still good taste to exhibit them. If the reception takes place at the bride's home, the gifts may be shown at a tea before the wedding or placed on display on white damask-covered tablecloths in some room of the house, so guests may view them during the reception. Where there are many valuable gifts private detectives are engaged to guard them.

Cards are now removed from gifts displayed, and gifts of more or less like value are grouped together to discourage comparisons. Checks are recorded on cards which are propped up for display. They read, "CHECK, $100" but the donor's name is not given, though the bride or groom often reveal the information, as checks usually come from close relatives.

THE BRIDE'S THANK-YOU LETTER

Even if the bride does not know the sender of the gift, who may be a particular friend of her husband's, she herself must write the thank-you note just as soon as she possibly can—within two or three weeks certainly, after receipt of the gift. At a large wedding, where hundreds of gifts must be personally acknowledged, an engraved card may be sent immediately upon receipt of the gift. It reads:

> Miss Penelope Kingsley
> wishes to acknowledge the receipt
> of your wedding gift
> and will write a personal note of
> appreciation at an early date

Stereotyped letters are never worth reading. You know just what they are going to say the minute you see a first line that begins, "It was so kind of you to send the lovely cake plate." If you were thanking Aunt Matilde face to face, would you say anything so stuffy? Wouldn't you be more likely to say, "What a lovely cake plate!" Here is how you can put such spontaneity in a thank-you note:

> Thursday

Dear Aunt Matilde,

The lovely cake plate arrived safe and sound. I always wanted Dresden and now I have a piece with which to start what I hope one day will be a real collection. When you see us in our new little apartment I think you will like the way I've used it in our decoration.

> Love,
> Frances

Your letters and you should be just alike. It's foolish to make the written expression of your personality old-womanish and out-of-date if you talk like a nice, alert, and friendly person.

Thank-you notes for wedding presents are signed, "Sincerely," "Cordially," "Love," or "Affectionately" (if the bride knows the sender well), "Mary"— or "Mary Kerr" with her new surname to someone to whom she would not be "Mary."

CHAPTER ELEVEN

THE HONEYMOON AND POST-WEDDING CALLS

Somewhere at some time I remember reading a stiff-necked interdiction against the term "honeymoon." Supposedly "wedding trip" is better usage. In French the term for this carefree period of adjustment is *"lune de miel,"* literally "moon of honey," and there is historic significance in the term. In Europe, in some countries, the couple drank a special beverage, or mead, called metheglin, a honey wine, for a month after the wedding—hence the "honey moon."

The modern honeymoon is much simpler, and usually much shorter, than that of previous generations. My mother's lasted three months and included a trip on horseback through part of the Rockies. In the 1860's a honeymoon could encompass a whole summer and might include the entire wedding party—at the bridegroom's expense. The depression following the Civil War put an end to such extravagance, fortunately, or it still might be the expected thing for the groom to take his and his bride's attendants along on what should be a most private holiday.

WHERE TO GO AND FOR HOW LONG

The place and duration of the honeymoon must depend on the amount of time available and the financial resources of the groom—for this is his expense. Unless, of course, either his or her parents, or perhaps both together, are able to give the couple a honeymoon as a wedding gift. A trip to Europe or a world cruise is, barring the interruption of war, a standard wedding gift on the part of parents who can afford it.

Even if both bride and groom must go back to work immediately after the ceremony, as so often happens in this tense society of ours, some sort of quiet getting away together should be planned at the earliest possible moment, before the two are caught up in the whirl of conjugal responsibilities. For suburbanites a week end in a nearby city can be honeymoon enough, if only that time can be spared. For city dwellers, a trip to the country may accomplish the same thing—a chance to be more or less alone during the first awkward stage of marriage, a time free of routine chores and of relatives and well-meaning friends.

Anything too different from the sort of thing each is used to may be a dangerous choice in the way of a honeymoon. A new husband who loves

to walk would make a mistake in choosing to introduce his bride to the
rigors of distance hiking if she's never trod on anything but city pavements
and doesn't know what it means to put her feet in low-heeled shoes. Too
many adjustments should not be made at once—to marriage, and, at the
same time, to a strange and perhaps too demanding environment or activity.
Instead, the couple should choose the kind of place where both will feel
comfortable and where, if they want it, there will be some sort of diversion
available in the company of other young people. It is helpful if the honeymoon isn't too—sometimes embarrassingly—private, for it then eases the
couple gently into married life as it really is, not two on an island of love
and kisses, but two as a unit in a community of friends and neighbors.

POST-WEDDING CALLS

In the days when formal calling was *de rigueur* everyone asked to a wedding was expected to call on the bride's mother within three weeks after the
wedding and on the bride and groom within a reasonable time after they
had returned home, especially if they had issued "at home" cards.

In actuality, if these formalities were rigidly carried out in our modern
society it would make for considerable confusion. Imagine the mother of
a bride, after a large, elaborate wedding to which anywhere from three
to five hundred guests have come from far and wide, having to receive
them all, or at least the women representatives of families, within three
weeks after the last bit of confetti has been swept out of the hall! She'll
want to talk over the wedding with many of her close friends, who would
call in the natural course of events. But to be at home to so many! And
the poor bride! It will be months before she has her home running in any
proper order. If she's like the average American girl, she knows less than
nothing about housekeeping and is either just learning to cook or is trying
her best to act mature with a servant or servants whose very functions she
hardly knows. Into the middle of all this, and with wedding gifts still being
acknowledged, no doubt, step two or three hundred callers? Ridiculous and
improbable, you say, but that's what is *supposed* to be correct.

As a matter of fact, the bride's mother, who has gone through considerable
in preparation for even a small wedding, expects to hear from no one who
attended the wedding and reception, with the exception of a few close
friends and relatives who let her know, by calling, dropping her a note, or
phoning, how well everything went and how pleased they are at the new
addition to the family.

If the bride and groom settle down in a new neighborhood they do not
expect their parents' friends who came to the wedding to come from another community to call upon them. They can hope that their immediate
neighbors will call, in time, usually in a most informal manner. The local
minister, in a small community, is certain to call.

The modern bride doesn't stand on much ceremony these days. If she's
just fallen heir to a country house and finds its intricacies too much for her,

she may merely poke her head through her neighbor's hedge and beg for advice, long before the neighbor has decided it is about time to run in and make herself known. It is certainly simpler to say to a neighbor, who may not yet be conscious that *you* are the one who's just taken the Murphy house, "How do you do? I've just moved in up the street. I'm Margaret Tillman. I wonder if I can ever achieve a garden like that?"

Of course, if a bride moves to New York, she may live in the same apartment house twenty years without knowing more than the face of the apartment holder next door. In this case, she *must* make every effort to establish contact with others in the city with whom she and her husband can begin a social life.

CHAPTER TWELVE

WEDDING ANNIVERSARIES

Today, most couples celebrate their wedding anniversaries in some quiet way as they come along. Some special attention is often paid the tenth, and usually the following are really celebrated with one's friends: the twenty-fifth, the fiftieth, and the seventy-fifth.

The same formality attends the wedding anniversary invitation as the wedding itself. Invitations may be, of course, engraved (see Correspondence Section) or handwritten or telephoned. They may or may not mention the occasion, in the latter instance merely asking friends to dine on the particular evening. Gifts should not be expected, except between husband and wife, but of course they may be given by close friends who wish to give them.

There is a tradition for the giving of wedding anniversary presents, though, of course, it need not be followed. Changing times, new fabrics, and products make it advisable to extend the list somewhat.

1st	paper, plastics	8th	bronze or electrical appliances
2nd	cotton	9th	pottery or china
3rd	leather or any leather-like article	10th	tin or aluminum
		11th	steel
4th	linen, silk, rayon or nylon or other synthetic silk	12th	silk, nylon, linen
		13th	lace
5th	wood	14th	ivory or agate
6th	iron	15th	crystal or glass
7th	wool, copper, or brass	20th	china

25th	silver	50th	gold
30th	pearls	55th	emeralds or turquoise
35th	coral or jade	60th	diamonds or gold
40th	rubies or garnets	75th	diamonds or gold
45th	sapphires or tourmalines		

FORMAL INVITATION TO A WEDDING ANNIVERSARY

Mr. and Mrs. Roland Purdy
request the pleasure of
the company of
Mr. and Mrs. Robjohn*
at a dinner to celebrate
the seventy-fifth anniversary of their marriage
on Saturday, the eighteenth of February
at eight o'clock
850 Park Avenue
R.s.v.p.

or,

In honour of
the fiftieth wedding anniversary of
Mr. and Mrs. Roland Purdy
their sons and daughters
request the pleasure of
the company of
Captain McMurray*
at dinner
on Saturday, the eighteenth of February
at eight o'clock
850 Park Avenue
R.s.v.p.
Mrs. Gibbs Purdy
88 Cricket Lane
Larchmont, New York

This form is used where listing of all children would crowd the invitation.

or,

Mr. and Mrs. Gibbs Purdy
Mr. Allan Nye Purdy
request the pleasure of
the company of etc.

*Handwritten

REPLIES TO FORMAL INVITATIONS TO A WEDDING ANNIVERSARY

Mr. and Mrs. Robjohn
accept with pleasure
the kind invitation of
Mr. and Mrs. Roland Purdy
to dine
on Saturday, the eighteenth of February
at eight o'clock

Captain McMurray
accepts with pleasure
the kind invitation
of Mrs. Gibbs Purdy
to dine
on Saturday, the eighteenth of February
at eight o'clock

CHAPTER THIRTEEN

CHRISTENINGS

WHEN THE BABY IS CHRISTENED

Usually only infants and very young children are given godparents, among those Protestants believing in baptism. When a child for some reason is not christened until he is eight or nine years old, presumably at the age of understanding and able to read the service with the clergyman, he may accept the sacrament on his own cognizance. His parents are present and he usually receives a baptismal gift of some significance.

INVITATIONS TO THE CHRISTENING   Invitations to a christening are always handled informally, by brief note, by phone, by telegram, or in person and should go only to those believed to be really interested in the event by reason of their relationship to or close friendship with the parents. Here is an example:

Dear Gertrude,

Cornelia is being christened this coming Sunday at church. Will you stay after the regular service for the ceremony and then join us at home for lunch?

Love
Norma

Even such an informal note is not necessary if a guest is readily reached by phone.

DRESSING THE BABY FOR THE OCCASION   The armful of petticoats and the long, embroidered christening dress are lovely but definitely a luxury, as the modern baby in everyday life is free of such bundling. If you have a christening gown that's been handed down or can borrow one or are given one, use it by all means, but a short white dress for a little baby—the kind all newborn babies receive from someone or other—will do for the christening. And shoes, even those little silk-topped and soled ones, are not necessary either. The baby wears white booties in cold weather and can be barefoot when it's warm. If he needs a bonnet and coat, it can be of any baby color, or white, but both are removed, as noted, before the ceremony.

WHAT OTHERS WEAR   Adults and children attending the christening, whether at home or in church, dress as for church, and the women's heads are covered—to be punctilious—even at home during the religious ceremony if covering the head is the custom for women in the church of the officiating clergymán. It is *always* correct for women to go covered to church or to any church ceremony such as a wedding, funeral, or christening, even when it is not actually required as, for example, among Congregationalists. Head covering is required in church by Catholics and expected by Episcopalians.

GODPARENTS AND THEIR RESPONSIBILITIES

Godparents chosen, according to the custom of various denominations, from among close friends and occasionally relatives of the baby's parents are preferably of the same religion as the parents. Or, if they are not, they must be willing to answer the baptismal questions in the prayer book to serve at an Episcopal Christening. Catholic children must have Catholic godparents. And Catholics may not serve as godparents to a child of another faith.

Godparents about the same age as the parents, or younger, should be chosen very carefully from among one's oldest and closest friends, as the association itself should be long and close with the child. In the service the godparents promise to oversee the spiritual education of the child and see that he is confirmed. They have an implied responsibility of parenthood, should the actual parents die before the child reaches maturity (although legal guardian arrangements are usually noted in wills). Once asked to serve as a godparent, a friend is virtually bound to accept.

The godparents need not be present at the christening but may be represented by proxies, who, too, are chosen from among close friends. Often various friends and relatives invited to the christening bring gifts to the baby, but the godparents always present him with something he can use and perhaps hand down to his own children—a silver porringer, a mug, or a fork, spoon, and pusher set. One of my children received a magnificent engraved Sheffield hot-water plate, fine for keeping his baby food hot but also fine for the time he begins entertaining in his bachelor quarters. The plate will be excellent for hot hors d'oeuvres.

CHURCH CHRISTENINGS

If the christening is to take place in church, arrangements are made with the clergyman and the time set. As babies are not always too happy about their christenings, it is best for them to be brought to the church just before the event is to take place. The godparents arrive either with them or shortly before and take their places near the font in front of the clergyman, with other friends and relatives near by.

If the baby has been dressed in cap and jacket for the trip to the church, the outer things are removed and, if the church is chilly, the baby wrapped in a white afghan and handed to the godmother, without his cap. As the clergyman takes his place, the congregation stands. At the proper moment in a Protestant ceremony the godmother hands the baby to the clergyman and, when asked his name, pronounces it very carefully. In the Catholic ceremony the godmother or a nurse holds the baby over the font to receive the holy water. If other than a godparent holds the baby, spiritual contact by the godparents is established by the godparents touching the child during the ceremony. If the name is at all complicated, it should be written down for the minister and handed to him just before the start of the ceremony, as the baby's baptismal name becomes his legally.

After the close of the service the clergyman signs the baptismal certificate, usually included in a little commemorative book where there are spaces for the names of the godparents, the parents, and the various witnesses to the ceremony. At a Catholic christening the baptismal certificate is not necessarily presented at the close of the ceremony but is available anytime. It is required for the child's first Holy Communion, for Confirmation, and for marriage.

THE FEE   As with other church sacraments, there is never any required fee, but parents usually do hand the minister an envelope containing an appropriate amount, anywhere from five dollars to fifty dollars or more, depending on whether or not the christening is to be followed by a large luncheon, tea, or reception—to which the clergyman and his wife or the priest must be invited. Of course, particularly on Sunday, they may find it difficult to attend.

CHRISTENING AT HOME

The baby is more likely to enjoy his christening if he may go through the short ceremony in the comfort of his own home, with as little change in his usual routine as possible. Some Protestant denominations permit home christenings. Catholics do not permit home christenings except in case of dire emergency before the administration of last rites.

The requirements are a pleasant, flower-decorated room with space for the assembled guests, a small, waist-high table on which is set a silver bowl to be used as the font. If the table has a high patina, it is often left bare, or it may be covered to the floor with damask. The base of the bowl may be placed within a circlet of delicate, white babylike flowers—sweet william, gypsophila, white violets, anemones, lily of the valley, or even fern. At a late afternoon christening followed by tea, white tapers in silver candlesticks, lighted of course, are suitable on the table if they don't crowd the arrangement.

At the home christening the clergyman is not necessarily in vestments, but if he is to dress he is shown to a special room. If the christening is followed by a reception he changes into his street clothes immediately after the ceremony before attending the reception.

If very young, the baby necessarily appears only briefly—just long enough for the ceremony. If he is older, and sociable, he may enjoy watching the celebration of the occasion by his elders from some quiet corner, where he may be occasionally admired but not disturbed by his well-wishers. He may even be able to enjoy a grain or two of his christening cake.

REFRESHMENTS

Champagne, plain or in a delicate punch, has replaced the traditional caudle cup at christenings. But at an afternoon christening a good dry sherry or, in winter, a hot mulled cider or wine might be very welcome.

A morning or early afternoon christening is sometimes followed by a luncheon, often buffet. But whether a tea or a luncheon is given, the food is more or less the kind one serves at wedding receptions. There is some kind of festive beverage for toasting the baby's health, and the christening cake. The godfather proposes the first toast.

The cake is a white cake with white icing. It may have white icing decorations and often bears the baby's initials or name and sometimes the date of the christening.

It should be kept in mind that this is a celebration in honor of the baby, following a formal religious ceremony. It has a character quite different from a cocktail party and should be kept on such a plane that even the most conservative baby could not object to the behavior and bearing of his elders.

CHAPTER FOURTEEN

DEBUTS

In Victorian days, when young girls up to the age of about eighteen were closely guarded at home their debuts or formal introduction to their parents' friends in society had some meaning. Today it is an empty form rejected by most young women whose families are in a position to launch them in the once expected manner. If a daughter of mine really wanted to make her debut, I'd insist on her joining a group in a mass debut. I cannot imagine buying a "list" of so-called eligible young men I have never seen to fill out the stag line. And I'd be disappointed if any daughter of mine would be interested in such shallow social success.

KINDS OF DEBUTS

The individual debut, as I've indicated, is growing rare indeed, and debuts, when they do take place, are often en masse. Debutantes make their bows in large groups at the various Cotillions and Assemblies in the large cities. These are charity affairs to which the girls' fathers make a contribution in lieu of spending a usually much larger amount on a private debut. The mass debut does, therefore, serve a useful purpose, besides giving a young girl a chance to wear a beautiful dress (usually white and diaphanous, though pastel colors are often permitted by the Committee). Often the debutante balls are preceded by private dinners in honor of individual debutantes. In many cities it is expected that each girl attending the ball subscribe for two escorts.

In the outrageous twenties, and even during the thirties, there were huge private debuts—especially in New York—whose cost and elaborateness were positively vulgar. Fifty thousand dollars for a debut was not an eye-popping sum by any means. And all this fuss for young girls who had been seen around in night clubs and all the most prominent restaurants and resorts almost since their emergence from pigtails!

While the private debut still occurs occasionally, it is usually in the form of a dinner party or perhaps a dance at home or in a hotel. However, the afternoon reception or tea during the winter and spring college holidays has its adherents, especially among the more conservative. The dinner party, which is usually given for the girl's friends rather than for those of her parents, may be given by her mother—or grandmother or other sponsor—together with the mother of another girl, as a joint effort.

Girls who do come out usually wait until they have finished school. But as more girls are now going to college instead of stopping their schooling at seventeen or eighteen, those who choose higher education often bypass a debut. For the debutante is officially on the marriage market, while the college girl with four years or more of education ahead of her is probably thinking in terms of career-before-marriage. So why should she make her debut?

THE EVENING DEBUT

The debutante at an evening debut may wear a bouffant dance dress, usually white, and her mother's formal evening dress may be dark in color but preferably not black. Both may wear some hair ornament—flowers or a diadem but not hats. The father, in full evening dress, does not stand in line but, as at a wedding, usually hovers in the vicinity to act as host. Friends of the debutante, in dresses similar to hers, who have been asked to "receive" with her do not actually stand in the line, either. They just feel a little more important and, at a sit-down supper, are seated with the debutante. (For details of formal dance see "Formal Dances at Home.")

THE DEBUTANTE TEA

The debutante "tea" is more properly a reception, as it is often followed by dancing, which naturally requires gentlemen, and the gentlemen, in turn, often prefer something stronger than tea. In this case, the tea table ceases to be the central theme and must cede honors to the bar. If the debutante tea dansant is in a club or hotel, champagne or cocktails may be passed by waiters or a table may be set up with a punch such as "Fish House."

There is a receiving line consisting of the mother of the debutante, or whoever the sponsor may be, and the debutante herself. Sometimes her father is in line for a short while in the beginning. She carries her father's bouquet and displays her other flowers in a floral background where she and the hostess stand, usually before a fireplace. Even though it may still be daylight, the curtains are drawn and the candles lighted. The debutante wears the kind of dress a bridesmaid would wear, usually white but perhaps a pale color. Her mother, or sponsor, wears an afternoon dress in a color other than black, preferably something fairly neutral, and they both are gloved but hatless. The debutante may wear a flower in her hair.

The debutante, as at an evening debut, asks numerous young men to act as ushers and tries to arrange it so that there are approximately eleven men to every ten girls. Some of her best friends are asked to "receive" with her. They wear fluffy, semiformal dresses, and perhaps the debutante may give them identifying corsages, but they do not stand in line. They do, however, stay throughout the reception.

The debutante's flowers come from her relatives, her best beaux, her family's friends, but it is not at all obligatory for all attending to send flowers and girls never do.

After all guests have been received the debutante may join the dancing, usually accepting her first invitation from her father.

Guests who must leave before the receiving line breaks up, wait their chance on the side lines, then say a brief "good-by and thank-you" first to the hostess, then to the bud. But every young man present at a tea dansant should seek a dance with the debutante, and well-bred young men remember to ask her mother as well as other older ladies present.

CHAPTER FIFTEEN

COURTSHIP AND ENGAGEMENTS

Eventually, in the course of things, a girl begins to narrow her interest in young men to one young man. A fairly long courtship and a brief engagement seem to be a safe formula. The courtship period is casual and informal, without pledges on either side. It gives each a chance to know the other better—and yet make a graceful exit if that seems expedient.

Wherever possible, a girl should receive an attentive man in her own home and not see him exclusively in the artificial atmosphere of the theater, restaurants, and other places of amusement. He needs, if possible, to evaluate her with her family, or at least in her own home, and to see her with her friends, to help him decide whether or not life with her would be comfortable and companionable as well as romantically satisfying.

If her relationships with her family are good and happy, no girl need be ashamed to bring a suitor into the most modest home, even if he be from a more prosperous background. And, conversely, a man should be highly suspicious of the girl who does not wish him to meet her family and her intimate friends. It is important, too, for the girl to know and become familiar with his background and interests.

It is impossible for a man and woman to know whether they are really suited to one another if they spend all their courtship time in the exclusive company of each other. Each should give the other an opportunity to expose to searching consideration his best and worst sides. They should see each other in the give and take of family life, or at least among close friends with kindred interests. Otherwise a resulting marriage is in for rude shocks and accusations of, "If I'd known such and such I'd never have married you!"

MEETING A MAN'S FAMILY AND FRIENDS

If a girl is taken to meet a man's family before he has said anything definite about marriage, she should be careful to be friendly and interested, but not *too* interested. Often a man is chary of introducing a girl into his own circle before he has very nearly made up his own mind about her, because either she or his family and friends might assume a seriousness about the relationship that may never develop. If he is wise, he might warn his family in advance not to jump to conclusions. And the girl must pretend not to hear any little inter-family raillery concerning John and herself. Nothing frightens a man more than presumption on the part of a woman. If ever a woman needs to be obtuse with the male it is when he is courting her but has not yet declared himself.

GIFTS BEFORE THE ENGAGEMENT

A man's gifts to any girl other than a relative, before the engagement is announced, should be relatively impersonal. In other words, they should never admit—or imply—intimacy or be so costly or conspicuous as to cause talk. He might give her a scarf, gloves, or handkerchiefs, but not a dress, hat, underthings, hosiery, or fur of any kind. He might give her a book, but not an expensive set of books. If she's a bachelor girl with her own quarters he might give her a cocktail shaker or a toaster, if she needed or wanted one, and he knew her well enough, but never a bed jacket or anything so intimate. He would, of course, pay for her taxi but never embarrass her by trying to pay the grocery or other household bill at the door or in a shop where they happen to be together. To do anything that puts a girl in an untenable position is to be less than a gentleman.

THE EXCEPTION IS LIQUOR   While a man visiting a woman at her own home may not pay for groceries or other household supplies should they happen to be delivered, he does pay for anything, such as liquor or food, he has ordered sent in, just as he would if he were the host in a restaurant. If, with his hostess' permission, he has ordered a special dinner sent in from a caterer, instead of taking her out, he takes care of the check. If he feels he has accepted her hospitality too often and wishes to replenish her bar supplies, he may do so—within reasonable limits. And always with her permission.

REFUSING A GIFT   A too-intimate or too-expensive gift is sometimes offered by a man who just doesn't know any better. If a girl receives such a gift she should be tactful. She should not show it nor try to explain it. She should, instead, return it to the donor with some such remark as this, "I know you didn't realize it, but I couldn't possibly accept such a gift from you, much as I appreciate your kindness in wanting to make me a gift." If she does this in a kindly way he won't be too embarrassed, and she won't be compromised.

THE PROPOSAL

The number of men today who ask, in so many words, that a girl marry them is probably very limited, despite the testimony of the movies and fiction. The engagement is usually approached by a very circuitous route, probably because young people now have ample opportunity to spend time in each other's company and to know each other well before any discussion of marriage takes place. Victorian times must have been very difficult for suitors, because it was only after they had proposed, and received father's consent, that they had any opportunity to know the girl of their choice. And even then contact was on the most restricted plane and sternly chaperoned.

Any girl with common sense knows when a man is trying to propose and either helps him commit himself or discourages him from doing so before he has gone too far. It is certainly unkind to encourage the expression of a proposal only to turn it down. Yet an obstinate coyness on the part of a girl who would really like to accept a proposal, were it offered, often deters a man, who fears he will be refused. In other words, it is up to the woman, at the right time, to let a man know that a proposal, if offered, will be accepted.

THE CONFERENCE WITH FATHER

These days people feel it is their right and privilege to become engaged and even to marry without the prior permission or sometimes even the knowledge of the bride's parents—or of the groom's. Perhaps the pre-proposal conference with father is archaic, but the well-bred young man will want to make some attempt to confer with his future father-in-law alone or in the presence of his fiancée. The reason for this is still the practical one. A girl's parents, especially if they have been supporting their daughter, have the right to know just how her fiancé proposes to take care of her after the marriage, in short, what his income is and his savings, if any, and what may be his future expectations.

Many young marriages need some subsidy. But for young people to assume blithely that their parents will go on bearing some of the burden of their support, without having had a complete understanding as to the extent of the help beforehand, is to court trouble.

In the ecstasy of love many a young pair vastly overestimate their ability to get along on the income available to them once they leave their parents' homes. They have little or no idea of what it costs to run even a simple establishment in the way they have been accustomed to living. A business-like talk with the bride's father or perhaps a conference with all four parents can help start a young marriage along the right path. If the bride's father knows, for example, that the attractive and promising young man Mary wants to marry has only five hundred dollars in the bank, he may be able to augment that amount with a substantial cash gift in lieu of an elaborate wedding. Or he might plan a very practical present, such as a major furnishing item for their living quarters.

I once knew a debutante who, given her choice of a $20,000 wedding or the cash, chose the wedding with its twenty bridesmaids, full orchestra, champagne, several hundred guests and all the attendant expense, and then went to live in a one-room apartment with her young husband, whose salary was fifty dollars a week and whose savings were nil. Most brides don't have such a choice—or so little sense, either—but they can be helped to face reality with the counsel of older advisers.

It is very comfortable to start married life on a sound financial basis. If you are marrying on a shoestring, there is no shame in admitting it to one's family and intimate friends. In this way the inevitable presents can have a more practical aspect, especially if the engaged couple prepares a list of the things needed—from a toaster to dinnerware—and leaves this list, providentially, with their parents.

HOW LONG SHOULD AN ENGAGEMENT LAST?

It is wise for a couple to fix a date for the expected marriage, as a too attenuated engagement is hard for both, but particularly hard for the girl should the marriage not take place and her other possible suitors slip out of her circle. Except under extraordinary circumstances, a formal engagement should not last more than six months. And any man or woman who lets the engagement run into a matter of years for any reason whatsoever is not a good marriage risk—at least not for that possible partner.

IS AN ENGAGEMENT IRREVOCABLE?

Engagements were made to be broken. Never, if you have just become engaged, assume that the engagement will necessarily terminate in marriage. If more engagements were honestly viewed before marriages are entered into there would be far fewer divorces. A man or woman should never be made to feel that by virtue of the exchange of an engagement ring he or she is irrevocably committed to the appointed marriage. This does not mean that an engagement should be lightly entered into or lightly broken. But an engagement is a tentative thing. It means, "If all goes well between us, we hope to be married at a later date."

THE ENGAGEMENT RING

Many a modern bride eschews a diamond or any other engagement ring. If she does want one, she should help choose it, with the kind of wedding band she wants in mind. If her wedding ring is to be wide, she may decide that it would be more attractive to have that inset with small diamonds or some other stone, making it engagement-and-wedding ring in one. Two rings on one finger don't always make an attractive or comfortable combination. Sometimes an eager fiancé, buying an engagement ring without his bride-to-be, selects one that can't be worn with an ordinary wedding ring, so that after she is married the bride can wear her engagement ring only if she takes off her wedding ring, or she must have a new wedding ring made to fit under the engagement ring setting.

If an engagement ring is given, the wedding ring should be of the same metal. A wedding band shouldn't be yellow gold, for example, and the engagement ring platinum.

HOW MUCH FOR THE RING? We used to believe a young man should buy the very finest engagement ring his circumstances permitted. I believe that if the engagement is to be fairly long and if a ring seems very important to the girl, she should have a ring. What it costs, whether or not it is a diamond, what size the stone is—are all irrelevant. Any girl worth her salt prefers a ring her man can really afford to one for which he must go into debt or which his father must buy for him. On the other hand, she will gladly accept a family heirloom, if she is offered it, in place of a newly bought ring. And it is quite possible she may really prefer some other article of jewelry, even when money is no consideration—a watch, bracelet, or pin.

THE GIRL'S WEDDING RING

Although the bride may help select her wedding ring, she does not rightly see it again until the wedding.

The engagement ring is not engraved on the inside, but the wedding band usually is—"J.W.M. to A.P." and the date, with the groom's initials first, or "A.P.—J.W.M." and the date, with the bride's initials first. If the band is wide, there may be room for anything else that may seem lovely to the betrothed ones. Inside my own for special reasons a tiny rose is engraved on each anniversary. Which reminds me that the modern bride doesn't worry about the occasional removal of her wedding ring—especially if she has one set with jewels that need professional cleaning.

THE MAN'S WEDDING RING

If the groom wishes to wear a wedding ring, he should select one that is plain gold and fairly narrow but definitely masculine. It is engraved as a gift from his bride "A.P. to J.W.M.," with the date and, if the bride wishes, any little phrase or motto that means something to them both.

IF THE MARRIAGE DOES NOT TAKE PLACE

If a girl decides to break her engagement she returns the man's ring, although legally it is hers to keep—a gesture that would certainly be considered mercenary. If her fiancé dies no one would expect her to return the ring to his family, if he has one, although if she does not know them well and has received a family heirloom as an engagement present she should at least offer to return it. If she has been given a new ring she can continue to wear it, but not on the engagement finger. She may wish to have the stone reset in some other piece of jewelry.

WHERE WILL THEY LIVE?

With very few exceptions, it is a very bad choice for a young couple to plan to live with either set of parents, even on what is intended to be a temporary basis. If their parents live well and the young people are reluctant to start out in the more modest kind of home they can provide for themselves, it is possible they are not yet adult enough for marriage. If it is impossible to find separate quarters, it is safer for the marriage if the newly married people share the home of strangers rather than that of either of their families. It is difficult for even the most understanding parents to think of their children under their own roof as anything but children. And even the youngest husband needs to *feel* he is the head of the house.

ANNOUNCING THE ENGAGEMENT

Many of us have regular or occasional dealings with the press. There is an engagement or a marriage to be announced, a garden club meeting to be reported, obituary information to be given, the announcement of a child's birth, or father's election to club office. Sometimes a public-spirited citizen will want his local paper to improve some condition or back some cause. How do we go about giving such information to the press?

One sure way to tread on everyone's toes is to try to give lists of names and other information to a newspaper over the telephone. Instead, typewrite, or have typewritten, what you would like to have published, remembering to give all the facts, all names and titles and addresses in full. It is easy to follow the form of these news items in the paper, avoiding nicknames and being sure that your story follows the basic rule of journalism so that when completed it answers the questions, "Who?, What?, When?, Where?" (and sometimes "How?").

Here is an engagement announcement that answers the newsman's questions.

CYNTHIA ANN TALBOTT
TO WED ASA G. SANTOS

Mr. and Mrs. Loring Talbott, of 10 Low Place, announce the engagement of their daughter, Cynthia Ann, to Mr. Asa Griggs Santos, son of Dr. and Mrs. José Santos of Havana, Cuba.

Miss Talbott is a graduate of Miss Hewitt's Classes and of Vassar College. Mr. Santos is a senior in the Yale School of Medicine and a member of Phi Beta Kappa. He will intern at Lying-in-Hospital, Boston. The wedding will take place in June.

It is a good idea to put some kind of heading on the news story so a busy editor can see at a glance what it is about. To look professional, the head should space out to the same number of "characters" for each line. Each letter and space is a character in the count. For your purpose you needn't be too accurate about it.

In the news story just given as an example, Low Place is, let us say, in the town in which the paper is published, so it is not necessary to give more than the street address.

HOW MUCH INFORMATION IN THE ENGAGEMENT ANNOUNCEMENT?   If an engagement is between very prominent people the engagement announcement may carry all the family information about the couple. But usually the engagement announcement is brief and the more detailed information, if it is considered newsworthy, is carried by the papers at the time of the wedding. But when it is given with the engagement news it is usually repeated when the wedding is reported, so if you think the papers will use it with either or both stories, furnish it yourself, don't leave it to telephone reportage.

THE RELEASE DATE

When an engagement is of sufficient news importance to warrant straight news and perhaps press association coverage to other cities, it is best to decide on the date you would like to see it appear in all your city's papers simultaneously. Then you furnish it to each paper in written form one day, or, preferably more in advance with the notation FOR RELEASE MONDAY, FEBRUARY 6TH typed in the upper left-hand corner in capital letters. To the city editor, to whom such a release should be directed, this means that you have put the same limitation on all other releases furnished his rival papers. If in his estimation the announcement does not merit regular news coverage, the city editor will route it through to the society editor, to whom such announcements are ordinarily sent. Weeklies need engagement and wedding announcements three or more days before their publication dates.

CHOICE OF THE RELEASE DATE   Why so many people send in their wedding and engagement announcements for the Sunday papers, I don't know. That is one way to have your cherished notice attenuated and lost in a sea of other notices or dropped entirely, because of the competition from announcements the editor may consider more newsworthy for one reason or the other. Even if your notice does get into the Sunday paper, it is very likely that your friends will fail to see it because so many are published that day. And the possibility of a picture being used on Sunday is very slight indeed—again because of the competition. But Monday is a slow news day. An engagement announcement sent to an urban paper for hoped-for Monday release should be so marked (FOR RELEASE MONDAY, FEBRUARY 6TH) so that it won't get into the Sunday paper by mistake. It should arrive at the newspaper office sometime Saturday, preferably in the morning before eleven. Wedding announcements should be timed to reach papers so the news can appear as soon after the wedding as possible. It is quite usual for early editions of city papers to publish details of an important afternoon wedding before it actually has taken place. It is convenient for the paper to have the story all set and ready to run before the wedding occurs. Wedding news that arrives very late must be very important to make the paper.

IDENTIFYING YOUR RELEASES If you send news to the paper or to radio stations, always place your name, address, and telephone number in the upper righthand corner of the page. This is so the editor will know who stands back of the story and to whom he may turn for additional information, if needed. Unidentified stories are often discarded by editors, unless they wish to bother to check the information by phone.

In a household where there is a social secretary, her name appears on social announcements from the family. Or the father of the bride or engaged girl can have his own secretary prepare and send out the information. She can refer to him or to the girl's mother any requests for additional information. Any member of the family or a close friend may act as spokesman with the press, but the bride or bride-to-be does not send out her own notices under her own name, even though she may prepare them for someone else to send for her. She may, of course, answer questions from the newspapers herself, but it is more usual for editors to call her parents for added information, if they are available for comment.

SENDING PICTURES If you wish, send a picture of the engaged girl with the announcement. The picture should have a caption attached, not written on the back of the picture. Type the information, "Miss Cynthia Ann Talbott whose engagement to Mr. Asa G. Santos has been announced," on a piece of 8″ x 10″ typewriter paper. Enclose picture, accompanying release, and protective cardboard in a mailing envelope and send "special" to papers of your choice or, better, have delivered by hand to either city or society desk as the news seems to warrant.

IS THE MAN'S PICTURE FURNISHED? Wedding pictures often include the groom, but pictures used with the engagement announcement usually do not include the fiancé. However, when the principals are page-one news the paper will usually request a picture of the fiancé if it does not have one of him in its files or "morgue." For example, if an unknown college student became engaged to the daughter of one of the wealthiest men in the country the papers would certainly consider the young man worth a picture and might, in fact, go to some lengths to secure one, if it wasn't furnished with the announcement from the family.

DIFFERENT PICTURES TO COMPETING PAPERS Newspapers prefer, if possible, to receive pictures that differ somewhat from those furnished to the other dailies in the same town or city. When the girl selects her pictures from the proofs, she should keep this in mind and try to choose several poses instead of having just one printed. Pictures for the press should be furnished on glossy stock, 8″ x 10″ size for easy filing. It is presumptuous to ask the paper to return them after use—or even if they don't use them.

DON'T CENSOR THE PRESS If you are a newsworthy person it is probable that all leading newspapers have a file of information on you or your family. If an announcement of your marriage is going to the papers and you have been married before, do not omit that information, as some paper is sure to include it, perhaps to the irritation of others that didn't check their files more carefully. The information does not have to be played up, but it is part of the story. A line or two at the bottom of the story can cover it: "This is Mrs. Morgan's second marriage. Her first husband was Robert Henry from whom she was divorced last year. She had two children by this marriage, Patricia and Ogden Henry."

The polite phrase "from whom she was divorced" is better than "whom she divorced," which sounds accusative. Even if her husband divorced *her*, the fact is never stated in social announcements. Never, ". . . Robert Henry who divorced her last year."

COMPLICATED RELATIONSHIPS

If a girl whose parents were divorced and whose mother has subsequently died has been brought up by her aunt and uncle, the announcement of her engagement reads like this:

Mr. and Mrs. Seth McClure, of 7 Fifth Avenue, announce the engagement of their niece, Sally Guthrie, to Mr. Penn Snyder, Jr., son of Mr. and Mrs. Penn Snyder, also of this city [often the fiancé's complete address is omitted from the engagement announcement]. Miss Guthrie is the daughter of Mrs. McClure's late sister, Mrs. Broadhurst Guthrie and Mr. Joseph Guthrie. [This indicates that Sally's father was divorced from her mother at the time of her mother's death and that he has married again. The phrasing is necessary, for to call her the daughter of Mr. Joseph Guthrie and the late Mrs. Guthrie would be, in effect, to kill off his second wife.]

When parents are divorced the mother makes the announcement but the father must be mentioned in the story. Let such an announcement read:

Mrs. French Weeks, of 1125 Park Avenue, announces the marriage of her daughter, Miss Pamela Weeks, etc. Miss Weeks is also the daughter of Mr. George Ranson Weeks of Asheville, N.C.

If this form is used no mention of the word "divorce" is necessary, as it is clear the parents are divorced and it is assumed, unless otherwise noted, that Miss Weeks lives with her mother.

If one parent is dead, the announcement reads:

Mr. James Muncie announces the engagement of his daughter, etc., etc. Miss Muncie's late mother was the former Geraldine Pew, descendant of

General Custis Pew, one-time business associate of Abraham Lincoln. (This is sheer fabrication, of course, but it is agreeable to give the mother some identification of her own in this case as she is obviously "the late Mrs. James Muncie," and some mention of her must be made. This is better than, "Mr. James Muncie and the late Mrs. Muncie.")

When a woman has reached "a certain age" she has the choice of letting her parents or some relative, such as her brother, if her parents are dead, announce her marriage or of doing it in conjunction with the groom. Formal engagements between people, one of whom, at least, has been married before, are rarely announced. The publicized engagement period does seem the prerogative of youth, along with the bridal veil and orange blossoms. Older or divorced people usually forgo both in favor of a simple announcement of their marriage. If a joint announcement is to be made it reads:

Mrs. Prime Holden, of 8 East 10th Street, and Mr. Rutherford Tyng, of Princeton, New Jersey, announce that their marriage took place Saturday, April 3rd, at the Church of the Ascension, Baltimore, Maryland. Mrs. Holden, the former Elsbeth Finn, is the daughter of Mr. and Mrs. Clarence Finn, of Baltimore. Her marriage to Mr. Harry Holden, of Tulsa, Oklahoma, was terminated by divorce last year.

Mr. Tyng, son of Professor and Mrs. Rufus Tyng of Princeton, is an instructor in mathematics at Princeton University, where his father heads the Physics Department. The couple will make their home in Philadelphia.

Under special circumstances sometimes a bachelor or an older, unmarried woman adopts a daughter who may or may not have taken her adoptive parent's name. In such cases the engagement notice reads:

Miss Wilhelmina Bosworth announces the engagement of her adopted daughter, Sybil Frank, etc.

Or:

Dr. Orrin Metcalf announces the engagement of his adopted daughter, Florence, etc.

When a child has been adopted by a couple, taken their name, and been brought up as one of their own children there is no reason why the adoptive relationship need be mentioned in the engagement or marriage announcements, even if the fact is generally known. But if the child bears another name it is necessary.

Occasionally you see an engagement announcement or a notice of a marriage where some mention is made of a legally changed name. For example:

Mr. and Mrs. Josef Greenberg, of 50 Central Park South, announce the marriage of their daughter Dorothy to Mr. Robert Harris, son of Mr. and Mrs. Chaim Hirsh, also of this city. Mr. Harris changed his name legally.

This clears up Mr. Harris's status but is not, I believe, strictly necessary so long as the notice states that he is the Hirshes' son. Readers will assume he changed his name, something he has a perfect right to do without legal recourse. And if the change did not go through the courts, it is certainly not necessary to mention the name change and the term "changed his name legally" is not used.

CALLING EDITORS

If a family is well-known to society editors, the news may be telephoned to each one. But there is the risk of having one paper "scoop" another on the news where a regular society column is featured, and details may be extracted from the person phoning during the course of the conversation that he may not realize he's giving and which may make him squirm when he sees them in print. The simple, typed, straightforward announcement containing all the facts and released simultaneously to all local papers is the safest way to handle engagement and marriage news. There are society and other columnists who may embroider news in their own fashion. But news once freely given out is beyond control, and one should be able to accept with grace any interpretation the press may wish to put on it, short of downright libel. To make an issue over some of the fatuous remarks that appear in the gossip columns is often only to blow something relatively innocent into a *cause célèbre*.

If it seems really necessary to set one of these scribes right, the offended person should do so in writing and with great dignity. But before doing so, he should consider that most of the incorrect statements gossip columnists make they never retract—or if they do retract, it may be in a manner that may be less pleasant than the original statement. For example, "Mrs. Borden Ring tells me" (this makes them seem very chummy) "she didn't shed her late husband in Reno, as stated here last week. He died. But weren't you in Reno at the time, Mrs. Ring—and for the usual purpose?"

IF THE FILES ARE WRONG   One reason it is a good idea to furnish complete family information, if it will be of interest to the papers and if they are sure to publish it anyway, is that very probably there is some incorrect information in the newspapers' morgues. When a person or a family is prominent, clips, sometimes extensive ones, are kept on all his or its published activities. If one story or item appears and some information in it is incorrect, that goes into the file, too, perhaps to plague the family or individual regularly from time to time as what he does makes news. I was once referred to as the niece —or perhaps it was the grandniece—of Mrs. Cornelius Vanderbilt, which I am not, but I expect to see that reference turn up from time to time because it is in many newspaper morgues.

IF THE ENGAGEMENT IS BROKEN

If notices of an engagement have appeared in the newspapers and the engagement is subsequently broken, additional notices are often sent, though not too hastily. Lovers quarrel, but they also make up. The announcement, if sent, is brief and to the point:

Dr. and Mrs. Richard Shawe, of 66 Riverside Terrace, announce that the engagement of their daughter, Celeste, to Mr. Bertram Farmer, has been broken by mutual consent.

As engraved engagement announcements are not sent out it is not necessary to retract the announcement to one's friends except in the most casual way—in conversation, in letters, "by the way, Bert and I broke our engagement recently." It is not necessary or wise to go into the reasons for a broken engagement outside of the family circle.

HOW NOT TO ANNOUNCE OR BREAK AN ENGAGEMENT   It s a travesty on marriage when young people, often under pressure from press agents, "announce" their engagements or the breaking of them in night clubs or restaurants. Such announcements should come from the girl's parents through formal notice in the press if the families are of sufficient interest to warrant publication of the news. Of course, an engagement may be announced at a party, possibly in a restaurant—but not in a night club. If an engagement party of some kind is given—a luncheon, tea, or dinner—it is more usual for it to be given at the bride-to-be's home and it is limited to the immediate families and very close friends.

SO-CALLED "ENGAGEMENTS"

It would seem axiomatic that you can't be engaged while still married to someone else. It is improper to announce an engagement while either member of the future union is still in the throes of divorce, Hollywood and café society dispatches notwithstanding. And for a woman to wear or even accept a man's engagement ring, even without announcement of an engagement, while her divorce from his predecessor is still pending is the height of bad taste.

BEHAVIOR DURING ENGAGEMENTS

If young people didn't want to make love most of the time during the period of their engagement it wouldn't seem normal. Everyone around them is conscious of how they feel and, up to a certain point, touched by their ecstasy. But if this joy becomes too tactile, onlookers are visibly embarrassed. Good manners always dictate that men and women be restrained about public demonstrations of their physical feeling toward one another.

For engaged people of all ages, society expects chaperonage of a kind.

They may, of course, spend long days and evenings together alone, but they may not go off for a week end or overnight unless adequately chaperoned. The company of another unmarried couple does not fill the requirement, but a married couple even somewhat younger than themselves is acceptable. So is a parent, guardian, or an older close relative of either sex—such as an aunt, uncle, grandmother, or grandfather—or any *mature* woman, married, single, widowed, or divorced.

If circumstances require it, an engaged couple may travel in a public conveyance overnight or even longer to get to some destination where chaperonage will be provided. But of course their accommodations are not in close proximity, such as an upper and lower berth or adjoining staterooms, and their behavior must be so restrained that they will be quite unremarkable to other travelers.

If these rules seem hard and conventional to modern young people they should remind themselves that the engagement is a trial flight which can easily end in a crash landing. It is best to follow the rules, for few young, love-bewitched people are invulnerable enough to bring down social criticism without harm to their relationship.

CHAPTER SIXTEEN

FUNERALS

It is not strange that when man faces the mystery of death he turns to religion for comfort and help. There are many civil marriages, but it is almost unheard of for us to bury the dead without at least a prayer. However unrooted we may be in our religious beliefs, the time of death turns us to the formalities of religion, to the clergyman, the priest, or the rabbi to perform the final, dignified rites.

The family's responsibility when death occurs is partly religious, partly social, partly legal.

IMMEDIATE PROCEDURES WHEN DEATH OCCURS

Every family should have an "emergency" file in its strongbox. In this file should be listed the name of a funeral director to be called when the need occurs. If the family owns a burial plot or a mausoleum, the deed should be in the file, as it will be required by the funeral director. If one or more members of the family prefer cremation, a note to that effect should be in the file, even if the request has been placed in the will. A copy of each birth certificate should also be in the folder (the Board of Health supplies photostatic or certified copies for family records at a small cost). Also included should be the names and addresses of all close relatives and friends who should be informed.

If these things are kept all together, whoever is placed in charge of the funeral—often a relative or friend—will be able to handle the many details. Without the birth certificate, for example, he would have difficulty in supplying the necessary information for the death certificate.

It is also important that a list of all bank accounts, social security numbers, bonds, notes, and mortgages of the various members of the family be listed, together with a notation on the whereabouts of safe deposit boxes, insurance policies, and wills. Many a friend or relative put in charge of a funeral has been in considerable doubt as to how much expense he should incur for the estate.

The name and address of the attorney or attorneys drawing the will or wills should be on file, and the person in charge of the funeral should notify the lawyer before the funeral takes place.

When death occurs and a doctor has not been in attendance, or when the person's religious beliefs preclude medical care, the county medical examiner—in some states the coronor—must be called to determine the cause of death and issue and sign the death certificate. This notification properly takes place before the calling of the mortician, who may not act without the medical examiner's permission.

ARRANGING THE FUNERAL

Whoever is chosen to make funeral arrangements should not be, if possible, any of the most bereaved. Our attitude toward funerals has changed very much for the better, and we now readily accept the fact that an elaborate funeral whose cost will leave the family in serious debt does shallow honor to the deceased. But a frightened young widow, unable to see ahead and perhaps ill-informed on her late husband's finances, can't be expected to make objective decisions concerning the various costs of the funeral.

For a long time the trend has been toward simple funerals, even among people who can afford elaborate ones. No one but the funeral director knows or cares about the fine details of caskets and their relative expensiveness or inexpensiveness. In fact, many people of sensibility shudder at the pretentious ugliness of expensive caskets, remembering that great heroes are often buried in simple, clean-lined pine boxes.

Whoever undertakes the responsibility of the funeral should realize that he or she is entering into a business contract—and under highly emotional circumstances—where those most involved may be of little help in making important decisions. Where expense must be regarded, he should discuss the necessity with the mortician and make as many decisions as possible himself. It is sometimes months before funds can be released for payment of bills he will incur, and in complicated cases it is sometimes necessary to get the court's permission to pay them. Therefore, all these matters must be handled with great care and conservatism.

If the deceased or his family has had some continuing religious affiliation, there is no problem concerning the choice of a clergyman to officiate. Otherwise a clergyman of any faith may, with the family's permission, be asked to read a burial service. When the funeral takes place in a city and the interment is in a family plot at considerable distance, one or more members of the family or its representatives go with the body to the place of burial and a local funeral director must usually be retained to handle the interment. He asks a local clergyman to conduct the brief service at the grave. A local florist may supply one or more fresh floral offerings.

CLOTHING FOR THE BURIAL

Among many people, and especially among Orthodox, Conservative, and some Reform Jews, the shroud is still used for burial. Otherwise, the person in charge of the funeral delivers to the funeral director the kind of clothing the deceased would have worn to church, choosing for older women soft materials in solid, quiet tones of lavender, blue, beige, gray, or taupe, with long sleeves and a high neckline. Evening dresses are unsuitable, and black is rarely used. Young girls are often dressed in white. Children are dressed as for Sunday school.

Clothes furnished for men should be, too, the kind they would have worn to church, usually something from their existing wardrobe. A cutaway is suitable, or a dark blue or dark gray or Oxford suit. Evening clothes are not suitable, nor are sports suits, although in the summer a white linen or any light tropical weave suit may be used.

People are no longer buried with their jewels, although many are with their wedding rings. Directions concerning rings or earrings (in pierced ears) are expected by the funeral director.

HANGING THE BELL

The custom of hanging the bell goes back to the days when doorbells were bells with clappers hung on or adjacent to the door. When someone died, the clapper was muffled in cloth. This later developed into ribbon streamers in white, purple or black, with white or purple flowers. Like mourning, the bell hanging was for the protection of the bereaved, so that anyone approaching the house would do so with quiet dignity.

Today, few hang the bell. And it is never done except when the funeral is to take place in the home. When a family still wishes to adhere to the old custom it so instructs the funeral director, who orders the flowers and has them hung just below the doorbell of either apartment or private house.

WHERE THE FUNERAL TAKES PLACE

The telescoping of our living quarters has brought into existence more and more "Funeral Homes"—some simple and functional like the old-fashioned funeral parlors, where a funeral was held only if there was no suitable home from which it could take place, others elaborate establishments with their own private chapels and pipe organs. Today it is very usual indeed for a funeral to take place in a mortuary chapel even when home facilities are quite adequate to accommodate a large attendance at the services.

The use of the funeral home is usually included in the over-all cost of the funeral, with the occasional exception of a charge for music.

If the funeral takes place at home, the largest room is usually selected, one preferably which can be shut off from the rest of the household. Folding chairs are provided by the mortician.

DEATH NOTICES

The person in charge of the funeral prepares the death notices, which are then inserted, often by the mortician, in one or more morning papers, in large cities, and, if thought advisable, in any evening papers that carry these notices. If the death takes place in a suburb the notices are carried by the nearest large dailies likely to be read by friends of the deceased. These notices are placed at regular space rates, and when it is desired that friends in distant cities be notified publicly the line is often added "Chicago (or Houston) papers please copy." Such out-of-town papers then may run a news item on the death.

When the person who died has been very well-known socially or otherwise it is probable that major papers in his city already have a prepared obituary on file which may need merely to be brought up to date through telephone checking with a member of the family. Each paper has an editor in charge of this kind of news, and the placing of the obituary notice is his cue to get the facts from a family representative, if the paper considers the death generally newsworthy.

As in the case of weddings and engagements sure to be considered news, it is wise for someone familiar with the details of the deceased's important activities to prepare that information in written form as soon as possible, as such news runs the day of the death or, at the latest, the day the obituary notice first appears. Although the information is usually called for over the phone, it is certainly better to have it written out for ready reference, as in many cases all papers call, as well as the wire services. Additional stories, when a person has been prominent, often run on the actual day of the funeral.

A paid death notice may be phoned to papers selected, but it should always be *read* from carefully checked information. Where it is given over the phone the newspaper's classified department usually calls back for re-check, to be certain the notice is legitimate. The form is:

Volkman—Lawrence Karl, on November 23 (year optional), husband (or beloved husband) of Helen Schroeder Volkman (his wife's maiden name is always given to aid identification) and father of Louise and Peter Schroeder Volkman (the daughters are listed first). Funeral at (name of church and address, if necessary), at 2 P.M., Tuesday.

Sometimes, especially when there was no generally known preliminary illness, the word "suddenly" may be added after the names of the immediate family. If a man was married his wife is always listed first, not his parents, whose names, in this case, usually do not appear in the paid notice but who are mentioned, of course, in news stories, if any.

A woman's death notice reads:

Jardine—Diana Minor (her maiden name), wife (or beloved wife) of, etc.

If the funeral is to take place out of town, friends are so notified in the death notice "Funeral at Emmanuel Church, Rye, New York. Train leaves Grand Central at 1 P.M."

The age is usually not given in the death notice, except in the case of a child. It is often mentioned in accompanying news stories.

ATTENDING A FUNERAL

Unless the words "Funeral Private" appear in the death notice, any friend or acquaintance of the deceased or his family may attend the services, as do interested strangers if the funeral is in church. Close friends or relatives may ask the person in charge of arrangements for permission to attend the interment if they are able to provide their own transportation or if there seems to be adequate room in the funeral cars. They should be very certain that their presence at so difficult a time will be of real comfort to the immediate family, which usually prefers to be alone with the clergyman at the last brief rites.

SENDING FLOWERS

Sometimes the death notice reads "Please omit flowers," and this request should be scrupulously respected. At some Protestant funerals the family prefers that the casket have one floral offering, that of the family. They sometimes request privately or in the death notice that flowers be sent to hospitals and, of course, this is thoughtful whenever a notice reads "Please omit flowers." Flowers then may be sent to hospital wards "In memory of— from—" and the family may be so notified by note or when the funeral call is made.

It is important, however, to know that one *never* sends flowers to an Orthodox Jewish funeral. Often they are not desired at a Conservative or a Reform funeral. And it is preferable not to send them to a Catholic funeral, as they may not be taken into the church (only the family's one spray and occasionally an altar arrangement are permitted).

When flowers are sent to a funeral a plain white card is attached with the name of the sender, "Helen Murray" or "Mr. and Mrs. Frederick Wallace," or a visiting card (a husband-and-wife card) may be used with a line drawn through the names in the case of intimate friends and the message, "Deepest sympathy from Jean and Hugh," written in ink. The envelope is simply addressed to:

> The funeral of Mr. Lawrence Karl Volkman
> Silvan Funeral Home
> Greenpoint

Where the funeral is to take place in church but the body is at a funeral home, friends may choose to send flowers immediately on hearing of the death, and to the funeral home, if calls are being received there, or to the church in time for the funeral. In the latter case the flowers are addressed to:

> The funeral of Mr. Lawrence Kárl Volkman
> Emmanuel Church
> Rye, New York
> Funeral 2 P.M., Tuesday

FLOWERS AFTER THE FUNERAL It is a growing custom for close friends to send flowers to the family of the deceased sometime during the weeks following the funeral (except to Orthodox Jews). They should be addressed to the hostess and the accompanying card should avoid reference to the bereavement. Instead it may read: "Kindest thoughts from us all, Peggy and John."

MASS CARDS

Most Catholics prefer mass cards to flowers. When a Catholic dies his friends and relatives, Catholic and non-Catholic, go to a priest and arrange for a mass to be said for the soul. The priest accepts an offering for the mass and presents a card to the donor stating that a mass is to be said for the repose of the soul of the deceased, its method of celebration—High or Low—and sometimes indicating the exact time of the mass. The card is given or sent by the donor to the family of the deceased, usually before the funeral. These masses may be arranged, too, for a year after the death on its anniversary or at any time immediately after the death has taken place.

FUNERAL CALLS

Now that the mortuary chapel has so much replaced the home in the laying out of the dead, people are often confused as to where they are expected to make their funeral calls. If they are close friends or relatives they may call both at home and at the chapel if they wish, leaving their cards or signing the register at the funeral chapel. If calls are received at the funeral chapel some family representative should be present at least during the afternoon and early evening, when calls are likely to be made.

THE FUNERAL SERVICE

It is a matter of family choice whether a casket is left open or closed before the funeral. At State funerals the open casket is optional, but it is always closed during Service for Episcopalians and Jews. At Catholic services, which must take place in church, the casket is open only for the clergy and occasionally for a high-ranking layman.

PALLBEARERS   Among Christians pallbearers are always men, and, today, merely honorary in that they seldom actually carry the casket and serve only at large funerals of distinguished *men*. There are never less than four and rarely more than ten chosen for this honor from among those personally and professionally close to the deceased. Jews have pallbearers for both men and women.

The pallbearers are usually chosen by the person in charge of funeral arrangements, after he has received suggestions from various members of the family. The family itself should be represented among the pallbearers, and the other men chosen must accept the honor unless there is some very valid reason for refusing, such as illness.

Sometimes the casket is already in place before the altar and the floral offerings are arranged on and around it by the time the congregation gathers. In this case, just before the start of the service, the family may file in from the vestry and into the front pew, usually to the right of the center aisle, or, more usually, may enter from the front of the church just before the start of the service. The honorary pallbearers sit in the front pews to the family's left. At the end of the service after the family has retired to the vestry, the pallbearers, walking two by two, are first to leave the church, marching slowly in front of the casket if it is to be carried from the church at that time, or marching out slowly alone and into the waiting cars that carry them with the family to the cemetery.

If the casket is carried into the church the pallbearers precede it, marching slowly, two by two, and stepping into the left-hand first pews as they reach the front of the church.

Pallbearers who have come from out of town and who may not be able to make their funeral calls upon the family before leaving often call briefly at the vestry, before or after the service, to pay their respects.

USHERS AND SEATING ARRANGEMENTS   While the mortician has men in attendance at every funeral who may act as ushers, and the sexton in a large church has a staff for the purpose, it is preferable that men relatives likely to know many of those attending the funeral act in this capacity. In church, like wedding ushers, they escort those attending the service to their seats but do not offer their arms, except to the old or infirm. They do their best to place relatives and close friends toward the front of the church, keeping the front left-hand pews free for the pallbearers or, if there are no pallbearers, for themselves. When there are no pallbearers the ushers precede the casket in the same manner as the pallbearers, or march up the aisle, two by two, just before the service is to start. They march down the aisle at the end of the service ahead of the casket, if it is carried out, before the rest of the congregation leaves the pews.

At Roman Catholic funerals the family does not enter from the vestry but follows up the aisle in the order of relationship to the dead when the casket is carried into the church, preceded by altar boys, priest, casket, and pallbearers. After the service they file out the same way behind the casket.

Funerals are never held in Orthodox synagogues, which do not permit the prescribed plain wooden casket to enter the place of worship. Therefore, Orthodox Jewish funerals are held in mortuary chapels or at home, with men and women assembling side by side and with the men hatless.

INTERMENT AND GRAVE MARKING

The minister, rabbi, or priest goes along with the family and pallbearers, if any, to conduct the brief graveside service.

A grave is marked with the name of the deceased and the date of his birth and death and, frequently, his family relationship, "beloved father of," "beloved son of." Sometimes a line or two of epitaph is added. The footstone or monument bearing this information is ordered by the family from a monument maker shortly after the funeral at minimum cost, but, of course, elaborate monuments with sculptures can run into thousands of dollars. The monument maker installs the monument or marker at no additional fee. If no monument or footstone is to be erected, the funeral director, if instructed, can place on the grave at time of interment a simple bronze plaque costing considerably less than a footstone and bearing the essential data.

Most cemeteries provide perpetual care of graves as part of the purchase price, but families usually visit and tend their plots from time to time, especially among Christians on Memorial Day, Easter, and Christmas, and arrange for special care of plantings.

FEES TO CLERGYMAN, SEXTON, AND ORGANIST

It is usual for the minister to be given a fee for his services. Sometimes an appropriate amount is sent to him by the funeral director, who includes this expense on his bill. More often it is sent by a member of the family in a letter of appreciation for his comfort and help.

The amount should be based on the family's ability to make a contribution. Simplicity of the funeral is today no indication of lack of funds. And certainly if the funeral has been large and expensive the officiating clergyman should not receive less than seventy-five to one hundred dollars. For the average funeral he usually receives from five to twenty-five dollars. When checks are sent they are made out to the clergyman rather than to the church, as these fees are expected to contribute to his own expenses.

The sexton in a large church is on the church payroll and devotes full time to church business affairs. He receives up to twenty-five dollars for opening a big church and overseeing the work of his assistants at a large funeral. In a small church this office, if it exists, is voluntary, but the sexton usually is sent a fee, which, if his own circumstances permit, he may contribute to the church. The organist receives a similar amount.

ACKNOWLEDGMENTS

If the funeral takes place at home, some member of the family makes a careful note of the flower offerings as they arrive, removing the cards and recording, either on the back of each or in a notebook, a description of the flowers, "yellow roses" rather than "roses" or "dark red carnations" rather than "sheaf." The flowers of those nearest and dearest should be placed close to and on the casket, even when those from civic organizations or others are more impressive.

When the funeral takes place at a funeral home the funeral director's staff collects the cards and makes the necessary notations for the family. At a church funeral some member of the family arrives in time to place the flowers and remove the cards when the coffin is to be in place before the start of the service.

Flowers, donations to charity in memoriam, and mass cards should be acknowledged within a reasonable length of time. Morticians usually supply as part of their service printed acknowledgment cards to be sent out by the family. These should not be used instead of a handwritten note, however brief, although the use of engraved cards for large public funerals, where thousands of letters and floral offerings are received, is quite understandable. Mrs. Roosevelt found it necessary to use them after the death of the President.

The note acknowledging flowers, a mass card, charity contributions, or a telegram need not be more than a few words, such as:

Dear Mr. Scott,

You were kind indeed to think of us at such a difficult time. Your violets were beautiful and comforting.

Sincerely,
Helen Volkman

LETTERS OF CONDOLENCE AND REPLIES

Social letters of condolence, always handwritten, need not be long. In fact, "Deepest sympathy" may be written on your visiting card. But they must be sent very promptly. Telegrams are often sent and follow the usual telegraphic form:

DEEPLY SHOCKED AT YOUR SAD LOSS. ALL OUR SYMPATHY. LOVE.

HELEN AND TOM

You address your letter to the widow of the deceased, otherwise to the parents or a sister or brother of the person who has died—always addressing the nearest relative, whether or not you are acquainted.

To the mother of a friend you might write:

Dear Mrs. Volkman,

It is several years since I have seen Larry, but it was with a real sense of loss that I heard the news. We were very close at college, as he may have told you, and have always kept in touch with one another even though we lived at such a distance.

I hope when I am in New York again that I may call upon you and, if possible, be of some service.

Most sincerely,
Gregory Burns

It is better to avoid the words "died," "death," and "killed" in such letters.

It is quite possible to write the kind of letter that will give a moment of courage and a strong feeling of sympathy without mentioning death or sadness at all. For instance:

Dear Jeanette,

For me Gale will remain the happy, dancing child I saw for the first time on her fifth birthday. She will always be with us in spirit.

Lovingly,
Mary

Of course, in replies to letters of condolence one may write at any length one wishes, but it is quite understandable that the note be brief, even to a close friend. Today it is usually on plain white rather than on black-bordered paper. Mourning paper is much less used now and quite unnecessary.

MOURNING

Visible signs of mourning—the widow's bonnet, the black clothes even for little children—are, I think happily, rarely seen these days. We all mourn the deaths of those we love, but the healthful thing is to accept the loss as well as we can and gradually make our adjustment to the life we must live without this beloved person.

Black has lost much of its meaning as the badge of bereavement ever since, in World War I, Chanel decreed that all fashionable women should mourn with her for her own war-loss when she launched the "little black dress," which has since become an essential of the wardrobe. Prior to that women seldom, if ever, wore black except for mourning.

Black dresses from the regular wardrobe and in a dull material are usually worn by women members of the family at a funeral. Children wear Sunday-school clothes in quiet colors or white. Someone usually divests dresses to be worn at funerals of any bright-colored ornaments, but they may be trimmed with white. Pearls may be worn and any functional pin of silver or, possibly, dull gold or an heirloom piece of jet. Simple pearl button earrings are acceptable, but any costume jewelry, diamond rings, bracelets, or anklets should be dispensed with, at least for the period before and during the funeral, in deference to conservative feelings in these matters.

The black chiffon veil is often worn by the bereaved women at a funeral. Stockings worn with black dresses at funerals are usually gun-metal or black, but dark, neutral tones are worn, too, if the mourner does not plan to go into conventional mourning. Ordinary street clothes such as one would wear to church are acceptable for others attending a funeral.

Men of the family wear cutaways for a large church funeral or dark business suits in navy or Oxford, with black shoes and socks, black or gray ties and white shirts. (See "Men's Clothes.") Boys wear dark blue or gray suits, white shirts, dark blue or gray four-in-hands.

THE TRADITIONAL IDEA OF MOURNING   Essentially, the wearing of mourning (not necessarily black—it is white in the tropics) was to give protection to the family as well as to honor the dead. In great families even the retainers were often put in some degree of mourning, and social activities even for tiny children were rigidly circumscribed for as much as two years. It was frequent for the older women in the family, especially elderly widows, to remain in mourning, more or less, for the rest of their lives.

We are getting away from the harsh idea that a strong will to live happily in spite of personal loss is sinful and disrespectful to the dead. We are developing a more positive social attitude toward others, who might find it difficult to function well in the constant company of an outwardly mourning person. In time of war it is often advised by governments that the putting on of mourning by war-bereaved families is an aid and comfort to the enemy and a decided detriment to home morale.

Another reason, I believe, for the little use of mourning today is the rapid spread of news. When death does occur everyone concerned is quickly informed by telephone, telegraph, and the daily papers. There is little possibility that the bereaved family will not receive tactful consideration on all sides, and it need not publicly proclaim its loss by the wearing of black, the use of black-bordered note paper, the strict withdrawal from any merely social activity.

Today when a girl returns to her office desk the day after her mother's funeral wearing her usual workaday clothes and a man goes forth after the death of his son without an armband to proclaim his grief, their co-workers know and understand. And no one considers that they mourn any the less.

Still, a few stores have mourning departments and advisers who may be consulted, free of charge, on the use of mourning and semi-mourning for those who wish to cling to a rapidly passing tradition.

RESTRICTION OF ACTIVITIES

Those who have just lost someone close to them naturally feel disinclined toward public festivity. Scheduled events, such as weddings, are, however, permitted to take place (see "Weddings"). Most of us pursue, or try to pursue, our usual social course within a week or so after a funeral in our immediate family, with our own feelings and convictions governing our behavior rather than "what people might think."

Today we go to small dinner parties, to concerts and the opera, to the theater and the movies. We play games, including cards, and listen to the radio and read novels, all as an aid to regaining our ability to function normally. We try to remember that our own state of mind affects those around us and aids or interferes with their ability to face life's daily problems.

The activities of young children should never be restricted after a death has occurred in a family. Children have, if anything, even more need to run and jump and play when their parents are weighted with sorrow and strange things are happening in the house. The fact of death must be faced by everyone, and children, unless they are very tiny indeed, cannot be shielded from it. They can understand the tears and the immediate grief, but continuing sorrow is not the pattern of the normal child. Let him run off his tension in uninhibited play and noise—away from the mourning house if there are those who cannot understand a child's needs.

2 DRESS AND MANNERS

Men's Clothes   140

What's What in Various Sports   161

The Well-Groomed Man   171

A Man's Manners in the Business World   176

The Masculine Graces   183

The Well-Dressed Woman   190

The Fastidious and Well-Mannered Woman   200

The Social Pleasantries   212

The Smoking Problem   219

Clubs   222

Manners at Table   228

Our Community Relations and Interfaith Courtesy and Understanding   243

The New Citizen and His Particular Problems   250

DRESS AND MANNERS

Good manners and appropriate dress are, or should be, part and parcel of gentle people. Notice the word "appropriate." Clothing need not be expensive or of the finest needlework or tailoring, but it must suit the occasion on which it is worn. We are not born with the knowledge that French heels are in poor taste with a classic tweed suit, that boisterousness is out of place in church. Precept and example show us how ladies and gentlemen should look and act. And feel. Outward conformity to a code is never enough.

The finest rules for behavior are to be found in chapter 13 of First Corinthians, the beautiful dissertation on charity by St. Paul. These rules have nothing to do with the fine points of dress nor with those of superficial manners. They have to do with feelings and attitudes, kindliness, and consideration of others. Good manners have much to do with the emotions. To make them ring true, one must feel them, not merely exhibit them.

CHAPTER SEVENTEEN

MEN'S CLOTHES

Two world wars have made both male manners and manner of dressing more casual. A man is certainly more comfortable, and his clothing, even for the relatively conservative, more colorful and varied. He goes to business vestless (in a double-breasted suit which can do away with the extra garment), in a collar-attached, often colored, shirt, in a suit which may differ greatly from the Oxford, navy, or black one his father considered a gentleman's business uniform. His hat may be a soft, snap brim or a rolling Homburg, but it needn't be the derby, a headgear not universally becoming. He is no longer a dun-colored bird. Even if he is properly cautious about the use of color in town (if he's not completely sure of his taste), he can indulge his long inhibited love of it in undergarments whose patterns and colors often rival Tahiti's sarongs. His slack suits at home, his bathing outfit, his pajamas, his clothes for active sports, his country wardrobe may all proclaim a peacock—if he can get away with it gracefully. But he'd better be able to live up to it.

It takes a good figure, perfect carriage, and tolerable looks as well as an inborn style for a man to wear some of the modern clothes well. If he hasn't these attributes he's better off minimizing his defects by sticking at all times to conservative habiliments designed to call no special attention to themselves or him.

SUITS

A man's profession, the kind of work he does, must necessarily influence his choice of suits. If he's a gentleman farmer, an artist, or a writer and rarely goes into the larger cities near his home, he may get along nicely with one sack suit, filling out his wardrobe with slacks and sports coats to please his fancy and satisfy his needs. Such a man may even look quite appropriately dressed if he comes to town attired in his customary clothes— a sports jacket and slacks or peaty tweeds—if he keeps to such masculine haunts as his club, men's bars, offices, or the homes of his understanding friends. He is dressed *informally*, albeit quite possibly more expensively than some on whom he might call. So attired he does not belong in pretentious restaurants, at receptions, funerals, weddings, or directors' meetings.

A man whose professional or business life takes him on frequent trips to parts of the country where life is less formal than it is in New York, and where his activities may take him more out of offices than in them, is justified, too, in wearing slacks and a sports jacket or tweeds to town if his travels will carry him more or less immediately out again. Slacks and sports jackets and of course tweeds are more and more worn for travel, as rumpled they look less unattractive than does a sack suit. A commuter, who comes in for a short day—a half holiday, say—and who has no plans for any appearances in town that require a more formal outfit, can conceivably choose to wear slacks to his office. But the wearing of this costume indicates the country gentleman who invades the city, if only for a short time. For a city dweller to choose it for office wear when he is not planning to leave the city that day seems posey. For other than executives to select such a costume for office work might seem pretentious to an employer.

THE BUSINESS SUIT

The suits a man wears to work should avoid being too distinctive in pattern, fabric, cut, or color unless he has a tremendous wardrobe from which to draw. I remember one young executive with whom I shall always associate a sharkskin suit, although he may have had several others with which to spell it. But he had to wear it much too often. As sharkskin can't be cut on the easy lines of tweed or Cheviot, my mind always sees him poured into that piscine garment.

It is safer to be dressed for any business occasion that might occur than to go to the office in clothes that might be out of place if an important client should turn up or a vital meeting be called. The beloved rainy-day suit looks shabby when the sun comes out at noon, the old tweed jacket throws a man off stride if he's suddenly precipitated into a group of men wearing directors' jackets (double-breasted, sometimes single-breasted black, short sack coats).

In winter, worsteds, flannel, the softer tweeds, Saxony, and Cheviots are office wear. In spring and summer, gabardines and the various light-weight fabrics are correct, with more latitude in the matter of mixed outfits. Summer social activities don't center in cities, so the man who must work in town is permitted clothing comfort—within reason. He is still expected to wear a coat, if only a seersucker one, even though his own office etiquette may permit him to be coatless at his desk while not engaged with visitors or his superiors.

His suit colors may be gray, black, any of the toast browns, grayed greens, blues. The strong reddish-browns (except in Harris tweeds), the yellow-greens, and the strong green-blues had better be bypassed except in an extensive wardrobe. A man's suit should be of good enough quality to last four or five years, if he alternates it with at least three others of the same quality. If any one suit is too assertive it automatically telescopes his wardrobe. The same is true of a too vibrant plaid, a too broadly striped one, a very pale color, or a check that doesn't fade into gray at a short distance, or too shaggy a tweed.

The double-breasted suit is considered more comfortable by some men for business wear, because it does not require a vest. Unless it is carefully tailored to his measurement with certain *trompe l'oeil* details, it can be most unbecoming to the man of less than average height or to one who, though tall enough, has too generous girth or too short a waist. The suit has become so popular, not only because it permits doing away with the vest, but because it suggests the American "wedge of cheese" sartorial effect. To be effective, it requires a trim waistline and it must be kept buttoned when a man is on his feet.

If it is worn by a short man with a short or large waist the broadening effect of the suit's cut foreshortens the wearer. But a man with less than an Adonis figure can wear the double-breasted suit if the buttons are not so far apart as to carry the eye to the outside outlines of the figure, and if the broadened shoulder line is on the conservative side and begins high enough to give an illusion of waist. Slanting the top buttons outward helps the effect. Lengthening the coat doesn't usually simulate height. On the contrary, it shortens the legs. The length of the coat is determined by the shape of the man. A suit coat should always be long enough to cover the seat of the trousers, but on a short man it should not be longer than that, no matter what the current fashion. A man who is tall and very thin looks better dressed in a coat of medium length. A too short one puts him on stilts, and one too long accentuates his thinness.

The single-breasted suit requires a vest except, perhaps, in the hottest weather. Even for the most conservative business occasions, the vest need not match the suit in fabric or color. The black-and-white, black, blue, and white, or black, white, and yellow-checked Tattersall waistcoat on light ground flannel is correct even with plaid or pin striped suits, as is the natural-color chamois waistcoat (weskit). It takes a man knowledgeable and easy with his clothes to wear them well, however. False moves with a tie, a shirt, or socks can make the wearer of a contrasting waistcoat look like a drummer. Fancy waistcoats call for white shirts, paisley, foulard, or solid color ties. They should be the sole accent note of the costume. The bottom button of the vest is nearly always left unbuttoned.

The trousers of the sack suit may have cuffs or be pressed straight down, depending on preference. If they are tailor-made and cuffless, the bottoms should be finished so they can be turned up in stormy weather. Length of trousers is again a matter of individual taste, but, fashionably, those with permanent cuffs should hang straight and not break over the instep. The trousers width should be medium, avoiding the sloppiness of the English "bags" and the narrowness of the Continental trouser leg. The short man improves his appearance by wearing his trousers cut fairly high, comfortably above the hipbones.

All trousers hang better when suspenders are worn and when a minimum is carried in the pockets. The carefully groomed man limits his trouser pocket contents to his small change and his keys. The keys should be in a flat key case. A used handkerchief, folded as flat as possible, can be returned to his hip pocket, but his wallet there may make an unsightly rear bulge (and may be an invitation to pickpockets who are not deterred by a button). A distinguished man, former President Miguel Alemán of Mexico, noted for his excellent taste in clothes, once told me that he carried an absolute minimum in his suit pockets so his clothes would fit as they were tailored to fit. He pointed out that a man who must take along with him the familiar assortment of papers, checkbooks, pens, pencils, photographs, credentials, and the wealth of small-boy items he manages to collect would make a better appearance if he carried most of them in a brief case rather than on his person.

REFINEMENTS OF TAILORING   The notch on the collar of a business suit should be almost a right angle and the lapel in recent years has tended to be cut a little broader than the collar, especially on a single-breasted coat. On double-breasted suits the lapels are definitely wider than the collar and are frequently slightly peaked instead of right-angled but should always avoid the pixylike exaggerated peak. (See illustration.)

Side pockets, except occasional patch pockets, should have flaps (which for good grooming should always be worn out). Trouser pleats may be long

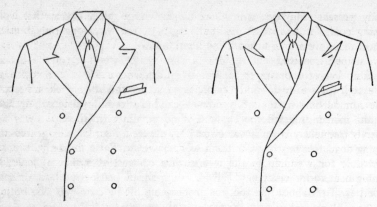

BUSINESS SUITS *Left:* Moderate peak, double-breasted suit. Good shoulder line merely improves slightly on natural contours except to correct defects— such as one shoulder lower than other. *Right:* Exaggerated peak like pixie-ears. Not recommended. This is often teamed with impossibly athletic shoulders and an over-long coat. Theatrical.

on the tall, slim man, but on the average or short man unpressed pleats not too generous, extending a few inches below the waistline, are more becoming. The buttonhole on the left lapel should be usable. In custom-made suits it is sensible to have the sleeve buttons completely functional, so the cuffs may be turned back if desired. British tailoring features this, together with colorful suit linings meant to be seen occasionally. The sleeve length should permit one half inch of shirt cuff to show when the arm is at the side. Visible hand-stitching on collar and lapels advertise the tailor-made suit and insure careful workmanship.

THE MORNING COAT OR CUTAWAY AND ACCESSORIES

This is an expensive accouterment for a man who does not lead a fairly active social life, but it is often a necessary one. It is the proper costume for a really formal daytime wedding, when the bride wears a veil and has bridesmaids. It is the usual costume of the church usher. In fact it is worn at any daytime function, until six o'clock, that makes any attempt at being impressive or festive—a wedding, a public funeral, a debutante tea, a call at the White House or at a governor's mansion, a concert, a christening, a city church service, any daytime ceremony.

Many a man who owns a morning coat rarely thinks to wear it, yet its acquisition need not be the extravagance it seems. Once acquired, formal daytime dress should be worn frequently, so a man feels at ease in it. His coat need not be the cutaway but, more modernly, may be the short, even double-breasted black or Oxford sack coat, or "director's coat," unless the suit must be bought especially for a formal wedding or other use where the wearer is expected to be attired the same as other members of the group who already possess cutaways. But where all the ushers, say, are buying new morning coats for a wedding, it might be better to suggest the short and, I think, more wearable jacket to be worn with the usually, but not necessarily, striped trousers.

It is no longer necessary, nor even usual, to wear spats with a morning coat except for a formal wedding, where white or sand linen spats are worn in the summertime with a white or sand-colored waistcoat. The correct hat with the morning coat is the black silk hat, although in England the gray topper is frequently worn at Ascot and for coaching. In summer, ushers in morning coats frequently go hatless and straw or panama hats are now quite permissible for wedding guests in cutaways. A top executive, wearing a morning coat to his office or the slightly less formal sack coat with striped trousers, will probably feel less conspicuous on the street in a black Homburg or a black soft felt hat than in a silk one. He wears a black or dark blue outer coat. Spats, if worn at all with the outfit (and they should never be worn at funerals), should be light or dark tan or light gray. Black socks, plain or ribbed, are worn with black calf, plain-tipped oxfords. Except at funerals, the black socks may be figured or clocked in white.

In winter the waistcoat, which may be single-breasted or (usually, except on distinctly older men) double-breasted, may be pearl gray or light or darker tan, or may match the black or Oxford gray of the coat.

Shirts worn with the morning coat should be with single or French "double" cuffs, white with pleated or plain bosom. The collar is wing or turndown, again depending on whether one is dressing like others in a group or not. The Ascot in a variety of materials from rep silk to broadly striped grosgrain, in grayed effects or plain black, white or lavenders (more mature), is the formal type of tie but the four-in-hand is often worn, and always worn in black for funerals. With the sack coat, the four-in-hand suits its somewhat lesser formality. With the Ascot, a pearl pin or an antique or modern gold scarfpin set with moonstone, amethyst, or other light stones is worn but is nowadays usually dispensed with on the four-in-hand. Pearl studs are *de rigueur* for the shirt, and gold cuff links—which may even be large, striking antique, jeweled ones—fasten the cuffs. The boutonniere may be any small, suitable flower—a dark red or white carnation, a cornflower, or bridal flowers at a wedding (orange blossoms, white violets, gardenias, lilies of the valley, etc., with the groom alone wearing a sprig from the bride's bouquet). At a funeral no boutonniere is worn.

Garters and suspenders are conservative gray or black-and-white, the handkerchief pure white, the scarf gray, white, or black, and the gloves light gray mocha, except at a funeral where dark gray suède gloves are substituted.

THE DINNER JACKET AND ACCESSORIES

A man, especially a young man, may be able to do without a morning coat, but he needs a dinner jacket (even if he never owns a tail coat). Here is a suit that should do duty for five years if it is well chosen, of good quality, from a good men's shop, if ready-made, or carefully tailored by a recognized tailor. Unless a man can afford two or more dinner jackets, he should stick to the conservative black, for if he appears in it time and time again, no one knows but what he may have two or a dozen like it. If he chooses his one tuxedo in the newer midnight blue, it would seem inconceivable to the observant eye that he had two such alike. And there are occasions on which he might feel slightly conspicuous in the slightly less formal blue. As for dark red or other colors in dinner jackets which may have seasonal popularity, it's better to shun them unless he has an extensive evening wardrobe. No girl wants her beau to turn up in a red suit, no matter how excellent the cut and quality, every time she goes dancing or dining with him. Whereas his one black dinner jacket, the fully accepted evening uniform of the semi-festive male, is never too remarkable.

Modern dinner jackets are single- or double-breasted, the latter to be worn with or without a vest. The vest usually matches the suit but may also be of white piqué, marseilles (or marcella), or black or midnight blue silk, ribbed or figured. Small braid matching that on the trousers may trim the vest in a custom-made suit. It is fastened with self-covered or smoked pearl buttons, not links. The vest is always dispensed with with a cummerbund (silk, rib-hugging sash which hides the top of the trousers), but this somewhat dashing accessory is no asset to a gentleman of expanded girth. The cummerbund is now best worn in black, maroon, or midnight blue. The cummerbund is particularly attractive, and certainly more comfortable, in summer and may be topped by a summer dinner jacket in white, with or without lapels or shawl collar in the same fabric. Or, if a man's figure can stand it, a white linen mess jacket, but this has come to be considered theatrical.

Dinner jacket lapels may be more peaked than those of business suits but should avoid eccentricity. A shawl or a notched collar, considered more casual, is preferred by some, and the facing of either type may be satin, grosgrain, or of the same fabric if the jacket is white.

The lines of a dinner jacket should be about the same as those of an easy, comfortable business suit. Avoid the too-fitted waist and the too-narrow Latin-style trousers as well as the absurdly built-out shoulders, although some padding is advisable for most men.

BRAID ON TROUSERS It is not entirely necessary to have a different pair of trousers (always uncuffed) to be worn with a tail coat, as there is only a shade of difference between the braid on the trousers worn with full dress and those meant for a tuxedo. Specifications differ very slightly over a period of years, but, generally speaking, the braid for full dress is double or triple width while that on dinner jacket trousers narrower and usually coarser. Sometimes a very broad braid in satin finish is worn with dress trousers, and at times some men affect no braid at all on trousers with a dinner jacket (though there is some possibility they might be accused of aping their butlers—who wear no braid).

For a man with heavy social duties two pairs of trousers to go with his dinner jacket and one pair of full dress trousers might be an economy. But the average man, unless he has pretensions to being a fashion plate, can get along with one pair of evening trousers, matching his dinner jacket and to be worn, as needed, with it or his full dress coat.

THE SHIRT A revolution has taken place in the past twenty-five years in the matter of the proper shirt to wear with a dinner jacket. No longer is the old, and to some torturous, "boiled shirt" and stiff collar strictly necessary. Even for quite formal occasions the best-dressed men wear white soft front, pleated, or plain collar-attached (or separate starched collar) shirts and, in summer, even button-down collar shirts with buttoned wristbands. Soft dinner shirts may even have the usual ocean pearl buttons but can be had to accommodate small real pearl, onyx, gold, or small smoked pearl studs (two or three of them). Cuff links may match the studs, or, if a man possesses them, he may wear handsome antique or modern jeweled ones.

THE TIE The tie for a dinner jacket is always a bow in black (or sometimes midnight blue, with midnight blue dinner jacket) dull silk, rep, grosgrain (seldom), or satin. Maroon rep is sometimes worn but, if so, looks better in summer with matching cummerbund and a dark red carnation.

THE BOUTONNIERE As a dinner jacket is a semiformal outfit, there is leeway in the selection of boutonnieres, although the carnation in red or white is most popular. White flowers other than carnations usually seem bridal, but certainly a miniature dahlia in white or any other color would be quite suitable, as are cornflowers, pinks, strawflowers, holly, or snowberries (in the right season) or any little flower—even a tiny orchid or modest gardenia—that can go through an evening in such service without early collapse.

Any woman would prefer no boutonniere at all to one of the permanent-duty feather ones. (Of course, the wearing of a decoration, such as the Legion of Honor, precludes the wearing of a boutonniere.) How would any man like her to wear a corsage of imitation orchids? There is always the tender implication that the woman a man is escorting has placed the boutonniere in his lapel with her own hands—as she very often does.

EVENING SOCKS Socks worn with dinner or full dress clothes are solid black silk or nylon, ribbed or plain. With the dinner jacket they may be self clocked or even clocked in white.

THE TAIL COAT AND ACCESSORIES

This is the winter, formal evening outfit of the, usually urban, gentleman— "white tie," it's called on formal invitations. A man wears it to the opera—at least to the opening or when he sits in a box with others similarly attired— to an evening wedding (which rarely occurs in New York), to formal dinners where it is requested, although the modern hostess knows that many men do not possess this garment and will either stay away if it is required or ask if they may wear "black tie." It is worn at balls, evening debuts (but here, especially if the hostess hopes for a turnout of young, dancing men, a choice of "black or white tie" may be given on the invitation), and for any elaborate evening entertainment. The host at a dinner party, at home or not, is never incorrect when so attired, when the hostess has given a choice to the men of black or white tie. It is possible that a man might be requested in some communities to wear a tail coat to a formal evening wedding in the summertime, but generally speaking it is winter wear.

Like the dinner jacket, the tail coat may today be black or the deep midnight blue which reputedly looks blacker than black at night. The trousers worn with it may be the same as those for the dinner jacket, for economy's sake, or have the somewhat wider, finer braid usual for full dress. The lapels are satin or grosgrain (of course grosgrain is so dull that one might almost as well wear a dark blue or black sack coat), always conservatively peaked and never the shawl collar sometimes seen on dinner jackets. If he can possibly afford it, a man should have his tail coat made to order, unless he is of average proportions, because it is almost impossible to alter a ready-made tail coat so that it fits as if it were made for him. A man somewhat under average height may shun the tail coat, because he feels it makes him look shorter. Yet if the tails are proportioned to his height by an expert tailor the suit can seem to give him several inches in height. A ready-made tail coat—or a rented one—for such a man can make him look like a small boy masquerading in his father's clothes. But, tailored to fit, "white tie" can give any man a special dignity and distinction as do no other clothes.

THE WAISTCOAT, TIE, AND SHIRT The full dress waistcoat is always white—piqué or marcella, with white or antique pearl buttons which may be inserted like studs for washability. It is made with or without a revers and with the bottom cut on the straight line preferably—although this is usually possible only on the custom-made suit with high-rise trousers—and is worn with a white pique bow tie. The shirt is a neckband one with one or two studs (small white pearl, gold, platinum, or certain antique studs with light colored stones permissible).

BOUTONNIERE, GLOVES, AND MUFFLER For full dress the boutonniere is, for conservatives, always white, usually a carnation, unless for a wedding, ball, or other very festive occasion when small gardenias are suitable. Dark red carnations are often favored, too. Gloves worn on the street are white doeskin or chamois. Today the white kid gloves, ultra-correct for indoor wear with formal clothes, are seldom seen, although some fastidious men don them for dancing, to avoid having to place a moist hand on a woman's bare back. Actually, a man's white kid gloves worn this way are not removed even when he is acknowledging introductions or having supper. The muffler worn with formal dress is white silk, woven or knit, initialed, possibly, in black or white—in fact, all formal evening accessories are unrelieved white or black or a combination of these as, for example, in garters and braces, which may be white or black with contrasting woven or embroidered design in black or white.

FORMAL HATS There is more choice of a hat to wear with a dinner jacket than of one to select for tails. If you don't own a black silk hat or an opera hat, don't wear tails at all. With a dinner jacket one may wear an opera hat (preferably with an overcoat), a soft black or, in summer, a gray felt hat, a black Homburg, or, in summer, a straw sailor or a panama. Despite the rigidity and severity of the derby, it is not considered suitable for any but business suits, even though you do see it worn sometimes with a dinner jacket. It might be more acceptable, this way, with a shawl collared dinner jacket (somewhat less formal).

THE FROCK COAT

This is a rare item these days in an American man's wardrobe and is found only if he admits to his years or is perhaps a clergyman or fox hunter. It used to be considered the preferred coat for the bride's father to wear with striped trousers, even though the other members of the wedding party wore the usual cutaways. Today's father has more spring in him, I guess. At least he seems to like wearing the cutaway instead. And as both these formal daytime uniforms seem unyouthful to me, I can see why he might prefer the less restrained cutaway, unless, of course, there is entirely too much length to his watch chain.

THE EVENING HOUSE SUIT

Most men balk at dressing for small dinner parties in their own or their friends' homes, although they are relatively willing to do so if the program includes the theater, a restaurant, or a night club or, perhaps, all three. Left to himself, even the well-dressed American male will come to dinner in a dark sack suit, and if he's more comfortable that way, I say, let him. In the country, depending on the temper of his wife and what his neighboring males get away with, he may even arrive in a loud plaid flannel shirt and corduroy trousers, even though his wife prefers to get out of her wool dress or pullover sweater and into a print, a little black dress, or, in her own home, dinner slacks, pajamas, or hostess gown.

Into the breach between the business suit and the tuxedo steps the double- or single-breasted smoking jacket or the silk or gabardine house suit. The smoking jacket is cut like a shawl or notch-collared dinner jacket and is made of dark blue, black, or maroon velveteen or corduroy with satin facing. An old pair of tuxedo trousers goes admirably with it; dark gray slacks do, too. This outfit, worn with a soft-bosom shirt and a turndown, buttoned down collar and a bow tie (black or maroon preferred) is quite acceptable for off-duty lounging and the small, home dinner when other men present are not wearing dinner jackets. The silk choppa or some casual silk scarf in polka dot, paisley, or other design may be used in place of the collar and tie by the man who can wear it with the right air.

Even more *chez lui* than the smoking jacket is the silk, gabardine, or, in summer, cotton-weave lounge suit (this in a large variety of colors from forest green to terra cotta) worn usually without a coat, although with the silk or gabardine suit the coat is sometimes cut smoking jacket style to be worn with a white soft shirt. It seems to me that men should be encouraged to acquire any such aids to more comfortable home attire. All fastidious people change from street or daytime clothes to fresher ones for dinner if it is possible to do so. In his own home a man should be given time to change from his business clothes into something easy and comfortable or quite festive before dinner, and, as men's clothes are trending, these two ideals are not incompatible even if he dons a dinner jacket.

With the smoking jacket, which is the most acceptable of the male lounging outfits, black patent pumps are worn or leather house slippers that fit like a pump, although they are cut away at the side and are sometimes of black patent and red or black soft leather. They should be hard-soled and have a heel.

OVERCOATS

Practical for the average man is the black, Oxford gray, or dark blue chesterfield with a black velvet or self collar. (The latter may have silk-faced lapels but then would be restricted to evening use or to wear with a cutaway.) The chesterfield may be single- or double-breasted and is equally useful for day as for semiformal or even formal evening wear.

The black satin-lined evening cape, an elegant garment, is still seen on gentlemen who take their clothes very seriously and who like to keep alive the niceties of Victorian dress. It is usually tailored to measure but is sometimes featured by the best men's shops in lush seasons. Once you own it, you can presumably wear the same cape the rest of your life with complete confidence.

THE DAYTIME OVERCOAT   For town wear with business or semiformal daytime clothes the blue, black, or Oxford gray double- or single-breasted chesterfield is always right unless the business suit is, say, a heather mixture or any rather woodsy tweed becoming to certain big-boned men. The chesterfield goes with the smooth surface fabric or herringbone, but tweeds need a more loose-lined topcoat, not only for comfort's sake but for congruity.

RIDING CLOTHES—FORMAL AND INFORMAL

The term "pinks" refers to the light pinkish-sand whipcord officers' trousers worn by army officers. But the "pink" coat cut as a frock coat, shadbelly (or Pytchely coat), or cutaway as worn by members of the hunt is really vivid scarlet. It may be worn by anyone joining the hunt even though he may not be especially asked to wear it by the M. F. H., unless the club has a special, colored collar (but Oxford or black is better unless you are asked or are a quite famous man to hounds). Supposedly, the coat was devised by an English tailor named "Pink" and was intended to be worn by riders in the hunt who were particularly familiar with the terrain so that they could lead the chase. Other worthies wore, instead, the cutaway or the black frock coat, but most hunt clubs now put on an occasional show of "pink" on all their members, although for most hunts ordinary riding clothes are worn. Riding breeches in white or sand whipcord are worn with pink coats, and "brick" red or "pinks" with the dress riding sack, and must be accompanied by black, not brown, boots with tan or champagne color tops. *All* boots have black soft legs.

The hat worn with a pink coat is a high hunting silk hat. A black riding derby which is shallower than the street derby may be worn with the dark cutaway or frock coat, or the black velvet beagling cap of the English foxhunter. Caps are worn only by the master, honorary whippers-in, the huntsmen, and professional hunt servants. The waistcoat is a tattersall or canary wool flannel, or may be of any distinctive color adopted by the hunt.

Traditional, too, for formal daytime riding clothes is the white stock worn with an appropriate scarf pin, white or buff chamois or calf gloves. The stock is said to have been designed to act as a bandage in case of accident, and it thus is a truly functional bit of men's wear still.

FOR EVENING HORSE SHOWS For night horse shows, a dinner jacket is often worn, especially if the owner is showing his own horse. Trousers may be the usual ones, or evening trousers cut slightly narrow in the leg with elastic straps under the insteps. The black evening oxford is correct and the hat is preferably a soft black felt.

To me the dinner jacket topping even the most blue-blooded mount seems incongruous, and I prefer the black or, usually, Oxford gray riding habit with black boots. However, correct though this is, it is less often seen even in Madison Square Garden than the more usual brown or tan riding jacket with matching or contrasting trousers or jodhpurs, usually in putty color or sand and worn with well-burnished brown boots or jodhpur shoes.

INFORMAL RIDING CLOTHES In the show ring jodhpurs are considered incorrect, although they are often worn by women, but this Indian importation is attractive on the man of average or more than average height. The bulge of the jodhpur trousers might be less flattering than ordinary ones on the short man, especially if his waistline isn't trim. The jodhpur, because of its close fit and lack of boot (it is worn with a special pull-on shoe), is certainly not the garment for the bandy-legged man or one who can't "show a good leg." Boots will cover his shortcomings more adequately. Jodhpurs must fit well and if ready-made must be altered so they fit smoothly over the calf and break correctly at the knee, so they will be entirely comfortable whether you are on the horse or off him.

The easiest, most universally becoming riding outfit, suitable for park or country riding, is the tweed jacket (cut slightly longer than an ordinary one, although the usual tweed sport jacket will do) and twill, cord, linen, drill, or gabardine riding breeches, worn with brown, polished boots with a rounded toe and normal heel. (Fancy, high-heeled boots are fine on a dude ranch or for the younger fry, to be worn with the usual riding pants or tucked in or out with Levis.) Shirts may be open at the neck (except for formal park riding, when a button down collar and four-in-hand tie or a stock are usual), in white or in colored flannel. For informal cross-country riding many men wear plaid flannel shirts or in summer polo shirts, with or without coats. A derby may be worn with the complete riding habit (not if you go coatless or wear a shirt open at the neck), or a soft felt in brown, gray, or green. A pork pie looks fine, and so does a green tyrolean, brush and all. Caps are considered correct and are probably comfortable, but they remind me of Dick Merriwell and the Rover Boys. Formal hunting dress, by some called "livery," whether worn by amateur riders or hunt "servants," is rigidly prescribed and is a subject in itself.

TIES, HANDKERCHIEFS, AND JEWELRY

TIES, EVENING AND OTHERWISE Not every man is dextrous nor can every man, attiring himself for a social evening, be valeted. Hence, into being came the pre-tied bow tie, for evening as well as for day wear. It seems to me a sad little invention, like the old-time celluloid shirt and the sleeve garter that, I gather, compensates for the ill-fitting shirt sleeve. However, I suppose the pre-tied tie is better than a self-tied one that is askew most of the evening. Most men wear bow ties so seldom they have little chance to practice tying them, but a man with a nimble-fingered wife has no excuse for turning up with his bow tie in a dreary little lump or in the startling butterfly perfection of some of the pre-tied ties. If a pre-tied tie must be the choice, be careful to wear it with a turned down collar if it has an observable fastening in the back, otherwise the coat collar will eventually ride down enough during the evening to reveal this little sartorial deception.

The daytime tie, usually a four-in-hand, is developing into an often gaudy creation which is giving the long color-repressed male a chance to exhibit his taste—or lack of it—in the choice of ties suitable for his wardrobe. While I deplore the "poached egg" and hand-painted, as well as the explosively geometric schools of tie design, I suppose it is the privilege of the male to wear them. It used to be that women who knew little about men's canons of taste were responsible for the gift purchase of such ties, but there is an alarming trend among men themselves to buy and wear such horrors.

If a tie has any design but a variation of the stripe, the paisley, the polka dot, or the small square, it had better be of exceptional quality and style, with cost no real indication of either. Any woman will tell you that it is much easier to combine one or more plain colors with not more than one figured one than to combine several figured ones, which takes some knowledge of color and design values. It is quite possible for a man to wear a colored, striped shirt, a tattersall waistcoat, a Glen plaid suit, and a bright, figured tie and a fancy handkerchief, but he needs either innate or acquired taste to do so. A man who is not sure of his color sense is safer wearing plain colored or white shirts with a suit that is either striped or plaid, plain ties and shirts with "horse-blanket" sports jackets or patterned suits, a single bright accent rather than several. This is, admittedly, the ultra-conservative point of view. There are men who can wear bright green suits with pink shirts and sunburst ties and still look all right, I guess— but not to me.

There is nothing shameful in being either color blind or, let us say, color unsure. It is only the foolhardy male who, knowing nothing about color harmony, goes right ahead and buys his clothes without any attempt to co-ordinate them acceptably—and without seeking advice. Perhaps it was the lack of opportunity to wear bright colors for generations that has made the male uneasy in the presence of the wide assortment of colored and figured garments he finds even in the most conservative shops. He sees even his most reactionary friends attired in colors and color combinations quite unthinkable except in Bohemian or Broadway circles a few years back, and he wonders if he'll have the audacity himself to brighten up the old routine of the blue, gray, or brown suit with the white, blue, gray, or tan shirt and the plain blue, brown, maroon, or (more daringly) green ties that have been his safe choice for so long. Perfectly acceptable males are wearing yellow, for example, and not only in canary waistcoats in the hunting field or in the generations-old chamois ones. They wear yellow wool mufflers and, in the country, yellow knit gloves and cheerful bright yellow wool socks and polo shirts. The old maroon tie in variations of pattern is always good, but the reddest of red ties now appear on sound, aggressively masculine men and with good effect, too. Green suits and hats, always considered tasteful in English and Continental tailoring circles, have captured the imaginations of the most conservative American ones. Green clothes need still to be chosen with caution and with a careful eye to a man's coloring. If he has a sallow, yellowish cast to his skin he can look mighty bilious in a green hat or suit. Forest green, gray green, and Lovat green are the safe ones to choose in wools and felts and go best with the well-tanned skin that has underlying color. The pinkish skin with ruddy accents can wear the various greens, too.

If a man decides to put a little more life into his wardrobe, he will find that women will approve and, with their usually more developed color sense, be able to advise him if he feels he needs advice. They will be able to help him find what is right for *him*—irrespective of what Jones at the club turned up in yesterday. It may be some comfort for him to realize that men have dressed so dully and conservatively for so long that the relatively slight changes going on in men's fashion circles (and there are male style leaders who exert a considerable influence on what men wear, you know) go almost unnoticed, and not only by other men but even by the more fashion-conscious women, the majority of whom know nothing of what is considered good, tasteful male attire from a technical standpoint. But women, generally, know what "looks good" on their own or other males, and many a man who has improved his financial and social position over the years gets some help from his wife in the selection of his clothes. Many men, in fact, leave entirely to their wives the purchase of handkerchiefs, socks, underwear, and shirts and ask their wives to go along when they are choosing a ready-made suit or overcoat or selecting material from which they are to be made.

HANDKERCHIEFS I feel about decorative silk handkerchiefs for men exactly as I do about chiffon squares for women—they in no way replace the good white linen or lawn handkerchief and, when worn for decoration, must not be used for the handkerchief's true function—for wiping one's face after exertion or blowing one's nose. Such handkerchiefs must, usually, be dry-cleaned or at least very cautiously washed, so they are not suitable for sanitary purposes at all. In fact, I prefer to see them knotted around the throat for sports wear rather than poking out uselessly from a breast pocket.

When a handkerchief with a colored border or initial is worn (and avoid these, of course, with formal day or evening dress unless, on an initialed handkerchief, the initial is in black or white) the color should be geared to the socks and tie, preferably. A man wearing a gray suit, a light gray, white-striped shirt, a maroon figured tie, and maroon wool socks would be better off choosing a handkerchief initialed in maroon rather than one with a gray initial.

The handkerchief in a man's breast pocket is supposed to be a clean, completely unused one, folded and placed casually so that it shows about two inches above the edge of the pocket. Once a handkerchief from the breast pocket has been used (after the spare one in the hip pocket has been exhausted), a man is not supposed to put it back in the same pocket, because it is no longer suited for display and stuffing it down out of sight produces an ugly bulge. The Englishman shoves it up his sleeve (not a bad idea), but the carefully groomed man does not make himself a walking laundry bag by carrying two soiled handkerchiefs. He shifts one to the bottom of his brief case or his desk drawer, to be taken home for laundering. A man who travels a lot on his job does well to locate a good hand laundry near his office where he can have laundered the extra supply of handkerchiefs, shirts, and underwear he keeps in the office to take care of unexpected out-of-town trips or freshenings-up he may want to do when he goes directly from the office to a social engagement. Even the very young executive can usually find a bottom desk drawer or the back of a file drawer—or, better, his locker—where such accessories may be kept. Let him not be embarrassed over his little caches—some top executives keep entire wardrobe changes in their private offices and have dressing rooms attached to private baths, where they may groom themselves as is expected of them.

INITIALS ON HANDKERCHIEFS I like initials or monograms (two or more initials) when they are not too ostentatious, because they give a custom-made look to clothes. And, as this is the function of initials, they should never be machine done. In buying handkerchiefs be sure the initials are hand-embroidered and the hems hand-whipped or hemstitched, the material of good quality. A man spoils the effect of otherwise good grooming by bringing out a handkerchief that is sleazy or not immaculately clean. If a man asks a woman what constitutes good quality in handkerchiefs she will gladly show him what to look for in buying his own. Then he might go through his present collection and consign to use in spading the garden all those he bought in vending machines when he ran out of handkerchiefs on various business trips. Or give them to his young son whose ability to lose all handkerchiefs promptly will solve the problem of how to get rid of them.

INITIALS ON CLOTHES AND VARIOUS ARTICLES The rule for monogramming or initialing of handkerchiefs applies, too, to those on shirts, pajamas, and leather articles. Initials should never be ostentatious. If a man has his shirts custom-made and wants a monogram in white or color (and it should never, in this case, be a single initial [the last one] as is often used on handkerchiefs), he might have it put on the sleeve about three inches above the cuff rather than on the shirt front or pocket. Two or three little block initials—white, maroon, black, gray, or blue, preferred—are better than a scrolly monogram with an embroidered border. Initials on leather articles, such as a brief case or portfolio, are quite functional and should be readily readable, not just a fancy decoration. As only a man's family, intimate friends, or servants see him in his pajamas, he might have a fancy monogram in any color his heart desires, if he wants. It is usually placed on the left breast pocket. To monogram or initial everything one owns, from a car to a pipe, may seem feminine, so it's a good idea for a man not to let the women in his family overdo it in giving him monogrammed gifts.

JEWELRY What jewelry a man has should be of precious metal, good, simple design, and as expensive as his pocketbook permits. When he adds up the sums he has paid for the male equivalent of "junk jewelry"—tie clasps, tie pins, tricky cuff links, make-do studs, collar buttons, and watch chains, all of which eventually lose their plating or drop their ersatz stones—he will see that the gradual acquisition of good jewelry is good business as well as good taste. Before hurrying into the nearest men's shop and paying five dollars or more for brightly plated cuff links, because the last pair, costing the same, looks like something from the dime store, he might look through the jewelry his father or grandfather wore. He may find a beautiful pair of heavy gold links or some intricately enameled ones that he couldn't buy today from a dealer in antique jewelry for a hundred dollars or more. These "old-fashioned" things are often in far better taste than the machine-made jewelry most men must wear, either for lack of the price of anything better or because they don't know that heirlooms like these are never out of fashion.

Today a man doesn't wear diamond rings or stickpins, but he may find an old-fashioned stickpin that will be really distinguished in an Ascot tie—even if it does have a tiny diamond somewhere in the setting. Never discard these things on the ground they're not "modern."

If a young man's social life is relatively limited by the exigencies of bringing up a family, he might consider that some day he may be a man whose clothes are all made to order and who will be able to find the leisure for the kind of social life that almost requires such niceties as real jewelry. Grandfather's heavy gold watch chain may not look like the delicate platinum one someone else received when he served as best man at that expensive wedding, but it will have meaning to a grandson and even give him a little edge over the young man whose grandfather had no gold watch chain to leave him and who has had to work up to a platinum one himself.

A man with a big, long-fingered hand can wear a ring better than the man with a short pudgy one. If he has an antique seal ring—usually heavy gold with a coat of arms or a well-devised monogram—it may be worn on the little finger of either hand, although he's less likely to wince in handshaking with hearty individuals if he wears it on the left hand. A ring with a stone, if worn at all, should be flat and preferably unfaceted, set in a simple gold setting. Some class or fraternity rings are so badly designed that a man often discards them a few years after graduation. There is no reason why when a very young man demands a ring (usually as he enters prep school) that it can't be tasteful enough for him to wear throughout his lifetime if he wishes. To be avoided are such things as "Chinese style" initials, imitation rubies, garnets, or emeralds set in the signet. If the ring is not going to be especially made for the boy don't overlook the pawn shops or the little jewelers who sell antique jewelry. There may be found the kind of man's ring (or studs or watch chain) of which he will never cease to be proud.

Wedding rings for men came into considerable use during World War II, and it is probable that the men who started wearing them will continue to do so and so influence later bridegrooms to follow suit. It used to be thought incorrect for a man to wear his wedding band on any but the little finger of his right hand, but the modern wedding-ringed husband prefers the same finger the bride's ring circles—the fourth finger of the left hand. And it does seem to me that his wearing it there does make it seem unmistakable that he is a "married man."

Rings worn on the index finger or on the second finger are just plain theatrical and affected, no matter how they were worn in Victorian days.

Watches and cigarette cases may be gold, silver, enamel, steel, or platinum, and the cigarette cases should not be set with precious or semi-precious stones. Wrist watches, unless of delicate design and without a leather strap, are less likely to be worn with evening clothes. Instead, a thin watch, in gold or platinum, on a thin gold or platinum chain (or grandfather's good gold chain, which may be monumental but impressive) is worn. If any ill-advised woman should try to give a man a platinum chain with tiny diamonds between the links, he should return it to the jeweler who was talked into making it and go to Palm Beach on the proceeds or put them on the nearest fast horse.

BAD WEATHER WEAR

Whenever possible, waterproofed shoes are preferable to rubbers for street wear in bad weather, but where rubbers are necessary the kind that covers just the sole of the shoe certainly looks better. For heavy duty in the country, elk-hide boots are more attractive than bulky galoshes, but the latter must be the choice of the commuter in snowy weather. Raincoats and hats (or plastic protectors over hats) are more practical than umbrellas, but there are times when every man needs to carry an umbrella. It should be large and black with a wooden crook handle and should be carried furled in its case when not in actual use. It may have a gold or silver initialed band on the shank of the handle.

THE RAINCOAT   The good old British raincoat, belted trench-coat style or fly-front, has been taken to the heart of the American male, who, like his English cousin, wears it as a light extra topcoat in the city or country, rain or no rain. In London this practice makes more sense, as any bright day is likely to turn into a rainy one before teatime, anyway. There is one injunction I should like to make—that the American not wear his raincoat when it is so dirty it embarrasses the women he escorts. An Englishman feels that his raincoat *must* be dirty—in fact, I am sure he tramps on a new one before he wears it for the first time—but in the United States a dirty raincoat is just a sign of careless grooming. In fact, it's just as repulsive as any other garment worn once too often.

WHAT EVERY MAN SHOULD KNOW ABOUT
VESTS, SOCKS, AND SHOES

The vest is, quite obviously from the look of the back of it, a piece of apparel to be worn under a coat. If a man does remove his coat, when given permission to do so for reasons of comfort, he should remove the vest, too. If he is wearing suspenders it is better to keep his coat on or, if he happens to have on a belt, too, to unhitch the suspenders when he removes coat and vest. A coatless man is more agreeable to the eye than one in a vest or one whose suspenders show. Need anything be said about the abhorrent custom of wearing sleeve bands? If a man can't buy shirts that are the right sleeve length, he should have the sleeves shortened or have fewer but better shirts, custom-made.

White cotton or lisle socks are never worn except with white shoes or sneakers. Heavy white wool socks, on the contrary, may be worn with country shoes and clothes—with tweeds, flannels, linen suits, or wool slacks— and for active sports. Argyle socks, even the most vivid patterns, have invaded urban areas and may be worn quite appropriately with such business suits as Glen plaids, wools, cheviots, flannels, and tweeds. Socks should be chosen with an eye to the tie worn, but exact matches are more cautious than interesting.

SHOES   There was a time when a rigidly well-dressed man would have looked askance at the wearing of brown shoes with a blue suit. The ultra-conservative still wear black shoes with a blue suit, but brown are certainly correct, and with any tweed or rough-surface mixture more suitable, in my opinion. I'll grant that a hard-surface blue serge might conceivably limit one to black shoes.

Brown shoes are also worn with all the varieties of gray with the exception of Oxford which looks better accompanied by black. Gray suits are more conservatively teamed with black shoes, but the combination would be unthinkable in the country, which is definitely brown shoe terrain.

Suède shoes in brown reverse calf or buckskin are permissible in the city with tweeds, and the monk shoe, moccasin and rough brogue, once solely country foot covering, are now seen in the city with tweeds or slacks.

White shoes are certainly not a good choice for town wear, because they soil immediately. The same is true of brown and white sport shoes. It is difficult to find a shoe that looks right with the informality of the summer suit made of seersucker or the various cotton mixtures so needed in our cities in hot weather. The monk's shoe or the moccasin seem nearest to being acceptable, especially as the cotton suit coats are now often worn with gray or brown-tone flannels or with gabardine slacks in a variety of muted colors from sand and grayed greens to slate blue. Black-and-white shoes, while they are still made for the best men's shops, are somewhat theatrical and pretty Victorian.

Formal shoes fall into two categories, the patent, bowed, dancing pump, and the laced patent evening oxford. The pumps are worn with tails, at home with a smoking jacket, or with a dinner jacket. They are preferred over the other types when the wearer expects to dance. The laced patents should not be pointed in toe or spade, and they look better without a toe cap. Black oxfords worn with morning coat should have a plain tip and preferably should be calf, avoiding the heavy-duty look of black street oxfords. These are the shoes in which a man is married when he dons the full regalia of a morning coat. Patent shoes of any sort would seem too frivolous for such an occasion. Nor are they suitable for funerals.

THE HATLESS AND GLOVELESS MAN

Frequently in winter you see even well-dressed men going gloveless and hatless. Perhaps they feel hardier that way, but an ungloved hand is, in the winter, usually a chapped and roughened one. For summer there are available loose, stitched, cotton chamois gloves, which give a finished look to the costume and keep hands from getting grimy in the city. Only the man whose hair stays put should attempt to go hatless in town. If he has no hair, letting the sun beat down on his pate doesn't stimulate the hair follicles, it seems. And he'll probably look better-dressed wearing either a light-weight felt, a panama, or some kind of straw hat. The traditional sailor is becoming to any man with a good figure, medium to tall in height, and preferably with a long or oval face. But let him be careful not to choose one with a band associated with a club or fraternity to which he does not belong. These color combinations can't be patented by the organizations in question, but wearing such a band when not entitled to do so makes one seem like a gate crasher. Before a man buys a band, he would do well to ask the clerk if it does belong to some specific goup. Adorning a hat band with fish flies or bright litle feathers is amusing for country wear or, if he's the type and can afford it, he may choose bands made entirely of pheasant feathers—but only for sports wear.

Needless to say, going hatless to formal events, to city weddings, to funerals, even to business calls is not very appropriate. Yes, there are men who affect a certain boyishness by going hatless winter and summer, rain or shine, but if a man wears a suitable hat, he is always right. This can't be said if he barges in everywhere hatless. Especially if he accompanies a well-turned-out woman.

WHEN NOT TO WEAR EVENING CLOTHES

It is not correct—no matter what you occasionally see—for a man to wear dinner jacket or tail coat in the daytime unless, perhaps, he's being buried! (And to follow up this lugubrious aside, if the family does decide to attire the deceased in formal clothes, it should give him the dignity of full evening dress for a night funeral and of a morning coat in the daytime. A tuxedo doesn't seem quite right.)

The only other possible uses for evening wear in the daytime are an audience with the Pope and certain Continental State functions when full evening dress is worn, not a tuxedo. Evening clothes should not be worn before six o'clock, unless, for example, a man is leaving the city for a suburban dinner or vice versa and can change only at home. But even this means he would be likely to emerge in his bedecked state between five and six. The ideal is not to appear in dinner or evening clothes in broad daylight, although in spring and summer this is usually quite unavoidable.

A tuxedo, essentially a frivolous garment, should not be worn in church for any reason. For a night wedding, even at home, full dress should be worn by members of the wedding party, unless they prefer the alternative of dark sack suits. In summer they may wear white flannels with blue coats or for an evening garden wedding, white dinner jackets.

WHEN WHITE FLANNELS OR PASTEL DOESKINS
MAY NOT BE WORN

A man should not wear easily soiled trousers, such as white flannels or pale-colored doeskins, in the city or on a train. Possible exceptions might be some urban, outdoor activity such as dancing on the Mall in Central Park or a Stadium concert if he's going on foot or by car or taxi. Flannels are worn, at least by the host or by house guests, in a penthouse, because of its pseudo-rural atmosphere. The trousers will get even more sooty on the penthouse terrace than they would on a train, but the fun of a penthouse is its carefully nurtured atmosphere of country or at least suburban living.

WEARING DECORATIONS

THE LEGION OF HONOR Most countries grant various orders to distinguished citizens and non-citizens who have performed some outstanding service to the State. Among those often seen internationally are the various buttons and ribbon of the French Legion of Honor (Légion d'honneur).

There are five grades of the Legion of Honor, each distinguished by its insigne as follows:

First Grade, Knight (Chevalier): Red ribbon at buttonhole, worn from the buttonhole to the outer edge of the left lapel.

Second Grade, Officer (Officier): Red rosette in buttonhole.

Third Grade, Commander (Commandeur): Red rosette on silver bar.

Fourth Grade, Grand Officer (Grand Officier): Red rosette on silver and gold grosgrain covered bar.

Fifth Grade, Grand Cross (Grand Croix), highest rank: Red rosette on gold grosgrain covered bar.

The highest rank that women achieve in the Legion of Honor is that of Commander (Commandeur). Women wear the red ribbon of the Knight on tailored suits, sewn on the left lapel just as men do. On street dresses they may wear it through the collar or neckline on the left side.

The insigne of Commander is pinned to the left shoulder as flowers would be.

For formal wear, women Commanders wear a white-lacquered five-pointed star on a circlet of gold attached to a large red ribbon worn necklace fashion.

Male Commanders for formal wear wear the same cross on a gold circlet on a large red ribbon tied around the neck beneath the white tie.

The Grand Officer has for formal wear a ten-pointed silver plaque worn on the left side of the breast. The Grand Cross (generally given to sovereigns and chiefs of state, occasionally to commanders in chief) is worn with red sash draped across the chest from right to left.

Holders of various ranks of the Legion of Honor may use the following designations or initials after their names: Knight ✳ ; Officer (O.) ✳ ; Commander (C.) ✳ ; Grand Officer (G. O.) ✳ ; Grand Cross (G. C.).

RULES FOR WEARING DECORATIONS BY CIVILIANS A U.S. civilian possessing any U.S. war decoration wears it on the left side, always above those granted him by any other country.[1] Other decorations are worn in the order in which they are received, except that those of any one country are always grouped together. This is true even when one has been received after a decoration from another country has been awarded.

The possessor of many decorations need not wear them all at the same time on formal occasions. But an American possessing an American decoration wears it at any time that he also wears a foreign one, with, as has been noted, the American one always taking precedence.

American decorations are worn in order of their particular importance, irrespective of when they were bestowed. Foreign decorations are worn in order of their bestowal, irrespective of their relative importance.

The rule that foreign decorations are worn according to order of bestowal has the following exception: at a reception or dinner abroad in honor of a foreign official or any distinguished citizen of a foreign nation, any decoration an American has received from that country takes precedence over his other foreign decorations for the occasion.

CHAPTER EIGHTEEN

WHAT'S WHAT IN VARIOUS SPORTS

GOLF

Golf courses fall into two categories, the private club to which one must be invited by a member and the public course open to all upon payment of a fixed green fee and caddy fee. On both public and private courses the caddy fee varies greatly as does the green fee.

At a private club guests usually pay their own green fee and caddy fee. At the "nineteenth hole" (the bar) it is usual among men for the loser or losers to pay for a round of drinks, but often each player picks up his own check.

[1]Exceptions: The Medal of Honor and the Presidential Citation ribbon are worn on the right. With evening dress the Medal of Honor is worn on a broad blue ribbon around the neck, hanging just below the tie. The Presidential Citation ribbon is worn, by both men and *women,* on the right, in miniature, for full evening dress. The Navy, in uniform, wears even these decorations on the left.

At the first tee there is no special order of precedence except that a guest or guests would be asked to tee off first and a woman or older player would usually be given the first drive. Thereafter, the winner tees off first. Sometimes on crowded courses, when eight or ten players arrive at the first tee at once, there is a ball slide into which players are expected to place their first ball as they step onto the green. When their ball emerges it is their turn to tee off. This system was devised to obviate dissension at the first tee. A player who is unaware that it is used, however, and who does not put his ball in the slide may miss out on the play entirely or at least be delayed.

Two players supposedly take precedence over a foursome, which must necessarily play much more slowly. It is good golf manners for a foursome to allow a twosome to go through. On the other hand, a twosome that is playing a leisurely game always permits a businesslike foursome to play through. Any other combination of players, from the lone golfer to the "gang"—over four—must allow the twosome or the foursome precedence. On many courses, especially public ones, only twosomes or foursomes are permitted on crowded week ends.

Even non-golfers should know the rules concerning quiet as a player tees off. Other players should stand still—not even make practice swings with their clubs nor speak to their caddies as another player addresses the ball. When a ball is lost other players in the group help look for it, but the search is never drawn out to such an extent as to hold up the play—a few minutes is enough. If he wishes, a player who has lost a ball may go on to the next hole, leaving his caddy to make a further search.

Great care must be taken not to tee off when others are in line with what a player hopes will be the flight of the ball and certainly never until the players ahead have each had their second strokes. The warning "fore" may not carry sufficiently against even a light wind. It should be used infrequently. Instead, a player should wait until golfers immediately ahead are well out of range.

CLOTHES   The most comfortable trousers for golf are slacks, usually in gray flannel or the tannish gabardines. In winter a regular tucked-in sport shirt with a light pull-over is the conservative choice with the slacks in pleasant weather. In cold weather a windbreaker or leather jacket is worn over a sport shirt with or without the addition of a pull-over. Socks, summer and winter, are best in wool, argyle, white or bright colors such as canary. Hats are always of the sports type, a snap-brim, unbound felt, a rough straw, a cap or a turned down duck hat such as is worn sailing. Shoes should be rubber-soled (not sneakers) or regular cleated golf shoes.

In hot weather loose sport shirts, not tucked in, in conservative solid colors are worn by some (depends on the man) over light, often blue, linen or duck slacks. Shorts are definitely taboo, and, of course, neckties if worn must be suited to sport shirts. They may be knit wool, cotton, or string or perhaps a gay cotton bow tie. A golf tie should not be silk, but a silk choppa, knotted beneath the collar of a sport shirt, is attractive for sports wear.

TENNIS AND BADMINTON

White clothes are so traditional on the tennis court that it is obvious that there must be a reason for them. Dark colors, even in light-weight cotton or other fabrics, under a beating sun would absorb the rays, while white deflects them. That is why white clothing is worn in the tropics. The extravagant white flannel trousers that used to be *de rigueur* for the well-dressed tennist are certainly dreadfully hot, despite their lack of color, but that is because of the weave rather than the weight of the material—and the same may be said of the white ducks that have always been considered correct. In tournaments—especially the internationals—white flannels are still worn, but more often on juniors white knee-length shorts are seen too. Any comfortable white sport shirt or a polo shirt permitting full play in the shoulders and arms is worn on the court for the warm-up, if the player wishes, or to be thrown over his shoulders, or donned, when he comes off the court. White wool socks are preferred, even in the hottest weather, as affording the best protection to the feet against the pounding on the court. Wool socks, as a matter of fact, are superior at all times of the year to rayon, cotton, or nylon for any active wear, because they allow for the evaporation of perspiration. (Some men even wear very sheer black wool evening socks, ribbed or plain, for dancing, for this reason.)

The tennis hat is usually soft white duck, sometimes with a green underbrim to protect the eyes from glare. Such hats are usually washable, although to see those worn by most men, you wouldn't think so. Tennis shoes are the flat, rubber-soled, heelless ones developed originally for the game. Wearing any other type of shoe, rubber-soled or not, generally calls forth a severe reprimand from the grounds committee and removal of the offender from the court.

Lawn tennis courts should not be torn up by leather or composition soles, either, but rubber-soled shoes or other types than the tennis shoe are often worn for badminton.

Many men prefer the knee-length English tennis shorts, in white or sand, to flannels or ducks for both badminton and tennis. They are comfortable and look well on most men. They should not be too short. An initial investment in shorts of excellent quality, properly tailored (they are usually pleated at the belt-line like well-fitting English slacks) will mean a long-run saving. In buying them, look for durable, closely woven material, slide fasteners, reinforced seams, sufficient leg length to cover the thigh to the knee, the absence of metal on fabric belts or half-belts, and a hem that is generous enough so that it won't fray out at the first hard laundering. Don't try to substitute white or tan bathing shorts for tennis shorts. Really proper with English shorts are long white wool, turn-over socks that come just below the knee and which are worn, of course, without garters. The alternative is the white wool anklet, with or without a cuff. Ordinary length white wool socks, worn necessarily without garters, look sloppy and tend to ride into the heel of the tennis shoe.

BEHAVIOR ON THE TENNIS COURT   A sociologist—or a psychiatrist—could glean considerable information about any tennis player's personality defects by watching his behavior on the tennis court. There is something about this game played in its sun-baked, circumscribed area with its inevitable gallery that spotlights character more quickly than any other except badminton. In these games each man stands revealed, even in a game of mixed doubles. He has plenty of room in which to throw a tantrum—or his racket—lots of space in which to yell and hurl taunts at his opponent, many opportunities to cheat when there is no referee and his word as a sportsman and gentleman decides whether ball or shuttlecock are "in" or "out." There is sufficient opportunity for watchers to observe the apologist whose "bum serve" is loudly explained by all kinds of things except his lack of technical skill at the game. We see here the man whose anxiety about himself carries over to the court—a man who doesn't dare to lose a game and who, if he does come out the loser at the end of the set, derives none of the relaxation the game should supply, but only adds to his inner anger and aggressions.

People cannot be taught by rules alone how to behave in any game so that others will not be disturbed and inconvenienced by their actions. This is because what a man *is*, he is most likely to express in the way he plays, and no list of rules is going to change the unconscious attitude he brings to the game. But if he can't or won't get in tune with the rules, social pressure usually effects his compliance with them. No man can play tennis, badminton, or table tennis by *himself*, as he can play golf, hunt rabbits, or shoot clay pigeons. He needs at least one opponent, and if he is consistently objectionable as a player he finds everyone worthy of his mettle either hostilely unwilling to play with him or else having other commitments— often suspiciously far into the future. When this goes on too long an intelligent man finds out what's wrong with himself, the boorish one quits the game —and then belittles it—and the stupid or unyielding one resorts to playing with the professionals—at a fee—or with any members of his family unable to say him nay.

Here, then, are the rules of the tennis or badminton court, and many apply equally well to many other sports—even the British cricket. In fact, the phrase "it isn't cricket" has come to epitomize all things unfair and uncomfortable to others in social, political, business, and even amorous behavior.

1. Come decently attired to the court, in clean, acceptable clothes appropriate to the game.

2. If no court is immediately available, await your turn courteously, making no attempt to disturb a play setup until a set has been completed by those in possession of the court and there is ample indication that a determining set is not to follow. If a set of singles has just been played, any suggestion that the court be given over to doubles must come from the players already on the court, although on a crowded day any considerate players would make such a suggestion, even if the club rules didn't require fair sharing of the courts on Saturdays, Sundays, and holidays.

3. Inexperienced players should not demand to share court space with crack players on crowded days, but should team up with those in their own class. If week ends and holidays are the only times they can practice or learn the game, they should try to occupy the courts either very early or late or at any time when others more proficient are not waiting for them. But fast, able players, in turn, should be satisfied with fewer sets on busy days. If they play more than three, they should break up the foursome to include some fresh player or players.

4. Each court is an island. Keep your activities and remarks and conversation within it, so as not to disturb other players or make a boiler factory of the club house porch or the side lines. Spectators, presumably dues-payers too, have the right to watch the game without being jolted by loud hoots of triumph, yells of despair, swearing, shouted imprecations, racket throwing, or other unseemly exhibitionism.

5. Toss rackets for first serve, or choose any other method of deciding pleasantly who should start the service, but don't assume the service yourself, unless asked to do so. A first serve, unless you know your opponent expects and can meet vigorous competition from the start, should be a moderate or slow one to indicate that this is a pleasurable game of give-and-take you are initiating, not a would-be one-sided slaughter.

6. If the sun will be in the eyes of a player or players on one side of the net, you may offer to take the sunny side in the initial game yourself, especially if you have invited your opponent to play, or determine the side each takes by toss.

7. Don't alibi your game in any way. Play as well as you can, except in a friendly game against a decidedly unworthy opponent and then if you do relax out of fellowship and to make the game a little more interesting and encouraging for him—or her—don't be offensively obvious about it. If you let anyone beat you—or nearly win—never say so. Don't take the wind out of the other fellow's sails. Leading on a coming player this way may develop him into exhilarating competition later on, to your own advantage.

8. Be a cheerful loser and a modest winner. Don't crow over your triumphs or sulk or exhibit anger over your defeat. If you are constantly defeated and feel angry or discouraged about it to such a degree that the game is not a pleasure to you or your opponents, take more lessons, play only with other players in your class, or change your game to something else that suits you better physically or emotionally than this exacting, competitive game. Insisting on playing a game for which, after a fair amount of time, you show no natural aptitude is frustrating to you and annoying to all but the most complacent opponents.

9. While spectators have their rights, they also are subject to rules guaranteeing the rights of the players. Spectators should make no comments, critical or otherwise, from the side lines during the course of play. They must not distract the players by invading the court for any reason or dodging past the back line while play is in progress. They should not lean on the

posts, climb on the fence, leave the gate open, or touch the net. They should not throw anything onto a court or behind it—such as a burned-out cigarette —as this can cause a player to fall or miss a shot. Drunkenness is no more desirable on a club porch than it is on the court itself. The function of a tennis club is to provide playing opportunities for members who expect to play tennis. Any spectators there happen to be, from small boys to old gaffers, must respect the players' right to play without interference or distraction from the gallery.

10. When you ask your opponent to keep the score you have no alternative but to accept his count. If you know he has colored the scoring to favor his own side, you are privileged not to play with him again or, at least, not to permit him to keep score again, but don't make an issue of it publicly or even privately.

11. At game and set, thank your opponents or opponent. You needn't apologize for winning nor explain why you lost—a matter that is usually obvious enough. It's not necessary, Wimbledon style, to leap over the net to show the winner how magnanimous you feel about being trounced. In fact, easy give—and especially—easy take seems the essence of good sportsmanship in social games. Even where stiff competition for the sake of a cup or other honor is involved the same rules of courtesy hold sway.

YACHTING

The word "yacht" comes from the Dutch verb *jagen*, to hunt. Essentially a yacht is a pleasure craft, a light sailing vessel meant for racing, but the term can refer to any pleasure craft that is not propelled by oars, whether it derives its power from the wind or from steam or electric power.

Anything over one hundred feet is technically a ship. All sailboats—with the exception of skiffs (light rowing or skulling boats)—are correctly called yachts, but seasoned yachtsmen casually refer to anything under sail as a "boat" and to themselves as "sailors." To refer to one's own sailboat, whatever its size, as a yacht, seems pretentious, even though, again technically, a boat is actually a dinghy, a launch, tender, rowboat or skiff, none of which is in the yachting, or racing class.

There are numerous yacht classes, some distinguished by the class mark on the mainsail—the Star, International, Atlantic, Lightning, all racing classes —several by meters and others by their length. Yachts of the same class usually race together or, if they are unevenly matched, they are raced on a handicap basis.

A fanatical sailor spurns any auxiliary power in a sailboat, preferring to get in and out of harbors and yacht basins under sail and to take his chances on a homeward-bound wind. When yachtsmen become fathers and there are children aboard to consider, this fanaticism is often tempered for a time and a "kicker" is added to the gear—at least until the children can be taught to sail.

Because the space aboard a yacht is circumscribed, the rule of the sea concerning neatness must be observed by guests. Everything must be ship-shape. No one should come aboard a yacht with a stiff suitcase. Stowable gear is always canvas. Guests on any owner-sailed yacht should be prepared either to lend a hand or to find a way to keep out of the way, especially at those crucial times when the sails are being hoisted or lowered, the course is being changed, or a jib is being broken out. Guests who have never been on the sea before can learn to do the small jobs such as pumping out the bilge or polishing the bright work.

Smoking aboard a small boat must be limited to the times when the boat is on its course—that is, for working hands. Cigarettes must not be thrown on the decks and stamped out or tossed over on the windward side, which would cause the sparks to fly back aboard. Garbage, too, must never be disposed of to windward or, of course, in a yacht basin or harbor.

On large yachts with a paid hand and crew, guests do not fraternize. Their relations with the crew are formal, and they call the men by their last names. A professional captain is called by his title and is treated with respect due his highly technical calling. On a very large yacht the stewards who attend the cabins and saloon are called either by their last names or simply "steward."

YACHTING CLOTHES What one wears aboard depends on the size of the yacht and where it is tied up.

A man invited to lunch or dine aboard a large yacht (with a saloon and cabins) tied up at a city club would wear just what he would wear in town. If he is to join the same yacht at an out-of-town mooring he would wear suitable country clothes and rubber- or rope-soled shoes and some kind of cap or hat that would not blow off in a wind. Warm sweaters, even in mild weather, are essential and shorts, preferably of the longer variety, often comfortable, but they should be worn with knee-length, cuffed wool socks.

On smaller yachts under fifty feet, or even on those over fifty feet where there is no paid crew, male guests (and sometimes female ones) should be prepared to lend a hand. This requires hardy clothes—never span new ones. Duck, sailcloth, or denim trousers are best with T-shirts and pull-over sweaters, pea jackets, or wind-resistant jackets. For sailing in sloppy weather parkas are ideal; otherwise a raincoat, preferably an oilskin with hat, is a necessity. Socks are best in white or light wool. Sunglasses or a sun-peak cap are advisable as a shield against the glare. Sunburn cream or lotion is needed, too, unless the skin has acquired a protective tan, for sunburn hazard is far greater on the water than on land. If the boat is very small, it is a good idea for a man to wear bathing trunks under his trousers, if he plans to swim. No one, needless to say, should dive overboard except from the stern or sides of the boat and then only with the captain's permission and only, too, when there is a tow line out the back if the boat is under sail. At all times the captain is responsible for the safety of the passengers.

CUSTOMS, DRESS, AND TABOOS IN OTHER SPORTS

Sportsmen have very stiff notions of what constitutes a gentleman, and unless you know these shibboleths you may be guilty, in your enthusiasm over a sport new to you, of offending, of being classified as a boor rather than, more fairly, as a mere ignoramus. Sportsmen are notably intolerant about non-conformist behavior.

In playing all games and pursuing all sports in a team or group you must abide by the accepted rules—unless, of course, the majority of players or participators agrees to relax the rules in some way or adopt other ones pro tem. For example (to the horror of experts), on our own badminton court, we prefer to score in the manner of ping-pong rather than use the regulation scoring as set down by the American Badminton Association. We do this because we think the ping-pong scoring speeds up the game and is easier to keep track of for both spectators and players. But on neighbors' courts where the usual rules are well-established, we follow them and allow our host the privilege of keeping the more complicated score.

When swimming, you do not swim beneath the diving board, for reasons that should be perfectly obvious, or jump off a raft into the midst of water-treading or floating bathers—instead you slip off backwards to create the least possible backwash. On most beaches bathing trunks without tops are now permitted, as are the briefest of trunks. A man should be perfectly objective about his figure, however, before deciding in favor of extremely attenuated costumes.

Swimming in the same ocean does not give a man the right to force his conversation or attentions on other—usually feminine—swimmers or sun bathers. Exhibitions of water-splashing, porpoising, wrestling, and sand-throwing, often engaged in by very young men to attract feminine attention, usually make them offensive in the very eyes of those they seek to attract, and certainly make them loathsome to the run-of-the-beach bather in search of a little peace.

There are various sports followed solo or in groups or teams, for which unwritten rules exist. If you hunt in the deer-shooting season, for example, you must not wear a white shirt or show a white handkerchief—or anything else white, for that matter—for it might be mistaken for that little patch of white on a deer's tail and so call forth a shot by another hunter stalking game in the same terrain. Loud talking or even noisy movements that frighten away the game limit not only your own possibility of making a kill but that of other hunters. In bagging small game, such as partridge or grouse, determine the legal limit before setting out and stay within it. It is not good sportsmanship to go over the permitted bag, even when there is little possibility of being caught at it. In shooting small game, never fire until the birds are on the wing, never shoot down a treed animal or one in cover, never horse in a fish without playing him on the line—give all a sporting chance to escape. In a wild turkey shoot, the sportsmen often camp under the trees in which the birds have roosted for the night, but any man who tried to wing one before it left the roost would be considered no gentleman. When you are working with dogs, wait until they have flushed the birds well out of cover and never shoot too low or you may pepper the dogs instead of the birds.

Guns, even in the hands of experts, are dangerous weapons. Look well before you aim, check the position of others in the party before you shoot. Carry guns, when not actively hunting or shooting, with the safety catch on. In the field, except when actually shooting, and en route, carry them with the muzzle down or with the gun over the shoulder with muzzle pointing up, or "break" the gun. Unload your gun when you enter the shooting wagon or car and when you stack it. Never lean on a gun.

In shooting with dogs, give orders only to your own. If another hunter's dog retrieves for you by mistake, don't take the bird from him yourself. Ask the owner or the handler to do so, as game retrieved by a dog is considered the property of the dog's master rather than of the man who shot it down. Also, a hunting dog must, more than any other, be a "one man dog." He is not a pet in the usual sense but a work dog and should receive his orders and his commendations only from his owner or handler, from whom he is trained to expect both. Shooting is like tennis in one respect—you don't take another man's shot. If a bird comes within range of another huntsman's gun, leave it to him. Don't "reach" for it, even though you, as a better marksman, are certain he will miss it.

CLOTHES FOR HUNTING AND SHOOTING

Comfortable, loose-fitting clothes—corduroys, flannel shirts—are wanted. A red hat, a patch of red for the sleeve or back of a jacket, or even a red handkerchief knotted around the cap, is a necessary safety device. High-laced boots, waterproofed, are needed for marshlands and snake country. Otherwise any heavy, comfortable shoes cushioned by wool socks will do. A hunter who goes into a blind inadequately prepared to withstand hours of cold and damp will be *persona non grata*. If you have never owned long woolen underwear, prepare to wear it now—and if you're a novice, maybe two pairs are better than one. A man in a blind who complains unendingly of the cold because he isn't dressed for it is in the same class as the pariah who ruins the fishing trip because he has not developed the fisherman's quiet philosophy of "watchful waiting" and can't sit still for what may prove to be fruitless hours without a catch.

In fishing and in duck hunting, you hear much about the need for being quiet so as not to frighten off the quarry. Low conversation is permissible in deep-sea fishing but not in surface fishing, as fish can hear and they feel vibrations such as are made by throwing an empty beer bottle into the water, by rocking the boat, by banging of any sort. Ducks' hearing is very acute, even when they are high above the blind. Fish take fright at violent movement, if they are surface swimmers. It takes a certain philosophical state of mind, a rigid self-control to make one a good fisherman or duck hunter, and especially an acceptable companion in these enterprises.

In the matter of terminology, one "shoots" other birds but "hunts" ducks. You "hunt" deer and other four-footed game. The serious hunter and fisherman may cling to the superstition—as does the actor stepping on-stage—that you spoil his luck if you wish him good luck as he starts out.

DISTRESS SIGNAL   People handling guns should know the distress signal—three shots fired at three-second intervals.

SKIING AND SKATING

The traditional ski costume consists of special baggy leg, ankle-hugging ski pants with elastic that goes under the arch of the foot to hold the pants in the heavy ski boots. The idea is to keep them both warm and dry, so the new water- and wind-resistant fabrics of treated cotton are more effective than plain wool. A coat, sometimes hooded, of matching material is worn over a wool shirt or sweater. A ski cap with ear tabs is a requisite, too, as are two pair of thick wool socks (the outside one worn over the trouser leg and turned down over the top of the shoe) and warm, gauntleted mittens or gloves in wool or ski cloth. The ski outfit for both men and women is good for many other winter sports such as tobogganing, outdoor skating, and hiking on snow-covered roads.

Skiing seems to be one sport that requires careful instruction from professionals or friends. The tyro skier is a menace to himself and others if he blunders onto a difficult run or discards his poles Swedish style before he is ready. He must do his practicing on the simpler slopes and behave as modestly as the beginner in other sports in the presence of accomplished skiers. It is tiring for one whose muscles are unaccustomed to the effort, but the beginner must herringbone up the slopes or use the ski or rope tow and not walk up, breaking the crust and so make the slope perilous or unusable for others. Every skier falls sometime, but the beginner seems to be mostly on his derrière. As he makes his precipitous way down the trail, he shouts "track" to warn others of his approach. On the slalom run, when he graduates to it, he is thoughtful to put back any gate poles he dislodges—right away, not on his ascent. His conduct on the ski tow or rope tow should say very plainly, "I'm a beginner and I want to learn the rules of this sport." If in his embarrassment at being a beginner he acts the cutup, he will be considered crass, to say the least. Generally speaking, this is a sport that must be learned on locale, although it is sometimes possible to take a few lessons from professionals indoors. If you decide to learn to ski, don't spoil the fun of professional skiers or of others out of your strictly amateur class. Mind your own quiet business and take your lessons seriously, or there is a fine chance that you may break your neck.

Almost anyone can skate if he has strong ankles. I've seen babies skating almost as soon as they learned to walk, and I've seen men and women in their seventies showing a gay blade. It all depends on how you go about it. There's always the skater who looks as if he's skating to a fire—round and round he races, frightening all the timid ones. There's the old gentleman in the middle of the rink performing graceful figure eights and bothering no one. There's the little boy on the double runners shuffling a foot or two at a time while clutching desperately at a hockey stick held by his father.

The clothes you wear for skating should be warm wool or wind-resistant and waterproof material. Skates attached to shoes are safer than the kind you attach yourself and, of course, better-looking. An older man may cling to his knickers for skating, and at that they are more comfortable for the purpose than cuffed tweed trousers, I am sure. A young man wears ski pants or slacks.

On an indoor rink you soon find your place among the slow or fast skaters —the fast ones are usually on the outside of the rink, and heaven help you if you stray in their path. As on the street, a man takes the outside position when he's accompanying a lady. Tripping a skater through your own awkwardness or foolish interference is grounds for mayhem. Loud shouting or games of tag disturb the philosophical skaters on a metropolitan indoor or outdoor rink, and usually an official puts a stop to them if they occur. If you cut any capers, be sure they are graceful ones that will be appreciated by the inevitable onlookers.

CHAPTER NINETEEN

THE WELL-GROOMED MAN

The well-groomed man looks clean, his clothes fit him comfortably, his shoes are well shined and their heels in good order, his tie is neatly tied so that it covers the collar joining and the short end lies well under the longer one if he's wearing a four-in-hand. If he ties his tie in a Windsor knot, the knot should be small and tidy, not theatrically large. If he wears a bow tie, it should be solidly foursquare, not a droopy little blob or with the ends tucked under the collar.

If he can help it, the well-groomed man never wears a suit the second day without having it pressed, unless it is of a material—such as tweed—or a nylon or other synthetic mixture which shakes out overnight. To facilitate this, he hangs his trousers over the bar of a valet stand when he takes them off or puts them immediately in their hanger—one for each pair of trousers. His coat is hung on a hanger or on the valet stand and buttoned so it will fall into shape.

A fastidious man never wears the same underwear or socks the second day, and he is never without a clean handkerchief. He keeps his nails clean and short with the cuticle pushed back. If he has his nails professionally manicured, they may be buffed but should never have any colored or even colorless polish applied.

A man who's unduly hirsute should have his barber clip the hairs in his ears and nostrils (but, of course, for safety's sake, never tweeze them). If his eyebrows run rampant they can be cautiously weeded out to give him a more groomed appearance, although any tweezing should be restricted to stray eyebrows or to the heavy hairs between the brows—a man's brow line should never be thinned or obviously shaped.

For the man with the blue jowl there seems to be no other course than that of a twice-daily shave. Powder doesn't really cover that bristle. The husband who gives himself a shaving holiday on a day at home is in the same class as the wife who doesn't put on her make-up or take her hair out of curlers until afternoon.

The well-groomed man never allows his hair to get so shaggy his new haircut is all too apparent. His hair is trimmed as often as necessary to keep it from colliding with his collar or his ears. He has it scissor-trimmed, not clipped, so as to avoid an ugly ridge across the back of his head. His side-burns are worn short but should be scissored rather than closely clipped or shaved. They are needed to give balance to his face. If he is bald he should realize that letting his side or back hair grow long enough to drape stickily over the bald spot deceives no one and usually produces a peculiar parting in the hair. And, let him be sure his bald pate is washed as often as he washes his face, because it is just as vulnerable to dirt.

I have a particularly soft spot for bald-headed men because so many of them suffer so obviously and needlessly from what they consider a handicap. Anthropologists have pointed out that baldness is often hereditary, that it is a very male type of complaint because usually it comes from overactivity of the pituitary gland, one of the glands that make men men. Scientists have pointed out, too, that eunuchs are very seldom bald. On the other hand, we associate luxuriant hair with femininity. And satyrs are depicted as bald. Perhaps women's intuition tells her these things, because you rarely find a wife concerned over the baldness of her husband. If he could understand this, he would sweep his hat off on the street, not lift it timidly or touch the brim in an effort to keep his secret shame to himself. And when he goes to a photographer, he will not insist on being photographed with his hat on —a dead giveaway. Instead, he will get help in making up his bald spot for the occasion, so that it will not be high-lighted in the picture. Any woman can show him how this is painlessly and quickly done.

Some men perspire quite heavily, winter and summer. If this perspiration is excessive enough to stain his suits under the arm a man should have re-course to any of the commercially available deodorants and perspiration checks offered for both men's and women's use. (If hatbands show perspiration marks they should be changed as often as necessary.) Daily or some-times twice-daily baths or showers should be routine for any man, but for the heavy perspirer they are obligatory. No cologne or powder can possibly cover the need of thorough daily cleansing.

Mention of cologne brings me to the observation that custom has changed in this respect, too. A few years back no American he-man would have con-sidered using a bit of cologne on his handkkerchief or after his bath. A man didn't use perfumes—or so he pretended. But American men, nevertheless, were inundated in a sea of ill-blended effluvia—violet hair tonic, mint, lilac, or carnation after-shave lotion, lilies of the valley or some such in their talcum, pine or geraniums in their bath soap. Now there are matched sets of these preparations for men or mercifully odorless items that won't conflict with a little good-quality men's cologne. True cologne, spicy and fresh, was always used by well-groomed men and women abroad, and there are many muted odors that suit even the most masculine male a lot better than do the violent odors in many popular hair tonics and lotions. Used restrainedly, simple colognes and toilet waters of the spicy variety (one at a time) are attractive for men and increase the impression of careful grooming.

Most men's hair does need some dressing to keep it in place, but daily application of such preparations eventually leaves the hair heavy, sticky, and inclined to pick up odors of tobacco smoke, even if a man doesn't smoke himself. If these various pomatums aren't shampooed out once a week, on a minimum, they may even take on a rancidity, of which the gentleman may be quite unconscious. Every shower should have handy to it a bottle of sham-poo. Just letting the shower soak the slightly soaped hair is not enough. Hair that has been heavily oiled needs several soapings and rinsings. Using liquid castile or a detergent shampoo prevents bits of soap from sticking to the hair.

The man who wants to make the proper appearance wears clean clothes always—even those items which by some are considered proper only if well dirtied up. Most men look better after their new hats begin to conform to the shape of their heads, but the battered old hat, no matter how dear to the wearer, contributes a careless rather than the hoped-for casual effect. As for shirts, they must be clean daily. It is good for a man to cultivate a very necessary vanity—the kind that is well this side of fussiness, of course.

My grandfather used to say that he judged a man by his shoes. Perhaps he was saying that our external effect is often the only one most people see and judge us by.

It takes time and care for a man to dress well. He can't do so if he throws his clothes over a chair at night and gets up so late in the morning he hasn't time to give any thought to what he'll put on. He grabs a shirt from the drawer, puts it on before choosing his suit for the day, lifts a tie from the rack with no consideration for his socks, shoves his feet into his untreed shoes without undoing the laces, gulps his breakfast, hustles into his top-coat—which hasn't been pressed all season—puts on his hat and is off. His pockets are bulging with yesterday's handkerchiefs, his heels need lifts, his hat could do with a blocking or at least a brushing. He's a pretty average American businessman. If he ever does catch sight of himself in the mirror, he decides that nothing can be done about it anyway. He hasn't a valet, he hasn't time, and very probably—or so he imagines—hasn't the money.

One of the best-dressed men I know went through a period, after years of military service, when he had two presentable suits, one pair of gray flannels, a sport jacket, two pairs of shoes, one tie, a gabardine raincoat, and a snap brim brown hat. The clothes he had he bought with great care and paid as much for each item as his budget could stand. His shirts were all light blue, both suits gray—one a flannel and the other a fine Glen plaid. His tie was blue, red, and white, always pressed, always spotless, and worn with the air of a club tie whose style and color would always be the same, too. His hair was always well-trimmed—and he learned to trim it himself to save money. He alternated the wearing of his two pairs of shoes and kept them handsomely shined and carefully repaired. His handkerchiefs were plain white linen, always fresh. His clean shirts he hung on hangers to keep the collar tabs and the cuffs from rumpling.

There is more to good grooming than good, clean clothes, of course, but cleanliness, neatness in dress has much to do with the outer integration of the man. Taste in dress is innate in some, acquired in others—but it can be had by any man who wants it. Top business and professional men usually dress well because certain standards of dress are set them by the circles in which they move. But money alone doesn't determine the final effect.

COSMETIC DEFECTS   There are men who, if they look in the mirror except to shave, either fail to notice certain obvious cosmetic defects or else think that it is effeminate to consider them seriously. Among these are chapped lips, blackheads, pimples, unsightly moles, dirty, stained teeth, and scaly scalp. Ordinary yellow vaseline or a bit of cold cream applied nightly or in the morning will relieve chapped and cracked lips. Blackheads and pimples may be in the province of a dermatologist if they are very evident, but thorough scrubbing of the face with hot water and plenty of soap at least once a day may stimulate the skin so it can police itself. A good barber or a loving wife using a sterile comedo extractor and a hot towel can keep blackheads at bay if utmost care is taken. Pimples should not be opened, especially on the face, as a resulting infection can be serious. Instead they should be dried up with a lotion or salve for the purpose. If true acne occurs, see a doctor about a possible change in diet or other corrective regimen. A diet high in fats and carbohydrates can cause this unsightly disfigurement. Moles, especially if they interfere with shaving, should be removed surgically or by the electric spark or other accepted method by a regular doctor treating such things, not by a barber or cosmetician. Barber treatments of really serious scalp disorders will probably make the situation worse. All scalps are somewhat scaly. Vigorous daily brushing with clean brushes help carry this flaky refuse off, as does a careful weekly shampoo. Even a bachelor can learn to clean his combs and brushes as often as necessary in a solution of ammonia and cold water.

UNATTRACTIVE TEETH   Some teeth gather tartar because of smoking, some because of improper and hurried cleaning, and some for reasons no dentist can determine. Teeth that do stain in this way should be professonally cleaned, probably every three months, otherwise the tartar gathers mouth acids, causes unpleasant breath, and, if not removed, can loosen teeth by causing pyorrhea. Aside from this medical reason for having clean teeth, there is certainly the cosmetic and social one. You may have the kind of teeth that don't show when you smile or talk, but they do show—perhaps in all their dreariness—when you laugh. And your breath depends on the condition of your mouth and teeth to an important extent. Offense here can have a deleterious effect on business, social, and, yes, especially love life. Don't let your oral hygiene go unchecked. See your dentist and dental hygienist as often as they deem necessary and learn, as an adult, how to wash your teeth and how to keep the spaces between your teeth free of food particles through the use of dental floss or dental picks (the professional kind dentists suggest) preferably after each meal. There is no nostrum that can disguise the need for dental attention or hygiene.

THE BACHELOR'S SOCIAL PROBLEMS

At first glance, from a feminine standpoint at least, the bachelor seems to have no problems whatsoever. He may be fat, bald, poor, homely, and dull, but someone will corral him as a dinner partner. The bachelor to the desperate hostess seems as rare and wondrous as the cigar store Indian and as worthy of collecting. A hostess without an almost inexhaustible list of fairly presentable bachelors on her list is really up against it.

The superior, highly eligible bachelor, of course, needs but to keep himself in clothes. Just enough to cover him decently, at that. Unlike his unmarried sister, he need give no thought at all to his appearance, as his appearance at all is enough. Everyone knows that a man can always marry even if he reaches 102, is penniless, and has all faculties gone. There is always some woman willing to take a chance on him.

However, bachelors, I am told, really do have problems. One of them told me all hostesses treat all bachelors like supernumeraries. "They invite me to fill in at their dinners at the last minute, never thinking I might like, for once, to bring a girl of my own. I always get stuck with someone's unwanted relative. I am expected to fetch her and take her home. And act exhilarated during the proceedings."

Bachelors tell me, too, that motherly women assume they are lonely, especially over week ends, and invite them to spend such free time in the child-ridden country or suburbs, but neither provide attractive, young, feminine company nor suggest that they bring some along.

It can be very expensive to be a bachelor if the young ladies he escorts insist on going to night clubs and to the to-be-seen-in restaurants. If he says frankly he can't afford such places a girl with any sense will settle for places he can afford. Actually, he may sensibly return to the time-honored custom of calling on a girl at home and leaving the responsibility of feeding her up to her parents.

CHAPTER TWENTY

A MAN'S MANNERS IN THE BUSINESS WORLD

The encouraging thing about etiquette is that it can be learned, that it doesn't necessarily have to be bred in the bone—though that is, of course, the way it would come easiest.

Professor Arthur M. Schlesinger of Harvard in a learned discussion of etiquette throughout American history points out that Andrew Jackson, elected to the presidency in 1828, was our first President not in the Adams-Washington aristocratic tradition. He was the son of a desperately poor Scotch-Irish immigrant, who through native ability rose to highest office, correcting his rough manners as he went along to such a degree that, as Schlesinger puts it, he "excited the admiration of both friend and foe by his urbane and courtly demeanor."

Knowledge and instinctive practice of accepted good manners does not, of course, make the gentleman. A real gentleman, a man with a heart for the kind, considerate, decent thing may have no manners at all, in the usual sense. Polished manners and a scurrilous character can well be encountered in the same individual—just as a man may dress like a gentleman as a result of careful imitation, yet be far from a gentleman in his daily actions. At the same time, it is highly desirable from a social and business point of view for every man to know and practice the accepted manners of his time—to err, perhaps, on the side of punctiliousness in such things.

Learning to make good manners almost innate makes life easier at home and in business. Young men who want to become executive material must do more than apply themselves to the technique of their jobs. They must school themselves in social as well as in business manners if they want to get ahead. They must learn how to dress, how to conduct themselves on various social and business occasions, how to communicate their ideas to others in concise, well-chosen language.

We have all known successful businessmen whose grammar was bad, whose taste in clothes was atrocious, and who broke every rule of good manners, if indeed they knew any existed. But this is doing it the hard way. It takes considerable business or professional genius to overcome the destructive effect of boorishness and uncouthness. Top executives, if they must endure these drawbacks in a key man, are uncomfortable and apologetic concerning him. Often such a man is replaced, if he can be, with another who fits more smoothly into a growing business. The day of the hell-for-leather individualist in American business is passing, if it isn't completely over.

I have often noticed that the great corporations invariably practice a most formal business etiquette. Their façade is imposing, they employ well-dressed, soft-spoken receptionists, they provide private offices and interoffice communications to cut down unnecessary noise and traffic. They usually exercise considerable control over the behavior and appearance of their employees for the sake of improved efficiency and of their public relations.

In such offices you don't see men put their feet on desks or sit around with their hats on and their coats off—although in some offices there is relaxation concerning coats during the hot weather. But even so, employees are expected to don their coats when leaving their desks to welcome visitors, to go elsewhere in the building, or to attend conferences. In the latter case, they may remove them again at the invitation of their superiors and with the permission of any women executives present.

WHEN DOES A MAN RISE?

Gone are the days of the quill pen and communication by letter only. Business pace is fast, and the courtly manners of old-time business offices are often impractical now and few expect them.

In business a man does not rise when his secretary enters his office to take dictation, although if she is newly assigned to him as his personal secretary he does rise to greet her and to shake her hand if she offers it.

He rises if he has a woman caller—unless she is a job applicant for a non-executive position. If he is on the telephone or dictating when she enters, he nods, indicates a chair, and rises when he has concluded his conversation, which he makes as brief as circumstances permit. If he must receive other phone calls, during the course of the interview, he excuses himself each time for the necessary interruption.

If he is at his desk and a superior, man or woman, enters, he rises and waits until he is asked to be seated again or the caller leaves.

If a male co-worker enters his office, he does not rise unless, perhaps, to greet him after an absence, for gentlemen *always* rise to shake hands—even with a man—or excuse themselves for being unable to do so for some reason.

It is courteous for a man to rise for any man caller except a job applicant in the non-executive capacity. He certainly rises for all "gentlemen of the cloth" and for men very much older than himself, although, if seated, he may acknowledge an introduction to another contemporary joining a group of men, merely by nodding or saying anything that seems to come naturally such as "Happy to see you here," or "Nice to see you," or even a smiling "Hello."

If a woman executive is in the group joined by a man, the man who makes the introduction rises, unless he is the chairman (who *may* remain seated by virtue of his dignified position), as do the other men at the meeting if the group is of a reasonable size. Otherwise, only the men in the immediate vicinity of the woman to be seated rise for specific introductions if any are necessary. If an introduction would interrupt the meeting, the man next to the nearest chair rises to seat the woman, unless he is in the midst of a report or discussion. A general introduction of the woman to the group may be made, if convenient, by the chair, "Gentlemen, this is Miss Helena Coyle, from our advertising agency." In such introductions it would only cause confusion for all to rise.

WHO PRECEDES WHOM?

In leaving a room in a business office a man always steps back to allow his superior to go first if the other is about to leave too, or, if there seems to be some delay, asks permission to go first. From the standpoint of superiority, the top executives certainly have the privilege of leaving before their inferior women employees, but I have noticed that, even in business, most gentlemen step aside, no matter what their capacity, to permit the women present to go first, even women in non-executive capacities. It's not a bad idea, for if a man gets into the habit of stalking through doors ahead of his secretary he is likely to forget that women take precedence in this respect in social life. It is difficult to have one set of manners for business and another for home.

The rule that a woman precedes men through doors is a set one, with the exception that a man goes ahead if the couple is walking the length of a train, opening the heavy doors and holding them open until the woman passes through. A woman, however, passes through a revolving door first after the man has set it in motion for her.

SMOKING IN THE OFFICE

A superior, man or woman, calling upon another employee may, of course, smoke without asking permission, but an outsider may not smoke in the office of someone else unless he is asked to do so. It makes a bad impression for such a caller to ask permission to smoke if he is there in his own behalf, asking for, say, a contract, a job, or an introduction.

A MAN'S SECRETARY

A really experienced and urbane executive keeps his relations with his secretary on a friendly but purely business basis even after years of association. In very informal offices a secretary is sometimes called by her first name, especially in small towns where everyone knows everyone else. But to the outsider—and, remember, such businesses may grow to be big, impersonal corporations in time—it seems less than businesslike and sometimes a shade too intimate for a man to call his secretary "Mary" instead of "Miss Jones," at least in office hours. The temptation is for everyone else, in and out of the office, to call her Mary, too, so that she is deprived of the dignity of her title. When everything goes smoothly it may be comfortable enough for a man to call his secretary by her first name and—as is often the case in these instances—for her to reciprocate by using his first name, but it is very difficult if Mary must be corrected about something or has to be fired.

If in your office a first-name precedent has already been set, at least refer to the women on your staff as "Miss So and So" to visitors to the office. Let it be, "Miss Ross will show you out, Mr. King," not, "Mary will show you out." Otherwise Mr. King, who may be no better than he should be, may get the wrong idea entirely about Mary and make things very embarrassing for her.

THE PRETTY SECRETARY   It is only human for a man to want his secretary to be neat, attractive, and, if possible, pretty. He has to look at her all day long. But the more attractive she is, the more, for his own and her protection, he must treat her with careful, polite objectivity. The quickest way to trouble, a straight line into the maze of gossipy office politics, is for a man to pay more than business attention to his secretary. If it happens that both are free to have some social life together, if they wish, they should still maintain formal relations in the office if their efficiency is not to suffer. Even at that, it is difficult for the woman, especially, not to show others that she has her boss under rather special control.

LUNCHING AND DINING WITH ONE'S SECRETARY   A secretary has a right to lunch as she wishes, in welcome solitude or with some friend in or out of the office. For her employer to make a frequent practice of asking her to lunch with him so he can catch up with his work is slave-driving. Occasionally, it may be a good idea for a man to take his secretary to lunch for business or purely social reasons, to smooth their working together, but it should always be kept in mind that it is easier to work with those with whom we do not have a close emotional tie.

If a man and his secretary are traveling together, the man may well offer to take his employee to dinner if otherwise she faces dinner alone. But he should be careful—if he is married or she is—to avoid any but the most dignified restaurants. If a married man takes his secretary to a night club, for instance, or some honky-tonk, whether or not they actually eat a meal, they are both open to some suspicion should they be observed by someone from home.

There is a delicate difference in the relations between a man and a woman associate in his business and a man and his secretary. Society might well feel that a secretary could not safely refuse purely social invitations from her employer, except at the possible risk of her job. A woman executive associate has more leeway. Supposedly she can control any difficult situation that might arise. She might well go to a night club in a strange city with an associate with whom she is traveling, although if one or the other is married, she would not do so at home unless others were in the party or there were some definite business reason for going.

TRAVELING WITH A SECRETARY

MAKING HOTEL RESERVATIONS In making reservations at a hotel for an executive and his secretary, the firm name should be used, not the executive's nor the secretary's, although it is correct for some other person in the organization to make the reservation if it is more convenient for return mail or telegrams to be addressed to an individual. Such a reservation might read:

HOTEL BLACKSTONE
CHICAGO, ILLINOIS
PLEASE RESERVE TWO SINGLE ROOMS THIS FIRM'S DR. ROGER GIDDONS
AND SECRETARY FOR DECEMBER 9. CONFIRM.

WM. TRAVIS, TRAFFIC MANAGER
HUTTON BROTHERS
444 MADISON AVENUE
NEW YORK

Although such a message makes it clear that the two should be assigned to different floors, a mistake, if it is made by the reservation desk, should be tactfully corrected by whoever signs the register if other rooms are available. If they are not, there need be no reason for panic. *Honi soit qui mal y pense,* which could be translated that you are your own best protection.

HOW SHOULD THEY REGISTER? It is usual for a secretary to check into the same hotel as her employer, so she will be available when he needs her. As his secretary, she may sign the register, "Henry Murray," with his firm name and address (rather than his social address) and beneath that, "Miss Bernice L. Wisner, secretary, same address." The clerk, unless asked to do otherwise, will usually assign the two to different floors. If the employer signs the register, he signs the same way, giving the business address and making his secretary's relation to him clear by entering the information on the register. Any verbal explanations to the clerk may embarrass all concerned quite unnecessarily.

DOES A SECRETARY NEED A CHAPERONE? It is obviously impossible for a secretary traveling with her employer to insist on a chaperone or to refuse to take dictation in a hotel room. It is not always possible for either a man or woman executive to secure a hotel suite, even if such extra expense is willingly borne by a firm, and it is often necessary for dictation to be given when executives travel.

A man should not hesitate to ask his secretary, traveling with him, to take dictation or do other office work in his room, though not in hers, once the rooms have been made up. (If it is impossible to get the chambermaid to do the room in time, at least the bed should be pulled together, not kept open.) The door should be unlatched, although it is not necessary now that it be open.

An employer may order lunch (but preferably not breakfast) in his room for his secretary and himself if necessary to conserve working time, but not drinks. He should not ask his secretary to dine with him in his room if it is at all possible for them to go to the hotel restaurant or some other one. Even while working, he should keep his coat on while his secretary is present, and she should be careful to be as completely groomed as she would be in her office at home. Needless to say, no man should ask his secretary— or even a public stenographer—to take his dictation when he is not fully dressed, unless he is ill and the fact is well-known.

THE EXECUTIVE ON THE TELEPHONE

In a personal service organization—one that depends on its daily contact with others for its business—an executive should answer his own phone, if at all possible. Many a deal has been queered by a snippy secretary's self-important announcement to the telephone caller, "This is Mr. Brown's *secretary* speaking. What did you want to talk to him *about?*" It is always that awkward and infuriating past-tense phrase, too. Mr. Brown is probably right there swaying back in his swivel chair and quite able to pick up the phone himself. If he's any kind of an executive, he can dispose of unwanted callers with tact and dispatch and he does not run the risk of cutting off his business blood supply.

But in case a man or woman executive is really busy, actually out of the office, or for the moment can't be disturbed, it is vital in almost any kind of business for the intermediary to handle the call in a way that will not hurt the firm's public relations. If the secretary can say, "Oh, Miss Johnson, Mr. Brown will be so sorry to hear he missed your call. I can't reach him just now, but where may he call you? Or is there something I can do?" Humanly enough, many secretaries build up their employers' importance in their own minds in order to bolster their own egos, and this reluctance to let the outside world—no matter how important the call—at the Great Being is all too apparent. In all my years of business experience I have yet to see anyone who really wanted to do business with an executive through a secretary. Where the procedure is absolutely necessary in order to conserve a busy person's strength and time, the utmost discretion must be observed by his go-betweens, from the switchboard operator to the executive's secretary. And it is a business axiom that the bigger the executive, the more approachable he is. I have always found it much easier to deal with the heads of corporations than with third assistant vice-presidents.

MAY I ASK WHO'S CALLING? If either the switchboard operator or an executive's seceretary is assigned to the job of keeping unwanted calls from him, we hear the phrase, "May I ask who's calling?" Now this really means, "If you're important, I'll locate him." If your name is unknown to the board or to the secretary, you will probably then be told, "He isn't in, just now," which you probably suspect, and rightly, is not so.

If this sort of thing must be done, let the explanation come first, "Mr. Brown *is* in this morning but he is in a meeting and I have been asked not to disturb him. I can give him your message when he comes out, if that will help, or if your call is in the nature of an emergency, I can put you through to him." Not even the most avid charity collector will insist on speaking to a man under those circumstances, and you have made someone feel he is important enough to be courteously treated no matter who he is.

The minute an executive gets too "important" to see people he is in danger of losing touch with the realities of the business world. He makes enemies of big and little people when he might just as well have been making friends. It is an even greater temptation for a woman who has risen to the top to put herself in an ivory tower, because power for her is a relatively new experience. For that reason, the gracious, relaxed woman executive who finds time to see people and to talk to them earns respect for her ability to get along in a tough, competitive world. No one really likes the tense, terribly important woman, no matter how talented, and it is only human nature for those she has sloughed off so rudely to rejoice if she falls by the wayside in the scramble to the top.

WHEN RELATIVES VISIT THE OFFICE

Men or women in offices, whether as business principals or not, should discourage members of their families from using the office facilities in any way. Even when staff members or other executives seem polite enough when relatives of their associates come in to use the office because of its convenience on trips to town, the interruption is often resented. If secretaries, bookkeepers, or the office boy are enlisted in any way in the service of such outsiders, they should be compensated for their trouble, and they should never be taken from their appointed tasks for such errands or favors without the consent of their immediate superior.

IS IT NECESSARY TO MEET SOCIALLY WITH ONE'S EMPLOYEES?

From the employer's standpoint it is rarely essential—except perhaps in a small community—for him and his wife to pay serious social attention to the families of junior executives. Business luncheons, an occasional drink, perhaps, with a younger man, or a few rounds of golf often suffice. Executives who are too close socially often work less well, rather than better, together, for they lose their objectivity or at least feel they should repress it.

It is a good thing in business to be able to speak out fair and valuable criticism without thought of close friendship. Staff promotions, too, are better handled when the owners are on relatively formal terms with all employees rather than intimate with a chosen few. To paraphrase Ben Franklin, "Love your business associates but don't pull down your hedge."

LETTERS OF RESIGNATION

Resignations from business firms are usually given in person but even then are frequently followed, for the sake of the record, by a brief, polite note of resignation, stating the cause of the resignation only if it in no way reflects on the firm. Such a letter is always pleasant, even if the parting has been stormy.

June 1, 1952

Mr. Abel Cressman
Premier Products Ltd.,
99 Lake Street
Green Bay, Wisconsin

Dear Mr. Cressman,

It is with great regret that I must tender my resignation as vice-president after so many years with Premier. As you know, I have long wanted to locate in New York and an excellent opportunity to do so has presented itself.

I am leaving, as you know, with the warmest regard for you and my fellow officers. I hope to renew the bond whenever I pass through Wisconsin, which may be frequently, as my new duties call for considerable travel.

Sincerely,
Robert Murray

CHAPTER TWENTY-ONE

THE MASCULINE GRACES

SENDING FLOWERS

Too many men use little or no sense in the sending of flowers. Confused, they buy something expensive and therefore, they believe, impressive, but it may be quite unsuited to the occasion or to the costume the girl is wearing. A corsage of purple orchids looks foolish at a football game, whereas a shaggy chrysanthemum, a bunch of violets, or orange calendula, or even a charmingly arranged spray of bittersweet would be in tune with her sport coat, lap rug, and stadium boots.

A woman is much more impressed when her escort makes an effort to find out what kind of flowers she would prefer to wear than if he just leaves it up to the florist.

If a man can't determine for himself whether a girl is the orchid or gardenia type and can't bring himself to ask her what she plans to wear, he is safe in sending white flowers—lilies of the valley, gardenias, chrysanthemums (for daytime wear), rosebuds (but they are perishable for an evening of dancing), carnations in a tight little round bouquet. But he should be careful not to have so many flowers in the corsage that a delicate gown will be pulled out of place by the weight of it. And for a short girl, never, under any circumstances, should a corsage of more than one or two orchids be sent. A girl with taste—and a taste for orchids—would prefer one little green, yellow, or white spray orchid to half a dozen ostentatious purple ones. But, orchids or cornflowers, corsages should be free of ribbon trimming, and rose corsages should not have any greenery but their own as background.

Flowers are worn various ways with evening clothes. (If they are to be worn on the shoulder for dancing, the right shoulder keeps them fresh longer.) A girl with braids or a chignon might prefer a red or pink camellia or a single gardenia for her hair rather than a corsage. A girl under five feet five might prefer a small arrangement to be worn on her back décolletage—rather than one to be crushed at the waist or on the shoulder during dancing—or a tiny nosegay to pin to her gloves or bag. Tall girls can stand the big impressive corsages men love to buy, but little girls often abhor them.

Flowers should be arranged in corsages so that they will be worn the way they grow, with the heads up. They should be sent with several florist's pins so they can be anchored firmly in place.

Bouquets of flowers should always be sent with some thought of where and how they will be arranged. Several dozen towering dahlias, chrysanthemums, or gladioli, sans container, will not always be welcome in a hotel room, in the compartment of a train, or aboard ship in anything less than a suite. A potted plant is impractical for a transient. Flowers—corsages or arm bouquets—sent to trains and planes are usually just a burden to the recipient.

It is a very nice thing, however, to send flowers for decoration to a girl who is giving a party. I once knew a charming gentleman with imagination enough to do that. He filled my apartment with flowers the afternoon I was giving a large cocktail party—and sent along his Filipino butler, too, to help out.

A man who is laying siege to a girl's heart does well not to systematize his flower-sending. I knew one man who could be counted on to send two dozen long-stemmed red roses every Saturday, rain or shine. And another who might send a gay red geranium in a simple clay pot or turn up with a single gardenia in a twist of green waxed paper—or a new recording or some fresh catnip for the kitten—one never knew. Any woman could tell in a minute which was the more interesting man.

LATENESS

If one is meeting a lady at an appointed place, lateness of five to ten minutes is acceptable, but it is always better manners to be there slightly before a guest's arrival. Greater lateness than this can be acutely embarrassing to a lady, and if some emergency has arisen an explanatory message should be sent, if possible.

LIGHTING WOMEN'S CIGARETTES

If he is seated or standing near her in a social group, a man leans over and holds a light to a woman's cigarette, if she has made the gesture of taking one herself. A thoughtful man, though he be a non-smoker, carries matches for this purpose or even a lighter. One very correct man-about-town I know carries both lighter and cigarette case, although he never smokes himself.

If a man wishes a cigarette himself, he must first offer one to the ladies in his immediate proximity, or at least to the one to whom he is talking. If she doesn't smoke, and he remembers the fact, he needn't make the offer, but if she says, "Not now, thank you," he should offer her a cigarette each time he takes one himself. A man or woman refusing a cigarette should never make a speech about it, although anyone may say, simply, "Thank you, I don't smoke."

SHAKING HANDS

A handshake is as much a part of personality as the way we walk, and although we may modify and improve a poor handshake if someone calls our attention to it, it will still usually be just like us, assured or timid, warm or cool.

Bad handshakes include the bone crusher—the grip that makes the other person, especially a woman wearing rings, wince. Or a limp, damp handshake that seems to say, "I am not really happy to meet you at all!" Or it may be the kind of straight-arm shake that seems to hold the other person off, or the octopus grip that draws you inexorably toward the shaker, who never seems to want to let go. Then there's the pump handle, or country bumpkin shake, and the very Continental style—reserved for women—which, though not a hand kiss exactly, is cozy and overlong, ending in an intimate little squeeze.

The good handshake is elbow level, firm and brief. A man does not offer to shake hands with a woman unless she makes the move first. Outdoors, it is no longer necessary for him to keep her waiting awkwardly while he removes his glove, nor need he apologize for taking her hand with his glove on. Whether he is shaking the hand of a man or a woman, the shaker must look the person he is greeting firmly in the eye and, at least, *look* pleasant, if he doesn't actually smile.

HAND KISSING

In this country hand kissing is an intimate rather than a social custom. But an American man encountering a European *married* woman who extends her hand to be kissed will certainly feel foolish if he doesn't know the technique. He should take her fingers lightly in his, *bow* slightly over her hand (not lift it to his level), and merely touch his lips to the back of it, not really implant a kiss. It is a great breach of etiquette to touch or kiss the palm of the hand, no matter what certain ill-bred foreigners do in taking hand-kissing liberties here for which they would be ostracized at home—all because *we* don't know the rules.

It is not correct to kiss the hand of an unmarried woman unless she is very definitely "of a certain age." It is plain silly for an American man in our own social circles to affect hand kissing. On the other hand, he should not stiffly insist on shaking hands in circles where hand kissing is usual—whether here or abroad.

A MAN'S HAT

A man's hat should sit more or less squarely on his head, not be pushed toward the back or tipped too jauntily to the side. It should never distort the natural position of his ears.

In the corridors and elevators of public buildings a man may keep his hat on his head. In crowded public elevators he is more considerate to keep his hat on, as holding it in front of him will require more space. If he approaches an information desk where a woman is sitting, it is polite of him to touch his hat when asking directions, though he need not remove it until he has actually entered an office. The same gesture—that is, of touching his hat but not removing it—is expected of him if he accidentally jostles a woman in some crowded place. He touches the crown of a soft hat or the brim of a stiff one, such as a derby or a sailor, but he does not actually lift the hat off his head for such encounters. The schoolboy yanking of the brim of a fedora, instead of gracefully touching the crown as if to lift the hat, has a certain servility about it and should be avoided. A man may well, however, greet another man with a casual salute in which the side of the hand touches, or nearly touches the brim.

In greeting a woman friend in the street or in some public place, once she has bowed first, a man actually lifts his hat from his head, turning his head slightly toward the woman and smiling, if he wishes, but not stopping unless she stops first. He must certainly not stop dead in his tracks and stare after her. If they do stop and talk, he should guide his companion out of the way of traffic after shaking hands—if she has made the first gesture to do so. He may return his hat to his head without apology if they are in the open and the weather is bad, but he must not smoke.

CONDUCT IN PUBLIC CONVEYANCES

A man touches his hat but does not look more than briefly at a woman to whom he gives up his seat. He then stands as far away from her as possible and does not look in her direction. It is certainly not expected that a tired businessman relinquish his seat in a crowded conveyance to any woman who happens to strap-hang over him (but let his conscience be his guide). But decency dictates that he give it up to a tired mother with a young child or a baby in her arms, to a pregnant woman, or to an old or crippled one— or to an old or disabled man. The relaxing of the rules has led to too many men jumping up for pretty girls who can well stand on their own two feet, while women who obviously need seats are left standing. Needless to say, no boy or girl should occupy an unreserved seat on a public conveyance when older women or women with babies in their arms are standing. A boy touches the brim of his hat and moves away from the person, man or woman, to whom he gave his seat. The person to whom the seat has been given says, "Thank you," but never opens a conversation with his or her benefactor.

If a man gives up his seat to a woman accompanied by another man, both men should touch their hats without actually removing them.

ALIGHTING FROM CONVEYANCES Men sometimes mistakenly allow the women they are accompanying to go first when alighting from various conveyances. This is incorrect as the man should go first in order to assist the woman to alight. Strangers, however, have no responsibility in the matter, letting women alight as best they can, unless it is obvious some difficulty is involved. A man may help a woman with baggage or a small child if no driver or conductor is on hand to do so, but he must be very casual in such offers of assistance, open no conversations, and, once he has helped, not seek to prolong the contact unnecessarily.

SUMMONING OR SHARING TAXIS If his time allows for the courtesy, a man waiting for a taxi permits a woman waiting in the same place to take the first to stop, but he never offers or asks to share it unless, of course, he has some acquaintance with the woman and they are going in the same direction. If his acquaintance is very slight and the woman is perfectly willing to share the cab (when there is obvious difficulty in getting one), each pays his portion of the fare, with the one getting out first paying the fare up to that point and leaving the usual tip. Under the circumstances, conversation is not expected, and it is never opened by the man.

If her escort summons a cab for a woman whom he is unable to accompany to her destination, he asks the driver what the approximate fare will be and pays him in advance, including the tip. He does not thrust the cab fare at the woman. If the appointment was a business rather than social one, he has no such responsibility, but, on the other hand, if the woman wants a cab, she should ask him to summon one and she should pay her own fare.

A man should never ride part way with a woman in a taxi, whether they have been on a social or business appointment, and leave her with the whole fare, if he alights first. If he has ridden in the cab at all, he should be willing and able to pay the entire fare. For a man to put a woman into a cab she has not requested with the assumption that she has enough money with her to pay for it is to place her, perhaps, in an embarrassing position.

A MAN'S BOW

A man's bow, a slight, graceful inclination of his body from the waist up, is the grown-up version of the boy's dancing class hand-on-heart one. He must not merely duck his head or, worse, pull in his chin in greeting, like a turtle, or give it a backward jerk, like a wet dog. He must modify to modern usage the courtly, sweeping bow of the knight-errant, and the only way he can master it is to practice it in front of a mirror until he knows how he looks. His bow must then become as much a part of him as his skin and should be so geared as to be suitable for men and women alike. It should be a democratic bow, as gracious to the little girl down the street as to the British Ambassador.

You must return any bow directed to you, whether or not you know the person bowing, or whether or not you have a friendly feeling toward the bower. Sometimes a person bows under the assumption that he knows you—and such a bow you must return, though if you are certain a mistake has been made you do not stop, if you can pretend you haven't seen the other person hesitate, in order to save him or her embarrassment. You never "cut" another individual who greets you publicly, no matter how much you may wish to do so. There are other ways of protecting yourself from unwanted acquaintance without doing that.

It is accepted that a woman bows first, but in this crowded world, today, a woman usually prefers to have the man indicate by his expression that he expects her to bow if she doesn't at the moment recall him—perhaps not in that place or under those circumstances. This is particularly true in the business and professional field, where it is hard to distinguish those we have met or had introduced to us from those we merely recognize because we see them so often in the places we frequent. A suburbanite may not instantly recognize a neighbor if she runs into him on a city bus and may feel very embarrassed later because she has failed to bow after he has looked directly at her but without showing he knows her.

MANNERS ON THE STREET

In America it is customary for a man to walk on the curb side when accompanying a lady on the street, but the rule is not so hard and fast as it used to be. In Europe the man walks on the woman's left, which may, of course, be the inside. When a man is accompanying two ladies he may walk between them or, conservatively, on the outside, moving to the center position to assist both across the street. He does not offer his arm to a lady, except to an elderly or infirm one, in the daytime, although he does do so at night or in bad weather. He offers his arm to assist her across the street but does not propel her by the elbow. The only time he does touch her elbow is when he is helping her *up* into a conveyance. If he precedes her—for example, down a train step—he offers her his hand to steady her descent. He may never take *her* arm.

KISSING IN PUBLIC   The Victorian gentleman shook hands gravely with his wife and family if he met them in a public place. But now, if it is usual for us to kiss our relatives or close friends, we do so, in greeting and farewell, in public or not, so long as the gesture is sufficiently brief so as not to attract the attention of passers-by. The senseless public kissing when women meet, particularly those who see each other frequently, should be discouraged. From the way they go about it, it is obvious each is afraid of getting lipstick smeared on her careful make-up or having her hat knocked awry. But if you feel like kissing out of real affection and pleasure at seeing someone, go ahead, so long as you avoid too public a display of your emotions. Even boys and girls who have no romantic attachment for one another sometimes kiss in public, on occasion, without anyone being embarrassed by their spontaneity. It isn't the kiss, it's the too obvious enjoyment or prolongation of it that should be avoided in public places. Love-making should be a private pursuit. Of course, if a man does greet a woman in public with a kiss, he must remove his hat entirely.

MAKING APOLOGIES   In disturbing anyone by passing in front of him or her—if there is no other course—say, "Please excuse me," or "I beg your pardon," or "I'm sorry," not the curt, imperative, "Excuse me," "Pardon," or "Sorry." Where possible, ask permission to pass first—as in a theater row—don't barge past people or over their feet without first giving them a chance to make way.

OPENING CONVERSATIONS   A gentleman does not open conversations with women he encounters in public places or conveyances unless there is some sound reason for doing so. If a woman leaves her seat in a hotel lobby and forgets her fur piece, a gentleman picks it up and goes after her with it. As he catches up with her, he touches her arm lightly, hands her the forgotten scarf, tips his hat, and turns away immediately, as she thanks him.

CAREFUL ABOUT NAMES   Never call out a woman's name in a public place, or in conversations use the names of friends, clients, or employers where they may be overheard by strangers. Talking in public places should always be keyed low, though it must never seem too intimate, either, where a woman companion is concerned. A gentleman does nothing to make a lady conspicuous in a public place.

A FEW BRIEF REMINDERS

Do not—

enter a room before a lady unless it is dark and you wish to make it ready for her

seat yourself while ladies are standing

speak or bow to a lady before she has given some sign of recognition. (There are exceptions, of course. A man passing a very good friend on the street or in some public place, and being sure that she had not seen him, might catch up with her and place his hand lightly on her arm or, if they are on a first-name basis, might call "Mary" softly when within hearing, but never "Miss Thayer!" as no lady wishes to have her name publicly called out.)

smoke without asking permission of the lady you are accompanying or seated so near (as in a train) that the smoke might annoy her

call any but your contemporaries or children by their first names

keep your hat on while talking to a lady (unless asked to replace it) or fail to touch your hat or to lift it when necessary

take a woman's hand, touch her face or body in the course of conversation, nudge her or take her arm except to help her up *into* or *out of* vehicles or, if really necessary, across the street

speak intimately of any girl or woman to other men

fail to pull out a lady's chair for her or fail to serve her or to see that she is served first

speak of repulsive matters at table

criticize another's religion, belittle his race or country, or refer unnecessarily to his color in his presence

enter any place of worship without removing your hat (if its removal is expected) and without speaking in reverent tones

laugh at the mistakes or misfortunes of others

fail to give due respect to a clergyman of any faith, to a woman of any religious order.

CHAPTER TWENTY-TWO

THE WELL-DRESSED WOMAN

The best-dressed women I know pay very little attention to the picayune aspects of *fashion*, but they have a sound understanding of *style*.

There are smart women who haven't changed the length of their skirts in twenty years, whose hats are always more or less the same shape although they vary in color and material with the seasons. Such women often wear their hair exactly the same way from girlhood on, wearing it short or long as most becomes them, despite current agitations one way or the other. We may envy such women. They have such a sure sense of what is good for them. They save time and temper assembling their wardrobes. Often they are considered among the best-dressed women in the world, although they might not make the famous list because, while they have style, they are superior to mere fashion.

This sureness is, sad to state, not for all of us. Instead, we are pushed hither and yon by the shallow dictates of fashion, often to a degree that is truly wasteful and silly. While fashion, if you can afford it, is fun, it is no fun to feel you must discard an expensive dress you have worn only a few times because it is no longer "high style." Unless you can really afford it, or because of your position must afford it, it is better to avoid all the expensive aspects of radically new fashion ideas until they have been sifted enough for the sound ones to emerge and have a fair existence.

The basic wardrobe has a theme which often carries through from year to year. If you have one winter cloth coat you must consider its color as your guide for all the seasons you wear it. The same is true of the accessories you bought for it. Such long-range planning means that you can buy better quality, for the investment is to be spread over more than one season, as it must be if you are an average woman not engaged in the fashion business—which lives on quick changes.

PLANNING THE BASIC WARDROBE

COLORS The woman who has no basic color scheme in her wardrobe must have considerable money in order to be well-dressed. She will need many more accessories than the woman who plans each season's clothes around what is still good and usable in her existing wardrobe, who has accepted the idea that there are certain basic colors becoming to her and to which she should adhere if she wishes to dress well on a controlled dress expenditure.

Basic colors are black, blue, brown (with all its variations), and gray, possibly green and wine. On the first four a good wardrobe can be built, allowing for much variety (although brown, itself, is difficult for formal clothes; the beige tones are better). The last two, as basic colors, are more limiting, except for a season or two. This doesn't mean that you shouldn't buy a plum or wine suit or a green one, but you should accept the fact that after two seasons such suits are readily recognizable if worn too frequently and that if accessories are bought to match them they will not be easily worn with other colors.

It is the interchangeability of accessories that makes for interesting variety in the wardrobe, not a large number of dresses and suits. Even extravagantly well-dressed women follow the basic plan, sometimes never varying the basic color from season to season.

As a young girl's taste in clothes develops, she will find that she turns again and again to certain accent colors because they make her prettier or happier. Eventually she is guided almost unconsciously to these colors, and variations of them, in choosing, say, a print dress or flowers for her spring hat. She will have decided early which of the basic colors go best with the accent colors she likes to wear, and she will buy her shoes, bags, belts, coats, and hats in basic colors that will complement or match anything she is likely to buy.

COATS For summer wear, a loose-fitting white or natural camel's hair coat is a basic that will have years of use if it is bought in a classic style. A black evening wrap is a sound conservative choice, but it is surprising how well one in flame red will go with almost anything a blonde or brunette is likely to wear in the evening if she doesn't go out too much, and especially if she has a dressy fur coat for a change-over.

If only one fur coat or jacket is possible on your budget, let it be a dress coat—preferably three-quarter- or full-length, with a shawl or roll collar. Avoid the high-fashion models. Mink in good quality is a long-term investment, and caracul, Persian lamb, the new muskrats in mink tones, seal, sheared beaver, and skunk (for a jacket) are among the hardier furs that should have a life of at least five years. When you consider that a good cloth coat is expensive and more likely to show wear or go out of fashion in less time than this, a fur coat is often a better buy. You consider its cost as amortized over five years.

If you live in a cold climate and in the country, a tough fur sport coat is often a better long-term investment than even the heaviest cloth coat suitable for bad weather—the upkeep is small and it *looks* warm. Among the best for the purpose are mouton (processed lamb), lambskin, the new sheared raccoon, leopard, or leopard cat (suitable for town, too). Almost a uniform for both men and women in smart country places is the trim, windproof, lambskin- or pile-lined belted coat of gabardine in basic tones. A well-tailored fabric raincoat makes a good extra topcoat between seasons.

If your budget is limited, beware the spring coat. It is often too high-styled and relatively too expensive for the use you will get from it. If your climate calls for some slight protection in early spring, a fur piece or little cape or jacket will have a much longer life and be usable day and evening. A classic camel's hair or a good simple, tailored coat and a dual-duty raincoat will be of use spring, summer, and fall for many seasons.

HATS If you are a country dweller your need for hats is usually limited. Instead, you need scarves, colorful bandannas, berets, a hunting cap for your belted sport coat, a duck snap brim, if you're the type, and a good dress hat or two each season that will carry you smartly into town on your occasional sorties into the more sophisticated world of clothes. In winter a becoming fur hat, well-made and expensive, to go with your dress coat—to match it or its scarf, collar or muff, or to contrast—say, a mink hat and muff with a black Persian lamb or broadtail—can have a long and fashionable life. The original investment is high, but you are sure of getting a hat that can take hard winter weather, stay on your head in a high wind, keep you warm, and be becoming for as many seasons as you will wear your coat. Its style can be varied from time to time by an adroit milliner, but, here, if there ever was one, is a basic hat.

In the summer your basic town, dress hat will probably be a well-designed, simple black, navy, or white straw or one in toast or natural tones, depending on your going-to-town wardrobe. The body should be the best you can buy, so that it is worth while to have the trimming changed from season to season. I have such a hat, whose original cost was forty dollars but which I have worn three summer seasons with three changes of trimming. Each season I have been complimented on my wonderful new hat. Considering the little I wear a hat in the summertime, it would be wasteful extravagance to have even one new, startling hat each summer (and I like them to be striking), so the remodeling of my basic summer hat is the answer and satisfies my desire for silliness in headgear at low cost. This would never work with a hat cheap to begin with—and it's better fashion policy to spend relatively more for a hat than for the dress with which it's worn.

A simple, round soft felt hat (or perhaps a good crocheted wool one) that goes with tweeds is another basic that fills in the seasons. Such a hat should match or complement the topcoat with which it is to be worn rather than the suit. If you have several tweed suits in varying colors, all to be worn with a camel's hair or other neutral topcoat, you can have removable hatbands or scarves that will pick up the color of the suit or accessories so that the same hat will serve several changes of wardrobe.

SUITS Every wardrobe needs at least one good wool or tweed tailored suit. It should be cut on classic lines, so that with minor shortenings and lengthenings from season to season it will be good for from five to seven years—or even longer. A cheap dressmaker suit, cut in the latest fashion and color, is an extravagant abomination. A good tailored suit should cost usually at least seventy dollars and be sufficiently conservative in color, line, and fabric that it is entirely unremarkable. A tailored suit is a uniform. A good dressy suit is a short-run extravagance, nice only if you can afford it.

The perfect tailored suit can be worn both in town and in the country with a change of accessories. Shoes may be walking pumps for town (not high heels), and ties, brogues, moccasins, or any other solid country shoe out of town. Beware the effect of too light a shoe—in color and heft—with a dark tweed. The feet should be darkly shod, too, to furnish a base for the soundness of the suit. Two-tone shoes, especially of black and white or brown and white, should be avoided with tweed suits, except those in pastel shades, and should not be worn in town.

Too sheer blouses look just as bad as too delicate shoes with tweeds.

A slipover sweater or wool shirt or some heavy fabric with body is best with tweed for the country. In the city a simple, non-sheer tailored blouse with a round collar or a turnover collar on a shirt neckline is most appropriate. White is usually best, or soft pastel tones, but avoid brilliant contrasts which destroy the effect of the classic suit which should be, as I said, unremarkable.

UNDERTHINGS Underwear should be simple, washable, and of excellent quality, devoid of imitation lace, sleazy ribbons, and machine embroidery. Hand-made real silk or fine nylon underwear is lovely, but machine-made underwear of good quality can do nicely, too, in a well-conceived wardrobe.

Nylon, unless it is the perforated knit variety, is hot in summer as perspiration cannot evaporate beneath it readily. Sheer cotton, fresh and crisp every day, is the coolest during a hot spell. Fine quality silk, well-made, with strong, French seams, costs a lot initially but can last years with careful laundering. Cheap rayon, knit or woven, can look fairly good when you buy it, but proves expensive in that it does not keep its finish and becomes limp and drab after a few washings.

The most comfortable girdle is the two-way stretch, which allows free body movement and which is made at least partly of lastex. Its loose weave permits evaporation of perspiration. Any girdle that pulls you in unnaturally, into some semblance of the currently fashionable figure, is likely to make you so uncomfortable and irritable that any striking effect your new clothes can make is nullified by your tense expression. If you are conscious of your girdle, it's the wrong one for you. The most you should ask of a girdle, anyhow, is that it hold in your stomach somewhat, give a smooth line to your hips, and support your stockings. If it does more than that it is merely displacing fat—pushing it from one spot, say your abdomen, to another, to your thighs or your diaphragm. And don't think the new bulges don't show.

Brassières have come a long way since Aunt Nellie was an adolescent and they bound her flat with a straight, tight bra which eventually broke down her muscles and, in her otherwise attractive forties, made her droopy. For young people brassières are not necessary except perhaps for active sports, unless support of abnormally heavy breasts is actually needed. For problem figures the various types of new brassières may be carefully fitted with wire, but never pressing on the soft tissues. No woman need look droopy today, either in a dress or a bathing suit, or flat-chested either. Ready-made clothes fit better if the bust line is something like the ideal—even if this approach to perfection is considerably helped along by uplifts or falsies or both.

DRESSES Here, considering to what a degree fashion plays a part from season to season, we can talk about line and fabric, color and suitability, rather than what is current at the moment. The basic rules of good grooming don't change.

The first rule is to accept what you are. If you are medium height—five feet three or so—with small bones, the heavy, masculine fabrics and bulkiness of line are never for you, no matter how much they are in style at the moment. You should dress to the lines of your body. If the line from the hip to your knee is relatively short, even if you have moderately long legs and an average waist, you will look overdressed in heavy tweeds, loosely cut clothes, large inverted or box pleats. Any next-to-the-body wools should be very light weight. Dress coats should be fitted and sport coats only moderately loose, or you will seem lost in bolts of material.

Most ready-made clothes are designed for the model figure—the long-legged, long-thigh-boned, and long-waisted type who can drape herself in a portiere and look chic. The little woman, or even the medium-height one should choose clothes which have been scaled to her proportions, or she should have her clothes carefully altered to suit her figure, first avoiding too heavy fabrics and too dramatic lines.

On the contrary, the tall, rangy creature should avoid too fine, too closely fitted materials and concentrate on bulky, rough-textured fabrics, loose line, pleats, bold plaids and stripes, contrast in skirt and blouse, tall, even staggering hats, and those handsome, tongued brogues that make the little woman seem rooted to the good earth.

A short or middling woman should strive for continuance of line. A red hat, a white jacket, and a navy skirt will cut her in three pieces. She can have the patriotic effect, if that's what she yearns for, by having jacket and skirt the same blue, by having a white blouse relieve the neckline, and by trimming her blue hat with a red cockade and carrying a not too large red bag.

Large, obvious accessories—such as huge bags, brightly colored gloves, bulky costume jewelry—and bright box jackets, heavy embroidery, enormous hats are only for big women, preferably the big-boned ones. A slender, medium-height woman can get away with one of these things at a time, occasionally, but she should beware of the dumpy effect they can give.

EVENING CLOTHES

Evening clothes for small and medium women should follow the body line and not be of heavy, bulky, or too stiff fabrics unless the wearer is very slender. Chiffon, satin (not heavy slipper satin on the plump), crepe, velvet (for the slender), moiré, taffeta are all suitable if simple in line and very restrained in trimming. Trains, panniers, bustles, wide sashes, bordered fabrics, and bouffant effects, when in style, tend to cut height and increase girth, as do all bold, two-or-more-color effects. The tall woman can wear heavier, bolder materials, unless she is heavy. In the latter case darker tones, lighter weight materials, smaller, but not tiny, patterns are more suitable.

Except for the very social woman, an evening dess is a luxury worn only a few times during a season. If a new dinner or evening dress is velvet its season is very short indeed—it begins to look outmoded by late December or January when the new Palm Beach prints make their appearance and it is not smartly worn after the end of February. Prints worn much before January first seem to be left over from the summer. But they are worn by smart women from January until the end of August. Print street dresses, especially in challis, often appear in the early fall, of course.

The best choice for an evening dress, if it is to have real use, is crepe, chiffon, or cotton lace in a non-assertive color or black. It can be worn in any season and can be changed by various accessories—a scarf, a bright sash, or colored elbow-or-longer evening gloves in doeskin or cotton doeskin or glacé kid, loosely fitting and with bracelets (but never rings) worn over them. Such gloves are part of a costume and are not removed during the evening, though the hand of the glove is pushed back over the wrist when one eats or drinks and the gloves should be removed entirely at the dinner table. To be avoided, usually, are embroidered or fancily stitched gloves and any made of weird materials such as silver or gold tissue or, to anticipate wildly, fur fabric. Gloves should be background, not bull's-eye, for a costume —except on an entertainer.

A wise woman never discards an evening or dinner dress that's been becoming to her, no matter how often she's worn it around home. If she goes first class on an ocean liner or cruise ship she will want to dress for dinner most nights, and a well-chosen evening dress five years old can look brand new to people who have never seen it before. Good evening clothes for women approach the uniform and date very slowly.

DINNER DRESSES A dinner dress has short cap or long sleeves but rarely leaves arms and shoulders completely bare, though arms and shoulders may show through net, lace, or tulle. It is usually cut on body lines and except for its length could be a formal afternoon dress. It can be worn either with an evening wrap or, better, with a fur coat or jacket or in summer a short, simple fabric jacket or fur scarf. It is worn with or without an evening hat to the theater, to informal dinners (where men wear dark suits or tuxedos), to restaurants. It is best in dark or neutral colors—beige, taupe, moleskin, amethyst, blue—and is not necessarily evening-length, though it is longer than daylength. The satin dinner suit, a little longer than street-length, is good for town wear and a fine solution for suburbanites with no *pied-à-terre* in town who must catch the eleven-forty home after the theater. Unlike evening-length dinner dresses, which are not worn before six, dinner suits can appear from four-thirty on and are very convenient for cocktail parties that lengthen out into dinner and the theater.

CLOTHES FOR ACTIVE SPORTS

TENNIS AND BADMINTON Unless she's playing on her own court at home, a woman wears white for tennis or badminton to keep from distracting other players on adjoining courts with bright colors. She may wear shorts—knee-length or above—loosely fitted for real playing comfort. Really classic is the short-skirted, pleated tennis dress in white cotton piqué or broadcloth, linen or sharkskin, knee-length or shorter, round or slightly V-necked, sleeveless or short-sleeved. To keep the hair and sun out of her eyes she wears a white duck or flannel green-lined visor or tennis cap, or just a clean, white linen sports handkerchief tied in a bandeau, or a simple ribbon. Shoes must be white, flat-heeled with rubber soles. Regular tennis shoes—sneakers—are best with white anklets, preferably light wool for comfort, but with one-inch leeway in the toes to allow for foot expansion during play. For badminton there are special shoes, which provide a little more support than sneakers. Hair flying loose, clanking jewelry, uncomfortable shoes or socks, shorts that are too tight can all ruin anyone's game.

SKIING Men and women wear the same kind of clothes. (See "What's What in Various Sports.")

DUCKSHOOTING (See "What's What in Various Sports," for this sport. This is no time for glamour, and warm underpinnings are most important.)

GOLFING The classic shirtwaist dress for golf is the cotton, flannel, gabardine, or linen golf dress loosely cut for swing action, pleated at the waist in back, and fastening down the front. The neckline is that of a regular shirt, and the belt is usually built in. A golf dress is usually in white, pastel, or neutral shades and is worn with traditional golf shoes with rubber soles or cleats to prevent slipping. The rubber-soled saddle oxford (but only in brown and white) is suitable, as is any sturdy brown leather walking shoe. No heel-and-toe-less play shoes or aboriginal sandals, please.

In cold weather a loose pull-over sweater worn with a shirt and comfortably cut wool or flannel skirt is best. A loose tweed jacket or a windbreaker may be worn on top if you choose to play when it's *that* cold. Brown leather gloves or the doeskin golf gloves with reinforced palms may be more comfortable than bare hands. Good English lisle hose may replace the usual anklets or be worn with them. Thin wool stockings are a good idea. The reliable, soft round felt in a neutral color or brown is helpful on a windy day.

SKATING The ballerina-type costume is only for the young and shapely. For others good, active-length wool skirt, slacks, or ski pants are best, with a sweater or jacket and wool stockings (lisle stockings with wool ankle socks are appropriate with skirts).

SWIMMING Any woman less bony than a shad looks ridiculous in a bra-top bathing suit and one that doesn't at least partly cover her thighs. If she has anything even slightly resembling a rubber tire around her middle, let her choose a bathing suit that will cover, or better, mildly control it, as do well-cut lastex suits. The dressmaker suit is a boon to less than perfect figures.

To swim is to make a very public appearance. Legs and underarms should be meticulously groomed, and feet should be carefully pedicured.

YACHTING Your costume depends on whether you are crew or mere passenger and, in the latter case, the size of the boat. Best guide, as always, is what the hostess, if any, is wearing. On a big craft, with regular captain and hands, ordinary country cotton, flannel, or gabardine sport dresses are suitable with rubber-soled shoes to prevent marking of the deck. A sweater or a sport coat, a bandanna, beret, or snap brim duck hat are advisable even if you start out on a hot day in a relative calm. A bathing suit and cap may be welcome. If the yacht is to put ashore at a club for dinner, inquire as to the advisability of taking a simple dinner dress and accessories. There may not be room aboard for such refinements—or no one may wish to bother with them. On large steam yachts with cabins you take the kind of clothes you'd take for a cruise, good country clothes, shorts and slacks if you wear them. Nicely tailored gray flannel slacks or a gray flannel skirt with a jersey and a jacket or blazer are comfortable and appropriate daytime wear. On an elaborate ship, ports of call and duration of the voyage determine your wardrobe. Inquire what others are taking. Any ship-side wardrobe should be reduced to an absolute, functional minimum, be of materials that won't need constant attention and stow away in limited space, if necessary.

RIDING In the real country, favorite costume for the ever-growing young is blue jeans and a plaid shirt or pull-over sweater, with moccasins. Properly, one wears good brown, well-fitting flat-heeled boots, that hug the calf and come, like men's boots, up to just below the knee, or, with jodhpurs, simple, English-type, undecorated brown walking shoes or regular ankle-high jodhpur boots with strap closing. Breeches worn with boots have a slight flare and should fit very comfortably. Jodhpurs should be tailor-made or carefully altered to fit, to look well. Fabrics for breeches and jodhpurs is whipcord in that pinkish beige called "pinks," or a cream or woodsy brown. Breeches or jodhpurs turned out in strange colors for the dude-ranch trade are best avoided, but color for cold weather riding can run rampant in waistcoats and ties, the latter always of the sport type usually in solid color wool or challis or, in summer, cotton.

The riding shirt—a turtle-neck sweater in neutral colors is acceptable, worn without a coat, if desired—is tailored like a man's (try the boys' department for small sizes at lower cost than you'd find in riding departments). It is best in white cotton, linen, or light wool. Bright or patterned shirts should be avoided except with blue jeans. In the country women riders wear a soft, round felt hat in a neutral tone, devoid of any bright trimming, save perhaps a bird's pinfeather stuck in the band on the knot side. Bandannas are acceptable in the country, but not for park riding. If the hair is well anchored or cut very short, hatless riding is usual in the country. But flying hair or hair that might come loose during a fast gallop can cause an accident.

The riding jacket is always tweed, single-breasted and cut on man-tailored lines. Fussy, pinch-waisted jackets in any but neutral, woodsy tones are anathema. Good, sturdy brown leather, chamois (cotton or leather), or heavy string gloves are a necessity to keep the reins from cutting into the fingers. A good brassière with wide, flat straps and loosely cut soft wool, rayon, or nylon open-leg panties that allow plenty of freedom are necessary. Never wear any kind of girdle or any jewelry, except a wedding ring and a gold safety pin for the tie or stock.

A standard riding crop, always plain, leather covered or bamboo, is not a necessity, nor are spurs. Any good horse will respond to a light touch of the unspurred heel or a slap of the hand on his flank. Some horses shy when they see crop or spurs, so inquire concerning various idiosyncrasies of a strange horse before mounting him. Unless you are a very experienced rider, you may not enjoy having to hang onto the crop as well as to the reins.

There are kinds of riding clothes for special occasions, but they are optional. For example, the side-saddle outfit sometimes affected for show riding or the Oxford gray habit worn with a stock and bowler. But even for show riding in the evening, the traditional, conservative tweed jacket and proper breeches or jacket are always correct.

If you join a hunt club and are an experienced enough rider to enjoy the formal hunt, special hunting clothes in the traditional style are called for. But if you are just to be a guest of the hunt you certainly wouldn't invest in a formal hunt outfit for one occasion or so. Instead, it is understandable for you to ride in your usual jacket and breeches with a white, collarless shirt and well-tied and anchored stock, plus the hunting derby. If the Master of the Hunt is a great stickler for form, he may frown on your informality. Ask your host to determine his stand on the matter before you accept. If you have had no experience with jumpers, do not accept a hunting invitation.

Handsome, correct riding clothes are never fussy-feminine. They should be worn with a certain, restrained air in deference to their masculine character. Never wear anything like lapel jewelry with a riding jacket, though a small boutonniere such as a man might wear—a little bunch of bright berries, a cornflower, a pink, or a small carnation—is acceptable. Mandarin-long, brilliant red fingernails look peculiar, though a pinkish polish that looks relatively natural seems horsemanlike enough. Those *femme fatale* nails, by the way, look odd, to say the least, for any active sport and lead to the suspicion that the cultivator of them is more at ease on a chaise longue than on a horse.

SHOOTING Upland shooting where birds are flushed by dogs and fly in front of the guns at some distance from the hunters permits the wearing of other than neutral colors. A gay flannel shirt may be worn with khaki breeches laced below the knee or with regular riding pants. Comfortable leather boots, field boots, or those high-cut, or moderately high-cut elkhide, waterproof boots with leather, not rubber, soles are needed. Wool socks prevent blisters, and cautious people wear a thinner pair inside heavy ones. In snake country, for example in Florida and Georgia, boots should always come just below the knee. (You learn to look down each time before taking a step, too.)

For clay pigeon shoots, dove shoots, and turkey drives (in open country, not in the Florida or Georgia woods) an English wool or tweed walking skirt with jacket or loose pull-over sweater (over a collared round-necked white blouse) is often worn instead of breeches.

If a hat is needed, it is, again, the trusty neutral soft, unbound felt with a dull-colored ribbon. Hair should be very neat, in a net if it is likely to fly loose.

In thickly wooded country briar-resistant trousers are advisable and white duck jackets are sometimes worn, or white duck visored caps, for visibility. Otherwise, for safety, you can tie a clean, white, man's handkerchief around the left, or shooting, arm.

For big game hunting—deer and moose—neutral-toned, heavy-duty breeches, boots, and hunting jacket are necessary with either a red hunting cap or a red patch on the back of the jacket or a red handkerchief tied around the shooting arm. White must not be worn, as a flash of white might be mistaken by another hunter for the white of a deer's tail.

CHAPTER TWENTY-THREE

THE FASTIDIOUS AND WELL-MANNERED WOMAN

A PRACTICAL BEAUTY ROUTINE A woman is well-groomed when she looks fresh, neat, clean, and well-pressed. This means a daily, and often twice daily, shower or bath, fresh underwear and stockings daily or twice daily, competent home or professional hairdressing at least once a week, well-manicured hands, no chipped nail polish, runless, wrinkleless stockings, and shined shoes at all times, even for housework.

Beauty care must be on a regular schedule, not just when social activities are planned. Excess hair must be kept invisible by one method or another at all times. Feet, pedicured and with toenails painted or not, must be kept soft and attractive, knees and elbows must receive their regular attention with emollients, and eyebrows be kept neat, though not obviously plucked. A good deodorant must be used daily or on recommended schedule.

Hair must be brushed morning and night with a clean, firm brush and combed with a good comb that, like the brush, is frequently cleaned in cold water and ammonia, then warm suds. A dirty comb or brush is as repellent as a bath towel used beyond its initial freshness.

A well-groomed woman is carefully girdled, if necessary, from the time she gets up until she undresses for the night. If she has heavy work to do she protects her hands with rubber gloves or work gloves and uses hand cream. For dusty work she covers her hair with a clean kerchief and she wears clean aprons or smocks to protect her clothes. Her handkerchief is always clean and when not in use, safely on her—not left on chairs or tables around the house or office.

The fastidious woman understands how much the appearance of her hair has to do with that of her whole person. If her hair is fine and hard to manage she arranges it many times a day, if necessary, to preserve the required neat look. She has it styled in the way that stays neat and attractive longest, and she never combs her hair or does her nails in public.

HOUSE DRESSES

It is far better to wear a simple, starched house dress, a clean one daily, if you must do housework, than to wear sweaters and skirts or wool or other dresses that must be dry-cleaned, unless you make up your mind to send them to the cleaners the minute the first spot appears (and if you are caring for young children, this may mean fresh outer clothes daily, an expensive proposition). There are now dark, winter cottons that can be styled like wool clothes, which are perfect for housework, topped, if necessary, with a sweater or wool jacket. You can make them in a becoming style, or have them made, with matching bibless aprons and feel like a well-dressed "lady of the house," no matter what dirty work you're up to.

CHANGING FOR DINNER

Every woman should change for dinner, if only into a clean house dress. Dinner is the high point of the day, the forerunner—it is to be hoped—of a free evening. Every little girl should be clean and in fresh clothes, even if they are just clean pajamas and bathrobe for nursery supper, every night, so that the idea of changing for dinner is inculcated at the earliest possible time. Fresh clothes and make-up, even if you are to be alone with the children for a simple meal, are psychologically sound and bring a needed change in the day's pace. Fresh grooming for evening is one of the criteria of gentility.

MAKE-UP

Our idea of what's permissible in make-up has undergone a drastic change in recent years. It is rare to see a woman over eighteen without lipstick and powder.

Lipstick should follow the natural lines of the mouth. Colored nail polish is more usual than not, although it is attractive to see well-groomed, healthy nails that have merely been buffed.

Mascara, once used only at night by some women, is frequently worn day and night and in a variety of colors, from blue and green to various shades of brown or black. Heavy black mascara is often hard-looking, but the others, properly applied (to the upper lashes only in the daytime) and of the non-smear variety, can help the appearance very much, especially that of a person with pale lashes. Eyebrows, if they need darkening, should be lightly rubbed with an eyebrow pencil the reverse of the hair growth, then brushed back into place, never drawn on. The eyebrow pencil can be used adroitly with an upward stroke, especially at night, at the far corners of the eyes to give them depth and to elongate them, but the line should be blurred with the finger tips.

Rouge, when used (and the older we grow the older it makes us look), is often best *not* on the cheeks. It can bring a glow to some faces if it is lightly applied above the eyelid, shading toward the temples. A little on the vertical planes of the nose bridge, on the chin or the ear lobes can play nice tricks, but experiment is needed.

Eye shadow is perilous stuff. It must be applied with a light touch, if at all. If nature has darkened your lids naturally, that is a cue, often, that you can wear eye shadow. If your lids are small and light, shadow often makes you look dead tired. You'll be better off with mascara.

It is often more youthful to leave all but the nose unpowdered and to allow a little shine on your face. Pancake make-up, or a good powder base, helps at night to keep make-up fresh, but daylight hours too often disclose its masklike properties.

A pocket-sized magnifying make-up mirror is a requisite for every woman. It should be consulted regularly.

COSMETIC DEFECTS AND PLASTIC SURGERY

EXCESS HAIR Unwanted hair, that which is not routinely removed after the bath, as necessary, should be professionally removed as soon as it appears or, if fine and downy, bleached. Even quite young girls often have excess facial hair which causes them embarrassment, yet it is simple and relatively painless to have it removed by electrolysis. Unattractive hair lines or too heavy eyebrows can be permanently corrected the same way. The operator should be recommended by the family doctor, as inexpert, careless work can cause infection and scarring.

Hair removal over large areas, such as the legs and thighs, is lengthy and expensive, but, where necessary, certainly feasible and often advisable. It should never be tweezed, especially around the mouth or nose, not only because tweezing injures the roots and may make permanent removal by electrolysis impossible, but because there is often the possibility of very serious infection.

MOLES AND WARTS   Brown moles, unless they begin to grow or are subject to constant irritation, are harmless and need be removed only if they really constitute a blemish. Often they are considered natural beauty spots. But when they are unattractively placed or in danger of irritation they should be removed by a competent doctor, not by a beauty operator. The commonest method, which is quick and painless, is for the doctor to cauterize them with an electric cautery after first anesthetizing them. After one or more treatments, they turn black and drop off, leaving, usually, an indefinable scar. Hairy moles should never be tweezed, though the hairs around them may be carefully cut off, as needed.

The horny warts that are so familiar on children's hands sometimes appear on those of adults, along with the difficult-to-treat palmar or plantar warts on hands or, in the latter case, the soles of the feet. These warts often disappear without treatment, but sometimes respond to X ray or acid, professionally administered, as does the common child's wart.

BIRTHMARKS, MALOCCLUSION, NEEDS FOR PLASTIC SURGERY   There are various kinds of birthmarks, some not in the least disfiguring, and all usually subject to modification by make-up or correction by X ray or plastic surgery. Birthmarked infants now usually receive CO_2 (dry ice) treatments which eliminate or greatly reduce the newly made marks.

Many a girl or even older woman can improve her appearance by having protruding or crooked teeth corrected by orthodonture. Although this is an expensive and lengthy proposition—taking usually two years in most cases—it often pays for itself in lessening decay and delaying of gum troubles, not to mention the increased self-confidence resulting from often dramatically improved appearance.

Plastic surgery has made fantastic strides as a result of two world wars. Its cosmetic uses are really wonderful. It corrects ugly, pendulous breasts, usually during fairly brief hospitalization, it removes the dowager's dewlap and takes layers of fat off the flabby abdomen, all with the minimum of trauma, as the surgery is connected with a sound rather than sick organism. Truly disfiguring noses are tailored to one's face, protruding ears are fastened back, and harelips made whole, all to the benefit of the ego. But this delicate work must be done, of course, by real experts approved by one's own doctor, members of recognized medical and surgical societies. Most of our physical defects need only the correction of our point of view, however, and plastic surgery, dramatic as it is, is not always advisable or really needed.

HOW TO SIT COMFORTABLY AND GRACEFULLY

You never see a product of Victorian days sprawled in a chair. Women trained in the austere etiquette of that time will invariably select the straightest, most uncompromising-looking chair in the room and sit on it, spine straight, hips flush with the back of the seat, feet parallel and flat on the floor. It was taught that a lady never crossed her legs or sat with her stomach protruding.

Today with fewer and fewer uncompromising chairs being manufactured, we are more or less forced to lounge as we sit. Sofas—the modern ones—are often so deep that the only way we can get back support is to boost ourselves onto them with our feet sticking straight out in front of us or curled as gracefully as possible under us. If we have short legs, we have a terrible time with most modern furniture. It throws us into unlovely attitudes, and sometimes we can't get up without help.

On entering a room, try to select a chair or sofa that suits your height and figure. If you are overweight and short you will not look your best on a high spindly chair that leaves your feet dangling and causes you to bulge over the seat. If you get down into one of those modern bucket seats you will need a strong arm to get you out again. If you sit on a sofa with a wide seat you must perch on the edge—which makes both yourself and others uncomfortable—or more or less sink back into the depths until you can be helped up again. Those low, deep-seated chairs, if they do not have bucket seats, are good for you but bad for a long-legged woman, who has no alternative but to stick her feet straight out in front of her or else sit jackknife fashion.

In sitting, be sure to look at the chair before bending your knees. Before your knees actually bend, the back of your leg should actually come in contact with the chair. When you have received this indication of the chair's position, you should bend your knees, lean forward slightly and go gently into the chair, maintaining careful contact with the floor. This way, if the chair is deep or tippy, you won't be thrown backward or forward.

The deep, wide sofa, modern style, is supposed to accommodate your entire thighs and all or part of your legs. The position of the cushions is an indication of where your spine is supposed to be. But if you are not supple, avoid such Turkish traps. If you do sit on them, don't flop, then squirm back into position. Instead, seat yourself on the edge, then, placing your hands on the sofa, ease yourself back with a lifting motion. A woman is more comfortable on such articles of furniture if she has on an evening-length skirt, slacks, or lounging pajamas. But sometimes it is possible to rearrange the pillows on such a couch so that there is less width and it can be used comfortably by someone who does not wish to lounge.

Crossing the legs is no longer considered masculine in women, but there are good reasons to avoid it is much as possible. First, unless one has slender legs, it creates unattractive bulges on the leg and thigh crossed over. Secondly, it is said to encourage varicose veins by interfering with circulation. So if you do cross your legs habitually, change the cross from left to right and from right to left at frequent intervals. It is much more graceful to sit, model-style, with the toe of one foot drawn up to the instep of the other and with the knees close together, if one wishes to vary the position of the feet. Further, crossing the legs *is* informal. It should not be done at the dinner table, in church, or at any formal occasion—or when a girl is trying to make a businesslike impression in applying for a job.

When the legs are crossed, attention should not be called to the fact by bouncing the free foot. And skirts should be full enough and long enough not to make the position a burlesque on how a lady should look seated.

WHEN WOMEN REMOVE THEIR HATS

In the country, when hats are worn at all by women, they may be removed with coats if desired. It is usual at house christenings, weddings, and funerals to treat the house, for the occasion, as if it were a house of worship and for women to keep their hats on. This, however, is not technically necessary, either for guests or for the woman of the household. At garden parties or garden weddings it is purely a matter of preference whether a woman, who has been shown to a cloak room first, decides to remove her hat or leave it on as an important part of her costume.

In town at formal receptions, teas, luncheons, and meetings women guests usually keep hats on if they have worn them. However, except perhaps at the home of an elderly and very conservative woman, on such an occasion the lack of a hat would not be in any way remarked these days. In fact, even at formal luncheons the modern hostess often suggests that guests leave their hats with their coats, if they wish. Certainly if most of the women at such an affair are hatless, one or two women who cling to the older convention in the matter will seem inelastic, to say the least.

Hats worn with dinner suits or dinner dresses are intended to remain in place throughout the evening and are usually tiny enough not to obstruct the view of those behind one in the theater. If there is any doubt about a hat obscuring someone's view at the theater, the movies, or a meeting, a woman should remove it promptly. If she's asked to remove it by someone having difficulty seeing beyond her, she should do it immediately with murmured apologies.

A WOMAN'S MANNERS IN THE BUSINESS WORLD

However competent she may be in business no woman should conduct herself in any but a dignified feminine manner. The brusque, unwomanly woman is anything but attractive in or out of business. And, equally, of course, the overly-feminine, coy female is just as uncomfortable to have around.

One time after I had addressed a directors' meeting the chairman, seeking to be complimentary, said, "We enjoy having her with us. She's just like one of the men." I was not complimented and replied, pleasantly, I hope, "Mr. X, I may be able to meet with you on your own ground professionally, but I am not like one of your own men and have no desire to be." He got the point and from that time on I had my place and the men had theirs. My professional standing was improved, and my femininity politely accepted. Every woman who refused to become "one of the boys" in business and who insists she be treated as a lady in the human rather than in the drawing room sense does her share toward a better understanding between the sexes.

Business leaders are quite conscious of the fact that women in business are also pulled in the direction of domesticity. Either they are in the marriage market, with few exceptions, or involved in the dual and difficult role of marriage plus a career. Today more married women than single women are in business. They are there to earn their livings or to help out the family income. And most of them have the complete management of their homes as well.

The married woman with a job in and out of the home is working under pressure, even if she is efficient and relatively relaxed about both home and job. There are always the unpredictables to cope with—Johnny's measles, the maid who leaves without notice, her husband's possible transfer to another city. A woman must be superlatively good at her job to give her employer full value while working as well as a head of a family. Her personal problems must be kept carefully in the background, and she must necessarily work more efficiently on her two or more jobs than does the man by her side, who traditionally is always protected against personal encroachments upon his business or professional life.

The woman who runs a job and a home often feels she deserves all kinds of special consideration from both her family and her employer. Of course she never can get it, because, despite the material benefits her job brings, her family is always resentful of mother's time away from home and employer or associates are necessarily coldly objective about her ability on the job. "Miss Barnes didn't get that report done for Mathewson because her husband's home with the flu" seems an untenable excuse to someone paying well for Miss Barnes's supposedly undivided attention.

It's hard to face this, but no woman can find happiness in putting career above her husband and family. Once she has taken on woman's natural responsibilities, whatever work she undertakes must be done in a way that deprives the family the *least*—for some deprivation they must endure if she works at all. Once encumbered she must have something very special in the way of talent to offer an employer to make hiring her worth while, at least while her children are young. Everywhere we meet women who seem to overcome the difficulties of the dual role, but the hard truth is that more women with young children fail at making happy homes while working full time than succeed.

With this in mind let us go on to the problems of women in business.

Secretarial schools send forth their fresh young graduates well equipped with elementary rules of office etiquette. As a result the American secretary is usually a well-mannered, poised young woman. The girl who has not gone through business school, however, and who comes to a firm in a junior executive capacity often has much to learn.

APPEARANCE Appearance is of primary importance, of course. Neatness and quietness of apparel are important. Conservative hairdressing, make-up, and a minimum of jewelry are equally so. Sunback dresses, evening-sheer stockings, French heels, Mandarin nails, sweaters, and overwhelming perfume are taboo.

PROMPTNESS Employers are paying for time on the job, so women executives, junior or senior, should get to their work promptly and once in the office start the day with a minimum of primping and coloquy in the restroom. Make-up repair should be in private, never at a desk, except in a private office.

TAKING ORDERS One of the most important things a woman in business can learn is to take an order and carry it out. This requires listening to the order without interruption, then asking any necessary questions that may clarify it. The woman who cultivates the ability to listen, to grasp instructions, and to carry them out without chatter or argument gets on in a man's world.

SMOKING AND EATING IN THE OFFICE Most organizations have rules concerning smoking on the job and eating at desks. If smoking is permitted, women should smoke in such a way that it does not interfere with work output. A chain-smoking woman is much more likely to be criticized than is a man with the same habit. Candy eating or coffee drinking, when permitted at a desk, should be done during a work-pause, then wrappers or containers removed from sight.

TELEPHONE CALLS Even a well-placed woman executive limits her incoming and outgoing telephone calls. Social chit-chat in an office annoys other workers and, even when indulged in by an employer, sets a poor example.

PERSONAL LETTER WRITING AND CALLERS Personal letters should not be written on office time, unless they are done during lunch hours. Friends and relatives should be strongly discouraged from visiting employees or even top executives. When such a visit does occur it should not be made a general social occasion.

THE WOMAN EXECUTIVE

A woman who achieves executive status of some kind must guard against being dictatorial at home as well as in the office. Men meet with their frustrations on the way up but not to the same degree, that is, on the ground of sex, as women. Therefore when a woman does arrive she tends to become irritatingly important. When she gives an order she wants action, and never mind the human element. It is very hard sometimes for a woman to continue to be warm and feminine and kindly once she has received business or professional recognition. Actually, she needs all these qualities more than ever if she is to keep on advancing and if her marital chances or relations are not to be harmed.

The very important woman is a tempting target for a jealous male associate. She rubs him the wrong way, threatens his position, overrides his suggestions, and tramples on his pride. She forgets the feminine graces and cajoleries and tries to meet him man-to-man. This leads to inevitable defeat. If women in business would only remember that they are *women* in business they would meet so much less resistance from men. No amount of professional conditioning will ever overcome the very real fact of femaleness.

ATTITUDE TOWARD OTHER WOMEN   It has been said many times that women have difficulty as executives because they treat other women business associates as implacable rivals, as if they were competing on a sexual rather than an intellectual level. This does seem to be true, that there is little real solidarity among women. I believe that with woman's increasing sense of security a more generous attitude toward women co-workers will come too. At any rate, it helps to be conscious of the competitive feeling and thus make an effort to modify it. (See "A Man's Manners in the Business World.")

WHEN THE WOMAN PAYS THE BILL

Occasionally in business it is necessary for a woman executive to pay entertainment or other bills for men clients or to take their share of checks when lunching with men business associates. In all cases (for the sake of the man) a woman tries to avoid a public display of her financial arrangements. Onlookers cannot know the circumstances, and men are easily embarrassed by a career woman's usurpation of their traditional role. Even if she is lunching a junior executive, it is courteous to allow him the dignity of seeming to pay the bill.

The arrangements for the preservation of male pride can be made in several ways. With an important client, whom the firm wishes to entertain but who would certainly not permit a woman to pay the bill, the obvious solution is the selection of a restaurant where the firm maintains a charge account for entertainment purposes. Even the tip is included in the bill, and the woman signs the check on the way out. She may ask the room waiter in advance that the check not be presented at the table but be left for her at the desk. When such tact is not necessary and the co-worker or client are on easy terms, the woman can quietly lay a bill on the table toward the end of the meal and say, "Settle the check for me please. Of course it's on my expense account." She should not actually pay the waiter, pick up the change, and leave the tip herself. (Any change the man gives her on the way out or elsewhere tells her the amount of both bill and tip for her expense record.) Or, if she's sure the client or co-worker can pick up the check and will willingly settle with her later—*not* outside on the street—she can say, "Let me know what this comes to when we leave. You are the firm's guest today."

THE SINGLE WOMAN

HOW TO MAKE FRIENDS IN A BIG CITY   Men have less trouble than women adjusting socially to big city life because, presumably, they are aggressive, while women are supposedly passive in such contacts. A girl living in, say, New York, after being brought up in a small town, can grow very lonely, waiting until she is asked out by the all-too-few unattached males she may meet in her office or elsewhere. A young man need not be even passably attractive to have as much social life as he wishes in such a metropolitan center. The competition for him, at least as an escort, is very keen, even if his prospects are meager and his spending money minuscule.

The girl who can surround herself with some sort of home background has the best chance of a full social life in a big city. Entertainment outside of the home is so expensive that a girl who has a home to which a man may come and be entertained has a better chance than the siren who lives in a hotel room and must be taken out continuously to meals, movies, theaters and night clubs. Such a girl costs too much and is too wearing. And, even if she is really interested in a man, she never gets to know him as she should in such an artificial atmosphere. The less beauteous girl with a stove and fireplace of her own has the advantage.

SHOULD A GIRL LIVE ALONE?   Living alone in a big city is for most girls who try it a disillusioning experience. Even if they are able to find and furnish—and support—attractive apartments all by themselves, they find that the drawbacks to living alone are, among other things, loneliness, inertia concerning household chores, and lack of at least implied protection.

A girl with her own apartment in a city is not insured against loneliness. Often she tries to be out every night or to have guests to combat loneliness. If she does stay home alone she listens for the telephone, and if it doesn't ring she feels abandoned. If she takes advantage of her ability to act as a hostess and invites a young man home to dinner she runs the risk of not being able to keep the rest of the evening on the easy, pleasant basis she desired. Too many young men, finding themselves in a girl's bachelor apartment without the steadying presence of other guests, imagine that more than conversation is expected of them.

TEAMWORK   The girl who has a good time in New York or other large cities is the girl who lives co-operatively. She finds one or more other congenial girls (preferably not more than two) approximately her own age, and together they rent a furnished or unfurnished apartment, which they run on the basis of their individual capabilities.

As often as they wish, such girls cook at home, thus keeping down expenses and eating better meals. They have more social life with men, because they can freely invite attractive ones they meet to come to their home without fear of being misunderstood, as there is always a "roommate" at least in the background to dispel any mistaken ideas. And, on nights when there are no dates or prospects of them, the household tasks can be done co-operatively in short order and can be relaxing rather than annoying. Too, by pooling their expense money such girls can usually afford a little outside help for heavy cleaning.

Such living can prepare girls, who have always had everything done for them at home, for future homes of their own if they go about it in the right way. They can learn what it is to serve dinner to guests, to manage a budget, pay household bills, and meet regular obligations such as the rent. They learn, too, how to divide the labor so that no one person does most of it.

CHOOSING A ROOMMATE   When a girl decides to share an apartment with another girl she should try to find someone from more or less the same background as her own, preferably a long-standing friend whose crotchets and personality she knows all about. They should have approximately the same income and be able to share the financial responsibilities of the venture on an even basis. If the income of one is considerably larger than that of the other, the living should be scaled to the lower of the two incomes so there never need be the feeling that one girl has more right to the place than the other.

If possible, the apartment should have at least two rooms, with the bath accessible to both the living room and the bedroom. A floor plan that requires anyone entering the bath to go through the bedroom is poor for sharing, as the girls' social activities are not always simultaneous. A girl who must sit up when she's sleepy because her roommate is entertaining is not going to enjoy such an arrangement for long—especially if she has fewer dates than her friend.

FINANCES   In such a shared apartment there is usually one girl who is better at money matters than the other, or who has more time for these details. A budget must be worked out, and a part of each salary turned over each week to the treasurer for necessary disbursement. One girl should never carry the other, but all debts should be settled with alacrity if the working arrangement is to prosper. The most important obligation, the rent, must be paid promptly each month and the receipts kept if cash has been paid. Food bills for shared meals are evenly divided, but each girl takes care of her own extra entertainment costs.

The lease for such an apartment is better taken out in the names of the co-operating lessees, where the landlord is willing. But where he prefers one signee, the other tenant or tenants should hold a brief written agreement on the length of their shared tenancy and the terms of it from the holder of the lease. It is also well to have duplicate or triplicate lists of all the belongings and effects in the apartment that are being shared, with a notation as to ownership, whether joint if they were bought out of pooled funds—and what the cost was—or individual. Such a businesslike view right at the beginning helps to keep the arrangement on an even keel, and, in the event one girl decides to leave for one reason or another, it makes her responsibilities clear.

Such a shared home needs house rules, too, drawn up by the participants. Perhaps the girls will agree to let each have one set night to have the apartment alone without the other or others. Maybe one night will be put aside as a "no visitors" night, when hair can be set, bureau drawers straightened, and the housework finished up. Certainly essential tasks must be assigned—the cooking, the bedmaking, dusting, and cleaning, laundry, shopping, and bookkeeping, the division of the chores dependent on the amount of time each girl can give and her abilities.

A little box by the telephone should remind visitors to pay for their own calls and encourage the girls to deposit their tolls for out-of-town calls right away or at least make a record of who made them. Only the base rate for the telephone should be equally shared by each.

If all the rules of courtesy are followed, such living can be most congenial. It can lead to a full and happy social life, with good possibility of marriage, even in a crowded unfriendly city where the competition for the eligible males is much fiercer than it would be in the small town that seemed to offer little in the way of career or romance.

DOES BECOMING A "JOINER" HELP?

Suppose for some reason, perhaps her inability to find a congenial girl with whom to share a home, a newcomer to a large city must live in a girls' club, a boarding house, or a small hotel. What are her chances of having a pleasant social life? Unless she makes some definite and continuing effort to meet people, even a pretty, attractive girl may be lonely during her free hours.

Before going to a place like New York, Washington, or Chicago to work, young people—men and women—should attempt to find someone who can give them social introductions in their new home. It makes much difference if there is someone to take a stranger in hand and see that he or she meets others of the same age and background. If there is at least one real home where such a stranger may go occasionally, it can help him find his own niche among new friends.

If there is no one at all to whom one may go in a big city for advice and companionship outside of working hours, the next best thing is to find one or two groups one can join. But to become a "joiner" in the sense of mapping out a continuous plan of activity in an effort to escape loneliness may mean that with so much to do a newcomer really enjoys nothing, gets to know no one well enough in her rush from club to club and classroom to classroom.

A church with a real and youthful social life can bring sound interests, as the stranger is always welcome and can quickly be made to feel at home in familiar activities. A hobby group is a sure way to find congenial friends. Adult education courses keep free hours busy and productive and may lead to new skills and friends. A college club—any group that brings something of a former background into the new life in the city—helps orientation.

Often an out-of-towner feels a little awkward at first in a metropolis. After a while she will realize that a certain polish may be acquired. Anything that makes her feel she "doesn't belong" can usually be corrected, from a broad regional accent (helped by diction lessons) to ungainliness on the dance floor or an unsureness about clothes. The "Y's" abound with all kinds of self-improvement courses for people who suffer from feelings of inadequacy one way or the other. Such courses are of great help, especially in big cities where on all sides others press for advantage.

BIG CITIES ARE STIMULATING

Once the effort to break in socially is made, the newcomer finds most big cities culturally stimulating and financially rewarding, as small towns can rarely be. A city like New York is full of people expressing or trying to express a wide variety of talents, talents for which there may have been no market at home. One needs only to make oneself a small part of the profession or business that appeals to find satisfaction and a feeling of "belonging," even in a city of seven million, plus. And once this feeling is achieved, the stranger is one no longer but able to realize that New York, especially, is made up of millions like himself who came from other places in the world. One may walk for miles in the city before finding a true "born New Yorker," and it is rare to number many among one's friends.

CHAPTER TWENTY-FOUR

THE SOCIAL PLEASANTRIES

A GUIDE TO TACTFUL CONVERSATION

In greeting people we say, "How do you do?" We do not really expect an answer, but it is proper to reply, "Very well, thank you," even if it is a blue Monday and you feel far from well. No one wants a clinical discussion in response to this purely rhetorical question. In fact, you may answer Socratically with "How do *you* do?"—expecting, and getting, no answer. In farewell, say simply, "Good-by," or something you really feel, such as, "Let's meet soon again" or "It was so nice running into you." Don't use some current banality such as "Good-by now." It is obvious it is *now* you are saying "Good-by"—not an hour previously nor an hour hence. Watch these clichés. Up to a point they can lend a little color to your conversation, but they can easily become second nature, so that you seem to be a person of little imagination, one suffering from a sad poverty of language. These innocuous slang expressions sound partciularly inept from a grown man or woman, unless one is using them quite consciously and in fun.

WHEN TO USE A FIRST NAME

Be slow to use people's first names and try to let the other person take the initiative. A man must never call a woman of his own circle by her first name unless he is asked to do so. Usually she indicates her willingness to be on a more familiar footing simply by calling him by his first name without any explanatory preliminaries but she may say, "*Do* call me Joan."

If a much older man or woman calls a much younger man or woman by his or her first name, that does not, of course, indicate that the junior should return the familiarity, although if the relationship continues over many years it is possible that in time it will be appropriate for the younger person to call the older one by his or her Christian name, but even then it is best to be asked to do so.

IF YOU CANNOT REMEMBER NAMES

No one is ever pleased if you say, "I know your face—but I just can't recall your name." Tactful people who aren't infallible about names work out a technique for coping with these bad moments. If you are warmly greeted by someone whose name—or maybe whose face, too—you can't recall, say something harmless such as, "Nice to see you" or "You're looking well." Then while looking quite attentive, let the other person do the talking until he or she gives a clue as to identity. Let us hope he doesn't ever say, "You don't remember me, do you?" for your own expression should always indicate you remember him well and favorably.

If you have trouble remembering the names that match the faces, always help out the other person who is probably suffering from the same thing. Never say, "Do you remember me?" or "You don't know who I am, do you?" Instead, in greeting people you haven't seen for some time or whom you are meeting outside of your usual place of encounter, identify yourself quickly and gracefully, "How do you do, Mr. Burton. I'm Joseph Bye of Arbor Mills. We did a little business together last fall." Or, when a woman has stopped and is obviously confused as to who you are, "I'm Joseph Bye, Miss Fox. We see each other at the Advertising Club." It is certainly more modest and tactful to assume that you aren't remembered than to presume that you are. I well remember the effect on me when my partner at a public dinner sat down, turned to me, and said, simply, "My name is Hoover." It was Herbert.

PERSONAL QUESTIONS—WHAT ARE THEY?

Sometimes I feel that understanding of what constitutes a personal question is innate rather than acquired. There are people who seem to have been born tactful and others who, no matter what they are told or how often they offend consciously or unconsciously, continue their stream of personal questions to the discomfort of all those with whom they come in contact.

We should not, for example, ask the cost of everything. If your neighbor wishes to volunteer certain information in the course of conversation—the amount he paid for his house, the cost of his son's school tuition, how much he paid for his new lawn mower, that is his privilege, but we should not ask these intimate questions unless there is some very valid reason for doing so. If you plan to send your child to the same school, you might ask the tuition your neighbor pays, but even then you might embarrass him, as some private schools have a sliding scale based on the parent's ability to pay, the desirability of the child from a scholastic or social standpoint, etc., and if he pays less than the regular tuition he may well be annoyed at the question.

Unless you have some business reason to do so, you shouldn't ask a man or woman the amount of insurance he or she carries, the amount of their mortgage or rent, the salaries of their servants. You might ask a man's age—though many men are less than anxious to divulge that information as they pass forty—but you never ask that of a woman over twenty-one, except for official reasons. Even then, the courtesy of letting her say "over twenty-one" usually is accorded a woman—except by the U. S. State Department, the various Motor Vehicles offices, and other sternly realistic representatives that must know all. So even though many women are frank about their ages—sometimes aggressively so—it really is no one's business, and it is, I think, a permissible conceit for anyone to shave off a few years if her face doesn't belie the amputation. But in her very late years a woman usually takes a belated pride in her longevity and brags that she is eighty-one or ninety—except a great aunt of mine who at ninety-six refused to admit it and blithely said, when queried about her great age by a caller on her birthday, "Oh, I guess I'm about ninety." (She lived to just three months short of one hundred.)

Most women are equally sensitive about their weight and dislike being asked to name the figure, with which they are doubtless displeased.

Men and women of less than average height are often diffident about references to the fact. Surprisingly enough, it seems to me, very tall men usually are far from flattered at references to their height, and, of course, no very thin or fat man likes to have his deviation from the norm commented upon in public, no matter how much inured he seems to friendly raillery. The very fat and the very thin are sensitive people, easily hurt.

Many of our ways of thinking are changing, so that a six-foot girl today might not bat an eyelash if you asked her how tall she was. If she carries herself straight and tall, is not afraid of high heels and dramatic hats, you can be sure she has no complex about her height. If she goes around in flat heels, walks stoop-shouldered, and wears itsy-bitsy accessories, you can be equally certain she'd hate to be asked her measurements and that to her such a question would be highly "personal."

And while practically all American girls—and men, too—have big feet these days, many like to pretend their feet are smaller than they actually are, in deference, perhaps, to the Victorian idea that small hands and feet denoted gentility. A woman who wears an 8½ D might get on the defensive if you asked her shoe size.

I'd never ask my best friend whether he or she had dyed hair, false teeth, a wooden leg, or a glass eye. I wouldn't ask anyone who his legatees would be or how he had made out his insurance, how much money he had in the bank or how his marriage was going.

DANGEROUS TOPICS OF CONVERSATION

You may be Helen Burke's most intimate friend, and she may have half-confided in you many times that she and Herbert are not getting along any too well. But for you to ask her a direct question as to the status of her relations with her husband is dangerous business. If you are cast in the role of confidante, willingly or unwillingly, avoid asking direct questions or referring to a former confidence when perhaps the crisis that precipitated it may have passed. All married people have their moments of incompatibility. Never take them seriously until and unless you see separate residences established. And mentioning any such acrimonious scenes to which you may have been witness is a good way to close the doors to reconciliation between the couple. Somehow if all her best friends keep reminding Helen that Herbert's behavior has been unforgivable she will find it harder to forgive than if no one but the most discreet among her friends is mutely conscious that there has been a little fuss.

When people are angry and abusive toward some friend, associate, or member of their family, don't take sides. Listen, refrain from expressing an opinion, and stay objective, though vaguely sympathetic. If angry friends ask for, get, and take your advice they will not like you better. On the contrary, they may resent your interference, well-meaning though you may have meant it to be. The role of mediator is hard and thankless, and most of us are not really equipped for the task.

HOW TO PARRY DIRECT QUESTIONS

Personal questions can be unsettling unless you develop enough sophistication to cope with them gracefully. Sometimes they are brutally asked with intent to wound. A naturally witty person knows well enough how to reply. An author who was asked by a jealous contemporary, "Who *wrote* your book for you?" replied, "Who *read* it to you?" This is the Socratic question-for-question defense which had best be left to professionals.

The safer way is to pretend that no offense was meant—and often the poser of personal questions is just a blunderer and doesn't really mean to be malicious. If you are a woman who does not care to advertise her age, whether it be twenty-five or forty-seven, you might reply to someone who asks how old you are (when it's none of his business), "You know, the women in my family have always been ageless and I like to keep it that way." Women are expected to lie about their age, anyhow, so even if you bared your sensibilities and told the truth the chances are your interrogator would, mentally, add another five or ten years.

When no tactful answer seems to suffice and the personal probing goes on, the only solution is to be quite frank. Say, without getting angry, "I know you don't realize it, but that is a personal question I don't feel willing to answer." If he then takes offense, he deserves to.

THAT WORD "LADY"

The word "lady" is suitable in the discussion of etiquette—"A gentleman stands behind a *lady's* chair until she is seated," but the use of it in conversation is very limited, unless we wish to imply our own humbler position.

A woman caller being announced in an office or in your home by an employee—or at home by a child—is a "lady," not a woman. A secretary will announce, "There is a lady to see you, Mr. Zachary. Here is her card." Or, "There is a Miss Long to see you. She's from the Grolier Society" (if she's presented no card). A child at home would say, "There's a lady to see you, Mommy."

A secretary or other white-collar employee never says—at least not in the hearing of the caller—"There's a *woman* here." Neither, ushering in the caller, does she say, "You may come in, lady." Instead, she says, "Please come in," adding the visitor's name, if known.

In a shop no one should ever use the word "lady" to a customer to get her attention, although in referring to the customer in speaking to someone else it is proper to say, "This lady would like to know if we carry——" In cases where a man or woman, no matter what his or her station in life, does not know the name, or doesn't wish to use the name of a woman to whom it is necessary to direct a remark, it is proper to say "Madam," never "Miss," unless the title is followed by her last name.

I have heard men in high business positions say, as a domestic properly does, "Please come in, *Miss* (to an obvious 'Miss')." Even with office personnel whose names they don't know, they should not use this form of address. A pleasant "Come in" is all that is necessary.

Remember, the King of England in his abdication speech referred to Wallis Simpson as "the *woman* I love." The word used properly has great dignity and meaning. A man, speaking of his wife, should refer to her as a "woman" to his friends, as a "lady" only to tradespeople and various others in service capacities. He may say to his new client, "I'd like you to meet my wife sometime—a charming *woman*." To the station porter he should say, "Will you help the *lady* over there with the bags while I buy the tickets?"

A woman does not refer to herself as a "lady" to her social equals. She does not call on the new neighbor explaining she is the "lady" next door. Instead, she says, "I am Mrs. Birch, your next door neighbor." To the butcher in the chain store she might say, "I am the *lady* who ordered the turkey last week," but I like better the more democratic, "I ordered the turkey last week." From your way of addressing him, the tradesman can see for himself how you should be catalogued.

HOW ABOUT "MISS!"?

Whenever possible the word "Miss" as a summons to someone whose name you don't know should be avoided. If you are being served by a waitress and fail to catch her eye, "Waitress!" is better than "Miss!" If you are trying to catch up with a woman friend in the street, never call out her name—which might embarrass her. Certainly you can't call "Miss!" after her, although if you are near enough and are on a first-name basis, you might call her first name softly in a crowd, if you fail to catch her attention any other way.

Salespeople nowadays avoid "Miss" in speaking to customers, although many well-trained ones say "Madam," if necessary, except to a very young girl. It is undignified for a matron, however young, to be spoken to as "Miss" by someone waiting on her—"Will you try these for size, Miss?" The "Miss" should be omitted and if any title is used, it should be "Madam." A customer, failing to catch a salesperson's eye, may call out "Miss," however.

INTRODUCTIONS

In America when men are introduced to each other they shake hands standing, without, if possible, reaching in front of another person. They may smile or at least look pleasant and say nothing as they shake hands, or one may murmur some such usual, courteous phrase as "It is nice to meet (or know) you." To which the other may reply, "Nice to meet you" or merely "Thank you."

In shaking hands, men remove the right glove if the action isn't too awkward because of the suddenness of the encounter. If they shake hands with the glove on they say, "Please excuse (or forgive) my glove." If the introduction takes place on a ballroom floor and the men are wearing white kid gloves, the right glove is not removed, even for an introduction to a lady, and no apology is made. The purpose of the glove, in this case, is to prevent damaging the ladies' gowns with a (possibly) perspiring palm.

Men who meet or are introduced to each other outdoors do not remove their hats unless a lady is present. Nor do men who know each other raise their hats when they pass on the street unless they are escorting ladies.

When a man is introduced to a lady he does not offer his hand unless she makes the move first, as it is quite correct for a lady merely to bow in acknowledgement of an introduction—in fact the usual thing. There is much less handshaking in this country, less between women, and women and men, than between men. A hostess, however, greets all her guests by shaking hands, and all guests should seek to shake the hand of the host.

When women are introduced to each other and one is sitting, the other standing, the one who is seated does not rise unless the standee is her hostess or a much older or very distinguished woman. The rising of one woman for another in this country indicates great deference. It is often a delicate matter to decide whether or not a woman is sufficiently older than oneself to be worthy of the gesture. If not, she may be offended rather than honored. Any young girl in her early teens, however, should rise when introduced to any matron and to any older man of her parents' circle, but she shakes hands only if the older person so indicates. Of course, any woman seeking employment rises when presented to her prospective employer, male or female, and permits the interviewer to make the move to shake hands, or not, as he chooses.

A woman or man introducing husband or wife to another person says, "This is my husband" or "May I introduce you to my wife?" A man's wife would, however, be introduced *to* a much older woman, to a woman of great distinction, or to an elderly and distinguished man.

Neither spouse refers to the other socially as "Mr. Brown" or "Mrs. Brown." Nor does a man say "the wife" or "the missus."

No one properly says "Charmed," "Delighted," or "Pleased to meet you" when presented to anyone. In fact, under ordinary circumstances a casual "Hello," or "How do you do?" (to which no answer but a repeated "How do you do?" or a smile is expected) is sufficient. A spontaneous "It's so nice to meet you" or "I am *so* glad you came" or even "I have heard so much about you" is fine when it is really meant—but it is never obligatory. All introductions may be acknowledged with no more than a pleasant glance and a slight bow except those between men, where a handshake is usually expected.

DUTY DANCES

At any dance, each man guest asks the hostess to dance at least once and also asks her daughters, if she has any, or her women house guests. A well-brought-up young man seeks out each lady of the household, including house guests, at a private dance, even grandmother, if she is present, and courteously asks for a dance. The phrase he uses is, "May I have this dance?" or "May I have the pleasure of this dance?" Between very young people this is often abbreviated to "Dance?"

At a supper dance those who have come together sup together. It is the expected thing. As suppertime approaches a girl's escort seeks her out if she is dancing with someone else and at the appropriate moment says, "Shall we have supper?"

REFUSING A DANCE

No lady need dance with anyone if for some reason she doesn't care to. But she must always be polite in her refusal. If she is hoping for another partner she may say, "Thank you, but I don't believe I'm free right now." Or if she is tired she should say so, "Thank you, but I'd like to rest a little. Won't you join me?" (if she really wants him to.) At a large dance where there is a floor committee or stag line a man can always signal adroitly when he thinks he has danced enough of a duty dance or if he is stuck with a wall-flower.

Girls, of course, get stuck too during interminable dances when no one asks to cut in. If no relief seems in sight either partner can suggest leaving the floor, usually under the pretext that there are too many couples danc-ing, that a drink, or a talk, or a walk in the air might be more fun. If either partner feels inept at a particular dance and the music strikes up in that tempo that is another quite acceptable excuse for sitting out a dance. But a man never escorts a girl from the floor and leaves her unaccompanied, though she may always give him some polite excuse for leaving him once they are off the floor.

CHAPTER TWENTY-FIVE

THE SMOKING PROBLEM

CIGAR SMOKING

There are men who will agree with me—and most women will, too—that cigar smoking has certain definite perils, esthetically. To me a large fat cigar in the mouth of a young man has about the same effect on his appearance as would a pince-nez. The smaller, slim, mild cigars seem preferable. At least it seems to discourage the unattractive habit of a man's leaving a half-smoked cigar around for later relighting. And a small cigar is usually treated like a cigarette and not allowed to stay overlong in the mouth. A chewed cigar end, only too apparent when the cigar is removed during the course of conversation, is enough to repel all but the most hardy females. If you do smoke cigars, treat them as if they were cigarettes. Don't exhale vast and, perhaps, offensive clouds of smoke. Remove the cigar when you talk, take brief puffs to keep the cigar dry and relatively sightly. Be sure a large enough ash tray is at hand before you start, so that you won't get cigar ashes all over the floor, furniture, and yourself. Never even ask to smoke a cigar during a meal (I suppose some men might). At table bring out cigars only at coffee time and even then, when the cigarettes are passed, be sure to ask if your stronger-odored cigar is permissible. Ask for a larger ash tray if the cigar you are to smoke is a large one.

If you are smoking your cigar in the living room, you will be considered very thoughtful if you don't leave the butt in an ash tray. If you know your way around the house, put the dreary remains in the garbage can. Or, first running it under water, wrap it in paper and drop it in a waste basket. Of course, if servants are on hand to empty ash trays the minute they get over-crowded, one cigar butt more or less will make no difference. But it will make a terrific difference in a party-crowded room where all the ash trays fill rapidly and are not being emptied as soon as desirable.

We might as well face it: the man who is a constant smoker of heavy cigars stains his teeth, lips, and fingers to a degree seldom encountered in cigarette smokers. But any heavy smoker—whether of pipes, cigars, or cigarettes—should at least be conscious of the fact that his over-all powerful odor of often stale tobacco can be very offensive, especially to women.

Heavy smokers—men or women—should be sure their clothes and they themselves are frequently aired. They need at least one thorough shampoo a week and regular trips to the dental hygienist to remove stains from the teeth. Finger stains can be taken care of at home with a few drops of peroxide on the nail brush or a rubbing over with pumice stone. But yellow-stained fingernails just have to grow out, I gather.

It is well known that every animal—including us, has his own special natural odor. Ours should be an attractive one, but it is easily distorted into something less than attractive by oversmoking, overdrinking, or too great consumption of certain foods—fatty ones, for example. Delicate colognes and perfumes should enhance our natural odors, not overshadow them. Scrupulous physical cleanliness and a cultivated fastidiousness about our habits, such as smoking and drinking, will make us more attractive.

It is well known scientifically that humans, as well as animals, are attracted or repelled by the odor of another person even when they are not actually conscious such odors exist. Perhaps we have more in common with the hound than we imagine.

THE PIPE SMOKER

Pipes are generally becoming to most men of any age—with the possible exception of well-colored meerschaums, which to me at least seem a little elderly.

But the pipe smoker must watch his manners, too. Pipe cleaning is a messy operation even in the hands of an expert and should be done in relative privacy. The discarded contents of the bowl and the used pipe cleaner should be quickly disposed of, not left in the ash tray to befoul the atmosphere. And if the smoker feels the necessity to improve the pipe's draw through loud sucking or blowing, or whatever it is that's so noisy, let him step outside the door, unless he is quite alone at his task.

There is pipe tobacco and pipe tobacco. It's safer perhaps to go by the judgment of friends in the matter of which blend to choose than to pick one by taste alone. It is not possible that tobacco that smells so bad can taste that way, too. Let your friends' pleased or pained expressions when you light up be your guide.

WHEN NOT TO SMOKE

With smoking so common, we sometimes forget there are times and places where one never smokes, even though not so reminded by a "No Smoking" sign. Members of the assemblage in any religious ceremony taking place at home, a wedding, a christening or a funeral, do not smoke—just as one doesn't smoke in church or, if he has any consideration, in elevators. Getting into an elevator "palming" a lighted cigar or cigarette is threatening yourself or fellow passengers with possible burns if the elevator becomes crowded or there is an accident.

You may not smoke in an airplane while the "No Smoking" sign is lighted, although you may when the plane has reached a certain altitude and the sign goes off.

Smoking is not allowed in court or in most public meeting places such as concert halls, movies, and theaters except in sections set aside for smokers. Many of the better restaurants prohibit smoking or restrict it.

You do not smoke on busses, street cars, or trains unless you are seated in a smoking section, so labeled. Do not even pass through non-smoking areas carrying lighted pipes, cigars, or cigarettes.

You never walk, smoking, into a sickroom or into a nursery. In a sick room, if the patient is smoking, you may smoke if invited to do so and are careful not to leave ashes and butts behind you to make the atmosphere unpleasant. It is incredible how many people not only smoke while visiting a young baby in his nursery but also use any available receptacle for the ends of cigars and cigarettes—from silver porringers to diaper pails—with no thought at all for the baby's possible reaction to the ensuing fumes.

Business firms have varying rules concerning smoking, but, even when employers don't consider the matter important, employees seated where they receive visitors to the office should not smoke on the job. Where office employees are permitted to smoke at their desks, they should not allow ashes and butts to pile up in receptacles but should dispose of them from time to time—and not by dumping them loose into the waste basket. Some employers, in desperation at the amount of time lost if employees are allowed to smoke in rest rooms only, permit smoking on the job. But a cigarette or cigar resting on the edge of a desk can ruin the finish. Close work interrupted by drags on a cigar, pipe, or cigarette can suffer badly, and production can be slowed down to the point of serious inefficiency if the worker is a constant smoker.

Women should not smoke while walking on city or town streets, although on open country roads they may if they wish (being careful to put out matches and smokes carefully before discarding them, to prevent fires).

No one riding with others in a taxi or automobile should smoke without permission of the others. And used matches and butts should not be ground out on the floor. If no receptacle is provided, snub out the light against the sole of your shoe and discard the butt out the window. Do not throw lighted cigarettes or cigars out of the window, not only because they may start a fire or burn a passer-by, but because the wind may blow sparks or the smoke itself back into the car and cause damage.

If you smoke on a sailboat, flip your ashes or discard your cigarette on the side the sail is on so the wind won't blow sparks or ashes or butts back into the boat.

CHAPTER TWENTY-SIX

CLUBS

MEN'S CLUBS

A good club is not a social necessity, but it is a social convenience. It is, usually, a place where one meets men of similar interests and background, a comfortable *pied-à-terre* in town where a man can stay overnight, put up another man guest, receive messages and entertain in private, if he wishes, as if he were in his own home.

Any man with enough money to pay the dues can list a long string of clubs after his name, even a long list of the best ones if he stands muster with the membership committees. But the man of substance prefers to be associated with usually not more than two main clubs, one in the country and one in town, depending on his interests. He avoids taking membership merely for the prestige in a number of clubs in whose affairs he can take little or no part.

Actual, active identification with his club is to a man's benefit, because it permits him a say in the running of it. Absentee, inactive membership, widely practiced, means that a club is taken over by a small clique that runs it for its own benefit and often against the interests of the membership as a whole. Furthermore, if he really understands what his club represents, what the thinking is as reflected in the by-laws, a man can protect himself against being classified as something he really is not, by fighting what he doesn't like or getting out.

JOINING A CLUB   It is part of our snobbism that we don't want to join a club everyone can join. For that reason, a man never openly asks that he be put up for membership in any of the exclusive clubs, although he may tactfully indicate his interest to members among his friends. Then, if he seems eligible, they may propose him, first making sure that he understands what membership entails as to initiation fee, dues, rules, and regulations. It is, of course, highly embarrassing to the sponsor or sponsors if the proposed new member is rejected for any reason. Their explanation to him of such a rejection must be accepted gracefully and without probing. It is often possible for him to qualify for the same club later, especially if his reaction to the first refusal has been sporting. It is an axiom that it is easier for a well-introduced stranger to get into a good club than a well-known man-about-town who's had ample opportunity to gather enemies as well as friends.

TIPPING IN CLUBS   In the major clubs the employees are tipped by the members at Christmas, or at the holiday time members may contribute to a kitty for the staff. In addition, most clubs now add a service charge to all bills. Guests of members do not tip unless they have been put up at the club, though the service charge is usually added to bills. Resident guests or members using private rooms for large parties may, if they wish, tip additionally the employee with whom they have had the most contact—on the same scale one would in a first-class hotel.

PROPOSING AND SECONDING   In large clubs new members are usually proposed by letter, although sometimes the proposing is done in a brief interview with the club secretary, who then usually posts the name, with the names of the proposer and seconder, after the suggestion has cleared the membership committee. The posting of the name gives members who might object to the inclusion of the proposed member a chance to protest to the board of governors. Such protest is often verbal to one or more governors or, preferably, by letter to the board of governors, stating one's objections to the proposed member. These objections are, supposedly, kept confidential and should be. It is foolish not to make them if they are merited and thus possibly admit a member who will not be agreeable.

LETTERS OF PROPOSAL AND SECONDING   A friend writes to the board of governors of his club to propose a new member somewhat in this manner, including relevant material:

September 15, 1952

To the Governors of the Town Club
Gentlemen:

It gives me much pleasure to propose for membership my friend Dr. Norman Benson, Jr., a former college classmate. Dr. Benson is a graduate of Dartmouth College and of Harvard University where he received his M.D. His late uncle, Judge Timothy Way, was a long-time member of the club.

Dr. Benson is married (to the former Lola Ferris) and lives at 800 Park Avenue. He is chief of research staff of Botts Pharmaceutical Company at 700 Fifth Avenue. He is in his early forties, a good squash player and a sound man in every way.

I hope you will agree that he would be a most desirable member.

Respectfully,
Norris Lanson

321 Park Avenue
New York, N.Y.

The seconding letter merely states that the writer is seconding the proposal and adds a few words of commendation, general or specific. It is always wise for a sponsor to get more than one other member to endorse his candidate for admission to the club if there seems any possibility of refusal. Often outsiders who can vouch for the candidate—his clergyman, his banker, or his lawyer—write to the board. Also, the sponsor sees to it that the proposed man meets as many of the board of governors as possible in brief calls upon them at their offices. The candidate makes these calls alone, after the sponsor has made the necessary appointments. He meets usually four governors in this way, two of whom are on the membership committee.

THE LETTER OF OBJECTION Voting on the candidate takes place in committee, with two blackballs counting against admission and no explanation required. All objections have usually been weighed before the election meeting. So any letter to the board is sent soon after the posting of the name. Such a letter should be reserved, but explicit enough to permit the board of governors to consider your objection properly. It might read:

January 12, 1952

To the Board of Governors of the Town Club
Gentlemen:

It has come to my notice that Mr. — — has been proposed for membership. In my opinion Mr. — — indulges much too frequently and heavily in alcohol. I have seen him garrulous and contentious to a degree that would, I am sure, disturb our relatively conservative membership.

Sincerely yours,
Signature

62 Sutton Place
New York, N.Y.

PUTTING UP A GUEST Most club by-laws have a limitation on the number of times any guest may be admitted to the club over a certain period. They also limit the length of stay of a house guest, in most cases to two weeks. Only out-of-town guests may be put up at a club, not local residents.

A letter putting up a guest is addressed to the club secretary. For example:

February 6, 1952

To the Secretary of the Town Club

I should like to put up my business associate Mr. Thomas Putney, of Chicago, for the week of March 18th. Will you be kind enough to send him a membership card at our Chicago office, whose address is on this letter-head.

Sincerely,
Norris Lanson

321 Park Avenue
New York, N.Y.

It is well understood that a member never asks to have a guest put up who for some reason would be quite ineligible for even non-resident membership in the club should he wish to join. A member would not ask to put up a prominent Socialist in the Union League, for example.

RESIGNING FROM A CLUB The loss of an influential member from a club is usually regrettable. If he is resigning " in protest," that is known by his conduct in the club prior to his resignation. His actual letter of resignation is brief and merely for the record. If he must resign after bills for dues for the new year have been received, he pays his dues even if he does not plan to use the club. A letter of resignation is always formal and makes some polite excuse for not continuing membership. For example:

June 16, 1952

To the Governors of the Town Club
Gentlemen:

Pressure of work makes it most difficult for me to take advantage of club privileges at all this year. I should like to resign with the thought that at some later date I might be able to continue the many pleasant activities and friendships the club afforded me.

Most sincerely,
John Robert Barbour

321 East 76th Street
New York, N.Y.

GUEST OF A PRIVATE CLUB A guest of a member must never "take over" a club. He should make himself agreeably inconspicuous and no more criticize the service, the furnishings, or facilities of the club than he would criticize these things in his host's own home. As in a private home, too, he asks permission to use the outside telephone, as he is required to give the member's name to the operator who is making the call. If he makes out-of-town calls or many local ones, he asks for the charges and quietly reimburses his host. He should not attempt to entertain his host in the club but should take him elsewhere, except possibly for a drink. Members, by the way, do not pay for meals and drinks at time of service but sign checks submitted and pay their bills monthly.

Men's clubs sometimes have certain rooms or sections where they may entertain women guests or where women friends or members of their family may meet members or lunch or dine without them. These facilities should not be used without the express knowledge of the member, who then arranges for the courtesy. The bill is signed by the guest, who places beneath his or her signature the member's name. The bill may then be settled later with the member, if that is the understanding. No tip is left, as a service charge is included.

Also, in most men's clubs, there are rooms for members only. Guests are expected to meet members in the public rooms, only by appointment.

WOMEN'S CLUBS

Women have far fewer resident clubs than men have. In formal clubs where there are full facilities the rules are much the same as those governing men's clubs. In such organizations as the Junior League, dedicated to social service, there are in addition certain work requirements before a candidate is eligible for membership.

The Women's Club in communities throughout the country concerns itself at least in part with local improvement. It is usually tied in with the national organization, the General Federation of Women's Clubs, and open to any local resident who wishes to join. There are, too, many special interest clubs, many of them affiliated with such larger entities as the Garden Club of America, the League of Women Voters of the U.S., and the various women's divisions of political and fraternal organizations, all of which are of social and civic importance.

HOW TO OBTAIN MEMBERSHIP In such clubs as these it is perfectly proper for an interested woman to write the club secretary and ask for a membership blank. Or she may be taken to the club as a guest of a member, who then asks the secretary to give her a membership blank. Dues are usually nominal. They should be paid promptly, and, as in a very formal men's club, one pays her dues anyhow if the bill for them has arrived before a letter of resignation has been received by the club.

In all women's clubs that make any pretense at formality the parliamentary procedure is followed. Women members should familiarize themselves with the rules, so that the business affairs of their club may be conducted in a dignified and efficient manner. (See "Simple Parliamentary Procedure.")

THE ELECTIVE CLUBS Such organizations as the Daughters of the American Revolution are elective to the extent that a candidate's qualifications for membership are rigidly fixed—in this case certain ancestral participation in the American Revolution. Anyone who believes she qualifies may apply for membership, and her application is then passed upon after the necessary historical checking.

CLUB TEAS It is usual for women's club meetings to be followed by afternoon tea, with the tea presided over by one or more club officers, who thus serve as hostesses. The tea table, always properly covered with a white cloth, is set up with a silver tea service at one end, the water kept boiling by a spirit lamp. Cups and saucers are arranged within reach of the hostess, each cup on its saucer and a teaspoon to the right of the handle. For a limited number of guests the cup and saucer is stacked on a small cake plate with a tea napkin (usually paper) between saucer and plate. Generally only finger foods are served, so no fork or butter knife is needed. For very large teas the cake plates are stacked at the other end of the table with napkins between, or adjacent to, them. Guests go for their tea to the person pouring, telling her whether they wish sugar, lemon, or cream, then pick up their plates and serve themselves to little tea sandwiches or cakes. Frequently coffee is served at one end of the table and tea at the other, with a hostess presiding over each beverage.

Guests usually take their tea standing and place their empty cups and plates on a sideboard or serving table for removal by committee members or available waitresses. As at any reception, one speaks to anyone who happens to be standing near, whether or not one has been introduced.

COUNTRY CLUBS, BEACH CLUBS, AND YACHT CLUBS

Under "Men's Clubs" and "Women's Clubs" I have discussed the procedures of becoming members and of resigning from clubs. The rules for behavior in all clubs are much the same, with consideration of others of major importance. In the section, "What's What in Various Sports," I discuss specific rules in sailing, tennis, swimming, etc., for spectators and participants.

If you move into a community, it is best to inquire tactfully whether or not it is necessary to be proposed for membership to any local clubs that interest you. In general, community clubs are fairly informal, and one may apply to the club secretary for membership without being proposed by a sponsor and seconder. Yacht and golf clubs maintained by the municipality are open to all able to pay the small fees or dues for maintenance.

Country and beach clubs are always family clubs and thus necessarily more relaxed than formal town clubs. The family uses them during summer week ends and sometimes in the winter, too. During the summer the younger generation—infants with their nurses, sitters, or mothers, the subteens and teen-agers—takes over during the week. From Monday to Friday there is not much point in trying to keep the noise down to a bearable level, except late in the day when adult members may wish to use the club, too. Infants obviously need their own little paddling corner, safe from the older children. All the children need some adult supervision even when there is no water. They must be taught early to use their own equipment, to return borrowed toys, boats, rafts, balls, and other things when they have finished using them. They should not be allowed to dig up turf or courts, throw sand, or misuse anything in the club house.

Week ends, when weary adults hope for some relaxation, children must settle for less than the full facilities of the club. Parents with young children should try to keep them away from the club on Saturdays, Sundays, and holidays to give older people a chance.

Club bills should be settled promptly and dues never be allowed to accumulate. Even club members in good standing should remember they are there by sufferance, by tacit consent. The club itself with its rules and its by-laws creates an atmosphere wherein even a founder member has the status of a guest the minute he steps on the grounds.

CLUB GUESTS

Most family clubs have few regulations concerning the bringing of guests, but good taste and good sense enter into consideration here, too. No one should bring so many guests that the facilities of the club are thereby taxed insofar as the members are concerned. For example, no member with consideration will fill all the badminton or tennis courts with his guests to the exclusion of members. Limited guests over week ends should be an unwritten rule if guests are to use the club facilities such as locker and steam rooms, game courts, pools, beach, or golf course. If they are invited to be spectators, that is another matter, but they should always be the kind of people the club might welcome as members. A private club is no place on which to inflict one's own private little social crosses.

CHAPTER TWENTY-SEVEN

MANNERS AT TABLE

A man or woman may take on a superficial patina of breeding, but it is very difficult to overcome slipshod table manners. And poor manners at table can be a real deterrent to social—and even business—progress.

Gentle people are often acutely embarrassed by the table manners of those with whom they find themselves eating. A carefully bred wife may suffer much inner torture because her husband—always when manners seem very important—forgetfully leaves his spoon in his cup or absent-mindedly licks his fingers. It is the job of a good wife to help an ambitious husband overcome these poor manners in a tactful way if she can—not solely because they offend her and are a poor example for the children but because good manners can help him advance in his work or profession. Of course, it is sometimes the other way around, and people are even less willing to overlook bad table manners on the part of women, who are expected to be fastidious about such things.

Some of the things necessary to know about behavior at formal meals are discussed under "The Guest at Formal Meals." But there are many more:

WHO IS SERVED FIRST?   The hostess is *not* served first unless she is the only lady at the table or is alone with her husband and children. If grandmother or even a young girl guest is present, the dishes are first presented to her after inspection by the hostess. When the hostess is serving at least part of the meal from in front of her place, with or without the aid of a servant, she is served next to last and her husband last. For her to serve herself earlier will mean her food will be cold and her filled plate in the way.

WHEN TO BEGIN EATING   After several people have been served, guests begin eating, so their food will not be cold. But children wait, if they are old enough to understand, until at least several guests have been served before beginning to eat, too. When children are alone with their parents it is considerate of them, at all meals but breakfast, to wait until their parents begin eating before beginning themselves, unless they are told to go ahead. And, except at breakfast, the polite husband waits until his wife has been served before beginning himself to eat.

THE USE OF THE KNIFE AND FORK   Knives and forks may be used American or Continental fashion, but a combination of the two systems is now often seen and is quite acceptable. Even when one uses the American zigzag method, it is sensible to convey food one has just cut to the mouth with the fork in the left hand, if one wishes. In other words, if you have cut off a bit of chop, it is not necessary, even conservative American style, to lay down the knife, place the fork, tines up, in the right hand and convey the meat to the mouth. Instead, one may use the fork in the left hand, with the tines of the fork down. Also, in eating a bit of bread and gravy—by impaling the bread on the fork (in either hand), tines down, and sopping up the gravy—it is now more usual than otherwise to convey the bit to the mouth with the fork tines down rather than up. Of course, nothing that would leak off the fork—apple pie or other things needing a shoveling technique—should be eaten this way. In the European fashion, food eaten with fork and knife is piled with the knife on the back of the fork, held in the left hand, and pressed down so it won't fall off—or in the case of meat, impaled on the tines. The fork is then conveyed to the mouth, upside down, with the left hand.

DRINKING BEVERAGES AT THE TABLE   In drinking any beverage at table, a sip is never taken until the mouth is empty and has been wiped with the napkin. This keeps cup and glass rims free from food marks.

THE NAPKIN   Napkins are placed on the lap—entirely open if they are lunch-size or in half if they are dinner napkins. Guests wait until the hostess has taken up hers before placing their own. Napkins are tucked in only for children. They are never refolded; at the end of the meal, they are gathered and laid casually to the right of the place setting. Paper napkins are preferable to napkins to be used for more than one meal and placed in rings, but, if rings are used, they are given only to the family. A guest staying over should have a clean napkin each meal. Napkins reused are as incomprehensible to me as beds which have only one sheet changed. There are so many more sensible ways to economize.

TIPPING OF DISHES   The tipping of soup or dessert dishes is acceptable if the plate is tipped away from the spoon, not toward the eater.

THE SOUP OR BOUILLON CUP   Soup or bouillon served in a handled cup or even in a small cup-size bowl (Oriental fashion) is drunk. If there are dumplings or decorative vegetables or other garnish floating on top, these may be lifted out first with the spoon before the soup is drunk. Noodles or other things which may be in the bottom of the cup are spooned up after the liquid has been drunk.

TESTING LIQUIDS   Coffee or tea may be tested for heat or sweetening by one sip from the spoon, then drunk. If it is too hot, it must be allowed to stand until it is tolerable—it may not be blown, spoonful by spoonful, until it is cool enough to drink.

"STIRRING" FOOD   Nothing should ever be stirred up or mashed into a conglomerate heap on the plate. Gravy—unless it is a gravy in which meat, fish or other protein is incorporated (rarebits, curries, blanquettes, chilis, etc.)—is never poured or ladled onto rice, noodles, or other than meat on the plate. It is an insult to the cuisine to inundate everything on your plate with gravy —or with that American favorite, catsup. If you want to eat your potatoes with gravy, you dip a forkful into the gravy that has escaped from the meat.

CONSERVES AND JELLIES   Conserves and jellies (jam and marmalade are for breakfast and tea) may be served at dinner or lunch with meat and are placed on the side of the plate, as are horse-radish, cranberry sauce, apple butter, relish. They are incorporated onto the fork as the food is taken into the mouth. Hard sauce is placed on the side of the dessert plate and incorporated with the pudding with dessert fork or spoon. Dessert sauces are ladled onto the dessert. Liquid sauces (mint, Chateaubriand, Worcestershire, etc.) meant for the meat are poured only onto it.

WHEN FOOD IS TOO HOT Too hot foods taken accidentally into the mouth are never hastily spit out in any way but are quenched with a drink of water before being swallowed (exception to rule against drinking with anything in the mouth).

"SPOILED" FOOD Nothing, not even a bad clam, is ever spit, however surreptitiously, into a napkin. But it is sheer masochism to down, for the sake of manners, something really spoiled, once you have got a goodly mouthful. Anyone with experience in those foreign countries where such things are common knows it is better to seem unmannerly than to brave ptomaine or worse. Certainly, a partly chewed mouthful of food looks unappetizing to one's dinner partner if it has been necessary for you to deposit it from your fork on the side of the plate. It should be screened, if possible, with some celery leaves or, perhaps, a bit of bread. And, in taking it out of your mouth, try not to look as if anything were the matter. After all, if you were eating stewed or canned cherries, you would place the pits in the spoon with which you were eating, then place them on the side of your plate without anyone thinking the procedure disgusting.

COUGHING AT THE TABLE Ordinary coughing at table is done behind the hand, without excuse, but a coughing fit, brought on by something being caught in the windpipe, indicates that you must leave the table immediately without excuse (you can't talk, anyhow). If necessary, your partner at table offers help in the next room—a pat on the back or a glass of water. If there is a servant present he or she attends to this unless the hostess indicates to some member of the family or to a nearby guest that help might be better from that source.

BLOWING ONE'S NOSE AT THE TABLE If the nose must be blown at table, it is done as quietly as possible, without excuse to draw attention to the fact.

"FOREIGN MATTER" IN FOODS Foreign bodies accidentally taken into the mouth with food—gravel, stones, bird shot—are removed with thumb and forefinger, as are fish bones and other tiny bones. If a gnat gets into a beverage or some other unappetizing creature turns up in or on a diner's food, he fishes it out, unobserved (so others won't see it and be upset), and then either proceeds or leaves the drink or dish untouched, depending on the degree of odiousness of the intruder. A gnat or a tiny inchworm on lettuce shouldn't bother anyone, but most fastidious people draw the line at a fly or worse. If the hostess notices an untouched dish, she may say, "Do let me serve you a fresh portion," and she has the dish or drink removed without remarking clinically as to the need for the move. Or if a servant notices, she asks if the guest would like a fresh serving. In a restaurant, if host or hostess does not notice (and both should be alert for this sort of thing) that something is amiss, the guest may tactfully murmur to the waiter that the dish or drink needs changing—preferably when host or hostess's attention is directed elsewhere.

WHEN YOU NEED SILVERWARE   Your own wet spoon should never be placed in a sugar bowl, nor your butter knife in the jam or butter dish. If the serving utensils have been forgotten, pause long enough for the hostess to notice what's happened.

TASTING ANOTHER'S FOOD   Sometimes a couple dining in a restaurant wish to taste each other's food. This is informal but permissible, though only if a fresh fork or spoon is used, with the possessor of the dish then handing the "taste" implement, handle first, to the other person. The other must not reach across the table and eat from a companion's plate, no matter how many years they have been married. If one of the two has had included some item —say French fried potatoes—in his order and doesn't wish them, he asks the waiter to serve them to the other, if desired—he doesn't take them on his plate, then re-serve them.

USING BREAD AS A "PUSHER"   A bit of bread, if available, is used to push food onto a fork—never use the fingers. At formal dinners when bread is not served one may always switch to the Continental style, if one is adept, and chase the peas onto the back of the fork held in the left hand, pressing them down before conveying the fork, upside down, to the mouth. Or, holding the fork in the right—or (French and Italian fashion) left—hand, tines up, on plate, one may guide difficult food onto it with the side of the knife.

REACHING AT TABLE   Reaching at table is now preferred to asking neighbors to pass things one can well take up himself, but one should not have to rise out of his seat.

CONVERSATION AT THE TABLE   Conversation and laughter should always be modified at table. Loud guffaws are disturbing at any time but worse from a dinner partner. General conversation, though it should never fall to a too confidential tone between diners, should never be so loud that the hostess cannot make herself heard, if she wishes to address the table. As it is she who guides the conversation, it is necessary for guests, even at a distance, to watch her for possible conversation breaks in the general talk. The modern hostess no longer does what her Victorian predecessor did—that is, at some point halfway through dinner "turn the table" by turning and talking to her dinner partner on the other side, with everyone, no matter where he was in his conversation, expected to break off and turn in the same direction to talk to the partner on *that* side. Instead, well-bred men and women talk pleasantly across a narrow table and whenever a partner on one side seems disengaged may draw him or her into the conversation on the other side. No two partners ever allow themselves to become so engrossed in conversation as to exclude everyone else, especially partners on the other side, throughout dinner. And it is the host and hostess's task to prevent such a thing.

What is deemed proper table conversation today? Almost anything except highly controversial (religion, politics) or squeamish topics (accidents, illness, operations, real scandal, unaesthetic things), but many sophisticated people are able to discuss once taboo-at-table subjects in a manner that is quite inoffensive, because they know how to employ polite euphemisms in the same or a foreign language—being sure they are comprehensible, of course, to the others at the table. For example, one of the funniest anecdotes I ever heard at table was told by a man quoting from an English magazine. In an English paper there appeared the heading:

John Longbottom
Aged 3 mo. Dies

The English magazine's trenchant comment in Latin, "*Ars longa, vita brevis,*" would be impossibly vulgar, if explained.

POSTURE Elbows on the table are permissible between courses but not while one is eating. Feet should be kept well on the floor, not stretched out under the table or wound around chair legs to possibly interfere with others.

TAKING PORTIONS FROM A SERVING DISH When a serving dish is passed with toast or patty shells beneath some food in a sauce, one takes toast or patty shells, too. While their function is sometimes to absorb excess liquid (toast beneath poached eggs), they may, of course, be eaten, cut with fork or fork and knife, never in the fingers.

When a dish is presented with serving fork and spoon, the spoon is used to cut or take up a portion, the fork is placed beneath it for the transfer to the plate. Where food is already portioned—for instance, planked steak—the guest takes the whole portion, does not (in this case) scrape off the potatoes and take just the steak.

ADDITIONAL BUTTER In eating potatoes or other vegetables, if additional butter is desired, it is taken from one's own butter plate with the lunch or dinner *fork*. The butter knife is only for the buttering of breads.

HOW TO HOLD GLASSES Large, stemmed glasses (water or wine goblets) are held with the thumb and first two fingers at the base of the bowl. (Exception: If they contain chilled white wine, they are held by the stem so as not to heat the wine with the fingers.)

Small, stemmed glasses are held by the stems. Tumblers are held near the base, but, except by a child, never with both hands. A brandy snifter, of course, is held in the palms of both hands to warm the liquor. The delicate fragrance is inhaled, and, finally, the contents drunk, almost drop by drop.

SAYING GRACE

The saying of grace is, unfortunately, not the daily matter it used to be. But in many homes throughout the land grace is said always on Friday night before and after the meal by Orthodox and Conservative Jews and at Sunday dinner, the major meal of the week, grace is often said in Christian homes,

especially in rural communities. Sometimes we hear grace said only on
Christmas, Easter, or Thanksgiving, when the family is all-inclusively
present. It is usually said, at least on Sunday, in clergymen's homes.

A guest at the table is often given the honor of saying grace. Sometimes
a child is asked to say it, or it is the expected privilege of the head of the
house (i.e. father—mother is head of the table).

Grace is usually said after everyone is seated and before anything—
napkins or even water—is touched on the table. A guest, of course, waits
for the hostess's signal before unfolding his napkin, thus he can tell whether
the table is waiting for all to be quiet so grace may be said. Heads are
bowed and the grace is said by one person at the table with the "Amen"
intoned by all. In Jewish homes all say ritual grace, led by the father.
Christian graces, like prayers, may be extemporized, of course, but there are
many lovely, familiar ones.

Here are two for children—the first an old Scotch one suitable for all
religions:

> Thank you for the world so sweet
> Thank you for the food we eat
> Thank you for the birds that sing
> Thank you God for everything.

Blessing for a Christian home:

> Bless this food
> And make us good
> For Jesus' sake.
>   Amen.

In religious Jewish homes after the father leads the general prayers before
food, a child may say this grace:

> May the All Merciful bless my
> father, my leader, the master
> of this house, and my mother,
> my teacher, the mistress of
> this house.

Here is the most familiar grace of all, acceptable to all religions:

> For what we are about to receive,
> Lord, make us truly thankful. Amen.

An eighteenth-century grace from Charles County, Maryland, is for
Christian homes:

> O Lord, forgive us our sins and
> bless these refreshments in
> Christ's name. Amen.

A simple one for a guest is Ophelia's blessing from *Hamlet*:

> God be at your table.

Various denominational prayer books, too, give graces.
Catholics are instructed in the saying of grace both before and after meals.
A Catholic grace before meals is:

> Bless us, O Lord, and these Thy
> gifts, which we are about to receive
> from Thy bounty, through Christ
> Our Lord. Amen.

HOW TO EAT VARIOUS FOODS

ARTICHOKES A finger food. The leaves are pulled off, one at a time, the fleshy base dipped in the accompanying sauce, then dexterously pulled through the teeth to extract the tender part. The inedible part of the leaf is then placed at the side of the plate so that by the time the choke (the fuzzy center) is reached there is a neat pile of leaves which, if the artichoke is very big, may be transferred in part at least to the butter plate, for greater convenience. When the choke appears, it is held with the fork or fingers and the tip of the knife neatly excises this inedible portion. Then the reward of all the labor comes—the delicate *fond* or bottom of the artichoke, which, if large, is cut in manageable bits, then dipped in sauce and enjoyed thoroughly.

ASPARAGUS It is not taboo to eat this in the fingers, but it is messy, so a fork is better. Use the fork to separate the tender part from the tougher end of the stem, then, again with the fork, reduce the edible part to manageable lengths to be dipped in sauce. Do not chew up and then discard, however delicately, the tougher ends, though you may bite off anything edible that remains on the ends by holding them in your fingers, not with the fork—but this is an informal procedure.

BACON Very crisp bacon may be eaten in the fingers if breaking it with a fork would scatter bits over the table. Bacon with any vestige of fat must be cut with fork or knife and eaten with the fork.

BIRDS, FROGS' LEGS Tiny birds, such as squab and quail, and the bones of frogs' legs may be eaten in part with the fingers when the legs or wings are so small as to defy all but the most expert trencherman. Such small bones are held in the fingers by one end while the other end is placed directly in the mouth. The impression of gnawing the bone must be avoided. It is no shame, by the way, for a lady confronted with a squab or half a broiled chicken to ask assistance from the gentleman with her in dissecting it—unless perhaps she's at a formal dinner. This is better than running the risk of having the meat land in her lap or, on the other hand, going hungry, if she is really inept.

CAKE   Sticky cake is eaten with a fork. Dry cake, such as pound cake or fruit cake, is broken and eaten in small pieces. Tiny confection cakes (served at wedding receptions, etc.) are eaten in the fingers. Cream puffs, Napoleons, and éclairs, all treacherous as to filling, are eaten with a fork.

CELERY AND OLIVES   Celery and olives are on the table when guests are seated if there is no service; or they are passed by a servant during the soup course. They are no longer considered essential even at formal dinner. They are taken in the fingers, placed on the side of the plate or on the butter plate (and see "Salt"). Olives, if small and stuffed, are put all at once in the mouth—otherwise they are bitten in large bites and the stone put aside but not cleaned in mouth.

CHICKEN   (Broiled and Fried) Chicken must be eaten with fork and knife except at picnics. Bones are not put into the mouth but are stripped with the knife while being held firmly by the fork. Joints are cut if one's knife is sharp enough and it can be done without lifting the elbows from the normal eating position. Chicken croquettes should be cut with the fork only, as are all croquettes and fish cakes, then conveyed to the mouth in manageable pieces.

CORN ON THE COB   This is only for informal eating and, unless one's teeth will not permit, is best eaten on the cob, with the fingers of each hand firmly in control on each end. A long ear may be broken in half, but only a row or so at a time is buttered and seasoned, never the whole ear at once. Salt already mixed with butter, pepper, and perhaps paprika and shaped in little pats or balls may be provided by the considerate hostess, but a mixture of salt, butter, and pepper may be made, unnoticeably, on the side of one's plate, then smeared a little at a time on the corn as you are eating it. If the corn is to be cut off the cob, the cob is held on one end with the left hand and the kernels cut off a few rows at a time with the dinner knife (which had better be sharp for the purpose). The kernels are then seasoned and eaten a forkful at a time, as one eats peas. There are small silver spears for holding corn, but if they are provided you are quite free to ignore them for the more trustworthy fingers-directly-on-corn technique.

FISH   Small fish, fried, are usually served whole (though cleaned) with head and tail (smelt, sunfish, butterfish, etc.). The head is cut off first, then the fish is held in place with the fork and slit with the tip of the knife from head to tail and laid flat. The tip of the knife is then inserted under an end of the backbone, which with the help of the fork—in a serving motion—is gently lifted out, bringing with it many of the tiny bones in the fish. This skeletal material is laid on the side of the plate or possibly on the butter plate. The balance of the fish is then cut with the fork, or with the knife, if need be, for manageable portions. Any tiny bones still in the fish when it gets into the mouth, after being thoroughly cleaned in the mouth, are taken in thumb and forefinger, and are laid on the edge of the plate or on the butter plate if there is one. There is no objection to anyone hardy enough eating the head, and very tiny fish, such as whitebait (too small to clean), are eaten head and all in one bite. Never one for enjoying the sight of a fish-eye on my plate or in my chowder, I prefer to have even boiled fish (cod, haddock, salmon) come to the table with the head removed, but it is quite proper to serve it whole, with a lemon filling the gaping maw.

FRUIT   *Apples and Pears*   Informally eaten in the hand, but at table they are taken onto the fruit plate and spirally peeled, or quartered with a knife, then peeled. The sections are then cored and eaten with the fingers or with the fruit fork. Lady apples, tiny as crab apples, are eaten in the fingers like plums.

Apricots, Cherries, Kumquats, Plums   Apricots, cherries, plums are eaten in one or two bites, and the stones, cleaned in the mouth, are dropped into the cupped hand and placed on the side of the plate. Kumquats are bitten into or eaten whole depending on size.

Halved Avocados   In their shells these are eaten with a spoon, scooped out and taken spoonful by spoonful, with the dressing (perhaps lime juice and powdered sugar, or a little lake of French dressing) provided. Halved or quartered avocados in salads or on fruit platters are eaten with the fork after being broken into manageable bites.

Bananas   Very informally (at picnics and by small children) bananas are peeled down with the end of the skin as a protective holder. When eaten at table from a fruit dish they are peeled, then broken as needed into small pieces and conveyed to the mouth with the fingers.

Berries   Eaten with a spoon. Large strawberries are sometimes served whole with their stems on. These are grasped by the stem and dipped in powdered sugar on the plate, then eaten in one or two bites, with the stem remaining in the fingers.

Grapes   Cut a bunch or section of bunch from bunches in bowl with knife or scissors (never absent-mindedly pull off grapes from centerpiece or ar-rangement of fruit). Eat one grape at a time, after placing bunch on serving plate. Grape skins, if you can't eat them, should be cleaned in the mouth but not chewed, then removed in the cupped hand with the pits and placed on the side of the plate. Or, holding the grape with the stem end to the lips, pop the inside into the mouth and lay skin on side of plate—if they *will* pop.

Grapefruit   Eaten, halved, with a pointed fruit spoon. Sections should be loosened with grapefruit knife before serving. Do not squeeze out juice at table, except *en famille* if the family can stand it.

Mangoes   Wits say the only place to eat them is in the bathtub. But they may be used in a fruit bowl and eaten at table, even though the best way to serve them is peeled, quartered, pitted, and chilled. A whole ripe (spotted) mango should be cut in half with a sharp fruit knife, then quartered. Then, with the quarter turned skin up and held in place with a fork, the skin should be carefully pulled away rather than peeled from the fruit. The juicy sections are then cut in one-bite morsels. Finger bowls or at least paper napkins are necessary, as this fruit stains badly.

Oranges Peeled with a sharp knife in one continuous spiral (if you're adept), then pulled apart into segments and, if the segments are small, eaten segment by whole segment. If segments are large they are cut in half cross-wise with the fruit knife and eaten with fingers or fruit fork. Navel oranges are sometimes more easily eaten if the skin is quartered, then pulled down toward the navel and pulled off. The navel is then cut off and the orange segmented or cut in slices and eaten with the fork. At breakfast, oranges may be served halved like grapefruit, with the segments loosened, and are eaten with a fruit spoon.

Peaches Halve, then quarter with fruit knife. Then lifting the skin of each quarter at an edge, pull it off. Eat sections in small pieces with fork, prefer-ably, as peach juice stains table linen.

Persimmons Often served as a first course with the top cut off well below the stem and the base cut flat so the fruit stands firmly on the plate. Grasp-ing the persimmon with the left thumb and index finger, scoop out and eat a spoonful at a time, keeping the shell intact. Avoid the skin which, unless dead ripe, is puckery. The large pits are cleaned in the mouth, dropped into the spoon, and then deposited on the side of the plate. Persimmons in salad are peeled and quartered—too difficult a procedure to attempt at table, and persimmons in a fruit arrangement firm enough to be decorative are likely to be all but inedible anyway. They should be dead ripe and slightly spotted.

Pineapple Eaten with a spoon if served cut-up for dessert. If served on flat plates in quarters or eighths, peeled pineapple is eaten with a fork, after being cut with fruit knife.

Stewed or Preserved Fruit The pits or bits of core of cherries, prunes, plums, apples, etc., eaten in compote form with a spoon are dropped into the spoon, then deposited on the side of the plate.

Tangerines Stripped of their skins, segmented, and eaten in the fingers without cutting or breaking the segments.

Watermelon If served cubed and chilled (often in white wine), eaten from a compote with a fruit spoon. Otherwise eaten with the fork. If seeds are present, the fruit is taken seeds and all into the mouth, then the seeds are cleaned in the mouth, dropped into the cupped hand, and placed on the side of the plate, entirely dry.

PICKLES AND RADISHES Whole pickles are take with the fingers, as are radishes. These are never conveyed from the serving plate directly to the mouth (nor is anything else where a serving plate is provided) but are laid on the side of the dinner or lunch plate or butter plate. (And see "Salt.")

POTATOES   *Baked*   These should be rubbed with fat before baking and be presented immediately on coming from the oven, a cross having been cut neatly on the top to allow the escape of steam and to permit the pre-service insertion of a lump of butter, plus a sprinkling of salt and paprika. Then it is simple to hold the potato with the left hand while one explores its innards with the fork. But if a baked potato is presented whole it is taken from the dish with serving fork and spoon, then broken apart with the fingers for buttering and seasoning. It is then eaten with a fork, and if one wishes the skin may be cut up with a knife and eaten (never cutting it up in pieces all at once, any more than one would meat). If the skin is unwanted, the mealy part of the potato is eaten right from the skin with each portion seasoned just before entering the mouth. Except for a child, *do not* scoop out all the potato, set the skin aside and mash the contents all at once with butter and seasoning.

Chips   Eaten in the fingers.

French Fried   Eaten with the fork after being halved with the fork, if necessary. Poor manners to hold any food with the fork and nibble off a manageable mouthful.

Shoe String   If really dry and impossible to eat with fork, may be eaten in the fingers.

SALAD   A quarter of iceberg lettuce may be eaten with knife and fork, though gourmets and nutritionists both frown on the cutting of lettuce in salad preparation. Lettuce for mixed salad should be *broken* in bits and mixed at the last minute—to preserve the vitamin content.

SALT   If there is only one saltcellar on the table (as there is when a condiment set is used or when there is a master salt), the salt is always sent down the table to the honored guest, if there is one, or to the hostess before making the rounds of the family. If salt is needed for dipping radishes or celery or for corn on the cob it is placed on the edge of the plate, *never* on the table cloth. If open salts are used and no salt spoon provided, use a clean knife to take salt from a common container. If individual open salts are at each place, salt may be taken between thumb and forefinger.

SANDWICHES   Small tea sandwiches and canapés are taken in the fingers and bitten into or, if bite-size, placed whole in the mouth. Double- and triple-decker club sandwiches, though served cut crosswise, are eaten at least with the *aid* of knife and fork. If they are not too unmanageable, they may be cut into fourths and eaten in the fingers. Otherwise, they are eaten with the fork, after being cut into small bits.

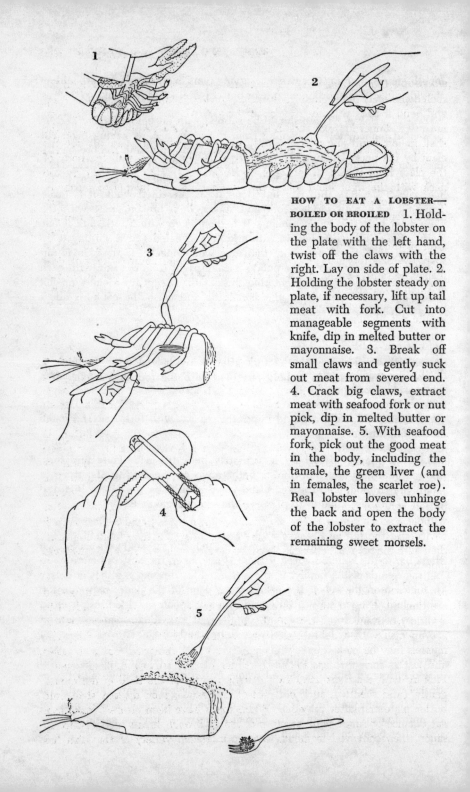

HOW TO EAT A LOBSTER—BOILED OR BROILED 1. Holding the body of the lobster on the plate with the left hand, twist off the claws with the right. Lay on side of plate. 2. Holding the lobster steady on plate, if necessary, lift up tail meat with fork. Cut into manageable segments with knife, dip in melted butter or mayonnaise. 3. Break off small claws and gently suck out meat from severed end. 4. Crack big claws, extract meat with seafood fork or nut pick, dip in melted butter or mayonnaise. 5. With seafood fork, pick out the good meat in the body, including the tamale, the green liver (and in females, the scarlet roe). Real lobster lovers unhinge the back and open the body of the lobster to extract the remaining sweet morsels.

SEAFOOD   *Clams (steamed)*   The steaming process is supposed to open the shell completely but sometimes doesn't. If a shell is not fully open, take it up and bend it back with the fingers. If this doesn't work, forget that one—do not use a dinner knife or fork as an opener. With shell fully open, take the shell in left hand just over the dish and with the right hand lift out the clam by the neck. Holding the neck with the right hand, pull the body of the clam from it and discard the neck sheath. Holding the clam by the neck with the right hand, place the whole clam first in melted butter or broth, or both alternately, then in the mouth in one bite. As empty shells collect, remove to butter plate or shell plates provided (and as clam-eating of this kind is always informal, it is an excellent idea for the hostess to provide platters or bowls for empty shells as well as finger bowls with hot soapy water afterward). Do not spoon up remaining liquid in soup plate—it may be sandy—but drink the broth separately provided in a bouillon cup or small bowl (but not if it is in a little dish). If clams are fried, eat with fork after breaking into two pieces if necessary. As these are greasy they should not be taken in the fingers, even by the neck.

Lobster and Hard-Shelled Crabs (broiled or boiled)   The claws of both of these require dexterous handling. They should be cracked in the kitchen but further cracking at table (with a nutcracker) may be needed. Then the shells are pulled apart by the fingers and the tender meat extracted carefully so, if possible, it comes out whole. A nut pick is useful for this, but an oyster fork may do it, too. The claw meat, if small and in one piece, is dipped in melted butter or, with cold crab or lobster, in mayonnaise, then put all at once into the mouth. Larger pieces are first cut with a fork. The green material in the stomach cavity, called the tamale, along with the "coral" or roe in the female, are delicacies and should be eaten with the fork. The small claws are pulled from the body with the fingers, then the body-ends placed between the teeth so the meat may be extracted by chewing (but without a sucking noise). The major portion of meat is found in the stomach cavity and the tail and is first speared, one side at a time, with the fork, then with the help of the knife, if necessary, lifted out and cut as needed into mouthfuls, then dipped in sauce or mayonnaise with the fork.

Mussels   Served pickled or smoked on toothpicks as cocktail titbits and are thus taken via toothpick directly to the mouth. Served shells and all in a variety of soup styles, too—Moules Marinières (Mussels mariner style) in a soup dish with a delicate thin souplike sauce redolent with garlic. The mussels may be picked out with small oyster fork provided, but it is easier and just as correct to use the shells containing the mussels as small scoops. Pick up with the right hand and, placing the tip of the shell in the mouth gently (and silently), suck out mussel and sauce, then discard shell onto butter plate or platter provided. When shells have been cleared from dish, eat balance of sauce with spoon and bits of French bread used to sop up sauce, then conveyed to mouth with fork. Italian variety of this dish has tomato, is eaten the same way, often as a main dish with salad. Finger bowl essential.

Oysters and Clams (half shell)   Hold the shell steady with left hand and, using oyster fork, lift oyster or clam whole from shell, detaching, where necessary, with fork. Dip in cocktail sauce in container on plate, if desired. Eat in one mouthful. Oyster crackers may be dropped whole in sauce, extracted with oyster fork and eaten.

Shrimps, Scallops, Oysters (fried)   Eaten like fried clams, except that oriental fried shrimp (French fried with the tails on) are to be taken up by the tail and dipped in sauce, then bitten off to the tail, which is then discarded. Unshelled shrimp are lifted in the fingers, shelled, and conveyed whole to the mouth.

Snails   Usually served on a hot metal plate. A special hinged holder with which to grip the hot snail shells is usually provided (or hold the shell with your napkin protecting the fingers), as snails must be dug out. The holder grips the shell with the left hand while the right pulls out the snail with a pick or oyster fork. Snails are eaten whole, like raw oysters. When the shells have cooled, it is proper to tilt them into the mouth to get the garlic butter and snail liquor, or one may sop this up with bits of French bread, which are then conveyed to the mouth with the fork.

SPAGHETTI   The *aficionado* knows that the only graceful and satisfying way to eat real Italian spaghetti (which comes in full-length or perhaps half-length rounds) is to eat it with a large soup spoon and a fork. The spoon is placed in the left hand more or less upright in the plate (or often platter) of spaghetti. The right hand uses the fork with the tip of the prongs against the spoon to wind the spaghetti into a manageable mouthful. It should not drip off the fork. The forkful of spaghetti is then conveyed to the mouth while the spoon remains in the hand and on the platter. As with any sauced dish, it should be eaten without stirring the spaghetti, grated cheese, and meatballs (or other garnish) all together, infant style. The timid way to eat spaghetti is to cut it into small bits with knife and fork and eat it with fork alone. Thick macaroni can't be eaten rolled on a fork so readily and is better cut with a fork as one goes along. Remaining sauce of each dish may be eaten with a spoon or sopped up with small bits of bread, which are then eaten with a fork.

TORTILLAS   These are laid flat in the left hand or on plate, filled slightly with *frijoles* (kidney beans) or other appropriate mixture, rolled up and eaten like a rolled sandwich, endwise.

CHAPTER TWENTY-EIGHT

OUR COMMUNITY RELATIONS AND INTERFAITH COURTESY AND UNDERSTANDING

If we know nothing of our neighbor's beliefs or background we may unwittingly offend him. If we have only a vague idea of his religious customs and taboos we may seem discourteous by our failure to respect them in our contact with him.

Courtesy is a superficial name for actions that can have a very important place in the character building of a human being. Both children and adults should know about the often unthinking cruelty inherent in intolerance of other religions than their own. And how intolerance often stems from our primitive suspicion of anything that is different or not a part of our own experience.

Many educators believe that one way to help children and adults toward better relations with their fellow man is to give them some knowledge of others' beliefs and customs as a purely educational activity, not with the idea of disturbing their own religious affiliations. There are important differences and similarities between denominations, between the belief of the Roman Catholic and that of the Jew—and among Jews themselves—between what the Quaker believes and what guides the Buddhist or the Greek Catholic. If we think less of the *differences* and inform ourselves of the *similarities* I believe we will have a warmer, more understanding attitude toward our neighbors.

The wise parent, I feel, teaches his child that no matter what people's beliefs are, all who follow religion are seeking the same thing, the strength to be good. Or what in their religion teaches them is good and worthy in their day-to-day communion with their fellow men.

Our country may be predominantly Protestant, but the lives of all our minorities are intimately connected with our own, many in very subtle ways. If our Italian tradesmen shut their shops to celebrate the Feast of St. Anthony, we may be affected. For that day at least we must find other places to shop, just as on Yom Kippur much business throughout the country slows down or stops or is in some way affected—through the absence of personnel or the closing of some key business houses. If every fourth or fifth person we meet on St. Patrick's Day is wearing the green, we are conscious of the Irish-descended among us, of their predominantly Catholic adherence.

Every community has its minorities. A Methodist is in the minority in an Irish or Italian neighborhood. A white man is in the minority in the China-towns or in the Harlems of America. The key to comfortable community life is courtesy—true courtesy that respects the rights and feelings of *all*. Courtesy and friendly knowledge about your neighbor help prevent tensions. As America grows we'll need, more and more, to use courtesy in our community life.

SHOULD A CHRISTIAN SEND A CHRISTMAS CARD TO A JEWISH FRIEND?

I think that depends on whether the friend is a deeply religious Orthodox Jew or one who thinks of Christmas and perhaps celebrates it, especially if he has children, as the national, gift-giving holiday it has become. It is per-haps better to avoid cards illustrating the Nativity. Many Jews now send non-religious Christmas greeting cards, have Christmas trees, and give and receive gifts.

DIETARY LAWS OF VARIOUS RELIGIONS

What about food restrictions of Jews and the fast days of Roman and Greek Catholics and some Episcopalians? What about Lent? As almost everyone knows, Catholics do not eat meat on Friday and on certain fast days or during Lent, the forty days commemorating Jesus's wandering in the wilder-ness. During Lent all Catholics and many Protestants keep certain Holy Days through special church attendance and fasting. Individuals often make token personal sacrifices by giving up candy, smoking, or other non-necessi-ties of life as a form of self-denial during this period.

If a Catholic is to be your guest on Friday, it is considerate to plan your meal around non-meat dishes, if such a solution is acceptable to the majority who will be at table. On the other hand, to abandon the roast beef everyone has been looking forward to in favor of fish is, perhaps, to make the guest un-comfortable. When such a guest arrives unexpectedly and there seems no solution for him but to eat meat or go hungry, his Church does not expect him to do the latter but will make dispensation available to him. But for a non-Catholic hostess never to consider this problem with Catholic guests is thoughtless, to say the least. Where special food must be served a guest, whether he be an abstaining Catholic or Episcopalian, a non-shellfish eating Jew, or a man with an ulcer, let it be done without drawing the table's at-tention to the fact.

An Orthodox Jew, in the minority among American Jews today, has many rigid restrictions concerning food and its preparation, but naturally no non-Jewish home is equipped to follow them. However, it is important to know that people who at home keep kosher will usually not feel free to eat the following foods away from home: any fish that is without gills, fins, or scales —the scavenger fish such as eels; any seafood, and this includes oysters, crabs, lobsters, mussels, clams, crawfish; reptiles—turtles, for example; or pork in any form. On the other hand, never assume that your Jewish friend adheres to the old restrictions. It is better to ask. I have known Conservative Jews who, as my guests, would condone the garlic butter on the steak, eat baked ham, but refuse a lobster. Reform Jews have no food restrictions, but they do have fast days.

Moslems, many of whom are racially Semites, have many of the same food restrictions. They may not eat pork in any form or shellfish. The old religious leaders knew the peril of eating improperly cooked or cured pork, the danger of trying to keep it without refrigeration, so they forbade it. The equally perishable shellfish they prohibited too, not on the ground that there was anything basically impure about it, as I understand it, but because unless it was handled in a most sanitary way and eaten almost as soon as it was caught it was dangerous.

It is interesting, too, that the mere proximity of these foods to permitted foods is forbidden. In my own home, we often give buffet suppers when there is a large crowd. Among my guests on one such occasion was an old friend, an Arab sheik. Both a ham and a turkey were on the buffet table, and, as the meat was carved, someone passed the sheik a plate containing a slice of ham and a slice of turkey. He sat politely with the plate of food untouched until I noticed what had happened and took the plate from him. Then, not completely understanding the problem, I merely removed the slice of ham and returned the plate with more turkey. Still he ate nothing, and when my attention turned to him again I realized at last what was the matter. The whole plate had been "contaminated" by the ham. I got a clean plate and served him again, omitting the ham, of course, and all was well. As he was a devout Moslem, my friend did not take alcohol in any form, although some Moslems do, and many smoke, although the Prophet forbade smoking as well as drinking. In place of occupying himself with a cigarette, the Moslem will often run his prayer beads through his fingers as he talks with friends or he will consume interminable cups of the sweet, thick "Turkish" coffee drunk demitasse without cream.

RELIGIOUS HOLIDAYS

The first day of Lent, Ash Wednesday, is kept by the Catholics and the Episcopalians, particularly, and their churches have special services on that day. Then both Catholics and high church Episcopalians may be seen with a smudge of ashes on their foreheads where the sign of the cross has been made by the officiating priest with ashes from the preceding Palm Sunday's palms burned for this Holy Day.

On Palm Sunday, the last Sunday before Easter, you will see Catholics, Episcopalians, Presbyterians, Methodist-Episcopalians among the worshipers coming from church with palm leaves or strips of palm to commemorate the palms carried on the entry of Jesus into Jerusalem.

No matter what our own religious beliefs, in heterogeneous America we are conscious of many of the major religious festivals—Ash Wednesday, Palm Sunday, Good Friday, Easter, Christmas. In some areas we note Chinese New Year with its paper dragons on parade, its firecrackers to warn off evil spirits, Russian Easter and the New Year that follow the Gregorian calendar in the Greek Orthodox Church. We are conscious, too, of the traditional Jewish Holy Days—Hanukah, which corresponds in time to Christmas and is an eight-day festival of lights and daily gift-giving, Purim, the Spring festival celebrating the victory of the Jews over the tyrant Haman, Passover, the Jewish freedom day. This is a time of joy and great preparation, new clothes for the family, special feast food, and even something comparable to the Easter egg hunt, the hunt by the father for any leaven in the house (with the mother always arranging for him to find it, to add to the fun). This mock hunt commemorates the fact that in the Passover the Children of Israel were ordered to flee Egypt, as is told in the Bible, without taking time to leaven their bread. Then, of course, there are Rosh Hashana, the Jewish New Year, and Yom Kippur, the Day of Atonement. And in big cities, at least, it is possible that we might meet a Moslem who, though in Western clothes, is keeping a special one-month period like Lent, Ramadan, as did a Persian prince I knew, by wearing a mourning band on his arm and leaving his collar open at the neck. He fasts from sunrise to sunset, denies himself, and ends the period with a happy festival.

CEREMONIES OF MANY FAITHS

There are many similarities in our various religions and sects. Both Catholics and Episcopalians celebrate the Circumcision because the baby Jesus, like all Jewish boy babies of religious parents, was taken to the synagogue on his eighth day of life to be named and circumcised with the appropriate ceremony. Among religious Jews (and Moslems, too) the day of circumcision is the same day as the boy child's naming. On this day, like many Christian children, he is given godparents. (Non-ritual circumcision is now practiced very generally, whenever the obstetrician deems it necessary or where parents desire it as the health measure the ancient Jews knew it to be.) A girl receives her name when her father goes to synagogue as soon as possible after she is born, usually on a Sabbath (which is from Friday at sunset until Saturday at sunset) and, reciting a little prayer at the altar, states her name. Jewish girls of Conservative or Reform congregations may have godparents, too, like their brothers.

Among Catholics the baptism—which joins the child to the Church—takes place as soon after the birth of the child as possible, during its first month of life, usually on a Sunday afternoon. Catholic children have just one set of godparents. Some Protestant demoninations permit two godfathers for a boy or two godmothers for a girl. And some wait until the child is of an age to understand the baptismal ceremony before performing it. Other Protestants don't baptize at all.

Catholic children often receive multiple names, one of which is that of a Saint, perhaps that of the Saint on whose day he was born. These names are not always all used when the child grows up, but they are his officially, nonetheless, even though he may use a shorter form of his name for legal and social purposes. Greek Orthodox children have just one given name. A Jewish child of traditional background is rarely "Jr.," "2nd" or "3rd" because it is not customary for Jews to be named for living people. If any meaningful name is used, it is usually that of someone recently dead, although the Biblical names are popular among Jews, too.

The children of Congregational parents may be baptized at any age, and godparents are not traditional, though permissible. Often Congregationalists of Episcopal or Lutheran background like to have godparents for their children.

Some Baptists—depending on whether they are liberal or conservative—dedicate their children to the Church soon after birth. Actual baptism with complete immersion takes place any time after the age of twelve, when the individual is believed to be able to make a free-will decision to come into the church. After this, as in most of the "gathering" denominations, he is elected to church membership.

Presbyterians baptize at any age, without godparents, then, after the age of twelve, the individual is elected to the Church. There is no confirmation. Lutheran baptism is similar to that of the Episcopalians, with the child having at least one sponsor. As with Episcopalians, the Lutherans accept the child into the Church at the time of baptism and confirm the pledges, made by the godparents at the time of baptism, when the child is twelve years old. The Eastern Orthodox confirm at the time of baptism in early infancy.

Methodists baptize at any time, and the child has at least one sponsor. The parents make a statement at the time of baptism promising to bring up the child in the Christian way of life. Then as the child approaches adulthood, any time from twelve on, he is prepared for admission to the Church through an affirmation of faith.

PARTICULAR COURTESIES

Does a Protestant walking with a Catholic lift his hat, too, as he passes a Catholic church? He may if he wishes, out of courtesy, but no one would expect it.

Does a non-Jew attending a wedding in a synagogue wear his hat if the congregation follows the old custom? Of course he does, just as non-Catholic women entering a Catholic house of worship, even as tourists, cover their heads, if only with a scrap of handkerchief, out of respect for the church custom.

Should a Catholic attending a wedding in a Quaker meeting house cross himself and make obeisance before sitting down? Probably not, as there is no altar.

How does one reply to a Quaker who uses "thee" and "thou"? The use of "you" would be more natural, I believe.

Should the Christian Scientist kneel at the funeral Mass for a friend, or should he merely bow his head as is his usual custom?

These are difficult questions for anyone to answer. We might say, "When in Rome . . . ," but there are religious practices such as crossing oneself, lighting votive candles, or repeating the Creed that seem out of place or even hypocritical in one for whom such rites or statements of faith are not usual.

It is not necessary to stretch courtesy to the point of offending one's own conscience, yet one may stay within the form of the service one is attending, sufficiently to show proper respect for the traditions and rules of that particular house of worship, standing when others stand, bowing the head at least when prayers are said, covering or uncovering the head as is customary. Communion, except among Catholics, who administer it to children before confirmation, is usually not taken by those who have not been confirmed, although in some Protestant churches the individual minister may administer the sacrament to the baptized at his own discretion.

In some Protestant churches the single chalice used in the Communion service of the Episcopalians has given way to individual cups of sacramental wine or, with some denominations, grape juice. Or it has become customary for those taking Communion to dip the wafer in the cup (intinction) instead of touching the chalice to the lips. There are other variations used under certain circumstances. However, in many parishes such modernization of the ceremony, though now permitted, is not really welcomed.

In taking Communion in a strange church take your place on the left of the rail—when it is given at the altar—so you may observe the custom of the church before accepting the sacrament or cup yourself. Catholics never offer Communion to non-Catholics, and only the priests partake of the wine.

What is the meaning of the Greek letters IHS which we see on Catholic and Protestant altars and of the INRI often seen especially on crucifixes? IHS is the Greek contraction of Jesus's name in that language. INRI stands for Jesus (Iesus) Nazarenus Rex Iudaeorum, Jesus of Nazareth, King of the Jews, and is used only by Christians. The sign of the fish stands for Jesus, too, for the letters of the word in Greek for fish, *ichthys,* are the same as those in the Latin phrase for "Jesus Christ Son of God the Saviour."

On their confirmation day, the day which for many is the day they join the church, you will see little girls of eleven or twelve walking to or from Catholic, Greek Catholic, and some Episcopal churches all in white, wearing miniature wedding veils and carrying flowers. On the Jewish boy's *bar mitzvah,* his confirmation day, you see him dressed as soberly as the Christian boy who goes to his confirmation at about the same age. His sister in the Conservative temple may have her bas mitzvah, for which she, too, dresses in white, although she is not veiled. The basic idea for all is the same, the admission of the child to the church or temple after a period of special preparation for the ceremony, a marking of a certain spiritual maturity and acceptability to the elders.

In some parts of our country the largest minority consists of Orientals. Many are Christians, both Catholic and Protestant, especially among the Filipinos and Chinese. Japanese conversion is still fairly rare.

One of the important things the Jews gave to many religions, including the Christian, is the Sabbath. Before the Mosaic law (that man should work six days and rest the seventh, the Sabbath) was handed down, men and women of the world then worked from daylight to darkness without having a specific day of rest. In fact, the expected thing was that they work a full seven days. The Sabbath, set aside for physical and spiritual replenishment, doesn't fall for all of us, not even for all Christians, on the Sunday of the Julian calendar. Seventh Day Adventists, for instance, celebrate it on Saturday. In many places of the world, there still is no Sabbath. Religious worship may take place daily or several times daily before household shrines or in special calls to prayer. Work goes on around the clock, seven days of the week, and these peoples' places of business stay open even when they are transplanted to predominantly Christian Sunday-Sabbath communities unless local ordinances forbid it.

As the Christian Sunday is not the Sabbath of religious Jews, you will often find Jewish businesses in Jewish neighborhoods open on Sunday but closed on Saturday, for the convenience of their regular customers and to permit employees and business owners to attend religious services.

CLERICAL DRESS

Greek Catholic, Roman Catholic, high church Episcopalian priests and some other Protestant ministers wear the clerical collar and rabat (pronounced raby) outside of church. Rabbis do not wear the clerical collar and neither do Christian Science readers. Members of Catholic and Protestant brotherhoods and sisterhoods wear their garb at all times.

Catholics, in general, carry and display the crucifix. The simple cross is more often used by Protestants, though the crucifix is used in many Protestant churches. When the cross is worn as jewelry, it is always the plain cross.

Both Catholic and Protestant brotherhoods and sisterhoods are celibate, and some high church Episcopal priests take vows of chastity. Confession, too, is not limited to the Catholic Church but takes place as well in high church Episcopalian services.

CHAPTER TWENTY-NINE

THE NEW CITIZEN AND HIS PARTICULAR PROBLEMS

OUR ATTITUDE TOWARD NEWCOMERS TO THE U.S.

Every generation has its immigrants. Many of us are descendants of the Irish who emigrated here during the potato famine in the nineteenth century, of Italians who came to supply our labor pool or bolster our artisan class in the nineteenth and twentieth centuries, of early Dutch settlers dissatisfied with opportunities at home and who came to trade and colonize in New Amsterdam. We are all, no matter how impressive our family trees, descended from immigrants of one kind or the other, if we are Americans. Even the American Indian is now known to have emigrated here from Asia.

Millions of us are the children or grandchildren or great-grandchildren of those who took refuge here to escape political, social or economic upheavals in their own lands or who fled from religious persecution. The Pilgrim fathers, now so revered socially as ancestors, were the first refugees, fleeing religious persecution, just as in the twentieth century refugees from Hitler—Protestants, Catholics, and Jews—sought not only the right to worship as they please among us but the very chance to stay alive. The Pilgrims faced the Indians, who, being here first, resented any encroachment on their hunting grounds. Every new settler today has us to face—the entrenched Americans, who, like the Indian tribes, forget sometimes that they came (or their grandfathers or great-grandfathers) to this land of opportunity because, for some reason or other, things were not good at home. It is only natural for every man to regard the stranger, the possible economic encroacher, with a wary eye. But we need to remember our own sources and realize that the vigor and progress of the country is stimulated by each such influx of new Americans, who bring with them talents, trades, ambition, and even wealth America can use.

Let's examine some of our attitudes toward refugees in our century.

One hears the criticism "Why do they all have to live in one neighborhood —all the Italians, all the Poles, the Scandinavians, all the French, the Germans, the Jews in tight little settlements?" The answer is that our ancestors, even if they came here at the time of the founding of our country, tended to do the same thing—for reasons of solidarity. The melting pot that is America doesn't immediately gobble up the new citizen. Any American who was born abroad must, of necessity, have mixed feelings about his new homeland.

The old living patterns, morals, social habits, and language are all part of him, and it is his children or perhaps his grandchildren who will first have the feeling of being uncomplicatedly "real Americans." Even after generations of assimilation there tends to be this gathering together of Americans with like backgrounds—the Irish in Boston, the Germans in St. Louis, Milwaukee, and Chicago, the Italians and Jews and dozens of other ethnic groups in New York, the Scandinavians in the Midwest, the Pennsylvania "Dutch," (really German) in Pennsylvania. Newcomers, quite understandably, gravitate toward these centers, where they can hear their own language, eat their own food, go to their own houses of worship, and receive assistance in their adjustment to a new and strange—and often unfriendly—land.

It is true that the young do move out and into other circles, through marriage or business opportunities, but it is human and understandable that the older and less adventurous often prefer to make their way in a more familiar atmosphere.

We should all remember that, no matter how American we are now, our ancestors, even if they were English speaking, had their own problems of adjustment here too—physical, social, and economic. Even well-bred English who settle here today feel our hostility or experience our ridicule of their manners and customs—as any English-born bride of an American can tell you. So it isn't language that is the principal difficulty at all. It is just the perversity of human nature. We all hate to move over, as others had to move over for us.

WHAT DO THEY THINK OF US?

All our new citizens or citizens-to-be have their own opinions of us, collectively as well as individually, and some of them quite unflattering. We are said by some Europeans to be noisy—which some of us are—scream-eaglish, that is, insular in our point of view, unsophisticated, often vulgar, and, worst of all, lacking in culture and inherent good taste.

These things so often said of us by foreigners are to some degree true, but not all so reprehensible as some of us in our indignation may feel. We *are* a very young country in the eyes of older, wearier civilizations—hence our frequent naïveté. We Americans are in the process of developing a culture of our own, and some of it we have adopted from all the peoples who have come to make up our country. Our language, taken from the English majority among our settlers, is in many ways quite different from the English of England, because it has been influenced by the melting pot. Our music, our art, our literature are all trending toward a recognizable American culture. The fact that we are young and learning—and yearning—should not be held against us. But we, in turn, should not feel superior to the older, established cultures and rich traditions, understanding and appreciation of which can make our own lives immeasurably more interesting.

DIFFERENCES IN MANNERS

TUCKING-IN THE DINNER NAPKIN In this country the napkin is never tucked in at the collar or in the vest, but must be put in the lap and opened lengthwise so that it is folded double across the knees. As it is used throughout the meal to dab the mouth, the napkin does come out of its fold but it should not be shaken out that way at the start of the meal (as you sometimes see waiters do). At the end of the meal or if, for any reason, you must leave the table during the meal, place the used napkin casually, not refolded, to the left of your fork. Little children may have their napkins tucked-in to save their clothes, however.

SILVERWARE The placing of silverware on the table here is quite different from the placement in Europe (see "Table Setting"). The dinner knife is always on the right side of the plate, and the necessary forks are on the left, with the one to be used first at the far left. If an oyster fork is used, however, it often appears on the knife side. When your dinner plate is to be removed either for a second helping (when the host carves at the table) or to go to the kitchen, place the fork and knife you've been using side by side on the right side of your plate with the blade of the knife facing in and with the prongs of the fork up. The knife should be placed on the right of the used fork.

THE AMERICAN AND CONTINENTAL USE OF KNIFE AND FORK I see no real reason why a person who all his life has employed the Continental style in using his fork and knife should change to the American, unless he feels needlessly self-conscious about the difference when he's eating with Americans. Here, the knife is used for cutting and is never used to pile food on the back of a fork which then, European style, is conveyed to the mouth upside down and with the left hand. In America the fork is mostly used in the right hand, so that it corners the food by itself with little or no help from the knife, whose function ceases after it's cut the meat (and here potatoes may be cut, too). A bit of bread may be used to coax the food onto the fork or to blot up gravy (but then the gravy-soaked bread must be conveyed to the mouth by the fork). The knife may be used to steer food onto the *front* of the fork but, if you are eating American style, never convey the fork to the mouth upside down with food *packed* on the back, though you may use the fork this way with a manageable mouthful, say, of waffle, impaled on the prongs. The knife must be left, preferably blade in, on the right side of your plate when you are not actually using it.

THE USE OF THE TOOTHPICK In Europe if a bit of food catches in one's teeth at dinner it is quite proper to remove it adroitly with a toothpick, using a table napkin as a screen. In America, however, one suffers. If you can't dislodge the offending bit with your tongue (and even such maneuvers must be unnoticed by the assemblage), leave it there until you can remove it in privacy. If something desperate happens—such as a bit of oyster shell threatening to puncture your gum—excuse yourself quietly from the table and make no report on your excavations when you return. The well-mannered person never inquires, even by the lift of an eyebrow, as to why someone else has left the table.

"THANK YOU" Many who come here knowing some English have learned it from English governesses, tutors, or instructors. They may never become conscious of many little Americanisms, ignorance of which can cause some social confusion. In America when you are asked, either at table or elsewhere, if you want something and you say "Thank you," this means you *do* want what is offered. In England it means the opposite. Here it is expected that you will say "Yes," or "No, thank you." A shake of the head is all that is necessary if you are offered something you do not wish by a servant at table although you may say, "No, thank you" to him or her quite properly.

ACKNOWLEDGING A COMPLIMENT Americans often disconcert the foreign-born by exclaiming, "Thank you!" when given a graceful compliment. This is an Americanism, of course, and the Continental manner of acknowledging a compliment—a gentle, protesting smile—is quite acceptable here.

INTRODUCTIONS AND SALUTATIONS In English the wife of a man bearing a doctorate does not receive his title as she does in some other languages. She is merely Mrs. So and So, not Mrs. Dr. So and So. This applies to letters addressed to her, as well as to oral address. If in introducing her you wish to indicate that Mrs. So and So is the wife of a doctor, you say so. "May I present" (if you are introducing her to another woman older than herself or of her own age and social status) "Mrs. So and So. Her husband, as you may know, is Dr. John So and So." For further information on introductions, see "Dress and Manners."

WHO IS "DOCTOR"? Europeans, by the way, tend to use doctorates, socially, more freely than we do. In America we commonly address as "Doctor" only persons holding the following degrees: M.D. (Doctor of Medicine), D.D.S. (Doctor of Dental Surgery), D.D. (Doctor of Divinity), and, optionally, Ph.D. (Doctor of Philosophy), and Sc.D. (Doctor of Science). The latter doctorates, along with LL.D. (Doctor of Laws), are more likely to be courtesy rather than professional titles, to be used socially or not as the holder prefers. Veterinarians, chiropodists, and chiropractors (in some states) who actually hold professional degrees use the title "Dr." both socially and professionally.

USING THE PHONE The Continental is frequently puzzled about the accepted way of using the phone in English—just as the American is often struck dumb if he must cope with a foreign operator or try to make himself understood in another language by means of the phone alone. When the phone rings, pick it up and say "hello." It is not necessary to announce your own name to the person calling. If you are calling someone else you do, of course, announce yourself by saying *"This is* Mr. Paris" or, if you feel a need to identify yourself more clearly, "This is Jacques Paris speaking," *not "Here is,* etc.," European style. Give your whole name without "Mr., Mrs., or Miss" if the person you are calling answers himself and is your social equal. You do this even when you do not use each other's first names in conversation. If a servant answers you say, "Mr. So and So is calling," giving your first name, too, only if your last name is rather common—a woman would say, for instance, "Mrs. *John* Jones calling." With other than a common name she says, "Mrs. De Paris calling" or, if someone other than a servant or secretary or child answers, "Norma De Paris calling."

The older, British form of telephone greeting between men—"Black of the National Bank calling"—is not so frequently heard. To a man client such a man would announce himself as "George Black."

If you give a number to the operator orally a zero is pronounced "o." If you are spelling a word or name the "z" is pronounced "zee" in America, *not* "zed" as in England.

GREETINGS Don't translate your reply to the polite greeting, "How are you?" into "Fine, how's yourself?" Instead you should say, "How are you?"— answering the question with a question, as the whole greeting is a formality anyhow, or you may reply, "Fine, and how are you?" or "Very well, thank you—and you?"

THE USE OF "LADY" AND "GENTLEMAN" In conversation we do not refer to a woman of our own social status as a "lady" or to a man as a "gentleman." Don't say, "I went next door to see the lady who lives there." Say, "I went next door to visit Mrs. Brown." You might add that she is a "charming *woman*" or that someone else is a "nice *girl.*" Somehow the term "*young* lady" doesn't fall into the same servile classification as does that of "lady." In speaking of a male friend it is preferable to say that he is a "fine man" rather than that he is a "fine gentleman," as the latter phrase places you a step below him socially. Again, however, the use of the adjective "old" or "young" furbishes the word. You might refer to a "fine *old* gentleman" or a "gay *young* gentleman" and still indicate that they are of your own circle.

A child, however, in referring to a grown-up says, for instance, "Mommy, may I offer the candy to this gentleman?" or "Does the lady always carry her doggie with her?" When a child knows the names of his parents' friends he should refer to them as Mrs. or Mr. So and So, if old enough to master surnames. I know a little boy of four who, if he forgets your name, refers to you simply as Mr. or Mrs. "Somebody." Very young children in America are often permitted to call their parents' intimate friends by the names they hear their parents use—"Joe" or "Mary"—because we may never use "Mrs.," "Mr.," or "Miss" alone without the surname as one does so simply in foreign languages. As children grow older they tend to decide for themselves where such intimacy is unwelcome and where it is preferred. To insist that a child call older people who are familiars of a household "Aunt" or "Uncle," when there is no reason for such a title, seems foolish and often irks the child.

CHANGING YOUR NAME

What justification is there for changing your name? If you are handicapped with a name that is almost impossible for English-speaking people to pronounce or spell—some of the Russian, Polish, or Slavic names are good examples—or are the possessor of a name that may leave you open to possible ridicule because of its association (Schicklgruber) or its connotation in English, you may do well to change it. Beware however of picking a surname at random only because its first letter is the same as that of your own. A man with a strong accent and the pleasant Italian name of Guglieri, who wearies of the way Americans mangle it, makes a mistake if he hits on—to be a little far-fetched—Gallagher, a typical Irish name. The combination of an Italian accent and an Irish name might make him the butt of many jokes.

Wherever possible simplify your name (the Welsh name Ijams to Iams is a good example) if need be, rather than choose a totally new name. Opera star Risë Stevens's Vienna-born husband did it nicely when he simplified his name, Szurovy to Surovy, easily spellable for us. Such a change permits you to keep your own identity, too. Try to have your name match your background. It should not be too obvious that your name has been changed, if it's to fit you comfortably. If you go too far afield in your selection of a name people will have trouble associating you with it. If a man named Otto Schmeller, to choose a Germanic name at random, settles on Arthur Washington when everything about him is Germanic, including his accent and appearance, he will find his new name more of a handicap than he thought his original name to be.

WHO CAN HELP WITH YOUR NAME? First, don't change your name just to become Americanized or because the naturalization clerk suggests some banal name or names to you which you seize on without careful consideration. A name is important. If you change yours, get help in choosing one that fits. Don't be afraid to keep the name you were born with, even though it is a little difficult, if you like it. You may come from a distinguished family abroad and, in your heart, want to remain identified with it. America is peopled with men and women who bear other than Nordic names. I'd rather have a difficult name any day which, once mastered, is not easily forgotten, than one so common it has no distinction at all.

If, after talking the matter over with your friends and family, you decide to change your name, discuss it further with a librarian, a genealogist, or an English teacher, so you will find the name that suits you best. Try wherever possible to keep your original first name. If your friends call you Hans or Rudolph or Jean, it will be confusing if your new legal name is anglicized to John, Ralph (let us say), or James, and when you bring old friends together with new ones, or with business acquaintances, there will always be the impression of duality. When you change your name, if you do, it should be used socially as well as in business.

HOW DO YOU ANNOUNCE A CHANGE OF NAME? When people change their names by legal means there need be no more confusion about it than there is when a woman changes her name to that of her husband. A formal announcement may be sent to friends and business associates to simplify matters, or you may let everyone know informally by letter, as the occasion arises, or casually in conversation. A formal announcement reads like this:

Mr. Casimir Wojciechowski
announces that by permission of the court
he has changed his name to
Cass Wiecks

A graceful announcement of the change may be made in a way that includes the juniors of the family, too. It is not, by the way, necessary to secure a court order to change your name, so long as you can, if challenged, prove you had no intent to defraud. A family adopting a new name may do so this way:

Mr. and Mrs. Ulrich Uhrmachermeister
Miss Gerda Uhrmachermeister
and Master Karl Uhrmachermeister
wish to inform you that they have adopted the surname of
Urman

If first names have been changed you should list all the changes so the announcement reads:

Mr. and Mrs. Ulrich Uhrmachermeister
Miss Gerda Uhrmachermeister
and Master Karl Uhrmachermeister
wish to inform you that they have adopted the names of
Mr. and Mrs. Richard Urman
Miss Gertrude Urman
and Master Charles Urman

The phrase "wish to inform you that by order of the court they (or he) *will be known as*" is also used.

Simple white cards are engraved with or without plate marking in black script or in any of the restrained English-style types. Where a very small list makes engraving of the cards extravagant, you may choose to have them printed, but the formal style should be the same. It's a serious matter to change one's name, and the procedure should be treated with due dignity.

If no such formal announcement is made, seasonal greeting cards, if usually sent, could be signed "the Urmans (formerly the Uhrmachermeisters)," but here again dignity should be the objective.

THE NEW CITIZEN AND THE ENGLISH LANGUAGE

The new citizen has at least a beginning understanding of his new language. It is more than courtesy to his adopted country that impels him to continue to study it carefully, even after his papers have been granted to him. If he is satisfied with a small vocabulary and a few idioms, or if, after many years in the country, he continues to translate his own language literally into English, he will continue to be considered a "foreigner" despite his American citizenship. He will have difficulty expressing his ideas fully in his business or profession. His children may feel some embarrassment at his unfamiliarity with English.

Many foreign born who become American citizens may find it impossible to lose an accent—a matter of little importance, I think, for foreign accents in English can be very attractive. It is the very rare American remember who learns to speak another language without accent. While there are methods of "de-accenting" the foreign born, it is not the accent itself that is of concern but the ability to make oneself understood and even to achieve real fluency in the language by thinking in it.

If you, as a new American, speak as much English as possible even with business associates of your own original nationality, you will find that you do begin to think in English and can express yourself readily. If, however, your social life is spent largely with those of your own original nationality, something quite natural because of a community of interests, you may for years make the same errors as they do in speaking English. You may also lose the ability to hear the important differences when you speak with native-born Americans—presupposing, of course, that they speak correctly themselves.

FOREIGN WORDS IN ENGLISH   It isn't easy to know what foreign words have become anglicized and which have not except by listening to the pronunciation of cultured people. Even here it is possible to become confused, for in England the French word "*garage*" has gone native and becomes the ugly "ga-rahge," with accent on first syllable. "Hors d'oeuvres" is pronounced in the French way. "Valet" is preferably pronounced as it is spelled, although in the Middle West if you phone for valet service in a hotel the operator will probably correct you—"Vallā service?" she will query. But you may rightfully stick to your pronunciation, backed by even the Oxford Dictionary, which, by the way, can sometimes lead you sadly astray on American pronunciation. "Chauffeur" becomes "shofer," losing its French twist somewhat, while "aide-de-camp" is pronounced as if the words were English. "Buffet" is pronounced as the French meant it to be and is never anglicized.

WRITING LETTERS   When you write a letter and use the form of address "My dear So and So," you are, strange to relate, using the more formal not the less formal term. In writing to intimates say, "Dear So and So," not "My dear."

In speaking, too, if you say "My dear John," or "My dear fellow, would you pass me the salt," you are being patronizing rather than affectionate.

If you are writing to someone very intimate you close your letters with something less formal than "Cordially." You say "Yours," "With love," "Love," "Affectionately," "As ever," "Always," or some other phrase to indicate your closeness.

3 HOME ENTERTAINING

Informal Entertaining 261

Formal Entertaining 271

The Guest at Formal Meals 283

The Ritual of Drinking 286

Entertaining Indoors 293

Entertaining Out of Doors 298

Hosts and Guests 300

HOME ENTERTAINING

An Albanian proverb goes, "Every guest hates the others, and the host hates them all." Too much entertaining is exactly like that, with no fun intended.

It is a good thing for a family to set aside its home for itself and its friends. When guests are invited to break bread for other than purely friendly reasons the entertainment is too often a failure, unless it so happens that such business acquaintances turn out to be congenial. A good rule to follow is: don't try to do business over your own dinner table.

So entertaining at home should have no strings attached. Occasionally we all accept invitations we prefer not to accept and thus incur a social obligation we must repay in kind. The successful hostess never includes too many new or difficult guests at what should be an intimate little dinner. Eight people who never saw or heard of each other before—and hope never to see or hear of each other again—can do social violence to the most adequately planned evening.

If host and hostess themselves can, through the careful selection of their guests and through sufficient advance preparation, look forward with pleasure to an evening or a week end, then the party is virtually assured of success. Whether trained servants present platters of peacocks' tongues or the hostess herself dishes up a good spaghetti dinner is quite immaterial. If the house looks as if it expected and welcomed guests, if the host and hostess are relaxed and smiling, the guests will feel at home and at ease, no matter what superficial accouterments of entertaining may be missing through necessity or design.

Entertain and enjoy it!

CHAPTER THIRTY

INFORMAL ENTERTAINING

THE COMPANY OR SEMI-FORMAL DINNER PARTY

The truly formal dinner in all its stiff elegance is not what the average American thinks of as formal dinner. What we encounter most in the way of special entertaining is the semiformal or company dinner for which the household puts its best face forward. This is the seated dinner of four to eight guests (who may or may not be in evening dress) or even more, depending on the dining room's ability to contain them all comfortably. Entertaining at home of more than eight at dinner usually must be buffet style or at bridge tables, informally.

INVITATIONS   Invitations to the company informal dinner are usually phoned or are given by word of mouth, and, of course, may be extended by informals or calling cards (see Correspondence Section). The hostess always tenders the invitation. On occasion, for convenience's sake, her husband may do so *in her name*, where close friends are concerned. For example, if he is a commuter and the friends are in the city he may phone them for his wife. He says, "Mary would like you to come to dinner on Friday at seven-thirty. Black tie." A hostess who asks her men guests these days to wear black tie in the suburbs or in the country, however, is very optimistic. She is safer to suggest that her women guests wear dinner dress and let the men come in their preferred dark suits, especially on a week night.

Invitations to company dinners are not lightly treated. The hostess obviously is going to considerable trouble, especially if she has little or no help. Guests should not disappoint her at the last minute without a believable excuse such as illness. Neither should they ask to bring another guest, with the possible exception of another single man for whom most hostesses have need.

ARRIVING GUESTS   No guest should be allowed to arrive without greeting. Both host and hostess should be on duty in the living room five minutes or more before the appointed time. When an invitation is issued for seven o'clock, guests may arrive at that hour, promptly, or up to ten or fifteen minutes later. At a large dinner party lateness of as much as half an hour is virtually expected in metropolitan communities, but frequently in the West and Midwest when a dinner invitation is for seven, guests begin to arrive at six-thirty as it is assumed that they are to be seated at dinner at seven or shortly after.

Once dinner is announced the hostess should not be expected to wait more than a few more minutes for late comers, unless one includes the guest of honor, who ideally should never be late but without whom it is certainly peculiar to sit down. If the lateness is really very serious, guest of honor or no, the hostess proceeds with the dinner. A late-comer enters the dining room as quietly as possible, goes briefly to the hostess (who remains seated so as not to disturb the table), makes an apology, and sits immediately in the indicated place. If the late one is a woman, the man to her right rises, or semi-rises, to seat her. Any long explanation of the reason for the lateness is uncalled for and should never draw in the others at the table. The hostess, no matter how she really feels about it, always minimizes the inconvenience to her as well as to the other guests. She says something such as, "It's really quite all right. I knew you would expect us to go right ahead."

ENTERING THE DINING ROOM   Where dinner partners have not been assigned by card (see "Formal Dinner" for example of place card) the hostess, when the meal has been announced, usually leads her women guests into the dining room with the men following, the host bringing up the rear. The men step forward and hold the chairs as the hostess indicates where each lady is to sit—with the woman guest of honor placed to the host's right and the male guest of honor placed to the hostess's right. At a cue from the hostess the men then seat themselves. For parties of more than eight, place cards simplify this little procedure. Even at a smaller party cards should be used if the hostess is likely to become flustered or forgetful of names—she must never resort to a little memorandum at her own place, as did one nervous hostess I knew. For seating at the semiformal dinner, see "Seating at the Formal Dinner."

THE MENU FOR THE COMPANY OR SEMIFORMAL DINNER PARTY   The season, naturally, must be considered in planning dinner for guests. Availability of produce and meats, too, is a factor, as is the seasonableness of the weather. Foods with rich sauces are less appetizing in hot weather. In winter a main dish *en gelée* would seem unsubstantial.

One of my favorite cookbooks, "Thoughts for Food" (Institute Publishing Company, Chicago), gives complete menus for each meal with accompanying recipes. The recipes for Informal Dinners as compared with those for Family Dinners show the degree of difference in the choice of food. A Family Dinner might have paprika schnitzel with noodles as a main course. One of the book's suggested Informal Dinner menus for guests is as follows:

Avocado Cocktail
Chicken Valenciennes   Asparagus Polonaise
Grape Compote
Chocolate Profiterolles

A formal dinner always has a soup course, always fish or seafood (which may come first, as in oysters à la Rockefeller), always hot meat with vegetables as the main dish, a salad, dessert, little cakes (petits fours), and demitasses served in the living room. Each course is served separately. The informal dinner is not so complicated and consists of an entrée of some kind, which may be hot or cold soup and which may be served in a handled cup, pottery bowl, or cream soup bowl, whereas at a formal dinner, soup is always in a flat soup dish. The main course may be fish instead of meat, since usually not both are served. Second helpings are often offered. At formal meals they never are. Salad may well be served at the same time as the main dish rather than as a separate course. There is dessert, and "after-dinner" coffee is often served at the table with dessert or just following it and is usually poured by the hostess (who adds sugar and cream for those who wish it) and passed around, though it may be poured in the kitchen if there is a waitress and passed on a tray with cream and sugar.

THE TABLE   A damask cloth may be used for an informal dinner, but place mats are becoming more usual. Candles are on the table and may be colored, rather than the white of the formal table. There is a centerpiece (which, if the table is against the wall, is centered against it rather than in the middle of the table), and it may consist of flowers, greenery, or a ceramic of some kind. A small table may have to dispense with a centerpiece entirely and use its main serving dishes—a lovely tureen, a handsome casserole—as focal points of interest.

The old idea of white cloth and white napkins, matching fine china, clear matching crystal kept solely for "company," made for monotony. Hostesses who made a fetish of such things often had set company dinners, too, devoid of imagination and deadly dull. Actually there is considerable precedence for gay dining cloths. Those of the early Saxons were bright crimson, gold-fringed.

At today's informal or semiformal dinner the guests may sit down at a bare, gleaming table, on occasion. Napkins may be almost any color, almost any material. Thick pottery mugs may be used for the summer iced tea, or frosty beer may come on in beer glasses, tankards, or steins. The dishes, the glassware, and the table covering if any, are more likely to be geared to the choice of food than to the fact that this is a company dinner.

Imagine the visual effect of cold boiled scarlet lobsters in a big wooden mixing bowl in the center of a round table covered with fringed woods-green cloth. Think of the mayonnaise in yellow and turquoise majolica, the chablis in chunky clear glass, the napkins big, lobster-printed paperlike cotton bibs. The salad, of course, is served in individual wooden bowls, and the dessert is chilled mixed fruit—whole red cherries, rosy pears, purple plums, crackling apples on a bed of crushed ice. Such a dinner is a far cry from grandmother's hushed Victorian party meals. And a lot more fun for everyone.

DINNER WITH ONE MAID

Pretension is so very uncomfortable. If a family has just one servant it is foolish to try to turn her into cook-waitress-nurse and lady's maid. Rarely these days do servants stay on one job the years it requires to function flawlessly at it. Pretrained servants coming on to a job are equally hard to find. The best thing in a one-servant household is for the mistress to face the fact that she cannot expect too much.

Entertaining causes extra work. Unless she is willing and able herself to take on some of the extras—such as making the butterballs and canapés, preparing the dessert, getting out the extra glassware, dishes, and silver and cleaning it, if necessary (special pieces can be sealed away in pliofilm, by the way, to appear bright as new for parties), a hostess is expecting too much of one maid, except, of course, when the family is small and adult. But there is still the usual routine of the household before party preparations can begin. Perhaps extra help is needed from outside, either during the day or to wait on the table and help with the cleaning up.

A company dinner that is to be both prepared and served by one maid should be kept fairly simple—three courses. Having a freezer makes it easy to have some dishes prepared in advance. Canapés can be frozen, then thawed or put in the oven (for those requiring broiling) just before the guests arrive and so can the dinner rolls. Frozen vegetables cut down on preparation time. The dessert—even pie or cake—can come from the freezer.

If you have no freezer, use the freezing compartment of your refrigerator wisely. It can store a dessert for a dinner party a day or more in advance, and it also can yield the vegetables. Rolls can be of the brown-and-serve variety or little glazed dinner rolls from the bakery. Don't ask Anna to bake fresh rolls, along with everything else she has to do.

A simply prepared solid piece of meat for carving at the table or to be passed from a platter cuts down work. A roast, steak, broilers, or chops are more convenient for a dinner than fried chicken, veal scallopini, fried fish, or seafood. Avoid foods that require last-minute preparation and prompt consumption—fried things and soufflés for example. Roast beef is everybody's favorite, and everyone, too, likes steak, plain or dressed up. But steak is difficult if dinner has been preceded by more than three cocktails. It just can't be held indefinitely. If there is any doubt about the exact time of sitting down to dinner, roast lamb, roast pork, roast veal, baked ham, roast chicken are far wiser choices than steak or roast beef.

THE FIRST COURSE If a first course is to be served at the table (it could have been served in the living room and at such a dinner it may be omitted) a place plate is in place with the folded dinner napkin on it or the first course is actually on the place plate. In summer the first course may be crème vichyssoise, in winter a fish ramekin or hot soup in a bowl, a cup, or in a flat plate, with the folded napkin to the left of the forks. For utmost simplicity, if there is no first course, the heated dinner plates are at each place.

A first course may be served by the maid once guests have been seated and have opened their napkins. All serving procedures described are intended to simplify work, save steps, and speed service. The maid comes in from the serving pantry or kitchen with the soup or other entrée in her left hand, and at a dinner of no more than eight, beginning with the lady at the host's right (never with the hostess), she serves clockwise, ending with the host. Everything is served to the *left*. Or, if there is no first course and place plates are on the table, she exchanges the place plates for heated dinner plates, taking off the place plates with her right hand to the guest's left *or* right and putting down the hot plate with her left on the guest's left side. Then she brings in the main dish and sets it before the host if it is to be carved. She passes it (first showing it to the hostess for inspection) to the woman guest of honor, at the host's right, if it is a made dish such as a casserole or if it is meat or fish that has been portioned in the kitchen. This is balanced on her left hand on a clean, folded napkin, steadied, if necessary, with her right. Then she brings in the vegetables, one dish in each hand on the serving napkin. (A two- or three-compartment dish is excellent here, too.) She offers first the dish in her left hand, then that in her right. In each dish is a serving spoon and fork face down with handles toward the person to be served. (Forks may be omitted if the vegetable is something like peas. However, with a vegetable like asparagus or a vegetable that actually needs to be lifted, both implements are provided. Asparagus, by the way, is often on a folded linen napkin in the dish if a sauce is to be served separately, otherwise it must be well strained before being placed on the platter. Sometimes toast, too, is used as a moisture-catcher for asparagus.)

The dish or platter should be held at a level comfortable to the guest, never too high and never so far to the side as to cause him to twist around in his chair. Sauces or gravies should be served immediately after the dish they accompany. Hot dishes should be very hot, cold ones chilled. No lukewarm gravies, tepid chops, or cold biscuits.

IF THE HOST CARVES If the meat is to be carved at the table, or the fish apportioned by the host, the maid stands at the host's left. Either she has removed his place plate and put before him a stack of hot dinner plates or he has before him one hot plate which he fills and which the maid then takes with her left hand and places before the guest of honor, first removing his hot plate with her right hand, to the left or right. She then returns to the host, puts the new hot plate in front of him, serves it and gives him another. The host ladles on to each portion the accompanying sauce or gravy or this may be passed separately by the maid before the vegetables. Or she may place it on the table to be passed by the guests.

If the host has before him a stack of hot plates the maid may stand at his left and take one filled one at a time, or two, if the table has been set with no place plates. Or she may let the host pass the plates right and left, as convenient, and she may bring the vegetables from the kitchen and serve them. With one maid, this is the best way to serve when the meat is carved at table. It assures that the food will be served hot.

IF THE HOSTESS SERVES   A made dish or one to be portioned at the table, such as baked fish, may also be placed before the hostess. Or the host may serve meat or fish, and the hostess serve the vegetables. The maid first receives the plate from the host, takes it to the hostess' left for vegetables, sauces, or gravy, then serves it to the guest of honor and so on around the table. If the dining room is so tiny as to make any service awkward or if the maid is inept at service, the best thing is to let her bring in the dishes for the host and hostess to serve, remove them at the right time, crumb the table, perhaps pour the water, and serve the dessert and after-dinner coffee, letting it go at that. Better no service than the bumbling kind.

SERVE LEFT, REMOVE RIGHT?   At my school in Europe each girl had to wait on table certain days in the week. Everything was served to the left and, formal style, *removed* from the left. This was to teach us how to train our servants when we had our own households. The removal of plates from the left is strictly correct, but in America to speed service with limited help it is quite permissible to serve *left*, remove from the *right*. If this is done, however, the waitress never reaches in front of a guest to remove from the *right* anything such as a butter plate on the guest's extreme *left*. These things are removed from the left, always.

SERVING AND REMOVING TWO PLATES AT A TIME   Where a service plate need not be considered, particularly after the table has been cleared for dessert— of all soiled plates, of salts, of condiments, of bread, of crumbs, and of relishes, of wine glasses unless one wine is serving through to dessert—two plates at a time may be served. This is done by placing one dish with the right hand to the left of a guest and the other dish with the left hand to the left of the next guest.

In removing dishes the same procedure takes place, with the soiled dishes being removed right, or left, with the maid using both hands. But if dishes are being removed from the left, all should be removed consistently from the left, so as not to confuse the guests. They should not be removed sometimes left, sometimes right.

At the end of dessert, the coffee may be served at the table, with the hostess pouring, adding cream or sugar as indicated, and passing the demitasses to guests, or after-dinner coffee may be served in the living room. In either case the hostess gives the signal to rise, first catching the eye of the lady guest of honor. She then leads the way to the living room.

INFORMAL LUNCH

The term "luncheon" is not properly used in conversation, as it is supposedly reserved for formal and ceremonious use. A servant announces, "Luncheon is served," but the hostess might turn to her guests and say, "Shall we go in to lunch, now?" Hotels and restaurants use the term, but unaffected people use the verb "to lunch" instead. "Yesterday I *lunched* with Muriel," not "Yesterday I had luncheon with Muriel." In writing, especially in etiquette books, lunch and luncheon are more or less interchangeable, however.

Lunch in a household with one maid is simple—at most three courses, sometimes, in consideration of dieters, only one.

The first course, which may be soup or an entrée, is in place on a place plate as the guests enter, hostess first to indicate the seating. Soup is served at lunch in a cup bowl or covered casserole. However, if it is to be the main course—a thick soup such as bouillabaisse or French potato soup—it is often served in flat soup plates from a tureen, with thick slices of French bread, fresh or toasted, in the semicut long loaf with garlic butter. Butter plates are on the table, and the maid either passes a variety of breads, often small hot ones, or places the bread basket or dish on the table for passing among the guests. A long French loaf may come to the table on a cutting board with a bread knife.

When summoned, the maid removes the soup and place plate together from left or right and immediately replaces them with the plate for the following course, which may be a salad plate arranged in the kitchen or a luncheon plate with an individual casserole on it or a warm plate for a dish that is to be passed or served by the hostess.

She then brings in the main dish, if there is one to be served, and either holds it on the flat of her left hand on a folded napkin, serving to the left of each guest, or places it in front of the hostess, then stands to the hostess' left to receive the filled plates. In small dining rooms or where the maid is less than perfection it is much simpler for the hostess not only to "dish" the main course but to hand around the plates herself, serving the lady on her right first. Better complete informality than ceremony that doesn't quite come off.

During the main course the maid pours water, when needed, and perhaps wine. In the summer, iced, sweetened, and lemon-flavored tea or water and wine are placed on the table, so the guests may help themselves at the hostess' suggestion. If iced coffee is served, hot coffee is poured over ice cubes into the glasses at the table and sugar and cream are passed either by the maid or by the hostess, so guests may add either or both to taste. At the end of the main course the plates are removed, left or right, and off come the butter plates, bread tray, condiments, and any serving dishes. The water glasses remain and so do wine glasses if wine is to be served through dessert. If sherry was served with the soup the sherry glasses are usually removed with the soup. Before the dessert comes in the table is crumbed.

Dessert may be portioned in the kitchen and served, left, to each guest, with dessert spoon and fork left and right on the plate, or the dessert implements may be at the top of the plate throughout the meal, European style. Or the dessert, say, charlotte russe, may be served by the hostess who has to her left the plates on which to serve it. Either the maid stays to place one plate at a time before the hostess from a stack at the left or the hostess does this herself, placing the dessert silver from the neatly arranged spoons and forks on her right before passing each dish. Hot tea, never served after iced tea, of course, or after iced coffee, is served by the hostess at the table. If it is convenient and she has the equipment she may make it right at the table over a small electric burner or, traditionally, over a spirit lamp. But, more usually, the teapot is brought in from the kitchen on a bare tray with the necessary cups and saucers, the sugar, milk, hot water, basin, and lemon slices. (See "How to Make Tea.") The little ceremony of making tea is always reserved to the hostess, who, in turn, unless there are many at table, hands each cup directly to each guest. She may add "cream" or lemon and/or sugar as indicated by the guest, or these may be passed separately by the maid. Tea is never, never served in the kitchen and passed on a tray. It should be made with loose tea leaves, never with what Louise Andrews Kent (Mrs. Appleyard) refers to as "the mouse in the teacup," a tea bag. These little horrors are, I suppose, a necessity of cafeterias, but they do a great disservice to tea.

There is no further disturbance of the guests by the maid while tea is being drunk. Tea is one of the most pleasant digestives. Its good offices must not be hurried by a busy little maid clearing away the dessert dishes.

INFORMAL TEA

Afternoon tea as a gentle means of relaxation should be encouraged in this country. Surely it is a pleasant, and incidentally inexpensive, way to repay small social obligations, even though husbands, unless they happen to work at home, can rarely be included.

Invitations to simple teas at home are usually given personally by the hostess or by phone. For elaborate teas a calling card or an informal may be sent but this would be done only for some special occasion. For debutante teas the invitations are engraved. (See Correspondence Section.)

The actual tray on which the tea is served has no cloth, although the table on which it is placed usually does. (See "Service of Tea, Coffee, and Candy" and "How to Make Tea.") All silver should be gleaming. Tea plates are in a stack, a folded napkin between each one. On the tea tray are the following: pitcher of hot water (for those who like diluted tea), teapot in any heat-holding material, silver or silver plate being the most decorative, a bowl for waste leaves, sugar, milk (not cream), lemon slices with pick or small fork, tea knives and forks if necessary, cups and saucers, conveniently stacked if necessary, buttered thin bread, jam, cookies, small cakes, tarts, or pastries, sugar tongs for lump sugar.

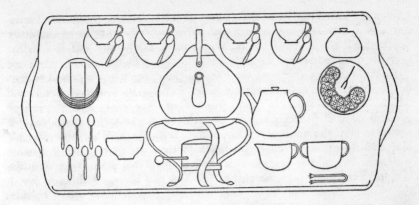

SETTING UP THE TEA TRAY   The tea tray is always set up without a cloth and with all the things on it arranged in pleasing symmetry. *Shown lower left to right:* Teaspoons (optional, otherwise on saucers as shown), basin for leaves, teapot on alcohol lamp, sugar, cream (really milk), sugar tongs, hot water. *Upper, left to right:* Tea plates stacked with tea napkins, tea cups with spoons shown on saucers to right of handles, jam pot, lemon slices stuck with cloves.

One dresses for tea according to neighborhood custom. In the country and even in the city a tweed suit and sweater might be appropriate. In some houses and with some people a simple daytime dress might seem more apropos. In the summer a fresh cotton or linen such as is worn in hot weather is correct, of course, for tea. Hats may or may not be worn by guests.

COCKTAIL PARTIES

Cocktail time is usually past the tea hour—from five to seven. But on Sundays and holidays, especially in the country, cocktails are often served before the lunch or noon dinner hour, not necessarily followed by a meal at the home of the host and hostess.

Any hostess who gives a large cocktail party where many guests are jammed in a relatively small area may expect a certain amount of damage. The space should be cleared as much as possible of footstools, *objets d'art*, delicate plants, small children, and pets. Large, inexpensive ash trays should be provided in every spot where a careless one might feel prompted to abandon a cigarette.

A table or bar should be set up, close to the festive scene, where drinks may be mixed and picked up. This may be a pantry, a porch, the dining room —or any place but the kitchen if a meal is also in progress of preparation. It is inevitable that most of the male and some of the female guests will stay in more or less fixed positions in the vicinity of the refreshments.

On or near the bar should be a continuous supply of clean glasses and a tray, too, for the used ones. People are supposed to keep track of their own glasses at cocktail parties in anticipation of refills, but they never do. Therefore a wise hostess equips herself with three times the number of glasses as guests. Such glasses need not be expensive at all. In fact, she had better save her good glasses for the intimate little dinner party.

No cocktail party ever ends on schedule. The people you expected to stay on for dinner frequently disappear early, probably because they can't wait out the bores who refuse to depart without one more drink. The experienced giver of cocktail parties plans to have dinner out to give himself a good excuse to clear the decks at a fairly definite time. He is, of course, under no obligation to extend a dinner invitation to those remaining, but it usually works out that all the stragglers go along if the dinner place is a restaurant and there the men share the check. The host and hostess wishing to avoid the cocktail guests who linger until midnight providentially make outside dinner engagements at friends' homes where they cannot take last-minute guests. Or they bring out a cold supper when the party has dwindled to the diehards.

INFORMAL DANCING AT HOME

Large dances at home are becoming rare except for weddings, when an orchestra may be brought in and a dancing pavilion erected. In many homes there are occasions when the rugs may be rolled back and the room cleared for dancing to the radio or phonograph or to the music of an accordion.

Graduation parties often are built around a home dance. Porch or living room floor is sprinkled with wax or even corn meal, a refreshment table is set up, music of some sort provided, and the evening is under way. Punch is the most suitable beverage at a dance as it is a pre-mixed drink and refreshing between dances. Nothing is served with it, but a dance is usually followed by a late supper, simple or elaborate as the occasion demands.

No matter what the age group, certain rules are always followed at dances. A man or boy always asks his hostess for a dance during the evening. And he literally dances attention on the girl he has brought to the party, dancing his first dance with her and seeing that she is never without a partner or never left alone on the sidelines. A girl, too, has the obligation of paying proper attention to the man who has brought her, not allowing herself to be whisked away the minute she enters the door, never to see her escort again during the evening until it is time to be taken home.

A host tries to dance with each woman guest at his party sometime during the evening. In a small group if some of the men do not dance he dances first with a guest, then with his wife if she has not been asked to dance. If all wish to dance, host and hostess often start off the dancing.

No guest, of course, leaves a dance without a brief farewell to host and hostess. A man who has come alone always asks his hostess if he may be of help in escorting an unaccompanied lady home. A hostess never allows such a guest to go home alone.

CHAPTER THIRTY-ONE

FORMAL ENTERTAINING

THE FORMAL DINNER

Very few homes in the land these days can accommodate the traditional thirty-four guests at one dinner table—or even half that many—in comfort. Who indeed has the space to store all the silver, glassware, and china for such dinner parties, and where are the trained men to serve them, one man to each three guests? Queen Victoria's dinners required three servants to each six guests. Present-day monarchs have one footman to each four or five guests. At large embassies there is, in addition, often a *sommelier* to serve the wines.

Formal dinners are so much trouble and so much expense that even in their heyday they were given by great establishments only three or four times a year. Important hostesses today feel that formal dinners at home are best replaced by smaller, more frequent semiformal and quite informal dinners or, if occasion really seems to demand formal dinners, that they be given in a private suite of a hotel or fashionable restaurant. However, as the occasional formal dinner does take place, let us see how the hostess must marshal her forces for such an undertaking.

First, of course, she must have the room to seat all her guests at one dining table. The minute she deviates from this arrangement, or makes do with female help at table, her dinner can no longer be considered formal.

Then, paramount, of course, is a chef or real *cuisinière* who can turn out *to perfection* the food that, of itself, proclaims a formal meal. Finally, she must have a butler who will function as major-domo, commanding his men—trained footmen perhaps hired for the occasion but preferably true house servants rather than restaurant waiters recruited for the event. These are usually best supplied by a catering service, along with any additional kitchen help that may be needed. Of course all must be properly attired (see "Dress and Duties of the Household Staff"). The hostess who can give such a dinner with only her own staff is fortunate indeed, as she will then have a smoothly functioning organization on whose service she can count.

Just before the arrival of her guests, usually a few minutes before eight, though sometimes formal dinners start at eight-thirty, the hostess checks the

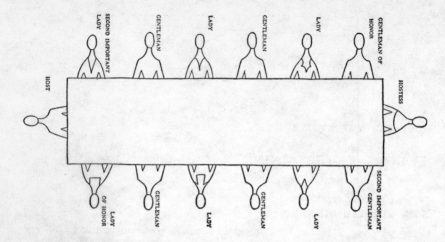

SEATING AT FORMAL LUNCH AND DINNER and the Informal Dinner Party

dining room and gives any last minute instructions to the butler. He, in turn, makes his tour of the footmen and inspects their apparel, their shoes, hair, and fingernails. In earlier times such serving men wore white cotton gloves, because of the danger, as one writer put it, of a dirty thumb in the soup. The butler sees to it that there are no dirty thumbs or anything else that can't pass muster.

ARRIVAL AND INTRODUCTION OF GUESTS AT THE FORMAL DINNER   As he removes his coat and hat each gentleman takes the small envelope bearing his name and containing the name of his dinner partner, from a conveniently placed hall tray. If the lady is unknown to him he arranges to be formally introduced before dinner is served. At very large dinner parties there is often a table diagram in the hall, and he should locate his and his partner's seat on this before going in to dinner.

At such a formal dinner the "roof" is not sufficient introduction, and guests must be formally introduced to one another. Obviously at very large functions guests necessarily meet only a limited number of other guests.

ENTERING THE DINING ROOM   At formal dinners the host offers his arm to the woman guest of honor and leads the way into the dining room followed by the other guests, teamed, with the hostess and the male guest of honor entering last. Host and hostess stand behind their chairs, and the hostess indicates (if no diagram has been provided) where each guest is to sit. The hostess then is seated by the male guest of honor, and everyone else follows suit.

SEATING   The seating at formal dinners is the same as that at informal ones at which guests are present. Host and hostess are seated more or less opposite each other, with the hostess preferably near the entrance through which the

Mr. Goodkind

FORMAL PLACE CARD.   Monogram, in this case, in gold with matching border. Name of guest is handwritten without given name.

food will appear. To the right of the host is placed the honored woman guest. If a young engaged girl is to be feted, for example, she is given this place despite the fact that older women are present. If among the guests there is one woman who has come some distance and is rarely a visitor to the household, it is she who would be given this place of honor. Ordinarily, among people who see each other frequently, the hostess places to the host's right any woman who has obvious seniority over the rest or, if none has, any woman guest who will bring out her husband conversationally if he needs special incentive. To her own right the hostess places the husband of the guest of honor, if there is one, the man who has come the greatest distance and is an infrequent visitor to the household or a man who may be a little shy or difficult conversationally.

To the host's left is placed the next most important woman guest and to the hostess' left, the next most important man guest.

At a long banquet table host and hostess need not sit at opposite ends but may sit across from each other at the center. The same seating of guests of honor maintains, however.

PLACE CARDS AT THE FORMAL DINNER   At each place will be a guest's name. The cards are usually plain white with beveled edges gilded, although in a household using a heraldic device the host's full coat of arms may be embossed in gold or the crest alone without the motto may be used. A widow or an unmarried woman may properly use only a lozenge for menu and place cards. (See "Heraldic Devices.")

Place card names are written "Mrs. Roberts," "Miss Sweeney," "Mr. Prudhomme" at formal dinners. At diplomatic dinners titles are abbreviated, "H. E. [for His Excellency] the Norwegian Ambassador," "The Secretary of Defense." Dinner partners refer to these gentlemen as "Mr. Ambassador" and "Mr. Secretary" in direct conversation, by the way.

MENUS AND MENU CARDS   Menus, printed, occasionally engraved, in script, or written in scriptlike handwriting in black ink, are always in French, as we

Dinner

Beluga Caviar
Saumon Fumé de Nova Scotia
Pâté de Foie Gras Naturel

Consommé Printanier
Celeri   Radis   Olives

Terrapin à la Union Club

Filet de Boeuf lardé rôti
Pommes Parisienne   Asperges Hollandaise

Salade du Jardin   Petit Roquefort

Gateau St. Honoré   Petits Fours

Moka
Chocolats   Fruits   Noix

Harvey's Bristol Dry	Kentucky Bourbon
Liebfraumilch Auslese 1945	Old Pugh 1882
Chateau Marquis de Terme 1923	Old Jordan 1891

Cognac

Dom Perignon 1928   Spring Hill 1894

April 26, 1949

see them at large, formal, public functions in the best hotels. Sometimes a menu, with or without a heraldic device, is in its holder at each place, but one is always in front of the host and hostess and others are placed down the table with one for each three guests.

THE SERVICE BEGINS

The butler takes his stand behind the hostess. He moves from this vantage point only when a footman needs direction or when he, himself, pours the wine. He actually serves food only if there is not sufficient additional staff to do the serving, and then serves the main dishes only.

In a smaller household a butler and a footman can efficiently serve a formal dinner for from eight to twelve guests. If he is quite adept, with adequate kitchen support a butler alone can handle a formal dinner for eight. At dinners larger than twelve it is necessary to have duplicate serving dishes presented simultaneously to each six or seven guests. In this way all food will be served so that the guests may eat more or less at the same time and hot food will be properly hot. The service begins with the lady at the host's right, and at a large dinner dishes are presented simultaneously to the ladies nearest, right and left, of the hostess. Butler, if he serves, and footmen present dishes with the left hand, right hands behind back.

At a very large dinner it is, naturally, not possible to wait until each guest has finished eating before the clearing of plates begins. In lavish service where a man was behind each chair, for instance at royal banquets, each plate was removed the minute the diner indicated by placement of the silver that he had finished with it. Today, the butler directs the removal of plates, or begins the removal himself, when the majority has finished, bypassing the slower diners, but there must be no sense of hurry and certainly no clatter or audible staff directions.

At only one period is there ever a moment when there is not a plate before a guest. That is just before the service of dessert. Until then, beginning with the place plate with its folded napkin upon it, there is always a plate. Sometimes there is still another on top of it, as in the case of, say, a crabmeat cocktail which would be in a stemmed double container, the "suprême" glass (sometimes silver) surrounding the "liner," on a small service plate. This complete unit is placed on the place plate. It is replaced, on the place plate, with the soup course—always in a flat dish. At the end of the soup course place plate and soup dish are removed, and, at a formal meal, removal is *only* from the left, except for those parts of the setting that are on the guest's right. As the place and soup plate are removed together, the warm plate for the fish course is immediately substituted. After the fish course has been removed the "*rôti*" appears, always hot, though not necessarily "roasted" at all. It is always completely arranged on a beautifully garnished platter or platters, often with its accompanying vegetables, such as tiny pan-roasted potatoes. Or green vegetables follow on a separate serving dish, sometimes on the partitioned kind where vegetables such as new peas, julienne carrots, and buttered pearl onions may each occupy a section. The whole course is passed to each guest who takes what pleases him but (at a formal dinner) nothing is offered a second time, aside from water and wine replenishments.

In Victorian days a sherbet, or "sorbet," followed the roast or came between entrée and roast as a separate course. In the West and Midwest I found this custom still in vogue, though the sherbet appears with the meat course and I seem to recall being served a piquant pineapple sherbet with fish in Chicago.

In Victorian days, too, a ten-course formal dinner was quite customary with game following the roast. Today, the roast, which may well *be* game, is the climax of the formal dinner and is followed by salad, dessert, and fruit. The salad course is often quite elaborate, perhaps *pâté de foie gras en bellevue* served without dressed lettuce because its delicate flavor must be kept intact. Its garniture, therefore, is more likely to be plain watercress or bits of aspic. Or the salad may be of exotic, green hearts of palm with thin slices of cold smoked turkey.

Where there are plenty of servants the fingerbowl may not come in on the fruit plate but may be brought on its own serving plate, replacing the used fruit plate before the guests leave the table for coffee. Otherwise, at a formal dinner, fruit plate, fruit knife and fork, finger bowl, and doily arrive as one unit. (See "Presentation of the Finger Bowl.")

TURNING THE TABLE   The "turning of the table" at a formal dinner is supposedly done by the hostess somewhere midway during the meal. She gently terminates her conversation with the gentleman on her right—the gentleman of honor—and turns to the gentleman on her left. Others are supposed to watch for this "turn" and do likewise. In actual practice people try to converse right and left throughout the meal, and even across a sufficiently narrow table, in a normal way. "Turning the table" makes for conversational artificiality.

LEAVING THE DINING ROOM   At the end of the fruit course, the hostess catches the eye of the lady of honor or some other lady at the other end of the table, bows, and slowly rises. The gentlemen rise and, where there are not enough men servants, assist the ladies. The hostess then indicates where coffee is to be served. English style, the men are served at the dining table with cigars, port, liqueurs, and demitasses, the latter offered today with cream and sugar, though once it was *de rigueur* to serve *café noir* at a formal dinner. Or the men may escort their dinner partners to the living room, then leave them for the library or wherever else the men are congregating for coffee. The women then have coffee and liqueurs alone and, before the men return, repair their make-up. Or, Continental fashion, men and women leave the dining room together, the men offering their arms, and together enjoy their coffee and liqueurs and smoking in the living room. This is the pleasanter method, it seems to me, and helps prevent that dismaying banding of men together that so often occurs at American dinner parties.

DEPARTING AFTER THE FORMAL DINNER   Except for some very good reason discussed previously with the hostess, no guest may leave after a formal dinner in a private home in less than two and a half to three hours and even then, not until the guest or guests of honor have departed. At formal public dinners guests who must leave early go quietly either before the speeches begin or between them, never while a guest of honor is speaking or while a national anthem is being played. Those who must leave, leave by the nearest exit without stopping to talk or bid farewell to guests encountered en route, except to bow briefly.

THE FORMAL LUNCHEON

In the 1880s formal luncheons, feminine to a degree, were very elaborate, with hand-painted satin menu cards, illustrated place cards, fantastic pastoral centerpieces.

An etiquette writer of the day, speaking of such affairs, found it necessary to admonish, "To eat with gloves on is female snobbery. Young women who go out to parties may be indifferent to smearing them with lobster salad, or to have the first finger and thumb darkened where the spoon touches them. But nothing is prettier than the freshness of a woman's hand, and the best fitting glove is, after all, but an awkward thing. Gloved hands that feed, to keep up the whole dignity of the thing, should find mouths which were hidden behind veils." Ladies lunching in those days were snugly hatted, without exception, including the hostess. It is interesting to note that Queen Victoria was reported as dining *gloveless*.

Today, although the formal lunch at home is rare, it does occasionally take place, especially at country places, resorts, and in diplomatic circles.

Invitations to a formal luncheon are usually telephoned, but those to official luncheons are engraved. At official luncheons and at Sunday, Saturday, or holiday ones, men and women guests are usually equal in number; otherwise a formal luncheon is essentially a feminine occasion.

Again, a formal luncheon is not possible without an adequate household staff. A hostess may not serve it herself, although if butler or houseman is lacking a waitress is quite acceptable at a formal lunch, though not at a formal dinner.

GREETING GUESTS   The guests are met at the door by a servant who indicates where coats may be left. He or she then usually precedes the guest to the living room (unless all guests know the house well), walks to within speaking distance of the seated hostess, and announces the guest's name. The hostess rises in greeting, but there is no formal receiving line.

Sherry and "biscuits" are often served. Occasionally cocktails are served before luncheon, but usually the hostess offers an alternative of vegetable juice of some kind.

After all the guests have assembled, the butler or waitress announces luncheon. The hostess leads the way with the guest of honor, if any, and the others follow along in any convenient manner, with any gentlemen present *not* offering their arms as at a formal dinner. If there are no place cards the hostess from behind her chair indicates where each is to sit, with the guest of honor at her right. If a host is present and the guest of honor is a woman, she is seated, of course, on his right.

PLACE CARDS AND MENUS   At official luncheons both place cards and menus may be used, and place cards at other formal luncheons are convenient when more than eight are to be seated. The place cards are placed upon the folded napkin, which is, in turn, *on* the service plate. A menu card, engraved or handwritten, is placed in its holder or flat on the table, either one for

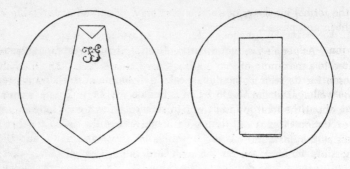

FOLDING OF NAPKINS *Left:* There are many ways to fold napkins (*see text*), but simplicity is usual now. To dramatize initialed dinner napkins, first arrange napkins with loose edges upward on the plate. The fold of the napkin will then form the point of a triangle. Now fold over the loose edges to form a small triangle above the monogram, then fold under the other two points of the napkin to make the arrangement shown. Lay flat on service plate. *Right:* The simple fold of a large dinner napkin. The square is folded over left into a rectangle and placed flat on the plate. A small hard roll may be placed in the fold or on top of it, or to the left of the forks.

each place or one for each two or three guests. There should be one before the hostess and another before the host if he is present.

THE TABLE Damask cloths are not used at formal luncheons. Place mats of the more formal variety, usually white, or an embroidered cloth which does not overhang the table are customary.

There are no candles on a luncheon table, but there are flowers or some other centerpiece. Butter plates are used, even at a formal table. Most formally, the butter is passed, rather than being in place when the guests sit down. The butter is in decorative curls or decorated balls or pats, not merely sliced off a quarter-pound bar. The butter decorations may be a bit of parsley or other herb. Various hot breads are passed during the meal.

If the table is large, decorative dishes of fruit, candies, or nuts may be spaced down the length of the table. A large epergne may contain both fruits and flowers, and on a long table the flower motif could be repeated in tight little low flower arrangements strategically placed. Sometimes there are place corsages for the ladies on some very special occasion, such as a debutante luncheon.

The luncheon napkin is smaller than that used for a formal dinner. It is folded with an eye to the usual corner monogram (see illustration). It has been folded by the laundress in a square. This square is folded into a triangle with the embroidery at the top. Then the other two points of the triangle are folded in under the napkin, which is then placed on the place plate, monogram up, of course. The napkin may also be folded in half lengthwise, as it comes from the linen supply, so that it forms a neat rectangle. This is placed on the place plate with the fold on the left.

At the formal luncheon no food is portioned or carved at the table but is brought in and passed.

THE FOOD As people prefer lighter luncheons today, even a formal luncheon is limited to a maximum of four courses, more usually three. The food should be chosen for its seeming simplicity and deliciousness. Each course should balance well against the one to follow. There is expected to be a certain distinction about the food for any formal meal, and that for a formal luncheon is no exception. Menus are written in French, and the service must be as faultless as the linen and silver.

A possible winter menu for a formal luncheon could be:

Consommé à la princesse
Red snapper à la dauphine
Pommes duchesse   salade de concombres
Fromage de Roquefort
Fruits assortis
Café

Usually not more than two wines are served at a formal luncheon, but one throughout is correct, too. Sherry, at room temperature, may be served with the soup (but not with fish). It may be poured from a decanter by the servant, who, however, must not lift the glass from its place. The sherry glass is at the upper left of the knives, with the glass for any subsequent wine to its right. (See illustration of place setting for the formal luncheon.) A dry white wine is served with the fish, and possibly a liqueur after the coffee. Champagne, for some very special occasion, could be the only wine, served from soup to dessert or introduced with the entrée.

A suggested summer menu for a formal luncheon:

Bisque d'écrevisses
Filet de volaille glacé à la Périgordine
Tomate nouvelle farcie   Choufleur à la Polonaise
Asperges froids sauce vinaigrette
Pêches à la crème
Café

A well-chilled white wine might be served throughout the meal. Sherry could be served with the soup, but, as it is fortified, it is not always the best choice on a hot day.

FORMAL TEAS

Occasionally there is an official tea or perhaps a large tea for a visiting celebrity where the guests are mainly feminine. In these cases, formal tea follows a traditional pattern. (See "Debuts" Section—for the Debutante Tea.)

THE TABLE AND THE LIGHTING The tea table must be large enough to accommodate two services on trays, at opposite ends of the table, one for tea, the other for coffee or chocolate. On the table, too, are placed buffet style, the necessary cups, small plates, and silverware as well as the special tea foods. The tea table, opened to its ultimate length, may be set in any convenient room to which passage to and from is easy and where groups may stand about, or occasionally sit, and have their tea with access to the food, which they serve to themselves. (See "Club Teas")

On the table itself is a white tea cloth, but the trays, usually silver, are bare. Each beverage service—a large urn is usual for coffee, a samovar good for the tea—is presided over by a hostess. The tea is set up farthest from the entrance, the coffee closest to it. At a large tea the hostess herself often reserves her energies for seeing that her guests enjoy themselves, and she delegates the actual "pouring" to two friends well-acquainted with the ritual. These ladies seat themselves at opposite ends of the table before the trays and serve each guest as he appears. The conversation may be limited to "Sugar?" or "Cream?" (actually this is, or should be, milk or nearly so, but it is usually referred to as "cream"), "Lemon?" In a crush, the guest may volunteer this information, and during a lull he may stand by and exchange a few courteous words with the "pourer," who despite the honor is probably in for a dull period. The guest always says, "Thank you," on receiving the proffered cup. It is permissible to return as many times as one wishes for more tea, coffee, or chocolate, but one waits until any who have not yet been served have received theirs before asking for more.

Very occasionally at a large tea, the tea, chocolate, or coffee are poured at the table but passed by servants on trays. This is not very satisfactory. The rule is that the tea should come directly from the hands of the pourer to the receiver, that it should be made, if possible, before one's eyes, as it was in the days when the kettle came directly from the hob and the guests had the pleasure of watching the steam rise and the full fragrance of the steeping tea filled the room.

Of course, if gentlemen are present they may offer to get tea for the various ladies, but a tea is, essentially, a self-service repast, and aside from the receiving of the cup from the hands of the tea-maker, guests are expected to help themselves to the various things upon the table.

The room in which formal tea is served is always artificially lighted, with the curtains drawn as if for an evening entertainment. Candles, tall and white, are most formal and, of course, most becoming.

THE FOOD Tea refreshments are quite different from those served at a cocktail party, and it is not wise to try to combine the two. People who love tea begin with some simple, bland thing like thin, very fresh bread with butter and jam. (For this plain bread and butter the crusts are left on, for sandwiches they are removed.) They may pass on to more complex combinations, such as watercress sandwiches, chopped candied ginger and cream cheese sandwiches, little hot, toasted cheese rolled sandwiches, open-faced rounds of crab or lobster mixture on soft white or graham bread—the tea kind of food, not the cocktail appetizers.

BIDDING FAREWELL There is no obligation on the part of a tea guest at a formal tea to stay more than the half hour needed to consume his tea. He has chatted with anyone taking tea in his immediate vicinity, not necessarily introducing himself first if he is a stranger. He has thanked the "pourers," if they are courtesy hostesses, as he received his tea, so in leaving he need not approach them again. If his hostess is not pouring he seeks her out for a few appreciative words in farewell. He also says good-by to the host if there is one. If the hostess herself is pouring she does not, in this case, rise to bid a guest farewell. She bows from behind the tea table, offers her hand, perhaps, smiles, and says a few words. The guest may be shown out by a member of the family, but more likely he makes his departure alone.

FORMAL DANCES AT HOME

The very formal dance or ball at home, frequent in the "season" abroad in the great houses, is increasingly rare here because of our telescoping living arrangements. Still, in the South, the Southwest, the Midwest, and sometimes in the Far West there still exist the houses that can accommodate large numbers of guests—and hosts and hostesses who enjoy giving such elaborate parties. They begin late, and invitations state the hour as ten-thirty or eleven (rarely on the quarter hour for formal invitations). They really get under way around eleven-thirty. (See Correspondence Section for dance invitations.)

The exterior of the house is always specially prepared for the occasion. A red carpet usually runs from curb to front door and there is an awning. A floodlight is on for the convenience of arrivals. The family chauffeur assists guests from their cars, and there may be private detectives or a policeman to protect arriving, bejeweled celebrities, all most formally attired.

A caterer and florist have taken over the house. There is a room set aside for racks on which coats are to be checked, and a caterer's man in house livery gives each guest a ticket for articles checked as he enters. A gentleman accompanying a lady accepts her ticket and, on leaving, collects both garments and takes care of the tip (twenty-five cents apiece). In an extensively staffed house there may be a rack in the ladies' dressing room under the supervision of a ladies' maid. In the gentlemen's dressing room a valet may be in attendance, but in any case tickets are given. When house servants perform these duties they are not tipped in this country unless they perform a special service of some kind.

The butler announces all guests as they enter the ballroom, or other large room cleared for the dancing, ladies, of course, preceding gentlemen. Hostess and guest of honor, if any, stand together receiving until the last guest seems to have arrived or until supper is served—about one o'clock.

The host, as at a wedding reception, stays in the vicinity of the line and introduces guests to one another whenever his kindly offices seem necessary. He may actually stay in the line briefly early in the evening. The hostess, too, has had the foresight to invite a stag line of ushers, theoretically one *extra* man to each nine or ten girls, and they wear identifying white boutonnieres which are usually awaiting them on a tray in the hall. Ushers come early and stay late and see to it that there are no wallflowers.

As extra men are always welcome, those invited frequently phone the hostess and ask for permission to bring a friend. If such men arrive without their sponsors they say to the hostess on arrival, "George Whitman asked if I might come. I am Andrew Tierney." Needless to say, no one, not even a friend of a friend, should "crash" any private party. To prevent this, many hostesses include in their invitations admission cards which must be presented at the door.

As at all formal affairs, the "roof" is not sufficient introduction. A man who has not been introduced to a girl may not ask her to dance, but of course he may ask someone to introduce him. An usher may ask a girl to dance even if he has not first been introduced, but that is because he is an acting host. In going on the ballroom floor a man leads the way through the crowd and once arrived stands ready to receive his partner. In crossing the floor to leave it he walks on the girl's left. Then, if there is a crush, he goes first, as in a restaurant where there is no headwaiter, to the group where he found her or to the refreshment table or to her waiting next partner. He never leaves her stranded.

SUPPER   At a formal dance or ball, supper is always served either buffet or at small tables supplied by the caterer. There are never place cards, and guests seat themselves as they wish, usually with friends. A girl's escort always takes her in to supper. Ushers see to it that unescorted girls are seated in congenial groups with young men who will serve them supper.

Abroad, sometimes the reception line re-forms for "good nights" when it is time to go. But in this country, after a dance or ball, this might mean that the guest of honor, if any, might have to stay on duty until dawn. Therefore after the receiving line breaks up at a late affair, it does not re-form. Guests say "good-by" to host and hostess if they are still about or to any member of the family, and, of course, a debutante stays up until the last guest departs.

At an official ball no guest departs before the guest of honor. The party call after balls and formal dances has virtually disappeared, except in Washington (but, of course, it always *may* be made). In Washington guests leave cards upon the hostess and host (if a man is calling—see "Card Leaving") within a week, but even there such calls have become the emptiest formality. It is not unknown for even a diplomat to give his card to some trusted cabby, with instructions that he leave it at the hostess' door within the stated time. He doesn't even necessarily bother to remain seated in the cab, himself, any more. (Naturally I can't endorse such a procedure.)

CHAPTER THIRTY-TWO

THE GUEST AT FORMAL MEALS

When a guest receives a formal invitation to lunch or dine he should know the various procedures of this kind of stylized entertainment. If he knows exactly what to expect he can be at ease. It is only the quite unknown that tends to shake our poise. So let us examine the guest's part in formal entertaining.

When a butler or waitress is serving at table, the persons served pay sufficient attention to the service to be ready to take their portions when dishes are presented to them (from the left) and, at a crowded table, to move aside, left or right, slightly, to aid the service or removal of dishes—the latter virtually always to the right, except for butter plates.

SECOND PORTIONS   At formal luncheons or dinners second portions are not properly offered (nor asked for) because of the usual multiplicity of courses. But at meals where they are offered, any guest who wishes more may serve himself from the proffered dish or platter even if other guests have abstained. The hostess then takes at least a token amount to keep him company, or she has eaten so slowly as to have a little left on her plate from which to eat while any guest consumes a second helping.

GUESTS DO NOT ASSIST   Unless asked to do so by the hostess, a guest does not assist in the service of anything at the table while there are servants in attendance. He never stacks dishes nor hands an empty plate or glass to a servant but permits these to be removed or replenished for him. At a formal meal there should be no need for those at the table to pass anything. There should be salt and pepper, ash trays, matches, cigarettes (if the hostess wishes) at every place, or at every other place. Bread or rolls are passed at luncheon, or rolls are in place on or in the napkin at a formal dinner or to the left of the plate, if they are served at all.

SMOKING AT TABLE   It is poor manners for any guest to sit down to a table, formally set or otherwise, with a lighted cigarette in his hand. At a formal table he may well find no place for the ashes or finished cigarette (if the hostess takes pride in her cuisine) and will be forced to leave the table with his cigarette or cause a certain amount of stir asking for an ash tray. At formal dinners cigarettes are usually not placed on the table until the dessert is served, if then.

THE PLACEMENT OF USED SILVER is optional—either of these two ways best as-suring that the plate, when removed, will have the utensils firmly upon it.

GREETING SERVANTS AT TABLE   A guest at table pays no particular attention to the servant waiting upon him. He never carries on a conversation with even an old family retainer while being served. He may, however, quietly say, "Good evening" or "Good evening, Johnson" (or "Nellie") as the butler, houseman, or waitress approaches to serve him, if this is the first time he has seen him (or her) since entering the house, and then only if he has been a frequent guest.

THE TOKEN PORTION   A guest takes at least a little of everything offered him at a formal dinner or luncheon and makes some pretense at eating it. This is done so the attentive host or hostess will not imagine he has been over-looked in the presentation of dishes. It is necessary neither to eat every bit on one's plate nor, again, to leave a little so as not to seem gluttonous.

PLACEMENT OF USED SILVER   When a plate of food has been finished or the diner has had all he wishes, he places the fork and knife (but only if he has used one or both) on the right side of the plate, sharp side of the blade facing in, the fork tines up, to the left of the knife. They should be so placed as not to slide off as the plate is being removed. Dessert spoon and fork are placed on the empty plate, as they were when the plate was pre-sented, that is, fork on the left, spoon on the right with tines of the fork up and facing, with the bowl of the spoon slightly toward the center of the plate, and securely enough so they won't fall off when the servant picks up the plate. No used silver is ever placed on the table or left in a cup. A soup spoon is left in a large soup plate. An iced tea spoon is left in the glass if no service plate is beneath. Unused silver at the place is left on the table, to be removed to a tray by the servant before the dessert course.

CRUMBS AND SPILLED FOOD When there is full service, crumbs and bits of bread are left on the tablecloth by the guest and are removed by the servant when he or she crumbs the table. But if any semi-liquid, such as a bit of jelly or sauce, has been dropped on the cloth, the guest, at the time, if he sees it, quietly retrieves it with some convenient utensil—butter knife, fork, or dinner knife—and places it on the side of his plate. If anything is spilled while a guest is being served, then the servant attends to it. The guest should make no more than a murmured apology, if any, and the hostess should take no notice of it except, if necessary, to instruct the servant in the proper procedure. In the case of a spilled beverage, it may be necessary for the servant to remove the place setting and put down a clean linen napkin over the cloth or replace the mat with a fresh one. But on either side, the accident should be minimized as much as possible.

PRESENTATION OF THE FINGER BOWL Finger bowls are rarely seen in understaffed or unstaffed households these days, but of course still do make their appearance in homes where perfect service is still possible. (It is interesting that as early as the thirteenth century silver finger bowls were presented with flowered linen towels.) They are filled three-quarters full with cold water and placed on the table in either of two ways, one of which requires the slight co-operation of the guest.

If the finger bowl on the dessert plate and, if one is used, decorative doily (never paper) is placed before a guest with dessert silver on each side, the guest is expected to lift bowl and doily and small glass plate, if any, adroitly with the right hand and place it in front and slightly to the left of his place setting. He then removes the silver and places it, fork left and spoon right of the plate. If the finger bowl is presented with no silver flanking it, this indicates that there is no further course and the guest does not remove it from the plate. Very occasionally, a small underplate on the dessert plate, topped by doily and finger bowl, is intended for use. For example, strawberries Romanoff is a difficult dessert for a flat plate. The menu or the hostess gives the cue.

In using a finger bowl, the guest dips in the fingers of one hand, then of the other, lightly, then dries them on the napkin on his lap, but all so briefly as to avoid the impression that this is a serious ablution. He may, too, of course, touch his lips with his moistened fingers, then pat his lips lightly with his napkin, which he then places, unfolded and unarranged, to the right of his place. He never leaves it on his chair or tosses it onto a plate.

Finger bowls, even without service, are almost necessary after the serving of boiled or broiled lobster or steamed clams. In this case, they are filled three-quarters full with warm water, often with a slice or half-slice of lemon in it (but only in this instance, though flower petals or tiny blown-glass fish, etc., are often used at the end of the meal in finger bowls).

THE SIGNAL TO RISE   As coffee is not served at the table to gentlemen and ladies together at a formal dinner, the guest should be ready for the hostess' signal to rise at the end of the fruit course. (See "Service of Formal Dinner.") If the gentlemen stay in the dining room for coffee, cigars, pipes, and liqueurs they move up in a companionable circle near the host—and all stay. For one robustious Lothario to make off after the ladies is considered bad conduct. And in equally poor taste is the young lady who leaves the gentlemen with a reluctant backward glance. Needless to say, if the gentlemen move on to the library for coffee no lady allows herself to be persuaded to join them. Historically, the stories that are sometimes told at these stag moments after dinner are unfit for shell-like ears, and, at any rate, the other ladies would frigidly resent such a defection. As insurance, perhaps, against any such encroachment on masculine preserves, the doors were locked upon the gentlemen after dinner in the early nineteenth century, and it is said many never did eventually "join the ladies."

CHAPTER THIRTY-THREE

THE RITUAL OF DRINKING

WHAT KIND OF DRINKS FOR GUESTS

If you are having people to dinner, mix only one kind of cocktail and offer, in addition, sherry, and scotch or bourbon or rye and soda—with vegetable or fruit juice for possible teetotalers. Old-fashioneds are a nuisance to fix for more than four or five. The safest choice seems to be martinis, which have the virtue of being relatively inexpensive, more or less foolproof as to concoction, and mixable well in advance. In fact, they may be bottled and stored full-strength for a week or more in the refrigerator—but don't bother to save diluted ones. They may also be varied—a tiny pearl onion in the glass instead of the usual unstuffed olive makes a gibson.

A martini should always be dry, never sweet. It should have a twist of lemon peel in the container in which the martini is stirred, or the peel may be twisted over each glass so a bit of oil drops in. Some experts insist that the ingredients be stirred all in one direction with the cracked ice—never shaken—but as I, with many another woman, am unenthusiastic about martinis (except for their convenience), I cannot say whether this is really vital. I have even seen a very knowledgeable gentleman of the old school shake his martinis vigorously, with a loud snort at all the talk that they must be stirred.

A prominently placed home bar, with the makings of a wide variety of drinks on demand and a host who can oblige, takes away the emphasis on dinner and puts it untastefully on what should be only an incidental procedure. Only at a really large party should more than one kind of cocktail be served at home, and then the host is usually not acting as bartender.

Esoteric cocktails should be avoided at dinner parties unless you are certain your guests have such preferences. An alexander, for example, would be a poor choice, especially with men present. Fancy mixed drinks are usually frowned on by men, though beloved of some women who like to order them in restaurants. But the standard cocktails are the wisest choice—and don't let the person who mixes them do so without following an exact formula. Nothing is so horrid as a martini with too much vermouth or an old-fashioned with too much bitters. A bacardi or daiquiri that is sickish-sweet will kill appetites for the best-conceived dinner.

Generally, gin and rum cocktails are preferred in hot weather to whisky cocktails. Eggnog is a cold weather specialty and is not served before dinner. It is an afternoon drink, always served with fruit cake and sweet biscuits, usually on New Year's Day.

Such drinks as hot buttered rum, glög, hot spiced wine are winter between-meal drinks often served after outdoor sports. They do not properly precede dinner.

Rum-and-Cola, tom collins, punch (milk punch perhaps excepted), bishop, bowles, swizzles, juleps, spiced wines are afternoon or evening libations, not appetizers before dinner. Stingers are served liqueur-fashion as a digestive after dinner.

You make no mistake when you choose one of the following cocktails to serve before a dinner party—martini, bacardi, or daiquiri (especially in summer), whisky sours (good any time and well-liked by both sexes), manhattans and old-fashioneds (with a minimum of garnish for male tastes).

Cracked ice—easy to make with a canvas bar bag and mallet or a little ice-cracking machine—makes cocktails cold fast without undue dilution. It is preferable to ice in cubes but is not used in most tall drinks. One exception is the julep, which requires crushed ice and plenty of it.

MAINLY ABOUT WINES

The subject of wines is a fascinating one—so fascinating that mountains of material have been written on it, thus frightening more than instructing, I sometimes think.

In Victorian days no gentleman of fashion could possibly be ignorant of all the fine points of vintage and temperature, vintner and *endroit* of the wines at his table. He kept a proper wine cellar and tended, or had tended, each precious bottle on schedule. He knew enough not to permit his butler to wipe off a fine old, dusty bottle of, say, Chateau Mouton Rothschild of a superlative year and wrap it in a napkin to hide the details of its lineage from interested diners. (None but a possibly dripping champagne bottle should be served wrapped in a napkin. Red wines never are.) His fine sedimented wines were kept on their sides at proper temperature and never put upright even before service. They could be decanted into beautiful clear glass decanters, slowly after the cork had been eased—not yanked out—until the sediment was reached. Or they could be poured from a cradle or wine basket that held the bottle almost horizontal so that wine and sediment would not mix. Some experts, however, say a sedimented wine may rest upright half an hour before serving, if no basket is available.

The *table* wines are those served at meals. The reds range from the hearty, full-bodied French burgundies (in infinite variety), the more delicate, ruby red, tart clarets to the blushing vin rosé, so light in body that, unlike the others which are served at room temperature or slightly warm, it is chilled and thus is most agreeable in warm weather. Of the myriad American varieties of dark red full-bodied wine, most with French names, not all, naturally, are burgundy, though burgundy they are often commonly called merely because they are red. I think it is advisable to know a little more than that about wines. The major wine merchants are interested in improving your wine education. Go to one and ask him to explain to you the fine points of difference in the red wines. Compare those pressed from the cabernet, the true grape of French clarets, with the delicate bouquet of some of the fine table wines from vintners in California's Livermore, Napa, Soma, and San Bernardino Valleys.

DRY REDS The dry red wines are those whose sugar content is low—red chianti, berbera are among the many types. These are preferable for service during main courses, although sweet red wines, and even some of the sweet sauternes, are said to be becoming popular in America as dinner wines—but mainly, I suspect, in the less pretentious restaurants and, I suspect, too, at the insistence of the ladies. But people who know food—and wines—will tell you that a sweet wine served before or during a meal takes the edge off the appetite and so defeats a dry wine's whole function, that is, to supplement rather than overshadow the food.

DRY WHITES It has become acceptable in our more simplified way of living to serve one dry white wine throughout a meal, even as an accompaniment to red meat. But on a more elaborate basis for dinner it is pleasant and formal to serve sherry with the soup, a dry white wine—perhaps hock or chablis— with the fish, chicken, brains, sweetbreads, or seafood, and a dry red or sparkling burgundy with red meat, duck, goose, or game.

At luncheon the one-wine theme is delightfully carried out with an alsatian, a moselle, a white chianti, or white orvieto, all imported. Or their American counterparts—reisling, sylvaner, scuppernong, semillion, pinot blanc, traminer, and the Ohio and New York State white wines—all merit consideration as do the South American rhine types and, of course, the true rhines, of which some, like liebfraumilch, are worth much penny-scrimping in other directions.

SWEET REDS The sweet red wines are dessert and between-meal wines. They include port (excellent with nuts and cheese), the sweet sherries (neither of which are ever referred to, by the way, as sherry *wine* or port *wine*), muscatel and madeira.

SWEET WHITES The sweet white dessert wines include malaga, semidry champagnes, white port from Oporto, Portugal (very delicious and not enough known), tokay and angelica, an American dessert wine originated in California.

And then there are the delicious homemade wines, white and red, whose acquaintance should be made by those gentlemen who enjoy showing off their culinary talents. What better way than to learn to make grandmother's dandelion, elderberry, or blackberry wine, or even to brew a real, authoritative ginger beer, English style? Old cookbooks give all the essential directions.

FILTERED DOMESTICS Some American wines are excellent, some poor—just as some imported varieties from the wine countries fit into both categories. Judicious experimentation is highly recommended so you may find what wines suit your needs, your palate, and your pocketbook most adequately. Experts tell us that there is less sedimentation in American red wines but that this isn't to their credit, as overfiltering to remove the sediment robs them of some of their character.

WINES IN PLACE OF COCKTAILS The true gourmet is horrified at the blatancy of cocktails before exquisitely planned and executed meals. He much prefers wine with canapés, *foie gras*, or caviar. Chablis—really a French white burgundy—is commendable in place of cocktails, as is a chilled dry (American—the French ones are sweet) sauterne. Most elegant, of course, is champagne, straight if it's the best imported, as a champagne cocktail if it lacks final excellence. Any of these, including the champagne, may be refrigerator cooled at about 45° for home service, as this is a less drippy procedure. And a partly used bottle of champagne or any other white wine, restoppered with a *different cork* will keep for weeks in the refrigerator, and even champagne will stay lively for days the same way (and good for champagne cocktails), though such refrigerated wines should not be allowed to freeze.

Partly used bottles of red wine should be recorked and kept in a cool place, rather than in the refrigerator. If they start to turn sour before they can be used, never discard them but permit them to turn to wine vinegar. A little from a bottle of wine vinegar added to leftover dry red wine will start the vinegaring process.

Port, sherry, and madeira are all available dry, as well as sweet, and the dry types are all suitable for service in place of cocktails. A good dry sherry is usually served from a chilled bottle rather than from the decanter at cocktail time.

Both dry port and sherry are good with bitters—orange or Angostura—in place of a cocktail. Dubonnet and vermouth at room temperature and served with a twist of lemon peel appeal to many palates, as does Amer Picon, but Dubonnet may be served frappé, i.e., with finely crushed ice in a cocktail glass, and the vermouth makes an attractive pompier highball, or vermouth cassis, to those who prefer appetizers low in alcoholic content. A vermouth cassis is made with 1½ to 3 ozs. of French dry vermouth (it's the Italian that's sweet and which is not good alone as an appetizer) plus ½ oz. of crème de cassis (a French currant juice liqueur) plus lump-ice and club soda, in a small thin highball glass filled ¾ full and gently stirred.

In some South American countries a cocktail party is called "a vermouth," and vermouth you get—no cocktails!

STORAGE OF WINES　All table wines should be stored on their sides, to keep their corks moist (and uncrumbling), in a cool cupboard, away from the light and from steam pipes. A wooden wine rack to hold them reduces chance of breakage, but they can be placed sidewise on narrow shelves of any kind.

WHAT KIND OF GLASSES　You may be the possessor of your grandmother's be-nobbed and overlaid green hock glasses or handsome ruby wines and will certainly want to use them. But any connoisseur of wines will hold out for the use of clear thin glass for all wines, as wine itself is sufficient decoration. The table wines should be served preferably in a fairly large glass—just under goblet size and more than twice cocktail size. They should be shaped to bunch the bouquet under the nostrils—in other words, the rim should be narrower than the base of the bowl with the exception of v-shaped (they *needn't* be this shape—any 3-oz. stemmed glass will do) sherry glasses, which, by the way, are the only ones to be filled almost to the brim. Others are filled about one half or two thirds to permit the inhalation of the bouquet. Champagne glasses are best without hollow stems, which are decorative but which permit the warming of the drink, as a chilled white wine is always grasped by the stem. (Red wine is drunk with the hand grasping the bowl.)

TO DECANT OR NOT　Sherry served with soup or between meals (this the sweeter type) may be decanted, though service from a good bottle is always right, too. Tequilla, aquavit and vodka (not wines, of course, but served often enough straight from the refrigerator, ice-cold as an appetizer) are not decanted.

Claret, madeira, and port may be decanted, though many like the appearance of the bottle—especially if the vintner's name means anything. All but the claret (unstopper this, by the way, an hour before serving) are safe in the decanter almost indefinitely, though sherry may begin to cloud up if decanted and not kept fairly cool.

Burgundy is not decanted but served from a wine cradle or at least from its side if it is an imported, sedimented type. It should be brought into the room and unstoppered an hour before serving. American filtered types may be served decanted or from an upright bottle. Sparkling burgundy is served at room temperature in its own bottle, upright like champagne. In very hot weather these wines are served "cellar" temperature, cooler than the room, though not chilled.

White sparkling wines are served from their own bottles, upright and slightly cold but not chilled.

Liqueurs are served at room temperature with the exception of crème de menthe (green or white), which is served frappé or in a stinger, though any cordial, especially a fruit one, may be served frappé, especially for ladies, or for all in the summertime—try Southern Comfort or cointreau frappé, for example.

POURING   A decanted wine may be poured first into a guest's glass—though host should check flavor sometime before serving. An undecanted wine, which might harbor traces of cork, is poured—just a little of it—into the glass of the *host* or, if there is no host, into that of the *hostess* to drain off bits of cork, if any. Host or hostess left with bits of cork in his or her glass is not expected to finish the pouring on top of cork after others have been served. A servant, if present, pours off the bit of wine-with-cork, or if there is no servant the cork-receiver may carefully lift out the offending bits with, say, the blade of a clean knife or a spoon and lay the bits on the side of his plate. Or he rises, glass in hand, and empties the offending inch in the bar or kitchen.

TO PREVENT SPILLING   To prevent spilling a drop of wine on the tablecloth when pouring from a bottle, give the bottle a deft little twist before lifting the mouth away from the glass. The bottle mouth may also be wiped with a clean napkin between servings.

TOASTS

Weddings, christenings, bachelor dinners, engagement parties are always occasions for toasts. But there are other occasions—formal dinners, anniversaries, birthday parties, intimate dinners—where men, in particular, may wish to propose a toast. While it is nice to be able to extemporize gracefully on such occasions as the rare man can, it is pleasant to know most of the standard toasts and to be able to tender them with ease.

The person toasted, if present and if not the President of the U.S. or other high dignitary, usually returns a toast. A woman, except when she is a bride, usually accepts the compliment of the toast simply with a smile and lowered eyes, remaining seated if the others stand and holding her wine, but not sipping it until the toast has been drunk. In fact, the person toasted never touches the drink to his or her lips until the others have drunk the toast, otherwise he or she would be drinking to himself or herself, an immodest procedure.

A man drinking a toast across the table to his dinner companion may do so merely by catching her eye and raising his glass. He doesn't rise unless others are at the table and there is a real occasion—such as her birthday—to propose a toast to the lady. If the two are alone the gentleman may actually say the words of some gay little toast, "À *vos beaux yeux* [To your pretty face]" or suggest they drink together "To a wonderful evening" or "To happy times."

A dinner chairman at, say, the Democratic National Committee dinner would propose the first toast to the President. The President, if present, merely remains seated and bows slightly in recognition of the standing toast by the others.

Important toasts, to rulers, to the President, to a bride, etc., are properly drained at one drink. The glasses used often to be thrown in the fireplace or at least snapped at the delicate stem, but today no dishonor to the toasted one occurs when the glasses are, sensibly, left intact. It is, by the way, rude to the point of insult to refuse to drink a toast to anyone. If you can't drink wine, you pretend to do so. A toast with water is no toast at all. It is not really correct to toast with cocktails, but a toast with punch or beer, ale or whisky is usual.

In England some drinks still have a bit of toast placed in them in the traditional style. In drinking a toast, one had to drain the cup to get the "toast," which, saturated with the drink, sank to the bottom. Toasting is a very old custom, indeed, predating the Caesars.

Many charming toasts to women are in French or other foreign languages because toasting is the expected thing abroad, relatively unusual—except for special occasions—here. If you can't master a toast in a foreign language so it sounds the way it should, don't attempt it—translate it into English, and it will be appreciated just as much. But it is convenient to understand what these familiar toasts in other languages mean. In addition to the one I've given, there are many more, often heard. Commonest are:

"À votre santé!" (Fr.) "To your health!"—suitable for anyone, of course.

"Sköal!" (Swed.)—"Your health!"

"Prost!" or "Prosit!" (G.)—"To your health!"

"Here's to your good health and your family's good health, and may you all
    live long and prosper!"—from "Rip Van Winkle," by Washington Irving.

"May you live all the days of your life!"—Swift.

FIVE REASONS FOR DRINKING

If all be true that I do think,
There are five reasons we should drink:
Good wine—a friend—or being dry—
Or lest we should be, by and by—
Or any other reason why!
—HENRY ALDRICH, c. 1700

At a small private dinner a toast may be informally proposed by anyone as soon as the first wine has been poured. The company stands only if the toaster rises. More than one toast may now be drunk with the same glass of wine—though a toast in champagne is often drained at one drink, especially at wedding receptions. Toasts are not drunk with liqueurs, although the dessert wines, sweet sherry, port, marsala, or angelica, would be suitable.

At public dinners toasts are not proposed until the end of the meal just before the speaking begins. The first toast is proposed by the toastmaster, and others may be proposed—with his permission—by honored guests at the dais but not by members of the general assembly.

CHAPTER THIRTY-FOUR

ENTERTAINING INDOORS

I never fail to be somewhat alarmed at the extent of my correspondence from people who want to know how to entertain their guests after dinner or luncheon. "What games should we play?" they ask.

Now an occasional game of bridge, canasta, mah-jongg (which still has its devotees), backgammon, or even poker can be enjoyable if everyone is in the mood, but certainly I'd like to be warned before accepting an invitation to dinner that it is to be followed by serious bridge. I wouldn't want any hostess to count on me for a fourth, for I asserted myself concerning ritualistic parlor games long ago.

The best after-meal entertainment though is stimulating conversation. Constant, organized card playing can kill off any attempt at conversation in a group of people who regularly see each other. They may have their bridge luncheons and suppers for years and never really get to know each other at all or get very much out of such meetings.

Of course, the nervous hostess and the awkward, inexperienced host are terrified of just an evening of "conversation." They feel they must do something. They rush around filling glasses, dumping ash trays, pulling up chairs, fiddling with the radio dials, or, willy-nilly, turning on the television.

The good hostess is careful to invite people who have some common thread of interest. She tries to have one, at least, known to be an eager conversationalist. Even if he spends the evening talking interestingly about himself, he can save the evening in a group of semi-mutes. People are always at their best, anyway, talking about themselves and their experiences. The adept hostess knows how to get them going and how, when others grow restless, to turn the conversation so that everyone else gets a chance to put in his oar. Above all, a hostess should not, herself, feel she must provide all the conversation, no matter how witty or erudite—or capable at conversation—she is. The essence of good conversation is to get others to talk.

CONVERSATION

The talk-talk kind of conversation does little but fill time better left unfilled. The chatterbox, usually feminine, rattles on very often because she is really ill at ease socially and in this way tries to make herself felt.

In conversation it is not really necessary to have a ready opinion on everything. On the contrary, good conversation develops opinions and thus depends on an ability to listen as well as to express oneself.

The bane of every hostess' life is the guest who falls into complete silence, who won't be brought into a conversation, but who, on the other hand, remains in the company. Such people feel shy, superior, or plain tired, I have often found, and should not be forced into conversations they are plainly trying to avoid. Often they enjoy themselves just listening, or they will suddenly come alert and make an interesting contribution later on.

An ability to converse comes with general social ease. The relaxed person, comfortable in his surroundings, is able to parry the conversational ball with little assistance. He should be himself and not try to fit his conversation in some stilted way to the company. If he finds himself well beyond his intellectual depth he can be an alert listener and he can ask a question now and then. His companions will usually be only too pleased to enlighten him.

A host and hostess should try to develop skill in bringing out their guests conversationally. They should know, or find out, the interests and hobbies of each and bring together those with kindred interests. From then on they keep the conversational fires kindled by helping the quieter guests to express themselves from time to time.

A hostess should never try too hard to get her party going. If she relaxes and lets her guests become acquainted, general and group conversation will normally develop. I know one hostess who carried clenched, in one hand, a little black notebook containing the tag lines of what she deemed appropriate stories. Whenever a lull came in conversation she would leaf nervously through it and come up with a story. She succeeded only in making her ineptness as a hostess even more apparent.

No two evenings of conversation are ever alike, even with the same people. An open fire, the preliminary of a good dinner, music perhaps, the little ceremony of evening refreshments—all help to make people comfortable together and expansive.

ICE BREAKERS

Occasionally, however, even the most astute hostess will find gathered under her roof—perhaps at a birthday party where relatives and friends are of varying ages—a group of people it is difficult to entertain. In this circumstance games are often very helpful as ice breakers. "The Game" is very popular even among intellectuals. "Ghosts" is also entertaining. I remember playing it when our electric power went off for four days and we wearied of trying to read by candle, lamp, and flashlight. Even a spelling bee can be fun in a large crowd of young and old. A book of games is probably an excellent addition to anyone's home library.

MUSIC IN THE EVENING

Good music is often a stimulus to conversation if it is kept in the background. If everyone, or nearly everyone, is interested in music, classical or otherwise, the hostess may ask if certain records or special programs will be welcome. Then conversation may—or may not—cease. Many a delightful evening with friends can be spent with hardly a word exchanged if all are listening to music.

Few people can or want to talk against the blare of the radio or the glare and chatter of the television screen. If you plan an evening of radio, bridge, poker, or television, say so and give any guests who prefer a different evening the opportunity to leave approximately one hour after dinner.

TELEVISION

The hostess with a television set should never assume that her guests are willing or eager to look at it. It is safer to assume that callers came to talk with their friends, not to enjoy their television. They probably have a set at home they could have turned on.

If unexpected guests arrive during the course of a telecast that the family is obviously enjoying, the hostess may say, "We like this program and look at it each week, so I hate to shut it off, but perhaps you would like to see it? If not, let's go into another room and any of the others who care to may join us." It is certainly not fair, for example, to drag father away from a championship boxing match, if that's what he's glued to, to help entertain Mr. and Mrs. George, who just dropped in from the next block. What probably happens is that Mrs. George and the hostess retire from the din and the two men have their television.

If the hostess, on the other hand, has television in mind as a means of entertaining expected guests, she should tell them so in advance. If they consider a whole evening of watching television lost, they have an opportunity to refuse the invitation. They wouldn't hesitate to say they don't feel like a movie. They may even be quite frank and say, "We hardly ever turn on our own set, except for a program or two we occasionally enjoy. Please ask us some other time when you're planning something else."

Guests who do accept a television invitation are ill-mannered, however, if once settled they keep up a continuous chatter that prevents the others from hearing what's going on. Trying to keep up conversation while watching television is impossible. They should be still and look and listen or remove themselves thence.

BRIDGE

If it is agreeable to a majority of the guests—enough to make up tables— to play bridge after dinner, the tables are set up as needed half an hour or more after coffee has been served. It is always best, when possible, to put the bridge players off by themselves in another room if at least half the guests prefer to talk. If space permits, the tables can be set up during dinner and placed in such a way that it doesn't seem essential for every guest to take part. It is quite possible for two or more guests not wishing to play to have a pleasant evening by themselves in a roomful of bridge addicts. But unlikely, I should say, and of course kibitzing is very dull indeed. The desire of the majority decides the evening, but non-participating guests should be helped by the hostess to do something they enjoy—to listen to the radio, read a book or the evening papers, play chess, or take a walk if they must stay to the end.

No one should play cards against his own real desire or he will probably make a miserable partner. No hostess should worry about a guest who has named his preference for evening entertainment. I once had a non-bridge-playing friend who spent his evening with me in the kitchen learning how to make a delicate dessert soufflé, while his wife played bridge with an interest he couldn't even feign.

COVERS FOR BRIDGE TABLES   Bridge tables should not be covered during play. The surface should encourage the easy deal of the cards. Two packs of unused cards, or at least very fresh ones, should be on each table, with a score card and a well-sharpened pencil with an eraser. When luncheon or supper is to be served on the tables, the tables are then covered with square luncheon cloths, preferably in white damask or linen and as alike as possible.

BEHAVIOR AT BRIDGE   My own feeling is that bridge is a game you should play well or not at all if the others are skilled players. You may be beautiful and witty, intelligent and glamorous, but if you sit down to a table of bridge with only a faint interest in and a hazier understanding of the game itself you make yourself worse than foolish. Very few people like to teach the game as they play. So if bridge is played much in your circle, go to a professional teacher and learn the latest methods. Read the bridge columns in your daily paper, and study a good book of modern rules. Don't let yourself be persuaded to sit in at a serious game whose progress your own inept playing will only hamper.

Not everyone, by any means, has a real feeling for cards. If you are one of those that no amount of teaching can improve, let it go. You will not be a social leper if you prefer to sit by and knit or read while the others really enjoy themselves. It is just as irritating to good players to have someone with poor card sense join them just to be agreeable as it is to an excellent tennis player to have a halfhearted one inflict himself on a game of doubles. You can't be too modest about your card playing. Always state frankly whether you are considered a good, middling, or poor player, and let the others decide whether to risk you. They, in turn, may very well suggest another game in which you may be more skillful. Certainly if you are to play any card game with a partner for stakes you are honor bound to explain your card status, even if *you* can afford to lose.

If you do play bridge, be attentive to your partner's signals and exercise judgment in taking bids away from him. Even if you are dummy, sit by quietly and pay attention to the play. Don't carry on constant chatter with the players at your table or with others in the room while you are playing.

Bridge seems to breed its own disagreeable mannerisms—the player who "takes all night" to make up his mind which card to play, the drummer-on-the-table, the slammer-down of the trick-taking card, the chair-teeterer, the whooper who takes loud pleasure in the opponent's defeat or discomfort. Then there is the historian who does an autopsy of every game, mainly to show how the others would have played their cards had they been he. Bridge is no different from other competitive games in that the rules of sportsmanship are the same—play quietly as well as you can, and win or lose without making your opponents feel uncomfortable.

CARDS FOR MONEY

A host or hostess planning to follow dinner with poker or bridge for money should say so when he or she issues the invitation. If a certain number of players are actually required and one guest, for reasons of his own, prefers not to play for money it can create an awkward situation.

Few of us like to admit, publicly, that we can't afford to gamble. We don't even like to admit that, if we play, a certain limit must be placed on the stakes. The danger, in that event, is always that as the heat of the game gets us we tend to permit a raising of the stakes with a possibly ruinous result. No one should enter any game of chance with the thought that he will win. He should, instead, face frankly the thought that he has an excellent chance to lose, and he must predicate his refusal or acceptance to play on that premise.

It is not good sportsmanship to agree to play for stakes that are possibly perilous to you and then be unable to pay off to the winner in the necessary, casual manner. Many people as a matter of principle always say, "We don't play for stakes," even when they can well afford to lose. If you are young people on a budget, play for stakes, if you enjoy the thrill, only if you are budgeted for the losses. Never anticipate the possible gains.

THE PAY-OFF   If you play for stakes, be prepared to pay off your losses then and there, preferably in cash. If you get beyond your depth and can't meet the obligation at the game's end, tell the winner when he may expect your check in full settlement. And don't make it necessary for him to remind you of your obligation. If you don't pay he can't go to law about the debt but he can ruin your reputation for decent sportsmanship so that others will be warned not to play for stakes with you again. The moral is always: *If you can't afford to lose, don't play for money.*

CHAPTER THIRTY-FIVE

ENTERTAINING OUT OF DOORS

There are picnics and picnics. There's the kind you may see at South-ampton, with dowagers sitting gingerly under beach umbrellas, the food being served by their chauffeurs. On the other hand, a picnic to be a good one does not necessarily mean that sand be in your sandwich. But it is more fun done in a quite informal, albeit, comfortable style.

The picnic on your own grounds probably makes use of a barbecue. The equipment can be anything from a simple charcoal burner on wheels to a handsome barbecue with wrought-iron grills, an oven and a chimney to blessedly take away the smoke. Whatever it is, so long as it's fire you can depend on the men to enjoy tending it.

With outdoor cooking facilities it is easy and pleasant to entertain rela-tively large groups at home. But, as with buffet, it is important to have a comfortable place for guests to eat the food so appetizingly prepared within view. A round table is very friendly. Sometimes one can be built around a tree well to leeward of the fire. Or a long pine picnic table with benches is convenient. An old-fashioned heavy oak or walnut round table with exten-sion leaves is easily found at a secondhand shop and rubbed down, painted, and waterproofed for an outdoors picnic table.

The adept-at-picnics hostess uses colorful, partitioned plastic picnic dishes or sturdy, waterproofed discardable paper plates, also partitioned. They hold food safely and cut down table clutter by making it possible to put meat, vegetable, and salad attractively on one plate. And men, I think, are more comfortable with such a sturdy plate—plus a place to put it.

While the old stand-bys of hot dogs and hamburgers are perfectly accept-able at a picnic, guests are usually grateful, especially if it's a picnic supper, to be served something a little more substantial and partyish. There is noth-ing better, of course, if the budget permits, than charcoal-broiled steak and baked or fried potatoes (these with onions). Charcoal-broiled chicken is another favorite. Spareribs, southern style, may be prepared outdoors or in the kitchen. Like the chicken, they should be eaten "in the rough." Finger food including, of course, corn-on-the-cob is most enjoyable at picnics.

PICNICS AWAY FROM HOME

Automobile picnics—with the food eaten by the side of the road while the party is en route, or at some planned destination such as the beach—require special equipment. The confirmed picnicker usually invests in a hamper—the basket kind is light and long-lived—and equips it, or buys it equipped, with picnic "silver," plastic or aluminum plates and cups, a vacuum bottle or so, and a corkscrew and beer opener. Waterproofed paper bags for leftovers, paper napkins, and such are a wise precaution if there is no time to burn trash and then to see the fire well out.

THE ART OF PACKING A PICNIC HAMPER   It's an art to pack a picnic hamper with the kind of food that makes the picnickers glad they didn't stay home. Cold fried chicken or little cold veal or ham pies, English style, make delicious out-of-hand eating. Chicken or potato salad in a glass jar combine easily at the picnic spot with crisp lettuce which has been brought separately in a damp towel and like the other foods mentioned are, to my mind, more palatable than a much-traveled sandwich. There are all sorts of good things that can be put in picnic jugs and served piping hot hours later—spaghetti with mushrooms and chicken livers, for instance, or baked beans or even thick fish chowder.

If you are going to a distant picnic ground, it is preferable to take food in vacuum jugs and bottles rather than to light a fire, unless specific camp sites have been set up in safe places. Or, if there are really able woodsmen in your party who can manage a camp fire so it doesn't smoke up the guests and ruin the food, be sure every spark is extinguished with water or loose dirt before you leave. And obliterate all signs of your presence so others may enjoy the woods or beach as you have.

ALFRESCO MEALS

Eating outdoors in pleasant weather is a delightful and relaxing thing and, of course, needn't resemble a picnic in the least. Alfresco meals are merely less formal, even when they are served, with fewer courses and those substantial ones. A luncheon in the garden, with no picnic atmosphere at all, would be set out under the trees or on the terrace table on colorful mats or a luncheon cloth, with matching napkins. A first course of tomato juice or vegetable juice cocktail might be passed with crisp crackers before the guests are seated. Already arranged salads of chicken or lobster and tall glasses of iced tea could be in place before the guests take their places. The hostess or a servant clears this main course—perhaps onto a rolling tea table—and the dessert is served and passed by the hostess. Even where service is available, host and hostess function informally in serving their guests and servants are not kept constantly in attendance to spoil the rural effect.

CHAPTER THIRTY-SIX

HOSTS AND GUESTS

ARRIVALS AND DEPARTURES

The street door is opened to guests by butler, houseman, or maid, or by some designated member of the family. At a dinner party, for example, in a one-servant family it is unlikely that the servant can attend the door as well as serve and prepare the meal.

Whoever opens the door takes the guest's coat and hat and leads the way to the living room, stepping back to let him enter. The hostess excuses herself to any guests she may be with, rises, and comes forward to greet the guest, man or woman. The host comes forward, too, and both host and hostess shake hands with the newcomer. This same little ceremony is repeated when the guest departs.

Often there is an awkward pause in conversation when a new person is introduced into the group. Large-scale introductions in which the possibly already somewhat self-conscious stranger is introduced to many people all at once, and vice versa, should be avoided. Instead, when there are more than five or six present, introduce the new guests only to those in his immediate vicinity, after host or hostess have greeted him. From there on as he moves about he introduces himself to those he hasn't yet met, or someone to whom he's been talking takes him in hand and presents him to others he may find congenial.

SEEING THE GUEST OFF   Whether a servant or the host or some other member of family sees a guest to the door, the door is never closed until the guest is actually underway, on foot or by car. In apartment houses a servant or the host summons the elevator and waits until the guest has entered it before closing the apartment door. If a taxi is needed, host or servant phones the doorman as the guest prepares to go or asks the elevator operator to see that the guest is taken care of.

WHERE THERE IS NO HOST

A single woman entertaining alone without servants delegates the role of host to some male guest—a relative or close friend—at a party, or if it is a party of women and there is no servant to greet guests at the door a friend may be asked to do so, so that the hostess will not have to leave her guests every few minutes at a large party to go to the door. The friend, if he or she doesn't know the guest, introduces him or herself and leads the way to the living room. Or if many guests are arriving all at once, the person at the door indicates where coats are to be left and guests, when ready, find their own way to the living room and greet the hostess before joining any friends who may be present.

SHOULD A GUEST BE CALLED FOR?

If a guest is coming for a visit to the country and the hostess knows the time of his expected arrival but has said nothing about meeting the train or bus, then the guest is expected to get to the hostess' home by any available public transportation. The guest does not phone and ask to be met unless some transportation breakdown or great delay has occurred.

A guest, already resident in the country where transportation is necessarily by car, doesn't ask to be called for unless every conceivable way of getting himself to the hostess' house has failed. If transportation is really a difficulty, the matter should be mentioned at the time the invitation is tendered, and the hostess may then suggest that the guest be picked up, either by someone else coming by or by the hostess' own car. Or she has the opportunity of withdrawing the invitation under the circumstances. Certainly the guest who must be picked up and returned by the hostess must be very attractive indeed to justify the inconvenience, if it really is one.

ACTING HOST FOR A BACHELOR GIRL

The man, other than a relative, who is asked to take on some of the responsibilities of host at the home of an eligible woman may open the door to guests and see them off, fetch chairs, mix drinks, help serve, and clear dishes where there are no servants and, in general, help make the guests comfortable. If he does seem very much an intimate of the household in this way, there is, possibly, some speculation concerning his exact relationship to the hostess. To allay such speculation, a bachelor girl may designate more than one "acting host" from among her men friends. But if only one serves, he is careful to leave with the last guest if it is late in the evening. Even if the relationship between "host" and hostess is quite intimate, a gentleman must always go to elaborate lengths to avoid anything that might appear to be compromising. Even an announced engagement doesn't free him of this obligation.

HOW A GUEST TAKES LEAVE

It is never necessary to make elaborate and lengthy excuses for leaving a party. A reluctance to leave should always be shown by one's manner or words, of course, no matter what kind of time you've had. One may say, seeking out the hostess first, "I'm so sorry but I must leave now. It has been such a pleasant evening." If it is still a reasonable hour, your hostess will probably reply, "Oh, can't you stay a little longer? We hate to have you go!" If you really wish to stay after such urging, do so, but you are under no obligation to and may, instead, gently and at least seemingly reluctantly go on your way, again without meticulous explanations. Even if other guests seem entrenched for the night, your hostess may be silently blessing you for your good sense in leaving at a reasonable hour.

When a man guest wishes to leave early he excuses himself to the group in which he finds himself without stating his intention of leaving and, going quietly to the hostess, makes his farewell. If saying farewell to his busy host might break up the party, he may say, "Do say 'good night' to Fred for me" to his hostess. He then is shown out to the street door by a member of the staff or some member of the family. If he is an intimate of the family, he will probably see himself off. The hostess will go with him at least to the door of the living room.

An early-departing woman guest leaves in the same tactful fashion, except that the host or some male member of the family must be summoned by the hostess to see her to her car or to a taxi if there is no servant to take her in hand after the hostess has escorted her to the living room door.

PROBLEM GUESTS—DO'S AND DONT'S

THE SELF-INVITED GUEST How much responsibility does a hostess have towards a self-invited guest, one who drops in without warning at mealtime—other than at teatime, which is traditionally open house? Aside from exercising her usual courtesy, the hostess has no definite obligation toward such a guest. She may invite him to stay to the meal, or she may quite unembarrassedly not do so if it is inconvenient. If he or she shows no sign of going, she says, "I do hope you will excuse us. Our dinner is ready. We're busy this evening or I'd ask you to join us. But perhaps some other time . . ." If she gives in, time and time again, to these thoughtless people who arrive, I am sure by intent, at mealtime, she might as well open a boardinghouse. Of course, there is always the exception—the quite intimate friend who feels free to invite himself or herself occasionally. Life would be dull if all meetings were strictly by appointment.

TAKING STRANGERS TO YOUR FRIENDS' HOMES Another deplorable habit is that of taking your own guest—or more often several ill-assorted guests—to a neighbor's home in the evening or at cocktail time without even so much as an advance warning. Your guests may be charming people, but your neighbor may have a headache and wish fervently for an evening to himself in the bosom of his family. If you turn up with your crew and he is obviously without the slightest excuse to escape you, you have done a thoughtless thing. You probably won't even think to offer to leave after twenty minutes or so but will make yourself at home by his fireside and with his best scotch, no doubt, till far beyond what he hoped would be his bedtime.

Under such circumstances and with a frequent offender, it is certainly justified for the host or hostess to take aside the ringleader in this assault on their privacy and say something like this, "It was nice of you to bring the Snodgrasses over, but Joe (or Mary) has had a hard day today and there are a couple of things we want to go over this evening before I get him (or her) to bed. I know you understand and do let us *know* [hint!] when the Snodgrasses visit you again and perhaps we can plan a little something."

Try to train your friends to call you before dropping in, without or with friends. If they wish to bring friends, they should explain who they are. Many a difficult situation could be avoided if we could ward off uncongenial people in time.

Suppose Bill Adams next door calls (because you've trained him to do so) and says, "Say, Mary, my cousins, the Mears from Philadelphia, are here for the week end. I'm desperate. You know what they're like. May I bring them over and we could listen to some of your long-haired music. That will interest them." You can always say you're busy (no explanation required), and how about taking the Mears for a brisk walk or to the movies. Given advance notice, you are not required to receive anyone in your home you do not wish to see. If they arrive unannounced, you can dispose of them in any tactful way after twenty minutes or so by treating them as formal callers.

INVITING A GUEST TO ANOTHER'S PARTY   There is practically no excuse for breaking an engagement for a formal dinner party—not even the sudden arrival of your favorite aunt. Extra women, even attractive and relatively young ones, are anathema to the hostess who has slaved over getting a man for every woman invited to her dinner. But even a decrepit "extra" male may be very welcome to her, so give her a chance to reject or accept him, but, in either case, go yourself even if your guest has to spend the evening at your home playing cribbage. If he has any upbringing he knows all about the sacredness of such an engagement, arranged a good two weeks, usually, in advance.

It is less heinous to ask to have your house guest included in a cocktail party, a buffet meal, or an informal dinner, unless you have observed your hostess' home to be small and ill-staffed or running under her power alone. Sometimes just one extra guest, especially one with nothing in common with the others, can put a drag on the best-planned little party.

If, when you are invited, you know you will have a house guest, give the hostess a chance to invite you some other time, instead. Say, "Mrs. Mills, I'd like to so much, but that week Aunt Belle will be with me and I'm not at all sure she'd fit in." Any hostess with aplomb knows just what to do with that opening. Let's hope she means what she says, either way. There is little that makes a hostess more ill at ease than the presence of a guest she would have preferred not to include. And the guest suffers, too.

304

THE GUESTS WHO WON'T GO   We all know the sitters. They are the ones who want a nightcap after all sensible people have indicated a desire to call it a day. If it's Saturday night with no workday ahead for father, there's little hope. But there is one thing a host can do. He can rather pointedly not join them in that one more drink. This ought to make them drink up fast—but I don't guarantee it.

If the guests really are impervious to all delicate hints, such as the gathering up of used glasses and ash trays and the host's reluctance to put another log on the fire, the hostess can always say, "Joe's been working pretty hard lately and I (or the doctor) want(s) him to get plenty of sleep week ends. So let's send him to bed now." The inference being that she'll stick it out on the sofa if it takes all night.

There are inveterate talkers and serious drinkers who won't even notice old Joe's departure but, usually, this technique works. The one unbreakable rule is that the hostess must stay, even though the host, as breadwinner presumably, may be excused after a decent interval. The only exception is when the guests are house guests. If, as I have mentioned elsewhere, they are intimate friends, they may stay on in the living room, talking or listening to music or playing cards, after their hosts have retired at a relatively early hour. But they should not make so much noise as to keep the rest of the household awake. Other than intimate friends or relatives take the host's and hostess' lead concerning bedtime.

THE GUEST WITH A DRAGNET   We are all acquainted with the guest who no sooner arrives than he's on the telephone making contact with all his friends in the area. While this is permissible within reason, if the guest is from a distant point, his attention should be directed to his host and hostess and the plans they have for him. He may not invite other friends to call upon him at his host's home. He may tactfully mention that he knows someone in the vicinity, and if the hostess makes the suggestion herself that the friends be invited for some time during his stay, she may invite his friends herself, by phone. The guest may speak to them first, then introduce his hostess, who extends the invitation.

Under certain circumstances a guest may be asked to be excused to make a brief call in the neighborhood, but he should not involve his hosts in it nor ask for transportation. Host and hostess are on duty in their own home while entertaining and should not be asked to chauffeur their guests on various personal errands.

Again because a guest must focus his attention on his hosts, he may not ask any friends in the vicinity to invite him, with his hosts, to their home. An exception might be some one whom his hosts have expressed a real desire to meet or whose gardens they would greatly enjoy. A guest then might ask permission to call with his hosts. Or if his hosts are new in the neighborhood and are really anxious to meet neighbors with whom he is well acquainted, the guest could ask his friends to call upon him at his hosts', if he feels he will be promoting a mutually attractive future association. The thing to avoid is any suggestion that what his hosts have to offer in the way of entertainment is meager compared with what he could have at any number of nearby friends' and why not just join up with the friends and have a really good time?

PROBLEM DRINKERS   Many of us number among our friends a certain number of problem drinkers of whom we may be fond but who are difficult and often unpleasant to entertain at home. Where others stop after a social drink or two before dinner or in the evening, these people who have the alcohol habit to a dangerous degree go right on drinking. How far can a host or hostess go in an effort to control the situation?

In discussing this all too common problem with some of my wisest friends, I found that the best course seems to be to consider the problem drinker among one's guests right from the start. Bring into the living room or out onto the terrace before dinner a cocktail shaker with just enough for two drinks for everyone or pass a tray of highballs you have prepared at the bar or in the kitchen. Do not place bottles and soda so guests can mix their own. After dinner, again pass one highball or possibly two, then lock the liquor cabinet and say nothing whatsoever about the possibility of any more alcoholic refreshment. The moderate drinker rarely will take more than one highball after dinner, if any. The immoderate drinker must not be allowed to ruin the evening for everyone else.

This procedure I have outlined does not, of course, attempt in any way to reform the uncontrolled drinker, who has probably arrived sufficiently "fortified" so that even these rationed drinks take considerable effect.

Should others present voluntarily forget alcohol to save the problem drinker from himself? I think not. But at the same time no one should urge alcohol on someone who is trying to stay within reasonable limits.

The most agreeable solution, naturally, would be to omit from our guest list anyone who is a problem drinker. But, as this is rarely possible for business or family reasons, the only thing we can do, as hosts and hostesses, is to keep a sharp eye on the source of supply, keep track of each round, and lock up all alcohol, including wine and beer, after a reasonable amount has been dispensed.

THE OBNOXIOUS GUEST   The hostess with any experience avoids asking a guest who might well turn out to be a thorn in the side to other guests present. If it is necessary to entertain such a burr, she restricts others present to her immediate family, whose reactions she hopes she can control with signals. She does not take a chance of fitting such an unpredictable guest—if she knows about him or her—into an otherwise intelligently assembled group.

When it does happen that a hostess finds she has erred in asking someone highly and unamusingly contentious to a party, she and the host must spend the evening trying to keep the conversation away from explosive topics—explosive to the particular guest. If he gets under way, and others are growing angry or hurt, the host or hostess breaks in with, "Perhaps we'd better continue this some other time," and then attempts a diverting technique. Best of all is to give the arguer something to do. If you have a game room, get someone to take him on at table tennis. Or take him for a brisk tour of your grounds, ostensibly to show him something, but really to get him to work off his aggression physically. If this can't be done, get the troublemaker into a card game or get him to show off some specialty of his, magic or card tricks, piano playing or tap dancing. A man or woman who feels mean and aggressive in company can often be brought pleasantly into the group by being permitted to shine in some acceptable way. A clever hostess can say in the midst of a heated argument, "Joe, we can't all follow you in debate, but I know *I'm* dying to hear you beat out that boogie-woogie." He takes this much better than other methods of shutting him up, because, interrupted in the midst of an argument, he can save face by immediately doing something to attract favorable attention.

MAKING YOUR OVERNIGHT GUESTS FEEL AT HOME

City apartments and suburban homes are growing ever smaller. Perhaps in time there will be no such thing as the overnight guest. As it is now, it's a rare house that has a guest room. If the guest gets a room to himself at all, it is usually a room ordinarily devoted to sister Susie or to mother's sewing and mending. Never planned for a guest's comfort, it seems geared to send him on his way in despair first thing in the morning.

Wherever you tuck him or her, be sure your overnight or week-end guest has the following:

Night clothes, including bathrobe and slippers
Face towel, wash cloth, bath towel, soap
Razor, shaving cream, clean brush and comb
Adequate bedclothes—more than adequate if there's any doubt
A bed light for reading
Current magazines, a mystery, or any preferred bedtime reading
Facial tissues, cold cream, toothbrush and toothpaste
Enough pillows to permit reading in bed
Cigarettes and ash trays, though put your foot down about in-bed smoking
Hangers for clothes, including trouser-skirt hangers
A bedtime snack—offer it anyhow but a dish of fruit, a plate, knife, and a paper napkin add cheer on a bed table

THE WELL-APPOINTED GUEST ROOM   If you can set yourself up a permanent guest room and are not reduced to tucking the poor guest into the pull-out couch in the library or on the sun porch, here are some additional desirable attractions:

A full-length mirror with a make-up mirror, attached or separate, that shows the sides of the face

Free drawer space, enough of it so a week-end guest needn't dress from
his bags

Shoe racks and trees, hat boxes or stands, clothes brush, spot remover,
sewing kit

Manicure equipment

A well-equipped shoe-cleaning box

A plug-in radio

Writing equipment of all kinds, including post cards

Hamper or laundry bag

Drop-down ironing board and folding iron

Luggage rack and bed tray

Aspirin, milk of magnesia

"Don't disturb" sign

An electric hot pad or hot water bottle

Scrap basket

BEDS FOR GUESTS   Never assume that a couple who are your guests would
prefer twin beds to a double bed or vice versa. In planning a guest room from
scratch it is probably more sensible to choose twin beds, preferably the
kind with a double headboard so that couples used to the security of
sleeping in one bed won't feel isolated in twin guest beds. It is thoughtful,
if you have only a double bed for guests, to ask a couple if they would
prefer single sleeping arrangements—if you can shift things around and
provide them. Many couples, unused to sleeping in one bed, no matter how
commodious it may be, spend sleepless nights when so forced to share
a bed together.

TURNING DOWN BEDS   In a well-staffed household it is the duty of the chambermaid to turn down beds for the night. If a party is in progress and the
guest room or the master bedroom is to be used as a cloak room, it looks
better, I think, to delay the removal of the spread and the turning back of
the covers until after the party is over. Then, if the servants have retired,
the hostess should prepare the guest's bed for the night, although under
the circumstances a thoughtful guest will attend to the matter himself or
herself but, please, according to Hoyle.

A double bed which is to be occupied by one person has the spread
removed or neatly folded lengthwise at the foot of the bed if it is very light
and won't be a weight on the feet. If it is removed, it is not tossed on a
chair but is folded neatly to preserve its freshness and to keep the room
restfully in order. The top sheet, which should extend as much as twelve
inches over the tops of the blankets, is turned, with the blankets, in a
right angle with the center of the bed forming the perpendicular side of the
resulting triangle. This turn-back should be on the side from which the
guest is expected to enter the bed. If two people will occupy the double
bed, turn back the other side the same way, on the other side of the bed, so
that you now have two right-angled triangles with the center of the bed

a common side. This makes a neater effect than does the more usual method of simply turning back the coverings half way down the whole bed.

The pillows, which have been pressed into a roll under the bedspread, should be plumped up and resettled on the bed with the borders to the outside edges of the bed, seams toward the center. If a bolster has been used, it should be removed and sleeping pillows substituted. If you have a closet or chest in which to place unneeded bedding for the night, you will help create a restful atmosphere by getting the bolster out of sight. If you use a day bed, try to create space in drawers, closets, or built-in ends to house the box spread and the cushions, so that they may be kept out of sight during the time the bed is used for sleeping.

SHADES   When a bedroom is prepared for the night by a maid or someone else it is usual for shades or venetial blinds to be drawn sufficiently to shut out the morning sun if it strikes that side of the house. Many people have them drawn because the coming of daylight disturbs their sleep. However, this depends much on individual sleeping habits, and a new employee who is expected to prepare bedrooms for the night should be instructed on the family's preferences. Shades in guest rooms should be drawn when the bed is prepared for the night as a matter of course. Or if all the house shades or draperies are drawn at dusk, as is necessary in crowded communities, the guest room has its shades drawn then if it is to be occupied.

In the country where a house is off by itself and the neighbors and passers-by can't look into the windows, shades, blinds and even draperies and curtains are often dispensed with except in bedrooms and bathrooms. Awnings or sometimes venetian blinds, which ordinarily are kept tightly tied at the top of the window, keep out unwanted sun as necessary, but the modern tendency in decoration is to include the outdoors as much as possible in your interior decoration if the view is worth anything at all. It is certainly not necessary to curtain all your windows with the traditional glass curtains and draperies if in so doing you are shutting out a clear view of your garden and keeping out needed natural light. Wherever possible, instead, keep the whole window expanse free so the window may perform its purpose of admitting light and air. Of course, if a window faces a blank wall or overlooks a dump yard or alley, the more you shroud your windows, the better. Light, airy (never skimpy) organdy, marquisette, or other sheer glass curtains draped to frame rather than cover a window or group of windows can be very effective in the right surroundings, but never feel obliged to curtain your windows these days unless the curtains are really necessary. If a downstairs window does not need to be covered most of the time, it may not even need an ordinary shade or a venetian blind if it's on the north or east. Morning sun, even in the summer, is usually cheerful and desirable in a house in most climates.

THE LENGTH OF DRAPERIES AND CURTAINS   Sheer glass curtains used to cover a window usually look best when they end at the sill if they are to hang straight. If they are to be looped back under draperies they look better when they are the same length as the draperies. Draperies of chintz or heavier material used with or without glass curtains do not necessarily have to be floor-length at all but in an informal house may come just to the window sill and may or may not be looped back. It is convenient, if you can use enough material, to make heavy draperies really usable—so they can be pulled over windows. In cold climates such curtains can be real fuel savers when used this way at night. But hang them so they don't obscure light, if light is available, or the view, if it is pleasant.

Modern decorating practice even approves draperies that differ in length in the same room. For example, they might go to the floor on most windows with a little extra to drape gracefully on the rug, but at a big window-seated bay window they might come just to the sill. Or where a radiator's placement might make an ugly bulge under the draperies on one window, they might be kept short there, long elsewhere in the room. It is also quite acceptable to use draperies and, perhaps, glass curtains on some of the windows of a, perhaps, many-windowed room and glass curtains alone or no curtains or drapes at all on others in the same room if the use of them would give an overcurtained, fussy effect, especially where bold chintzes are used or where the view is so lovely it needs only the simplest framing.

GUEST HOUSES Guest houses vary in size and facilities all the way from the one-room pine shack to the five-room house complete with kitchen and oil burner.

Never put a guest off by himself in a primitively equipped guest house unless you are sure he has everything—such as extra blankets, drinking water and at least rudimentary toilet facilities—to make him relatively comfortable. Don't introduce a city-dweller to a guest house heated by a wood, kerosene, or coal stove without fully instructing him on the management of it. Otherwise he may asphyxiate himself with a coal stove, burn the house down with the wood one by building too hot a fire or allow a kerosene stove to smoke. Always equip your guest house with one or more fire extinguishers, anyhow, and show the guests their location and how to use them. Be sure to buy the right kind of extinguisher, discussing with the vendor just where and under what conditions it may have to be used.

A small guest house equipped with bowl, pitcher, and *pot de chambre* may, from time to time, be occupied by more than one guest, so provide whatever privacy is possible—a screen or a curtain for the lavatory section.

If wood fires are used—in fireplace or stove—remember it takes a little time in the morning to get them going, especially if a guest is not very familiar with such routines. An auxiliary heater such as a small kerosene stove or an electric heater will be convenient if it is placed close enough to the bed so that he can warm the room before he puts his feet to the floor.

Kerosene stoves need very careful handling and so do oil lamps. Never assume that a city guest knows the perils of them—he may not even know how to extinguish an oil lamp—or even how to light it. If he needs a night light in a guest house that has no electricity, it is safer to let him burn up the battery of a small flashlight than to suggest he leave a lamp or candle burning. Every guest house dependent on non-electrical lighting should, in any case, have a good, preferably large, flashlight for emergency use and to light the guest back and forth if the grounds aren't illuminated.

If you live far off in the country dependent on a volunteer fire department for protection, always warn city guests of any possible fire hazards, especially if they are to be quartered off by themselves. City-dwellers, used to flipping lighted cigarettes out of high windows (which they shouldn't risk, either) often do the same out of country house windows, never thinking of the peril or possible grass or woods fires or, at least, the disorder to gardens and walks their discarded butts bring.

IF YOU LIVE IN THE REAL COUNTRY Country living often has specific problems that should be promptly explained to guests—aside from the matter of transportation.

If your hot water supply is limited, for example, it is important to explain that to a week-end guest so he won't waste water by taking overly prolonged showers or letting the water run while shaving, for example, as he might in the city.

If you have a septic tank or cesspool, you need to explain that insolubles such as facial tissues and cotton should not be thrown into the toilet bowl but should be placed in the paper-bag-lined wastepaper basket you have provided in each bathroom. If the guest is going to help around the house during his or her stay, explain that with such plumbing facilities a minimum of such household aids as ammonia and chlorine must be put down the drains because they inhibit the necessary growth of bacteria in the tank, bacteria which in turn consume the waste and make it unnecessary to have a septic tank cleaned out more than every few years—and that's an expensive process.

If you are turning a country house (or even your city home) over to a guest or guests, even for so short a time as overnight, don't imagine he will know exactly what to do in the event of an emergency. Suppose there is a power failure, or the telephone wires go down in a storm, or the furnace goes out, or the oil burner breaks down? What if he needs a doctor or the police or the firemen? At all times, every home should have prominently placed near a telephone the following information to aid family, servants, and possible guests in-charge in case of an emergency.

INSTRUCTIONS IN CASE OF EMERGENCY *Fire:* Pick up phone. Say "I want to report a fire." (Or use the firehouse number, if given.) You will be connected with the nearest firehouse. Give your name, the exact address—floor and apartment number, if any—and the nature of the fire, general, localized, stove, or whatever the origin may be, if you can determine it. The fire department may be able to instruct you on what is to be done until they get there.

If there is no phone available, run to the nearest fire alarm (explain its location). Pull it and *stay* there, or have someone else do so, to give the firemen the address when they arrive.

Fire Extinguishers: Explain their location in your home and how to use and on what kind of fire to use specific ones.
Police: Pick up phone and say "I want the police." Speak to the desk sergeant.
Doctor: List your various doctors—pediatrician, if any, general practitioner, your dentist, and your veterinary if you have pets—with their addresses and telephone numbers.
Plumber:[1] List name and phone
Electrician:[1] List name and phone
Repair Man:[1] List name and phone
Laundry: List name, address, and phone
Dry Cleaners: List name, address, and phone
Tailor: List name, address, and phone
Beauty Parlor: List name, address, and phone
Household Employment Agency: List name, address, and phone
Drug Store: List name, address, and phone
Liquor Store: List name, address, and phone
Names of People to Call in an Emergency: Explain who they are
Husband's Business Address and Number
Wife's Business Address and Number if any
School Address and Number
Fuse Box: Give location in house and place where extra fuses are kept. At the box itself, have a diagram of what fuses serve what rooms and utilities. Instruct servants and members of the family on how to change fuses. It is frequently impossible—and certainly unnecessary—to summon an electrician to perform so simple a service.

THE WEEK-END GUEST

INVITATION AND REPLY FOR A WEEK-END VISIT In extending a week-end invitation it is very necessary to be specific about the date, the time you are expecting the people to arrive, and whether or not you will be able to meet them if that is necessary. In replying to a week-end invitation it's a good idea to mention both the time and date of your arrival so that no misunderstanding is possible.

August 3rd

Dear Nell,
    Will you, John, and the children spend the week-end of the 21st with us.

[1]If your city home has a superintendent he may be in charge of these matters. If so, list his name and apartment number.

There's a train that leaves town at 12:30 which we plan to meet. We'd be so happy to have you.

Love,
Molly

August 5

Dear Molly,
We'd love it. Count on us on the 12:30 on the 21st complete with children.
As ever,
Nell

Let's take the country hostess, in this case, who plans to have guests for the week end. Unless she runs the equivalent of a hotel, it is vital that she know long before the week-end just who is coming and when, so she may apportion her beds and plan the entertainment. If everyone says airily, "Oh, I'll call you Saturday morning," or "Let's see what the weather's like —maybe we'll be out," she may be left high and dry with one lonely bachelor and a large leg of lamb on her hands or she may be flooded with guests—because of the sunshine—and have to make one small chicken do for Sunday dinner. In the real country there is no such thing as a delicatessen open twenty-four hours a day and not everyone has a freezer, especially not people who, themselves, go to the country only on week ends. So, then, the first requisite of the guest is that he respond to his invitation promptly and permanently and be specific as to when he'll arrive. To accept and then later turn down an invitation to the country because of a cloudy sky is to belittle your hostess's ability to entertain you, no matter what the weather. Or it shows that you are more interested in the terrain than the people.

ARRIVAL AND DEPARTURE   The hostess herself should suggest the time of the guests' arrival and any guest or guests who can't make the train or bus indicated should at least offer to get themselves from the station to the hostess' house by cab. Otherwise the host, hostess, or, if he exists, the chauffeur may have to make countless trips to the station where one would have done. For the same reason, the hostess, who is herself run by the railroad's timetable if she's a country dweller, can certainly suggest the time of the guests' departure so that all can make the same train in something less than breakneck speed. Any guest who drives himself to the country week end and removes himself the same way is doubly blest if he offers to bring and return other guests from his own bailiwick.

GIFTS TO THE HOSTESS   If you are a frequent guest at a home, you are not expected to take a gift to the hostess each time, but on the first visit for a week end it is thoughtful to do so. And throughout the year, if you go often, take an occasional gift. This gift need never be elaborate or expensive. In fact, if it is obviously beyond your means it will embarrass everyone. Many women are pleased if you take some small gift to the children rather than to them. Children are so often pushed aside by all the grown-ups on week ends this little sop to their presence is helpful—maybe a box of lollipops, modeling clay, a game, or a soap bubble set.

Men, in particular, seem to be at a loss as to what constitutes a suitable gift to a week-end hostess. Taking her flowers is often like carrying coals to Newcastle, but if she has a collection of house plants she will always be pleased to have one more. African violets, geraniums, especially the rarer ones such as rose or lemon, begonias, that charming little plant, the pick-a-back (that should always be watered from the saucer beneath it, like all fuzzy-leafed ones), or a hydrangea are all welcome. An original gift in the early fall is a dozen or so tulip or narcissus bulbs. Go to a good seed store and buy the best varieties and be sure you know the color so she can plan her border accordingly. You may not know a daisy from a cactus, but you can get all kinds of agreeable information on gifts suitable for your country hostess, if you will describe her garden to the man at the florist shop, greenhouse or seed store. At the moment I can think of nothing nicer than a spring week-end guest arriving with a few pansy plants to set out in the annual border. They wouldn't cost as much as the usual fancy box of chocolates and would give pleasure for weeks to come. There are estates you might visit, however, that have their own greenhouses, and their own corps of gardeners might think you presumptuous if you turned up with a box or two of pansies and might let them wither, out of sheer spite, behind the carriage house.

Thinking up a gift for such a hostess, for one who seems to have every material thing, is always challenging. There's little use just buying something *expensive*. Anything you might think of she probably has. In such a case, I usually fall back on gourmet foods, things like imported English ginger beer, a smoked turkey, Stilton in port, or a brace of partridge. For some reason, people who have all the money in the world to buy any food they wish esteem such rare and relatively expensive specialties. A hostess may have a famous cellar but she will love you extra well if you turn up with a dusty bottle of fine champagne or one of Lacrima Christi.

In every well-appointed household things are always wearing out or getting broken. If you're an observant person, note well what a house needs if you are a frequent visitor. Perhaps the bar could stand a more efficient bottle opener or corkscrew—in fact, extra ones are received with joy in most homes. If the summer season is coming on, maybe a dozen or even half a dozen commodious beer glasses will anticipate eventual breakage of those in current use. Maybe the place could use a little bird house or a bird feeding station, some large ash trays, pretty aprons—who ever has enough?— a poultry shears (for the host's convenience in carving—especially duck), or some cocktail napkins. Gay books of matches in quantity, and with the covers initialed or not, fit in anywhere. Some of the things you can get in stationery departments make pleasant gifts—memo pads for the kitchen or the telephone stand, office-style pencil sharpeners (wonderful for a boy's room or a study), those lovely Swiss, floral post cards or thank-you notes, paints and crayons for the children or their art-yearning elders. Gifts of books are good if you are sure of your hostess's reading taste. The latest novel, chosen for its hot-off-the-griddle quality and nothing else, may just offend her sensibilities. A non-fiction book on some subject that interests you may bore her. If she's an enthusiastic cook, she can never get enough cookbooks. If she gardens, the newest gardening book will always interest her. If she loves music, a symphony she doesn't already own (know if her record changer is automatic or manual or takes L.P. records and get what's suitable) or some unusual records—European or South American imports— or new pressings of Caruso may be fine.

The storage problem in the average small or medium-sized house is always difficult. Think twice before you take your hostess something that will just clutter up her house and which, because of your frequent presence, she won't be able to tuck away or, in desperation, discard. Many of these white elephants grow in gift shoppes. Consider well before you buy gadgets or ornaments of any kind. Be careful in choosing pictures or actual furnishings for another's house—in fact, I wouldn't do it unless I had the hostess with me.

The bathroom suggests many suitable little gifts—big, fragrant cakes of bath soap to a friend you know very well, luxurious little guest cakes of soap (I remember some shaped like succulent strawberries that once delighted me in someone's powder room), bath salts and bath mitts, if they are not from the bargain counter in a drug store but are, too, in the luxury class, bath cologne, bubble bath, or a pair of hand-embroidered guest towels in a color that will blend with the bathroom's color scheme or in good, safe white linen.

If you are a guest in the country you can give yourself instead of a money-costing gift and be blessed for the thought. You can arrive with the news that you would like to rake the leaves, help build the rock garden, mow the lawn, or clear the brush—if you know any of these activities are on the calendar. In a help-short household you can offer to get a meal if your talents lie in that direction, paint a boat, take the children on a picnic, do odd jobs around the house, or wash the car—all this, of course, if you know your host and hostess well enough to take official notice that these things are in need of being done if someone just had the time to do them. I don't mean to suggest that you should imply in any way that the lawn's a mess, the meals terrible, the children underfoot, the house and its accouterments falling apart from lack of attention, all of which may be quite true.

Whenever you offer to do any such personal things, you must do so with great diplomacy, giving the idea, if possible, that the suggestion that the things should be done by someone came from the hostess or host themselves. For instance, if you're a woman—or one of those rare males who can get a good meal without wrecking the kitchen and calling for a score of helpers— say something like this, "I think you said Ida would be off Sunday afternoon. Let me get Sunday night's supper, won't you? I've found out where I can get some good clams for a chowder." If you want to put on an epicurean feast that will make more work for the hostess in the getting of ingredients she doesn't already have in the house, your offer may not be received in too grateful a spirit unless you fetch the missing things yourself.

WHAT CLOTHES TO TAKE The good guest arrives on time and knows, or quickly finds out, when he should leave. If he doesn't know the customs of the household and neighborhood he's visiting, he should find out in advance what wardrobe is expected of him. Find out if you are to dress for dinner, if you will need tennis, golf, riding, or swimming outfits. It is sometimes possible for a hostess to equip a guest for these various activities out of the family wardrobe and game closet, but she prefers to have you come equipped with your own things.

The size of the house and the bank account of your host are no indication at all of how his family entertains in the country. On some large estates the entertainment may be quite formal, with dinner jackets and dinner dresses the expected thing every evening except Sunday. On the other hand, taking a cue from the host and hostess, the guests may wear sport clothes all day and continue to wear them at dinner, fresh clothes preferred, of course, but still sport clothes—sweaters and skirts or slacks or flannel, wool, silk, gabardine, or cotton sport dresses for the women, slacks and sport jackets for the men. It is not "correct" to sit down at anyone's table in the evening in such informal attire, but in many, even elaborate, country homes it is an accepted and comfortable custom.

But how do you find out what to bring? You ask your hostess or your host by phone or by note when you accept the invitation, "Will I need my dinner jacket?" or, for a woman, "Should I bring a dinner gown? What are you planning for us—shall I bring along my tennis racket, my swimming or riding things?" When, for some reason, it isn't possible to ascertain these things in advance it is better to be safe than sorry—pack dinner clothes, take your tennis racket or your skis, as the case may be. Men should take a dark suit for dinner, if tuxedos aren't worn but slacks won't do. A woman should take at least one dinner dress for the week end and one or two non-sport-type dresses suitable for dinner. It is better to have your clothes a little on the formal side than overly casual. I am thinking of a suburban dinner party I once attended where the men wore dark suits and the women appropriate silk dresses. One male guest, a well-known "character" about town, came to the table without his coat and sporting bright red suspenders. His theatrically casual appearance may have been forgiven by his hostess, who knew, and was amused by, his idiosyncrasies, but to the others who didn't recognize his peculiar genius he was boorish.

RULES OF BEHAVIOR The rules for country and city week ends are about the same. You are prompt for meals, you let the hostess plan the activities and you fall in with those plans as well as you can. If she projects a long walk and you are a poor walker, she will understand if you prefer to stay home with your book. If you are the only guest, she will counter with a more suitable activity you can share with the family or maybe, mercifully, she'll take them on their brisk walk and leave you in peace.

I am an advocate of the English style of entertainment—I don't believe in the close organizing of guests' activities but like to let them entertain themselves in whatever manner that pleases them most. If they want to sit up listening to recordings with other congenial guests until four in the morning, I feel no compunction against going to bed myself and telling them to enjoy themselves without me. If they prefer to lie in hammocks, sleep late, or read in the garden instead of attending the hunt breakfast or the Yankee Doodle Fair, it's all right with me, so long as the entertainment, whatever it is, wasn't planned especially for them. If they turn up for meals on time or skip them entirely (if they don't request sustenance at odd hours—although they are free to raid the refrigerator), I am quite happy. But I realize that more rigid hostesses might be put out, to say the least, by a guest who felt so much at home as to say he wanted to sleep late or go to bed early. She couldn't leave him, with good conscience, to munch an apple during his sun bath while everyone else went blueberrying. She might even feel forced to stay home with him or make everyone else go sun-bathing to keep him company, which, alas, was not at all his idea.

There are people who can't stand having their leisure time organized to the nth degree—and I am one. And the hostess who works so hard at keeping every guest unremittingly busy having a good time is usually so tense and full of drive she spoils everyone's fun. On the other hand, someone has to be at the helm, to see that everyone is comfortable and that entertainment of some kind is at least available, to keep down domestic insurrections by getting people to the meal table on time to keep soufflés from falling and hollandaise from curdling. Why is it that, despite adequate warning of the approaching dinner hour, all men disappear "to wash their hands" the moment dinner is announced—while the soup and the ladies' heels cool?

GREETING SERVANTS   If you are a familiar of the house you are visiting you may say, "Good afternoon, Perkins," to the butler or houseman who opens the door and greet by name other servants you recognize if you wish. Housemen and butlers are usually addressed by their surnames, chauffeurs preferably by their surnames but often by their proper names (never nicknames). Maids and cooks are "Ella," "Katherine," or "Katie," whichever they prefer, although in some formal households the woman servants are called, English fashion, "Murphy," "Keene," etc. Chinese men servants are called by their last names, which, Chinese fashion, are always given first. A man who tells you his name is Fu Wang expects to be called Fu, his last name. Housekeepers are often dignified by being called "Mrs. Jackson" or "Miss Lang" by the staff and their employers, as is the cook, very often, in a house with a large staff. To the staff the butler is always "Mr. Perkins," for he is the household's executive officer. A chef is "Chef" or else is referred to by his surname alone. A French chef is usually "Monsieur Robert" (his first name).

PROFESSIONAL PEOPLE IN A HOUSEHOLD A registered or practical nurse, is, preferably, "Miss Cranford," never "Mildred," though sometimes "Nurse," especially if visitors don't know her name. A governess, tutor, or companion is "Miss Romano," "Mr. Robertson," "Mrs. Grayson," and a social secretary is accorded the same courtesy.

In many long-established country communities where a small household's help is drawn from neighboring homes, employees (more often in the "mother's helper" or housekeeper category than not) are frequently called "Mrs. Willis" rather than "Mary," because the calling of such neighbors "Mary" would encourage the use of the employer's first name by the employee or else make the employee feel herself to be in a class socially to which, in the eyes of the community, she does not belong.

Tenant farmers are "Mr.," though a hired hand or handy-man gardener may be "Peter." A full-time or visiting professional gardener is "Mr. Swenson," not, usually, "Ole."

HOW TO INFURIATE YOUR HOSTESS Bachelors, no matter how attractive, seem to bring with them on week ends somewhat heinous faults. While the things I'm about to discuss seem rather masculine failings, they are by no means entirely so. Many a non-housekeeping or just thoughtless girl can set a hostess' teeth on edge the same way. For instance:

Using cups, dishes, and decorative ornaments, not meant for ash trays, as ash receivers or throwing dead cigarettes in the dregs of tea, coffee, or cocktail. If the hostess hasn't put ash trays on the dinner table it is probable that she prefers to have you smoke after you leave the table, but if you feel very much at home you may ask for an ash tray—but please wait until dessert has been served, even if ash trays and cigarettes have been provided. Smoking throughout the meal is messy and an insult to the cuisine. It seems to indicate a background of lonely living. Good talk and good food should be comfort enough. When you do smoke at the table, ask permission of the hostess first unless she is smoking, too.

Leaning back on the rear legs of your chair. If your hostess owns antiques she hates you doubly for this. Do it, at the risk of your neck, with the kitchen chairs or garden ones, preferably those of cast iron, but sit on the others as they were meant to be sat on.

Putting your shod feet on the bed or on an upholstered chair. There are times, places, and rooms where feet may find some level other than the floor, but watch where you put them and let the house owners lead in any such informality.

Flicking ashes onto the floor, into vases, and into the fireplace, followed in the latter case by the butt, SANS DOUTE. If you don't see enough ash trays around, ask for one, don't improvise. The fireplace, lighted or not, that is turned into a garbage incinerator by the guests is not exactly an attractive hearthside.

Using the table silver for purposes other than that for which it was intended —drawing on the tablecloth, opening clams. Now that isn't at all farfetched. One of my best silver knives bears the ineradicable scars it received while being used as a clam opener by a guest who got a steamed clam that hadn't unhinged itself in the cooking process. I had it resilvered but the deep marks can't be removed.

Standing on the furniture to reach something. Every well-equipped household should have a kitchen step-stool. Your full weight on the loveseat springs (and by the way, don't sit on the arms of chairs no matter how tender your motives) may cause them to collapse in despair at such treatment.

Leaving the bathroom in a mess. Not every household has a chambermaid lying in wait for you to emerge from the bathroom so she can tidy up after you. In there somewhere, perhaps under the basin or in a cabinet, is a can of cleanser and a cloth or brush for cleaning the porcelain. Use it instead of leaving a childish ring in the bathtub. Men should clean the basin too of their shaving lather and bits of beard (run the soap under the water, too, to clean it of lather).

If you have been provided with a towel rack in the bathroom instead of in your room, use it, folding the bath towel first in three, lengthwise, then neatly over the rack. If the rest of the towels are folded in another manner, try to duplicate it. If you are using a guest hand towel, discard it in the hamper if one is available or refold it neatly and lay it somewhere to be discarded. Don't leave used towels and washcloths thrown around the bathroom or draped over the bathtub or basin. This makes the room unpleasant. Leave it as you found it or better (if you have been preceded by a guest who has never been told these things).

Disciplining the children. Never reprove a small child in front of its parents —let them do it if they deem it necessary. Child-raising methods are different now than those to which you were exposed yourself, very probably. If you don't like children, see your friends away from their home or wait until the children are somewhat grown before you week-end. Happy, healthy children must make a certain amount of NOISE. If you can't take it or the family can't isolate it, stay home.

Giving orders to servants or disrupting them in any manner. If you have been told that Mary will be glad to help you in any way, give her something to press, if it's unavoidable, but remember all guests make extra work for the household. If it's a one-maid household and you know how to press, ask to use the ironing board yourself, but never when the kitchen is in an uproar. A good rule is to keep out of the kitchen unless you've been invited in. Many a good cook has left in a huff because a guest has made a highhanded invasion of her sacred domain to show her how real tea *should* be made or to tell her, in a friendly way mind you, what's the matter with the coffee.

Some people really do things like that. Be even more polite to servants than to your friends. Rudeness to those who have much less than we have is the mark of a person who was not raised with privilege. The good people of this world are born with a kindly understanding of others' problems and, no matter how they prosper materially, treat everyone else, especially domestic employees, in a decent democratic manner without being either condescending or overfriendly. While servants want to be treated in the same way as any other kind of employee, they often resent the jocular, personal remarks sometimes made by guests—usually the male ones. Any servant will enjoy an appreciative word about his or her work, a tip for extra consideration, an occasional personal gift from a frequent visitor—never liquor—but cigarettes, candy, toilet water, playing cards, a mystery story, writing paper, and hosiery (from a woman only) are all good choices.

Strewing papers, turning down book leaves. If you are reading the papers—especially those monster Sunday papers—in the library, living room, on the lawn, sun porch, or in your bedroom, for goodness' sake keep them neat. When you finish, put all the sheets in order and fold them in the proper fashion. Place them in a magazine rack or on a table, don't leave them on a chair or on the floor. Even if no one else is going to read the papers after you—and how can you be sure of that?—it's easier to store them if they are nicely folded, and this keeps the room inviting. Many households, especially country and suburban ones, keep newspapers for housekeeping purposes or save them to aid various causes, such as the Boy Scouts, who put on wastepaper drives from time to time. Crumpled and torn paper is hard to handle this way. As for books, anyone who turns down a leaf to mark a place or bends a book back to make it stay open is out-and-out destructive. Let him read paper-bound books, but it is good to treat them decently, too, so others will enjoy them. They are easy to mail to friends or to pass on to the hospital wards or club rooms. Why destroy them?

Rising early. You don't come on the hearty ones so much any more, somehow, but sometimes a week-end houseful gets an early riser who is up and out for a walk before the family knows Sunday has come around. Let him go quietly, that's all, I say.

The breakfaster-in-pajamas. If the family breakfasts week-end mornings in dressing gowns, pajamas, nightgowns, you are free to do so too. But don't take the informality so much to heart that you fail to comb your hair, wash your face and teeth, and generally make yourself attractive. No woman guest should appear too *negligée* or with her hair unarranged (neat, newly braided pigtails are all right, if you're the type, or a ribbon around your hair) and her face unmade-up, if she's in the habit of using make-up—and most of us are. Be sure your dressing gowns or negligees are fit for public appearances. Otherwise get dressed. Don't stay in this temporary costume a minute longer than the others in the group. But it is better to come to the breakfast table so attired, but freshly groomed, than to keep everyone else awaiting breakfast, if you haven't been called in time. But ask permission first. If you prefer to dress fully or if you should because the others have, ask them not to wait breakfast for you. Remember you may be interfering with the routine of the household if you delay getting to the table too long.

HUNGER PAINS The week-end guest sometimes is weak from hunger between meals, or so it seems. Fruit, nuts, candy left around in containers are meant to assuage such hunger pains, and it is not necessary to ask the hostess's permission before taking them. Most hostesses attempt to overfeed the guests, but sometimes it's the schedule of meals and the guests' own eating habits that make it hard to get from meal to meal without someone wanting a snack. If you can't bear more than fruit juice and coffee for breakfast on Sunday—or any other day—it will be difficult to get through until dinnertime at night in a two-meals-on-Sunday house, quite a comfortable arrangement for the others who have had a well-rounded late Sunday breakfast. In this case, ask for a sandwich and milk to tide you over when hunger hits you. Offer to make it yourself, as Sunday schedules, even in fully staffed households, are sometimes sketchy. Whatever you do, clean up after you and make as little public hue and cry about it as possible. If something to eat or drink before bedtime is your usual habit, ask for it quietly, if it isn't offered—maybe others will be delighted you brought up the matter. There is little more pleasant than an informal, friendly snack in the kitchen late at night with interested excursions into the refrigerator. But, again, clean up afterward. The servant—or the hostess—who's finished the last dish and put it away won't want to face a pile of cups and saucers, dishes and silver on the early morning after.

HOW CAN YOU HELP? Whether or not you lift a hand around your host's home while his guest depends very much on the staffing of the place and the personality of the hostess. There are fastidious housekeepers who would rather have you sit with your hands folded than see you stack their fine Wedgwood china and waltz with it to the kitchen when you're the type who puts it, scraps and all, into the dishwater. I am one. There are hostesses who are (I think rightly) distressed when all their guests rise as one man—or woman—and start clearing the table, just as everything was going so well, conversationally. A good hostess wants the mechanics of meal-getting and serving to go as smoothly as possible. If you want to help—if she's obviously bogged down—fall in with her system. She's captain of the ship. Never mind how you've always washed the dishes. Maybe you never had anything like these dishes and this crystal to wash, and it does make a difference.

If you do offer to do the dishes in a household without help, your hostess assumes you will do it in proper fashion. She may even leave you completely alone with the task—often a grave error, considering possible breakage and inferior washing where tyros or untrained housekeepers are concerned. But there is a right way, and no housekeeper, no matter how careless she may be herself, will be offended if you treat her dishes with this respect:

HOW TO WASH DISHES If you are using an electric dishwasher—God bless the inventor—get proper instruction from whoever knows how to operate the particular model you're to use. Then do your brief work and be grateful.

For the usual and much disliked hand dishwashing there is only one correct, really sanitary method. Scrape the plate scraps into a garbage can or onto several folds of newspaper (which you later roll up and discard) or give the contents to the pets, if so instructed. Save all food from the serving plates, putting it whenever possible into covered icebox dishes. Don't store it in the plate in which it was served unless the dish is pyrex or pottery, and then only if there is enough food left over to make the use of so much storage space sensible. Save cold coffee and leftovers from butter plates for cooking use if the hostess approves. Clean bits of butter can go in an icebox dish or in a piece of wax paper.

If you have only one sink to work with, rinse each dish in running hot water, then stack before beginning the real washing. Remove any garbage from the sink, clean the porcelain if it has absorbed grease from the rinsing. Now run in the hottest water your hands can stand (maybe there are rubber gloves to be had) with enough soap powder—a detergent is ideal—to do a good cleaning job. Never put pots, pans, glasses, silver, and dishes in together! Do the dishes first, rinsing each as it emerges. Place them in the dish rack to dry by themselves. This is really more sanitary than towel drying, according to the American Medical Association, in case anyone is unduly critical. You will need to dry the silver well, otherwise it will spot or rust. Don't put plastic-handled knives, forks, and spoons into the water. Wash just the metal part with dishcloth or dish mop. Otherwise the handles will eventually come off.

Unless there is some limitation on the hot water—and if it is heated by a separate heating unit there may be—wash the glassware in fresh, clean hot water with plenty of soap or detergents, then rinse in hot water. Washing it in with the dishes will often streak glassware, and no amount of rubbing with the towel will improve the situation. It is better to use a detergent for glassware, especially, and let it dry itself. This prevents lint sticking to the glass. To test your efficiency, hold the glass up to the light. You can see that running glasses under a stream of cold water, bachelor-girl-and-boy fashion, isn't acceptable. Who wants to encounter a lipsticked rim?

A special blight on the guest who offers "to do the dishes," then leaves the greasy pots and pans for the hostess. Pots are washed last, first rinsed of any food that may be sticking to them. They should be scoured inside and out wherever necessary. A good dishwasher leaves the bottom of the pot as shining as its sides. Pots should be rinsed and dried, preferably over a low flame, or with paper toweling, not with the best glass toweling. They should be put away, if possible, nesting if they are meant to nest, but it is better to leave them on the top of a stove or cabinet than to tuck them in

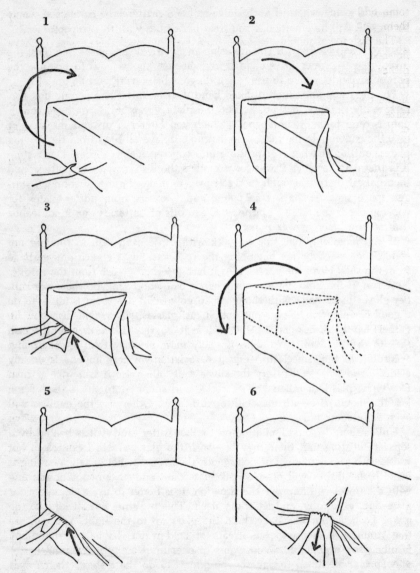

MAKING A BED, *placing the under sheet*   1. Grasp sheet as shown, raise. 2. Let fall on top of mattress. 3. Tuck in hanging part of sheet smoothly. 4. Drop corner of sheet. 5. Tuck under, being sure to catch fold coming down over head of mattress. 6. With fists uppermost, hands together, pull diagonally and tuck under, holding onto roll as far as it will go. Repeat this along entire length of bed.

some odd place where the cook can't find them at hand when she wants them.

The dish towel should be placed over the draining dishes, when you have finished, to keep dust from settling on them. If you know where to put the dishes and silver when they are dry, put them away, exactly as you found them, if your hostess has an orderly cupboard, not stacked any old way. If the cups have hangers, put them on all facing in one direction to minimize breakage. In putting away kitchen cutlery, be sure it's perfectly dry or it will spot or rust. Leave the kitchen like the laboratory it should be—drawers and cupboards closed, dishcloth hung on a rack or neatly folded over the sink, broiler pan back in the oven, all counters wiped up (with the dishcloth or a sponge, not the dish towel!), the stove shining and with all the burners turned off. A really good housekeeper sweeps the kitchen after each main meal to repel rodents and just to be neat and clean. Sweepings should go into the trash can, not out the window or into the yard.

MAKING BEDS   If you're a guest it's better to leave your bed strictly alone unless you are perfectly sure you can make it up at least the way you found it. If you are leaving before the next bedtime, just throw the covers back to air the bed, or, if your hostess would really appreciate a hand, ask for fresh linen for the bed and make the bed as nicely as possible.

Any man with military training knows how to miter sheets, even if he pretends to have forgotten. There are people who loathe having their sheets tucked in and prefer to tear apart any bed so made before trying to settle down for the night. But for the most part, sheets mitered at the corners, all the way around for the bottom sheet if it's big enough, and at the bottom of the top sheet make the best-made bed. Look at the hems of a sheet before putting it on. The bottom sheet should be placed with the hemmed side next to the mattress. The top sheet should be the reverse so that when the top of the sheet is folded over the blankets—to keep them from scratching, of course—the smooth side of the sheet will show. Your hostess will grit her teeth if you make up a bed with an initialed top sheet and turn down the sheet so the initial is on the wrong side—now what's the use of an initial that can't be seen in all its glory?

1. Center top sheet lengthwise. Allow for folding back over blanket. Leave loose at foot. 2. Place blankets on bed lengthwise at shoulder height. Allow blanket to hang over foot of bed. 3. Provide toe space by making a box pleat at foot of bed, upper sheet and blankets together. 4. Tuck sheet and blankets loosely under mattress at foot of bed. Retain pleat. Make loose corners. (Pleats provide space for toes.)

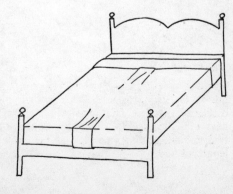

Pillows should be placed so that the hems of the slips are on the outside. To make a bolsterlike effect with the pillows, push them tightly against the headboard, put the bedspread on the bed, turn down a top fold just at the edge of the pillows, tuck this folded edge under the tightly placed pillows, then fold the edge of the spread back over them, tucking the fold in to give an unwrinkled appearance. The bedspread should hang evenly on the sides and on a bed without a footboard is usually best left hanging loose to cover the springs. The quilt, if any, is either put away for the day or folded attractively at the foot of the bed. One way to do it is to fold it in half, end to end, place it on the bed, then indent the folded side so the quilt looks like half a bow knot. Don't ever put a quilt under the bedspread—that gives a lumpy, unmade look to the bed.

DUTIES OF THE OVERNIGHT GUEST IN THE CITY

Most city-dwellers live in apartments. And in apartments the guest room is becoming archaic. The living room, the library, the dining room, or a child's room must serve for the occasional overnight guest in the usual city home. Because of this lack of privacy, overnight guests in town are usually just that. Week ends are usually too difficult for all concerned, and longer stays an impossible strain on the household. An overnight guest in a city apartment should leave as promptly as possible, be as neat as if he were operating from a footlocker aboard a naval transport, observe a strict meal-and-shower schedule and prompt rising and retiring hours compatible with the family's living.

He should not treat the apartment-dwelling friends as if they were running a hotel for his convenience, open all night and with latchkey freedom. He is a guest even on a daybed, and if he merely wants the convenience of a stop-over in town, without any social obligations involved, the real place for him is a hotel.

4
HOUSEHOLD MANAGEMENT

Furnishings in the Established Household 326

Setting the Table 336

Special Problems of Service 351

Employer-Servant Relations 358

Dress and Duties of the Household Staff 370

Gracious Living Without Servants 377

Financing the Family 387

HOUSEHOLD MANAGEMENT

This section is written mainly from the point of view of most of us. The day of the complete staff, of formal entertainment, except in a limited way, is about done. The most exclusive men's tailors in the country say they have no ready-made liveries any more because there are no longer customers to support the department. The few establishments with permanent men servants must have liveries made to order.

This is the day of the electric dishwasher, the storage wall, the dining ell, the deep freeze, buffet meals, day workers, sitters, the automatic washing machine, the mangle, and nursery school instead of Nanny.

Actual living space has become so expensive and difficult to obtain, that non-essentials in household furnishings are automatically ruled out in many a home. There are usually no attics, no pantries, and often no cellars for storage in the ranch houses mushrooming all over the country. The one-level floor plan itself is designed to make it easier for a woman to do the housework without a servant. All this simplifies our living and, necessarily, our entertaining. It often means that, even if we can afford help, we have no room for a servant to live in. Women with no previous domestic talents have found it necessary to develop at least the fundamental ones.

In many ways it's better, but whether we like it or not we can never go back. We must master the new ways, the new mores, and the new skills. I have tried in this section to show how this can be done most effectively.

CHAPTER THIRTY-SEVEN

FURNISHINGS IN THE ESTABLISHED HOUSEHOLD

FURNITURE

Many a fine and helpful book has been written on the subject of house furnishings. Many magazines deal well and extensively with the subject. If your taste is unformed, perhaps because you've never given the matter thought, you can and should learn from these sources. But best of all, move with your eyes and senses alert through the loveliest homes you can find. You might start with a trip to Charlottesville, Virginia, where Jefferson's majestic "Monticello" will prove an inspiration and delight. Drink in the colors of the walls, of the handmade brick, of the furniture patined by time. Enjoy the surprising freshness and frugality of the muslin curtains, the depth of the boxwood, the body to the silver. Then go to Williamsburg, to Mount Vernon, to New York City's Metropolitan Museum of Art, and Museum of Modern Art, to antique shops, to modern galleries, to the great silversmiths and glassmakers, to the beautiful homes in your own community that may be opened each year to the public through co-operation with the garden clubs.

Keep a scrapbook, collect swatches of material and samples of color. Develop your own taste from what pleases you in all this. Then build your own home around what you have learned with the help, if you wish, of a decorator. But never let a professional superimpose his taste on yours. You will never be comfortable in your surroundings if you don't understand them and if, no matter how perfectly conceived from a decorating standpoint, they don't seem in the least like you.

Never decorate in haste, trying to complete the whole picture within a four-wall frame at once. Homes grow from the outside in. We need to live in them a little and in relation to what belongings we have with which to start, before we know what is right for the house and for us.

Do not be misled by those who preach the necessity of "period." Nothing, to my mind, is duller than a room, modern or ancient in genesis, all keyed to one static note. Good modern rooms come to life with old glass, a piece or so of antique furniture, an old painting, a time-honored rug, a brass from ancient Syria or Ceylon. A room graced by antiques will be more comfortable for its present-day roomy sofa and its freedom from froufrou.

Whatever you do, remember that some things must be of as recent vintage as your purse will allow—sofas, beds (which if old may be lengthened, equipped with box springs and innerspring mattresses), kitchen and laundry equipment. The living room must have one or more really comfortable chairs, preferably with some equipment, such as hassock, that permits elevation of the feet. The sofa should be as big as the space will allow and have adjacent a coffee table for ash trays, cigarettes, drinks, a book or so, and flowers or ornaments. The furniture should be grouped with a main center of interest—the fireplace or the view—and subsidiary groups for conversations among two or three, so that they can join, without moving, conversation in the main group governed by the placement of the sofa or sofas.

In good decoration a room should never look too new. Do not fuss if you can't have every piece of furniture freshly reupholstered at one time. It will seem more comfortable for an occasional bit of genteel shabbiness.

Do not be misled by the vagaries of fashion in decorating. A good room can remain exactly as it began for many, many years, with occasional necessary refurbishing. To be a good, pleasant, and satisfying room, a living room should have shades or variations of each primary color—red, yellow, and blue. Our eyes unconsciously seek these colors. Of course they include all the greens, shades of rose, orange, gold, and dozens of possible combinations. Beware the startling and work up from the rug or the floor color.

The most livable rooms reflect the interests and hobbies of the owners. A friend of mine, proud possessor of a Sutton Place brownstone, has a pleasant masculine study whose chief decorative motif is a large airplane propeller over the Victorian marble fireplace. My friend is an aviation engineer and to him a propeller is just as beautiful, I suppose, as one of his Manets. At any rate, it looks right in the room because it expresses *his* interest, not one some decorator has thrust upon him.

Most important, our surroundings should take into consideration our physical appearance. The possessor of a six-foot-two, big-boned husband is plain silly to expect him to sleep comfortably in a spool bed she hopefully imagines is big enough for two. The small couple make themselves smaller still—if it matters—by surrounding themselves with massive furniture in large, open rooms with high ceilings. The plump family spills over on the seats of gilt salon chairs and looks even plumper in rococo rooms.

Colors are most important of all. Never try to live with a color you don't like and couldn't wear. This goes for men, too, who are notoriously uneasy in juxtaposition to pastel, fussy-feminine *décor*.

LINENS

Bed linen, special bedroom linen such as handkerchief and lingerie cases, tray sets, and bathroom linens are marked with the married initials of the mistress of the house. In modern usage these are her first initial, the initial of her maiden name, and the initial of her married name. Helen Fulton Jameson has initials HFJ. No longer is the old usage popular whereby her initials would be HMJ, for Helen May, her baptismal names, Jameson.

These personal, feminine initials may be as simple or as elaborate as a woman may wish. But as good household linens may last a decade or more, it is well to remember that simple things hold up best, fashionwise.

Downstairs linens, except those for lavatories, are usually marked in the same way silver and glass are when they are acquired during the course of the marriage—with the initials of both husband and wife in a monogram, in decorated lettering or in a simple triangle, or with a crest or crest and motto for small pieces and coats of arms or larger, decorative monograms for large pieces (see "Silver Marking").

Four complete linen changes for each bed and four complete towel sets for each bathroom are usually adequate.

ADDITIONAL IDENTIFYING MARKS For linens and in fact everything sent out to commercial laundries it is wise to have those excellent little name tapes sewn or ironed inconspicuously onto the foot of sheets, on the undersides of tablecloths at the hem, and on anything else where such marking can be done without being seen by the user. This can't very well be done on dinner napkins, which is sad. I have two damask sets, each with twelve napkins, that are unusable because a laundry returned them with assorted damask napkins belonging to other customers. No laundry is going to compare the design in a damask napkin, it seems, and most feel you are fortunate to get back twelve napkins of any design. Chaos reigns in many a linen closet as a result. The only solution is to have such expensive items done at home, if at all possible.

CHECKING LAUNDRY Commercially done laundry should be checked against the duplicate list as soon as it is unpacked—not only for the number and condition of pieces but for identification of the articles sent. A laundry may return the correct number of sheets, say, eight, but they may well be someone else's well-worn ones rather than the fine percale initialed ones you sent out. It is well not to settle laundry bills until each bundle is satisfactorily checked, and it is imperative for the person making out the laundry list to be detailed in her listing—and to make a carefully dated duplicate. Instead of writing "6 dish towels," she should write "6 red plaid linen dish towels." Instead of "14 shirts," "14 shirts, size (take this from neckband)," and for further identification she should list the color and the manufacturer of each. The manufacturer's name is also in the neckband.

NURSERY LINENS Linens for the nursery should be simple and sturdy. Coarser muslin or percale for sheets—eight per bed for the wetting ages—and terry cloth accessories stand up under the necessary heavy laundering. Cotton knit bottom sheets—four to six—with elasticized corners that fit snugly over mattresses are excellent for cribs and youth beds, for they stay in place and, of course, require no ironing. Children's towels and washcloths—four of each, minimum per child—are best tape-marked, but they may be marked with a single machine- or hand-embroidered initial (that of their surname) or with a first name, "Stephen," or a nickname, "Patty," sometimes amusingly machine-stitched in bright colored script.

Children should never be surrounded with ultrafancy bedroom accessories that can't take good, hard wear. I prefer simple white muslin curtains, rickrack trimmed, cottage style, to starched organdy, dimity, or dotted swiss. Denim, ticking, or candlewick bedspreads are better than those of delicate fabrics. As much as possible should be washable.

TABLE LINENS What kind of linens you regularly need depends very much on the living quarters you occupy and the life you lead. If your "dining room" is a tiny foyer of a small city apartment, dining must, of necessity, always be informal. Table mats are the best solution here—four or five sets, including one or two for breakfast, should be enough. A gay linen cloth or so will ring an occasional change. If you own a large house, beautiful linens, silver, glassware, and china, you may still live informally because of your inability to get the servants who understand formal entertaining or even those willing to be instructed in it. The trend is toward more and more relaxed living. It is both thrust upon us and, in most cases, gratefully accepted. Formal entertaining of all kinds is either on the wane or already gone and, like the value of the nickel, I don't see how it ever can return.

Modern hostesses set their dinner tables wherever it's convenient or particularly appealing. On a cold winter night a round table drawn up before the fire in the living room or library may seem ideal. In summer, dinner on a terrace, even one opening off a bedroom would seem inviting. Some people have all their summer, spring, and early fall meals on a porch or, weather permitting, fully out of doors. One of my friends has made a lovely, green dining place beside his dammed-up river. Built-in storage space houses simple dishes, glassware, and "silver." An old-fashioned ice box functions nicely at hand. The tablecloth is checked cotton or shiny green oilcloth. The whole family trails down, even for breakfast. The dining room in their little remodeled farm house is forgotten except on rainy days.

In one of the largest town houses I know the hostess is famous for entertaining in her huge, Victorian kitchen. On Sunday she dismisses her servants, dons an apron, and goes to work on one of her delicious specialties —spaghetti with clam sauce, chicken cacciatore, New England baked beans and ham with brown bread or thick, sizzling steaks with tender, pan-steamed onions, and bursting, hot baked potatoes. She could entertain in her dining room with all the éclat in the world, and she has the staff with which to do it. But everyone loves her kitchen fests. And she really enjoys herself.

Actually, variety in the service of meals makes them interesting. I would not care to dine formally every night—nor buffet-style every night, either. Dinner always served on the same china, with the same candlesticks or candelabra on the table, the same style of table covering, shows lack of imagination.

FORMAL TABLE LINENS Truly formal dinners require full-sized white cloths, that is, large enough to provide a generous overhang on the table for which they are intended. Damask ones should have self-color woven designs or simple bands. Large dinner napkins (approximately twenty-four inches square) should be hand-hemmed and match the cloths. Cream damask is also acceptable, but the delicate pastel colors are considered less than formal. Damask cloths are placed over silence cloths, felt mats that fit the table exactly. Delicate linen cloths with embroidery and lace are placed over a bare table. Large dinner napkins to match such cloths should be very simple. All machine-made lace should be rigidly avoided.

Finger bowl doilies are not necessary even at the most formal dinner, but if they are used they should be of fine linen or real lace. Paper ones are not correct.

Doilies in lace or embroidered linen are also needed for the bread tray used for dinner rolls, melba toast, cheese sticks, crackers—all dry finger foods—and for the plate on which petits fours are served. Except at formal meals these are usually paper.

INFORMAL TABLE LINENS As a ménage develops it will become more and more apparent that the most useful pieces of table linen are place mats. These come in every imaginable material and in every possible color. They may be tiny straw disks to fit under a dinner plate and not be seen, so that the effect is that of a gleaming bare table. Or they may be generous rectangles of self-fringed linen. If it seems likely that no use will ever be found for the two damask banquet cloths that were among the wedding presents, the clever woman will either sell them or convert them into four dinner cloths, two or three of which she may have dyed a pleasant dark color, such as ruby red or amethyst. Her napkins may remain white or be dyed to match or contrast. Out will go the table runners and the dresser covers, the embroidered rounds meant for occasional tables and only Heaven knows for what else. Off to the Thrift Shop will go the faded linens that seemed worthy of saving but are never quite presentable enough to put on the table, and they might well be accompanied by the giftee nightgown cases, the cross-stitched napkin cases.

CHINA

FORMAL CHINA China for the formal dinner is fine bone china or porcelain, never earthenware. Occasionally it is fine glass, antique or modern. One famous collector of early American glass has a complete set of Diamond Point, which, of course, could appear proudly on the most formal table.

But even on a formal table with fine china it is not necessary, nor even usually very attractive, to have a matching set turn up course after course. The effect may be varied with, say, antique oyster plates in iridescent oyster white on service plates of blue and white Copeland, followed by the fish course on lovely, fish-decorated Limoges. The dinner plates could be of the set, if one owns one, in any of the old or modern fine chinas from Lowestoft to American Lenox, perhaps in the gold and white wheat pattern. The salad course for formal dinner is always on a flat plate, perhaps on a beautiful clear or frosted glass in color, never in individual bowls, and is always passed on a flat serving dish, with or without cheese and crackers. In the Victorian era the cheese tray was passed between the dessert and demitasse.

The main thing to remember, at either a formal meal or an informal one, is that all the place plates at a single course must match. Serving dishes and butter plates may be silver or of a fine blending china or glass, but need not match the set. Of course, butter plates are not used at the most formal kind of dinner.

INFORMAL CHINA Into this class falls almost any receptacle for food placed on the table. It includes sea shells to hold deviled dishes or to be used as out-door ash trays, the Mexican glass salad plates, pottery ramekins and those in fine china, the everyday dinner plates (and one should have enough so that the same plates don't turn up night after night). In this group are the pitchers in pottery, china, glass, brass, copper, pewter, and silver that are part and parcel of every household. Serving dishes that come from stove to table are informal but may appear without a blush at the nicest company dinner. Wooden salad bowls, large and individual, belong here, along with wooden pepper grinders, nutmeg graters, salt grinders. Platters may be in wide, wide variety from great round porcelain or pottery wall hangings occasionally put to use, to wooden cheese trays and the tole trays which often can double as platters.

Butter plates are informal and come in dozens of materials from pewter and wood to ruby or amethyst glass. It is more attractive if they don't match a dinner or luncheon set.

GLASSWARE

FINE GLASSWARE Of all a young bride's household possessions the most fragile is the fine glassware and, though she is at first perhaps unaware of the fact, very expensive to replace. After a few sad experiences she learns to use it only when she herself is willing to wash it and put it away in its special storage section. A growing family makes so many demands upon an inelastic budget that somehow the broken sets seldom get filled out again. Therefore, fine glass, of all luxury furnishings, must be given the most special handling.

Perforated rubber mats in sinks help cut down breakage and chipping. Pliofilm covers over glassware help avoid extra washing, and washing of this glass should be done by hand. In hard water a detergent and perhaps a water softener in addition lessen the need for dangerously hot water. Glass must really sparkle. It should be rinsed in fairly hot water, hot enough so that the glass will dry without being toweled. When necessary, polishing may be done with a linen glass towel.

It is frustrating indeed to try to set a table for guests only to find that there is one too few really good glasses or that the best wine goblets have chipped rims here and there. By carefully husbanding her best glass, the wise hostess sees to it that she has at all times eight or more matching glasses for water and eight or more for one or two wines. A dozen or more really good cocktail glasses and eight nice sherries should be kept apart from the regular glass supply of the household. Twelve good highball glasses should be reserved for those special occasions when the hostess can't afford even to *feel* apologetic about such minor matters. Fine liqueur glasses are cobweb-frail and should be stored well away from casual gropers in the bar shelves.

Wisest of all is the careful hostess' habit of washing her party glasses herself after a late party, not leaving them to be done—probably carelessly—with the breakfast dishes.

The young homemaker who did not receive the kind of fine glass for which she yearns as her home takes shape, yet is appalled by the price of new glass, should patronize the auctions, treading carefully at first to learn what quality is and what the glass she sees would bring when new. The contents of estates out of town are more likely to yield what she wants than the auction rooms in town.

GLASSWARE FOR EVERYDAY USE   The established household usually includes children, and children mean breakage of glassware. Open-stock, inexpensive glass should be used for children's meals. Plastic and other unbreakable wares are attractive and sensible.

Along about the fifth year of marriage wedding glassware is often about gone, sad to state, except for the little-used fine glass such as champagne glasses, although these are particularly short-lived because of their delicacy. Glasses used in the summer for beer and for iced drinks have a very high mortality. They fall onto stone floors, are tipped over on the terrace, fall from ill-balanced trays. Most people soon forget their pride and replace them with inexpensive but attractive glass, with the realization that replacement will be necessary again the following season, anyway. Very practical for outdoor use, of course, are metal glasses—hammered or spun aluminum for example. They keep drinks very cold and are indestructible.

It is wise to put on a high shelf for special occasions whatever may be left of the fine cocktail glasses and replace them with heavier, open-stock ones in a pleasant pattern or in a simple, plain glass. At cocktail parties few give any notice to the glass in which the drink is served so long as it is the right shape and size. To be avoided, however, are inexpensive "hand-painted" glasses and overdecorated ones in somewhat doubtful taste.

In making replacements it is well to remember that blown "bubble" glass, interestingly irregular, cannot stand either rough handling or really hot water. It must be washed by hand, not put in the dishwasher. Pretty and practical are some of the plates, sauce dishes, sugars and creamers in reproductions of cut and pressed glass and other items in clear and colored glass which abound in the five-and-ten and in department stores.

One of my own hobbies is old glass and china, and I find it very rewarding to discover the things I love in antique shops and even in secondhand shops. A little study on how to recognize old glass and china will be very worth while. Ruth Webb Lee's *Handbook of Early American Pressed Glass*, kept for easy reference in the glove compartment of a car, will be of help in such treasure hunts. Her *Antique Fakes and Reproductions* may keep an "antiquer"—once the collecting bug has bitten—from paying a sky-high price for something now being turned out on the production line. In the library are all sorts of books on old china and glass, American and European. It is well to remember that antique blown glass, too, is perishable to a degree and was mainly meant for decoration. Using it will prove disappoint-

334

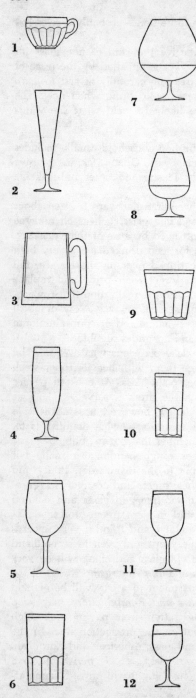

GLASSWARE

1. Punch glass, 1½ oz. Fill ¾ full.

2. Pilsener glass.

3. Beer mug. Shape optional.

4. Iced-tea glass. Shape optional.

5. Water goblet. Shape optional. Preferable at table for luncheon and dinner. Fill ½″ from top.

6. Water tumbler. Fill ½″ from top. Preferred for water served away from table except at breakfast.

7. Large brandy, approx. 8 oz. Fill only ¼.

8. Small brandy, approx. 2 oz. Fill only ¼.

9. Old-fashioned glass, 3 to 4½ oz. Fill ¾.

10. Juice glass, 3 to 4 oz. Shape optional. Fill ½″ from top.

11. Large bowl for white wine. Fill ½″ from top.

12. Crème de menthe frappé, about 4 oz. For stingers, too, and any frappé, such as Old Southern Comfort frappé or apricot frappé. Or a frappéed liqueur may be served in an ordinary cocktail glass. Fill about ¾ full.

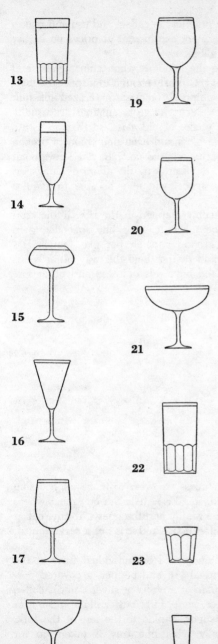

13. Delmonico or whisky sour (but ordinary cocktail glass will do).

14. Stem whisky sour or parfait glass. Fill ½″ from top.

15. Hock or Rhine wineglass, sometimes with green bowl, occasionally decorated (antique specimens). Should not be used except for hock or Rhine wines. Any table wineglass may be substituted. Fill ½″ from top.

16. Traditional sherry. Fill ½″ from top.

17. Optional sherries. Fill ½″ from top.

18. Cocktail glass, 1 oz. or more. Shape optional.

19. Large bowl glass, 4 oz., for red table wine.

20. Optional glass for table wine, 1 oz. or more. Fill ½″ from top. For white wine, port, and red table wines.

21. Champagne glass, solid stem preferred. Used for frozen daiquiris and champagne cocktails too. Fill ½″ from top.

22. Highball glass. Shape optional. Fill ½″ from top.

23. Shot glass, 1 oz. For whisky.

24. Liqueur glass, 1 to 2 oz. May be used for liqueur brandy too.

ing, but early pressed and cut glass is practical to collect and use and makes for an attractive table. If you're clever, you can have it at prices no higher than those asked for much modern glass.

It is a good idea, too, to patronize the auctions when china, glass, and other household items need replacement. Go early enough to inspect the merchandise, however, and do not buy chipped, cracked, or crazed glass or china. (See "Attending Auctions.") Dealers who go to auctions are usually interested only in the more valuable pieces of old glass, so that an astute buyer can often pick up fairly modern glass and even fine china in broken lots at such auctions at a fraction of its original cost. If you know what you want and are not distracted from the search by the allure of things for which there may be neither use nor space, you may be able to acquire lovely things indeed.

When expensive glassware does become chipped in the rim, if the chip or crack is not too deep it should be taken to some one specializing in grinding down glass. The cost runs around a dollar per glass—much less than the replacement value of most, and saving them this way often keeps a set intact. Collectors' magazines often have ads of these and other fine repair specialists.

CHAPTER THIRTY-EIGHT

SETTING THE TABLE

BREAKFAST

Breakfast is a simple, informal meal—unless we wish to make an occasion of it (wedding breakfasts, hunt breakfasts, etc.). It is the one meal where it is often not even expected that all the family and the guests, if any, eat at the same time. And even in a well-staffed household it is not a served meal, except in a sketchy sense.

For ease of service, breakfast is often served on individual trays at the table with each tray containing individual salt and pepper, a covered portion of toast (covered with a linen napkin or a china or silver dome), coffee or tea cup with the spoon on the saucer, knife, fork, butter plate and butter knife, fruit or fruit juice, cream and sugar, napkin to the left of the fork, jam, the breakfast dish and—especially when the tray is taken up for breakfast in bed—a simple low flower arrangement.

For the breakfast table the centerpiece may be simple flowers, a green plant in a silver or copper urn, or a convenient Lazy Susan. The table is

THE BREAKFAST TRAY always has a tray cloth, usually linen. It may have its own special china. *Shown top left to right:* Simple low flower arrangement if space permits, jam jar, toast or rolls in napkin or under dome, sugar and cream. *Below, left to right:* Butter plate, napkin, breakfast plate with cover for food upon it, salt and pepper, coffee cup with spoon to right of handle, coffeepot. The morning paper in an upright holder if room on the tray.

usually bare except for place mats, but on a beautifully surfaced table or in a breakfast nook where the table has a composition top even these may be dispensed with. The silver at each place consists of a small fork and knife, a dessert-size spoon for cereal, if needed, a butter knife on the butter plate, and a teaspoon on the saucer beneath the coffee cup or to the right of the knife to the left of the cereal spoon. Coffee cups may be before the hostess or at each place to the right of the knife. Jam or marmalade is served in a small serving dish or silver-topped or other decorative jam jar on a small service plate, with a spoon on the right side of the plate or in the jar or dish. Fruit or fruit juice is at each place on the breakfast plate. Water is at each place in tumblers, at least when guests are present.

When there is service the waitress or butler pours the coffee and asks each person how he wishes his eggs. If there is something else offered, plates may be arranged in the kitchen and served individually. If everyone is ready at once, a platter of, say, bacon and eggs may be passed or griddle cakes and bacon. Or foods may be kept hot on the sideboard along with the coffee, either over alcohol lamps or in electric *bains-marie.* Toast may be made on the sideboard or at the table if it is not brought in from the kitchen on a covered dish or beneath a napkin. The napkin is laid on the plate, the buttered or unbuttered toast on top, then the corners of the napkin are folded to cover the toast.

Breakfast is the one meal at which it is permissible to read the paper, mail, or anything else that suits our fancy. Many people are totally unable to function conversationally early in the morning.

AT BREAKFAST the first course, stewed fruit, is in place on the breakfast plate. Tumbler is used for breakfast water. Coffee spoon may be on saucer as shown, or at right of knife. Dry cereal is placed above place plate. Hot cereal is served from the kitchen.

INFORMAL LUNCH

As at breakfast, the basic silver for lunch is always a fork and knife, whether or not both are actually needed. To this is added a spoon for soup or appetizer, if needed. The table may be covered with a lunch cloth, elaborate or simple, depending on the degree of formality. But, as is the modern fashion, it is more likely to be set with place mats. Water is in the goblets at each place, or may be poured. The centerpiece can be simple garden flowers or an arrangement of fruit. There are ash trays, cigarettes, and matches at each place—unless the hostess is unalterably opposed to smoking at any meal. Butter plates are always used. Luncheons are usually limited to three courses—which may be soup (in cream soup or bouillon cups rather than soup plates) or appetizer such as shrimp cocktail or paté, a main course often combining meat and vegetable (shepherd's pie, casserole, stew, curry), salad with cheese or simple dessert, often with a fruit base. Sometimes there may be only two courses—a main dish, such as a cold sea food plate, and dessert.

Dessert silver may be on the table above the place plate or on the dessert plates, passed by maid or hostess.

Lunches may also be served buffet and are conveniently done that way even for only a few guests when there is inexpert or limited service—or none at all. The food is placed, buffet style, on the dining room table or on the sideboard if it is to be eaten elsewhere, or the table may be set with place settings and the guests may serve themselves from the buffet, then seat them-

INFORMAL PLACEMENT OF DESSERT SILVER, informal lunch and dinner: This is a convenient way to place dessert silver above the place plate. Without first course (or with first course served after guests are seated): Dinner napkin is on dinner plate (or on service plate if one is used) when guests sit down, as at a formal dinner. Note optional placement of dessert silver, easy when service is limited or when serving is done by the hostess.

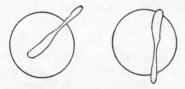

OPTIONAL PLACEMENT OF BUTTER KNIFE: Two of the three ways the butter knife may be placed on the butter plate. The third way is shown in many of the place settings illustrated and is more usual.

selves at the table. Service is limited to the removal of plates and to the replenishing of dishes as necessary.

When salad appears at lunch it is often not served as a separate course but may come to the table in a wooden bowl to be mixed and served—perhaps in small wooden bowls—to the delectation of the guests. Or it may be an "arranged" salad placed at the luncher's left immediately following the service of the main course if there is a maid. If there is no maid such a salad is often in place as the guests sit down and may be eaten by the guest with the first course, if any, if he wishes.

Dessert at an informal lunch depends on the season and on the menu, of course, up to that point. A rosy baked apple stuffed with nuts and raisins or topped with fluid or whipped cream, fresh cut-up mixed fruit in season, what I call the nursery puddings—tapioca, rice, rennet, cup custard, cornstarch, farina—all are pleasant at lunch. When men are present a sound fruit pie is always a good choice, as is fruit and cheese, but the fussier desserts such as charlotte russe or meringue glacé usually seem better suited to dinner.

In California it is popular to serve the salad first as an appetizer. It is beautifully done, often in individual wooden salad bowls or abalone shells in place as guests are seated.

In summer iced tea, iced coffee, iced chocolate, or a tall fruit beverage may be in place on the lunch table before guests are seated. At informal luncheons hot tea or coffee may be passed during the meal or with dessert. Or demitasses or large cups of coffee, to those who prefer them, are served after dessert at the table.

Lunch is an excellent time to serve simple dishes almost everyone likes, yet which are not exactly "party" fare. At an informal lunch in the winter the following would all be appropriate as the main course, preceded or not by an appetizer: fish chowder, French potato soup, bouillabaisse, *pot-au-feu* (all served from a tureen and served in generous portions in soup plates), baked macaroni and cheese, baked beans with salt pork served with raisin brown bread, tripe, potato and chipped beef or ham casserole, corned beef and cabbage, or frankfurters, sauerkraut, and mashed potatoes, eggs Benedict, scrambled eggs with kidneys and whole hominy or hominy grits, pancakes with creamed lamb, and rice, tomato, and ground meat casserole.

INFORMAL DINNER

At a semiformal company dinner party the silver is preferably sterling, but at a wholly informal or family dinner it may be a good plate or any of the wood or plastic-handled tableware in common use, so long as it is in good condition and all matching. Whatever the "silver," it is placed one inch or so from the edge of the table at place settings that are equidistant from one another on a table laid with care and precision. The napkin is placed on the place plate, unless the first course is in place, and then it is to the left of the forks, but it should not obscure them, nor should the silver be obscured by the plate. On an informal table the other appointments are geared to the size of the table, the amount of service available—which may be none at all—and to the number to be seated. At a small, round table, for example, a centerpiece may prove impractical if meat and vegetables are to be served at table. Perhaps all the table can conveniently hold at the center, in addition to the food, are the candlesticks or a single candelabrum. Candles may be in any color but should be above eye level and, if they are on the table at all, lighted. The silver is whatever is neded for the meal, though many prefer to introduce the dessert silver with the dessert. Otherwise

INFORMAL DINNER SETTING *First course:* The first course is in place when the guest is seated, usually. If not, the dinner napkin is on the place plate instead of to the left of the forks as shown (*see below*). The seafood fork is shown in one of the three accepted ways of placing it.

Second course: Informal dinners are very elastic. They may have as few as two courses but are usually limited to five. The soup course may well be omitted, especially if an appetizer is served first. At informal dinners the soup need not be served in the traditional flat soup plate.

Third course: The salad is usually served with the entree for simplicity's sake. The knife is optional, depending on the type of salad and whether or not cheese is served.

dessert spoon and fork or spoon alone may be above the plate (illustrated). The knives are usually limited to two—one for an appetizer, if any, one for the meat, as the informal dinner rarely has more than four courses. If salad is to be served with cheese a salad knife is needed. The silver is placed traditionally, that needed first, farthest right and left of the plate. The forks are usually two, for meat and salad, occasionally one more for an appetizer, but never more than three at once. The salad fork is inside the meat fork, unless the salad is served as a first course in which case it is the first fork in the setting. At informal tables iced tea or iced coffee may be served but not at the same time as wine. The iced tea spoon is placed to the right of the knives. Sometimes the iced tea or coffee is on its own small serving plate, sometimes placed directly on the (treated) table or on a small coaster. For iced coffee, cream and sugar are passed. Iced tea at a meal is best served sweetened and lemon-flavored and poured from a pitcher at the table over ice.

Spoons for soup or fruit are on the table, to the right of the knives. If hot coffee or tea is to be served at the table, during the meal or with or after dessert, the spoons for it are on the saucers, to the right of each cup handle.

On the informal table, butter plates and knives are used with the butter knife placed in a variety of ways—across the top of the plate, blade toward

Fourth course: The salad course may be served separately as a fourth course and, especially when accompanied by a cheese tray, may replace dessert.

Fifth course: When dessert silver is not in place above the place plate at an informal dinner it comes in on the dessert plate, or is so placed and passed with the dessert by the hostess from her place. When the dessert is in place, flanked by the silver *on the plate,* it is left that way. If the silver is on an empty plate with or without finger bowl, the guest places silver left and right of plate (*see illustration of dessert service and text*).

the user, across the top of the plate, tip toward the center of the plate, or occasionally parallel to the knives, blade to the left (illustrated).

Salts and peppers on a informal table may be in a wide variety of materials, from the wooden salt and pepper grinders of the gourmets to Victorian condiment sets with their pressed or etched glass and silver containers for salt, pepper, paprika, red pepper, mustard, and vinegar. At a large table a salt and pepper for each two guests is convenient. Little open dishes may be used, glass or crystal, even ceramic or pottery. They should be freshly filled, and unless there are individual salts and peppers for each guest little spoons are needed. It is well to remember that any salt cellar with a silver top must have the top removed and the threading washed completely free of salt after each use or the threading will corrode and the diner will get much more salt than he bargains for!

The informal diner expects to smoke at table if he is a smoker at all. Individual ash trays are best, but one larger one for each two guests is acceptable, too. Cigarettes may be on the ash trays or in any gay little container, such as an antique handleless teacup or a small, squat pottery or porcelain vase. Silver boxes are also used on informal tables, but there should be more than one and those used should match.

When carving of meat is done at the table the carving set with the sharpener is placed to the right of the carver above the place setting, so that when the roast is brought in the implements will be to the right of the platter.

When the hostess is to serve there are hot-plate mats, if necessary, in front of her place and to her right are arranged serving forks and spoons needed, the fork nested in the spoon. Silver (or china or glass) ladles for sauces are in the sauce when it is served, and the bowl or boat is on a serving plate. When jellies or condiments are in place on the table, to be passed, the spoon or fork for them is next to them on the table and is placed in them by the first person taking up the dish.

Wines at an informal meal are usually very simple—at most two, perhaps sherry with the soup and one dinner wine throughout the meal. Wine glasses are placed in order of use. The sherry glass is above the knives, the wine glass to its right in a variety of positions (illustrated). Sometimes the sherry glass is removed with the soup, sometimes it stays until dessert. At an informal table the dinner wine glass remains throughout. Sometimes, depending on the menu, beer replaces wine. It may follow sherry, but no sweet wine or liqueur should follow it. It is served in tall, cone-shaped beer glasses, in mugs, steins, or any tall glass.

Sometimes demitasses are served at the table by the hostess or even hot tea, after the meal, at the table. The spoons are on the saucers, to the right of each cup handle.

FORMAL LUNCHEON

The centerpiece for a formal luncheon may be flowers, a ceramic or crystal piece, or, perhaps on a modern table, driftwood or coral or any other decorative objects that express the taste of the hostess. Candles are not used, unless in winter illumination is needed in the room—then the curtains are drawn and the candles lighted.

The table may be bare (small round straw mats not showing beneath the place plates), but, of course, the table surface must be flawless. The napkins for a formal luncheon are usually white, often initialed, medium in size. They are to the left of the (not more than three) forks. They are damask, linen, grass linen, or on a modern table even some of the newer combinations, such as handkerchief linen with organdy bands inserted, or some of the rayon, metallic mixtures. Luncheon cloths that do not overhang the table, sometimes lace inserted or embroidered, are used without a silence

FORMAL LUNCHEON SETTING   *First course:* Above, crabmeat cocktail in suprême glass in place as guests are seated. Seafood fork placed in one of three
accepted ways, to the right of knives and parallel to them. Iced-tea spoon
above service plate may be placed to right of knives (*see below*). Salad knife,
optional, depends on type of salad and whether cheese is served (*see text*).
Second course: Below, at formal luncheon of four courses salad is served with
entree, here creamed chicken and mushrooms with border of puréed peas in
ramekin. Salad may be served in place of dessert. Dessert silver is brought on
dessert plates (*illustration of dessert service*).

cloth, but mats are preferred by many. A damask cloth is not used at even a formal luncheon in a private home.

The silver must be sterling, the china and glass of the best quality. Since everything is served, the silver on the table consists only of that which each guest requires for the menu, plus salts and peppers in silver, silver-and-crystal, or porcelain for each two guests. (See illustrated placement of these at formal dinner.)

If soup is served the soup spoon is at the right of the knife or knives (not more than two). If it is to be the less usual four-course luncheon, with the soup followed by an egg dish or fish, there is a small knife to the left of the spoon and next to it the larger knife for the main course. If it is a three-course meal beginning with an appetizer, the soup spoon is, of course, omitted. On the left of the plate go the necessary forks, not more than three, appetizer fork, meat fork, salad fork, with the one to be used last on the inside. The exception is the oyster fork, which usually goes on the knife side, either parallel to the knives at farthest right or slanting over with the tines upright and in the bowl of the spoon. Forks and spoons for dessert are not included on a formal table but are brought in with the dessert.

Butter plates are used on a formal luncheon table in the usual place (illustrated), with the butter knives in any one of the three accepted positions (illustrated). There are rarely more than two wines, often only one, and glasses for each wine may either match or just go well together for the two wines.

If the hostess wishes, individual ceramic or silver ash trays with their complement of cigarettes and matches (see illustration for formal dinner) are at each place, or cigarettes may be passed at the end of the salad course or at dessert or later in the living room after service of demitasse. Neat, "dress" pipes are now acceptable even in town in mixed company at any time other men are smoking cigars. No gentleman would light a pipe in the middle of any meal—or a cigar, either—even though many thoughtless people take the table cigarettes now appearing more and more on formal tables as an invitation to smoke between courses or even while eating. This can never fail to offend a hostess whose cuisine makes any claim at all to excellence.

FORMAL DINNER

The silver at a formal dinner must be sterling (gold plate at the White House!) placed, as is silver for all other meals except buffet, about one inch from the edge of the table, each piece lining up at the base with the one next to it. The silver should not be obscured by the place plate. The large damask dinner napkin, folded, is on the place plate, no matter how decorative the latter may be. But the place plate, if it is pictorial, is carefully arranged so that the design is toward the diner.

No butter plates or butter knives appear on a really formal table, as breads that are passed are placed directly on the tablecloth. The hard

FORMAL PLACE SETTING   The dinner napkin is on the service plate as the guest is seated. Shown are the usual number of glasses for formal dinner: water, sherry (for soup course), red wine for entree, dessert wine. Sometimes there is also a white wine for fish instead of sherry, sometimes both. Occasionally just champagne is served throughout the meal as the only wine. Note in this illustration the oyster fork is shown with the other forks, an optional arrangement, but no more than three forks may be in place at one time. In this case the salad fork and knife (if needed) will be put in place when the salad course is served. At a really formal dinner there are no ash trays on the table. There is no smoking until the service of dessert has been accomplished (*see text*).

dinner roll is in or on the napkin or to the left of the place plate as the guests are seated. It is unbuttered, and no butter is ever passed.

Silver and settings must be exactly arranged, just as they are for all settings except the buffet. A crowded table is never attractive, but a crowded formal table is impossible to serve. There must be a foot or more between each guest, the space accurately measured. But there should never be so much space between guests that conversation becomes difficult. At a long narrow table with few guests the seating is arranged so that host and hostess sit opposite each other at the center of the table with guests grouped right and left of each and with the ends of the table unset.

At a formal dinner all serving is from the kitchen or pantry, so no serving implements are on the table. As the guests sit down there is a centerpiece, usually of flowers, with four silver candlesticks, one at each corner of an imaginary rectangle described about the centerpiece a comfortable distance from the place plates. Or there may be one large candelabrum (sometimes

ALTERNATIVE PLACEMENT OF SILVER Here the silver is arranged for a first course of salad, California style. In the top illustration note that although the dinner knife and fork are the prescribed 1″ from the table edge the salad silver is paired with them at the junction of the handles. Below, the more usual arrangement is seen with the handles all lined up evenly 1″ from the table edge.

wreathed with flowers at the base) with its several branches holding tall, lighted white tapers. If the table is large, there may be two candelabra spaced carefully equidistant from the centerpiece the long way of the table.

At each place, in addition to the place plate, the roll, and the napkin, is the following silver: knives, to the right, never more than three—for appetizer, if necessary, fish, and meat or for fish, meat, and salad (if cheese is served with it or if the salad is difficult to eat solely with a fork). If more than three knives are necessary the additional one is put in place at the time the course is served. To the left are the forks, also never more than three at a time, one for the appetizer, if any, one for the fish, if needed, one for the meat, or the first for the fish, the second for the meat, and the third for the salad. If a fourth fork is needed for salad it is placed when the salad is served. If there is an oyster fork it is usually placed, not with the forks, but on the side with the knives with the tines of the fork placed, upward, across the soup spoon or parallel with the knives. With the exception of the spoons for soup or melon there are no spoons to the right of the knives, as at *all* settings, except buffet, silver is placed left and right so the diner works from the outside in toward the plate in choosing his implements. At a formal dinner, coffee is served demitasse and the spoons are in place on the saucers to the right of each handle. Dessert spoons with their forks are in place, spoon right, fork left, on the dessert plates when they are brought in. Sometimes the finger bowl, on a doily or on a finger bowl plate or on both, is on the dessert plate, too. Sometimes the finger bowl is presented with fruit silver after the dessert.

On the formal table individual silver or silver-and-crystal salts and peppers are, pepper first, directly above the place plate or a little below the line of the glasses, with one set for each two guests. At a large table larger sets may be used rayed out, pepper above, salt below, from the corners of an imaginary rectangle around the centerpiece. Open salts and peppers require little sterling, ivory, or mother-of-pearl spoons. Where many sets are used on a formal table they need not match but they should be somewhat alike—not "modern" with Victorian. Mustard pots are not set on a formal table but are passed, if needed, on the butler's tray. But I have even seen beautiful silver pepper grinders—two or more—on formal tables, where the hostess is one who makes a fetish of freshly ground pepper.

Formal glassware need not be in matching sets, but all glasses for a particular wine should match each other and all glasses chosen should look well together. A host might have a set of antique or modern light-green-bowled hock glasses for Rhine wine and like to see them used on a formal table with the, otherwise preferred, clear glass. Wine glasses may be large or small, but many who love wines like to see a generous one for red Burgundy, handmaiden of the equally substantial meat course. Beer is not served at strictly formal meals.

Glasses are placed in order of their use above the knives (see illustration) in a variety of ways. Each is removed with the course it accompanied with the exception of the dessert wine glass, which remains through the fruit and demitasse (when these are served to the gentlemen at table). At a formal dinner champagne may be the only wine served after the service of sherry with the soup.

On the really formal table there may be no ash trays and cigarettes at all during the meal. Or, as is becoming acceptable, in front of each guest is a small silver or porcelain ash tray, with two cigarettes laid horizontally across the top and a small box or book of matches below. The match box may be silver, containing tiny dinner matches, or a plain gold or silver or sometimes black packet of book matches may be used, the smaller the better. Otherwise, cigarettes and cigars are passed with the coffee. Sometimes the butler brings cigarettes in silver cigarette boxes and individual ash trays on a serving tray with a lighted taper or sometimes a large silver lighter and passes them to guests after dessert, lighting each cigarette and placing the ash trays to each smoker's right.

THE BUFFET TABLE

A buffet table is always informal in that, from it, guests serve themselves. But it can certainly have the aspect of formality when it is spread with damask, beautifully decorated with flowers, and sparkling with the finest silver, china, and glass. At a presidential reception in a foreign country I saw

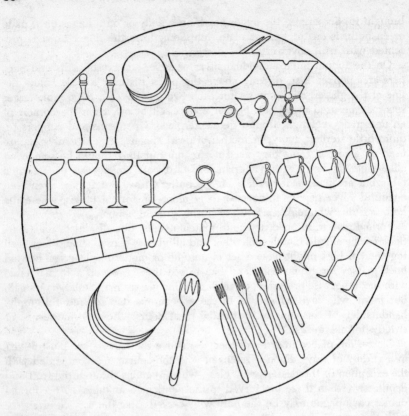

SETTING THE BUFFET Here a round table, always friendly, is shown with a buffet setting for a garden supper. Round tables look best when silver and other things in the arrangement radiate from the center. A buffet should not be too crowded. Additional serving tables may hold anything else necessary if the main table is not large enough.

such a table with serving platters on one side—and footmen ready to serve from them and actual place settings for guests opposite. The guests in full evening dress ate standing before settings that included glasses for two wines.

Usually, however, a buffet table is much less elaborate. Instead of places being set, the table, opened to its full length, is placed in such a way that guests may serve themselves easily. Sometimes the table is against the wall. Sometimes it is built up beneath a covering cloth, or cloths, into tiers for a *smörgåsbord*. Often a buffet table is bare, or it may have a bright linen cloth. Great leeway is permissible in a buffet setting, so long as it is not crowded. Large serving dishes are placed so they balance one another. Platters are complete with serving spoons and forks. Plates are in stacks near the main dishes and napkins are placed, one overlapping the other, in any agreeably symmetrical fashion. (Illustrated.) I like to see forks and knives (if necessary) arranged in neat rows, forks first, about an inch from the table, and I like to avoid any fanciful arrangement of them—an arc, for example. A pepper grinder and a salt grinder or salt cellar of generous proportions belong on a buffet table. Near by are ice water and glasses or cold beer or a container with assorted bottled drinks in cracked ice. Or wine may be passed. It is pleasanter to clear all serving and other dishes before bringing on dessert. This may be portioned, or guests may serve themselves. Demitasse is poured by the hostess or guests may serve themselves from the buffet.

DINNER AND SUPPER

The words dinner and supper are not interchangeable. Dinner is the main meal of the day. In Europe it is always in the middle of the day except when there is formal entertaining. The evening meal, following midday dinner, is supper or, in England, high tea, a relatively simple meal of usually not more than three courses and built, more often than not, around a main course of cold sliced meat.

In America we usually follow the midday dinner plan only on Sunday, since it is unusual for an American businessman to return home for his noon meal as the European so generally does. Our suppers, therefore, come on holidays or Sundays or after dances or other special evening entertainment or after an afternoon wedding. A supper table is set as for informal dinner with whatever silver is indicated by the menu. Buffet meals served in the evening are always referred to as suppers, never dinners, which are *served* meals.

CHAPTER THIRTY-NINE

SPECIAL PROBLEMS OF SERVICE

TEASPOONS

Teaspoons are not put on the table with the fork and knife, unless they are to be used in place of bouillon or cream soup spoons or for grapefruit. Otherwise they are placed on the saucers of tea and coffee cups on the side opposite the cup's handle (always to the right). At breakfast the cups and saucers, with their spoons, may be grouped around the coffee at the right of the hostess or on the sideboard, English breakfast style, or at the right of each place setting.

After-dinner coffee spoons, like teaspoons, are placed on the saucers

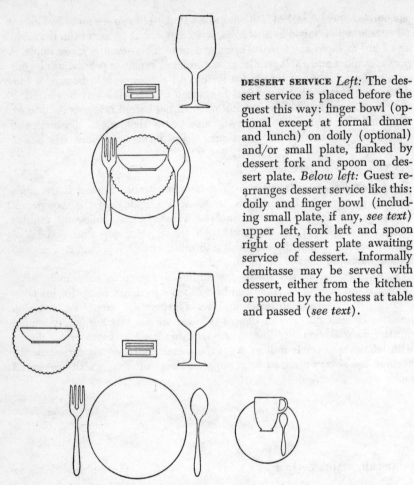

DESSERT SERVICE *Left:* The dessert service is placed before the guest this way: finger bowl (optional except at formal dinner and lunch) on doily (optional) and/or small plate, flanked by dessert fork and spoon on dessert plate. *Below left:* Guest rearranges dessert service like this: doily and finger bowl (including small plate, if any, *see text*) upper left, fork left and spoon right of dessert plate awaiting service of dessert. Informally demitasse may be served with dessert, either from the kitchen or poured by the hostess at table and passed (*see text*).

before the coffee is served, whether at the dinner table, after dessert, or, formally, in the living room.

THE ICED TEA SPOON

In the setting of the table the iced tea spoon is placed to the right of the knife. As iced tea is usually served without a small service plate beneath it many are puzzled as to what to do with the spoon, once the beverage has been stirred. When there is no plate beneath the drink the long spoon is left in the glass, with the handle held toward the far side with the first and second fingers while one drinks. This is an admittedly awkward procedure but the only possible one if there is no small service plate. Certainly a wet spoon may not be laid on the tablecloth or place mat. The same is true of straws, which are left in the glass.

WATER AT MEALS

At an informal meal where there is a cold beverage to be drunk in place of water—milk, iced tea, iced coffee, or iced chocolate—water glasses are not always placed on the table, though they should be. At a formal meal, even when wines are being served, the water glass is placed at the tip of the knife with the wine glass or glasses slightly below and to the right of the water glass (see diagram).

At family meals where there are no guests and service is limited or missing completely it is acceptable to omit the water—and usual to omit it at breakfast—if the members of the family do not ordinarily take it at meal times. But if guests are present water glasses are in place. The water, chilled, may be poured—in fact, usually is poured—before guests sit down, and, if there is service, butler or waitress replenish glasses as needed throughout the meal from a pitcher of ice water on the serving table or sideboard. Otherwise guests serve themselves from a pitcher on the table, or the hostess offers it from a pitcher on the sideboard.

SERVICE OF TEA, DEMITASSE, COFFEE AND CANDY

Hot tea is always gracefully served by the hostess or a woman friend acting for her, never by servants, except perhaps at an enormous tea. When tea is served informally at the luncheon table it is passed down the table from hostess to guests, not passed on a tray by a servant. Aside from the traditionally ceremonial aspects of tea-serving, tea is never poured out, then passed several cups at a time, the way coffee may be, because it cools very quickly. Instead it is always taken by the guest directly from the hands of the hostess or the woman friend or relative acting for her.

Actually, the only formal service of tea is the service of afternoon tea in the living room or elsewhere with due ceremony, eggshell-thin cups, the finest silver, and most delicate napery. But why worry about such formality when many people would enjoy tea at other than four or five o'clock and without the kind of preparation that makes tea-drinking a special and sometimes troublesome occasion. Tea may be served informally at any time of the day or night, so long as it is served hot, if it's supposed to be hot, and made properly with actively boiling water so it will not be the poor apology for a beverage it so often is in this country (see "How to Make Tea").

After formal luncheons—and how few and far between they are—demitasse in the living room, as after formal dinner, is the stiffly correct procedure. But the lessened formality of coffee at the table, with large cups for any who wish them, is much more popular, and among ardent tea drinkers tea with luncheon, formal or not, is a requirement (both tea and coffee may be offered at informal meals).

SERVICE OF DEMITASSE After-dinner coffee, unlike tea, may be poured by butler or waitress. After informal dinners when the guests take coffee in the dining room, if the hostess prefers it may be poured in the kitchen or at the sideboard and, with several of the demitasses on a serving tray (no tray cloth), be passed on the left of each guest. The sugar and creamer are on the tray and the servant may ask, "Sugar or cream, madam?" or else present the tray and permit each guest to add sugar or cream as he wishes. Sometimes, with a very experienced staff, the butler stands behind and to the left of the guest and pours the coffee into the demitasse (three-quarters full, only), then presents the freshly filled cup on the tray with the cream and sugar. At small dinners the hostess may pour the coffee at her place and the guests or the servant may pass it.

At formal dinners the coffee is served in the living room, with the hostess often pouring at a coffee table and passing the cups to women guests within reach, the others coming to her for theirs. A butler or second man or waitress or both, in highly formal households, may serve the after-dinner coffee in the living room, however. If two work as a team, the butler bears the coffee in its small pot on a tray with the cream and sugar (always lump or coarse crystals) and, standing before each guest, pours the coffee into a cup on the tray borne by his assistant and then holds his serving tray so the guest may help himself to sugar and cream.

If one servant is to do the serving, the cups—only a few at a time— are on a bare serving tray with the sugar and cream. The coffee pot is held in the right hand. The servant pours the coffee, then presents the tray for the guest to serve himself from it. Occasionally, filled cups are brought in on a tray from the kitchen, but this gives the coffee a chance to cool, and if service is limited it is preferable for the hostess to pour, whether or not a servant remains to pass the cups.

CANDY AT THE TABLE At a formally set table that is long enough, bonbon dishes may be placed between the candelabra and the end of the table place settings, but they are not essential. Candy may be passed after the dessert or with the coffee, usually informally around the table after it has been brought in and placed on the table. It may be formally presented, of course, too. It should not be nibbled by the guests before dessert time, by the way, though salted nuts, of course, are.

At holiday tables decorated for special occasions nuts and candies are often in little party favors at each place, especially at a family affair where there is a mixed group of children (who feel cheated without something of the kind) and adults. Little paper boxes or baskets at each place never seem suited, somehow, to even the most relaxed adult dinner, but then I can't bear paper hats and streamers at New Year's, either.

SERVICE OF FOOD ON TRAYS

Tray cloths or special tray mats or doilies are placed only on trays used in the service of meals—high tea, breakfast, luncheon, supper, or dinner (in bed or on individual trays on the dining room table or any convenient and attractive spot). Cocktails are served on bare trays with alcohol-proofed surfaces. A glass of water requested from a servant is brought on a small bare tray, just as a card or a letter is tendered on a bare silver salver. After-dinner coffee is on a bare silver tray, and tea is poured into cups—placed directly on the tea tray, which may be of course on a set table.

A man or woman dining alone might prefer a tray in the libary or on the porch rather than sitting alone at the table. Or a hostess might find it much more efficient to have week-end guests served breakfast trays in their rooms than to try to keep things hot in the dining room until all filtered down.

SETTING FOR CARD TABLE SERVICE

The amount of silver on a card table should be at minimum, because service at small tables is always relatively informal even at a big party. A crowded table is always unattractive. If wine is being served, omit the water glass and have water available to any who want it on a convenient serving table. If iced tea or coffee is to be served, water glasses are omitted and the beverage may be passed on a tray or be in place when the guests sit down. For supper or luncheon, tea or regular coffee cups may be at the right of each bridge table setting, with a spoon on the right-hand side of the saucer. Each table may have its own pot of tea or coffee, or the beverage may be poured by whoever is serving. Also to prevent crowding, hot buttered rolls may be passed and placed on the luncheon or supper plate instead of on a butter plate. Where there is limited service with one servant, or none at all, a warmed service plate is used for service of the entrée and the first course, if any, is in place when the guests seat themselves. Too many courses and too inconsequential food served at bridge tables—when there is a pretense at serving a full meal—is a mistake. A hot-dish pad in the middle of each table can hold one substantial hot dish from which guests can serve themselves. Or the tables can be used for a sit-down buffet supper, with guests serving themselves as they wish at the buffet table.

Much fussing over the service at little tables makes for confusion and destroys the feeling of intimacy they give. Even if you have a butler and a footman or waitress, keep the service at bridge tables very simple. Plates are removed with both hands, not one at a time, and courses are limited, usually to three. It is a good idea to have salad, arranged on each plate, as a first course, or to pass it with the main course—say of spaghetti and chicken livers. Finger bowls are not advisable, as the removal of them from the dessert plate creates a crowded table, already burdened with ash trays, salt and pepper, possibly nut or candy dishes, cigarettes, and beverage.

At luncheon on bridge tables a luncheon napkin is on the service plate or, if a first course is in place, to the left of the plate. In the evening if more than a dessert is to be served dinner-size napkins are used. Paper ones are quite acceptable if the hostess runs the household herself and the labor or expense of doing up a number of large dinner napkins is of some consequence.

THE FINE DAMASK CLOTH

The height of formality is a good damask tablecloth with matching dinner napkins. Most well-equipped households have several of these, one at least large enough to cover generously the dining table that is opened to its fullest extent. It should overhang not less than twelve, not more than eighteen inches.

Such a cloth is a luxury in that it can seldom be used more than once. It must never be put on the table with the slightest wrinkle or stain—far better to use table mats. It should be over a table pad or silence cloth, and it should be placed so carefully that the center fold is exactly down the center of the table, lengthwise, with the fold in the cloth tentwise to the surface of the table. In some establishments, where an expert laundress does up such cloths at home—a hard job—and the storage space is sufficient, the cloths are rolled on a cylinder to avoid any creases at all. Once on the table, the cloth's ends should be equal and so must its sides.

While pale pastel damask is acceptable—though not completely formal in the most exact sense—damask that has the design in one pale color and the body of the cloth in another should be avoided. The beauty of damask is always its elegant simplicity and the subtlety of the woven design.

A too fancy tablecloth is like a too assertive rug—in color or design—in that the things that go on it must be keyed to it rather than be used against a quiet background.

GARNISHES

Food should never be overdecorated, and whatever garniture there is should be perfectly edible. The obvious exception is the frill on the bone of a chop or chicken leg or the frill around the crown roast of pork. There is nothing modern about these, by the way. They go back to the days before the carving fork and were meant to protect a lady's hand from grease when she took up the bone in order to cut off a portion for herself. Today we use such frills sometimes to hide the bare bone where the meat has drawn back in roasting or frying. They are *not* an invitation to pick up the bone in one's fingers.

It is well to explain to a husband who carves that whatever is on the plate with the fish, roast, or chops, steak or other meat, should be apportioned too. He should not shove aside the parsley or the water cress, the thin lemon slices, perhaps neatly cut out in some way on the rind. Nor should he ignore the sauce on the dish. Of course, a serving spoon should be placed with his carving implements to facilitate the serving of gravies and sauces on the serving plate.

What constitutes garniture? Anything that trims the dish—minced parsley, capers, poached eggs on veal cutlets (schnitzel à la Holstein), a lump of appetizingly melting butter, a sprinkling of paprika, a grating of nutmeg, chopped, sliced, or quartered egg, strips of pimiento on asparagus vinaigrette or perhaps on a white fish such as sautéed filet of sole. Buttered bread-crumbs (à la polonaise) are also a garnish, as are the onion rings for ham-burger. The cook should avoid garnishing *every* dish, as this defeats the attempt at surprise. She should also learn different ways to garnish standard dishes. Spinach need not always be served in the leaf with quartered hard boiled egg. It is better in the opinion of many if it is finely chopped, then thickened (keeping its own juice), flavored with garlic salt and nutmeg, seasoned with butter and a pinch of sugar, and served with little croutons browned in butter or sometimes in bacon fat. Or it may have a garnish of crisp, crumbled bacon and chopped egg.

In garnishing a platter the cook strives for pleasing balance. If a rib roast is on a large silver tree platter her eye must tell her—and this takes practice —just where the parsley or watercress shall be and how much is needed to make a setting for the roast without crowding the platter.

Continental style, a whole boiled fish is served with the head on and with a lemon in the fish's mouth. As the head is not served, the lemon is not, either. The same is true of suckling pig, served whole with the head and with a bright red apple in the mouth. Actually, I have never cared to see food served in too anatomical a fashion.

WHEN ARE PLACE CARDS NEEDED?

Place cards are a convenience to the hostess who is seating more than eight guests. They may be used at any time—at a festive breakfast, at luncheon, at seated buffet suppers, and, of course, at large formal dinners.

For family affairs, birthday or holiday parties, the familiar decorated cards are quite permissible, with first names, if desired, written in black ink, "Julie" or "Tom," but formal place cards follow a prescribed pattern. (See the "Formal Dinner.")

Place cards, if flat, are propped against a standing dinner napkin or laid on a folded one. Or they may be placed above the place plate. If the double cards are used they are set above the place setting.

CHAPTER FORTY

EMPLOYER-SERVANT RELATIONS

THE HIRING OF SERVANTS

WORK WITH YOUR EMPLOYMENT AGENCY It is best, I believe, to hire domestics through an accredited employment agency with whom you regularly do business. The agency checks the applicant's references and lets you know what amount of work is expected in each category at the current wage. The agency helps you determine what is fair and expected in the matter of time off and vacations. If differences you can't seem to handle satisfactorily arise, a good agency will act as mediator between you and your employee, in the hope of keeping you a satisfied customer.

When complaints are put on a businesslike basis instead of being constantly tossed at a bewildered or resentful employee the results are often good. If you have a complaint to make—about wastage of food, lack of promptness, about attire or the handling of some household job—interlard the complaint with an encouraging remark before and after. For example, "Mary, I thought your service tonight was very good indeed, but I'd like you to be a little more careful about your sleeves. Be sure, if you shove them up for work in the kitchen, that you push them back in place and fasten the cuffs before you begin to serve. You always look so nice in your dress uniforms if they are quite in order."

The potential employer should keep in mind that the hiring of household employees is on a different basis from that of a generation ago. Domestic service has many drawbacks from the employee's standpoint, not the least of which is the thoughtless and unbusinesslike manner in which servants are often treated.

When you interview, have in mind, or better, have a list of the minimum duties you will require. Do not be vague in this first interview, full of enthusiasm over the pleasant job you are offering, and forgetful of the unattractive aspects every job holds.

WAGES State exactly when the salary is to be paid—weekly, semimonthly, or monthly. It is usual for the monthly wage to be given, but, if the employee wishes to be paid by the week, it is important to make it clear that the monthly amount is not merely divided by four, as so many seem to think it should be. To arrive at a weekly wage from the monthly figure, multiply the monthly wage by twelve and divide by fifty-two. This is the way it is done in the business world, as there are four extra pay days a year. If you pay by the week—basing your pay on a four-week month every month you are overpaying an employee one full month's wages.

YOUR REQUIREMENTS At the beginning of an interview, state the possibly difficult or unattractive things about the job first, or the things to which some domestic employees object. If, for example, you require a health certificate—and you should, especially with children in the house—say so immediately. Your interviewee may not wish to go into the interview any further—which settles an important point. If she has no health certificate and wishes to go to your doctor for examination, you yourself should pay the doctor's bill and wait the necessary time, usually three days, for results of chest X rays and Wassermann tests before taking on the employee even on a temporary basis.

It is better to conduct an interview in your own home, showing the applicant the house and explaining your requirements if after the first few minutes he or she seems a possibility. If you interview in an agency office, do not commit yourself until the applicant has seen your home and had explained to her, graphically, what will be expected. She should be satisfied, too, that the quarters you offer are as you represented them.

Where a servant sleeps, the privacy and comfort you can afford him or her are very important. If it is necessary for a nurse or maid to share a room with the baby, say so immediately. And make some arrangement for her to have occasional use of another room of the house or apartment for the entertainment of friends, if only on your own evenings out.

THE INTERVIEW Try to set the locale of your interview of a domestic at home in surroundings in which she will be more at ease than she might be in your drawing room. Choose a study, your office, if you have one, a sunroom, dinette, servants' sitting room, or even the kitchen if it is free and there are not other employees to overhear what is being said.

Establish immediately the employer-employee relationship. Put the interviewee at ease, but do not offer him or her a cigarette unless, if you hire him or her, you are going to permit smoking in your presence and on the job. Remember that everyone undergoing a job interview is likely to be self-conscious and not at his best. Know, too, that no matter how your questions are answered and what the first impression is, you cannot know how this potential employee will work out until you see the quality of his work.

The questions you ask depend on your own family and household situation. You can usually guess an applicant's approximate age, so it is not usually necessary to ask it, though you may. If you are interviewing many possibilities, jot down your impressions and the answers to your questions as you see each one, so you can make comparisons later.

If you have children with whom the applicant will be in contact if she is hired, it is not only necessary to ask her feeling about children but, if the answer is satisfactory, to see her with them and to see how they react to her. Often a child's response to an adult is more acute than yours can be. If the baby takes an instant dislike to a woman applying for a job as a nurse, don't hire her. The baby knows best. People who like children seem to telegraph that information to the younger generation by their warmth and unaggressive friendliness. Beware the efficient, scientific woman who knows all about children but whom children detest at a glance. Better to have an easygoing, ill-educated "Nanny" with love in her heart.

Be sure you are always in charge of the interview, that you aren't being interviewed yourself! Of course, an applicant for the job you offer has a right to ask a few questions herself, and, in fact, you should encourage her to do so. But never in desperation hire someone who has put you on the defensive, who, in effect, will do you a favor by taking the job. Such a woman will shortly be running you as well as the household, whether or not she is younger or older than yourself. In regard to age, by the way, some women make it a practice to employ only those younger than themselves so they can maintain executive control. To me, however, executive ability should not depend on seniority. It is quite possible for a young employer to employ a woman or man twice her age, so long as she knows, and knows well, how the job should be done and has the ability to see that it *is* done.

In describing the job never minimize the duties you will expect. Don't say "light laundry" when all the family's wash is to be done at home. If you have a non-automatic furnace that needs regular attention and the person you are hiring will be responsible for it, say so. If you expect windows to be washed and heavy cleaning to be done, describe the work in detail and save yourself trouble later. If you are in charge of the baby but plan to leave him with the maid a full day or more a week, establish that right away. Don't say she will have no care of the baby and then turn him over to her, unannounced, when she has many other things to do. Where small babies and their care are concerned, household matters often have to wait.

Among the questions you should ask are those concerning drinking and smoking. Make it clear that you will not permit drinking on the job. And make it clear, too, that you will not permit drinking on time off if work suffers as a result of drinking off the premises. If you permit smoking, establish in what parts of the house it may take place. Do not allow it during the course of actual work or you'll have burned table tops, holes in the rugs or linoleum, and ashes in the food.

It is usual in this country to permit servants to eat the same food as the family eats with the exception of expensive delicacies such as pâté de foie gras, candies, out-of-season foods, and other things the mistress may wish to buy only for entertaining or her family's own use. Where privilege is abused and special foods disappear in the kitchen before the family sees them, the only answer is a locked food safe, Continental style.

WHAT RECOMMENDS YOU AS AN EMPLOYER? An applicant for a domestic job wants earnestly to know—whether or not knowing how to ask—what kind of person is hiring him. Tell the applicant, reservedly of course, what you can about yourself and your family, what hours you keep, how much entertaining you do, how much you are away from home, how long other servants have been in your employ. If your employees stay a long time with you and leave only for good cause—such as marriage—say so. Most people prefer to work for kind, generous employees than for those who may pay better than standard wages but who are mean and faultfinding and who have a record of rapid turnover in help.

HOW GOOD ARE REFERENCES? The average employer who must let a servant go usually gives her a reference. Ask for these references when you interview. Usually you can tell whether they are perfunctory or genuine recommendations. If no address or phone of the reference-giver is forthcoming or the employment referred to was too far back and the explanation as to the interim occupations too vague, be very wary. Even when a written recommendation is unequivocally good, it is best to check it by phone, not, of course, in the presence of the applicant. People are more willing to tell you the faults or quirks of their former employees over the phone than in letters.

THE PART-TIME WORKER If you have part-time workers, it is virtually imperative that you get verbal recommendations from other employers. Many such workers, gotten through agencies, are floaters about whom the agencies know very little. You are better off finding someone who does such work for a friend who will vouch for her honesty and thoroughness, because, very probably, you will have to entrust her with a key and, perhaps, if you work yourself, rely on her doing her work without any direct contact with you.

INTRODUCING THE NEW SERVANT TO THE HOUSEHOLD

In introducing a new servant into the household, all members, including the males and even the baby, have the newcomer introduced to them, never the other way around. Children below their teens are called by their first names by servants, unless they are titled. In their teens they may be called "Master James" or "Miss Ellen," except by old family retainers who have known them from infancy or early childhood and who may be privileged at least until the children reach their majority. Children's nurses, governesses, and tutors call children by their first names, except titled children (and sometimes even then if the children are not of royal blood).

Wherever you can accord household employees the dignity of their surnames, do so. Many capable people have left the household field because of what they feel to be the indignity of their loss of identity. It is sometimes wise to begin a well-trained, full-charge houseworker in your one-servant, busy home as "Mrs. Childs" rather than "Nora" and to start her as a housekeeper rather than as maid-of-all-work, at least in appellation. Her morale may rise as a result, and children, especially, may immediately accord her relatively more respect, as may her friends. Don't, however, force such a change upon her if she's more comfortable being called just "Nora," as I have seen happen, too. But just being "promoted" to the executive classification has often persuaded a wavering Nora to stay in household work rather than desert it for the factory where she is, in her own point of view, accorded dignified treatment. Every human being needs to feel important, even Nora —wages or opportunity for saving, quite aside.

INTRODUCING SERVANTS AND GUESTS

In introducing guests and servants the servant is always introduced to the guest in this way, "Mrs. Hansen, this is Mona, my personal maid. She's going to look after you, too, while you are here, so call upon her if you need anything." You do not complete the introduction. If you call your visitor by her first name and have not had an opportunity to straighten out the guests' identities with the servants, say, "Sigrid, this is Mona, etc." Then to Mona say, "Mrs. Johanson will spend the week end with us and will be in the North Room." That takes care of the identification of the guest, although Mona will call her "Madam" or "Ma'am" rather than Mrs. Johanson.

THE FURNISHINGS OF A MAID'S ROOM

If a maid's room is furnished like a bed-sitting room she will probably feel more comfortable in it and can have an occasional friend in to visit her— a practice you should encourage, so that she feels part of the household in at least a one-room home of her own. She will never feel as free and as much of an individual as if she "lived out," and you must put yourself in her place. Give her as much freedom as her personality and integrity seem to merit, but never let down your regulations as to dress, punctuality, and manner or you will find yourself with the kind of problem only dismissal will solve.

If you are a kind and fair employer who treats her domestics as she would like to be treated were she in their place, you will occasionally be taken advantage of, but you will also have a better chance of keeping your employees. Constant domestic turnover is hard on you and very hard on your family. For that reason a pleasant, willing employee who may not be completely competent is better in the long run than a household martinet who must be handled with kid gloves and who makes everyone uncomfortable.

THE BED Anyone who has slept—or tried to sleep—on a hard, lumpy bed knows how he feels the next day. Therefore, no maid's room should have as its bed some family cast-off that can't possibly provide a decent night's rest. If you have doubts about the comfort and cheeriness of your servant's quarters, try them yourself and see if they would induce you to live in them, were you in your employee's place.

ACCESSORIES The modern maid's room needs a radio, a comfortable chair or so, some place for writing letters, for storing clothes. It must have a good bed, light, adequate heat and bedding, and as attractive general surroundings as you are able to provide. And you must see that the room is kept as spotless and orderly as the rest of the house. Many a servant, obliged to keep the rest of the house clean and tidy, lets her own room go. Her morale will be better if she must keep her own room attractive, too, and she should be encouraged to take pride in it as her part of the home. It must not be just an untidy place in which she can flop on her time off.

THE SERVANTS' SITTING ROOM OR DINING ROOM

Large houses are often able to provide a sitting room and a dining room for servants. These should be simply but comfortably and cheerfully furnished, not just repositories for the family's cast-off and battered furniture, dreary old pictures, holey rugs. It is worth while putting a slipcover, however inexpensive, over a worn sofa. The employee whose own surroundings are clean and comfortable is a better employee. The occasional one who mistreats his or her pleasant surroundings is outweighed by others who will be grateful, appreciative, and loyal. Again, a well-trained supervisory eye can help prevent damage.

If you provide the kind of quarters I describe it is wise to explain to a new servant or staff that the room is attractively furnished, especially for her or them, and not merely filled with worn-out things that are "good enough." Build up a pride in the job and what it offers—good pay, supplied work clothes, better living quarters than they might be able to afford on their own, full board, paid vacations, and no deductions for absence because of sickness. Actually, a household employee has every incentive to save proportionately more of her income than many an employer of her services.

IT IS YOUR JOB TO TEACH AND DIRECT

It is a rare servant who arrives in your household perfectly trained. If he or she is unique in having undoubted ability for the job it will still be necessary to train him or her for your job. And you can't expect the job to run itself without direction—and often some aid—from you.

The nagging employer who is never pleased with the cook's work but who can't cook herself will never have her household running satisfactorily so long as she remains ignorant of how to do the things she demands of her servants. Not unless she employs a managing housekeeper who, having these household arts at her fingertips, knows exactly how the household is going at all times.

It is hard to be sympathetic to a servant's problems if you have no real conception of what they are. If necessary, can you rise at seven or before, prepare breakfast—sometimes several breakfasts at differing hours—wash the dishes, clean the house, do the laundry, take care of the children, prepare and clean up after lunch, answer the phone, do the ordering, answer the door, cook and clean up after dinner, and sit with the children afterward—

all the while looking neat and clean yourself and keeping a civil tongue in your head? Many women, who had always formerly had servants, have found out in the past few years what it is like to do all these things day in and day out without much relief from monotony. And they also found out, perhaps, why generous wages and time off were not enough to compensate for the drudgery.

THE GENERAL HOUSEWORKER

Few families today can afford a staff of servants, and even the general house-worker, employed full-time, is becoming rare except in the upper income group. Most families with even much better than average income just can't afford her.

If you are among the relatively few who can afford a full-time maid—or who must have one whether or not you can afford it (and sometimes it is necessary, especially when there are young children, to have help even at the sacrifice of other things)—you must not expect the impossible of her.

Some women, perhaps previously without help at all, or long without it, become suddenly complacent when they finally are able to hire someone and expect to achieve, without lifting a hand to help, a perfection in their homes that has been expediently forgone up until then. They may expect a house-worker to do all the things they have themselves done—and done perhaps not too well—and to add to her duties certain frills of service that only overwork and irritate the poor maid to the point of dissatisfaction with her job. In desperation, if she doesn't quit, she may inflict a kind of bumbling slowdown on her employer that is worse than no help at all.

ARE YOU YOUR OWN MANAGING HOUSEKEEPER?

If you have a one-employee household and a busy family it will certainly be necessary for you to give your maid some systematic assistance, as well as careful supervision.

You will probably save money by doing the supply shopping yourself if you have a practical knowledge of cost and quality in food. Telephone ordering from charge-account stores is convenient but expensive. In some shops it is customary to rebate to the servant, who brings her mistress's business, a percentage of the monthly bill—which, in turn, is padded to take care of the rake-off. If you cannot afford runaway bills, watch these details. If you permit telephone ordering, have the kitchen save the sales slips for you. Be sure each package is checked to see that it contains each item for which you have been billed. Omitting items in a package, but billing for them, is another way some unscrupulous merchants gouge households whose servants do the ordering and, through connivance or carelessness, overlook such omissions. Don't be embarrassed at checking up. Your employees will respect you more if you are not "easy."

If you have a maid-of-all-work, you may decide you can help the household run more smoothly if you do the routine upstairs work every morning— if your own time permits. This may mean making the beds, tidying up and dusting. You may designate as your job—and in this you will be wise—the dusting or washing of valuable ornaments in the house. Perhaps you will make the day's dessert. It is probably certain that you will do the family mending—or arrange to get it done outside—attend to repairs, put out clothes for dry cleaning, keep drawers and closets tidy, and, unless you can hire someone to help take the burden off Mary, help in most of the regular work when you have guests.

KEEP YOUR DIGNITY

Try from the beginning of your relationship with a domestic to establish a dignified employer-employee relationship. Make your orders clear, and, whenever possible, put them in writing. From time to time review the work in a friendly manner, giving censure, encouragement, and praise, as needed. Avoid an apologetic attitude when telling an employee what must be done or improved. In your own manner and tone of voice, assume that what you are saying will be acted upon without difficulty or argument. Adult treatment of domestics usually results in responsible, adult behavior on their part.

NOTES TO SERVANTS AND TRADESPEOPLE

Notes left or sent down to servants should always be pleasant and clear. Criticisms should be made face to face wherever possible. If you have a part-time maid you rarely see, it may be necessary to leave a note of criticism from time to time, but it had better be tactfully phrased. The same thing said to her with a pleasant expression on your face will be much more tolerable. But such a note could read:

Emma—
When you do the silver today, will you use a little brush on the raised design so that no polish remains? It helps, too, as you know, if you wash it afterwards in hot water and suds before shining it. I am anxious to have it look especially nice tonight as I am having guests.
Also, while you are working with the polish, will you be sure to go over the light switches and the bathroom faucets and soap recesses.
                                                                          A.V.K.

This note implies that Emma has been a little remiss previously, but it should not make her annoyed. Try not to state a criticism except indirectly, unless you are there to hear what the servant has to say about it. There are often mitigating reasons for poor domestic performance

A note for a tradesman may use the same initial signature or simply be signed "Mrs. Knowles." For example:

Oil Man—
Please don't disturb me today. Just fill the tank and leave the slip on the porch table. I'll sign it and mail it in.

Mrs. Knowles

DON'T PRY

In all things that don't concern you or your family or that don't affect her job, a servant's life and activities should be her own business. In personal matters, don't give advice unless it is asked. The salary she earns is hers as inviolably as that of your husband's secretary. But if she gets into financial difficulties to the extent that her work suffers, that is your business and she may welcome or at least need some suggestions from you on how to manage her affairs. Help her, with your own care concerning expenditures of household funds, to value thrift and to seek security through regular saving of some portion of her earnings.

TIME OFF

In various communities the days for time off and the amount of free time differ. But your staff needs time off on one shopping day at stated periods as well as on the usual Sunday afternoon and evening. You should not dictate that a maid spend the night in on her free day, so long as she is on the job on time the following morning or whenever it is she is expected back. You should not, except in unavoidable emergencies, change her time off without adequate advance warning. She has, it is hoped, some social life too, which, because of the restrictions of her job, must be carefully arranged beforehand. It is unfair to her to tell her, suddenly, that you want her to stay in Thursday afternoon, without finding out if it is just as agreeable to her to take some other afternoon on that occasion. Normally, have regular days for time off and keep to them.

USE OF THE TELEPHONE

Where you have unlimited local service, servants should be given telephone privileges in moderation. They should not make or receive so many calls that their work is seriously interfered with or the family can't use the phone when it needs to. Records of out-of-town calls by servants should be kept and the toll charges either deducted from wages or settled at regular periods.

EXTENSION OF CREDIT

The employer who constantly gives an employee advances on his or her salary is doing no kindness. Everyone has an occasional emergency, of course, but no employee should be allowed to be constantly in debt to his employer. Such a practice encourages credit-buying and charged expenditures to a degree that the employee may be spending more than he or she makes. The existence of unpaid debts, especially to an employer, makes for a poor relationship, fraught with resentment. Avoid such situations by making your statement of policy concerning loans-against-salary, right at the beginning of employment.

WORKMAN'S COMPENSATION

By all means carry insurance to cover the possible injury of employees in your household.

There are personal liability policies issued by major companies that protect the householder against what might be financially crippling liabilities incurred through bodily injuries, sickness, disease, or death to employees, guests, or even casual visitors such as delivery boys on your property. If a housemaid falls from a stepladder, her injuries, under such a policy, are covered by the medical clause. If she sues, the employer is covered by the liability clause.

DISMISSING A SERVANT

It is always more efficient—and kinder—to give a servant another chance whenever possible than to be a hair-trigger firer. In business the careful office manager does everything possible to avoid wasteful turnover of personnel. Even if help is readily available, it takes time to train a strange servant in the ways of your own household, and despite excellent references, verbal and written, there is always the unknown factor of how he or she will work with you and with your other employees. Give me, anytime, a pleasant, cheerful, co-operative worker who's perhaps not quite perfect rather than a rigid paragon of virtue you hate to face in the morning.

There are times, of course, when a second chance might prove foolhardy, and circumstances must be considered. I once had a wonderful German country girl who came home once or twice noisy and considerably tiddly from beer drinking. She was genuinely repentant, and the slips were very infrequent over a period of several years. On the other hand, I had a Chinese houseman who was as quiet and respectful as a mouse but who somehow never seemed to be able to get his work done. Eventually I discovered he consumed nearly a quart of whisky a day—his own, it is true—and had been doing so for twenty years without ever being really drunk. He was a real problem, and I couldn't let him stay on.

In some of the places where I have lived abroad it is freely assumed that all the servants steal, given the chance. Firing servants for light fingers would mean a dizzy turnover of help. Instead, everything tempting is kept under lock and key and home-going servants are checked out like workers in a gold mine. Here, however, we usually feel uncomfortable and resentful if we are certain a servant is involved in even minor pilfering, and once guilt is certain it is usually better to let the employee go rather than try to circumvent him.

The employee who wears you out with his or her contentious reactions to routine orders is also usually not worth wasting your effort on, unless you are veritably desperate for help. Such people are usually resentful and hostile about the fact that they must do household work, and the only way they *can* do it is their own way. They usually get on better with bachelors or certain household-unconscious career women than with an employer who really knows what she wants. Just be sure, before throwing in the sponge, that you are not piling too many conflicting orders on such a servant and are not, perhaps, expecting too much. It helps to write everything out in proper order, and it is even better if the employer has an exact knowledge as to the length of time each of these assignments should take, all legitimate interruption taken into consideration.

THE LETTER OF REFERENCE

Withholding a letter of reference is a very serious matter. Whether or not a servant leaves of his own accord or is discharged, he should have one unless your experience has been very bad indeed. Another employer, in many instances, may find your ex-employee satisfactory—perhaps because her own requirements are much simpler. At any rate, you can usually write a letter that gives the worker a chance to earn a living elsewhere and which doesn't make you feel like a hypocrite. The thing is to write all the good things you can and omit mention of the bad. An experienced hirer can read between your lines and make her own decision, probably after phoning you for details concerning your obvious omissions as to honesty, sobriety, neatness, promptness, and training. In writing a reference for someone who has been unsatisfactory, keep in mind that for someone else he might be at least adequate.

Such a letter might read, on your house paper and preferably in your handwriting:

[No salutation, definitely *not* "To Whom It May Concern" unless a butler or managing housekeeper is writing the reference]

Hilde Dummkopf has been in my employ several weeks as a general houseworker [if it's been at least two, stretch your conscience] and has proven cheerful and prompt about her work. She is kind and patient with children and a good cleaner. I found her sober and honest. She is leaving me because our requirements call for someone with experience enough to proceed without supervision much of the time. But it is with real regret that we are parting with Hilde.

This letter covers the essential points of sobriety, honesty, and disposition and anyone, except possibly Hilde, will understand that here is a girl who is untrained and probably disorganized and who certainly should not be let near a stove unless her mistress stands behind her, as there is pointed omission of her cooking. Consider that many a woman will be content, indeed, if she can get a maid-of-all-work who is good with children, patient, prompt, and a good cleaner. And another employer's idea of good cooking may differ fantastically from your own.

Careful employers are always concerned, or should be, about sobriety, length of previous tenure, honesty, disposition, and ability or at least willingness to learn. They also wish to know why the person has left or been discharged from the job. Wherever discharge has been necessary, give the worker benefit of the doubt, and consider that under other circumstances things might have been quite different. If you cannot, honestly, say anything constructive, or some very serious infraction has occurred, withhold the reference. Never give an unreservedly enthusiastic reference to any employee who has proved to have serious faults, especially where morals are concerned.

When you find it really necessary to withhold a reference, say reluctantly to the departing one, "Hilde, I am sorry, but I am not able to give you a reference." Say why, of course, if an explanation seems necessary, but usually she knows only too well.

When you can really give an unreserved reference, don't be too formal and restrained, give the employee a good chance to better himself in the next job by being explicit in your praise. For instance:

[No salutation]

Mary Washington has been with us for the past five years as cook, and I can recommend her highly. She is sober, pleasant, honest and in five years was never late or absent from the job. We are most regretful that she is leaving us now that we are moving to the country. We wanted to take her with us, but she prefers to stay in the city near her family. I shall be most happy to answer any inquiries about Mary at any time.

[no closing]
Henrietta Forrest Bates
(Mrs. Mark J. Bates)

If the letter is not written on house stationery with the address at the top and on the envelope (left unsealed), the date and address may be written at the top right, as in an ordinary letter, or the date may be top right, and the full name of the employer may be written, with the address, in the lower left-hand corner:

Mrs. Mark J. Bates
12 Prospect Street
Forest Hills, N.Y.

But, of course, she signs the letter, too.

REFERENCES OVER THE PHONE

If someone calls you to get additional information concerning a written reference you've given, you can be somewhat more frank, but again, if possible, try not to be damning.

If you have omitted "honesty" in your list, say, perhaps, "We were careless about leaving loose change around and it disappeared, but if you keep that in mind, maybe James would work out for you." If "sobriety" is the issue, perhaps you can say, "I suppose we should have locked the liquor cabinet but we didn't and there were several rather embarrassing experiences with Theresa. But perhaps she's learned her lesson now. I had no such report from her previous employer and I checked carefully." Let the decision rest with the interviewer after you have been rigidly fair in giving facts. But do not withhold any truly important information.

CHAPTER FORTY-ONE

DRESS AND DUTIES OF THE HOUSEHOLD STAFF

MEN SERVANTS' CLOTHES

It is the rare household these days that boasts of a butler, that well-trained, English-style servant whose duties are quite circumscribed and who is chief-of-staff in an establishment. It is pretentious to refer to one lone male servant with no staff, male or female, under him as a butler. And he shouldn't be expected to function as chef, butler, chauffeur, and house cleaner attired in formal butler's clothes—which, by the way, are never liveries, the special house uniforms of footmen. And, of course, a household doesn't retain a footman or "second man" without a butler, as the footman always acts as the butler's assistant and himself has circumscribed duties. A household has *one* butler, if any, but it may have more than one footman.

Where a man and wife work as a couple in a small household with perhaps a nurse as the only other staff member, or no other staff at all, the man may be referred to as a butler but he is more properly a houseman because of his very general duties. He will assist his wife with all the household work, help with the dishes, possibly drive, wait on table, answer the door, and in the country often do some outside work on the grounds.

It is more usual in even a large American household to add female help to a butler's staff as needed than to provide him with a footman or footmen— except in Hollywood movies where liveried footmen, in breeches, *sans doute*, are an important fixture. But they are little seen elsewhere. Where they are used (outside the movies) they may wear livery with a striped vest—but no knee breeches. More usually, they wear a gray or black alpaca or, in summer, white duck or linen double-breasted white coat with plain black trousers, a soft white shirt with soft collar, black four-in-hand, black oxfords. Oriental men servants usually are dressed this way and often work in pairs as housemen rather than as butler and footman.

THE BUTLER

A butler usually provides his own clothes for his work. But, of course, they may be provided by the household, in which case they are the property of his employer. In very conventional households a butler has three clothing changes a day and wears in the morning a solid color, double-breasted sack suit in blue, black, or Oxford, a white shirt with detached, fold-over stiff collar, black oxfords, carefully gartered plain black socks (lisle or thin wool, silk or nylon, unclocked) and a dull black four-in-hand.

The formally attired butler serves luncheon in a cutaway differing from that of his employer in several ways. First, his waistcoat is black and double-breasted. His tie, whether a bow with a wing collar or a dull black four-in-hand with a stiff fold-over collar (less formal), is always black, whereas his employer would wear a black four-in-hand with a fold-over stiff collar only at a funeral. (See "The Morning Coat or Cutaway.") It is also quite permissible for him to wear his evening tail coat with a double-breasted waistcoat and striped trousers from noon to six. The butler wears black calf oxfords, plain black socks, and no spats.

A butler does not wear jewelry such as tie pins, rings, or conspicuous cuff buttons, nor boutonnieres or gloves. His evening shirt studs are like gold collar buttons or are white ocean pearl. He and other men servants are traditionally clean shaven.

After six the formally attired butler wears a modification of the tail coat. The difference between his formal attire and his employer's lies in his unfaced lapels, his black double-breasted waistcoat, his braidless trousers, and his button-like studs.

As a concession to summer heat even the formally dressed butler may be permitted a soft shirt and collar with a black four-in-hand, worn with the usual striped trousers from noon on. Replacing his cutaway is a single-breasted gray or black alpaca, or a white linen or duck coat, with either matching cuffs or contrasting ones in the livery color, plain or striped. In the evening the white coat is accompanied by a wing collar and white tie.

From all this it is easily understood why, with the fast disappearance of old family retainers, even wealthy families usually put their butlers into simpler garb.

DUTIES OF THE BUTLER   Where there is no housekeeper, the butler is in charge of all servants and is the household's major executive. He does not have authority over governesses, registered nurses, social secretaries, tutors, or, of course, companions. Valets, chauffeurs, gardeners, and lady's maids, usually under direct supervision of employers, are more or less on an equal basis with the butler, although they do not interfere with his direction of other servants.

In a really large establishment where there is an extensive staff supervised by the butler, most of the manual work is delegated by him to others. He answers the phone, saying, "Mrs. Sawyer's residence" (or sometimes "apartment"), takes messages and relays them to the member of the household for whom they are intended. If a guest is to be called to the phone, the butler so informs the hostess, who tells the guest, if they are together in the same room.

Where there is no footman, the butler opens the door to callers and, if necessary, asks who's calling. He no longer opens the door, card tray in hand, but has one ready on the hall table if a card should be tendered. He does not take a card directly into his hand. Even with family friends he recognizes, a butler is careful not to commit himself at the door as to whether the person inquired for is actually at home, unless he knows the guest to be expected. He says to a social caller, "Will Madam [or the gentleman] be seated [indicating a hall or anteroom chair]. I'll see if Madam is home."

A well-trained English butler always phrases things in the third person, but the more democratic American practice of servants' using the second person is now usual. An American butler answering the door may well say, "Will you be seated while I see if Mrs. Moore is at home?" He is still courteous and deferential, however.

A butler, even where there are footmen, is on duty in the hall whenever there is important entertaining. He, personally, helps the master into his coat, though a footman or parlor maid may bring it to him. He is always properly coated for front hall duty, although in a household with a small staff he wears a butler's apron for manual work.

In a household where there is no valet, the butler valets the master, adult sons, and gentlemen guests. If there is a footman, the butler valets only the master.

In the dining room the butler, when he isn't serving, stands behind his mistress's chair, attentive to any request she may wish to make. If he is assisted by a footman or waitress, either of these serves the vegetables, sauces, relishes, bread, and water. The butler usually serves the main dishes and the wines.

Where a houseman or maid does all of the work, he cannot be expected to be on duty in the dining room throughout the meal, and, actually, many families prefer not to have servants in attendance in the dining room. Instead, they are summoned by buzzer or silver bell when one course is completed and another is to be served or when more water or other beverage or bread should be passed again. An alert servant knows approximately when these replenishings should be and appears from the kitchen without being summoned.

THE VALET

A gentleman's gentleman is in the same circumscribed category as the lady's maid. He works under his master's orders primarily. He keeps his employer's clothes in order, does personal shopping, keeps shoes shined and every clothing item clean and in repair. Often he acts as household secretary— buying train and theater tickets, making reservations. On trips in the car he rides with the driver and acts as "man in the box"—opening the door, assisting those entering and leaving the car, carrying wraps and packages.

A valet wears his own dark blue or black double-breasted business suit, with white shirt and semi-stiff (or if permitted, soft) white collar and dull black four-in-hand. Sometimes on occasion he is expected to wait on table. If he then works under the butler he wears livery or black trousers and a black or gray alpaca three-buttoned coat or, especially in summer, white duck coat, white shirt, semi-stiff or soft collar, black tie. If he serves alone he wears the latter costume.

THE CHAUFFEUR

In most modern households a full-time chauffeur, where this relatively *rara avis* still exists, is expected to do more than drive the car or cars and care for them when they are privately garaged. Usually he doubles as butler or, in the country, as gardener or stableman. For this reason, the traditional chauffeur's livery with its leather puttees and uncomfortable coat is seldom seen. Instead, most private chauffeurs now wear a plain Oxford gray or black double-breasted suit (or, in summer, a neutral whipcord) with a white shirt, semi-soft collar and black four-in-hand, black shoes and socks, black driving gloves. The usual chauffeur's stiff-visored cap is retained. The chauffeur's black or Oxford overcoat, double-breasted and round-collared, is still worn, but fur collars are much less seen, as chauffeurs, even in town cars, are usually under cover.

Chauffeurs are usually on seven-day duty, on call day or night. The family must modify its own demands so that within this period the chauffeur receives the equivalent of a full day and a half of time—an occasional evening with no expectation of call and free mornings to counterbalance late nights. A tired man is an unsafe driver.

In those states that renew drivers' licenses merely on payment of a fee a chauffeur's employer should see to it that the chauffeur receives a thorough physical check-up at least annually, especially if he is an older man.

THE HOUSEKEEPER

A housekeeper is not a servant but an executive in household management. Sometimes she is a well-educated woman who comes into a motherless household and takes full charge, with or without additional help. She does all the household buying, its hiring and firing, its meal planning, bookkeeping, and, if necessary, she prepares the meals, takes full care of the house, and supervises the children. She is treated as a social equal and often has meals with the family. She wears her own dark clothes.

Only very large "establishments" these days, such as the White House or a Governor's Mansion, and a few large, private homes have managing housekeepers. They are knowledgeable, educated women, well-versed in home-making and able to supervise all the household service and purchasing, with or without the assistance of the household's mistress.

Such a housekeeper is always "Mrs. Todd," not "Mary." She has her own attractive apartment (or she may live out) and directs the household from a convenient "office" near the service quarter. Her meals are served to her by the waitress, footman, or butler. She associates and may often have meals with a registered nurse within the household or with a governess, tutor, companion, or social secretary but not with the servants over whom she has charge. Usually, the hiring of governesses, social secretaries, gardeners, valets, cooks, and butlers is done by the mistress or master of the household, but the housekeeper may be consulted or given full responsibility concerning at least the butler and cook, and in a mistressless home possibly concerning the others in the professional class.

THE COMPANION

Many gentlewomen in reduced financial circumstances turn to the profession of "companion." They are never servants but live in households as members of the family. Their duties usually concern only one woman member of the family who needs friendly company. A companion is often a friend or relative. She should be a good and cheerful conversationalist and a good reader, enjoy parlor games, and be able to adjust herself readily to the needs of someone else. Often she is expected to undertake light nursing duties, mending, and personal shopping.

A companion has meals with the family or on occasion with any other congenial professional person in the household, rather than alone.

She wears her own clothes and dresses for dinner whenever the family does so. If she accompanies her particular charge to formal entertainments, she, too, wears formal evening dress.

THE SOCIAL SECRETARY

The private social secretary has a difficult role. She is sometimes expected to live in the household she serves at least part of the time, especially when the family travels to various fashionable resorts. Her social life is often theirs, yet her paid status makes her participation strictly at the suggestion of her employers. At other times she must be available, appropriately dressed, for anything from a beach picnic—in her dual role as companion—to dictation of letters from her employers. The modern social secretary is an expert typist, usually takes dictation, and has a cultivated handwriting, rounded, legible, and of the English school. She is expected to be able to compose both social and business letters and to write them in longhand or on the machine as the situation demands. Her hours and her days off are usually dependent upon the household's plans.

Where a household employs a social secretary, much of the business it transacts passes through her hands, so she must have a head for figures as well as for the social graces. In a very high income family her financial activities may have the supervision of a visiting accountant. She keeps the books, handles the payroll, pays the bills, takes care of insurance, balances the accounts, and keeps careful records for income tax purposes.

In a household where there is no managing housekeeper, a social secretary, where engaged, is often expected to take on this role, as well. She is responsible for the planning of meals, especially those at which entertaining is done, unless the mistress assumes this duty. She may do the hiring and firing and in general she keeps the household in smooth running order.

When the family entertains, the social secretary, with the hostess, makes up the guest list, issues the invitations, compiles the replies, often orders the food and all the party accouterments just as the mistress would if the secretary were not there to take these details off her hands. If she is personable and living as a member of the family, she may even take her place at the party itself. When the family is alone she may eat by herself, with a companion if one is employed, or, when invited, with the family. She is in no way treated as a servant. She wears her own clothes, chosen with her duties in mind.

The public social secretary often has a small organization which works with her on the management of social events such as debuts, weddings, dances, and balls. She works out a guest list with the hostess on the committee—and even supplies a list in some cases—issues the invitation for those giving the party, collates the replies, often works with caterers and florists, and is present with her staff, if necessary, to check the guests at the door at large affairs. She charges a fee for her services and, in addition, may have an arrangement whereby she receives a percentage of various suppliers' bills.

THE COOK AND KITCHEN MAID

In the household boasting a professional cook, this important personage does virtually nothing but cook. The kitchen is her domain. She keeps it clean and sees to it that it is completely stocked at all times, whether she does the marketing or is just responsible for making out the shopping lists. She confers with the mistress of the house, or the housekeeper, on the daily menus. The cook provides her own white cotton dress and wears white shoes and neutral stockings.

In very large establishments the cook's assistant is the kitchen maid. It is she who does the scouring and scrubbing, the preliminary preparation of vegetables, the routine dishwashing. She wears a short-sleeved work uniform, like the morning dress of the rest of the female staff, but covers it with a utility apron.

LADY'S MAID

A lady's maid tends the person of her mistress and of women guests and older daughters of the household. She draws their baths, lays out their clothes, helps them dress. She sees to it that her mistress's wardrobe is always in order, with clothes properly cleaned, pressed, and, when necessary, repaired. Often she does her mistress's hair, nails, and personal laundry. Frequently she does her mistress' shopping and at parties is on duty wherever the coats of women guests are laid aside. On occasion, she may assist at large teas or cocktail parties when the downstairs staff is rushed.

A lady's maid may wear simple dark clothes of her own (unless she is doubling as waitress) or a dark, long-sleeved afternoon uniform (light colors for summer). She wears her uniform with or without dainty white collars and cuffs. In the evening she dons black silk or taffeta with or without a black bibless apron.

Orders for the lady's maid usually come from the mistress. Only if she is not needed by the mistress may she be drawn into other household chores by butler or housekeeper, though never to the neglect of her own responsibilities.

THE CHAMBERMAID

Upstairs is the domain of the chambermaid although she may also act as waitress—regularly in a household that has no regular waitress, or on party occasions as an assistant.

The chambermaid makes beds and keeps the upstairs rooms clean and tidy. She patrols the bathrooms so they are in order after each use. She keeps the household linen mended and is in charge of the linen room. She collects and prepares the upstairs laundry to be sent out—or done at home. At night after dinner she turns down beds, refills the water jugs on the night tables, brings fruit, crackers, or other expected bedtime snacks, and lays out night clothes (except for master and mistress if they have a valet and lady's maid, respectively).

The chambermaid wears the usual morning uniform—light, preferably short-sleeved, serviceable cotton with white collars and cuffs and white strapless work apron, white or black shoes, preferably oxfords, neutral stockings. Her dress uniform matches that of the waitress, but she does not wear a serving apron except when waiting on table.

CHAPTER FORTY-TWO

GRACIOUS LIVING WITHOUT SERVANTS

MANAGING THE SERVANTLESS HOUSEHOLD

I know many women who can afford full-time help who forgo it in these days of high wages and often quite inferior performance. They have faced the fact that the whole domestic employment situation is changing rapidly and that eventually the live-in worker will be rare indeed. Daily workers, instead, will do the work of each household, probably in four- or eight-hour shifts, where full-staffing is maintained.

With such electric equipment as dishwashers, mangles, automatic washing machines, power vacuums, home freezers, electric waxers, and modern clock-watching stoves, an intelligent, organized mistress can do the work of even a fairly large household more quickly and efficiently than can the average, often truculent maid-of-all-work. And the mistress will respect the equipment.

Heavy cleaning is usually more efficiently done by men day-workers where they are available, so the functional, servantless household often runs very smoothly indeed, even when there are small children. The meals are always a problem, of course, but even there a mistress who likes to cook and who prepares delicious meals in a relatively effortless manner can run a more agreeable household than does the woman who must depend entirely on the somewhat doubtful ability of her cook-houseworker.

Every household has its own specific requirements and thus its own schedule, but unless some daily plan is followed even in a servantless household good housekeeping is almost impossible.

In Victorian days, and earlier, the fine china never went to the kitchen for washing. Instead, a pan of dishwater and one of rinsing water were brought to the table after a meal and the dishes were washed and put away in their special china cupboards—or else returned to the table for the next meal. So, too, for the sake of efficiency, the lone homemaker can start her day the night before, by setting the breakfast table after she finishes the dinner dishes at night.

Everything that helps avoid the morning rush is advisable. It is important to start the day without hurry and tension, then things will seem to go in their proper, ordered way. So it really does help if the breakfast table is set the night before. Some even prepare the orange juice, grapefruit, or other fruit (if the prepared fruit is covered the vitamin loss is very slight). The next day's menus should be decided upon, perhaps written out as a guide, so that, in the sleepy early morning, preparation of the breakfast can be more or less automatic.

Most important is to avoid the last-minute search for mittens, schoolbooks, rubbers, caps, and father's brief case. These articles can be assembled the night before, or at least their whereabouts checked upon. Of course, they should all have their special place, but as it takes years of training to get children to "put things back," it is certainly not a good idea to count on everything being where it should be.

The whole family should be urged to arise early enough for a leisurely start on the day. There should be time for father's second cup of coffee, his pleasant walk to the station, his morning romp with the baby. If mother is to become family chauffeur, breakfast should be eaten by all at the same time so she has a regular, peaceful meal, too, and time to clear away the dishes, if not perhaps to wash them, before taking father to his train or the children to school.

LAUNDRY　It takes approximately twenty-five minutes for one load of wash to run through an automatic laundry. And if laundry is done at home, it is easier to do some laundry each day than to allow it to collect so that a whole morning must be devoted to the laundry project. If there are hanging facilities in the cellar or elsewhere, it is not necessary to wait for sunshine. In large households where there is insufficient indoor drying space it is often a great saving of work to have an electric or gas clothes dryer.

Daily sorting of laundry is another timesaver. This means that as the soiled laundry goes to the laundry room it is immediately put in separate hampers. Hampers are labeled "Woolens," "Lingerie," "White," "Colored," "Baby," etc., according to requirements. First chore of the morning, after breakfast is over, is to load and start the washing machine. If it is loaded the night before, it can be started before breakfast so that clothes to be sundried—weather permitting—can be put out early.

CLEANING ROUTINE　As the kitchen is the heart of the house, it should never be left untidy while other chores get prior attention in the morning. The best plan is to finish the kitchen first, then proceed to bedmaking (see "Making Beds"), if it is not possible for each member of the family to air and straighten his own room and make his bed before reporting to breakfast (the ideal arrangement in a servantless household).

After beds are made and bedrooms tidied, bathrooms are cleaned and put in order, then the living room tidied (if this was not done the night before). Now, with everything in order, dishes washed, and beds made, dusting and floors come last.

When all the work is done by the mistress of the household one room each day is chosen for thorough cleaning. This room, then, on the early schedule is ignored, except for bedmaking, if it's a bedroom. The objective is, of course, to set the entire house to rights as soon as possible, so that if further housework must be abandoned for the day, as so often happens, or unexpected visitors arrive, there is at least order, if not perfect cleanliness.

The room chosen for thorough cleaning, whether by a day-worker or the mistress, is first disassembled as much as is practicable. Furniture is pulled away from the walls, scatter rugs or carpets are rolled up, ornaments are removed from shelves, pictures taken down, draperies are folded back or taken down.

All walls and woodwork are cleaned first. Modern vacuums are good at getting at dusty surfaces, cornices, cobwebs in corners or on the ceiling. Everything washable should be washed as time allows—window sills, shelves, even furniture finishes benefit from careful going-over with a clean, soapy, not-too-wet cloth or nylon sponge occasionally, followed by thorough drying and waxing. As all dirt falls onto the floor as one proceeds, the floor is done last if it is to be washed and waxed or vacuumed. Floors to be swept are done before the dusting, obviously. Whether the floor is to be washed depends on its surfacing, but waxed wooden floors respond well to an occasional thorough cleaning with one of the modern cleaning waxes or a solvent such as turpentine (after sweeping). The waxer is used only after the freshly applied wax is quite dry. Old wax should be removed from time to time anyhow, even from linoleum, either with soap and water, a detergent, or a recommended liquid cleaner. (Windows should be open if the mixture is combustible!) In corners and inaccessible spots the floor should be lightly scraped with a paint scraper, steel wool, or a dull knife.

When the cleaning is finished, the room should be put in perfect order, not left for later reassembling. Too often schedules can't be completely adhered to in busy households, and it is dismaying to think of cleaning things to be put away, pictures to be rehung, and rugs to be put down at the end of a long day.

On sketchy days the minimum housework should consist of meal-getting, dishwashing, bedmaking, bathroom cleaning, and room-tidying. To neglect any of these things until day's end means coming home to an uninviting house and, usually, a feeling that a free day is hardly worth it.

MAIDLESS ENTERTAINING

It's a dull life without friends in one's home. Therefore the woman who gives up servants, or who never has depended upon them, must strongly resist the idea that entertaining without at least day-help is impossible, or at least very difficult.

Most households have no outside help whatsoever. It is the rare thing to have a full-time houseworker, rarer still to have anything approaching the full staff of even upper-middle-class living in the last century. But we can't all entertain away from our homes, and where the cost of outside entertaining is immaterial, it is still the warmer, friendlier thing to entertain in one's own home often, no matter how simple the hospitality must be.

It is obviously impossible for a woman doing all her own work and tending several nursery-age children to conduct her home on the same lines as her neighbor does who employs both cook and butler and whose half-grown children are away at boarding school. But such differences in household management occur constantly in the same neighborhoods and on the same streets. The woman with the small children does not, today, hesitate to invite her neighbor to tea or dinner merely because she cannot entertain her with traditional formality, the kind of formality that at one time was expected in upper-class neighborhoods.

If one must simplify one's living, it is important not to feel apologetic about it, or even try to explain it. Put away silver that is not regularly used, pack away the huge linen tablecloths for some easier time and use table mats instead. Streamline each room by removing from it all dust-catchers, keeping ornaments to a minimum. Slipcover the furniture with washable fabrics. Make the kitchen so attractive that work-saving meals served there —breakfast and the children's lunch—will be cheerful. Convert lost space in cellars and attics into play and work areas, to save traffic in the more damageable parts of the house.

Avoid the tension and trouble of extra preparations for company entertaining by living, daily, approximately the way you do when guests are present. This way, we cease to think of guests in terms of much extra effort, and so include friends more often in the family circle. Inviting one or two guests at a time this way makes living more agreeable and creates diversion for the family without too much work for the hostess.

THE LET'S-GET-IT-OVER-WITH IDEA

The kind of entertaining whose object is to pay off as many obligations as possible all at once is usually a social failure, even if it does accomplish the objective.

The cocktail party with guests elbow-to-elbow, unable to make ordinary conversation heard above the din, is an unbeautiful American phenomenon wise people avoid. If cocktail parties are to be the solution, let them be small and manageable—and more frequent. The cost of materials will be no more, and the saving in wear and tear on the furniture and nerves will be very great. For more information about cocktail parties see the section on Entertaining.

The buffet meal is often the best way for a staffless household to entertain six or more guests, but, again, too large a crowd defeats the purpose of social entertaining. Guest and host should be able to enjoy each other, not be separated most of the time by the very weight of the crowd.

THE BUFFET DINNER

There are several ways to serve a buffet meal—guests standing (large receptions), seated at one table, seated at small tables, or sitting any convenient place and taking plates on their laps. If the group is small—six to eight people—and the dining table large enough, the table may be laid with cloth or mats, silver, wine glasses, napkins, salt, pepper, nuts, candelabra, ash trays, and cigarettes (if the hostess wishes), and filled water or iced tea or coffee glasses (in summer) but no service plates.

The buffet foods are placed on the sideboard or a serving table along the wall, and guests form a line at one end, pick up their plates, and either serve themselves or are given servings from the main dishes such as baked ham, turkey, or a casserole by the host, hostess, or servant. Guests usually serve themselves to the secondary dishes, to buttered rolls, salad, cheese, and relishes, then take their places at the table. The guests, on finishing the main course (and "seconds" are quite expected), place their soiled dishes on the buffet table, from which they are cleared to the kitchen. Dessert is then brought in and served at table or the buffet by the hostess or each guest may serve himself and go back to the table.

Where the buffet meal is not seated at a main table, guests take their filled plates to any convenient spot in the living room or other indicated place. There bridge tables may be set up (see "Setting the Table for Card Table Service") or coffee tables may be available for those who dread to balance a plate in their laps. It is not necessary for all to be served before those arriving first start eating, though two or more guests usually form a group and eat together.

Any wines or after-dinner coffee at an informally seated buffet is passed by servant, host, or hostess. At a very large party a guest may serve himself to wine or coffee, although it is usually poured for him. If all guests are seated together, wine may be passed in its bottle, with each guest pouring his own into the glass at his place.

MANAGING A SIT-DOWN DINNER WITHOUT A MAID

There is absolutely no use, in a servantless household, in trying to duplicate at the table the kind of service one would have with a trained staff. Multiple courses that require the hostess to spend most of the mealtime rushing back and forth from the kitchen defeat the very idea of relaxed, effortless entertaining that should be the goal of a servantless home.

English-style service, with all the food for the course on the table or on adjacent serving tables within reach of host and hostess, is comfortable and intimate. The system is often followed in households employing an adequate staff, so if this must be your method of serving meals never feel embarrassed.

The active participation of host and hostess in serving food to guests at the table creates a fellowship that is often lacking at a table waited upon by

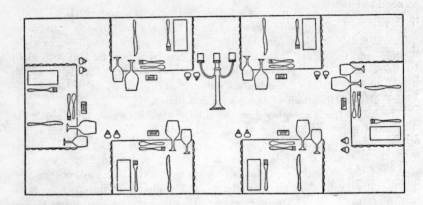

THE SIT-DOWN BUFFET This is the most comfortable way to dine buffet. The dinner table is set as usual, with the exception of place plates and serving dishes. On the table are all the silver needed, ash trays, salts, peppers, candelabrum, napkins, glasses for water and wine, possibly place cards and flowers. Guests serve themselves at the buffet, then take their seats at the table. Close-up shows informal placement of dessert silver.

butler or waitress. The constraint necessary when servants are in constant attendance is missing, and dinner becomes a friendly, leisurely matter, with no need to finish promptly so the table may be cleared by employees anxious to complete the day's work.

It is important, however, to so organize such a meal for entertaining that the family enjoys itself, too, and the guests never feel that host and hostess are trying to double as butler and waitress. The host, for example, does not rise to pour wine for each guest. Instead, he pours a little of any bottled wine in his own glass, tastes it, serves the guest on his right, then passes the bottle to the gentleman nearest him on the left, who in turn serves the lady to his right, as her wine glass is nearer to him than to the host. The other glasses are filled by the gentlemen, but without reaching or rising. The glass of the host is filled last.

If soup is desired, the easy way is to serve it from a tureen at table. Or filled soup plates, on service plates, may be in place when guests enter the dining room. Then, as many guests are confused by the ritual of the service plate, unless a servant has charge of it, service plates should be cleared with the soup plates, even if it does mean leaving a blank space in front of the guest for a few minutes. The hostess, actually, should not try to function as a maid would.

In small quarters where the dining area has been reduced to an absolute minimum the table is often unable to hold all the accouterments of a well-set dinner table that would be expected in a more commodious, though still servantless, dining room. If placing the roast on the table for the host to carve, family style, crowds the table, let him carve it in the kitchen or on the sideboard and place the carved portions on a serving platter furnished with serving fork and spoon. The platter is then passed around the table by the seated hostess, each guest serving himself. The meat dish and the serving dishes containing vegetables are then placed on a nearby serving table or tea table (if they can't be accommodated on the table), in a position, if possible, to be reached without the hostess leaving her place. This serving area also is used for clearing the first course, if there is one, without taking the hostess out of the room.

(At breakfast or luncheon, bread or rolls can be passed already thinly buttered, so that a small table won't be crowded by butter plates.) At family dinners bread is often not served, although crackers may be passed during the soup course and are placed on the serving plate beneath the soup or bouillon. A dinner roll, unbuttered, may be on or in the napkin on the service plate. Butter formerly was never served with the roll at dinner, but in recent years it has been accepted that most people don't really enjoy a dry roll and even at semiformal, served dinners a butter plate and pat of butter are often in place.

If a tea wagon is used as a serving adjunct guests pass their plates to the hostess, who refills them or at the end of a course, without obvious scraping, stacks them on the tea wagon, placing used silver on the top plate. After the salad course, if it has been separately served (but it is easier to serve it with the meal), all the things that were used at the meal—vegetable dishes, condiments, cruet set, unused silver, salad plates are passed to the hostess. Bits of bread are inconspicuously gathered up by each guest and placed on the used plates being passed to the hostess.

When the clearing has been completed for the dessert course, with no one but the hostess, if she must, having to rise, the table should have on it just the cloth or place mats, wine glasses (if a dessert wine is to be served or if a white wine is being served throughout dinner, including dessert), water glasses, and ash trays, nut and bonbon dishes, if any. Individual salts and peppers are left in place. Dessert silver may be placed on the dessert dishes before they are passed, or placed on the table at the beginning of the meal, above the dinner plate, Continental style. (Illustrated.) Finger bowls are dispensed with.

After-dinner coffee may be served either with the dessert—as many prefer —or when the guests have left the dining room and are settled in living room or library. If demitasses are served at the table the coffee tray is in front of the hostess, who pours and serves sugar and cream to each guest as indicated. Many people do not like black coffee, and it is certainly inconsiderate for a hostess not to offer cream with after-dinner coffee on the ground that it is unfashionable *not* to drink demitasse coffee black. How can fashion dictate what pleases the palate?

AFTER-DINNER TEA

An English custom brought back by many who have lived abroad is the after-dinner service of tea. The tea is served an hour or so after dinner, rather than immediately following it. It is served in the living room in thin teacups, with sugar and usually milk, rather than cream, if desired, or lemon slices. It may be accompanied by little cookies or shortbreads, which are passed and placed on the saucer. Late tea is a delightful custom, particularly welcome to those guests who are not after-dinner highball drinkers.

Hot evening tea may be served, too, Russian-style in tall glasses with lemon slices and lump sugar. For those who wish, it can be laced with rum or brandy. But whichever way it is served, the important thing is that the tea be properly made in the first place.

HOW TO MAKE TEA

One thing we prepare badly in this country is tea. Consequently, we think that the tea is at fault, that compared to coffee it is a characterless beverage. Anyone who has drunk tea prepared by the Chinese or the English knows what a fallacy this is.

The first rule in making tea is to have the water actually boiling. It must bubble-boil three to four minutes and then be poured immediately over the tea leaves. Tea made with water under the boiling point does not have its flavor liberated and is flat and insipid. The tea made in most restaurants and at drug store counters is tasteless, because the water for it is drawn from the coffee urn or from kettles kept hot for some time and is not fresh water, *freshly* boiled.

When the water is actually boiling scald out the teapot so that the metal, china, or pottery is heated through. Then *dry* the pot and set it near the heat to keep hot. Now measure one teaspoon of tea for each cup to be served and one for the pot. Pour in the boiling water, cover the pot and, if you have one, use a tea cosy, although there are excellent sturdy pots of various kinds that keep the tea piping hot. Let it steep three to five minutes. Stir before serving the first cup. Have a pitcher of boiling hot water available for those who like weak tea (or pour theirs first before it has had a chance to infuse very much). If more tea is needed, it is best to start the entire procedure again instead of trying to add the somewhat cooled pitcher of water to the tea leaves in the pot. The result is usually poor. However, if you have made the tea at the tea table and are keeping the water at a boil over a spirit lamp or small electric stove, you may add the actively boiling water to the leaves in the pot when half the tea has been poured. The result is usually satisfactory.

When guests are seated around the room, they come forward to take the tea cups from the hostess—she does not rise to serve the guests. Gentlemen present take tea to women guests, of course.

THE KINDS OF TEA The dark teas—sometimes with a little green blended in—are good for daily use. But there are delicious—and sometimes very expensive—mixtures one should try in tea-taster amounts to find preferences. It is well to know that people who know tea never put milk in a green tea (makes it *look* unappetizing), though they sometimes use lemon. The flower teas such as jasmine are horrid with milk in my opinion and also so special they should not be offered to conservative tea drinkers. If you serve them, it is wise to offer an alternative tea at the same time unless you are sure your guests like them. The herb teas, tisanes, are sometimes greatly liked, often as a nightcap, and are usually best with honey as the sweetener but because they are green teas, not with milk. Among the easier to find (always in drug stores) are peppermint tea, camomile tea, and anise. The latter is very good, I think, steeped in hot milk, strained, and sweetened with honey as a nightcap. Children and invalids—and people coming down with colds—often particularly enjoy these tisanes.

SUGGESTED MENUS FOR MAIDLESS DINNERS

As I've mentioned before, graceful efficiency is easy if courses served at table are reduced to an absolute minimum. That means the main course with salad and dessert. What about a first course? If you must have one, let it accompany cocktails, sherry, or appropriate wine in the living room. One good idea is to place oysters half-shell on a large platter of cracked ice. Place small serving plates nearby, with oyster forks, horseradish, and cocktail sauce, and let each guest help himself. Serve with oysters a chilled dry sauterne or Rhine wine instead of cocktails. Thin slices of buttered white bread cut in strips are good with this, or the usual oyster crackers. It is not difficult, by the way, to learn to open oysters with a regular oyster knife—the heavy steel kind—or you can use the simple home oyster-opener.

The same sort of thing can be done with shrimp. Shell them *first,* (Chinese style—it's easier) remove the black line, cook them in a small amount of bouillon, covered, with a bay leaf and a few black peppercorns. (Save the bouillon for stock.) Serve them on a platter, each impaled on a toothpick, surrounding a dish of cocktail sauce or one of mayonnaise, curry powder, and minced onion, to taste.

Hot fish ramekins or scalloped fish in shells or even antipasto can be served in the living room with cocktails or wine, too. Clearing the empty dishes on a tray from the living room before seating the guests for dinner is simpler than having to leave the dining table to clear dishes from there.

Any substantial hot hors d'oeuvre can double nicely as a first course. Many are simple to make but so effective and delicious that they give the impression that hours have gone into their preparation.

Many people, too, serve soup or bouillon in the living room in cream soup or bouillon cups. The course can be borne in on a tray, and guests can consume it sitting or standing.

A main course that is reduced to one dish is ideal for the kind of entertaining we have been discussing. If you are sure all your guests like it, a curry is festive and satisfying. Curried lamb, veal, chicken, or shrimps can be served on a mound of fluffy rice. It is good accompanied by small dishes of chopped peanuts, grated coconut, chutney, and chopped hard-cooked egg. A mixed green salad in a generous-sized salad bowl completes the course.

Other good possibilities—much liked by men—are deep-dish chicken pie cooked with peas, baby onions, and potatoes, beefsteak and kidney pie with potato crust or with a pastry crust and the potatoes combined with the meat. Old-fashioned chicken pot pie with dumplings and new peas needs no apologies, either, nor does a fine fish and potato chowder served with garlic French bread and plenty of green salad.

COOK BOOKS AND RECIPE FILE

Every woman who runs a home needs more than one cook book. She also needs an indexed recipe file. Not to refer to such adjuncts to good housekeeping is to limit the meals, company and otherwise, to a few stereotyped patterns. By using good cook books often and by building an interesting recipe file we can get away from the monotony of twenty-one meals a week.

There are many specialties easy to make that put interest into ordinary meals, yet many women hesitate even to try them. I'm thinking of popovers, homemade cream puffs (fine as a base for leftover meat or chicken, creamed, or they make a delicious dessert filled with ice cream), homemade soups in infinite variety, hot hors d'oeuvres, soufflés of all kinds, potatoes in the dozens of different ways they can be served, other than baked, boiled, and fried.

Proper acquaintance with interesting cook books, plus practice, can prove to any woman that it is possible to entertain frequently without the expenditure of much, if any, more money for food than one would use in the average, unimaginative family meal-planning by a routine-weary homemaker. The thing is to forget the routine things and explore the byways. Try königsberger klops instead of hamburger, ham jambolaya instead of cold, sliced, baked ham, potatoes boiled in bouillon instead of in plain water, a meat loaf made with beef liver instead of chopped beef. And thinly sliced apples or a cup of blueberries will do a lot for those ready-mixed pancakes that do save trouble.

EXTRA GUESTS AT THE DESSERT COURSE

An easy way to expand your entertaining painlessly is to invite a manageable number for dinner and then additional guests to join you for dessert and coffee in the living room. But, of course, it is not necessary to include for dinner or even dessert all the guests you may have invited for the evening. Some may be invited much later than others, although nine o'clock is usually the latest for which such an evening invitation is given.

CHAPTER FORTY-THREE

FINANCING THE FAMILY

CHILDREN'S BANK ACCOUNTS

The best way for any child to learn arithmetic is for him to have the actual handling and spending of some money of his own from the earliest possible date and with a minimum of interference from his parents. A child may have a savings account right from birth, either in his name alone or in trust for him. When it is in his own name he may draw against it himself as soon as he can sign his name, once his signature is on file at the bank. A child who knows he may deposit and withdraw from his savings account according to his needs is usually very reluctant to make any withdrawals except after lengthy and pretty mature consideration. A child in his teens who receives an allowance covering his clothes and school expenses should also be taught the management of a checking account and should learn the careful management of his funds as preparation for his future family life. More unions founder on the rock of financial difficulties than on any other.

LETTING THE CHILDREN IN ON FINANCES An understanding of money is always in terms of relativity to a child. Money itself, to a very young child, is just another thing to pile on his bureau or jingle in his pocket like nuts and bolts until he understands that it is a *medium of exchange:* for so many bright pennies you receive so many peppermint sticks. If you lose a penny en route to the store the man will not give you the extra peppermint stick just because you *did* have the money to pay for it.

Many parents despair because a young child speaks so lightly of a thousand dollars—or a million—or maybe ten dollars—as if they were virtually interchangeable amounts. The way to make him understand is to provide him with actual, realistic financial problems—those of his own family as soon as he is able to grasp them. Whenever possible, take him shopping with you. Show him what the relation is between the current price of eggs or butter and his allowance. Later he may be fascinated to discuss with you the matter of the rent or of the mortgage and its monthly payments and what they cover. A child who sees and understands how his home is paid for learns that spending is often saving and he learns to take pride in seeing an obligation reduced through careful financial planning.

DON'T CHILDREN TALK TOO MUCH ABOUT FAMILY AFFAIRS? Intelligent children entrusted with certain confidential information, such as the amount of the house money or the salary paid to the maid, seem to develop a certain good sense about the discussion of such things other than in the family circle. They need to know why something they desire can't fit into the family spending plan or why such a desire is unreasonable in the first place. The child who is kept in the dark about family finances is the one who makes wild and frequent requests for unattainables, who may state that his father is a "millionaire." On the other hand, a child who is constantly met with "We can't afford that" or "We haven't enough money to buy you things like that" merely feels the deprivation—however momentary his desire for, say, a live elephant. After years of hearing such remarks without further enlightenment, he may come to have a feeling of hopelessness, especially if he receives money in dribs and drabs as his parents think of it and has no set allowance on which to plan.

The child who understands why certain requests of his are unreasonable— because his parents have bothered to explain why—is the child who has a chance to gain a mature understanding of money matters. Suppose a five-year-old demands a full-sized boy's bike costing over forty dollars and refuses to consider his tricycle as an interim solution. To him forty dollars has no relativity unless you point it out in terms he can understand. How many years would he have to continue to get his present allowance in order to pay for that bicycle himself? What is the relation between the cost of that greatly desired thing and the monthly food bill or the rent? Maybe a five-year-old can't understand much of this—on the other hand it is surprising what he can understand. It may be only after he is seated on such a bicycle in a store that he can understand the other logical grown-up reason for delaying such a purchase—he couldn't ride his treasure anyhow until he grew considerably more, or, if he did ride it with blocks on the pedals, it might be at some danger, because his small body couldn't really dominate the machine.

A child who has a compelling and insistent drive to acquire something, no matter how strange such a need may seem to his parents, should if possible be given a chance to plan, through his own saving and earning, for its acquisition. When the time comes and the money is at hand, perhaps his urgent need for, say, a full-sized playhouse may have diminished some, especially when he sees exactly what his painfully amassed purchase price will bring him. But his dream has been allowed to grow toward possible fulfillment. And in the end it is he who decides whether or not fulfillment of it is really worth while.

JOINT CHECKING ACCOUNTS

Except for those rare couples who never have any trouble over their family finances and for whom everything rolls along in an ideally smooth fashion, with each careful and accurate about money, a joint checking account is a constant source of possible friction. Invariably one or the other fails to make an entry or list a check drawn, and there is a snarl or worse.

It always seems much better to me for the wife to have the handling of the house money and her own clothes and spending allowance through the use of her own checking account. She can handle such purchases with cash, but this involves more bookkeeping. To have husband and wife each drawing household expenses and their own expenses from the same account often makes for confusion.

Every man and woman needs a certain amount of money regularly to spend as he or she needs without having to give wife or husband, brother or sister an explanation of its disbursement. Once a husband gives his wife her house allowance, out of which she may or may not be expected to get her own clothing and other expenses, depending on what proportion of the family income can be spared, and after he has met obligations such as insurance and dues, he should not be held accountable concerning his own spending of what remains.

WHO SHOULD MANAGE THE FAMILY INCOME

The responsibility for management of income must be decided on the basis of who has the greater ability—husband or wife—to handle major expenditures. Sometimes—quite often—the wife is better equipped through training and inherent qualities to handle accounts than her husband is. Only in the most hopeless cases, it seems to me, should either wife or husband be denied the right to control some of the family's funds, at least. And even when one partner has an obviously good head for figures, plus the time to handle at least the major bills, it is often wise for the responsibility to be at least divided. On the other hand, a wife who constantly overdraws, lets bills slide, has to borrow constantly to make ends meet, and in general finds it impossible to keep the family's finances in some sort of order certainly needs help in the management of them. A husband, talented as he may be in his own field, may also have difficulty in the handling of money and, if so, should be helped toward the organizing of his obligations. He should be relieved of the detail of expenditure of the family funds as much as possible if his wife is more capable of taking over. But it should be well understood that difficulty in arithmetic is no sign of low intelligence. A general vagueness on the part of, say, a creative artist concerning the mundane matters of existence makes him in no way inferior to his mate who may be able to read a balance sheet at a glance. Their fields of comprehension are different, that is all, although their I.Q.s may be neck and neck.

DEFICIT FINANCING How many families in America live on extended charge accounts! The grocery bill just drifts along, somehow never quite paid up to date. Things are charged in anticipation of an improvement in the financial picture—which probably never will take place because no one faces the facts. Father borrows lunch money at the office because mother emptied his pockets the night before because she needed money to pay the laundry bill. She had somehow forgotten the laundry bill when she bought the new hat that suddenly loomed so alluringly in a Main Street window. A certain amount of unplanned spending is inevitable in every family, but for all spending to be unplanned leads to chaos, unceasing debt, and family anxiety.

CHARGE ACCOUNTS AND INSTALLMENT BUYING Charge accounts can be controlled in only one way: one person in the family, the one who budgets, must have full knowledge of what is being charged. If the whole family may run in and out of a store charging items at will without any central control bills are certain to get out of hand and budgets impossible to manage. No child, for example, should be permitted to use a family charge account without explicit permission for each purchase. When he violates the rule in the face of warning, the store must be notified that a limitation has been put on the account, that only certain members have the use of it.

In a family where finances are carefully controlled charge accounts are paid promptly when bills are rendered and discounts taken where offered. For your credit rating it is important that you keep your charge accounts in good order. If for some reason, as sometimes happens in the best of families, you cannot meet a bill when it is due or at least within sixty days, it is better to write to or speak to the tradesman than to allow the "duns" to come in month after month, while you avoid the store and make no explanation. If you are well-known in a small community, step into the store, see the credit man, if there is one, and tell him why you are in arrears, or write him a brief note on the bottom of the bill you can't, at the moment, pay. If he is put on the carpet as to why this account hasn't been paid, he thus has some explanation to offer. Too, if you can pay something on account, when it is inconvenient or impossible for you to pay in full, your credit standing is improved.

Never feel that you are disclosing anything tradespeople can't find out when you have to explain that you can't meet an obligation on schedule. All towns and cities have credit organizations, chambers of commerce, and other checks as to the credit standing you have, if you have ever asked for credit anywhere. If you have a smug feeling about yourself and consider that your position is such in the community that no one should really expect you to pay such things as your butcher bill when it's due, you may be in for quite a shock if you ask your bank or your lawyer or someone else with access to this information what your credit rating is. Sometimes the most intimate information turns up in these reports. You may find that you are rated "poor" as a risk and that every time your oil man delivers oil to you he mentally crosses his fingers. Conversely, it is nothing to be ashamed of if you discover that your rating is "slow but good," if there has been a bona-fide reason for your taking a long time to catch up with your bills.

Prolonged family illnesses, business failures, deaths can upset even the most carefully planned family expenditures. It is only when you have dropped into the habit of continually dragging out all your bills, never being paid up, that you are on the brink of that disastrous business, deficit financing.

As to installment buying, it is undoubtedly here to stay and is, with limitations, justified for many people if the spending is for needed things, not sheer luxuries. If mother would have to save money over ten years for a refrigerator but can meet five dollars a week out of the house money for one she can have now after a down payment, the burden of the debt seems justifiable. But all installments must be treated as fixed expenses which have to be taken into consideration in the weekly or monthly allotment of funds. These payments must be met immediately, like rent or utility charges. Nothing can throw a family into financial difficulties faster than a number of installment purchases that have not been considered in relation to total income. Never buy anything in the *hope* you'll be able to pay for it. *Know* you can pay for it before you obligate yourself. Have a backlog in case of the inevitable emergencies.

ESTABLISHING CREDIT   If you have never had a charge account or wish to start one or more in a new neighborhood it is usual for tradespeople to ask you the name of your bank or banks and the names of stores or firms with whom you have credit elsewhere. You may think you have no such references, especially if you have never had a charge account, but if you have paid utility bills—electric, telephone, gas, rent, coal, or oil bills where you pay by the month—you have used credit even when, as with the telephone company, the cost of the basic month's service is deducted in advance. That is why experts say it is highly important for families and individuals to pay utility bills promptly, even if others sometimes have to wait. A record of suspension of service for non-payment of bills is a pretty difficult thing to live down among credit managers. A utility bill unpaid in another city may serve as a prevention in getting service in your new home.

Never be too hasty in expecting immediate credit—your very haste may be suspect. Ask courteously for the extension of credit if it will be more convenient for you to pay tradespeople monthly, but expect some check into your past record, a matter that can take from a few days to a week or more, depending on the extent of credit you ask for and from whence records must come. Often a tradesman on his own would give you credit on the strength of your name or appearance, but he has behind him the stern reality of the bank, which may have considerable say in the way he undertakes new risks—which is what you will be no matter what your previous records. The best risks can change overnight.

POOR CREDIT RISKS   You may have an income in six figures and still be a poor risk whose business a sound tradesman doesn't want. I have known wealthy and prominent familes to live by deficit financing to the extent of letting the grocer wait a year for payment of his bill, while they kept up their club dues for fear of social ostracism if their names were posted for non-payment of dues. But such names are posted anyhow—in credit organizations—and many a tradesman takes business with that knowledge. If the tradesman has a whole collection of such families, as sometimes happens in wealthy neighborhoods, he must take slow payments or no payments (involving possible litigation or, at least, unpleasantness) into consideration when fixing his prices. And he must have enough capital to finance the easy living of people too slipshod to meet the everyday obligations which others must meet regularly to get along. So never imagine that just because you have social position and wealth your credit is automatically considered AAA. You or members of your family may have damaged it badly, and, although you have a probable ability to pay on which most tradespeople are willing to gamble, the sound, independent tradesman does well to encourage you to deal elsewhere while he concentrates on the substantial, creditable middle class.

YOUR CREDIT RATING CHANGES   There is a way out if you know yourself to be poorly rated as a risk. That is to prorate your payments on outstanding debts so that each creditor gets something at regular periods, plus information as to when he can expect the bill to be paid up. In the meantime, do not open new accounts. Continue to deal with your regular suppliers, unless their prices are really out of line with your normal income, but pay cash—don't pile credit on unpaid credit. Avoid paying just the bills of those who make the most clamor. Instead, be fair—divide what you have, to pay on back bills. Otherwise, you may find that a creditors' meeting has been called—if you are in a really bad situation—and bankruptcy proceeding begun, so that each creditor *will* get a fair share and none take precedence. I have known such unpleasantness to extend right into the family life of prominent individual men and women, much as we are prone to think of these legal proceedings as being limited to business firms.

LIVING WITHIN YOUR MEANS It is never a disgrace to say, "I can't afford it." And when you do have to make such a statement when you have been urged to spend beyond your means, it is certainly not necessary to explain why. Perhaps, in spite of a really generous income, you have obligations about which others don't or can't know—the support of an aged, distant relative, private charities, extensive savings programs or investments. It is never shameful to have to say, "I can't afford it." It *is* shameful to commit yourself to expenditure you know you can't really afford and shouldn't make—just because someone else urges you to go against your own better judgment.

I have real respect for the person who can say without any self-consciousness at all, simply and cheerfully, "I can't afford it." But I hate to hear a long-drawn-out explanation of why. As a matter of fact, we should never demand to know why a person can't spend money on something he says he can't afford unless there is a sound reason for his finding some way to afford it. Then you may, if you feel you should, try to show him that way, quietly and without irritating him.

CHECKING ACCOUNTS

Do you pay by check? It is the best way to handle your money and keep your records straight. It does take businesslike attention and special care, but then so does any handling of money.

HOW TO OPEN A CHECKING ACCOUNT An individual no longer needs to have a certain sum of money to leave in his checking account as a minimum balance at all times, although many banks still demand it, sometimes in quite large amounts, for a so-called regular account. But there are "special" checking accounts that may be opened for as little as one dollar. You are then charged a small amount for each check drawn and for the handling of the account. The statement of the account arrives periodically. When you open your account, see an officer of the bank and ask for instructions on how to operate your checkbook if you are not perfectly sure of the procedure.

AVOIDING ERRORS You don't need to be very good in arithmetic to avoid the snarls people so often get into with their checkbooks if you will just take the trouble to "prove" each bit of subtraction as you learned to do in school and to check your addition very carefully. If long columns of figures bother you, break them up into short ones, then put the results together. Do each page of your checkbook as you go along, totaling the stubs and subtracting the result from the balance as shown on the opposite page. It helps to make all deposit entries in ink to prevent any accidental erasures. However, only a bookkeeping genius does his addition and subtraction in *ink*.

Be careful to note the source of all deposits. If a sum you have just put in the bank came as a gift from Aunt Nellie write on the page where you note the deposit, "Gift from Aunt Nellie." Always list the date you deposited the check, together with the full amount. I once knew someone who so hated to add odd numbers that he always made his stubs and deposits in even numbers, no matter what the really correct amounts were. The income tax people take a sour view of such shortcuts.

Even banks do make mistakes—though only occasionally. When your statement comes, get right to work on it. First, put all the checks in numerical order. If you have a great many, divide them into convenient categories first—the ones to tens, the tens to twenties, etc. One good way to proceed is to check off, with a colored pencil preferably, the canceled checks against the stubs (marking the stubs) for that month. Where there is no canceled check for an issued check, note the amount of the missing check and its date in a neat column on the page opposite the last check drawn for that particular month—notations for which you have left convenient room. This is better than keeping information on a separate piece of paper which may become lost. Now add the sum of these outstanding checks to the balance you had in your own book after the last entry for this period. Take care to deduct from the latter amount vouchered bank charges of any kind which may appear on your statement. Your figures should then tally with the balance from the bank.

If they don't tally—and alas they often don't—first of all check all your deposits against those shown on the bank statement. I find errors are most often made here. Or be sure that you haven't forgotten to enter some blank or loose checks you drew. See that the amounts on canceled checks tally with those on stubs.

HOW ABOUT BLANK CHECKS? Blank checks or loose checks torn from your book and carried with you cause a lot of trouble but so do pocket checkbooks if you are keeping a large checkbook, too. However, if you carry a small checkbook with you at all times and draw any blank checks from it, being careful to enter these checks in your master book each time you return home, it will be much easier to keep accounts in order.

If you use a blank check furnished to you by a store, be careful to write in the full name and address of your bank plus your own address. If you use another person's check (a poor policy), cross out all information that does not belong on a check you issue—the name of the bank (you substitute yours with its address, of course,) the check number, if any, a printed name, if any.

PRINTING AND DATING CHECKS Many people, writing checks in a hurry, forget to number them. This makes it harder to have an accurate record and makes for difficulty in balancing the checkbook. For a small sum, any bank will imprint your checks with your name and address, if you wish, and they will number each check beginning with any number you choose. Such checks seem a little more acceptable to shops and individuals to whom you are unknown, too.

If your signature and handwriting are illegible the printing of your name on your checks is virtually a necessity, unless you wish to block-letter your name and address on the face (lower left) or reverse of your check each time such information is asked for.

WHO ACCEPTS CHECKS Almost any individual or firm will accept a check that comes to him through the mail or which is given in return for merchandise that is to be sent. There is opportunity to verify the existence and standing of your account should there be any doubt.

It is where you are about to take out merchandise with you immediately that questions may arise if you tender a check. It is best to ask, first, if a check is acceptable, at the same time offering cards of identification. A calling card is not proper identification, as anyone might have your calling card. Instead, have with you, always, club cards with your signature affixed, insurance identity cards, hospitalization, or driver's license. If you sign your business name differing from your married name, if you are a woman, to your checks, be sure you have necessary identification of yourself under that name—club cards are useful here.

Never get indignant if someone refuses your check. That is always a tradesman's privilege, and no personal slight is meant. He may have had some heartbreaking experiences in the acceptance of personal checks.

You can always leave a small deposit to hold your purchase, while you cash a check at some other place where you are known or where your identification is acceptable.

Never, unless you are well-known, ask for change on a check you are making out for merchandise. Many business establishments have a fast rule about this. They will accept a check for the correct amount but will not give change. If anything goes wrong, they might have some chance of retrieving the merchandise but the cash would be gone forever.

CHECKS FOR CASH Many merchants in your community have a constant daily drain made on them by customers who ask them to cash checks merely as a convenience and who do not necessarily buy anything at the time. Sometimes it is unavoidable for you to ask such a favor, but always realize it is a favor. Many such checks in the course of a day send a small merchant to the bank unnecessarily for funds with which to carry on his business. Maybe the bank isn't so far out of your own way as you imagine. And don't be offended if your grocer must refuse to cash a check for you from time to time. His cash drawer may be too low, and he must always be in a position to make change.

STOPPING PAYMENT ON CHECKS   If you lose a check that has been given you by someone else or if one you have sent out did not reach its destination after a proper length of time steps should be taken to stop payment. In the case of a lost check, notify the person to whom you sent it that you are stopping payment and sending another check (with a different number and date). This is in case a check that has been delayed in the mail arrives and the recipient tries to put it through, not knowing payment has been stopped. The bank is notified at the same time, first usually by phone, then by mail or by a call on the bank officer or a teller. You inform the payee of the amount of the check and the date it was issued. In your checkbook you write "void" or "payment stopped" on the stub of this check and the date you stopped payment.

Suppose, on the other hand, you have paid a workman for, let us say, the installation of a new bathtub and you find after he has left, check in hand, that the bathtub has been cracked during installation. A delicate point comes up here. You would, it would seem, be quite justified in immediately stopping payment on his check, pending adjustment of your complaint, but the burden of proof rests with you—that the bathtub wasn't cracked somehow after he left—and this may take you right into court. Right here is a good place to warn you against paying a bill immediately upon completion of labor and installation. Adjustments, if necessary, are more likely to be made before payment than after.

You can't just change your mind about merchandise and stop payment on a check you've issued for it. If you buy a hat, take it home, and don't like it, don't stop the check you gave for it or you can be subject to suit. Instead, return the merchandise to the store and go through the usual procedure for getting a refund or exchange on returned merchandise. Only in case of absolute, undoubted fraud is it permissible to stop payment on a check under these circumstances. For example, if a man came to your door and represented himself as a bonafide collector for a charity and you gave him a check, only to be informed by a neighbor, shortly, that he was an imposter, you would be justified in stopping payment—but only if you could prove that no part of that check was actually going to the charity for which he solicited.

DON'T DRAW AGAINST UNCLEARED CHECKS   When you make a deposit by check you receive a receipt by mail or, if you have made it in person, from the teller. This testifies only to the bank's receipt of that deposited check. It does not mean the money has been deposited in your account, for the check must first go through the clearing house. If it's an out-of-town check this procedure may take up to ten days or more. Always allow a suitable length of time for a check to clear before drawing against it or, good, honorable citizen that you are, you may be guilty of issuing bouncing checks. Here, as in all contact with the law, ignorance is no defense. Not only are you subject to bank fine if you draw a check against insufficient or uncollected funds, but you can be subject to immediate arrest in some states if the recipient of the check wishes to press charges, something that does happen sometimes and to the nicest people, who had no *idea*.

If, through some horrid accident of delayed mails, an unmailed deposit, faulty bookkeeping, or a bad check that you yourself have received, you find that you have overdrawn your account—if the bank doesn't tell you so first—immediately call anyone to whom you have just issued a check and ask him not to put it through until you can straighten out your account. This kind of tangle can happen to anyone, and straightforwardness at once can prevent a piling up of additional bad checks and resultant injury to your credit before you get to the bank with money to cover your error. If your credit is good and your intentions are known to be strictly honorable your bank will usually trust you for twenty-four hours, if that time is necessary for you to transfer funds to cover the shortage. If you are a rather absent-minded person or poor at arithmetic it is a good idea to tell your bank so. If yours is a small, personal service bank its officers may be willing to keep a paternal eye on your account and call you when it seems to be getting dangerously low. Or they will hold any overdrafts for you until you have been able to deposit so that you don't get a poor reputation with the community. But, if a check of yours is presented at a cashier's window when there are no funds to cover it, the bank cannot honor it.

IF ARITHMETIC STUMPS YOU What is the sense of spending hours on the balancing of your checkbook, piling error on error, in your anxiety to find what's wrong? For a small monthly fee an accountant will take over this function if you really have an extensive account, or, in an emergency, you can always take your bankbook and statement to your bank for assistance. For a large establishment an adding machine may save much time and irritation.

IF YOU LOSE YOUR CHECKBOOK The loss of a checkbook is serious only in that it means you must now reconstruct your accounts from canceled checks, bank statements, and memory—a terrific chore, sometimes. No one else can use your checks—unless, of course, he has your signature to forge. If you do lose your checkbook, notify the bank at once and immediately begin a new series of check numbers, telling the bank the number of the last check drawn, if you can, or at least the payee and amount.

If in reconstructing your bankbook you can't identify all your deposits, it is possible that your bank has a microfilm record of each check that has gone through your account and, in time, can locate the information for you.

WRITING, SIGNING, AND INDORSING YOUR CHECKS Your legal signature is your check signature. Harriet Moran, not Miss Harriet Moran.

If you receive a check made out incorrectly as to your name, what do you do? If you are Harriet Moran and the maker makes out his check to

Harriat Morgan or some other strange variation of your name, indorse the check exactly as written, putting your correct signature directly below.

CARE IN HANDLING YOUR CHECKING ACCOUNT Before depositing checks to your account, be sure the date has been properly filled in—it is preferable, by the way, not to date your own check on a Sunday or a legal holiday. Checks drawn on these days should be dated the day *before* (unless in the case of a legal holiday that day falls on a Sunday). Never *postdate* any check—that is, write a check dated ahead.

Always write checks in ink. If you make an error, make out an entirely new check and destroy the first one—don't try to erase or cross out. Be sure the figures on the check tally with the amount as you write it out in words. Be sure, too, the number of your check is the same as that on the stub. Always fill out the stub before the check, so you are sure of a record. Remember that it is safer to write a check to a person or a firm than to make it out to "cash," unless you are actually going to cash it to have money in your own pocket. A check made out to "cash," if lost, may be cashed by anyone who finds it if you haven't had time to stop payment on it—a difficult matter. Treat any check, anyhow, exactly as if it were cash. In extensive traveling avoid carrying large amounts of cash and eliminate the difficulty of using your personal checks by purchasing traveler's checks.

DON'T ACCEPT POSTDATED CHECKS Not only should you never issue checks in the expectation that by the time they clear there will be funds to cover them, but you should never accept postdated checks. If you do so, with the full knowledge that they are postdated and must be held for a certain time before being deposited, you are in reality accepting worthless paper to cover an obligation. In a court case of which I know, the accepter of such a postdated check lost his case against the issuer. The court ruled that he had accepted the check knowing it to be worthless and therefore had no ground for complaint when the debtor was unable to make it good.

5 CORRESPONDENCE

Stationery and Letters   401

Invitations, Acceptances, and Regrets   425

Correct Forms of Address   437

Heraldic Devices   464

Writing and Conversation Can Be More Colorful   467

CORRESPONDENCE

The art of letter writing has certainly been neglected as telephone and telegraphic facilities have spread. I cherish little notes from some of my old lady friends in their eighties, because they know how to turn a sprightly phrase in even the briefest notes while some of my contemporaries freeze up at the sight of note paper and put down only the most stilted expressions.

If you think of letter writing as conversation put on paper, it's much easier to produce a readable missive. We used to be told that it was ill-mannered to talk about ourselves and what we were doing, but to keep social letters on a high, impersonal level is to make them dull. While the "you" beginning is courteous, here, too, it is usually impossible to go on in that vein indefinitely without growing stilted, especially if your correspondent is at a distance and you really haven't too good an idea of what he's doing or thinking. Everyone likes to talk about himself and is usually more entertaining when he talks about what he's doing and what's going on around him, what touches him and moves him, than he is if he struggles to keep his comments away from strictly personal matters. Gossip belongs in social letters, gossip in the friendly, interested sense about friends in common, about births, deaths, successes, and little disappointments. These are the things you would tell a friend face to face, so why bore him with talk of the weather when what he wants to know about is you?

A bowing acquaintance with other languages and certainly a sound knowledge of our own are aids to stimulating correspondence and conversation. I hope the lists—which do not pretend to be complete—at the end of this section prove helpful in showing how both writing and speaking can be more colorful and exciting.

CHAPTER FORTY-FOUR

STATIONERY AND LETTERS

A WOMAN'S SOCIAL STATIONERY

When you choose your social stationery there are various factors to be considered. If you are a woman, is it for your personal use, or for the use of the entire household? If the latter, it should be of a comfortable size for a typewriter or for a man's handwriting—or for a woman's if hers happens to be large—monarch size, usually single sheets which fold twice. If it's for the whole family it should obviously be more or less neutral. Any conservative color will do, white, gray, blue, tan, usually with cut rather than deckle edges. The paper may have a simple colored border, in a sound plain ink—nothing iridescent or metallic. A die-cut city paper is more conservative than one for the country. It carries just the address and, if you wish, the telephone number, at the top center of the paper. The envelope usually has on the flap just the address with the apartment number, unless the sender lives in a house when just the street number suffices. Often the return address is simply handwritten.

A woman's personal note paper may be of any delicate shade, but I can't say I like pink, lilac, yellow, or apple green, and I definitely dislike the strong colors with vivid contrasting inks except for the school-girl set, if then.

If any heraldic device (see "Heraldry") is used, it should be small, engraved in one color. It may be centered at the top of a double or single sheet or in the upper left-hand corner. If a device is used, it is better to let it stand alone, not complicate the paper with an address. The envelope alone may carry that on the flap.

Paper bought with a single initial engraved, printed, or cut out is better avoided. Engraved initials may be used either in a decorative arrangement in the upper left-hand side of the sheet or in the upper center. They should not be so large as to dominate the paper and should be in one color. Engraved initials may be dye-cut, usually in one color.

Country paper often becomes very insouciant, without the least offense. I still prefer white, gray, blue, or some variation of tan, but a soft gray-green printed in white is very effective. My own best Tiffany paper is thin, faintly ruled, dull-finish gray paper, single sheets, with the place-name and address engraved in forest green. It has matching ink.

The telephone number is nearly always included on country paper and may even be pointed up by a tiny drawing of a telephone. Sometimes country papers carry maps to aid the visitor from town. (See "Informals.")

Every home, city or country, needs a special, excellent grade of white (preferably not engraved) note paper, standard note paper size and usually double fold, for handwritten letters of condolence. Many people of good taste prefer such paper, too, for replies to formal invitations. Dark blue-black or black ink should be used.

PRINTED VERSUS ENGRAVED STATIONERY It is nice, indeed, to have some stationery specially engraved for occasional use. But, considering the cost, it is impractical to carry on all one's personal and business correspondence on such paper. For this reason, most well-equipped households and most busy women with much correspondence to take care of have a secondary utility paper of no pretention whatsoever. I have mine done, a thousand sheets and envelopes at a time, at the local newspaper office because they will print in dark green. The same kind of single-sheet paper with unlined envelope may be bought at any department store stationer's or by mail with blue or black printing of a simple name and address, almost by the pound. The name, address, and often the telephone number appear on the paper, upper center, and the name and address are printed on the envelope flap. This kind of stationery does well enough for all routine correspondence.

LINED ENVELOPES Even the finest quality paper, engraved, is frequently unlined. A lining, if used, should not be giddy or garishly printed. A plain, darker shade of the same color as the paper is pleasant, as is a conservative contrast—a blue lining for white paper. The plaids and the polka dots amuse the youngest set, along with the magenta ink, the facsimile signatures, and the daisy borders. For them anything goes, so long as they are not writing to Uncle Ephraim.

INKS Conservative blue or black ink is still best, when in doubt. If, however, you have a specially designed paper printed or engraved in a certain color it is sometimes nice to continue the color scheme—if the effect is not too garish. I had a friend who went so far as to have brown ink for her typewriter ribbon, for use with a light brown paper, and she signed her name with brown ink. This I cannot recommend. Nor do I like purple ink or any shade of red, though I have known some very proper old ladies to pen their notes with purple ink, which may explain my prejudice. It seems elderly.

Personal letters should not look too arty. As do many of his friends, I treasure those from the late Hendrik Willem Van Loon, with the delightful elephants or little Dutch scenes in crayon on the envelopes, but genius can do many things unbecoming to the rest of us.

I would even go so far as to warn against the ultrafancy new typewriter

WOMAN'S SOCIAL STATIONERY

SCARLETT MORRISON
LIPPINCOTT SQUARE, PENNSYLVANIA

Type is Engravers' Roman. The 8 x 10 paper size is useful for large handwriting or for typewritten letters. Same die used on envelope flap. Or new
die includes "Miss" (more expensive).

Die-cut Note Paper. An appropriate combination of colors might be French
blue with die in darker blue, silver, and white. Border of paper light blue.
Envelope carries flap address: 15 Whippet Lane, Toledo, Ohio, for a house;
Mrs. Elton Gow, 119 Lake Ravine, Ohio, for an apartment. The name may
be used with the address of a house, too, in the same form as it would be
used on the face of a letter, Mrs. or Miss. A good size for this paper is
5¼ x 6¾.

ELYSIAN FIELDS
NEW LONDON
CONNECTICUT

Lozenge on Social Stationery. Type is Bankers' Gothic. The lozenge might be
in blue, gold, and black on blue-and-gray bordered white paper which is
5⅜ x 6¾. Address in matching blue.

type that looks like handwriting. Why should typewriting pretend to be
anything else but? As for handwriting personal letters, with certain exceptions I'll note, avoid it unless your penmanship is beautifully clear.

MAN'S SOCIAL STATIONERY

STEPHEN JOHN KNOX
14 BANCROFT PLACE. N. W.
WASHINGTON 8. D. C.

Type is Engravers' Roman. The 7¼ x 10¼ size is suitable for typewriter or longhand.

Norman Bell
14 East Fifty-second Street
New York 22
Plaza 5-0000

Type, Typo Script, is in black. Size of paper is 7¼ x 10½.

HOUSE PAPER

Westbury

Water Land, 75

Old Westbury

Cedar Hills

Type is Eve Italic. Paper size is 5⅝ x 6¾.

STICKERS While practical usage still calls for a return address on the flap of a social envelope, the post office likes return addresses on the front. When the return address is engraved or printed on the flap, the sender can facilitate matters by using a small printed return address alone, if feasible, on the upper left-hand corner of the envelope. Or, if his return address is not printed or engraved on the envelope's flap, he may write his return address on the face of the envelope, upper left, as small as possible.

A MAN'S SOCIAL STATIONERY

A man's social paper should look masculine—in size, in color, and in quality. He sticks to cream, white, or gray with engraving or printing in black, blue, dark green, or perhaps maroon. He may use his initials, dye-stamped in color or in simple block form at the top of his stationery or upper left, or his name, Geoffrey Lansing (no Mr., of course), with or without the address. Or, he uses the address, upper center, alone, with or without his telephone number. If he has the right to use a crest, he may have it engraved in one color, upper center or to the left, but in this country for an American citizen, male, it seems pretentious.

"PERSONAL" BUSINESS STATIONERY

Business executives often have their own personal stationery, which may bear no relation at all to the firm's. The best of this is in heavy white bond paper, sometimes watermarked, with an engraved or printed address:

40 Wall Street
Office of the President (title often omitted)

This is the generous size of a man's note paper, usually a single sheet. Women in business use this size, too, for personal notes dictated in the office. For such paper, engraving or printing is done in black or, for a woman, in any conservative color she likes such as forest green, maroon, or blue.

Envelopes carry the sender's name but not his title. For example, Miss Miriam La Jeune, 804 Broad Street, Dallas, Texas. Sometimes a suite number is added, but if an executive is important enough to have his own stationery he is usually important enough to be listed on his building's board.

BUSINESS STATIONERY

The best business stationery is white, even when it is the "personal" business stationery of an executive, the kind used for notes of a more or less personal nature sent from the office.

Good white bond paper in the standard 8 x 10 size with standard envelopes is best for business correspondence because it takes erasures well and fits standard file folders without dropping out of sight or extending beyond the confines of the folder. A firm should not try to save money on the stationery with which it faces the competitive world. It should not permit its letterhead to be designed by the office boy, either. It is worth while to have a simple, attractive letterhead laid out by a typographical expert. It should, if possible, be devoid of photographs, drawings of the plant, slogans, and

BUSINESS STATIONERY

DOROTHY PALMER LEIGH
DECORATOR
30 EAST 44TH STREET
NEW YORK
MU 1-0000

Professional Woman's Stationery. Type is Light Gothic. Paper size 7¼ x 10½. Preferred business practice is to use same die on both the paper and on the flap of the envelope (or upper left on the face of the envelope).

SHIRLEY LANG
1 WEST FIFTY-FOURTH STREET
NEW YORK

Business Woman's Personal Stationery with office address. Type is Light Gothic Extended. The paper size, 5¾ x 7¾ is large enough for the typewriter.

WILLIAM AUSTIN BENJAMIN
THIRTY ROCKEFELLER PLAZA
NEW YORK 20, N. Y.

Man Executive's Personal Stationery with office address. Type is Light Gothic Extended. Paper size 7¼ x 10¼.

DOUBLEDAY & COMPANY, INC., *Publishers* ⚓ 575 MADISON AVENUE, NEW YORK 22 · MURRAY HILL 8-5300

Well-designed Business Letterhead with full information, including phone. Size 8½ x 11. Type is Weiss.

extensive lists of officers' names. Lettering or printing is preferable in one color. Simple, clear black on white paper is most effective. To save the reader's effort, the letterhead should list the telephone number.

The envelope should have the name and address of the firm, simply designed, in the upper left-hand corner. The post office dislikes any return address on the flap, especially on letters of a business house.

Certain businesses such as those in the advertising, publicity, fashion, and novelty fields may feel a little leeway is called for in the matter of their stationery. But if they begin their business life by using attention-calling stationery, they may live to regret it if they grow to important proportions. There is nothing more conservative than really big business.

SIGNATURES ON CHECKS, LEGAL PAPERS, AND LETTERS

A woman who signs herself M. L. Gibbons (except to a domestic) seems a little masculine, to me, even on a check. A check signature may carry her given and maiden name plus her married name if her married name is a common one and her first one usual, too. For example, Elizabeth Green might better sign herself Elizabeth Grainger Green, or she may use her husband's name, signing herself Mrs. Bertram Green on her checks, unless her husband has an account in the same bank and this might lead to confusion. If she is a career woman and married, her personal checking account may carry either her married or her maiden name and she may use either as her legal signature. She often pays her income tax under her maiden name, if she uses it in business, because she receives most of her income under that name and is known to the Government as a tax source by her business name.

A woman should not sign business letters just Jane Woods, for example, or Mrs. Gordon Woods alone. A postcard order with no salutation could read, however, "Please send 1 doz. Green Star toothpaste. Charge my account. Mrs. Gordon Woods [address if not printed on card]." If she is leaving a note in a milk bottle for the milkman, she may sign it "Mrs. Woods." Naturally, he knows who she is and doesn't expect more formality than this. But she should never sign any letter, business or social, with a "Mrs." or "Miss" before her signature unless it is in parentheses before (for "Miss") or beneath her name. I prefer to see the married name used in full parenthetically, because it sometimes happens that the careless reader imagines that, although she signs herself "Jennifer Woods," she is perhaps Mrs. Gordon, rather than "Mrs. Gordon Woods," as she meant to indicate. It is better to make it very simple and clear by the writing of her full married name beneath her signature. If she is single she signs her name "(Miss) Jennifer Childress." If her signature is impossible to read she should type or print under her signature: (Miss Jennifer Childress).

In signing a social letter, sign it with one name even if it expresses joint interest or thanks. A thank-you note looks odd signed, "Affectionately, Betty and Joe." If Joe wants to send a message, let there be reference to the fact in the letter. "Joe and I both enjoyed ourselves so much." Or, "Joe joins me in thanks for the lovely week end. Cordially, Betty."

If your name is very usual and you are writing to someone with whom you are on first-name terms, but who may not be able to identify your first name signature too readily, sign yourself "Dorothy Preston," not just "Dorothy," for the recipient may know three or four Dorothys who might be writing such a letter to her.

ILLEGIBLE SIGNATURES Perhaps there is little, if anything, to be done about improving a signature that has evolved, or rather deteriorated, into an illegible chicken track. But you can help people with whom you deal by having stationery with your name and address printed on the envelopes, by using name and address stickers on envelopes, or by typing or printing your name beneath your signature together with your title—Miss or Mrs. (and very especially so if you have a name like Marion, Leslie, or Cecil, which may be masculine or feminine), by having your personal checks printed at slight cost with your name and address at the top or on one end, and by using postcards with your name, address, and, if you wish, telephone number printed on the top. This way you will save your own time as well as that of business people, and you will prevent costly delays and mistakes.

SEQUENCE OF PAGES IN A LETTER

The envelope determines how a single sheet of paper is to be folded for insertion, in one or two folds. Either way, the writing goes from top down, then again from top down on the other side, never crosswise of a single sheet. When a double sheet is used for a short letter the sequence is to write on page one, finish on page three. If all four pages are used they may be in the usual sequence, one, two, three, four, or the letter may go from page one to four, then be folded flat and balance written with paper sidewise down the full folded-out page. The sequence is not important but two things should be remembered: writing should not be written over, Victorian fashion, in the opposite direction, and if the envelope is transparent a protective sheet should be used if page four is readable through it.

ADDRESSING SOCIAL ENVELOPES

The addresses on social envelopes may be typewritten or written by hand depending on whether the letter within was typed or handwritten. Handwriting on the envelope should be orderly and legible, with names either written in full or initials omitted entirely. Either Mr. James Nathan Webster or Mr. James Webster, not Mr. James N. Webster. If an initial normally precedes the name and the full name it stands for is never used then it must necessarily read, Mr. J. Nathan Webster.

In a social address commas are omitted and there are no abbreviations. City and state occupy separate lines. An imaginary margin on the right-hand side may be perpendicular so the last letters of each line line up with those above this way:

Mrs. Ralph Webster Crooks
62 Morningside Drive
Reservoir Heights
Las Vegas
Nevada

or:

Mrs. Ralph Webster Crooks
62 Morningside Drive
Reservoir Heights
Las Vegas
Nevada

The latter is much easier to achieve.

Many people follow these rules very loosely, yet achieve distinguished envelopes. Small numbers may be written out—"Ten," "Twenty," "Eighteen." More complex numbers are nowadays put into numerals in consideration of the postman.

THE USE OF "PERSONAL" AND "PLEASE FORWARD"

It is always assumed that a letter sent to a person's home will be opened only by the addressee. It is therefore rude to other members of the family to mark such a letter "Personal." If, however, you are addressing a purely social, and perhaps quite confidential, letter to a person in his or her office where there is likelihood that mail is first opened by a secretary, then the use of "Personal" in the lower left-hand corner of the envelope is permissible.

If you know only a former address, not the present one, of the person to whom you are writing, you may write in the lower left-hand corner of the envelope, "Please Forward."

THE USE OF "MESSRS."

"Messrs." is the abbreviated form of the French for "Misters." It should be used only for letters addressed to brothers, never as an address for father and son. In sending a Christmas card or a wedding invitation to two young men in a family which includes several others to whom you do *not* wish to address the card or invitation, you write, "The Messrs. Guy and Donald Parsons." If there are merely the two brothers in the family you may address them as "The Messrs. Parsons" or simply "Messrs. Parsons." (See Wedding Section for further information on this point.) This form is usual in the United States, rather than the awkward English "Mr. Guy and Mr. Donald Parsons."

LETTERS THAT MUST BE HANDWRITTEN

Although the typewriter has come into social use, there are a few limitations on its use for such correspondence. No matter how poor your handwriting, don't type a letter of condolence. However, if you are writing a condolence letter from a business office to someone related to a person you have known mainly in business the letter may be dictated and typed.

Informal notes of invitation may be typed, but never formal ones, nor notes of invitation to a small wedding. Letters of congratulation—on the birth of a baby, on a girl's engagement, of felicitation to a girl on her marriage—all should be handwritten. People with social secretaries dictate much of their correspondence, but even the busiest people usually take the trouble to write such notes as these in longhand.

SOCIAL LETTER WRITING

THE CORRECT FORM FOR SOCIAL LETTER WRITING If no engraved or printed address appears at the top of the paper the writer writes her return address in the upper right-hand corner, unless her address is well known to the recipient, thus:

> 876 North Main Street
> Walpole, Massachusetts
> February 6th (year optional)
> (sometimes the date appears, lower left on the last sheet below the signature)

Dear Natalie,

> Affectionately (or sincerely, cordially, lovingly,)
> Prue

February 6th
(optional placement of date)

GETTING STARTED A quick plunge instead of a slow approach is better for any letter, business or social. Get to the point quickly in a business letter. In a social letter start with something that will lead the reader on.

If you have unpleasant but necessary news, try to prepare the way for it tactfully. Don't write, "Uncle Joe died suddenly last night and the family asked me to tell you immediately." Instead, write, "Something has just happened that was a great shock to us all and which will be, I'm afraid, to you, too. I am sorry to have to tell you that Uncle Joe, who hasn't been at all well lately, etc." Again, in such a painful instance, try to think what you would say to this person in his presence, and use the same form.

BREAD AND BUTTER LETTERS

The thank-you for entertainment is obligatory after any overnight stay as a guest. As I said in the discussion of calling cards, I prefer even the briefest little thank-you note to a laconic "Thank you for the lovely week end" scribbled on a visiting card and mailed to a hostess, although, mind you, such a thing is quite correct. A little more human, something that indicates a little more thoughtfulness, is a note, handwritten if your handwriting is legible, typed if it is not, but in any case graceful and friendly:

Monday

Dear Mildred,

Your party and the entire week end, as always, were great fun. I enjoyed meeting the Le Beaus and found them just as stimulating as you promised. In fact, just talking to M. Le Beau stirred me to dig out my French grammar again.

Love,
Josephine

THANK-YOU NOTES FOR ENTERTAINMENT

A note to someone who has never entertained you before, or with whom you are on formal terms, might read:

Saturday

Dear (or more formally, My dear) Mrs. Goodrich,

We have always wanted to see "High Ridge" in the peony season and so enjoyed your invitation last Tuesday, especially as you served cocktails in your really lovely garden. Thank you so much for including us.

Cordially, (or Sincerely yours
or Yours truly)
Josephine Mason

Here, because she knows you are Mrs. Fielding Mason, you don't put that information parenthetically under your signature, of course.

Technically, it is not necessary for you to do more than thank a hostess orally as you leave a luncheon, tea, or dinner party if you are not staying the night or longer. But if it is obvious that the hostess has gone to much trouble to arrange entertainment especially for you, it is certainly decent of you to drop her a line of thanks or to telephone her to express your appreciation. It is a little irritating to a hostess when she has gone to great lengths to entertain people to have them depart with a brief word of thanks and not send her any word again for weeks, months, or sometimes years. Yet that is what happens today, especially in our busy cities, now that the party call has virtually disappeared. But the little party note, even if it is on your card, can certainly take the party call's place if you have a certain sensitivity about such things. Even when you are entertained at dinner very often by the same people, it is courteous at least occasionally to bother to write a few words of appreciation, or to phone your thanks for an especially nice time. And to send a little gift to someone who entertains you often and whom, perhaps, you have no way of entertaining—at least in the same manner—is another pleasant way to say thank you.

Do not, however, send printed cards of thanks for anything. But you may use those charming little floral-bedecked informals or postcards, so long as no sentiments are printed on them. There is no objection to a penny postcard (especially ones specially printed for you) between old friends if they will speed up a thank-you for a happy time together and if they are used informally. You can hardly put intimacies on a postal card for anyone to read. I'd never use even an imported floral or art postcard for a thank-you for overnight entertainment unless I enclosed it in an envelope, and even then it should go only to a close friend, as others would expect more formality.

THANK-YOU NOTES FOR GIFTS

If a gift is given in person, the recipient makes his thanks then and there, though, of course, if he wishes to write a note after the donor has left, it makes a nice, spontaneous gesture. Thank-you notes should be sent just as soon as possible after the receipt of the gift, within a week preferably. A thank-you for such a gift may go on an informal or on a single sheet of paper or on a correspondence card. No one expects more than a few words, but they should sound sincere and really appreciative. Just the day of the week will do for the date, upper right or lower left below the signature. For example:

Dear Jon,

The melodious little alarm clock was exactly what this household needed. Now Allen won't have to rush to the station mornings without his coffee. Next time you come you'll see what a reformation you have wrought!

Cordially,
Nina

Tuesday

"ANGRY" LETTERS

If you are angry, be very careful how you express your anger in a letter. Remember it may travel many miles and that circumstances, or just time, may change your feelings materially. Almost as soon as you have posted an abusive or ill-tempered letter you may wish it back. We all need to have an outlet for our anger from time to time. Write exactly how you feel about something, let yourself go and be furiously vituperative, then "sleep on it." The next day rewrite such a letter and, in calmer tones, say anything that needs to be said. Try to begin your letter with praise, if possible, and end it the same way if you can. How?

Wednesday

Dear Genevieve,

It isn't often that I have any reason to complain about your treatment of the children. In fact, I sometimes think you are, if anything, too likely to overlook their faults but . . .

And end it:

I hate to bring this whole thing up and really wouldn't have except that it was troubling me very much, probably quite unnecessarily. I am sure you, who are usually so very considerate, can help me prevent such a thing happening again.

Get things off your mind. Anger that isn't expressed sometimes makes us vaguely or definitely anxious or depresses us. But, if you can, rehearse what you plan to say. Write it out, let it cool, then see if that is really what you want to say in the way you want to say it. Wasn't that putting it pretty strong? Was it really that way? Couldn't there be extenuating circumstances? Everyone has his bad days and perhaps you are damning a good friend or neighbor for life for something you could clear up with a firm, courteous objection. For instance:

A LETTER OF COMPLAINT TO A NEIGHBOR

June 12th

Dear Mr. Robbins,

You will be sorry to hear that our baby was snapped at yesterday by your dog. I am sure it was the baby's fault, as the dog is normally a friendly animal, but your children do bring him here unleashed and it isn't always possible to keep an eye on him. I wonder if you can ask the boys to leave Rags at home—at least until the baby is old enough to understand he mustn't pull a dog's tail.

With kindest regards to you and Mrs. Robbins,

Cordially,

Jane Doe

LETTERS OF APOLOGY

Occasionally there is need to send a letter of apology. Such letters should really be notes explaining some remissness, such as the sudden canceling of a dinner or failure to keep an appointment, though telephoned or telegraphed word has probably preceded the letter. Apologies of a more serious sort are difficult and sometimes useless to put in a letter. When some grave misunderstanding has arisen it is better, if possible, to settle it in person, as even the most carefully couched letter may merely add fat to the fire.

A note of apology need not be too definite. If you had sudden guests drop in the evening you had promised to play bridge with friends who were not near neighbors, you would write a note something like this if you had not been able to reach your hostess in person by phone:

Wednesday

Dear Carol,

Hope you received my message in time to get another couple for bridge Tuesday night. We had counted on it but had some guests from out-of-town show up unexpectedly just before dinner. Let's try again for next week. Will you plan to come here? Please let me know.

Love,
Ruth

LOVE LETTERS

Love letters are sometimes bombshells. It has often been said that nothing should go into a letter that couldn't be read in court. It seems hard to regard so tender a passion with so suspicious an eye, but life can sometimes distort the tenderest sentiments into something else. Letters are often opened by mistake, or by prying hands. A gentleman should never write anything in a letter which might damage a lady's reputation if his words should be read by someone else. Promises of undying devotion might give an unfriendly reader the impression of intimacies that had never occurred. Even where love is eagerly reciprocated, expressions of it are best not entrusted to the mails unless they are couched in asbestos phrases. Some of the greatest writers of all times have been able to write the subtlest love letters in such a way that the loved one may read anything he or she wishes into the words. But they are written, too, so that no direct promises are made, no reputations put in jeopardy, no intimacies exposed to ridicule should the letter fall into hands other than those for which it was intended.

LETTERS OF SOCIAL REFERENCE AND INTRODUCTION

Letters of social reference are never baldly requested by anyone, and the wise friend never gives one except obliquely. That is, she may write to friends in a community to which a close friend is going and ask them to look him up, stating why she thinks they may have something in common. This leaves a delicate matter entirely up to the friend-at-a-distance and gives her some protection, should entertainment not be convenient at the time. Otherwise, if a letter of introduction is actually written and presented she has little choice but to entertain the stranger in some way as a courtesy to the writer of the letter. The oblique letter of introduction goes this way:

Dear Margaret,

Our dear neighbors here, the Lionel Downings, plan to spend several weeks at The Rock, which seems to be fairly near you. While they are the sort of people who make friends easily, it might be interesting to you both if you could get together during their stay. Both Lionel and Anne play golf well and I think you'd enjoy a foursome. Don't feel this is a "must," of course. I haven't obligated you in any way and if you do call and introduce yourselves it will be a pleasant surprise for them.

Love,
Margery

A direct letter of social introduction has some point, perhaps, if a close friend—and only a close friend—is going abroad and you would like to make his social path pleasant for him where you have friends. You might then furnish him with a letter which he would personally present with his card on making a formal call.

My dear Henriette [this is the European *intimate* form of address]

This will introduce one of our dear friends, Henry Welsh Lanier. I could not let him go to Paris without at least the promise of a glimpse of you. He won't be there very long, something you are sure to regret the moment you all meet. How I envy him the chance to visit you and Paris in the spring.

Love,
Paula

The letter is given the traveler, unsealed, with the name of the friend to whom it is to be presented on the outside:

> Madame
>   Henriette Simon de Nouilly (note form)
> Courtesy Mr. Lanier

The address, presumably, is in his address book.

Give such letters only after mature consideration, for you are guaranteeing your friend's behavior and social acceptability. For this reason never allow a friend to extract such a letter for a friend of his own.

It is becoming common for people to say, even to chance acquaintances, "When you're in St. Louis, do call my good friends the Chases. Any friend of mine is a friend of theirs. They'll treat you royally." And doubtless on a dull evening this far from intimate friend will do just that. And the Chases, not considering this a casual matter, will put themselves out considerably for your sake. Try, always, to leave the initiative up to those in the home territory if you would keep their friendship. Sometimes, however, it is expedient to do something like this if people are traveling on an irregular itinerary and don't know exactly when they will arrive at a stated place. In this case write your friends, "My good friends the Milton Petersons are traveling in California this spring and I have taken the liberty of asking them to let you know when they are in San Francisco. If it is convenient do let them see your cliff gardens. They are ardent gardeners."

WRITING TO A CELEBRITY

No writer, author, public officeholder, artist, musician, or other person singled out because of his accomplishments is ever offended by your words of praise, oral, or written. He may even be stimulated by, and interested in, your criticisms decently given, if you care to give them. He may or may not reply to you depending on the warmth of his personality or the lack of it. He may actually not have the time to take care of such correspondence, especially if he has no secretary. But don't hesitate through diffidence to express yourself, if you feel you have something you'd like to say to such people. Encourage the expression of such response in your children, too. One of my sons at age eight read a charming children's book by a famous writer who had just made his first venture into the juvenile field. Much to my surprise, my son said, "I want to write that man to tell him how much I like his book." He'd never suggested such a thing before but was quite unself-conscious about writing to someone he didn't know. We got pencil and paper, and he printed his own little letter which, with the help of "Who's Who," I sent off to the correct address. Within two days back came a charming reply, which we all treasure and which will be kept in that particular favorite book for grandchildren to enjoy, too. (*Stuart Little*, by E. B. White.) I am sure the author enjoyed the bit of sincere appreciation, sent so spontaneously, quite as much as we enjoyed his delightful reply to a worshipful small boy.

Everyone, I am sure, enjoys appreciation of what he is trying to do if the words he hears or reads are sincere and given without thought of possible benefit to the giver of them. You need never feel constrained to keep your reactions to yourself. Even the President of the United States wants to know what you are thinking—even if you aren't necessarily thinking his way. Let's try some of these letters I'm talking about:

A LETTER TO THE WHITE HOUSE

(Your address
Date in full)

The President of the United States of America
The White House
Washington, D.C., U.S.A. (on the envelope if it's sent from abroad) or

The President
The White House (if sent from anywhere in the country)

Mr. President: (or, less formally, My dear Mr. President, and the tone of your letter can decide which you wish to use.)

Your address to Congress last week brought us new confidence in the quality of your leadership. While my wife and I are not members of your party and have previously taken issue with you on many measures you have endorsed, we now feel that your recent actions have shown us that we have been wrong in some of our judgments. I believe, sir, you are on the road to converting two hitherto hidebound opponents to your party's platform.

I have the honor to remain,

> Very Respectfully,
> (signed) Cyrus Tweedsworth

A LETTER TO AN AUTHOR

> (Your address
> Date in full)

Miss Gertrude Prince
Dogwood Heights
Lake Meadow, Illinois

Dear (or more formally, My dear) Miss Prince:

Your new book, "The Dinner Bell," certainly deserves the best-sellerdom it has achieved so quickly. It gave me so very much pleasure I wanted to tell you so. I am recommending it to all my friends as the best thing you have written. Let's have more about the Judge family.

> Sincerely,
> Lisette Ford Bowens
> (Mrs. Martin Bowens)

WRITING TO A PUBLIC OFFICIAL

Express your appreciation when you feel admiration for something someone has done, even if you don't know that person or have any hope of knowing him. If you disapprove of legislative activities or of pending bills, say so, too, to your properly delegated representative. It is senseless to vent your fury on your friends when there are—in Congress, or in your state or local legislatures, or other bodies, representatives elected by you who must listen to you, pro or con, concerning their actions. Here is a letter to a Congressman:

> June 1, 1952

The Hon. Paul Burns Tyng
House of Representatives
Washington, D.C.

Dear Mr. Congressman (or Sir, or Dear Sir):

May I add my protest to those that are pouring in upon you concerning your recent attack on the Moreland Bill (H.R. 267). I believe the passage of this bill is vitally necessary to the proper safeguarding of interstate motorists, and I urge you to reconsider your stand.

> Sincerely,
> (signed) Julia S. De Palma
> (Mrs. Guido De Palma)

So much righteous indignation which could be a vital and intelligent power in our legislative bodies is wasted by people who have no idea that they have a right and a duty to inform their Senators, Congressmen, their Mayors, and even the President himself, if they are so minded, of their own convictions concerning such vital matters as pending legislation. If you don't know the names of your state's Congressmen and of its Senators, call your local paper or library for the proper information. A postal card or a telegram (composed by you) will register your protest or support. A telegram, properly addressed, is even suitable to send to the President. Do it this way:

THE PRESIDENT
WASHINGTON, D.C.
RESPECTFULLY URGE VETO JENNINGS BILL DISCRIMINATING AGAINST SCHOOL TEACHERS.

> BURTON WHEELER GAINS
> PRINCIPAL, LAWTON HIGH SCHOOL
> BRIGHTON, KANSAS

In wiring the President or any other officeholder, always prepay the wire even where the telegraph company might slip up and accept a collect wire to such an individual. A Congressman might feel called upon to accept the charges because you are a constituent, but he has only limited funds for office expenses and will not appreciate your adding to them.

Always identify yourself if you hold some position, and, if possible, indicate in your wire what your interest is, if you have a biased one. Never misrepresent your interest or you may find yourself in an embarrassing position. If, as the wife of a man who will be deeply affected by the passage or non-passage of a piece of legislation, you appeal for or against it without stating your personal stake in it, it is possible you might be asked to testify for or against the pending bill. Also, your communication might be published, and your vested interest immediately revealed. Congressional committees are always very interested in what is behind a mass protest or support of a bill and whether or not activity has been professionally organized.

OFFENSIVE COMMUNICATIONS

You may be indignant or downright furious at something your representatives in Congress or in the state legislature have done but never send an abusive letter or wire. Try to be as objective as possible and to consider the respect the office deserves, even though you may at the moment consider the holder of it ill-advised, to say the least. An offensive, possibly libelous, telegram is usually refused by the telegraph company. A scurrilous letter can bring a libel suit, although if your Representative should reply in kind—and some have been known to do so—his congressional immunity prohibits legal retaliation by you. He can call you all kinds of a liar, special pleader, fellow traveler, or whatever suits his fancy if you attack him. But you are vulnerable to his wrath if you overstep the bounds of decency and at least relative respect in addressing him. Again it is the office that is protected against abuse, not the man.

DON'T TELEPHONE

A protest to a legislator by telephone is useless unless you, for some reason, have the privilege of talking to him personally. Put your reaction into writing. If he knows his business he will answer you, often with a brief personal letter or at least an acknowledgment of some kind. Before berating him or requesting he vote this way or that, determine what stand he has already taken on the matter. The League of Women Voters, your local newspaper, your local or national political headquarters all have this information, down to the most recent details. It is embarrassing to write a letter to a Congressman only to receive assurance by return mail that one look at his record shows he is on your side and has been battling all along for the cause you urge him to support.

CHRISTMAS CARDS

I think the spirit of Christmas is destroyed when a man and his wife sit down and address hundreds of engraved or printed Christmas cards, partly for business reasons, partly because they know that they themselves will be deluged with other hundreds of cards at which they scarcely have time to glance once the holiday season is upon them. But they will display the deluge, nevertheless, as a proof of their vast and friendly acquaintance.

When Christmas card sending begins to take on such gargantuan and impersonal proportions the time has come to take stock. You will not become a social pariah if you don't send a single Christmas card. If you don't send any at all a great many people will probably cross you off their own swollen lists with a sigh of relief, and like you none the less. If you pare your list to distant friends and leave out the close-by ones to whom you may wish a Merry Christmas in person, that makes sense, too.

If business and friendship have become so intermingled in so social a thing as Christmas card giving it is wise to separate the two anyhow. If business Christmas cards must be sent—and I have never seen much logic in that practice—let the business send them, not the executive and his wife. Better "The Jones Company (or Roy Jones) sends warmest wishes for a Merry Christmas and a Happy New Year" than "Mildred and Roy Jones wish you, etc.," especially when Mildred Jones is not a part of the firm and probably is unknown to most of the firm's clients.

The frenzied sending of Christmas cards to everyone who sent *you* cards the year before or who may be expected to send cards this year is really senseless. It takes courage to abandon the custom and to send cards, only if you want to, only to those people whom you are not likely to greet in person. I would infinitely prefer a card with the warmth of a signature and perhaps a little message for me alone to the most ornate engraved card.

It is, as they say in German, *gemütlich* to have a photograph taken of your children or of the family together or of your house, your pets, or a beloved part of your garden to send to really interested friends, who will often keep such historical cards year after year. These needn't be elaborate at all. They may even be printed on post cards and sent without an envelope, with or without a personal message. They needn't even be Christmassy. Everyone will understand that you are sending a little sentimental keepsake because it is a friendly time of year. A handwritten "Merry Christmas" is all that is needed. You never send such personal cards to people who would not possibly be interested in little Alex's first attempt to stand alone. Others may be sent little holiday informals with a note inside, or any engraved or printed Christmas card in good taste. Religious cards, unless recognizable Art—for example the Raphael Madonna—are often bathetic. Simple cards, not necessarily expensive ones, are best and should always be given the dignity of first-class postage.

ADDRESSING CHRISTMAS CARDS   Christmas cards should always be addressed to a husband and wife even if the sender knows only one of the couple. When a card is sent more or less for business reasons it may be sent to a man or woman's office, to him or her alone. Where a business and social relationship exists which has included the wife or husband, then the card, even a firm's card, may be sent to a home address, addressed to both husband and wife. In this case where the woman is in business under her maiden name, she must be addressed jointly with her husband—Mr. and Mrs. Robert Clawson, never at home as Miss Caroline Carter.

SIGNING CHRISTMAS CARDS   An engraved or printed card has the sender's name or names first: "The Robert Meyer Jobsons (or Mary and Bob Jobson) wish you, etc." A printed card without the name carries the signature at the bottom of the greeting:

Merry Christmas and Happy New Year
The Robert Meyer Jobsons
(Or, Mary [wife's name first] and Bob Jobson)

If Mary is writing the cards she would be more likely to write Bob and Mary Jobson, but it is quite optional. If a list of members of the family is to be given, the father's name comes first: Bob, Mary, Helen, and Peter Jobson. And on this occasion use red ink if you wish, even on the envelope.

Return addresses are often omitted from the envelopes of greeting cards, but it is helpful to add them in the upper left-hand corner of the face of the envelope as the post office requests. In this way you can often discover changes of address of which you might not otherwise be aware. If you contribute to charities that sell Christmas stickers as a means of raising revenue, it is nice to use the seals on your Christmas card envelopes and packages, to further such worthy causes and encourage others to think of Christmas, too, as a time for impersonal giving as well.

WOMEN'S BUSINESS LETTERS

WRITING THE BUSINESS LETTER Everyone has occasion to write a business letter from time to time. A woman's order to a department store, for example, should be a business letter in correct form in order to facilitate the filling of the order. If your handwriting is illegible except to friends, type or print your business letters. Using block letters may seem childish, but it's better, isn't it, than to leave considerable doubt concerning what you are trying to say?

SIMPLICITY OF LANGUAGE The perfect business letter is shorn of the phrases we used to find in text books on English usage. The good letter writer never uses such expressions as "Yours of the fifteenth inst. received and contents noted." Instead he writes, "Thank you for your letter (or for the information)," and goes on, briefly and succinctly, from there, putting in all relevant information and trying whenever possible to limit his communication to one page or less.

As in the social letter, try to avoid the "I" as an opening word and, instead, use some form of "you," if possible. Keep sentences short, avoid the semicolon and the use of quotation marks around words. Here is an awkwardly phrased letter:

September 25, 1952

Mr. Max I. Klug
Klug Inc.
600 York Street
Elizabeth, New Jersey

My dear Mr. Klug:

I am chairman of the board for the York Street Juvenile Society and I would like to know if your firm would, as it has on previous drives, be willing to contribute the sum of $500 for this worthy cause which is, as you know, supported by all the leading business firms in your area and has the endorsement of many prominent people who deal with your store. The Society looks after minor children of working mothers; it affords play space on Saturdays and Sundays; and gives psychiatric and other counseling to families and individual children when they get into various difficulties. May I count on your generous contribution? The enclosed envelope is for your convenience.

Sincerely,
Jane Doe

Instead of using such a self-important approach, the writer should have thought of herself as face to face with this businessman. Then she might have written as she would have talked, and thus produced a better letter. For example:

September 25, 1952

Mr. Max I. Klug
Klug Inc.
600 York Street
Elizabeth, New Jersey

My dear Mr. Klug:

Your firm has given generously to the York Street Juvenile Society each year at this time when our drive takes place.

As you know, the Society's work is to provide greatly needed facilities for the minor children of working mothers. It furnishes play space Saturdays and Sundays. It gives psychiatric and other counseling to families and individual children needing help.

We are sure Klug Inc. will want to continue its support of this work. I enclose a pledge for $500, the amount you regularly subscribe.

Sincerely,
Jane Doe

The constant use of the semicolon on any page, handwritten or printed, causes the eye to jump to the punctuation instead of concentrating on the subject expounded upon, just as a "river"—vertical space on a type page caused by inexpert setting—disturbs vision. Where a semicolon can't be replaced by a simple comma, it is often better to rephrase the thought into two or more separate sentences for easier comprehension.

In any writing avoid the use of quotation marks around words which you feel should get special emphasis for some reason—slang words, for example, which you have habitually placed in quotes to show that they are slang. Your correspondent probably knows slang when he sees it and will read your letter with greater facility if it isn't dancing with quotes, underlinings, exclamation points, and those irritating dots that advertising writers use to indicate a blank spot in their thoughts. If you want to use dots, use them as they should be used, to express an unfinished quotation or thought, "The time has come, the Walrus said..." "So I told Johnny if he ever brought a toad into the house again . . ." In letter writing I think the dash performs the same function nicely. But avoid having your letter full of dashes, too.

It is frequently necessary to write to department stores, shops, and local merchants.

Here is an example of such a to-the-point communication.

(use your address in full)

1482 Cricket Drive
Lake Forrest, Illinois
(date, including year)

B. Coons & Co.
Fifth Avenue at 34th Street
New York 1, New York

Gentlemen:
Please send me the dressing gown №79 listed in your current catalogue.
I would like it in yellow, size 16. My second choice of color is rose. Please
charge to my account.

Sincerely,
Jennifer Woods
(Mrs. Gordon Woods)

LETTERS OF COMPLAINT In writing to a business organization of some kind to
voice a complaint about merchandise or service, think of the recipient of
your letter as another human being like yourself and not just as a representative of an organization. For he will be affected pleasantly or otherwise by the tone of your complaint and inclined, quite possibly, to act
less quickly, or not to your benefit, if you are abusive. Even big companies
are fallible because of the human cogs in the machine. Most companies
want to keep your patronage by making good or at least by apologizing
when things go wrong. I had my first lesson in this when, as a very young
girl, I made, all by hand, an organdy dance dress. I had bought the imported French organdy and binding for the scallops in a highly reputable
department store and had spent weeks making the dress. Imagine my embarrassment when the first time I wore it the fabric began to disintegrate
even before I arrived at the dance. Evidently something had been wrong
with the dye, or the material had been on display in the sun. At any rate,
it was ruined, and so was the evening to which I had looked forward. The
next day I managed to write a good-tempered letter, which set forth all
the circumstances. I suppose it was a very naïve letter, but it was a tem-
perate one. I sent the dress along with it to prove my point and asked only
for enough material to replace the bodice, which was the only part of the
dress that had been so strangely affected. Almost by return mail I received
enough material to make an entirely new dress, plus matching thread and
binding. A letter with it said that the complaint department was so unused
to getting pleasant or humorous letters of complaint that they decided to
do more than I asked. Let's see how a friendly letter of complaint to a
store might read:

786 Decatur Road
Thomasville, Georgia
April 3, 1952

Nu-Fairbanks Seed Company
400 Bond Street
Richmond, Virginia

Gentlemen:

Your company has always given such excellent service that I regret having a complaint to make now. On June 22 you mailed me a package of grass seed I had ordered and which arrived with the carton open and most of the seed gone. I took the matter up with the post office here, and they informed me that the package had not been properly prepared for mailing, nor had it been insured. As the mistake seems to have been made by your shipping department, I am sure you will make good on the order by having the carton more carefully packed before sending it out to me again. Thanking you, I am,

> Sincerely,
> Jane Doe
> (Mrs. John Doe)

If you write politely and make it clear that you expect some adjustment or correction to be made, you will usually get prompt results. Contentious letters and abusive ones sometimes get delayed results or a refusal.

I had a self-important friend whose request for a passport was held up interminably because she was offensive to a government clerk. Somehow her abusive letters and complaints never seemed to get through to the right people. An irritated individual can usually find some way of being uncooperative, especially if he's a little, pushed-around cog in a big machine. Try approaching him with a pleasant letter or a friendly tone of voice and he will be so surprised to hear a complaint couched in such a human manner that he will often find a way to make exceptions in your case. People are people even when they are part of big, often bureaucratic, organizations.

MAKING RESERVATIONS When travel reservations are to be made, letters or wires may be sent by either the husband or the wife. In either case the term "my husband and myself" or "my wife and myself" are used to make clear the relationship of those desiring reservations. Such a letter reads:

285 Park Avenue
New York 21, New York
May 10, 1952

The Manager
The Pines
Pineville, S.C.

Dear Sir:

Will you please reserve a double room with double bed for my husband

and myself, and a single room for my son for July first for one week? If such accommodations are not available at present please let me know the earliest date you can take care of us.

> Sincerely,
> Myra Cox Castle
> (Mrs. Brion X. Castle)

On arrival, the husband registers, "Mr. and Mrs. Brion Castle and son," unless the son is grown in which case he is registered separately, Mr. George Castle.

Mrs. Castle traveling with a maid registers, "Mrs. George Castle and maid."

WIRING RESERVATIONS Husband or wife may wire reservations ahead:

AIR FRANCE
NEW YORK
PLEASE RESERVE TWO SEATS TO PARIS WIFE AND SELF FIRST AVAILABLE JULY DATE. REPLY COLLECT. BRION CASTLE.

In a collect wire the telegraph company has a record of your return address, but it does not accept collect cables. To insure a reply by cable you prepay the reply as well as your cable.

CHAPTER FORTY-FIVE

INVITATIONS, ACCEPTANCES, AND REGRETS

FORMAL INVITATIONS

Formal invitations, engraved or handwritten on conservative paper, are sent out on a number of occasions—for the formal dinner, the debut, the formal dance, and the official luncheon or reception. They are written in the third person and are sent approximately two weeks ahead of time. A formal invitation should be given that much leeway, but not more, as the occasion might be forgotten entirely with more advance notice. (For wedding invitations, acceptances, and regrets, see the Wedding Section.)

THE ENGRAVED FILL-IN INVITATION TO A FORMAL DINNER

Mr. and Mrs. Charles Smith Prescott
request the pleasure of
Miss Wing's [1]
company *at dinner*
on *Tuesday, the Second of May*
at *eight o'clock*
4 East Eightieth Street

R.S.V.P.

ENGRAVED INVITATION TO A FORMAL DINNER

Mr. and Mrs. Elliott Harrison
request the pleasure of your company
at dinner
on Friday, June the fifteenth
at eight o'clock
250 Park Avenue

R.S.V.P.

HANDWRITTEN INVITATION TO A FORMAL DINNER   The formal written invitation may be written on any personal formal writing paper, usually white. If the stationery does not have the address at the top the address is written at the bottom underneath the time.

Dr. and Mrs. Walter MacFee
request the pleasure of
Mr. and Mrs. Anderson's
company at dinner
on Wednesday, September the sixth
at eight o'clock

R.S.V.P.

Poppy Villa
Beverly Hills

[1] Italic type indicates handwriting.

FOR A DINNER IN HONOR OF A SPECIAL GUEST

> Mr. and Mrs. Gerald Fox Healy
> request the pleasure of
> *Mr. and Mrs. Buxton's*
> company at dinner
> on Monday, September the tenth
> at eight o'clock
> to meet Mr. Johnson Parker

R.S.V.P.
21 Sutton Place

INVITATION TO A FORMAL DANCE

> Mrs. Richard William Horst
> requests the pleasure of
> *Mr. and Mrs. Thompson's*
> company at a dance
> on Saturday the thirteenth of September
> at half after ten o'clock
> Lotus Beach Club

R.S.V.P.
One Silver Lane

**INVITATION TO A FORMAL DANCE WHEN THE REPLY IS SENT TO SOCIAL SEC-
RETARY**

> Mr. F. Vernon Osborne
> requests the pleasure of
> *Mr. Scott's*
> company at a small dance
> in honour of his daughter
> Miss Amanda Osborne
> on Monday, the twenty-ninth of December
> at eleven o'clock
> Montclair Country Club

R.S.V.P.
Mrs. Van Broeck
8 East First Street

428

INVITATION TO A DEBUTANTE DANCE

Mr. and Mrs. Macy Linde Turner
request the pleasure of
the company of
Miss Lippincott
at a dance in honour of their granddaughter
Miss Charlotte Gilchrist
on Saturday, the fourth of February
at ten o'clock
River House

R.S.V.P.   Dancing

or, if the parents give the dance:

Mr. and Mrs. David Filmore Gilchrist
Miss Charlotte Sue Gilchrist
request the pleasure of
the company of
Mr. Butterly
on Saturday, the fourth of February
31 Sutton Place South

R.S.V.P.   Dancing

Though on wedding invitations the "Miss" is virtually always omitted, it appears on social, formal ones. Note that the phrase "in honour of" does not appear when the debutante's name is listed under the parents. For an invitation to a small dance the guest's name is frequently not handwritten and the phrase "request the pleasure of your company at a small dance" is substituted. The debutante's name is sometimes omitted.

INVITATION TO A DEBUTANTE RECEPTION

Mr. and Mrs. David Filmore Gilchrist
Miss Charlotte Sue Gilchrist
At Home
Saturday, February first
at five o'clock
31 Sutton Place South

R s.v.p.

AN INVITATION TO AN OFFICIAL LUNCHEON

Mr. and Mrs. J. Peter Morton, Jr.
request the pleasure of your company
at a luncheon in honour of
His Excellency, the President of Chile
and
Señora de Martinez-Garcia
Sunday, the twenty-third of March
at one o'clock

R.S.V.P.   Aboard
17 Gracie Square   The "Mermaid"
New York City   Long Island Yacht Club

The abbreviation "J." is permissible when the first name is never used.

"AT HOME" INVITATIONS Occasionally a prominent bachelor of the old school will have formal "at home" invitations issued. The following card indicates cocktails followed by a buffet supper. These cards usually measure 4½ x 3½.

Mr. Frazier Gerard
at Home

Cocktails etc.
Hampshire House   5:30 o'clock

Older, socially established women still occasionally, too, have their formal "at homes." Cards for them may read:

Mrs. Cornelius W. Dresser
At Home

Tea and Sherry   R.S.V.P.
                                                          The Plaza

430

INFORMAL INVITATIONS

Invitations to informal or semiformal dinner parties, luncheon, tea, cocktails, buffet suppers, and children's parties may be extended by visiting card, informal, or may be telephoned. If the hostess desires an answer she writes R.S.V.P. on them. Otherwise, it is omitted. On the visiting card carrying a message you may or may not—as you wish—draw a line through the engraved name if the message is signed informally with a Christian name.

INVITATIONS ON VISITING CARDS

Lunch
Sunday, June 2nd—1:30 [1]

Mrs. Laurence Patton

R.S.V.P.   775 Park Avenue

Tea
Tuesday, Apr. 16, 4:30

Mrs. William Thayer

R.S.V.P.   *14 Maine Street*

Cocktails Tuesday
March 2nd, 5—7

Mrs. William Goode Harper, Jr.

10 Park Avenue

Birthday party for Lillian
Saturday, August 9, 5—7

~~Mrs. Henry Eugene Cox~~

Do hope you can come—
Love, Julia

R.S.V.P.   Cold Spring Harbor
               Long Island

[2] Italic type indicates handwriting.

Dinner
Friday, March 7, 8 P.M.
Mrs. John W. Klemin
R.S.V.P. 7 Pink Cloud Lane

INVITATIONS ON INFORMALS The "informal" is the fold-over card, once only permissible in white with black engraving, the latter usually from the calling card plate. Today's informals are exactly what the name describes and can be in almost any color and engraved or printed in contrasting colors. Often they bear amusing little maps, sketches of a country home, or initials. They often contain the address and telephone number of the sender, sometimes are gayly bordered, and may be plate-marked. The paper on which they are engraved or printed is often that used in the household's stationery. Colored inks may be used in writing messages on them. Informals have many uses but can't double for calling cards—they are abbreviated stationery and may be used for any short note (except one of condolence, for their informality—and the gaiety they have—would be out of place). They may be used for invitations and for a birth announcement. A double informal, with the joint names, may be used for sending and replying to informal invitations. It may be enclosed with gifts and flowers or used for Christmas messages.

Cocktails Sunday
Mr. and Mrs. Joseph A. Benet
Sept. 6th, 4–6

Bayside Avenue
East Islip, Long Island

Dinner Friday
Mr. Arthur Paul Banks
Nov. 10, 8 o'clock
Cedar Hills Road

R.S.V.P. *Black Tie* [3]

AN EMBOSSED CREST ON A MAN'S INFORMAL. A crest is sometimes used by women but it is not strictly correct. (See Heraldry)

[3] Unless black tie is written on the invitation the guest should assume that street dress will be worn.

MEN

Nov. 3

Dear Sabra,
    Won't you and John please
join us for brunch, Sunday,
November 10th?
                Love
                Natalie

A WOMAN'S INFORMAL WITH MONOGRAM

46 East Fifty-first Street

Mrs. Humphrey Arden Hanshaw

Tea, Saturday April 12th
4-6

INVITATIONS ON THE CARD-INFORMAL   There is a fairly new card that is being used these days—the card-informal. It is larger and heavier than a visiting card, about 3½″ x 4½″ and unlike the usual informal does not fold over.

INVITATIONS AND REPLIES BY TELEPHONE

In issuing an invitation to an informal or semiformal dinner party by telephone, a social secretary or a butler may leave the message with employees of the other households. "Will you please say that Mrs. Willott Meegs invites Mr. and Mrs. Carter to dine on Saturday, the eighth, at eight o'clock. White tie. Mrs. Meegs' number is [give number]." The person taking the message repeats "Dinner at Mrs. Willott Meegs, Saturday, the eighth, eight o'clock. White tie," and of course writes it down.

The reply by telephone follows the same form, "Will you please tell Mrs. Meegs that Mr. and Mrs. Carter will be happy to accept her invitation to dine on Saturday, the eighth, at eight o'clock" or ". . . regret that because of a previous engagement," etc. The wise hostess then sends a reminder in the form of her visiting card or an engraved reminder card to those accepting. If she uses her visiting card these words are written in ink at the top of the card, "To remind—Dinner, Saturday, the 8th at 8." If the address is not engraved on the card it should be written in the lower left-hand corner. Below is an example of the engraved reminder card—

This is to remind you that
Mr. Douglas Stewart
expects you for *dinner*[4]
on *Tuesday, May 2nd*
at *eight* o'clock
Heatherside Farms

In answering an informal invitation by telephone, try to speak to the hostess in person, saying, "We received your invitation for Tuesday and look forward very much to being with you."

If it is necessary to leave the message with a servant, say, "Will you please tell Mrs. Grant that the Bigelows accept her invitation for Tuesday?" Spell your name and be sure he has understood the message by having it repeated to you. It is unforgivable not to answer an invitation and so keep your hostess on tenterhooks. Giving your acceptance too casually to a servant or a person other than the hostess answering the phone, in the expectation that it will reach your hostess, can be equivalent to not answering at all.

INVITATIONS AND REPLIES BY TELEGRAM

FORMAL INVITATION

DR. WALDO BURNS REQUESTS THE PLEASURE OF DR. AND MRS. RICHARD LIONEL FLANDERS' COMPANY AT DINNER MONDAY JUNE SIXTH AT EIGHT O'CLOCK.

FORMAL REPLY

DR. AND MRS. RICHARD LIONEL FLANDERS ACCEPT WITH PLEASURE DR. BURNS' KIND INVITATION FOR MONDAY JUNE SIXTH AT EIGHT.

[4] Italic type indicates handwriting.

INFORMAL INVITATION

PLEASE JOIN US AT DINNER MONDAY THE SIXTH. BLACK TIE.

WALDO BURNS

INFORMAL REPLY

WE ARE DELIGHTED TO ACCEPT FOR MONDAY THE SIXTH AT EIGHT.

LUCY FLANDERS

POSTPONING OR CANCELING AN INVITATION

FORMAL POSTPONEMENT

Mr. and Mrs. Charles Smith Prescott
regret that it is necessary to
postpone their invitation to
dinner from Tuesday, the second of May
to Tuesday, the ninth of May
at eight o'clock
4 East Eightieth Street

R.S.V.P.

INFORMAL CANCELING ON A JOINT CARD

Sorry, we must cancel our
dinner for Tuesday the eighth
but will see you soon, we hope

Mr. and Mrs. Harold Clark Straghan

ACCEPTING INVITATIONS

Invitations are accepted with the same degree of formality with which they
are extended. Formal invitations receive a reply written in the third person
on the first side of one's most conservative stationery—never on informals or
on calling cards, though acceptances may be telephoned or telegraphed.
(See "Replying to Invitations by Telephone.") All invitations should be

answered as soon after receiving them as possible. In accepting a formal invitation or even an informal one where a meal is involved, it is better to repeat the day and the hour, so as to be sure there is no misunderstanding.

Following is a written acceptance in the third person. It follows the same general form whether it is to a dance, dinner, reception, or any other formal entertainment.

Mr. and Mrs. Frederick Walter Stevens
accept with pleasure
the kind invitation of
Dr. and Mrs. Newman
to dine
on Saturday, the fifteenth of June
at eight o'clock

In answering a formal invitation to a "small dance," your acceptance—or regret as the case may be—should omit the word "small." If the names of several people appear on the invitation they should also appear in your acceptance or regret. For example:

Miss Sarah Harrison
accepts with pleasure
the kind invitation of
Mr. and Mrs. John Cameron
Mr. and Mrs. Felix Schwab
to a dance
on Saturday, the tenth of March
at ten o'clock
The Baroque Room

ACCEPTANCES TO INFORMAL INVITATIONS When informal invitations are sent out on visiting cards or on informals and the date, time, and purpose of the gathering are briefly stated but the R.S.V.P. is *omitted*, the hostess is assuming that you'll come if you can. If you are a busy person, you might at least phone or drop your card saying you'll try to get there. If you don't make it, you've made an agreeable try in that direction, at least, and your hostess is conscious of the fact. Even if you don't get around to replying in time for the event, you might send a card later saying, "Hear the tea was a great success. I wish I could have been there—and thank you. Marie." For such little messages on visiting cards salutation and closing are never used and on informals are not necessary, although the inside of an informal is often treated as if it were note paper.

If the informal invitation on a calling card or informal has asked for a reply, of course you reply, as in the following examples:

We accept with pleasure for
the 6th at eight[5]
~~Mr. and Mrs. Lawrence Armitage~~
Lucy

Love to come Friday
~~Miss Laura Sue Ramsey~~
at five
Laura

IF YOU HAVE TO BREAK AN ENGAGEMENT AFTER YOU HAVE ACCEPTED   If an invitation which has been accepted must be broken, the best method is to phone or telegraph the hostess immediately and explain the circumstances. (Such excuses to the White House are written or telegraphed—see "The New Resident in Washington.") The usual social form is: (Telegram) MR. AND MRS. HAROLD CLARK STRAGHAN REGRET THAT MR. STRAGHAN'S ILLNESS MAKES IT IMPOSSIBLE FOR THEM TO KEEP THE ENGAGEMENT WITH DR. AND MRS. PRESCOTT ON MAY SEVENTH.

REGRETS

In regretting, as in accepting, an invitation you must reply with the same degree of formality in which the invitation was extended. A formal regret usually states briefly in a word or two the reason for the refusal—"because of our (my) absence from town," "because of a previous engagement," "because of illness"—but it is often better to omit the reason when illness is involved, except in refusing a most important summons such as one to the White House.

REGRET TO A FORMAL INVITATION

Mr. Preston Moore
regrets exceedingly (or simply "regrets")
that because of a previous engagement
he will be unable to accept
Mr. and Mrs. Treadwell's
kind invitation for the third of August

[5] Italic type denotes handwriting.

REGRETS TO INFORMAL INVITATIONS

So sorry I can't make

~~Mr. Francis Lapolla~~

it the 6th—my parents are
arriving for the week end.
                          Francis

So very sorry I
can't join you and

~~Mrs. William Johnson Peale, Jr.~~

Charles on the sixth—
I'll be in Paris!
               Love, Tabitha

CHAPTER FORTY-SIX

CORRECT FORMS OF ADDRESS

In the matter of correct form of address it is vital to be on sure ground. No one likes to be incorrectly addressed, verbally or in writing, and to so err, carelessly, is often to get off on the wrong foot. We all have at least occasional need of this information, for example in addressing the clergy, the military, or members of Congress.

We need to know the differences, too, in British and American forms of address. We cannot ever use the American formal form "My Dear" on a letter to a British person with whom we are not on intimate terms. In England, as I have explained, "Dear" is the formal form.

For Americans, British titles and forms of address, with all their complex ramifications, are very difficult to remember, especially as they differ very much from those on the Continent. In England there is no "Count," but there is a "Countess." Earl is the British equivalent of the Continental "Count." I have tried to make all the shades of difference clear in each category. When I asked an English friend how the British themselves keep all these distinctions clear in their own minds she replied, "My dear, when you're born into it, the distinctions seem perfectly simple."

GOVERNMENT OFFICIALS

CORRECT FORMS OF ADDRESS

In making *formal* presentations for banquets, etc., the form is always that of the full title: "Ladies and Gentlemen—the President of the United States; the Vice-President of the United States; the Honorable James J. Brown, mayor of Trenton; the Honorable Eustis Coates, Associate Justice of The Supreme Court.

THE PRESIDENT OF THE UNITED STATES

WRITING TO *For domestically mailed letter, address:* The President
The White House
Washington, D.C.

If his wife is included: The President and Mrs. Adams
For letter addressed from abroad: The President of the United States
The White House
Washington, D.C., U.S.A.

Letter opening: Mr. President: (*business*)
My dear Mr. President: (*social*)
Closing: Respectfully (*business*)
Very respectfully (*social*)

SPEAKING TO Mr. President. *In prolonged conversation, occasionally* Sir
INTRODUCING OR REFERRING TO The President, *or* Mr. Adams

THE VICE-PRESIDENT OF THE UNITED STATES

WRITING TO The Vice-President
United States Senate
Washington, D.C.

If wife is included: The Vice-President and Mrs. James
Home Address
Washington, D.C.
In letter addressed from abroad: The Vice-President
United States Senate
Washington, D.C., U.S.A.

Letter opening: Mr. Vice-President: (*business*)
My dear Mr. Vice-President: (*social*)
Closing: Very truly yours (*business*)
Sincerely yours (*social*)

SPEAKING TO Mr. Vice-President. *In long conversation, occasionally* Sir
INTRODUCING OF REFERRING TO The Vice-President *or* Mr. James

CABINET OFFICERS

WRITING TO The Honorable Percy Woods
Secretary of the Interior
Washington, D.C., U.S.A.
If addressed from abroad append "of the United States."

(*A woman is:* The Honorable Mary Fortune
        The Secretary of the Interior
        Washington, D.C.)
If wife is included, the form is: The Secretary of the Interior and Mrs. Woods
                Washington, D.C.
Letter opening: Sir: (*business*)
        My dear Mr. Secretary (*or* Madam Secretary): (*social*)
Closing: Very truly yours (*business*)
      Sincerely yours (*social*)
*All members of the Cabinet are so addressed, with the exception of the
Attorney General. Letters to him are addressed:* The Honorable Jared O'Neil
                             Attorney General
                             (*or* The Attorney General)
                             Washington, D.C.
Letter opening: Sir: (*business*)
        My dear Mr. Attorney General: (*social*)
Closing: Very truly yours (*business*)
      Sincerely yours (*social*)
When Cabinet officers are women, if husbands are included:
  The Secretary of Labor and Mr. Fortune (*diplomatic*)
  Mr. and Mrs. John Fortune
  Home address (*social*)

SPEAKING TO Mr. Secretary, Mr. Woods *or* Madam Secretary *or* Miss *or* Mrs.
Fortune.
INTRODUCING OR REFERRING TO The Secretary of the Interior, Mr. Woods.
The Secretary *or* Mr. Woods. The Secretary *or* Miss *or* Mrs. Fortune

ASSISTANT SECRETARIES

WRITING TO Honorable Benson English
        Assistant Secretary of Labor
        Washington, D.C.
        The Assistant Secretary of Labor and Mrs. English
        (*diplomatic*)
        The Honorable and Mrs. Benson English (*social*)

SPEAKING TO Mr. English
INTRODUCING OR REFERRING TO Mr. English

HEAD OF A DIVISION OR WASHINGTON BUREAU

WRITING TO John Gray, Esquire
        Bureau Address
        Washington, D.C.
Letter opening: Sir: (*business*)
        My dear Mr. Gray: (*social*)
Closing: Very truly yours (*business*)
      Sincerely yours (*social*)

SPEAKING TO Mr. Gray
INTRODUCING OR REFERRING TO Mr. Gray

CHIEF JUSTICE

WRITING TO The Chief Justice
The Supreme Court
Washington, D.C.
If wife is included, the form is: The Chief Justice and Mrs. Meigs
Home address
Letter opening: Sir: (*business*)
My dear Mr. Chief Justice: (*social*)
Closing: Very truly yours (*business*)
Sincerely yours (*social*)
For letter addressed from abroad:
The Chief Justice of the Supreme Court of the United States of America
Washington, D.C.

SPEAKING TO Mr. Chief Justice
INTRODUCING OR REFERRING TO The Chief Justice

ASSOCIATE JUSTICE

WRITING TO Mr. Justice Burke
The Supreme Court
Washington, D.C.
If his wife is included, the form is: Mr. Justice and Mrs. Burke
Home address
Letter opening: Sir: (*business*)
My dear Mr. Justice: (*social*)
Closing: Very truly yours (*business*)
Sincerely yours (*social*)

SPEAKING TO Mr. Justice *or* Mr. Justice Burke
INTRODUCING OR REFERRING TO Mr. Justice Burke

SPEAKER OF THE HOUSE OF REPRESENTATIVES

WRITING TO The Honorable Mark Ewing
Speaker of the House of Representatives
Washington, D.C.
If his wife is included, the form is:
The Speaker of the House of Representatives and Mrs. Ewing
Home address
Letter opening: Sir: (*business*)
My dear Mr. Ewing: (*social*)
Closing: Very truly yours (*business*)
Sincerely yours (*social*)

SPEAKING TO Mr. Speaker *or* Mr. Ewing
INTRODUCING OR REFERRING TO The Speaker, Mr. Ewing, *or* Mr. Ewing *or*
The Speaker

AMERICAN AMBASSADOR

WRITING TO The Honorable Frank Peabody
American Ambassador
London, England
If his wife is included, the form is:
The American Ambassador and Mrs. Peabody
American Embassy
Home address
London, England
In countries other than England the form is:
The Honorable and Mrs. Frank Peabody
Letter opening: Sir: (*business*)
My dear Mr. Ambassador: (*social*)
Closing: Respectfully yours (*business*)
Sincerely yours (*social*)

SPEAKING TO Mr. Ambassador *or* Mr. Peabody

NOTE: the wife of the American Ambassador is Mrs. Peabody. She is only occasionally given a courtesy title socially of "Ambassadress"

A woman actually appointed Ambassador is not referred to as Ambassadress, but as Madam Ambassador.

INTRODUCING OR REFERRING TO The American Ambassador, *or* Ambassador, *or* Mr. Peabody

NOTE: When an Ambassador or Minister is appointed from the Army his Army title is retained. He is addressed as General Frank Peabody, American Ambassador (or Minister). Letter opening (social) is, My dear Mr. Ambassador (or Minister) *or* My dear General Peabody. In making introduction, a Minister away from his post is identified, i.e., The Honorable Philip Gordon, American Minister to Switzerland.

AMERICAN MINISTER

WRITING TO The Honorable Philip Gordon
American Minister to Switzerland
Bern, Switzerland
If wife is included, the form is: American Minister and Mrs. Philip Gordon
American Legation
Bern, Switzerland
In English-speaking countries, the form is: The Honorable and Mrs. Gordon
Letter opening: Sir: (*business*)
My dear Mr. Minister: (*social*)
Closing: Very truly yours (*business*)
Sincerely yours (*social*)

SPEAKING TO Mr. Minister, *or* Mr. Gordon
INTRODUCING OR REFERRING TO The American Minister, *or* Mr. Gordon
NOTE: In presenting American Ambassadors and Ministers in any Latin-American country always include the phrase "of the United States of America" after Embassy or Legation. Avoid the terms American Embassy,

American Legation, even American Minister or American Ambassador. For the latter say, Ambassador of the United States or Minister of the United States. The reason for this is that Latin Americans consider the South American continent and the Central American states "America" too.

A woman representing the United States in either of these posts is Madam Minister or Mrs. Leeds. Letters begin, My dear Madam Minister (or Dear Minister) or My dear Mrs. Leeds.

AMERICAN CHARGÉ D'AFFAIRES, CONSUL GENERAL, CONSUL, OR VICE-CONSUL

WRITING TO Prentis Gates, Esquire
American Chargé d'Affaires, ad interim (*or other of these titles*)
Paris, France

If wife is included, the form is: Mr. and Mrs. Prentis Gates
Home address

Letter opening: Sir: (*business*)
My dear Mr. Gates: (*social*)

Closing: Very truly yours (*business*)
Sincerely yours (*social*)

SPEAKING TO Mr. Gates
INTRODUCING OR REFERRING TO Mr. Gates

JUDGES

WRITING TO The Honorable Jackson Adams
Presiding Justice, Appellate Division
United States Supreme Court
Washington, D.C.

If wife is included, the form is: Honorable and Mrs. Adams
Home address

Letter opening: Sir: (*business*)
My dear Mr. Justice: (*social*)

Closing: Very truly yours (*business*)
Sincerely yours (*social*)

SPEAKING TO Justice Adams
INTRODUCING OR REFERRING TO Justice Adams
NOTE: Judges of other courts are also The Honorable, but are referred to as Judge Jones. In presentations and introductions they are:
The Honorable Judge Jones,
Judge of the Murfreysville Court
Home address

FOREIGN REPRESENTATIVES

Ambassadors and Ministers are referred to as Ambassador or Minister, with name of the country, i.e., Ambassador of Ireland, Ambassador of Peru, with the following exceptions: Ambassador of the Argentine Republic, British Ambassador, Chinese Ambassador, Ambassador of the French Republic (informal form of reference, French Ambassador), Italian Ambassador, Japanese Ambassador, Ambassador of the Netherlands, Ambassador of Thailand, Ambassador of the Union of South Africa, Ambassador of the Union of Soviet Socialist Republics, Minister of the People's Republic of Bulgaria, Ambassador of the Federal People's Republic of Yugoslavia, Minister of the People's Republic of Rumania.

Ambassadors are addressed at their Embassies, i.e.: Ambassador of the Argentine Republic, Embassy of the Argentine Republic. Ministers are addressed at their legations, i.e.: Minister of Switzerland, Legation of Switzerland. Foreign Presidents, Ambassadors and Cabinet Ministers are referred to as His Excellency unless they have royal titles, in which case the royal title is used. Where they have titles such as Doctor, Lord, or Sir, etc., these titles are included.

FOREIGN AMBASSADOR

WRITING TO   His Excellency, The Ambassador of Brazil
                   Washington, D.C.
If wife is included, the form is:
   His Excellency, The Ambassador of Brazil, and Madame Lo Pinto
   Washington, D.C.
Letter opening: Sir: (*business*)
                  My dear Mr. Ambassador: (*social*)
Closing: Very truly yours (*business*)
           Sincerely yours (*social*)
NOTE: The wives of all foreign Ambassadors and Ministers, with the exception of those from English-speaking countries, are given the courtesy title of Madame and in speaking are referred to as Madame Lo Pinto, or Madame, rather than Signora, Senhõra, Vrouw, etc.

SPEAKING TO   Mr. Ambassador
INTRODUCING OR REFERRING TO   The Ambassador of Brazil. Mr. Lo Pinto, the Ambassador of Brazil, *or* Mr. Lo Pinto

FOREIGN MINISTERS PLENIPOTENTIARY AND ENVOYS EXTRAORDINARY

WRITING TO   The Honorable Theodore Lie
                   Minister of Finland
                   Washington, D.C.
NOTE: The designation is not used in addressing the Minister but is the most formal designation used in diplomatic and journalistic references and on visiting cards.
If wife is included, the form is: The Minister of Finland and Mrs. Lie
                                      Legation of Finland
                                      Washington, D.C.

Letter opening: Sir: (*business*)
      My dear Mr. Minister: (*social*)
Closing: Very truly yours (*business*)
      Sincerely yours (*social*)

SPEAKING TO   Mr. Minister *or* Mr. Lie
INTRODUCING OR REFERRING TO   The Minister of Finland, Mr. Lie. The Minister. Mr. Lie

UNITED STATES SENATORS AND STATE SENATORS

WRITING TO   The Honorable Angelo Cognato
      United States Senate
      Washington, D.C.
If wife is included, the form is: The Honorable and Mrs. Angelo Cognato
      Home address
Letter opening: Sir: (*business*)
      My dear Senator Cognato: (*social*)
Closing: Respectfully *or* sincerely yours
NOTE: A woman is The Honorable Genevieve P. Schuler (always with given name). If husband is included, the form is: Mr. and Mrs. John Schuler, home address. Official invitations read: The Honorable Genevieve P. Schuler and Mr. Schuler.

SPEAKING TO   Senator Cognato
INTRODUCING OR REFERRING TO   Senator Cognato

REPRESENTATIVES AND ASSEMBLYMEN

WRITING TO   The Honorable Lincoln Chadwick
      House of Representatives,
      Washington, D.C.
If wife is included, the form is:
   The Honorable and Mrs. Lincoln Chadwick
   Home address
Letter opening: Sir: (*business*)
      My dear Mr. Chadwick (*social*)
Closing: Respectfully *or* sincerely yours
NOTE: A woman is The Honorable Lucy Butterfield. If husband is included, the form is: Mr. and Mrs. Amos Butterfield, Home address. Official invitations read: The Honorable Lucy Butterfield and Mr. Butterfield.

SPEAKING TO   Mr. Chadwick
INTRODUCING OR REFERRING TO   Mr. Chadwick *or* Assemblyman Chadwick

GOVERNORS

WRITING TO   The Honorable Grover Welsh
      Governor of Connecticut,
      Hartford, Conn.

NOTE: Only three states—New Hampshire, Massachusetts, and South Carolina—have officially adopted the title, "Excellency" for their governors, but the term may be used as a courtesy in any state, viz.: His Excellency the Governor, Hartford, Conn., if the letter is from within the state. In a letter from outside the state, if his wife is included: His Excellency the Governor of Connecticut and Mrs. Welsh, Executive Mansion, Hartford, Conn.

Letter opening: My dear Governor,

Closing: Respectfully *or* Sincerely yours

SPEAKING TO Governor Welsh

INTRODUCING OR REFERRING TO Governor Welsh *or* The Governor

MAYORS

WRITING TO The Honorable Joseph Leach
          Mayor of Portland, Oregon
If wife is included, the form is: The Honorable and Mrs. Joseph Leach
                         Home address
                         Portland, Oregon
Letter opening: My dear Mayor Leach

Closing: Sincerely yours

SPEAKING TO Mayor Leach *or* Mr. Mayor
INTRODUCING OR REFERRING TO Mayor Leach *or* The Mayor

PROTESTANT CLERGY

PRESIDING BISHOP OF THE PROTESTANT EPISCOPAL CHURCH IN THE U.S.A.

WRITING TO The Right Reverend Peter Flagg, D.D., LL.D.
          Presiding Bishop
          Address
Letter opening: Right Reverend Sir: (*business*)
          My dear Bishop Flagg: (*social*)
Closing: Respectfully yours (*business*)
          Sincerely yours (*social*)

SPEAKING TO Bishop Flagg

INTRODUCING OR REFERRING TO Bishop Flagg *or* Dr. Flagg

NOTE: All church dignitaries in any formal presentation before audiences of any kind are given their full titles—for example, The Most Reverend Peter Flagg, Presiding Bishop of the Protestant Episcopal Church in America.
NOTE: Bishops of the Episcopal Church may be married, unless they belong to one of the religious orders of the Church. The social form for a Bishop and his wife is The Presiding Bishop and Mrs. Flagg.

BISHOPS OF THE EPISCOPAL CHURCH

WRITING TO   The Right Reverend Gideon Carew, D.D.
Bishop of Cincinnati
If wife is included, the form is:
The Bishop of Cincinnati and Mrs. Carew
Letter opening: Right Reverend Sir: (*business*)
My dear Bishop (*or* Bishop Carew) *or* My dear Bishop
Carew: (*social*)
Closing: Respectfully yours (*business*)
Sincerely yours (*social*)

SPEAKING TO   Bishop Carew
INTRODUCING OR REFERRING TO   Bishop Carew *or* Dr. Carew, the Bishop of
Cincinnati

DEANS

WRITING TO   The Very Reverend the Dean of St. Matthew's *or* The Very Rev.
John Brown, D.D., Dean of St. Matthew's Cathedral
If wife is included, the form is:
The Dean of St. Matthews and Mrs. Brown
Letter opening: Very Reverend Sir: (*business*)
My dear Mr. Dean: (*social*)
Closing: Respectfully yours (*business*)
Sincerely yours (*social*)

SPEAKING TO   Mr. Dean
INTRODUCING OR REFERRING TO   The Dean of St. Matthews *or* Dean Brown

ARCHDEACONS

WRITING TO   The Venerable Charles Smith
Archdeacon of Richmond
If wife is included, the form is:
The Archdeacon of Richmond and Mrs. Smith
Letter opening: The Ven. Archdeacon Smith
Venerable Sir: (*business*)
My dear Archdeacon *or* My dear Mr. Archdeacon: (*social*)
Closing: Respectfully yours (*business*)
Sincerely yours (*social*)

SPEAKING TO   Mr. Archdeacon
INTRODUCING OR REFERRING TO   The Archdeacon of Richmond *or* Archdeacon Smith

CANONS

WRITING TO   The Very Reverend Canon Charles Pritchard Thomas, D.D.,
LL.D.
Canon of St. Mary's Cathedral

If wife is included, the form is: The Canon and Mrs. C. P. Thomas
Letter opening: The Rev. Canon Thomas, D.D.
      Reverend Sir: (*business*)
      My dear Canon Thomas: (*social*)
Closing: Respectfully yours (*business*)
    Sincerely yours (*social*)

SPEAKING TO Canon Thomas
INTRODUCING OR REFERRING TO Canon Thomas *or* Doctor Thomas, Canon of St. Mary's

CLERGYMEN WITH DOCTOR'S DEGREES

WRITING TO The Reverend Joseph E. Long, D.D.
If wife is included, the form is:
 The Rev. Dr. Joseph E. Long and Mrs. Long
Letter opening: Reverend Sir: (*business*)
      My dear Dr. Long: (*social*)
Closing: Respectfully yours (*business*)
    Sincerely yours (*social*)

SPEAKING TO Dr. Long
INTRODUCING OR REFERRING TO The Reverend Doctor Long

CLERGYMEN WITHOUT DOCTOR'S DEGREES

WRITING TO The Reverend Frank K. Hanson
If wife is included, the form is: The Rev. and Mrs. Frank K. Hanson
Letter opening: Reverend Sir: (*business*)
      My dear Mr. Hanson: (*social*)
Closing: Respectfully yours (*business*)
    Sincerely yours (*social*)

SPEAKING TO Sir
INTRODUCING OR REFERRING TO The Reverend Frank Hanson

In addressing clergymen who do not have doctor's degrees, it is wiser to use as an invariable form "Reverend Sir" or "Sir," since this is always correct and will avoid giving offense to the several groups who are used to a particular form of personal salutation.

The use of Father, designating an Episcopal clergyman or a priest who is not a member of a religious order, is a matter of the clergyman's own preference. When Father is used in writing it is usually coupled with the surname of the clergyman—The Reverend Father Huntington, O.H.C., without the Christian name. In direct reference, it is Father or Father Huntington. However, in the Episcopal order of Franciscans, where there is a name conferred by the order—as among Roman Catholic religious orders—it would be The Reverend Father Joseph, O.S.F. in writing, and Father or Father Joseph in direct reference. Lay brothers are addressed in writing as Brother Charles, O.H.C., and in direct reference are Brother or Brother Charles.

RABBIS OF THE ORTHODOX, CONSERVATIVE, AND REFORMED
CONGREGATIONS   Rabbis of Orthodox Congregations preach in synagogues. Rabbis of Conservative Congregations preach in synagogues or
temples, depending on the term adopted by individual groups. Rabbis of Reformed Congregations preach in temples. The term "church" is not used.

RABBI WITH SCHOLASTIC DEGREE

WRITING TO   Rabbi Nathan Sachs, D.D., LL.D.
            Temple Emmanuel
            Bridgeport, Connecticut
If wife is included, the form is:
    Rabbi (*or* Doctor) and Mrs. Nathan Sachs (Some prefer Rabbi to *Doctor*)
    Home address
Letter opening: Sir: (*business*)
                My dear Rabbi (*or* Doctor) Sachs: (*social*)
Closing: Very truly yours (*business*)
         Sincerely yours (*social*)

SPEAKING TO   Rabbi Sachs *or* Doctor Sachs
INTRODUCING OR REFERRING TO   Rabbi Sachs *or* Doctor Sachs

RABBI WITHOUT SCHOLASTIC DEGREE

WRITING TO   Rabbi Harold Schwartz
            Beth David Synagogue
            New York, N.Y.
If wife is included, the form is: Rabbi and Mrs. Harold Schwartz
                                Home address
Letter opening: Sir: (*business*)
                My dear Rabbi Schwartz: (*social*)
Closing: Very truly yours (*business*)
         Sincerely yours (*social*)

SPEAKING TO   Rabbi Schwartz *or* Rabbi
INTRODUCING OR REFERRING TO   Rabbi Schwartz *or* Rabbi

CANTOR (Chief Singer of the Congregation)

WRITING TO   Cantor Chaim Levy
            Beth David Synagogue
            New York, N.Y.
If wife is included, the form is: Cantor and Mrs. Chaim Levy
                                Home address
Letter opening: Sir: (*business*)
                My dear Cantor Levy: (*social*)
Closing: Very truly yours (*business*)
         Sincerely yours (*social*)

SPEAKING TO   Cantor Levy
INTRODUCING OR REFERRING TO   Cantor Levy

THE ROMAN CATHOLIC HIERARCHY

THE POPE

WRITING TO His Holiness, the Pope *or*
His Holiness Pope Benedict I
Vatican City
Rome, Italy
Letter opening: Your Holiness *or*
Most Holy Father:
Closing: Your Holiness' most humble servant

SPEAKING TO Your Holiness *or* Most Holy Father
INTRODUCING OR REFERRING TO His Holiness, the Holy Father, the Pope, the Pontiff

CARDINALS

WRITING TO His Eminence Patrick, Cardinal Terrance (Archbishop of San Francisco)*
Letter opening: Your Eminence:
Closing: I have the honor to be, Your Eminence, etc.

SPEAKING TO Your Eminence
INTRODUCING OR REFERRING TO His Eminence *or* Cardinal Terrance

BISHOPS AND ARCHBISHOPS

WRITING TO The Most Reverend Peter Judson, D.D. (Archbishop of St. Louis) (Bishop of Dallas)*
Letter opening: Your Excellency:
Dear Bishop (Archbishop) Judson:
Closing: I have the honor to be, Your Excellency, etc.

SPEAKING TO Your Excellency Bishop (Archbishop) Judson
INTRODUCING OR REFERRING TO His Excellency Archbishop *or* Bishop Judson

ABBOTS†

WRITING TO The Right Reverend Abbot Henry J. Loester (add designated letters)
Letter opening: Right Reverend Abbot *or* Dear Father Abbot:
Closing: I have the honor to be, Right Reverend Abbot, etc.

SPEAKING TO Abbot Loester
INTRODUCING OR REFERRING TO The Right Reverend Henry J. Loester *or* Abbot Loester

*Title in parenthesis not needed in address, but may be used if desired.
†Members of the order of St. Benedict—The Right Reverend *Dom* Anslem McCarthy, O.S.B. addressed as Dom McCarthy.

PROTHONOTARIES APOSTOLIC, DOMESTIC PRELATES AND VICARS GENERAL

WRITING TO   The Right Reverend Monsignor Robert McDonald
Letter opening: Right Reverend Monsignor *or* Dear Monsignor McDonald:
Closing: I am, Right Reverend Monsignor, etc.

SPEAKING TO   Monsignor McDonald *or* Monsignor
INTRODUCING OR REFERRING TO   Monsignor McDonald

PAPAL CHAMBERLAINS

WRITING TO   The Very Reverend Monsignor Robert Ross
Letter opening: Very Reverend Monsignor *or* Dear Monsignor Ross:
Closing: I am, Very Reverend Monsignor, etc.

SPEAKING TO   Monsignor Ross
INTRODUCING OR REFERRING TO   Monsignor Ross

PRIEST

WRITING TO   The Reverend Father James L. Cullen
Letter opening: Reverend Father *or* Dear Father Cullen:
Closing: I am, Reverend Father, etc.

SPEAKING TO   Father Cullen
INTRODUCING OR REFERRING TO   Father Cullen

BROTHERS

WRITING TO   Brother William Shine
Letter opening: Dear Brother William *or* Dear Brother:
Closing: I am, respectfully yours

SPEAKING TO   Brother William *or* Brother
INTRODUCING OR REFERRING TO   Brother William

SISTERS

WRITING TO   Sister Mary Annunciata
Letter opening: Dear Sister:
Closing: I am, respectfully yours

SPEAKING TO   Sister Annunciata *or* Sister
INTRODUCING OR REFERRING TO   Sister Annunciata *or* Sister

EASTERN ORTHODOX COMMUNION Greek Orthodox clergymen choose before ordination whether they are to be celibate or non-celibate priests. All highest clergymen, i.e. archbishops, patriarchs, and archimandrites, are celibates. The supreme head of all Orthodoxy is the Ecumenical Patriarch of Constantinople—equivalent to the Pope among Roman Catholics.

PATRIARCHS

WRITING TO   His Holiness, the Ecumenical Patriarch of Constantinople
                      Constantinople, Turkey
Letter opening: Your Holiness:
Closing: Respectfully yours

SPEAKING TO   Your Holiness
INTRODUCING OR REFERRING TO   His Holiness
NOTE: There are three other patriarchs of the ancient sees of Jerusalem, Alexandria and Antioch. They are addressed, Your Beatitude, as is the Archbishop of Greece.

ARCHBISHOP

WRITING TO   The Most Reverend Michael
                      Archbishop of Cincinnati
                      Address
Letter opening: Your Eminence:
Closing: Respectfully yours

SPEAKING TO   Your Eminence
INTRODUCING OR REFERRING TO   His Eminence
NOTE: Metropolitans, who supersede suffragan bishops in rank, are found in large cities mainly among the Russian and Syrian Orthodox congregations but in Greece they function, as well, for the Church of Greece. They are addressed, The Most Reverend Peter, Metropolitan of Boston, etc., and like Archbishops are referred to as Your Eminence.

BISHOP

WRITING TO   The Right Reverend Basil Althos
                      Bishop of Chicago
                      Address
Letter opening: Right Reverend Sir: (*business*)
                      My dear Bishop: (*social*)

SPEAKING TO   Your Grace
INTRODUCING OR REFERRING TO   His Grace

ARCHIMANDRITE

WRITING TO   The Very Reverend James Papas
                      Address
Letter opening: Reverend Sir: (*business*)
                      Your Reverence: (*social*)
Closing: Respectfully yours

SPEAKING TO   Father James *or* Father Papas
INTRODUCING OR REFERRING TO   Father James *or* Father Papas

PRIEST

WRITING TO The Very Reverend Nicholas Kontos
Address
Letter opening: My dear Father Kontos:
Closing: Yours respectfully

SPEAKING TO Father
INTRODUCING OR REFERRING TO Father Kontos
NOTE: In the case of a non-celibate priest the form including his wife
would be The Reverend Nicholas Kontos and Mrs. Kontos in the U.S. or,
abroad, the Reverend Nicholas Kontos and Madame Kontos. At present
there are no Greek Orthodox sisterhoods in America, but they exist in
Greece and are very similar to those of the Roman Catholics.

BRITISH OFFICIALS AND INDIVIDUALS   It is exceptional for a private
individual to address a King, Queen, or other member of a royal family. A
foreigner should address them only through the regular diplomatic or other
proper channel.

An American citizen in addressing any member of the royal family or
nobility or any foreign official may use the American form of formal address
and close.

THE KING

WRITING TO His Majesty the King
Buckingham Palace
London (*England—on cables and envelopes only*)
Letter opening: Sir *or* Your Majesty:
Closing: Yours very respectfully *or* Yours respectfully

SPEAKING TO Your Majesty. *In prolonged conversation,* Sir
INTRODUCING OR REFERRING TO His Majesty the King
NOTE: In England the form for letter closing always properly begins with
"Yours." The term "My dear" is the intimate form of opening, "Dear" the
formal—quite the opposite of the American form.

THE QUEEN

WRITING TO Her Majesty the Queen
Buckingham Palace
London (*England—on cables and envelopes only*)
Letter opening: Your Majesty:
Closing: Yours very respectfully *or* Yours respectfully

SPEAKING TO Your Majesty. *In prolonged conversation,* Ma'am
INTRODUCING OR REFERRING TO Her Majesty the Queen

A ROYAL PRINCE OR A ROYAL DUKE

WRITING TO   His Royal Highness the Duke of Trent, K.G.
            Local address
Letter opening: Sir:
Closing: Yours respectfully

SPEAKING TO   Your Royal Highness. *In prolonged conversation,* Sir
INTRODUCING OR REFERRING TO   His Royal Highness the Duke of Trent *or*
His Royal Highness, Prince Thomas

A ROYAL PRINCESS OR A ROYAL DUCHESS

WRITING TO   Her Royal Highness the Princess Royal
            Local address
            Her Royal Highness the Duchess of Trent
            Local address
            Her Royal Highness Princess Anne
            Local address
Letter opening: Madam:
Closing: Yours respectfully

SPEAKING TO   Your Royal Highness. *In prolonged conversation,* Ma'am
INTRODUCING OR REFERRING TO   Her Royal Highness the Princess Royal

THE PEERAGE

A DUKE, NON-ROYAL

WRITING TO   His Grace, the Duke of Norfolk, K.G.
            Local address
Letter opening: Sir: (*business*)
            Dear Duke: (*social*)
Closing: Yours very truly (*business*)
        Yours sincerely (*social*)

SPEAKING TO   Your Grace. *In prolonged conversation,* Sir
INTRODUCING OR REFERRING TO   The Duke of Norfolk
NOTE: In England invitations are never addressed jointly (on the envelope) to husband and wife but to the wife alone. Christmas cards may be addressed jointly, however. (See "The British Use of Esquire.") In this case the form would be: Their Graces, the Duke and Duchess of Norfolk.

THE ELDEST SON OF A DUKE AND HIS WIFE

NOTE: The eldest son of a Duke has the highest family title below his father's, such as Marquess. His wife has the corresponding title, such as Marchioness.

454

THE YOUNGER SONS OF A DUKE

NOTE: The younger sons of a Duke have the title Lord with their Christian and family names.

WRITING TO   The Lord James Beaumont
             Local address
Letter opening: Sir: (*business*)
             Dear Lord James: (*social*)
Closing: Yours very truly (*business*)
           Yours sincerely (*social*)

SPEAKING TO   Lord James
INTRODUCING OR REFERRING TO   Lord James Beaumont
NOTE: The terms "My Lord" and "My Lady" are forms of address used mainly by servants and tradesmen, although the usage is not *necessarily* menial.

THE DAUGHTERS OF A DUKE

NOTE: The daughters of a Duke take the title Lady with their Christian and family name.

WRITING TO   Lady Bridget Beaumont
             Local address
Letter opening: Madam: (*business*)
             Dear Lady Bridget: (*social*)
Closing: Yours very truly (*business*)
           Yours sincerely (*social*)

SPEAKING TO   Lady Bridget
INTRODUCING OR REFERRING TO   Lady Bridget Beaumont

THE WIFE OF THE YOUNGER SON OF A DUKE

NOTE: The wife of the younger son of a Duke has the title Lady with her *husband's full name* or *Christian name* but not with his surname only.

WRITING TO   Lady James Beaumont
             Local address
Letter opening: Madam (*business*)
             Dear Lady James: (*social*)
Closing: Yours very truly (*business*)
           Yours sincerely (*social*)

SPEAKING TO   Lady James
INTRODUCING OR REFERRING TO   Lady James Beaumont

A MARQUESS

WRITING TO The Most Honourable the Marquess of Remington, *or*
The Marquess of Remington (*less formal*)
Local address
Letter opening: Sir: (*business*)
Dear Lord Remington: (*social*)
Closing: Yours very truly (*business*)
Yours sincerely (*social*)

SPEAKING TO Lord Remington
INTRODUCING OR REFERRING TO The Marquess of Remington, *or* Lord
Remington (*less formal*)

A MARCHIONESS

WRITING TO The Most Honourable the Marchioness of Remington, *or*
The Marchioness of Remington (*less formal*)
Local address
Letter opening: Madam: (*business*)
Dear Lady Remington: (*social*)
Closing: Yours very truly (*business*)
Yours sincerely (*social*)

SPEAKING TO Lady Remington
INTRODUCING OR REFERRING TO The Marchioness of Remington, *or* Lady
Remington (*less formal*)

THE SONS AND DAUGHTERS OF A MARQUESS

NOTE: The eldest son of a Marquess has the highest family title below his
father's such as Earl—his wife has the corresponding title such as Countess.
The younger son and daughter of a Marquess take the title Lord or Lady,
respectively. The wife of the younger son of a Marquess has the title Lady
combined with her husband's full name.

AN EARL

WRITING TO The Right Honourable the Earl of Leeds, G.C., V.O.,
C.M.G. (*business*) *or* The Earl of Leeds (*social*)
Local address
Letter opening: Sir: (*business*)
Dear Lord Leeds: (*social*)
Closing: Yours very truly (*business*)
Yours sincerely (*social*)

SPEAKING TO Lord Leeds
INTRODUCING OR REFERRING TO The Earl of Leeds *or* Lord Leeds (*less
formal*)

A COUNTESS, WIFE OF AN EARL

WRITING TO   The Right Honourable the Countess of Leeds (*business*) *or*
The Countess of Leeds (*social*)
Local address
Letter opening: Madam: (*business*)
Dear Lady Leeds: (*social*)
Closing: Yours very truly (*business*)
Yours sincerely (*social*)

SPEAKING TO   Lady Leeds
INTRODUCING OR REFERRING TO   The Countess of Leeds *or* Lady Leeds (*less formal*)

THE ELDEST SON OF AN EARL AND HIS WIFE

NOTE: The eldest son of an Earl has the highest family title below his father's such as Viscount. His wife takes the corresponding title such as Viscountess. The younger sons of an Earl and their wives have the title Honourable.

WRITING TO   The Honourable George Bird
Local address
Letter opening: Sir: (*business*)
Dear Mr. Bird: (*social*)
Closing: Yours very truly (*business*)
Yours sincerely (*social*)

SPEAKING TO   Mr. Bird
INTRODUCING OR REFERRING TO   Mr. Bird

WRITING TO   The Honourable Mrs. George Bird
Local address
Letter opening: Madam: (*business*)
Dear Mrs. Bird: (*social*)
Closing: Yours very truly (*business*)
Yours sincerely (*social*)

SPEAKING TO   Mrs. Bird
INTRODUCING OR REFERRING TO   Mrs. Bird
NOTE: The daughters of an Earl have the title Lady combined with their Christian and family names.

A VISCOUNT

WRITING TO   The Right Honourable the Viscount Bemis (*business*) *or*
The Viscount Bemis (*social*)
Local address
Letter opening: Sir: (*business*)
Dear Lord Bemis: (*social*)

Closing: Yours very truly (*business*)
Yours sincerely (*social*)

SPEAKING TO   Lord Bemis
INTRODUCING OR REFERRING TO   Viscount Bemis *or* Lord Bemis (*less formal*)

A VISCOUNTESS

WRITING TO   The Right Honourable the Viscountess Bemis (*business*)
or The Viscountess Bemis (*social*)
Local address
Letter opening: Madam: (*business*)
Dear Lady Bemis: (*social*)
Closing: Yours very truly (*business*)
Yours sincerely (*social*)

SPEAKING TO   Lady Bemis
INTRODUCING OR REFERRING TO   Viscountess Bemis *or* Lady Bemis (*less formal*)

THE FAMILY OF A VISCOUNT

NOTE: The eldest son of a Viscount and *also* his wife have the title Honourable.

WRITING TO   The Honourable Thomas Bemis
Local address
Letter opening: Sir: (*business*)
Dear Mr. Bemis: (*social*)
Closing: Yours very truly (*business*)
Yours sincerely (*social*)

SPEAKING TO   Mr. Bemis
INTRODUCING OR REFERRING TO   Mr. Bemis

WRITING TO   The Honourable Mrs. Bemis   *Omission of husband's Christian name indicates she is wife of eldest son.*
Local address
Letter opening: Madam (*business*)
Dear Mrs. Bemis: (*social*)
Closing: Yours very truly (*business*)
Yours sincerely (*social*)

SPEAKING TO   Mrs. Bemis
INTRODUCING OR REFERRING TO   Mrs. Bemis
NOTE: The younger sons of a Viscount and their wives also have the title Honourable.

The daughters of a Viscount take the title Honourable with their Christian and family names.

WRITING TO   The Honourable Gladys Bemis
                 Local address
Letter opening: Madam: (*business*)
                 Dear Miss Bemis: (*social*)
Closing: Yours very truly (*business*)
           Yours sincerely (*social*)

SPEAKING TO   Miss Bemis
INTRODUCING OR REFERRING TO   Miss Bemis

A BARON

NOTE: A Baron is addressed as "Lord" never as Baron.

WRITING TO   The Right Honourable the Lord Lancer (*business*) *or* The Lord
                 Lancer (*social*)
                 Local address
Letter opening: Sir: (*business*)
                 Dear Lord Lancer: (*social*)
Closing: Yours very truly (*business*)
           Yours sincerely (*social*)

SPEAKING TO   Lord Lancer
INTRODUCING OR REFERRING TO   Lord Lancer

A BARONESS

NOTE: A Baroness in her own right has the title Baroness but may *also* be addressed as Lady. The wife of a Baron who is not a Baroness in her own right is addressed only as Lady.

WRITING TO   The Right Honourable the Baroness Lancer (*business*)
                 or The Baroness Lancer
                 or The Lady Lancer: (*social*)
Letter opening: Madam: (*business*)
                 Dear Baroness (*or* Lady) Lancer: (*social*)
Closing: Yours very truly (*business*)
           Yours sincerely (*social*)

A BARONESS (not in her own right)

WRITING TO   The Right Honourable the Lady McGuiness (*business*)
                 or The Lady McGuiness (*social*)
                 Local address
Letter opening: Madam: (*business*)
                 Dear Lady McGuiness: (*social*)
Closing: Yours very truly (*business*)
           Yours sincerely (*social*)

SPEAKING TO   Lady McGuiness
INTRODUCING OR REFERRING TO   Lady McGuiness

THE CHILDREN OF A BARON

NOTE: All the sons of a Baron and their wives have the title Honourable. The daughters of a Baron also have the title Honourable.

A BARONET

NOTE: A Baronet has the title Sir and the abbreviation for Baronet (Bart. or Bt.) follows his name.

WRITING TO   Sir Thomas Riddle, Bart.
              Local address
Letter opening: Dear Sir: (*business*)
              Dear Sir Thomas: (*social*)
Closing: Yours very truly (*business*)
          Yours sincerely (*social*)

SPEAKING TO   Sir Thomas
INTRODUCING OR REFERRING TO   Sir Thomas Riddle

THE WIFE OF A BARONET

NOTE: The wife of a Baronet has the title Lady with her husband's surname only.

WRITING TO   Lady Riddle
              Local address
Letter opening: Dear Madam: (*business*)
              Dear Lady Riddle: (*social*)
Closing: Yours very truly (*business*)
          Yours sincerely (*social*)

SPEAKING TO   Lady Riddle
INTRODUCING OR REFERRING TO   Lady Riddle
NOTE: The sons and daughters of a Baronet have no title.

DOWAGER

NOTE: The term "Dowager" is used as part of a title in England to indicate the *earliest* surviving widow of a preceding peer. She is known as the Dowager Duchess of Wickham. A later surviving widow who might be the widow of the first earl's son, nephew, etc. would be known as Mary, Duchess of Wickham, retaining this usage for life even if the Dowager dies

A KNIGHT

NOTE: A Knight has the title Sir and the initials of his order or orders of knighthood, if any, follow his name.

WRITING TO   Sir John Waugh, G.C. M.G.
              Local address

Letter opening: Dear Sir: (*business*)
              Dear Sir John: (*social*)
Closing: Yours very truly (*business*)
         Yours sincerely (*social*)

SPEAKING TO Sir John
INTRODUCING OR REFERRING TO Sir John Waugh

THE WIFE OF A KNIGHT

NOTE: The wife of a Knight has the title Lady with her husband's surname only.

WRITING TO Lady Waugh
           Local address
Letter opening: Dear Madam: (*business*)
              Dear Lady Waugh: (*social*)
Closing: Yours very truly (*business*)
         Yours sincerely (*social*)

SPEAKING TO Lady Waugh
INTRODUCING OR REFERRING TO Lady Waugh

OFFICIALS

NOTE: Englishmen in England are not addressed as Excellency even when entitled to be so addressed in other countries.

MEMBERS OF PARLIAMENT

NOTE: A member of Parliament has no special title except that the letters M.P. are written after his name.

MEMBER OF THE HOUSE OF COMMONS WITH TITLE

WRITING TO Sir Henry Coakley-Smith, K.B.E., M.P.
           Local address
Letter opening: Dear Sir: (*business*)
              Dear Sir Henry: (*social*)
Closing: Yours respectfully (*business*)
         Yours sincerely (*social*)

SPEAKING TO Sir Henry
INTRODUCING OR REFERRING TO Sir Henry Coakley-Smith

WITHOUT TITLE

WRITING TO L. T. Needham, Esq., M.P.
           Local address
Letter opening: Dear Sir: (*business*)
              Dear Mr. Needham: (*social*)

Closing: Yours very truly (*business*)
　　　　Yours sincerely (*social*)

A PRIVY COUNCILLOR

NOTE: A Privy Councillor is addressed according to his title, if any, preceded by the title The Right Honourable. If without title, he is addressed simply as The Right Honourable, "Mr." in the salutation. (All members of the British Cabinet are members of the Privy Council and as such are entitled to the initials P.C. after their names.)

The wife of a Privy Councillor has no title as such.

WITH TITLE

WRITING TO　The Right Honourable Sir Percy Harron, Bart., D.S.O., P.C.
　　　　　　Local address
Letter opening: Sir: (*business*)
　　　　　　　Dear Sir Percy: (*social*)
Closing: Yours respectfully (*business*)
　　　　Yours sincerely (*social*)

SPEAKING TO　Sir Percy
INTRODUCING OR REFERRING TO　Sir Percy Harron

PRIME MINISTER (BRITISH)

NOTE: A Prime Minister (being a Privy Councillor) has the title The Right Honourable in addition to and preceding any other title.

WRITING TO　The Right Honourable Harley Asheden, M.P.
　　　　　　Prime Minister, London
Letter opening: Sir: (*business*)
　　　　　　　Dear Mr. Asheden: (*social*)
Closing: Yours respectfully (*business*)
　　　　Yours sincerely (*social*)

SPEAKING TO　Mr. Asheden
INTRODUCING OR REFERRING TO　Mr. Asheden

A BRITISH AMBASSADOR

NOTE: A British Ambassador is addressed according to his rank of nobility, if any, his title of rank being preceded by the diplomatic title His Excellency.

WRITING TO　His Excellency The Right Honourable Sir Harold Pim,
　　　　　　G.C.M.G.
　　　　　　British Ambassador
　　　　　　Rome, Italy
Letter opening: My Lord (*or* Sir, *according to rank*): (*business*)
　　　　　　　Dear Lord X, Sir Harold, Mr. Y: (*according to circumstances*) (*social*)

Closing: Yours very truly (*business*)
Yours sincerely (*social*)

SPEAKING TO   Your Excellency (*when at post,* Sir Harold *elsewhere*)
INTRODUCING OR REFERRING TO   Sir Harold Pim

A MINISTER

NOTE: A British Envoy Extraordinary and Minister Plenipotentiary is addressed according to rank of nobility, if any. Otherwise he is addressed:

WRITING TO   Edward Matheson, Esq.
Envoy Extraordinary
British Legation
Bogotá, Colombia
Letter opening: Sir: (*business*)
Dear Mr. Matheson: (*social*)
Closing: Yours very truly (*business*)
Yours sincerely (*social*)

SPEAKING TO   Mr. Matheson
INTRODUCING OR REFERRING TO   Mr. Matheson

THE BRITISH USE OF ESQUIRE

In addressing business or social correspondence to a British gentleman without title, use the abbreviation Esq. (for Esquire) after the name, but do not precede it with "Mr." or "The Honorable" or, of course, any title such as "Lord," "Sir," or "Dr." A British surgeon, however, is always addressed as "Henry Walters, Esq." and in conversation is "Mr. Walters," not "Dr. Walters."

In diplomatic and extremely formal correspondence "Esquire" is written out in full.

"Esquire" was originally used as a lesser title. It indicated a knight's eldest son and the younger male members of a noble house whose hereditary title was borne only by the eldest male heir. Now professional men and all those working in the so-called genteel callings—arts, letters, music —and members of the House of Commons and the landed gentry are addressed in writing with Esq. following their names. Often, too, older gentlemen of standing are called "Squire" in conversation.

Where a man's name is combined with his wife's, as in this country, the form is "Mr. and Mrs. Bertram Montgomery," but this form is rare in Great Britain except on joint visiting cards. Engraved invitations are addressed to the wife alone. Inside on the top, or in the blank space provided is written "Mr. and Mrs. Montgomery." Invitations written in longhand are also addressed to the wife. If a visiting card is used for an invitation the envelope is addressed to the wife alone and on the top of the card is written "Mr. and Mrs. Montgomery" (no Christian name).

Christmas cards may be addressed "Mr. and Mrs. Bertram Montgomery."

MILITARY FORMS OF ADDRESS

In the modern Army, rank is used in all grades for both men and women in the service.

Doctors in the service have a starting rank of Lieutenant, and common Army usage dictates that they be addressed by this rank, but junior officers are not infrequently called Doctor. Once, however, they reach Captain or above, they are generally addressed socially by the Army title so long as they remain in the Army. Officially they are always addressed by rank.

Chaplains in the Army and Navy are always called, officially and socially, Chaplain, no matter what the military rank. There is no ruling, however, expressed in regulations, which would prevent men from referring to Catholic priests as Father.

Non-commissioned officers are addressed officially by title, i.e., Sergeant for all grades of Sergeants—First Class, Master, Sergeant, etc.—but there is no regulation prohibiting the use of Mister socially.

A Warrant Officer in any branch of the service is called Mister officially and socially.

In the Navy, Commanders and above are addressed socially by their Navy titles. All below that rank are Mister. Properly a Lieutenant Commander is Mister, but recent custom accords him the courtesy title of Commander socially, with his actual status indicated to all by his two and a half stripes.

Any officer in command of a ship, whatever its classification, is Captain for the period of his command, no matter what his usual title may be.

Cadets of the U. S. Military Academy are Mister socially and in conversational references, but Cadet officially.

National Guard and Reserve officers not on active duty do not use their titles socially or in business affairs unless their activities have some bearing on military matters. Whenever the rank is used, the proper designation must follow the name, i.e., ORC or NG.

Socially and in ordinary military use Lieutenant Colonels, Major Generals, Brigadier Generals, and Lieutenant Generals are known as Colonels and Generals, respectively.

Vice-Admirals and Rear Admirals are Admiral.

CHAPTER FORTY-SEVEN

HERALDIC DEVICES

WHAT IS A COAT OF ARMS?

The subject of heraldry is very complicated, and what I shall say here for the purposes of etiquette is necessarily greatly simplified.

In the twelfth century the custom arose for warriors to emblazon their distinguishing devices on their shields so they could be recognized as friend or foe in battle. Armor was, of course, completely concealing when a man's visor was down as he prepared to engage. His device therefore became his trademark and was for further clarity also embroidered on the sleeveless jacket worn over the armor—hence "coat of arms." On his helmet a warrior wore a crest—say a falcon or dragon, forged to the metal headcovering. The helmet itself might be of a distinctive shape and design. Today a coat of arms consists of these three elements—the *shield* with its *coat of arms*, surmounted by the helmet, in turn surmounted by the *crest*. To these may be added "mantling," symbolic of the flowing cape or cloak which was attached to the warrior's shoulders and "supporters," which are generally animals such as lions, unicorns, deer, or even human beings, and the motto on a "ribbon." Mantling is mere optional ornamentation but permission for the use of supporters must be granted by the Heralds' College in London, which is the best-known authority on heraldry. Some other countries have such governmental heraldic authorities—Holland, for one, with its *Koninklijk Nederlands Genootschat Voor Geslacht-en-Wapenkunde Bleijenburg* in the Hague.

By the sixteenth century many families other than the descendants of Crusaders and Knights bore coat-armor—hence the term "armigerous families"—and some merely assumed arms. It therefore became necessary for the Heralds' College, or College of Arms, established by law in 1483, to make an official "visitation" of all the families in each of the shires and counties, recording pedigrees and arms. These pedigrees form the basis of the mass of records collected in the College of Arms.

If you are of English, Scotch, or Welsh descent the College for a fee (which may run to several hundred dollars) will examine your claim to the right to use a coat of arms. Or if that right cannot be established it will for a fee grant you a new coat of arms. If you are of Irish descent you may apply to a separate College of Heralds in Dublin.

To determine your family's right to a coat of arms, you need to know, not only the full name of your earliest American ancestor, but his connection with an armigerous British (or Continental) family and your own exact line of descent from him. If your name is Clark, Smith, Carpenter (all occupational names) or even as unusual as Blenkenship, Hungerford, or Cobleigh, you don't merely ascertain that there were coats of arms for these families and proceed to appropriate them for your own use. It may be happenstance that your name is the same. One Miller family, say, may have the right to use the coat as listed in Burke's *General Armoury,* another, quite unrelated, could not legally use that coat. Using a coat of arms not rightfully yours is like using another's trademark (as a matter of fact, some coats of arms actually are copyrighted in the United States).

The right to use a coat of arms was given in perpetuity to all direct male descendants *of the name.* In the early days of our country it was the younger sons who were more likely to emigrate from Europe than the oldest ones who inherited the title and lands. These younger sons sometimes came alone, sometimes with families, and with limited funds and even more limited experience in the kind of work they had to do in a new, rough country. In a generation or two perhaps former claims to gentility were forgotten, as all struggled together to build the new world. But the male heirs of the name, of direct descent from the original armigerous forebear, still had the right to the coat of arms, a right many a family here today doesn't realize it has.

THE LOZENGE

A woman who is an heiress or co-heiress (with sisters), i.e., an orphaned, female descendant of a line—without brothers or nephews of the same name —has the right to use her father's coat of arms (as may her sisters) in a

JONES   BROWN

Mr. Jones marries Miss Brown (an heiress) and their coats of arms are impaled

Their son has their combined coats of arms quartered, thus:

diamond-shaped "lozenge." (Illustration.) If she marries she may "impale" her arms with those of her husband—the shield is divided in two vertically and his arms are blazoned on the left side of the dividing line and hers on the right. (Illustration.) Her children may "quarter" their parents' arms. (Illustration.) Technically, if an "heiress" marries a non-armigerous husband she and her children lose their armigerous standing, but in this country there is considerable relaxation of this fine point. An heiress may continue to use the lozenge herself even though she marries a non-armigerous husband. But if she is not an heiress she is not correct in using her family's arms on the lozenge after her marriage.

HOW ARE HERALDIC DEVICES USED?

The commonest use of the coat of arms is on an *ex libris*, or bookplate, as a marking for silver or on fine china, on wedding invitations and announcements, on place cards and menu cards for formal entertaining, and, of course, the device may be painted and framed for wall decoration.

FULL COAT OF ARMS MASCULINE The full coat of arms—shield with crest and motto—or what is known as a "gentleman's heraldic bearings" is never properly used on personal belongings by a woman. Women in medieval days did not normally go forth in battle and therefore did not carry shields. It is proper form in England, to which we must look for precedent as we have nothing resembling heraldic authority in our own governmental setup, for a woman to use a *crest* on her stationery, on personal linens, etc., but never a coat of arms on a shield. The lozenge, however, is approved, and if a British woman is titled she uses the coronet of her rank above it. But a woman of an armigerous family, especially is she is unmarried or a widow, may use just the crest (Illustration) or the coat of arms itself—but only if blazoned on a lozenge. (Illustration.)

A MARRIED WOMAN'S USE OF THE DEVICE A woman whose father has a coat of arms, but whose husband has not, shows better taste, actually, in saying good-by to it and its feminine modifications once it has been used on her wedding invitations and announcements and, if she wishes, on silver her family has given her. A painted coat may be displayed on bedroom or library walls, not too conspicuously, but the device may not be adopted either by her husband or children. No woman ever uses a heraldic motto, for these were invariably aggressively masculine and unsuited to feminine social use.

CREST, *at left;* Full coat, *center;* Miss Brown's coat of arms on a lozenge, *right*

USE ON WEDDING INVITATIONS AND ANNOUNCEMENTS When the names of a girl's mother and father appear jointly on wedding invitations and announcements it is correct, if the father has a coat of arms, to use it in its complete form —shield, helmet, crest, and motto—embossed without any color at the top of the invitation. If the bride's mother alone—or some woman sponsor alone—has her name on the invitation or announcement she may not use her husband's or father's coat of arms. She may, however, use her lozenge embossed without color.

SILVER MARKING AND THE COAT OF ARMS When the bride's family gives her silver they may mark it with her father's crest and motto without the shield and helmet. Very large plain pieces such as soup tureens, punch bowls, etc., may carry a full marshaling—shield, helmet, crest, supporters, and mantling, with the motto on a "ribbon" beneath. If later silver is given to match the original set, it *may* be marked the same way, though silver given before the marriage or after it by the groom's family bears his crest. Additional silver purchased by husband and wife during the course of their marriage may, if they wish, have their respective arms, "impaled," on it, but the lozenge should not be used, except possibly upon the wife's personal silver—toilet articles, cigarette case, vanity, etc.

CHAPTER FORTY-EIGHT

WRITING AND CONVERSATION CAN BE MORE COLORFUL

A BOWING ACQUAINTANCE WITH OTHER LANGUAGES

Once I spent a challenging evening with a well-known writer, who seemed to question every other word spoken. In his adjacent study he had an unabridged dictionary open on a stand. He referred to it at least twenty times in the course of general conversation. It was a rather nervous way to chat, I thought, but the quality of this man's writing indicates that the dictionary is a good, close friend in the best sense. He does not use impressive words merely to seem erudite, but he uses words with an exactitude that is delightful.

We needn't be linguists to get along nicely in cultured circles. We do need to master quite a list of foreign phrases and words, however, so that we do not find ourselves beyond our depth.

In this country moneyed circles are not necessarily cultured ones at all. In Europe cultured people, threadbare professors or not, move in the highest social circles by virtue of their erudition and sophistication. Here, one is more likely to encounter learning at a level below that of millionaires and so-called social leaders. Certainly, to move in café society and its equivalent you need to know less than nothing about language—your own or those of contemporary or ancient civilizations.

The kind of society we should seek is that which stimulates us to express ourselves verbally, that spurs our intellectual processes, that makes us want to achieve our own ultimate. People who keep us on our social and mental toes are good for us and make us grow spiritually, socially, and, often as an end result, financially. Ours is supposed to be, but of course is not, a wholly democratic, classless society. A foreign student once remarked to a friend of mine that all Americans are in their own minds actually divided into three classes, their own, the one directly above them, and the one just below.

As we mature as a nation, as the world produces more balance between the haves and the have-nots, so shall we each seek our place among people solely on the basis of intellectual and social gifts comparable to our own— because of their congeniality. Actually, money should never be a determinant of "class," and with thoughtful human beings it can't determine real values. But young people should keep in mind that they should prepare themselves to move up, to widen their social circles, to move with greater ease among strangers, to be able to go any place and meet anyone without feelings of social inferiority.

As one form of insurance against the dreaded feeling of "not belonging" among educated people, I urge at least a bowing acquaintance with Latin and French, a slight knowledge, at least, of Greek roots, prefixes, and suffixes, an ability to pronounce German and Spanish words reasonably well.

While it is affected to interject foreign words and phrases into ordinary conversation at every opportunity, it is nevertheless true that such expressions are second nature to many intellectuals and it is more comfortable to be on terra firma with them than on terra incognita. You don't need more than good, native intelligence and a lively curiosity to build an interesting vocabulary. Even a college education is no guarantee that a man or woman can express himself in well-chosen words—he may be too lazy mentally or too unsure of himself.

A friend of mine who had to go to work at fifteen has one of the most excellent vocabularies I know, and he doesn't build it solely by consulting the dictionary from time to time. Instead, he has a flattering way—considering his job as head of a large organization—of asking you, during the course of conversation, what a word you have used means. Then the next time you meet him you will find him using this word correctly and easily in his own conversation. The very fact that you know he has built his vocabulary step by step himself, not just absorbed it as many of us do from our family circle as part of our cultural heritage, makes you admire his continuing drive for self-improvement.

In the following lists of foreign words or phrases which you'll very likely encounter as you enlarge your social circle, I have omitted instruction on pronunciation. I would rather have you hear how a word should be pronounced than simply read it, dictionary-wise. Learn how the word or phrase looks, how it is spelled, what it means, then find someone who can really tell you how it sounds. In this way, with a little practice, you will have made many good, useful, and descriptive phrases and words part of your vocabulary. You won't be afraid to verbalize them if you have learned how to pronounce such words and phrases from someone who really knows and if you have listened for them to crop up in conversation. Be like my friend—if you don't know, ask. People will like you all the more for it. If you hear a man say he's "suffering from Weltschmerz," don't mumble a reply and make a mental note to look that one up in the dictionary sometime—you'll probably forget to, anyhow. Instead, say, "Is that how you pronounce that word? I've been meaning to look it up but now you can help me. I'm not even too sure of what it means." This is certainly better than forming hazy ideas of new words just by listening, then never questioning or looking them up in a reference work. I have a relative who shied from the forthright "pregnant" and substituted her notion of the correct and seemingly more modest French term, which she thought was "*ancienne*," actually "ancient," when what she meant was, of course, "*enceinte*."

There are words which, politely speaking, are more acceptable in a foreign tongue than in our own sometimes brusque one. It is, therefore, possible to speak of a lady's *derrière*, the baby's *po-po* (German and French baby talk for "fanny"), a *pot de chambre* (decorators seize on antique examples as perfect flower vases these days), a *crime passionel*, a *cochon*, a *fille de joie*, a *maison close*. In fact, if you want, you can interject almost anything in a foreign tongue into an English conversation and what in English might be considered crude becomes in another language at least bearable. This phraseological distinction is also a device often used in best sellers to spare the ignorant and to give those who can translate some slight feeling of naughty superiority.

An interest in language—all language—is tantamount to an interest in people. If you go to your Italian grocer and ask him how to pronounce *pizzeria*, he will not only tell you, but instruct you in the making of the specialty, *pizza*. He will be delighted at your interest and will add to your store of Italiana on each subsequent meeting. Borrow your son's Latin primer and ask him to help you on modern Latin pronunciation and you will create a warm feeling of co-operation between you, and a feeling of being needed—through momentary superiority—on his part. Ask help from your librarian by telling her what you want to accomplish.

The library is full of foreign language textbooks, unabridged dictionaries with all kinds of foreign words and phrases, foreign periodicals. Getting away from the notion that English alone is enough for anyone widens our social horizons in a neighborly sense that can embrace the whole world. It increases our own self-esteem and so puts us on a better footing with others. Every added competence increases our social acceptability and makes new friends.

FRENCH WORDS AND PHRASES

À BAS down with

À CHEVAL on horseback, but also used in the sense that one can consider or look at a thing from two sides

À COMPTE on account, in part payment. You might hear a phrase like this: "Here's a few dollars, *à compte.*"

À DEMI half, by halves, or imperfectly. In the latter sense it is used in this fashion: "That man! He does everything *à demi!*"

AFFAIRE DE COEUR a love affair

À HAUTE VOIX loudly

À LA BONNE HEURE Good! Fine! An expression of approval

À LA CAMPAGNE in the country

ALLEZ-VOUS-EN! Be off with you! Used literally and also as we use "Get out" to indicate non-belief.

À MOITIÉ half

À MOITIÉ MOITIÉ half and half

À MON AVIS in my opinion

À OUTRANCE to the bitter end

À PROPOS timely, reasonably

À PROPOS DE BOTTES literally, about shoes. Used parenthetically to indicate an irrelevancy; *à propos* of nothing.

À REBOURS inside out, across the grain, wrong sense and, idiomatically, "Quite the contrary."

ARRIÈRE-PENSÉE mental reservation

AU COURANT up to date

AU LEVANT to the East, also the sunrise

AU PLAISIR awaiting the pleasure (of seeing you again)

AU PLAISIR DE VOUS REVOIR in anticipation of seeing you again

AU PREMIER the first floor above the street floor, our second floor

AU RESTE as for the rest, besides

AU REVOIR until we meet again

AU REZ-DE-CHAUSSÉE even with the street, the ground floor

AU PRINTEMPS in the spring

AVANT COUREUR forerunner

AVANT-PROPOS preface or preliminary

À VOLONTÉ at pleasure

À VOTRE SANTÉ To your health! A toast.

BAS BLEU bluestocking, puritanical

BEAU GARÇON fine, but not necessarily handsome, fellow

BEAUX YEUX pretty eyes, but often means a pretty or handsome face

BEL AMI a beau, a handsome fellow

BELLE DAME an elegant matron, rather than a pretty woman

BÊTE NOIRE stumbling block, bugbear

BIENTÔT soon

BON JOUR good day; how do you do

CARTE BLANCHE without interference

CHEF-D'OEUVRE a masterpiece

CHEMIN DE FER train, also a gambling game

CHERCHEZ LA FEMME Look for the woman. A phrase often used in connection with the solving of crimes.

CLIQUE small group with mutual interests; set. Often used disparagingly.

COMME IL FAUT the way it should be; correct

CONCIERGE desk clerk or door tender, sometimes janitor

COQUETTE a flirt

COUP D'ÉTAT political stroke

COUP D'OEIL a glance

CUL-DE-SAC dead end

CULTE a group following a particular leadership; clique

D'ACCORD in harmony; in agreement

DÉCOLLETÉ low-cut (usually said of a neckline)

DÉJEUNER À LA FOURCHETTE American- and English-style breakfast (requiring a fork)

DISTINGUÉ distinguished

EN FAMILLE together with the family

EN PASSANT in passing

FAUX PAS a social error

FEMME DE CHAMBRE chambermaid

FEMME FATALE an irresistible woman

GARÇON boy, waiter

GAUCHE awkward, left

GIGOLO male, paid dancing partner

GRANDE DAME dowager

HOMME D'ESPRIT witty fellow

HOMME DU MONDE man of the world

HONI SOIT QUI MAL Y PENSE Old French. Evil to him who evil thinks.

JEUNE FILLE a young girl, girlish. (For one of her age, her behavior is certainly *jeune fille*.)

JEUNESSE DORÉE young fashionables

JOIE DE VIVRE exuberance, joy of living

LÈSE-MAJESTÉ high treason

MAÎTRE D'HÔTEL headwaiter

MAÎTRESSE mistress, schoolteacher

MAL DE MER seasickness

MARIAGE DE CONVENANCE an arranged marriage

MAUVAIS GOÛT poor taste

MÉNAGE household

MERCI thank you

MIDI the South, noon. Le Midi—the South of France

MODISTE milliner

MON CHER (masculine) *ma chère* (feminine) my dear

MON VIEUX old man (in the complimentary sense—"That's quite a hat, *mon vieux*.")

MOUSSELINE DE SOIE very fine silk

N'IMPORTE it doesn't matter

NOBLESSE OBLIGE one's position implies decent behavior

NOM DE GUERRE a pseudonym by a writer of barbed material

NOM DE PLUME pen name

NOUVEAU RICHE newly rich and considered crass

OBJET D'ART collector's item

ON DIT people say, also literally, one says

OUI yes

PARDONNEZ MOI I beg your pardon

PARVENU a pusher, one who tries to crash into high circles

PETITE AMIE little friend (often used in the sense of "mistress")

PETIT À PETIT L'OISEAU FAIT SON NID Little by little the bird builds his nest. Nothing is accomplished overnight.

PETIT DÉJEUNER French breakfast of coffee and rolls

PIÈCE DE RÉSISTANCE the main dish, the incomparable

PIED-À-TERRE a temporary residence

POUR FAIRE RIRE to make one laugh (often used sarcastically)

POUR PASSER LE TEMPS to pass the time

PREMIÈRE first appearance of a play, movie, etc.

PRIX FIXE fixed price. A meal that is listed as *prix fixe* includes all courses at the indicated price.

RACONTEUR a (usually) witty storyteller

RAISON D'ÊTRE the purpose

RECULER POUR MIEUX SAUTER to retreat, the better to advance later

RÉPONDEZ S'IL VOUS PLAIT (R.S.V.P.) please reply

ROBE DE CHAMBRE   a dressing gown

ROBE DE STYLE   period gown

SALON   a meeting place for intellectuals in someone's home

SANG-FROID   composure

SAVOIR-FAIRE   knowledgeableness, sophistication, social awareness, social grace

SAVOIR-VIVRE   good breeding

SOIRÉE   an evening entertainment, usually at home

SOUPÇON   a little bit, a suggestion of

SUCCÈS D'ESTIME   polite acclaim out of respect alone, often a critical success rather than a monetary one

TABLE D'HÔTE   the whole meal at a fixed price

TÊTE-À-TÊTE   confidences, intimate conversation between two people

TIENS!   an expression of annoyance or surprise. Pshaw! Or, "You don't say so?"

TOUJOURS   as ever, always

TOUR DE FORCE   a thing accomplished by sheer determination

TOUT DE SUITE   right now

TOUT ENSEMBLE   all together, complete

VIVRE DE SON SAVOIR FAIRE   to live by one's wits

VOILÀ   There! Sometimes, "Here comes——" (Voilà la Princesse Maude)

VRAISEMBLANCE   likelihood, probability

LATIN PHRASES

AD NAUSEAM   to the point of nausea, disgust. We might say, "His complaints went on, *ad nauseam.*"

ARS LONGA VITA BREVIS   Art is long, [but] life is short.

AVE ATQUE VALE   Hail and farewell. This is a phrase that you very likely have noticed many times in obituaries. It frequently appears on tombstones.

CARPE DIEM   Make (good) use of the day, seize the opportunity.

CAVEAT EMPTOR   Let the buyer beware!

DEUS EX MACHINA   a wonderful, fortuitous and unexpected happening or circumstance that saves the situation

ECCE HOMO   Behold the man!

ET TU, BRUTE   You, too, Brutus. Caesar said this when he saw his great friend among his assassins.

It is used to indicate treachery—sometimes facetiously.

EX CATHEDRA   Usually used in connection with a pronouncement from the Pope. Literally, "from his chair" or officially.

EX LIBRIS   from (among) the books (of), a bookplate with the owner's name, coat of arms, etc., to be pasted on the inside cover of a book

HABEAS CORPUS   A writ or order permitting a prisoner to be produced at a stated time to determine the court's right to detain him. This is a phrase beloved by crime reporters and mystery writers.

IPSO FACTO   by the act itself

MARE NOSTRUM   our sea. A phrase used politically by the Italians to indicate the Mediterranean. And a phrase particularly liked by editorial writers.

MULTUM IN PARVO   much in little

NOTA BENE note well (often seen abbreviated: N.B.)

OBITER DICTUM a conversational aside; in law an incidental decision that isn't binding

OMNIA VINCIT AMOR Love conquers all.

O TEMPORA! O MORES! Oh [the] times! Oh [the] customs! (often used in a pseudo-shocked sense)

PATER FAMILIAS father of the family (very commonly used)

PAX VOBISCUM Peace be with you.

PER CAPITA each individual (actually counted by heads)

PER DIEM by the day, daily. "Department store workers are sometimes paid on a per diem basis."

PER SE by itself, intrinsically. "I do not object to television per se, but I do object to many of the programs supposedly suitable for children."

PINXIT sometimes seen on paintings after the signature—meaning "painted it"

POST SCRIPTUM the after writing, or thought. Abbreviated by P.S. when an additional message is appended to a letter after the signature. Sometimes when still another paragraph is added a P.P.S. precedes it, meaning *post post scriptum.*

PRO BONO PUBLICO for the public good

PRO PATRIA for one's country

PROPTER HOC because of this

PRO TEMPORE for the time being (abbreviated as *pro tem*)

QUID PRO QUO tit for tat

QUOD ERAT DEMONSTRANDUM The problem is solved, or demonstrated. A geometric term usually used in its abbreviated form,

Q.E.D. These initials appear at the end of a solved geometric problem but are often used conversationally to indicate that a matter is closed.

RARA AVIS a rare bird, a unique person or thing

REDUCTIO AD ABSURDUM reduced to an absurdity, silly

REQUIESCAT IN PACE Rest in peace.

SCULPSIT used after the signature of a sculptor—meaning "he or she sculptured it"

SIC thus. Indicates when used parenthetically that the quotation thus used, although quoted as it appeared is, of course, incorrect in some way

SIC TRANSIT GLORIA MUNDI So go the glories of the world; everything's so transient. (Often used)

SINE QUA NON without which nothing (is good or advisable); a necessary condition

STET Let it stand. An editorial indication that something which has been crossed out should be left as it was originally.

SUMMUM BONUM the supreme good

TAEDIUM VITAE boredom

TEMPUS FUGIT time flies

VENI, VIDI, VICI I came, I saw, I conquered. (Julius Caesar's report of a victory.)

VERBATIM word for word (very commonly used in conversation)

VICE VERSA the relations between things being reversed

VINCIT OMNIA VERITAS Truth conquers all.

VIVA VOCE by word of mouth, orally

VOX POPULI, VOX DEI The voice of the people [is] the voice of God.

FAMILIAR WORDS AND PHRASES FROM OTHER LANGUAGES

AUF WIEDERSEHEN (Ger.) Till we meet again.

DAS ALTER WACHT, DIE JUGEND WAGT (Ger.) Old age considers, youth ventures.

DOLCE FAR NIENTE (It.) It's sweet to do nothing.

EINMAL IST KEIN MAL (Ger.) One swallow doesn't make a summer (literally, one time is no time).

GEMÜTLICH (Ger.) friendly, appealing. "That fine restaurant has a *gemütlich* atmosphere that I like."

GESUNDHEIT (Ger.) To your health! Often said if someone sneezes.

GOLD VERLOREN, NIET VERLOREN; MOED VERLOREN, VEEL VERLOREN; EER VERLOREN, MOER VERLOREN; ZEEL VERLOREN, AL VERLOREN (Du.) Gold lost, nothing lost; courage lost, much is lost; honor lost, more is lost; soul lost, all is lost.

GOTT MIT UNS (Ger.) God is with us. God is on our side.

GRÜSS GOTT (Ger.) old German greeting. Literally, God greet you.

HOI POLLOI (Gr.) *the* common people. Don't use the article before it. "That is for hoi polloi."

KAKON KORAKOS, KAKON CON (Gr.) Like from like. (A bad crow lays a bad egg.)

LEBENSRAUM (Ger.) breathing space, space, space to live

NITCHEVO (Rus.) What's the use?

PRIMA DONNA (It.) first lady, used usually to indicate a top-ranking woman singer, and frequently to describe a woman who is not a singer but indulges in "temperament"

¿QUÉ PASA? (Sp.) What goes on? What's happening? What's new?

¿QUIÉN SABE? (Sp.) Who knows?

SHIBBŌLETH (Heb.) Now used to mean criterion, identifying word or action. Originally it was a word, meaning "stream."

SKOAL! (Swed.) Good health. Often used as a toast.

WANDERJAHR (Ger.) a year of wandering. University students often took a year off in Europe to discover the world around them physically and philosophically. It is in this sense the term is used.

WANDERLUST (Ger.) a tremendous desire to travel or wander

WELTKRIEG (Ger.) World War

WUNDERBAR (Ger.) wonderful

ZAPATERO À TU ZAPATO (Sp.) Shoemaker stick to your last.

ZEITGEIST (Ger.) spirit of the age

ZUM BEISPIEL (Ger.) for example. Abbreviation: z.B.

COMMON EXPRESSIONS FROM ENGLISH LITERATURE

In English there are innumerable phrases, many taken out of context, the understanding of which indicates at least a nodding acquaintance with the classics and unfortunately, ignorance of which leaves one very much in the dark, sometimes, as to the meaning of some spoken or written comment. Listen for such phrases, mark them in your reading, and discover their sources.

The information desks of large libraries, your local librarian, a well-read friend, a teacher, the inquiry columns of newspapers, Sunday supplements, and literary publications can help you classify and understand these myriad enrichers of our language. Some of the world's greatest writers have kept journals and notebooks—Arnold Bennett's were minutely kept—in which to record their day-to-day impressions, to capture an attractive phrase, to record a shade of meaning in a word or quotation for possible future use or inspiration. This is an excellent way to improve one's vocabulary.

Some of us are born with good memories and some seem to be unable to remember things easily, at least not exact quotations. Sometimes memory can be trained, but it can always be jogged by notes. Make good use of them in the building of your vocabulary and in collecting a usable background of quotations, allusions, and proverbs. It's pedantic, of course, to stud everything you say or write with such references, but you'll certainly need to recognize them and it is pleasant and interesting to be able to use them without self-consciousness after they have become as much a part of you as your everyday expressions.

It will be impossible for me to list more than a few of the common expressions and quotations, but the following brief list may suggest where you'll find more. The old and new books of the Bible are studded with quotations and references we meet, often unknowingly, every day. Shakespeare contributed immensely to cultured language. *Aesop's Fables, Alice in Wonderland,* Benjamin Franklin's *Poor Richard's Almanack,* Dickens, the great poets, the Greek and Roman legends, folk tales, and fairy tales are among the many, many sources of words and phrases that are dropped into conversations and that turn up with great frequency in our reading.

ENGLISH EXPRESSIONS COMMONLY USED, THEIR SOURCES AND MEANING

Achilles' heel   The heel of legendary Greek hero Achilles was the only vulnerable portion of his body. "When we know his background, we can easily detect his *Achilles' heel.*"

A prophet is not without honor, save in his own country . . .   Matthew 13:57. "A prophet is not without honor, save in his own country and in his own house." Oracles with whom we are on a familiar footing fail to impress us.

Augean stable   The cleaning of the Augean stable, terribly, repulsively dirty, was one of the tasks assigned to the legendary Hercules.

Barkis is willin'   From *David Copperfield,* by Charles Dickens. Barkis was willing to—and did—marry Peggotty, David's nurse.

between Scylla and Charybdis   The Greek poet, Homer, describes two opposing perils—a six-headed monster and a whirlpool—one on each side of the Strait of Messina, through which sailors had to steer their course. The phrase is used to indicate a great dilemma. "I was between Scylla and Charybdis, not knowing which way to turn."

Beware the Greeks bearing gifts   Virgil's *Aeneid*. A paraphrase of the line, "I fear the Greeks bearing gifts." The reference is to the Trojan horse.

Beware a wolf in sheep's clothing   From the Aesop fable about the wolf who, draping himself in a sheepskin, pretended he was part of the flock. "I thought him a friend but he turned out to be a wolf in sheep's clothing."

billingsgate   Invective. Refers to the imprecations of fishwives in England's Billingsgate market. "He was treated to some rare billingsgate."

blarney   Cajolery. In Blarney Castle, Ireland, there is a stone which, if kissed, is said to confer a cajoling tongue. "What a lot of blarney"—talk that is pretty obviously flattering. We also say, "He has kissed the blarney stone," meaning he can turn a complimentary phrase neatly—that we enjoy the blarney but don't quite believe it.

bread cast upon the waters   From Ecclesiastes 11:2. "Cast thy bread upon the waters: for thou shalt find it after many days." Literally, good deeds are rewarded in kind.

Brobdingnagian   Giantlike. From Swift's *Gulliver's Travels*. Brobdingnag was the land of giants.

By their fruits ye shall know them   Matthew 7:20. "Wherefore by their fruits ye shall know them." People are judged by what they do.

caviar to the general   *Hamlet*, Shakespeare. This means something is very unusual, special, not appealing to most people. "Orchid growing is caviar to the general."

country mouse   Know when you're well off. Aesop tells of the country mouse who yearns for the life of the city mouse, tries it and discovers its perils. "He thought he'd like San Francisco, but he discovered that he was just a country mouse."

"Curiouser and curiouser"   Alice's exclamation when she began to grow as she ate the little cake in *Alice in Wonderland* by Lewis Carroll. The phrase is used to express wonder. "Her actions are growing 'curiouser and curiouser.' "

Damon and Pythias   From the Greek tale of two devoted friends. "They are a veritable Damon and Pythias."

Darby and Joan   From an old English ballad, "The Happy Old Couple." "It's been a happy marriage. They are a real Darby and Joan."

Davy Jones' locker   Ancient seamen's expression for the deep, or a watery grave. Jones is thought to be a corruption of Jonah, the prophet who was thrown into the sea. "Captain Kidd's gold is in Davy Jones' locker."

dog in the manger   Refers to Aesop's tale of the dog in the manger who, though he didn't wish to eat the hay there himself, wouldn't let anyone else enjoy it.

Gordian knot   To cut the Gordian knot—to solve a problem by swift, direct action or by evading the conditions. Derives from the classical myth about Alexander the Great's cutting of an intricate knot. "To get through the red tape of Customs was like trying to cut the Gordian knot."

hare and tortoise   Slow but sure. From Aesop's fable of the cocksure hare who challenged a slow but steady tortoise to a race and was beaten because he idled by the wayside while the tortoise kept his eye strictly on the finish line. "Jones has made a good showing in the primaries, but remember the tale of the hare and the tortoise."

Her price is above rubies Proverbs 31:10. "Who can find a virtuous woman? for her price is far above rubies." This whole passage, 31:10–31, "The Praise of a Good Wife," is one of the most often quoted in the whole Bible.

hoist with his own petard From *Hamlet,* Shakespeare. Hamlet says "For 'tis the sport to have the engineer/Hoist with his own petar." A petard was an ancient variety of bomb. Shakespeare used the former spelling, now obsolete.

How are the mighty fallen! Bible. II Samuel, 1:23. Indicates the impermanence of established people and orders. "The democrats suffered a defeat—how are the mighty fallen!"

If the hill will not come to Mahomet, Mahomet will go to the hill. Usually we hear this quoted "the mountain." From Francis Bacon's essay "Of Boldness." "He may be stubborn but, after all, Mahomet can always go to the hill."

ill wind Usually quoted as "It's an ill wind that blows nobody good." From sixteenth-century Thomas Tusser's poem:

> Except wind stands as it never stood,
> It is an ill wind that turns none to good.

in the arms of Morpheus Asleep. Morpheus was the Greek god of dreams. This is a frequently heard, rather coy expression for describing a night's sleep.

Let sleeping dogs lie. Chaucer in *Canterbury Tales* says, "It is not good a sleeping hound to wake."

lean and hungry look From *Julius Caesar,* Shakespeare.

> Let me have men that are fat,
> Sleek-headed men and such as sleep o'nights:
> Yond Cassius has a lean and hungry look;
> He thinks too much; such men are dangerous.

Let him fry in his own grease. "In his owen grese I made him frie." Chaucer, *Canterbury Tales.*

little foxes The Song of Solomon 2:15. "Take us the foxes, the little foxes, that spoil the vines." Depredators, destroyers in a sly fashion. "Gossip of the little foxes sometimes destroys reputations."

milk of human kindness From *Macbeth,* Shakespeare. We use it in an approving sense—"Her kind actions reflected the milk of human kindness."

"Mine is a long and a sad tale." The mouse's plaint to Alice in *Alice in Wonderland,* by Lewis Carroll.

mumbo jumbo A grotesque idol of a tribe of the western Sudan, object of senseless veneration. When we say, "to me it's much mumbo jumbo," we mean it's incomprehensible.

Murder will out From *Hamlet,* Shakespeare: "For murder, though it have no tongue, will speak with most miraculous organ." Crime can't go undetected. (Shakespeare got it from the *Canterbury Tales,* where Chaucer wrote it "Mordre wol out.")

nemesis Nemesis was an ancient Greek goddess who personified retribution. "He met his nemesis"—he got what he deserved, his just due.

"Off with his head!" The Queen of Hearts' frequently voiced order in *Alice*

in Wonderland by Lewis Carroll. This is often used in a joking manner to indicate disapproval.

O, that this too too solid flesh would melt . . . From Hamlet's soliloquy. Although a somber thought in Shakespeare, this is often used facetiously by the overweight.

Pollyanna From the juvenile novel, *Pollyanna,* by Eleanor H. Porter. The expression is used to describe someone, male or female, who is saccharinely optimistic.

sour grapes From Aesop's fable of the fox and the grapes. The fox, unable to reach the grapes, covered his chagrin by declaring them sour, anyway.

Stygian night Taken from Greek mythology and referring or pertaining to the river Styx, over which souls crossed to Hades; murky, gloomy night. "It was a starless, Stygian night."

tender mercies Proverbs 12:10. "A righteous man regardeth the life of his beast: but the tender mercies of the wicked are cruel." A phrase used sarcastically, "I would not like to be subject to her tender mercies."

The best laid schemes o' mice and men gang aft a-gley The best laid schemes of mice and men often go wrong. From Robert Burns's "To a Mouse."

The left hand doesn't know what the right hand does Matthew 6:3. "But when thou doest alms, let not thy left hand know what thy right hand doeth." Go modestly about your good works.

Trojan horse Something that looks harmless but is really perilous. From Virgil's *Aeneid.* In the Greek siege of ancient Troy, Greek warriors, hidden in a great wooden horse, got inside Troy's walls by stratagem and overpowered the city during the night.

ugly duckling From Andersen's fairy tale of that title. The ugly duckling grows into a beautiful swan. Used to predict promise of beauty.

utopia An imaginary island in the book of that title by Sir Thomas More in 1516, epitomizing the perfect social and political state. From the Greek, meaning "no place."

Valhalla From the Norse myth. The souls of slain heroes feasted in Valhalla, the palace of Odin, which was the final resting place of such illustrious dead. "The hero went to his Valhalla."

voice of the turtle The Song of Solomon 2:12. ". . . and the voice of the turtle [meaning turtledove] is heard in the land." Spring.

WORDS AND PHRASES OFTEN INCORRECTLY USED AND PRONOUNCED

ABDOMEN The preferred pronunciation is ăb·dō'mĕn, not ab'do·men

ACCLIMATE Meaning to habituate and pronounced ă·klī'mĭt

AFFAIR Never used in connection with the word "social" or in describing any social activity such as a dance, dinner, etc. It is correctly used in the sense "concern," "It is no *affair* of his," or plurally in the sense of "business," "His affairs were in good order." It is also used to mean an extramarital relationship, "They are having an affair."

ALL THE FARTHER (I am going) Should be "as far as I am going."

ALLOW and **ALLOW ME** Do not use as a synonym for "agree." It means "permit." The phrase "Allow me" used as a supposedly polite offer of assistance to a lady is classed with "Permit me"—among the Victorianisms. A man offers such assistance without comment or with some more current phrase such as, "Do let me help you with that."

AN INVITE The noun is "invitation."

APPRECIATE Not to be used in the sense of "understand." Not, "I *appreciate* how you feel about it but . . ." Instead, "I appreciate the opportunity to go."

APRICOT Preferably pronounced ā'pricot. Ap'ricot is secondary pronunciation.

ARCTIC The first "c" is pronounced. It is ark'tic.

BETWEEN As a preposition used to make comparison between *two* things. When higher numbers are involved use *among*. Ex: "Between us two," "Among us three."

BUILD OR SHAPE These vulgar expressions should never be used to indicate a person's "figure," e.g. "Jane has a good shape."

CAN'T HARDLY No; "can hardly," instead of the double negative.

CARE TO Do not use for "wish to" or "want to" or "prefer to."

CHAISE LONGUE Means "long chair" in French and must be used in the two original words, never shortened to "chaise" (shāz) which just means "chair." Also note it is "longue," pronounced *läwng*, not as our word "lounge."

CONGRATULATE Be sure to pronounce the first "t." Often carelessly pronounced congradulate.

CONSENSUS Use alone. Do not add "of opinion." It means "agreement of opinion or testimony."

CORPUS DELICTI Mystery writers to the contrary, it does not mean "the body" but "the body of evidence in connection with a crime."

DAIS Speaker's platform—pronounced dā'is, not dī'as.

DISTINCTIVE The word means "distinguishing," "characteristic." Some people trying for simplicity translate the French term "*distingué*," meaning "of distinguished *air*" into "distinctive," which can't be done. "Distinguished" is the appropriate translation, but use of the French term is very common. "She was very *distingué*, I thought."

DRAPES Advertising term for "draperies" or "curtains." It should never be used in conversation.

EITHER Two pronunciations (ē or ī) and meaning "each of two."

EXPECTING The phrase "Is she expecting?" meaning "Is she pregnant?" is one of those little evasions that sound particularly vulgar. Even "Is she expecting a *baby*?" sounds odd to the purists. One of them used to rail against the common "*expectant* mother" for what doctors call a "primipara," one who bears a child for the first time. "She may be a woman expecting a child," he would fume, "but she is not an expectant *mother*."

FIFTH Not to be pronounced fith. The second "f" should be heard.

FINE, SPLENDID, EXCELLENT Often incorrectly used in adverbial form (plus the "ly") when they should be used as predicate adjectives referring to the subject. It is "I feel *fine*," "He looks *splendid*," "It really seemed *excellent*." But when these words modify a *verb*, then the following sentences are correct: "The comparison was *finely* drawn." "The music swelled *splendidly* out into the hall." "She rides *excellently*."

FOLKS Don't use for "family." But "folk" (plural for people, nation, race) is correct, of course, in such a sense as this: "The Lilliputians were imaginary folk."

GEMS A gem is a precious stone, especially one that is cut and polished. Therefore a "gem" is not "jewelry," and the two words can't be used synonymously.

GENT In the same vulgar class as "dearie," "girlie," "tootsie" (unless you're joking), "hubby," "little woman," "old man."

GIRL FRIEND, BOY FRIEND, GENTLEMAN FRIEND, LADY FRIEND True, our language is deficient in words for these combinations. There is something very low class about them all, especially "lady friend" and "gentleman friend." Etiquette has almost given up over "girl friend" and "boy friend" but in all cases it is better to substitute "man (girl, boy or woman), who is a friend of mine" or "woman friend" or "man friend," "sweetheart" (for young people) or "beau" for any man or boy who is courting a girl. A girl introducing a girl to her mother doesn't say, "Mother, this is my *girl* friend Jeanette." The word "friend" is sufficient, and it is obvious she is a girl. Even if the friend is not present, the use of the pronoun identifies her enough. "Mother, I have a friend at school I'd like to ask over today. She lives on Cabot Street."

GIVE ME, LET ME, GOING TO Enunciate these words carefully so they don't become, "gimme, lemme, gonna."

HAIRDO This ugly word has been admitted to American dictionaries because people have trouble pronouncing the more attractive French word *"coiffure"* (kwa·fūr′)and get that confused with *"coiffeur"* (kwa·fer), a male hairdresser. Word-sensitive people either use *coiffure* or some substitute, "Have you *arranged* (or fixed) your hair in a new way?"

HIGH-CLASS This is one of those phrases that seem to indicate social inferiority in the person uttering it. Instead, use "good, superior, excellent, distinguished, fine" to indicate something or someone of good quality.

HOSIERY This is a shop or trade term for stockings. It should not be used in conversation.

HOSPITABLE Preferred pronunciation is hos′pitable, but hospit′able is also correct.

HOUSE, HOME There is a delicate difference, and the two words are not interchangeable. You may be hunting for a house in which to live, but after you are in it, with your goods and chattels around you, it is your home. In referring to the style of its architecture, however, you would say, "It's a modern house," or, "Our house is the one with the pillars." You are, or are not, "at home," but some other resident of the house would, if in the garden, say, "Mother is in the house," never "in the home" or even "at home," which is in this case unspecific. Mother might well be boating on the pond yet still be "at home" to callers. But if you buy a television set, you have them deliver it to your "house."

INTEREST Pronounced in′ter·est or in′trist. Never pronounced in·ter·est′

ITCH If your foot itches, you scratch it. Be careful not to confuse "itch" for "scratch." The former is the sensation, the latter the action to lessen it. Of course, both words are nouns, too. You may have the itch. Or you may have a scratch on your hand.

LEAVE ME Not to be used for "let me." Say "let me go" not "leave me go."

LEND You lend something to someone who wants to borrow it from you. Never say "I want to lend it from you." You borrow from and lend to.

LIABLE Correct only when used to express legal responsibility as "He is liable to a fine for speeding" or an undesirable possibility, as "He is liable to fall on the ice." Never, "She is liable to grow into a pretty girl."

LIKE   It is colloquial—but ugly—to use *like* as a conjunction, as if it were synonymous with *as*. Not "It snowed like it did in January," but "It snowed as it did in January." Why give in to the vulgar without a fight?

LIMB   Don't use as a nice-nelly substitute for the forthright "leg."

LINGERIE   Probably one of the most frequently mispronounced words. It is lăn'zh'r·ee' (the "zh"="z" in "azure" and the heavier accent is on the last syllable), not *longeray'*.

LISTEN! UNDERSTAND? I MEAN   These words appear far too frequently in conversation. Sometimes you will hear them several times in the same sentence. Listen for them in your conversation and try improving your way of speaking so that you will not fall on these weak devices for trapping your listeners' attention.

LOAN   "Have a loan of" is very colloquial. Instead say "borrow."

MAESTRO   This is an Italian word used as the most distinguished title for a master of music—a composer, a conductor, or a great teacher. It shouldn't be used for every little tunesmith. It is pronounced "mä·ĕs'trō" in a liquid, rapid pronunciation which, sad to state, sounds to some like "mīce·tro." If you enunciate the second syllable carefully you avoid this.

MANUFACTURE   It is surprising how many otherwise well-spoken people turn this into "manafacture." The "u" is pronounced as in "unite."

NEITHER   Two pronunciations (nē or nī), followed by "nor." "Neither my son *nor* I could go."

NOTORIOUS   To be used only in the sense of "infamous." "The notorious Jesse James" but "the famous Disraeli."

OFF   Never use in place of "from." It is never, "I got it *off* him," if you mean he gave it to you.

PARDON ME   This is a rude order. One says instead, "Please excuse me" or "I beg your pardon" or "Please forgive me."

PERFECT   When used as a verb, the preferred pronunciation is per·fect'. When used as an adjective, it should not be modified by "more" and "most" as it is the superlative. "It's a perfect day," is the ultimate you can say. "The most perfect day" is really meaningless.

THE REASON IS BECAUSE   This should be—"the reason is *that*." The "because" is superfluous in this construction.

REFER BACK   The word "back" is redundant in this phrase. Say simply "refer," as in the sentence: "The President referred to his previous remarks before Congress." The "*re*" means back and "*ferre*," take.

RICH, WEALTHY   Supposedly it is "manners" to avoid these two terms indicating affluence, and, if one must be used, "rich" (tongue-in-cheek style) is supposed to be preferable. In speaking socially of people, it is more usual to say "They have a lot of money." To me "rich" seems more vulgar than "wealthy," but the dictionary has nothing against either.

SECOND   Be sure to sound the "d."

SORE   Correct and acceptable only to describe physical or mental hurt, not a state of irritation. "Was she sore at me!" is a vulgarism.

STRENGTH   All the letters are pronounced. It is often mispronounced as if the "g" were omitted.

TOMATO It is not more elegant to say "tomahto." In fact, though both pronunciations are correct, "tomāto" is preferred in American dictionaries.
VASE It seems affected these days to pronounce this as "vahz" instead of "vāze."
WHITE The *h* is pronounced.
WRAPS OR WRAP These are old-fashioned terms for outer clothing. "Coat" or "things" is more modern. However, "evening wrap" is correct and current.
YOU'LL HAVE TO EXCUSE ME Instead say, "Please excuse me."

MUSIC AND DANCE TERMS

ADAGIO slowly, also a balancing movement in ballet.

ALLEGRETTO musical term meaning quicker than "andante" but not so quick as "allegro"

ALLEGRO musical term indicating speed; brisk, lively

ANDANTE moderately slow, but flowing; quicker than larghetto, and slower than allegretto

ARABESQUE a ballet term meaning to pose on one foot; a musical ornament

AUX POINTES ballet term: on the toes, the half-toe position of the male dancer.

BALLETOMANE a ballet enthusiast

BOURRÉE a lively old French dance tune in 4–4 or 2–4 time

COUNTERPOINT contrasting musical themes, neither having dominance in a composition

DOLCE soft and smooth in execution

ENTRECHAT a scissoring of the legs in mid air with calves touching

FORTE loud, powerful

FUGUE in music, a theme repeated in such a way that the first theme seems to take flight from the repeating one, often played in another octave

GLISSANDO gliding effect of notes sounding in quick succession

LARGHETTO somewhat slow, but less so than largo

LARGO very slow, broad, stately

LENTAMENTE slowly

PAS DE BOURRÉE ballet term: tiny little steps on the toes, suggesting a glide

PIANO soft

PIROUETTE ballet term: to whirl or turn on the toes

PIZZICATO plucked—a direction to players of bowed instruments to pluck the string instead of bowing

PREMIÈRE DANSEUSE first lady of the ballet

PRESTO at a rapid pace

SUR LES POINTES ballet term: on the tips of the toes, toe dancing, the female dancer's elevated position

TOUR EN L'AIR a complete turn off the ground, in ballet

TOUR JETÉ leap and turn in ballet

CULINARY TERMS

It is nice, but not necessary, to be able to pronounce foreign culinary terms as you encounter them on menus in many restaurants. Often the waiter himself, unless he's French, can't pronounce them any too well, though of course he must know what they mean. But you can easily learn from the following list that *rognons* for example, are kidneys. It is perfectly sensible to ask, "How are the kidneys prepared?" Perhaps they are in a steak-and-kidney pie, or with red wine and mushrooms. You can remember that the word *"hachis"* means chopped-up, hence our "hash." So, *"pommes de terre hachis"* are our old friend, "hashed brown potatoes." A *"pomme de terre"* is, literally "an apple from the earth," so *"aux pommes"* means with apples, whereas *"aux pommes de terre"* means with potatoes. But often on menus the *"de terre"* is omitted. Fried potatoes become *"pommes frites,"* meaning *"pommes de terres frites."*

A girl can always ask her escort to choose a meal for her and leave the deciphering of those French terms to him. And he should know what they mean even if, as I said, he doesn't dare try to pronounce them. If he is confronted with something that stumps him completely he can always say to the waiter, "What is this please?"—but a working knowledge of a French menu is an impressive little skill. It must be no fun at all for a man to feel at a disadvantage before a pencil-poised waiter.

The reader wishing to go further in his French culinary education will enjoy the Escoffier cook book, for example, which gives recipes for the best-known French dishes. It has been translated into English with no loss of Gallic flavor. It is interesting to the novice cook as reading matter mainly, but the graduate cook, male or female, will find it inspiring. At last count my own cook book library numbered 300 volumes—not because we use them all constantly but because we like them for occasional reference. A knowledge of food and international cookery helps to add to the pleasantness of life and quite often to metamorphose everyday routine.

À L'ANGLAISE   roasted or boiled

À LA BÉARNAISE   with sauce of chopped onions, egg yolk, vinegar, oil or butter and seasonings—for meat or fish

À LA BIGARADE   with sauce made with orange juice or rind, usually served with duck

À LA BONNE FEMME   housewife style; thin meat or fish stock with vegetables. *Omelette à la bonne femme* is made with pan-browned potatoes or onions.

À LA BORDELAISE   sauce with Bordeaux wine combined with chopped mushrooms, garlic, shallots, or onions

À LA CAMERANI   usually a thick chicken liver soup

À LA CHATEAUBRIAND   steak or chops (usually) with *maître d'hôtel* butter

À LA CERFEUIL   with chervil sauce; usually with fillet of beef

À LA CIPOLLATA   with hot Italian sausage or forcemeat

À LA COCOTTE   heated and brought to the table in a shell

À LA CRAPAUDINI   chicken, squab, etc., with legs and wings removed and the meat flattened before broiling

À LA CRÉOLE   with sauce of tomatoes, onions, mushrooms, and peppers

À LA CROISSY OR CRÉCY   flavored with turnips or carrots

À LA DAUBE   little squares of bacon or salt pork cooked with sliced carrots, onions and turnips

À LA DAUPHINÉ   a thick vegetable soup

À LA DAUPHINE   with egg sauce

À LA DAUPHINOISE   dipped in sauce or batter, crumbled, then French fried

À LA FINANCIÈRE   truffle-flavored Spanish sauce

À LA FLAMANDE   Flemish style with sliced turnips, Brussels sprouts, and cabbage

À LA GODIVEAU   with meat balls, usually of veal

À LA LANGEDOC   cooked in or served with olive oil

À LA MACÉDOINE   with mixed fruits

or vegetables in unusual variety

À LA MAÎTRE D'HÔTEL in the host's style, plain substantial dishes with sauce of chopped parsley, melted butter, and lemon juice

À LA MARENGO with oil and garlic

À LA MARYLAND with a less rich Newburg sauce

À LA NEIGE snowy (as meringue)

À LA NORMANDE served usually with apples

À LA PRINTANIÈRE with spring vegetables

À LA PROVENÇAL Provence-style, with olive oil, garlic, tomatoes and, often, onions

À LA RAVIGOTE in an herb-flavored white sauce made with tarragon vinegar, egg yolk, mustard, and pepper

À LA REINE cream of chicken (soup)

À LA SERVIETTE served in a napkin —corn or steamed clams, for example

À LA TARTARE with a sauce of mayonnaise, chopped olives, and capers

À L'HUILE in oil

AU BEURRE FONDU in or with melted butter

AU BEURRE NOIR with well-browned butter

AU BEURRE ROUX with browned butter sauce

AU BLEU cooked to the blue point— refers to fish

AU GRAS with the fat or, with soups, containing meat

AU GRATIN with a topping of grated cheese and crumbs. Also refers to well-baked meat.

AU JAMBON with ham

AU VERT PRÉ with green herbs. Non-culinary meaning, grass.

AUX FINES HERBES with chopped herbs

BONBON candy

BONNE BOUCHE a titbit

BOUILLABAISSE thick fish and seafood stew, Marseilles style

CAFÉ AU LAIT coffee with hot milk

FOND D'ARTICHAUT artichoke bottom

MONGOLE in a sauce made of tomatoes and puréed peas and beans. Most frequently met with in *potage* (soup) *mongole*.

ROGNONS SAUTÉS sautéed kidneys

VIANDES meats

VOLAILLE poultry

REGIONAL ACCENTS

Many experts on the English language contend that the finest English in America is spoken in Boston. That is, I suppose, it most closely approaches English English. But to my ear there are many delightful regional accents I should hate to see disappear in some vast misguided effort to make us all speak alike.

In the various theater arts it is considered advisable to erase regional accents for the simple reason that an actor or actress usually desires to play a variety of parts. A person with a strong southern accent would necessarily find himself typecast in the theater or on radio or television. This problem does not exist for most people, but those who travel or live in a variety of localities find that their original regional accents become more or less cosmopolitan in time or take on the inflections, the tones, the idioms, the slurrings, or the stresses of the place in which they have lived longest. Often the widely traveled, cultured person has no ascertainable accent at all. He is a language-citizen of the world.

Of course there are ugly accents and regional idioms that may well be overcome. But before we condemn, for example, "foist," "erster," and "boid" as pure Brooklynese of the lower strata we should travel to the South, where the same distortions turn up among some of the native-born, politely educated citizens of New Orleans, among other places.

I like accents of all kinds. They help to make people different and interesting. Unless they are real handicaps, professionally, or from the standpoint of understandability, I hate to see them "corrected."

A WELL-MODULATED VOICE

The placement of the voice is very important. There are, naturally, all kinds of born speaking voices, some attractive, some unpleasant. But all respond well to efforts toward pleasant modulation. Vigorous people usually have voices to match, and they often wear us out just through the sound they generate. It is difficult to gear them to more pleasing tonal levels, but if they want to improve their voices they can do so consciously.

Childhood is the real time to do something about the tone and quality of the voice. The familiar reminders—"Not so *loud*," "Please *speak up*," "A little *slower*," "Don't *mumble*"—eventually have some effect, if only when the child is on his best behavior outside the family circle. But essentially the child will speak, when he becomes an adult, as his parents and siblings spoke, which may be well or badly—unless, of course, his higher education was completely away from his family. Even then, no change may ever come in his manner of speaking unless some special effort has been directed toward the changing of it, if that seems advisable.

The ideal speaking voice is placed low, is not nasal. If we speak too rapidly what we say loses much of its effectiveness. If we drag our words out in what seems an excess of caution we bore our audiences. If our voices drop at the end of each sentence we tend to depress our hearers. If we speak in a constant burst of enthusiasm we tire others and seem sophomoric. A goood speaking voice lifts slightly at the end of each sentence. It is not too rapid, nor too pedestrian. It comes through well-opened lips and from an open throat, from the chest rather than from the neck. Good speech requires good breathing, good posture, and essentially good health, mental and physical. Fear, anxiety and ill-health constrict our vocal chords and make our voices thin and tight or weary. Relaxation makes our voices round and easy to tumble out.

The sound of the voice and the way the language is used is often a deciding factor on the assay of a man's or woman's personality. A beautiful woman, beautifully dressed, carrying herself like a queen can destroy the effect in a flash merely by opening her mouth. A handsome, well-groomed man is ineffective if his voice has a weak, high register.

I once knew a very attractive artist whose wife told me his success as an artist and as a man came as a result of his lowering his high, thin voice to a resounding bass after special teaching.

6

THE FAMILY AND SOCIAL
EDUCATION OF CHILDREN

Manners in Marriage   489

Children and the Formation of Character   499

The Religious Education of Children   523

The Adult-Child Relationship   524

Adopting a Child   530

Traveling with Children   532

The Teen Ager   535

Divorce and Separation   541

THE FAMILY AND SOCIAL EDUCATION OF CHILDREN

The most important phases of etiquette deal with the comfortable living together of the family. The family's politeness to its individual members is vital to its happiness. One face to the world, another at home makes for misery. Of course in the family circle there is always some necessary relaxation of the rules of etiquette, but simple manners are always essential between husband and wife, between children and parents. It is important, too, to recognize the essential from the non-essential in the light of present-day psychology.

Rigid parents can, naturally, insist on a regime of strict behavior at home, but they will, by so doing, lose something very beautiful in the child-parent relationship. And the negativeness that must have some expression is sure to erupt outside the home, at least if the child is to be emotionally healthy. Better to have it at home to a certain tolerable degree than in school or elsewhere, where it may be less understandably dealt with and where it can really interfere with educational and social progress.

It may seem odd to include such things as thumb-sucking and bed-wetting in a book of etiquette. Actually, of course, they have nothing whatsoever to do with the subject of manners. But many people, especially those with no children or those who have raised children a generation or so ago, often contend vehemently that the correction of these things lies within the realm of manners, i.e., of teachable behavior. For this reason I am setting down the modern, pediatric viewpoint, which has effectively demonstrated that we cannot correct the sometimes embarrassing habits of children by treating them in terms of good or bad manners. We must dig down to the basic emotional causes of anti-social behavior.

Parents can help their children learn comfortable social practices by their own attitude toward each other. Again mere correctness of form is not the deciding factor. Warmth of spirit, kindliness in their dealings with one another, generosity, and elasticity are much more significant.

CHAPTER FORTY-NINE

MANNERS IN MARRIAGE

UNDERSTANDING THE WOMAN IN THE HOME

Great heat is generated over the discussion as to whether men can ever understand women—especially their own wives. Perhaps it is impossible for most husbands to understand everything about their wives, and it is equally true that even relatively uncomplex husbands are never completely understood by the women they've married. But both husband and wife can try to find the widest possible area of agreement, and each must eventually recognize that there are some traits, habits, anxieties, ambitions, prejudices, sentiments in the other that need to be accepted or made allowance for. That in almost everyone there is some immaturity, no matter what the chronological age may be. At certain periods in their cycles the glands of both men and women stimulate special needs, either for passionate expression or for understanding and comfort.

A few days before the beginning of her menstrual period, for example, the average woman is likely to have one of two moods: the first of great feminine activity—tidying drawers, cleaning closets, or, if she's a business woman, reorganizing her files, cleaning her desk, picking up stray ends of unfinished business. This mood is often fairly intolerable to the slower-geared male, who is especially resentful if the accompanying burst of activity extends to his own domain and results in the rearranging of his tool chest, his desk or his favorite chair. The second possible mood-change is one of deep or moderate and unaccountable depression, which lifts when the period begins. The more high-strung the woman, the more likely this is to be her reaction to the physiological change, just as in the menopausal period the neurotic woman may have physical and psychological upsets the happier woman rarely experiences.

Being married does not give women the right to be brusque or impolite in dealing with their husbands. But the man who does not take the calendar into consideration when he has serious problems or criticisms to thrash out with his wife, is plain foolhardy. If such problems can't wait a day or two, let them be presented very cautiously and quietly, with criticisms preceded by a nicely turned compliment, if possible, and followed by another. Let me give you an example:

Mrs. Birch has had discipline troubles all day with her four-year-old—he's reached that well-known negative stage and she's in no humor to cope with it diplomatically. She knows that force will only defeat her aims, one way or the other—and she's on the verge of the "weeps." Besides, she has a backache and a blemish on the tip of her nose, is pale, has circles under her eyes, her hair is limp, and her feet are swollen. She has a vague headache and a feeling of inability to contend even with the family puppy, let alone Junior. Home comes father, fire in his eye. She's overdrawn their joint checking account, and the bank had called him to make a deposit before three o'clock. (A pox on joint checking accounts, by the way.) Let me spare you the rest—tears, mutual accusations, slammed bedroom doors, father in the guest room for the night. One look at the calendar and Mr. B. would have buttoned up his wrath or worked it off somewhere else (chopping wood, punching the bag, boxing at the gym, weeding are all fine outlets for justified—and unjustified—rage). By next Tuesday he can mention the matter quite safely. Mrs. B. will be prettily contrite and manage to make her husband feel like a big, strong infallible male who never overdraws *his* account.

The truth is, women are people and should be treated as such, with time out for physiological interferences such as the well-known instability of pregnancy—another period in the female cycle intended by nature to bring out the supposed innate protectiveness of the male. However, many a woman sails cheerfully through those nine months protecting a quaking husband against his own pre-paternal anxieties.

THE AGREEABLE HUSBAND

A man who's easy to live with gets up in the morning in time to get to work without putting the house in an uproar. He does his best to be agreeable on arising, to help the whole family get off to a good start. Or, if he's one of those people who's grouchy before coffee, he explains his temperament to his family, so they'll know there's nothing personal about it. He either accepts what is put before him for breakfast or, if he has special preferences, states them in ample time beforehand. It is difficult for the cook—mother or a paid hand—to change the breakfast order from boiled eggs to hash while father drums on the table and watches the clock.

When things do go wrong at meal times he doesn't make a scene. The best cooks have their off moments. At the breakfast table, even when the family is alone, he makes some attempt at pleasant conversation with his wife—who may have a lonely day ahead of her—and with his children of whom he sees little enough as it is. He should make it a rule to avoid unpleasant and acrimonious discussions at the table any time for the sake of the family's collective digestions.

A man should come to meals shortly after he is summoned. It is difficult enough to time a meal for a specified hour, and it is even harder to have to hold it and still serve palatable food. The agreeable husband conducts himself at the table exactly as if guests were present. He is clean, combed, and generally presentable. If he wants to sit down coatless or tieless, he should ask his wife's permission just as he did in the days when he was trying to impress her. He should limit his smoking to the end of the meal, using an ash tray instead of dishes as ash receptacles. (I shall keep driving this point home.)

In all things he should consider himself a partner in the home, not its dictator, he and his wife sharing responsibility in the management of the family resources. He should give his wife some portion of their income for her own use without any strings attached, just as he keeps some funds to use at his own discretion without having to account for them.

Even in physical things—manners, appearance, behavior—he must remember that it is no longer he alone who is answerable for them. Society holds a wife accountable to a large extent for the presence or lack of agreeable attributes in a husband. If his manners are boorish, she is expected to correct them, one way or the other, to help him get ahead. If his clothes are ill-kempt and shabby, the fact is usually attributed to his wife's negligence or lack of thrift. If he's blatantly attentive to other women, society asks where his wife has failed—and it may be right.

It seems to me that one of the greatest difficulties a man meets in adjusting to married life, is the proper evaluation of his wife's contribution. Most men, while enjoying their work, hate the actual daily necessity of doing it and tend to think of their wives as having comparative leisure because they stay at home. Because of this fundamental misunderstanding, a husband is likely to minimize his wife's problems and not to see the need of adjusting to conditions in his own home as he would adjust in the office.

It is quite true that a woman's work is never done, while the average man, once he leaves his office, shuts his door on his work until the next morning. At five o'clock his wife, instead of having a long and peaceful evening ahead of her, must bathe the children, prepare dinner, make herself attractive for her husband's home-coming, serve dinner, get the children to bed, wash the dishes, and entertain her husband, and possibly guests, for the balance of the evening. Even after she gets to bed she may still have to rise up in the night to attend to the baby or comfort a night-terrored child. And she never, or rarely, knows what it is to sleep late or get a full day off without at least checking in to see what's going on at home—not if she has a growing family. If she is a career woman she has all these responsibilities, in some degree or other, added to those of her office. And, considering the number of women gainfully employed in this country, this means millions of women on double shifts—breadearners and homemakers. It is not always an enviable outlook for a woman in these days of high-cost and sometimes impossible-to-obtain household help, small quarters, and high tension. A husband needs to lend a hand not only morally but often physically.

HE LENDS A HAND The old-fashioned pater familias, whose dignity would have suffered if he lifted a hand toward the household tasks, is as extinct as the Stanley Steamer. Most modern fathers can change a diaper, feed and burp the baby, take a pulse, figure a temperature, bind a wound, make beds, oversee children's baths, and scramble together an emergency meal. Anything a husband does do, should be done in a spirit of comradery rather than of martyrdom. His wife should, I think, try her best to spare him the too feminine chores—washing the dishes, setting the table, or sweeping the floors. But he can and should help, if the household is literally on his wife's back, by picking up after himself and others (a neat bedroom induces rest), helping to clear the table occasionally, taking out the garbage (if there are no small boys around), doing small essential repairs and, if he can, intelligently helping with the shopping—a backbreaking and time-consuming job for a woman if she must use the cash-and-carry system to balance the budget. Any man can be a boon to a household in a nice, unobtrusive, and wholly masculine fashion. But a man who can't or won't see a woman's problems can be hard to live with despite his flashing eyes and all-American figure.

BUSINESS ENTERTAINING

"I'm bringing a client (or the boss) home to dinner." How often such news —usually delivered at the last minute—strikes terror into the young wife. She has not reached that phase of housewifely proficiency where the announcement that the President himself was about to descend for a meal would not fluster her overmuch.

No well-brought-up husband should ever bring *anyone* except a most intimate friend home to dinner without sufficient warning to his wife. It may be cook's night out—if there is a cook—or "economy night" when the family is to eat the remainder of the roast in a hash. The silver may be due for a cleaning tomorrow but will make the hostess self-conscious before guests tonight. It isn't that the average wife is unable to rise above such unimportant things herself, but she knows full well the critical eye of an outsider can light on these domestic deficiencies and imagine the household has no better standards. And apologizing only makes everything much worse. Every hostess naturally wants her home to look its best when guests come.

These last-minute business invitations are often psychologically correct from a man's point of view. He has made some progress with a difficult associate and feels now is the moment to apply a little personal pressure from the social angle. But he should never ask such an associate home to dinner— and certainly not for the week end—without forewarning his wife and having her enthusiastic consent to the invitation.

Suffice it to be said that running even a simple household is much more complicated than most husbands ever understand. Often everything goes wrong at once—a crisis with the plumbing, an accident to the baby, trouble with the help, failures in delivery of supplies—a thousand irritating household matters. Of course, all this can also happen when you are preparing for expected company. But when it happens and unexpected guests arrive, it is that much worse.

Business dinners are often best handled outside of a man's home unless he and his wife are really willing and happy to accept the business associate and, necessarily, his wife on social terms. This is very important. Home should really be home—not just a continuation of the office. A man should do all he can to avoid taking into his home business associates whom he and his wife cannot possibly enjoy socially. Instead, he can entertain such people semisocially outside of his home—often to their greater comfort. Perhaps they, too, prefer to keep social and business lives separate. A business man may invite a client and his wife to a good restaurant for dinner and, unless her presence seems vital, make a tactful excuse for his own wife. Of course he may freely invite the man to lunch alone or with other business associates.

Some husbands—or career wives—will argue that it is of inestimable business value to entertain important clients, prospects, or associates at home. But is it? Good taste prohibits the pursuit of business deals while the quarry is breaking bread under one's own roof. On the other hand, over dinner at a restaurant two men can come together on business matters easily enough, even when one is playing the host for reasons apparent to all concerned.

If business friends from time to time are to be brought into one's home circle, not because of what they can do, but because of what they are as people, that is a different matter. They should not be invited, however, when there are important business matters pending, as it will be too difficult for the host and probably the hostess not to show some strain.

THE AGREEABLE WIFE

Until you have been married you can't know what a marriage partner can do, or fail to do, that makes him or her less than attractive to have around constantly. It's a good idea before marriage for two people in love to discuss, good humoredly, all the possible things they would dislike in this close living-together. A man might remember some of his mother's habits that annoyed him or his father and so give any intelligent, co-operative wife a good idea of what he'd prefer her not to do. He might make it clear that he'd hate to see her come to the breakfast table with her hair in curlers—in fact, that he is quite repelled by curlers at any time, even after lights-out at night. And that he couldn't abide the sight of her face oiled with cream.

I wonder how many wives could resist rising up in unholy protest if husbands suddenly took to wrapping their heads up in wire and head rags, greasing their faces, tying up their chins, putting on oiled mittens for the night. If a woman has her own room I suppose she can safely dedicate herself to the pursuit of beauty in her sleep, once she is alone. But if she shares her sleeping quarters she is obliged to make herself an attractive roommate, not a banshee. Experts say that the skin absorbs in about twenty minutes all the cream it's going to absorb, so if you feel your skin needs some lubrication, why not use your bath time or a rest period, when you can be sure of privacy?

Bedtime should be a time for nice, feminine nightgowns, clean faces (traces of lipstick in the morning look very careless to a fastidious male and, besides, think of the sheets), well-brushed hair braided or tied back with a ribbon, perhaps—especially if you have a double bed and want to keep your curls out of your husband's face—and a touch of flower cologne. Isn't this from a man's standpoint more inviting in a wife than utilitarian pajamas, a face covered with grease, hair rigid with curlers?

MEETING COMMUTER TRAINS

All over America, morning and evening, is enacted the rite of delivering father to the train and picking him up at night. The appearance of the country-staying wife and the city-going husband at these times is often sadly incongruous. Too often the wife is under the impression that no one notices her as she delivers her well-pressed (we hope) husband to the 8:11. She may throw an old coat over her house dress and tie a bandana over her curlers or her ill-dressed hair. The baby beside her, if she has no maid to leave him with, may have traces of his morning egg on the face he offers daddy for the good-by kiss. Mother's shoes as she takes over the wheel may be anything she thought good enough for the approaching morning's housework.

Maybe only occasionally does a well-intentioned homemaker find herself downtown looking this way. But doesn't it invariably happen that if you are not looking as you'd be proud to look you will run into someone you'd rather not see under the circumstances—the man who holds the mortgage or that older woman who made the catty remarks about Johnny? Making yourself presentable on arising, whether or not you are going to make the trek to the station, is always a good investment in self-respect.

A man's last glimpse of his wife in the morning and his first view of her at night should be pleasant experiences. At the station he likes her to compare favorably with the other wives bound on the same errand, and he likes his children to be attractive too.

A man who has been surrounded all day by a trim, well-ordered office staff is never pleased to be met by a sloppy, preoccupied wife and his unwashed, uncombed brood, where any neighbor may see how things are at home. Father's home-coming should always be a respected occasion for which the whole family prepares as best it can, for father is certain to appraise it, though he may be unconscious of doing so.

SPECIAL ADJUSTMENTS

ANNOYING HABITS   I can think of any number of annoying habits, not exclusively the property of wives, which are mighty unattractive day after day. Do you put the cap back on the tooth paste? Are you careful to screw the covers on various bathroom-cabinet jars when you have finished using them? Do you close boxes, stopper bottles, shut doors? Perhaps doing so is a sign of an orderly mind, but these are certainly things you can train yourself to do if you think of them as being considerate to your mate or your family. A razor, used by man or woman, should be loosened in its holder, rinsed to remove the hairs, and replaced on its shelf. Any discarded razor blades should be carefully disposed of. If there is no slot for them in the bathroom, put them in their envelopes, if you still have them, or wrap in paper so that anyone emptying the wastepaper basket won't be cut. A used razor blade left to rust on window sill or basin is a proclamation of a careless and thoughtless member of the family.

No one should smoke in bed, ever, because of fire hazard, but where one mate is a smoker, the other a non-smoker, watch particularly the habit of smoking before going to bed or immediately on rising. Dead cigarettes and their ashes in a bedroom can be nauseating, and, if you ask me, any wife who smokes when her husband doesn't takes a long chance with his affections if she permits herself to be a chain smoker or a first-thing-in-the-morning and last-thing-at-night one.

You wouldn't think otherwise fastidious women would fall into the habit of biting their nails or pulling their fingers out of joint, but they do—and so do grown men. These are usually habits carried over from childhood and the nail-biting can be a sign of emotional disturbance in an adult. Nagging —as with anything else—is no help, but reassurance, affection, gentle reminders may be. A happy, relaxed marriage relationship can sometimes perform miracles in overcoming tense reactions to life. A well-balanced diet high in the B vitamins and vitamin A can assist, too, with the attainment of greater nervous stability. But where chorea (St. Vitus's dance), nervous tics, nail-biting, and other anxious habits are really distressing to the person having them as well as to his or her partner, something can be done about overcoming them through emotional re-education with psychiatric help. If such help is not possible, allowance must be made for them as such motor habits usually cannot be controlled by will power alone.

Suppose you are married to someone who drums his fingers on the table, snaps them while waiting for something or aimlessly draws on the tablecloth with his knife. These are just habits—not necessarily nervous ones. You might tackle the problem by suggesting tactfully that the particular habit is somewhat annoying to you and at the same time asking him to bring to your attention any habits that may be annoying to him. Perhaps you forget to put on your make-up before breakfast or you never let your husband finish a funny story, constantly interrupt his reading with conversation, or ask your relatives too often to meals.

All these things can be adjusted between two people desirous of living happily and fully together if discussion of them is friendly. It is better to run the risk of a little immediate acrimony by bringing the matter up when it first annoys than to let the irritation fester over months or years of married life. Out of such little, infuriating things can spring the seeds of actual or spiritual dissolution. There must always be a comfortable balance in marriage, with each partner giving and being given due friendly consideration.

There are times when even the most loved person is viewed objectively by his or her partner, and it is well if on these occasional days of—often silent —reckoning we pass muster in the most important things. But it is amazing how often the little things that are wrong in a marriage can make it less full and beautiful than it should be. We tend to think, "If she really loved me she'd remember I hate to see her nose shiny, she'd take a little more trouble about herself when she knows I'm on the way home." Or, "If he wouldn't make me ask for the house money, wouldn't keep me waiting dinner night after night without phoning to say he'd be late."

The little things that are too often overlooked are sometimes a sign that the whole marriage can do with a check-up. A husband or wife who begins to be careless about grooming or weight, for example, may feel unloved or at least less loved by his mate, rather than less loving himself. The over-weight is just a symptom.

OVERWEIGHT AND UNDERWEIGHT Many eating habits are social devices to make us more at ease with one another—cocktails before dinner, the eating of the dinner roll as we wait for the first course, the nibbling on mints after demitasse. The thoughtful meal planner provides substitutes for these things for anyone in the family on a reducing or other diet. Self-denial seems less heroic to the dieter if there is a fruit or vegetable juice cocktail for him on the cocktail tray and crisp celery, carrot or cucumber sticks at his place in lieu of bread. It isn't too much trouble to provide him with non-starchy breadsticks or rye wafers. Hot skimmed milk or evaporated milk will taste better in his coffee than cold skimmed milk, a little container of saccharine on the demitasse tray will cater harmlessly to his sweet tooth.

There is considerable modern medical literature devoted to the thesis that both underweight and overweight can have emotional causes. Some times the underlying factors are very complicated and not easily brought to light, but almost anyone with a weight problem—in either direction—will recognize that anxiety either causes his appetite to decrease and his weight to go down or that in anxious periods he becomes a compensatory eater. He may eat without waiting for his hunger mechanism to prod him, just for the sake of the vicarious satisfaction the mere act of eating gives him.

Many compensatory eaters take to sweets at such times, thus piling calorie on unwanted calorie and so making themselves as unattractive as they secretly feel. It seems obvious that anyone with a proper self-regard does not overeat or undereat to a degree that makes him or her unattractive. The desire to achieve and hold the proper weight must come from a real, consistent effort to do so if there is a tendency toward wide fluctuations. The happy, healthy, well-adjusted person is usually neither too fat nor too thin. He eats when he's hungry and abstains when he isn't. Food to him is pleasant and necessary, not something to give him satisfactions he misses in life, or something which he denies himself for some neurotic, usually unconscious, reason.

It is useless to try to stuff a member of the family who is sadly underweight or to limit the intake of another unless we have their real co-operation and can help them find satisfaction and security in their lives. Threats or nagging are senseless and cruel, but the meal planner can be a friendly ally once the individual announces that he wishes to lose or gain and seems ready to make a real effort to do so. He needs co-operation, and he needs bolstering of his ego. Tell him continually how noticeable the difference is from week to week, how much more attractive he is, how much better his clothes look on him, etc. When someone is on a reducing diet at the family board, help him to avoid making exceptions, too many of which will prolong the routine discouragingly. Don't be a tempter. If possible, try to set up a little friendly rivalry, pitting two dieters against each other.

SPEAKING OF DIETS Making a to-do about anyone's diet is a bore to everyone except the dieter, who may either delight in the extra attention or squirm under it. But the diet that works best, it seems to me, is the one that is taken as a matter of course by everyone without special comment or commiseration. Most diets are not life-time sentences. They are planned to accomplish a certain result in a specific time. Mary will not forever be denied her strawberry shortcake, so what does it matter if tonight she takes her strawberries plain? John, if he cuts some of the fat off his meat for another month or two, omits bread at dinner and lunch and substitutes fruit for the pies and cakes he loves, will soon be able to take in the desired notch in his belt. Genevieve, if she adds a little of the thick cream to her coffee each time, though she'd prefer it black, and takes that extra slice of bread and butter, may soon have the little padding here and there that will make her a prettier girl.

Both reducing and gaining diets are somewhat of a trial at first, but it is encouraging to know that, if we wish to gain, it is not necessary at all to increase the actual quantity of food we take. It is possible to gain by revising our diets to include the same quantity of food but food of greater caloric value, perhaps taken in more frequent meals. Reducers need to know that they may eat relatively huge amounts of low-calorie foods, to a degree that they need never be hungry, by substituting them for the high-calorie preferences that have been their downfall. But remember, diet-talk for those not dieting is dull business. Let the results do the talking, and the increased personal satisfaction and well-being will be the chief reward.

THE IN-LAW PROBLEM

THE MOTHER-IN-LAW With longevity increasing, the possibility of a newly-married couple having mothers-in-law is greater than it was twenty or thirty years ago. A mother-in-law in her late forties or fifties without enough to occupy her fully, now that her children have left home, can be a source of friction, especially if she is also a widow. Good and secure family relations are among the best gifts a man and woman can bring to marriage. But no family at all is better than an interfering one.

When we marry we literally must "forsake all others" and consider the marriage bond the paramount one. The whole process of growing up is that of growing away from one's parents in the physical sense and to a great degree in the emotional one, too. Young people need the freedom to make their own mistakes in their own way. They really never do believe their elders who want them to accept experience in life vicariously.

Where in-laws are to be considered, especially a mother-in-law who finds it difficult to relinquish hold on her child, the very first steps in the relationship are most important. A young son-in-law, for example, should not be made to feel like a culprit because he can't call this relatively strange and sometimes seemingly hostile older woman "mother." And, perhaps, despite the usualness of the term for her, the mother-in-law doesn't like it either. Both she and her son-in-law may be more comfortable with the modern "Mrs. Brown" or just "Jane" as if she were a contemporary. Then when the children begin to arrive, a pet name usually solves everything, and "Mrs. Brown" or "Jane" becomes comfortable old "Nanny" or "Granny"—or any other variation of a child's loving title for his grandmother—to everyone in the household. And somehow with little hands in hers she feels less shut out, more needed in the new living arrangement, and she usually is.

A COMFORTABLE DISTANCE   When it is necessary or advisable for a mother-in-law to live in the same house with a couple it should be remembered that she herself probably feels a certain diffidence if not an actual unhappiness at the upheaval in her own life. She is perhaps less adaptable than she was as a younger woman, used to her own way of doing things and probably to more privacy than seems possible in the new household.

Whenever feasible, she should have her own room, however small, furnished with at least some of her own things. It should be a bed-sitting room so that when she pleases she can get away from the family and have an inviolate place of her own, reminiscent of the home she has left. If certain contributions to the household are expected from her—a hand with the children or the meals—it should never be assumed that she has no plans of her own. Too many little chores constantly dropped on her shoulders without a by-your-leave make her feel imposed upon, and quite understandably. The smaller her own means, the more helpless and frustrated she feels under such thoughtless imposition. Older people (especially mothers-in-law) must always be treated like human beings. Happy ones who feel needed and useful can add immeasureably to a full, complete family life in the secure old-time sense.

REAL TROUBLEMAKERS   Sometimes mothers or fathers living with a young couple become impossibly difficult. They either can't or won't adjust to the new arrangement, and they become tyrannical. If the young people have moved into the older person's home, then they have no recourse but to move out again as amicably as possible, or, if possible, somehow divide the house into completely separate living quarters so there can be a minimum of contact between them and the difficult parent. In England during the acute housing shortage following the war, one small town solved its in-law problem by billeting parents with other than their own children, with a great improvement in everyone's morale.

WHEN A PARENT REQUIRES SUPPORT Many young married people have to support one or more parents or at least contribute to their support. Whenever possible, especially during the first few years of marriage, a couple needs to live by themselves. It is usually better for parents to live separately, no matter how simply, to ensure their own independence and that of their children. But whether the dependent parents live with their children or not, their bills should not be paid for them if they are at all capable of managing their own affairs. Unless they are undoubtedly senile, they should be treated like responsible people, no matter what their age, and permitted to handle their own expenditures for rent, clothes, food, and spending money. Unless they ask to be relieved of the responsibility, they should have their own checking or savings accounts to which their children contribute at stated intervals. They should know how much money they can count on and when. Even if the income is small and they must keep strictly within it, most old people feel more self-respect managing it themselves.

Even the very aged seldom are willing to consider that their remaining days are limited. They often have the fantasy that they will outlive those who care for them and then, without means, will be dependent on "charity."

Money in their own name helps them to feel that they have a little more time. And they need to make their own decisions on how to spend it. Most of them are more capable than their overcritical children wish to admit.

CHAPTER FIFTY

CHILDREN AND THE FORMATION OF CHARACTER

CHOOSING THE BABY'S NAME

Some babies' names are chosen in sheer desperation, it would seem, and too often they form an unlovely combination with the surname. And a baby who is saddled with a cumbersome family name as a first name, with the thought that he will be, conveniently, called "Buster" as a little boy, may never be able to shake his nickname. A sixty-five-year-old "Buster" is a somewhat ludicrous fellow, no matter how he tries to stand on his dignity.

Be careful that the first name you choose doesn't form some kind of pun when coupled with the last one. Parents, if they notice it, may think such a combination of names amusing, but the child probably will find it far from amusing, once he gets to school. A jaw-breaking first name—perhaps Montmorency—finds itself teamed with a family name of Drinkwater or Hasenpfeffer. Or a first name is chosen with little consideration of how it will sound when spoken aloud with the last name. A child named Brooks Scott will be referred to as Brook Scott because his name, spoken, doesn't indicate the two "s's." Be careful not to elide a child's name this way by having the last letter of the first name the same as the first letter of the last.

A name, even for a little baby, should strive for dignity and simplicity. If your surname is Gallic, German, or Italian try to find a Christian name that suits it, although most of the short English names such as John, Mary, Robert, Charles, Edward, Alfred, Frederick, Andrew, Henry, Ann and Peter go well with almost any surname. But don't overlook the pleasant possibility of giving such a child some variation of these or other good names that are in keeping with the surname. Carlos, Carlo, Henri, Mara, Frederika, Marie, Hans, Hannes, Jon, Roberta, André, Andrea, Jeanne, Edda, Pieter, Peta, Piet, are all possibilities. Many real Scotch or Irish names are strong and fine—Moira, Kitt, Sean, Timothy, Michael, Kim, Sheila, Terrence—but they belong with Anglo-Saxon surnames. Sometimes coined names are very effective. I have a friend who shortened her name, Charlotte Louise, as a child to Charlise and liked that so well she named her daughter Charlise. Another friend, christened Marie Nanette, made it a manageable and attractive Manette.

Each generation has its run on favorite names, which seem to repeat themselves in cycles. Old-fashioned names have taken a new lease on life, and at present every school roll has dozens of Sarahs, Janes, Marys, Catherines, Susans, Anns, Joans, Elizabeths, and Lindas. Before deciding on a name, talk to as many friends as possible and see if you are about to give your child one that may, at the moment, be greatly overworked. Be extra careful about this if you have a common last name.

HOW DO YOU FIND A NAME? The best place to find a suitable name for the baby is in your own family tree. It is my own feeling that wherever possible it is better not to name a boy "Jr.," because doing so sometimes has the effect of denying him his own full identity during his father's lifetime. He gets "little Tom" or "Junior" or "young Tom" instead of a good name all his own. He can be named for his father without becoming "Jr." if he is named, say, Thomas Briggs Macy instead of Thomas Gordon Macy, and he will then have a middle name that can be used as his first name to avoid confusion.

A little girl should never be called "Junior" even if she is named for her mother. She may come to resent "little Helen," too, and wonder why she couldn't have had her very own name. She can be "Helen II," but that does seem cumbersome. If it is ardently desired that she be named for her mother, it might be better to call her Helen Louise, so that she may use "Louise" to distinguish herself from her mother.

If a careful study of the names used in your family turns up nothing you think sufficiently attractive for the new baby, you can find lists of names in unabridged dictionaries and there are books devoted to possible names, giving their derivations and meanings. We needn't take the meanings too literally. A boy named "Christopher" is, today, not necessarily the child of Christian parents (the name means "one who carries Christ"), for the name has lost its original, distinctive meaning.

DOES YOUR CHILD NEED A MIDDLE NAME? Today the simpler a name, the better. With few exceptions, middle names, if used, get lost in a muddle of initials that people can't remember. Is the name Clarence R. Jackson or Clarence E. Jackson? When a man signs his middle name and if it is meaningful—as in Ethan Allen Jackson or, to use a real instance, George Washington Carver—people will remember it and use it. But more often than not a middle name merely elongates and confuses a signature and often weakens the name. Which is stronger—Virginia Jocelyn Framingham or just Virginia Framingham? Be careful a name you have carefully selected doesn't sound like a mouthful of hot potatoes when it is burdened with a middle one in addition to the surname.

BOYS' NAMES FOR GIRLS AND VICE VERSA Sometimes, especially in the South, a girl is given a boy's name when a boy had been expected and a name for him had been firmly decided upon. There are numerous examples of girls named "Charles" or "Peter" or "John" because of the rigidity of their parents, and one shudders to think of the possible psychological effect upon the children who, in name at least, are not allowed to be little girls. The same danger exists for girls whose names are derived from boys' names if their families shorten Andrea to Andy, Maxine to Max, Charlotte to Charlie, Josephine to Jo, Philippa to Phil, Frances to Frank.

There is a similar danger in naming boys with names used more frequently for girls—Leslie, Beryl, Vivian, Marion, Evelyn, Cecil, Jean.

A CHILD'S CLOTHES

DRESSING THE BABY Modern babies are dressed for active comfort, not for style. This is good social and pediatric practice. It's usually only the first baby, partly because of the mother's inexperience, that's in danger of being overdressed in weighty and too warm clothes and in overly fancy ones. It's the first baby who gets the lion's share of clothes from friends and relatives, who spend too much on frills and never give a thought to utility and ease of laundering—or to the baby's comfort. Gone are the days of long baby dresses with a matching, lacy slip—except for christenings and even then a short white dress will do nicely. Babies hate hats, so the rosetted ones, the ones with long satin chin ribbons, the layer-on-layer of georgette or organdy lovingly shirred into a bonnet are all a waste of time and money. In the winter, of course, the baby must wear a hat, and it needs to be something he can't pull off and which won't annoy him any more than necessary with bows under the chin. Often his snow suit has a functional hood that keeps his neck and head warm without restricting his movements or giving him something to chew on.

If you could ask a baby, he would tell you he wants clothes that allow a maximum of freedom. A very young baby is constantly having his clothes changed, and they need to be tough and absolutely washable. Little flannel bathrobes with satin binding and fancy trimmings are just silly if they can't go into the tub and after one or two wearings must go to the dry cleaner. Even in a household where money is no particular consideration this is certainly an unnecessary and foolish expense. The various cotton fabrics—corduroy, seersucker, piqué, cotton flannel, cotton jersey, Byrd cloth, and denim are sensible and comfortable.

The tiny infant is best dressed in a cotton knit nightie, and most babies I've seen don't care for the ones that make a restricting bag at the feet (if so the drawstring may be pulled out). Over the nightie goes a cotton sack—seersucker is fine, or cotton jersey or cotton flannel. Fine embroidered wool sacks or silk ones are an affectation, and in one or two washings they will be a shambles anyhow, especially if they've run afoul of some cod-liver oil, a certain eventuality. Under the nightie, with the inevitable diapers, is worn a plain cotton shirt, preferably without buttons or strings. The baby who is tiny through the winter or who lives in a drafty house should have long-sleeved shirts. Otherwise the short-sleeved or sleeveless ones are adequate and should be bought in year-old size, like everything else for the infant, because the rate of growth of a healthy baby is amazing and the tiny little garments offered for newborn babies in all the shops are rendered useless in a few weeks. All these items are relatively expensive, and friends and relatives should be encouraged to give them along with other clothing into which the baby will grow.

Few babies are put into shoes these days until they are actually walking. Stitched shoes in pink or blue silk will be wasted on the modern baby, no matter how much they appeal to Aunt May. Bootees, large enough to allow for inevitable shrinkage are fine for the infant who is tiny during winter and spring. Innumerable infant sweaters—all size one or larger—are welcomed by any mother and baby.

Satin, quilted coats or comforters are useless to today's baby. Cover him with light-weight, easily washable wool blankets. Receiving blankets are very useful, but only if they are relatively utilitarian—several should be in cotton flannel and the others should not be too elaborate because there is always the washing problem. Hand-knit afghans must be washed very carefully by hand and rolled in a towel to dry—a long process and something to consider when you think of the dozens of quick changes a baby needs daily.

One rarely sees today those delicately embroidered "dribble bibs" that were an accouterment of our own clothes-tortured infancy. Current cotton-clad babies aren't constantly be-bibbed, although a good, absorbent bib is vital at feeding time. For these, turkish toweling is best, as it prevents spilled food from soaking through to the underclothing and may be washed without ironing (so very important even if a mother has help, even if she has a baby nurse). Plastic bibs shed liquids onto mother but are useful later when more solid food is taken.

When the baby is big enough—from six months on—he or she goes into creepers or dresses, with overalls for ordinary rough wear (which means most of the time) standard for both sexes. Don't buy something that fits too exactly, for in a matter of two or three weeks it will have to be discarded. In buying baby clothes, take into consideration the weight and length of the particular baby, not just his age. Children's clothes are unfortunately not standardized, so one "size two" may be much smaller than another. An expensive "size one" pair of corduroy overalls may fit the baby from six to nine months and then have to be passed on to a younger child.

Even where there is plenty of help, a baby's clothes are often left unironed, except for dress-up ones like starched pinafores and dresses. It is better to keep a baby as clean as possible and sweet-smelling in fresh but unironed clothes than to have mother or a nurse busy most of the time ironing his clothes when there are so many more things that would be better for all, such as an extra hour in the open air.

Keeping the baby as clean as possible makes him feel comfortable when he's very little. But later on as he begins to crawl and toddle it is expected that he will gather considerable good clean dirt, and constant fussing at him over "dirtiness" tends to inhibit his adventurous spirit in an unwholesome manner. Any soiling that doesn't make him uncomfortable is certainly preferable, psychologically, to overstressing of cleanliness. At this time, the bath, often the second for the day, takes place before suppertime, for a baby can't be comfortable going to bed dirty. The warm bath, in which he should be given plenty of time to play, will help him settle down for the night.

DRESSING THE PRE-SCHOOL AND THE OLDER CHILD In what *style* (the cost of the clothes is unimportant) are the other children of your neighborhood dressed for school and for party occasions? That's the way you must dress your child if you aren't to interfere with his healthy emotional growth. If you make a little Lord Fauntleroy of your son, refusing to crop his charming little curls, or if your daughter wears velvet and taffeta to Sunday school when the other children wear clean, pretty washdresses even in the winter, then you are handicapping them. Children have a psychological necessity to be exactly like the others in their group. If they are made to be different by strong-minded, often highly individual parents, they miss something very important in their development.

This does not mean that you can't mention an eventual goal of tidiness and quality of dress to your growing son when he is at the stage where he won't wear anything but blue jeans, polo shirts, and dirty sneakers or sloppy moccasins. All the other children are at times poured into "Sunday clothes," wearing ties, shined shoes, garters (perhaps) and being expected to have clean nails and combed hair, so he won't feel too discriminated against if you insist on his conforming to community custom on these occasions, too.

From six on—sometimes earlier—he should have something to say about the clothes he wears. If he detests certain colors and textures or styles, try to avoid them. If he wants his hair long and you prefer it crew cut, try to effect a compromise.

Little girls are likely to be more clothes conscious than boys, and at an earlier age, but not necessarily so. Boys, if they get a chance to express them, have strong opinions on what is "the thing" to wear, and, within reason, parents should shut their eyes to the ridiculousness of current boy and girl clothing fads. Each generation has had its own fads, and to prohibit a child from following what is probably a quite harmless fashion, even if it offends your own and your friends' sensibilities, is to make the child "not belong" with his crowd, a hurtful thing.

HAND-ME-DOWNS AND MADE-OVERS   Even the last child in a large family has the right to at least a few clothes bought especially for him, if it is at all possible. The system of handing down clothes from one child to the next is necessary for most of us, and most children accept this economy in good grace. But a child who from infancy is clad only in castoffs can't develop the necessary pride of possession and of loving consideration he gets from having at least some things that were bought or made for him alone.

Children's clothes that are made over from those of adults should always be of fabrics and colors suitable for a child, and unless the remodeling can be done with an expert hand it had better not be done at all. Children always seems to know when they are being made to wear something that will cause them to be ridiculed by their peers, and they, very rightly, fight against it. A child is often secretly embarrassed at having to wear a coat made out of an old skirt of mother's or a dress concocted from some all-too-familiar garment of sister's. Swapping clothes with other mothers—and preferably with mothers whose children move in different neighborhoods—seems a good solution, for to most small children any article of clothing they haven't seen before is "new" to them.

As children rarely wear new clothes out before they outgrow them, a barter arrangement set up through the Parent-Teacher Association or just among the mothers themselves is a sensible and widely accepted idea now in even upper-income groups. Older children often love to sell their outgrown clothing through such outlets and use the money to buy other new or used things that suit them. Where such swapping is an accepted thing in a community, they don't even mind knowing whose clothes they are getting. In fact, they often are delighted to be able to buy or swap something for a garment or other article once owned by an admired older child. By setting up such organizations and encouraging all groups to contribute and exchange clothing through them, we do a social service that avoids the onus of charity for those children who must get their clothing this way or not at all.

WHEN DOES THE CHILD CHOOSE HIS OWN CLOTHES? I believe that a child should be at least consulted on his clothes preferences almost from the time he is able to state an opinion. Where he is making an obvious mistake, he should be guided, but within reason he should not be forced to wear clothes he obviously dislikes. He has his own, sometimes quite peculiar-to-us, ideas of what's becoming to him. And consideration of any strong opinions he may have on the subject is only fair if we wish to follow the modern ideal of considering the child as a person right from the start, not just a possession to jump at our superior commands.

His taste in clothes and in other things develops slowly, partly through example and partly through his own character growth, through enthusiasms passionately embraced, then quickly or gradually abandoned to be replaced by others. We can help children find their style by letting them, wherever possible, make their own choice if they seem ready to make one—a brown hat instead of the blue, a rose dress instead of the more practical tan. Mistakes will be made, but then they won't be made a second time if they have caused the child any discomfort.

Children's tastes in good clothes are usually conservative, perhaps because it takes an individuality they haven't yet achieved to choose something which, while still in good taste, is not just like everybody else's. The teenage girl who, despite gentle advice to the contrary, selects a dress that is too old for her or too impractical for the purpose will, after having worn it, learn the valuable lesson that something that looks fine in the shop under the sales person's blandishments may look all wrong viewed against her existing wardrobe or next to the party dress of her best friend. The older boy who uses up several months of his clothes allowance to buy his first tuxedo when he really needs school clothes more will learn to regret his hasty decision.

FORMING CONFIDENCE AND SELF-RELIANCE

HOW MUCH ALLOWANCE SHOULD THE CHILD HAVE? The amount of a child's allowance should depend on what he is expected to do with it and, when he's very young, on what others his own age in his community normally get. A child of wealthy parents should not have more pocket money than the children with whom he regularly associates. But neither are children expected to "keep up with the Joneses" if a large family, heavy responsibilities, or other circumstances make it necessary to give a child less spending money than is customary in the neighborhood. Children are much more realistic than we believe. They can accept all kinds of economies and deprivations if they are told quietly and sympathetically why they are necessary.

Whatever the allowance is, its entire use should not be dictated by his parents, because a child learns to use money intelligently only through handling it himself. If a six-year-old gets five or ten cents a week allowance and is made to put it all in his piggy bank, he gets no idea that the real use for money is as a medium of exchange. He gets the shiny coin and it promptly disappears. The idea of a bank account is much too abstract for so small a child, although he can be made to understand and enjoy saving his pennies—not all of them, only a part of what he receives—to buy something he especially wants. To expect any young child to save, say, for his college education is expecting entirely too much and is asking him to assume at least in part the responsibility of the parent. Instead he should be saving, earning, and spending suitable amounts all along in order to learn how to manage money and to keep him in a favorable status with his friends. The boy who never can "treat," who can't join the kids in a candy store occasionally, because he has to save every cent he gets or earns for some big dim project his parents have chosen for him, is a sorry child and likely to be left out of things.

Give the child a chance to earn some money around his home or in the neighborhood to develop his initiative. Give him a set allowance, expect certain not-too-difficult or time-consuming chores from him, and pay him for extra work you ask him to do. But let him spend his own money as he pleases after he and you have agreed to some saving and spending plan that leaves him leeway to move in his own little world as a sufficiently moneyed individual.

Children treated with this kind of understanding don't squander their money. They nearly always save and nearly always are solvent. They don't attach undue value to money, because it is not used as a weapon against them and they are not told what to do with each penny supposedly freely given them. Taking away some privilege is safer punishment for a serious infraction of discipline than withdrawal of his allowance, because a child's "social obligations" go right on and having no spending money might encourage a resentful child to pilfer or to impose on others in his desire to get the things "all the other kids have." A child wants to be able to depend on his allowance being given to him on a set day and to have nothing interfere with it, if that is humanly possible. To him it is a pay check and what he has planned to do with it is as important to him as the family income is to his father.

WITHHOLDING ALLOWANCES The only time an allowance should be withheld, if you want your child to have an understanding of money, is when he himself wishes to borrow in advance for an immediate purchase. Explain that loans must be promptly returned and that his allowance will be withheld until his contemplated loan is paid up. Usually he will prefer to save for the purchase, instead—a very good practice to encourage.

If allowances are withheld for the sake of punishment, his share of the family income ceases to be in the proper perspective for the child—instead, it is something he can't count on, which can be given or withheld according to what he thinks of as his parents' whims. An allowance riddled by fines, which are often levied at moments of parental anger, ceases to be the inviolate thing it should be.

There are other ways of punishing a child that are more effective than by using his allowance as a club. When he handles the money which he receives on schedule, money restitutions are often valuable in developing a sense of his obligation. Suppose a child habitually rises late, misses the school bus, and has to be driven to school by a harassed mother or father, thus upsetting their daily schedules. Sometimes the way to cure that is to give warning that the next time it happens the child must go by taxi and the fare must be returned to his mother, out of his allowance—no matter how long it takes. His actual handing over of that money until the debt is paid is more valuable educationally than the complete withholding of the allowance by the parents for the same period. And there is more dignity in such an arrangement for the child, especially if it is all done on a quiet, business-like basis devoid of scolding and moralizing about promptness. He will get the point very well.

CHILDREN'S TABLE MANNERS

A happy, year-and-a-half-old child may make efforts to feed himself with his spoon. If so, let him do as much as he can in some easily cleanable place, but don't expect him to take over the function immediately and don't let fussy grown-ups annoy him with their admonitions to keep his hands out of his food. A baby who puts his hands in his cereal or dabbles his fingers in his mug of milk is experimenting with self-feeding—not exhibiting bad manners. If he spills some on the tray before him—an inevitable result—don't be in too much of a hurry to clean up the mess, because to him it is delightful. He slides his fingers around in it, and it makes an interesting squishy sound. He likes the feel of it and needs this kind of play whether with mud pies, water or, under such circumstances, his food. A child who dawdles over food once he is competent to feed himself may want to attract his mother's attention so she'll sit with him or perhaps give him a hand with some of the less tractable items, like custard (and why not?), or else he's not hungry. In the latter instance the food should be pleasantly removed.

MUST A CHILD FINISH HIS FOOD?   At various periods in our culture we have heard diametrically opposite pieces of advice, which we, in turn, have drummed or tried to drum into our children. One is that a child must for discipline's sake "clean up his plate" at any cost—even that of an immediately rebellious stomach. No one knows why. Another is that it is "rude" to leave any food on one's plate. And then that it is "rude" to eat every last thing—on the ground that one should not be too interested in one's food if he is to be considered well-bred, a rather Victorian concept of nutrition.

Each baby is born with a built-in, well-functioning hunger mechanism. It tells him when he should eat and when he should stop eating. If this mechanism is respected by parents and baby, normal growth and appetite usually follow right along. But interference with this delicate adjustment can cause serious emotional difficulties in a young child that may continue into his adulthood in a very complex manner. Constantly coaxing a child or forcing him to eat beyond his capacity, beyond what his hunger dictates at the moment, puts this mechanism out of commission. It often results in an overweight child or one tense and thin, prone to car sickness and frequent digestive upsets.

SHOULD A CHILD CHOOSE HIS OWN FOOD? Suppose someone with quite different tastes from yours dictated every morsel you put into your mouth. Would you enjoy your food or would you feel frustrated and angry? Anger causes digestion to stop dead in its tracks. A chronic state of tension at mealtimes is the cause of many of our modern ills, especially ulcers. Unpleasant mealtimes must be avoided for the sake of the whole family and especially that of the children, whose attitudes concerning food are being set at this time. Insisting that a child eat food he doesn't like (and usually the dislike will pass) is bad for the child-parent relationship. The child knows instinctively mother is not right this time.

But if you let a child dictate what he'll eat and when, won't he fill up on sweets and never eat the things his body needs? There are many modern children for whom no problem about feeding has ever arisen—they are under the "permissive" or "self-regulating" system. Such children are not fussy eaters unless there is some particular reason for the fussiness—teething, oncoming illness, over-fatigue—which is respected by the adult in charge. The child is excused from his meal with no comment one way or the other. Conversely, when he eats well he is not praised for eating. Why should he be? It is important that the whole issue of eating to please a parent (or of not eating to displease) never arise and that happy mealtimes geared to the child's food preferences be the rule.

Where a child has a history of tension over meals and has been subjected to rigid rules of manners even in the nursery, he may when introduced to the self-regulating system of feeding start eating his dessert first or refuse to eat anything but sweets. This is because a premium has always been placed on these things—"If you don't eat your lamb chop, you may not have your ice cream!" This puts good, sound lamb chops into the class of something unpleasant but necessary, to be bolted quickly so the "good" child can have the "delicious" dessert.

Psychologists and psychiatrists working with children have found that children who have been exposed to this kind of handling may, once given the opportunity to choose what they want to eat, eat their dessert first. If they do, it's not important, not worth making an issue of, because shortly they will want to be like other people who eat their meat and potatoes first and finish with dessert. In experiments with very young children it was shown over a period of time that children have selective appetites—one day a child may want nothing but string beans for lunch and won't touch his milk. Another day he'll want the meat but not the vegetable on his plate; but careful graphing of such food intake over a period of a week will show that the normal child, allowed to select his food according to his preference, will instinctively consume a properly balanced diet if he has been offered, each day, the various elements in it. If he skips lettuce one day and eats twice as much of it the next, he is getting what he needs, isn't he? The body, given the chance, dictates what it requires for adequate nutrition.

In time, any normal, happy child wants to be like those closest to him. If his mother and father, his aunts and uncles, his older sisters and brothers break their bread into small pieces before buttering and eating it, cut their meat into manageable forkfuls, the littlest one will eventually cease trying to get a whole slice of bread or an entire chop into his mouth at one time. It does no harm to bring a child to the family table as soon as he can stand it and the family can stand him. But to expect him to sit like a silent little statue throughout the long adult meal or wait for late-comers is not to understand the immediacy of the small mind. In time, he'll catch up to our way of doing things. We did not ourselves arrive in the world full-fledged in the complexities of etiquette.

SHOULD CHILDREN BE SEEN AND NOT HEARD?   It would be a good idea for us to discard many of the old saws to do with the training of the young, and this, the idea that a child, having nothing to say—at least nothing of importance to most adults—should say nothing, is one of them. The ability to carry on a conversation at meals is an art, developed like any other through guided practice. Even the baby at table should have some conversation or attention directed his way occasionally, even if he replies with nothing more than "Goo." Otherwise, he will find some anti-social way of getting attention, such as spilling his milk on the tablecloth or dropping his spoon on the floor. If we have the children at the table at all, they should be treated with the same courtesy and consideration we give to the adults there. Of course children should not be permitted to monopolize the conversation or make everyone else uncomfortable by their noise or messiness.

If because of fatigue or the presence of too many strangers (other children as guests can sometimes upset the applecart nicely) the usually pleasant child begins to make a scene at table, remove him gently and let him have his food by himself, not as punishment but for his comfort—and, of course, yours. In fact, it is better to anticipate such possible crises and arrange, beforehand, to side-step them. But don't scold the child or apologize unduly to the adults about him. "This, too, shall pass." Don't expect too much of him, now.

OLDER CHILDREN AT TABLE   Later on, adolescence brings forth in children the same orneriness that we find in the four-to-six bracket. They are a little more amenable to reason but not much, because of their own physical and emotional upheavals. Again, don't exact more than the child can deliver, of manners or anything else. He should be made to understand that meals with the rest of the family are a privilege, that no one member should make the others uncomfortable by bickering, noisy behavior, lounging all over the table, lack of grooming, etc. If it seems impossible to get him to follow the house rules concerning meals, let him eat alone for a while until he is ready to return and conform, within reason. Making every mealtime a battle-ground of manners is a strain on everyone and usually does no more than stir up defiance in the child. But, while manners are caught, they can also be taught, gently, during the course of ordinary exposure to them.

A child is very interested at around ten or eleven in the reasons behind various food practices. He likes to hear, for instance, that primitive man eats out of a common dish with his fingers, that the Chinese invented the fork, then later returned to the dainty chopsticks so difficult for the Occidental to handle expertly. He is relieved to discover that, while most things on his plate should be eaten with fork or spoon, there are still many finger foods. He hates to seem awkward, so if he is to be confronted, for instance, with his first artichoke when there are guests present, show him in advance how you take off each leaf and dip it in the sauce, how you eat just the tender base of the leaf and place the rest at the side of the plate. Explain about the choke and how to remove it with knife and fork before coming to the reward of the heart.

Children like to eat with their fingers. Give them plenty of opportunity for it with between-meals snacks and in meals out of doors, in spring and summer where they may eat hot dogs, pie, cake, and fruit out of hand, with adults doing likewise and taking no time out for pleasure-spoiling lectures on manners.

AWKWARDNESS IN CHILDREN Children are beginners. They are starting a job in life. If we expect them to do everything expertly at once we are certainly going to be disappointed. It doesn't help for adults to be affronted or infuriated—as so many of them are—by childish errors at table. We should realize, for example, that awkwardness is increased by nagging—not only awkwardness in children, but in adults. When we are having difficulty in the carrying out of some motor act, criticism embarrasses or irritates us into further awkwardness. If the peas won't stay on Junior's fork, give him a spoon—quietly and pleasantly—and let him use it until he is ready to cope with the fork.

It is important to know that increased, very noticeable awkwardness, especially at table, shown in the dropping and spilling of food, the knocking over of glasses, can be a forewarning of one of the infectious childhood diseases—scarlet fever or measles, for example—which may be followed by chorea or St. Vitus's dance. But where awkwardness seems to be part and parcel of the child, then increasing his social poise and skills may help. In severe cases professional re-education, sometimes in handedness, may have to be resorted to, and for this school and medical advisors need to be consulted.

THE SOCIAL BEHAVIOR OF CHILDREN

TEACHING RESPECT FOR BOOKS AND OTHERS' PROPERTY   The public libraries each year report thousands and thousands of dollars' worth of damage to books. The damage is not all done by children, of course, but the damage done by adults—tearing out pages, dog-earing pages, doodling and scribbling, and breaking the backs of books—results from the lack of training during childhood.

A small child cannot be controlled with a constant stream of prohibitions. When he reaches the crawling and toddling stage, breakables like ash trays and ornaments must be put out of his reach wherever possible and his activities confined to areas he can't seriously damage. He should not be allowed to play with such things as phonograph records which he is bound to break. He will squall when he is removed from such enticing playthings with the words, "Those are Mother's, baby mustn't touch," but in time he will find it not worth his while to turn in their direction, especially if acceptable articles are given him immediately as a substitute. It accomplishes nothing to give him cracked or damaged records to break, for he cannot distinguish between the records he may treat with impunity and those he will be punished for breaking.

A baby should have his own books—with the first ones the undamageable kind. Later when paper books are introduced, they should be looked at only under parental supervision at first. Infant interest is very short, and in a matter of minutes the new book that was so bright and arresting may pall. The baby will throw it on the floor or start tearing out the pages. This should not be permitted. The mother should say, "We don't hurt books. Mother will let you see the book later." And the book should disappear until the next supervised reading. If this procedure is followed every time, eventually even a child of one or two will not destroy his books and won't harm those of his parents, should any be within reach. To give a baby old magazines to mutilate, or permit him to harm his own books, is inviting trouble. He can't know the difference between old and new magazines, between his books and his parents'.

When the child gets his first pencils and crayons he should be allowed to use them only under supervision until he learns how they are used and where. The minute interest lags and the crayon starts straying off the paper or coloring book, the little artist's equipment should be gently put away until the next time.

NECESSARY REMINDERS   It is often said that the manners of today's children are atrocious. Perhaps many parents are so sensitive to possible criticism that they fail to take into consideration that manners, where actually taught —aside from being almost bred in the bone through proper example—are never successfully imparted through constant nagging or physical reminders (a sharp crack on the recalcitrant elbow at table, for example). Such teaching makes most children resentful and unco-operative. The tension created by such parental tactics is a poor background for learning the social graces, to say the least.

There comes a time when even a headstrong child will want desperately to know how to do the right thing. The time to remind him of the rules of manners is *before* he comes to table with guests, *before* he goes to the party, *in advance* of his boarding the train. Constant correction of the child in front of others is irritating to all concerned and often reflects the parents' own lack of social poise.

A boy or girl studying American history will be amused and benefited by being referred to George Washington's fifty-four maxims on personal conduct, which for all their quaint phraseology do embody most of the things we all should know about accepted social actions and attitudes. The maxims, by the way, were probably translated by Washington from the original French while he was a teen ager, himself, and are not believed to be original with him. Any library can turn up frequent references to them.

Aside from Washington, whose advice is so basic as to refer to the picking of teeth in public and reading the letters of others, there are elemental codes of behavior and niceties of manners that should be implanted in all children in their years of close contact with parents, who, it is hoped, follow the same pattern of behavior. What are some of these? I believe a child should eventually come to understand that publicly in "polite society" we do not do the following things:

1. Scratch, pick the teeth, spit, comb the hair, or tend the nails.
2. Chew with our mouths open or with obvious noise or lip-smacking.
3. Leave a spoon in a cup, or eat with a knife.
4. Tuck in a napkin (unless we are very young indeed), suck our fingers instead of wiping them on a napkin.
5. Sit down to a meal unwashed and uncombed or improperly dressed.
6. Fail to greet others encountered in the household when we arise and when we return home.
7. Tilt chairs or push them back from the table with all our body weight upon them.
8. Lounge on the dinner table or put our elbows on it except between courses (and then preferably one elbow at a time, if any) or sit on our spines.
9. Go up and down stairs like elephants and bang doors after us.
10. Pass in front of others without saying, "Please excuse me" or "I'm sorry."
11. Use a flat "No" or "Yes" in answer to questions. Instead, "Yes, Mother," "Yes, Mr. Roberts (or, Sir)."
12. Speak ill of the dead or repeat damaging gossip.
13. Swear in a way that is generally considered offensive (though most children need a list of acceptable "swear words" with which they can blow

off steam—perhaps one list for use in the parents' presence, if absolutely necessary, and another list for away from home where there is likely to be more rigidity in the matter).

14. Put more than a manageable mouthful in our mouths at one time.

15. Burp, belch, sneeze, or cough without attempting to turn away from others and then only behind the cupped hand or a clean handkerchief.

16. Stick feet out into aisles and passageways so people may fall over them.

17. Behave noisily and conspicuously in public places.

18. Enter a room whose door is closed without knocking and waiting for permission to enter.

19. Interrupt a conversation except for an important reason and then only after asking permission to speak.

20. Speak unnecessarily loudly. Chatter incessantly.

21. Walk without actually picking up our feet.

22. Pull our finger joints, drum our fingers or indulge in any similar irritating little habits that set people's teeth on edge. (But see What to Do about Annoying Habits.)

Children and young people (and, of course, all men and women) should know and practice these things as an integral part of their daily lives, eventually without particular consciousness that they are following accepted precepts of gentlefolk.

Instead of constantly reading adolescents and pre-adolescents the Riot Act, let them study a list such as this at times when they seem relatively receptive. Often they will accept what is in books more readily than what they hear, perhaps too constantly, from properly concerned parents.

CALLING PARENTS BY FIRST NAMES

In ultra-progressive educational circles parents and even teachers are often called by their first names. The idea seems to be that this puts adults and children on the same level and increases rapport. To me it seems self-conscious, if not, in the case of parents, barbaric. To other children who call their parents "Mother" and "Father," or variation of these honored titles, in the traditional manner, children who substitute "Marie" and "Bill" seem peculiar, unless most in the group do likewise. The mother-father relationship is there, no matter what parents are called. Why shouldn't it be frankly admitted for the sake of children and parents? To me, such ultra-modern parents and children seem to be missing something very important. And to the uninitiated the children seem like foundlings.

"MAKING" CHILDREN MIND THEIR MANNERS

There are certain accepted manners which children should be continually encouraged to cultivate. Their attention should be drawn to the fact that, on various occasions, mother and father do certain things to be socially agreeable and these courtesies will be expected of them, too, as soon as they are able to cope with them.

The mother who makes a scene with her child because he won't shake hands with Mrs. Smith or thank a small hostess for a party he didn't in all honesty enjoy, does little but make everyone uncomfortable. It is far better to say, "Helen, Johnny would like to tell you what a nice time he had at your party. And he hopes to see you soon again," the minute one senses that a child is going to balk at the expected amenities. Most children eventually rise to the social graces in their own good time. In the meantime, they should hear us deliver the courteous phrases for them, without irritation. And they need to be told quietly, before and after social events, what will be expected of them as a matter of course.

If necessary a mother should say in a low voice to her young son with whom she is walking on the street, "Here comes Mrs. Smith, dear. When she stops to speak to me, remember, please, to take off your cap." She should avoid giving these lessons in front of others, unless the reminders can be made very privately.

I have never seen a child with well-mannered parents who grew into an adult completely devoid of social grace. But I have seen such a child, in rebellion at constant goading concerning his manners, go through a savage period during which the only conformity with social customs was enforced with damaging tension to both child and parents. Such a nagged child gets to believe he *is* a boor and that nothing can remedy the fact, so he might as well be as primitive as possible, just to show them.

A friend of mine with whom I was discussing these things said he and his wife taught his hoard of boys manners by taking them out very frequently, en masse. They quickly saw for themselves that the relatively relaxed manners possible at their family dinner table were not the manners for a fine restaurant in town. They were so thrilled at their parents' including them in grown-up parties that they were most anxious to conform to the code of proper public behavior.

A little friendly review of manners before and after parties and other events to which children go helps, too, to make such things second nature.

Real social polish is usually acquired away from parents, once the essentials have been inculcated. Children need plenty of opportunity to practice what they have been taught at home in the company of other children who are going through the same social exercises. Dancing class from eight to ten and on up is very helpful and for some self-conscious children a virtual necessity. Concert, museum, and theater attendance, the opera, if possible, "Y" classes, Boy and Girl Scouts, all the extra-curricular activities where manners, social form and co-operation can be taught and observed are very valuable, just because the lessons do not come from the often over-insistent parents.

MUST A LITTLE GIRL CURTSY?   The stiff, self-conscious little curtsy, against which so many little girls under ten rebel, is not essential to good manners to-day. It may be required in dancing class but it should not be insisted upon in the living room, and it looks Victorian outdoors. If a child enjoys the dramatic effect of the curtsy before adults in greeting them and saying good-by, as many do, that's fine. But many little girls come through these little social contacts more gracefully if they are just expected to bow or shake hands politely. And they should certainly not be expected to kiss a whole roomful of strangers, or in fact anyone whom it would not be quite natural for them to kiss without being reminded.

THE BOY'S BOW   Even little boys can be encouraged to come forward and, feet together, bow their heads slightly and shake hands with their parents' guests, so long as the occasional neglected courtesy is not made into a crisis. If the tiny boy says "No!" when asked to say "Good afternoon" to Mrs. Smith, Mother can say, "Well, next time I'm sure you'll shake hands, like Daddy." Usually he will want to emulate Daddy right then, if belatedly, if the mother is relaxed rather than humiliated. Sometimes childish coldness to guests is instinctive—they sense the guest does not like children. The warm, child-loving adult rarely has any trouble in such introductions. Children are attracted to them at once. Which is more valuable socially—for a baby to reluctantly go through a stiff little ceremony, or flatteringly crawl onto the stranger's lap?

EXTENDING INVITATIONS

Boys or girls, even those in their very late teens, should not extend invitations to other children to meals, for week ends, or for outings of various kinds except through their mothers. A boy of ten or so may phone another boy of his own age and say, "Peter, my mother would like you to come to dinner and stay overnight. If you'd like to come, she'll speak to your mother." It is courteous to let the children make the preliminary arrangements, as they invariably have their own plans and preferences in playmates. Mothers should avoid making such arrangements for their children's entertainment without their full consent.

An invitation from a boy to a girl (whatever the age) to visit his home for a meal or overnight should always be extended by the mother in the final stages of the arrangements. This may be done by note, if the children live at some distance, or by phone. In the case of a teen-age girl, the mother of the host writes to her or phones her, then asks to speak to the girl's mother in order to verify the invitation herself.

CHILDREN'S INTRODUCTIONS

A child bringing a strange child home says, "Mother, this is Billy Burnham. Billy, this is my mother." If his mother's surname is different from her son's, he says, ". . . my mother, Mrs. Fellows." The guest says, "How do you do," or perhaps just "Hello." If he is introducing a girl he follows the same form, introducing the guest to his mother as soon as possible after arrival. The mother then leaves the young people to their own devices in their own part of the house or apartment, but, in the case of very young children, she doesn't leave the house. Teen-age boys and girls are not left without acceptable adult supervision, that is, not solely with servants, even for short periods.

BIRTHDAY PARTIES FOR CHILDREN

It has long been clear to me that many a small child's birthday party is put on for the pleasure of the grown-ups around him rather than for the delight of the child.

Watch a party for a one- or two-year-old. He sits in the midst of piled-up packages but hasn't the tactile ability yet to open them himself. So some adult unwraps each thing and hands it to the baby. A profusion of playthings is troubling to such a small child. He likes to pick, up, examine, and play with one toy at a time in his own fashion. But he is not allowed, on this occasion, to make proper, slow acquaintance of each gift. Too many things and people come at him at once. By the time the cake and ice cream are triumphantly brought forth for his approval, he is probably in tears or has retired in self-protection to some quiet corner to play with some familiar, tattered plaything. He might as well not be at his own party.

There are exceptions, of course, but usually things don't improve much by the fifth or even the tenth birthday. In fact, many sensible mothers, with their children's complete agreement, make birthday celebrations very simple indeed. There are no big parties with magicians, donkey games, Mickey Mouse movies, and other exciting diversions. There is never the inevitable ice cream and cake spilled on the living room rug and the birthday celebrant too keyed-up and goody-stuffed to go to bed peacefully. Instead, perhaps, the older child is permitted the choice of one friend with whom he can do something very special. They may lunch in a restaurant and go to the zoo or on some little trip. Mother goes along and perhaps father does, too. There is never too much of anything—not too much rich food, not too much entertainment.

Very young children can't possibly understand what birthday parties are all about. But as the adults enjoy them, let there be ice cream and a cake after one of the baby's regular meals. Let just the family celebrate with him, with perhaps one other little friend arriving for the cake ceremony. As the baby won't appreciate more than one or two simple toys, let doting relatives give him things he needs—clothes or money for his bank account. If many toys arrive, some should be put away for the inevitable rainy day. They should never be showered on him all at once.

In my experience, most children prefer these quiet family celebrations of their birthdays without too much said about it all in advance. Certainly threats such as "If you are a bad boy, you won't get any birthday presents this year!" should never be used. We don't really mean such threats, but the child believes them, and even when his birthday arrives along with the presents much of the pleasure is dissipated because of his preliminary anxiety.

In the early teens, birthday parties begin to come into their own. Now the children can take real part in preparing for them, making up their guest lists, choosing favors, planning and conducting the entertainment.

WHAT HOURS FOR CHILDREN'S PARTIES?   Most mothers dislike the birthday party at which their eight- or ten-year-old gorges on ice cream and cake, arriving home at his normal suppertime unable to eat what's been prepared for him. Parties for young children, if they are given at all, should include a normal meal followed by the birthday food. This means that in the five-to-ten group parties should begin at three-thirty or four and terminate with an early supper, so the children will be home and ready for bed by six-thirty at the latest for the little ones and seven-thirty or eight at the latest for the older ones.

THE CHILD'S MANNERS AT HIS PARTY   No child, we know, learns manners or anything else at one fell swoop. So a child who is host at his own birthday party should not be goaded and corrected by an overanxious parent all during the proceedings. If he is old enough, he may be told just before the party that, as he has been taught, it is good manners to greet his guests as they enter, to thank them for gifts (even if they have brought something he doesn't like), to see that they have a good time and first chance at toys and games, and, finally, to bid them good-by and, if possible, to thank them again for coming and for their gifts.

All this ceremony is trying, even for adults at a party, so we should not dissolve in despair if our children forget a few moves in the complicated game of etiquette. We should remember that the child feels some embarrassment at all this focusing of attention on him. It is normal for him to take a playful poke at some incoming pal with a "Hi, Skinny! I was hoping you'd stay home." Children understand each other. Parents should, within reason, allow them to conduct their social intercourse without censure.

Of course, these occasions are valuable for learning. But correction—by means of gentle suggestion—should come before and after (much after) the party. The parents can watch how their child conducts himself, stepping into the picture only if things get too much out of hand. The next day they may find it desirable to go over some of the things that were less than perfect, taking into consideration that the child was under a strain at the time and that, at his age, it was instinctive for him to try to enjoy his own birthday party to the utmost, guests notwithstanding.

SPECIAL PROBLEMS

TAKING A CHILD TO THE DOCTOR'S OFFICE   You need your doctor as a ready ally in coping with the inevitable illnesses and emergencies of childhood.

Don't build him up in your child's mind as an ogre through senseless threats—"If you fall, you'll be hurt, and the doctor will have to come, so get down right away!" or "Stop eating that candy or you'll be sick and the doctor will take you to the hospital!" Doctors and hospitals are necessary. Children should know their functions but should never be threatened with them as a method of so-called discipline.

As far as a child is concerned, the doctor should be a familiar friend. The child-wise doctor knows this and, except when quick action is vital, takes time to let the child get accustomed to him as a person before examinations or treatments begin. When a mother can do so without anxiety she should tell the child what is going to happen. "Your throat is sore, so the doctor will ask you to open your mouth wide—like this—so he can see where the trouble is. He will hold your tongue down with a stick for a minute. If you ask him, he'll give you a throat stick to play with. It will come in handy if Teddy gets a sore throat."

Some mothers increase tension if they are present in the examining room, but most mothers can help the doctor materially in calming the child's fears. No good is accomplished by telling even the smallest child that something that will certainly hurt, won't. Instead say—or let the doctor say—"Now this will hurt just an instant but it will soon be over. Then I'll give you a lollipop." Try to make all contacts with the doctor or dentist have a pleasant ending, and do not build up unnecessary tension beforehand by talking unnecessarily about the coming session. The baby who is frightened because of his memory of painful inoculations needs to be reassured by his mother and, if possible, have an opportunity to make friends with the doctor before the next treatment takes place. A favorite toy or a lollipop should be ready to catch his attention and comfort him the minute he can be released. A calm, cheerful mother, not overly commiserative, helps the situation considerably.

THE CHILD IN THE HOSPITAL Where an operation is necessary for a child—a tonsillectomy, say—it is important for his mother or doctor to tell him quietly, not too far in advance, just what is going to happen, how long he will be away from home, to what degree it will hurt, and who will be with him. The young child should, if possible, have his mother, or some member of the family, and a favorite toy with him in the hospital at least the first night after an operation, especially when he first comes out of the anesthesia. He should be given a sedative before going to the operating room, if possible, to dim its terrors and, again, if it is permitted, the mother or father should go with him until after he is anesthetized to keep him calm and secure and to pass on the orders of the strange person who will administer the anesthesia. Needless to say, a frightened, anxious parent under the circumstances is worse than a calm stranger. But the right kind of parental reassurance is of tremendous assistance both physically and psychologically. A relaxed, trusting child, sure of a safe outcome for the operation and understanding the need and procedure of it reasonably well for his age, makes the best patient. A frightened child who has built up many nameless fears of an operation about which he's in the dark can cause complications for the surgeon, the anesthetist, and the nurses. An anxiety concerning hospitals and operations may shadow the rest of his life and, of course, delay his immediate recovery. An operation, well-handled in an atmosphere of parental reassurance and patience, can for the small child be something beyond recall a few years later.

CHILDREN IN THE DARK The end of the day should belong to parents and their guests, once the children have been put to bed. But many a family's troubles with a child begin with insistence that the child "learn" not to be afraid of the dark. Fear of the dark is often implanted by thoughtless grown-ups or older children who threaten a little one with the "boogie man." A tiny infant is not afraid of the dark, and its mother may be planting the seeds of trouble if she starts the baby off sleeping in a room which is always kept lighted.

Babies, right from birth, can be trained to sleep undisturbed either by the absence or presence of light. To pull down the shades automatically at nap time for a baby may be to make him too dependent on light conditions in a room. Instead, start the baby sleeping in an unshaded room not overly protected from the usual household noises so he will quickly learn to go to sleep under any conditions. Place his bed so he won't be disturbed by the sun shining full in his face, but don't pull the shades. An older child who has been conditioned to sleeping only in darkened rooms can be patiently encouraged to sleep in a room under different circumstances. If he learns to do so, he is laying the base for better adult sleeping habits.

NIGHT LIGHTS The happy child who has never had a night light normally takes "lights out" in his stride. A child who has been given a night light and then as he grows older is arbitrarily expected to do without it sometimes becomes frightened and prolongs his sleeping preparations endlessly because of a fear he is ashamed to express. Such a child may so infuriate his parents with his jumping out of bed, his demands for a drink of water, his needless trips to the bathroom that he brings undeserved punishment on his head. If continuation of a night light quiets such a child so that he goes to sleep promptly, isn't it better to give it to him than to try to force him to give up his fear by rational explanations to the effect that the dark is harmless?

Many adults are unable to sleep in a room that is completely dark, either because they have been accustomed to a night light since babyhood or because in childhood they were frightened by stories of the terrors lurking in darkness. Fear of the dark, of going to sleep is very usual and human. Think of the prayers that suggest it—because it has always been so elemental —"If I should die before I wake," "The pestilence that walketh in darkness." No one, child or adult, should be forced to sleep entirely in the dark if he is unable to do so easily and fearlessly. Showing a little child who is terrified of the dark that there is nothing to be frightened of by switching on a light when his fear comes on is one way to help overcome fear of the dark, if it is to be overcome at all. To insist that a child sleep in a dark room when such devices are ineffective and the darkness keeps him tense and sleepless defeats the whole purpose of putting him to bed and needlessly disturbs him and the household.

Being perfectly matter of fact about lights, one way or the other as the child seems to desire, right from the beginning is the best way to prevent fantasies concerning the danger of darkness. If a child knows he may have a light if he feels he needs it—and on special occasions even a child who has slept happily in a dark room from infancy may want a little light—he will be more secure and less likely to demand a light at all times. The child who is forced to sleep in a dark room, who is punished for not going to sleep on schedule will be a child who, when he does sleep, will have restless slumber and perhaps night terrors that will wake the whole family.

HANDLING THE SHY CHILD Most children, even the most confident and happy ones, pass through various periods of shyness. At these times don't use force. A young baby, who until now has been gay and friendly, may suddenly run to his mother and bury his head in her skirt at the approach of a stranger. Don't scold or ridicule in a mistaken effort to teach him "manners." Don't allow the visitor to force attentions on the child, either, but keep cool and objective yourself and direct attention away from him. He will then usually emerge with his normal amount of curiosity about a newcomer and, if let alone, will probably make friends in his own way. It is well to remember that even Daddy, suddenly appearing in hat and overcoat, may look quite different to a young child. Reassure him, lightly, and let him get his bearings himself.

THUMB-SUCKING, BED-WETTING Since many parents erroneously think of thumb-sucking and bed-wetting in children, nail-biting too, in terms of bad manners (see the Introduction to this section), I feel that presenting the modern pediatric viewpoint on this may be helpful. It is obvious that no mother wishes to see her child suck his thumb, wet his bed, or bite his nails indefinitely. But all these things are perfectly normal to a greater or less respect in most little children, and growing out of them depends much more on the happiness of the child and his adjustment to the difficult business of life in a grown-up world than on arbitrary "training." A child may be led out of these behavior patterns sometimes, but never coerced out of them by punishment, restraints, or ridicule, though rewards are sometimes helpful.

Some children have a greater need to nurse—for which thumb-sucking is a substitute—than others. Modern pediatricians warn that abrupt cessation of breast-nursing or, later, too early and complete insistence on the cup instead of the loved bottle can cause the child to thumb-suck in a compensatory manner. Even children who have had the most understanding care will, when they come up against frightening periods when something new or undesired is expected of them, begin to suck their thumbs again. Or they may do so when they are overtired, hungry, or under any tension. Most thumb-sucking stops, anyhow, by the time the child is five if no attention is paid to it.

Thumb-sucking in a child over five may be an indication of insecurity and may be helped by increased attention to the child's emotional needs through more companionship with the mother. Sometimes this may have to be done at the expense of a younger—and usually more relaxed—child who needs her less. The thumb-sucker "wants to be a baby." Give in to this desire for a little while through extra mothering. If a new baby has arrived, the older child may benefit from a brief (and private) return to the bottle if he expresses longing for it. If his need is handled understandingly, he will soon be reassured and realize that, while being a baby and dependent is comforting, being his own age and growing up is much more satisfactory. But don't be rigid and peremptory with a thumb-sucking child. Let him get his comfort from you rather than from his thumb.

Most dentists agree that thumb-sucking has little effect on baby teeth, that even if they do become displaced the second teeth push in and correct the malocclusion. If the second teeth are crooked, thumb-sucking isn't necessarily to blame at all and it is foolish to tax the child with the responsibility for it. Even proper nutrition and vitamin supplements don't guarantee straight teeth or even good teeth. Inheritance has much to do with it, although good nutrition and vitamin D, especially, can minimize hereditary tendencies toward crooked or protruding teeth and receding jawline (no sign at all, by the way, of a weak character. And conversely a bull-dog jaw does not indicate either strength of character or tenacity of purpose).

Never hurry any change-over to a more grown-up behavior pattern (such as making the child switch from a bottle to a cup) with a child. Wait until he indicates a readiness for the step.

THE BABY SITTER

YOU AND YOUR SITTER   Professional and amateur baby sitting has come into its own as a result of the servant shortage, women's independence, and smaller living quarters that can't accommodate relatives. Unmarried or widowed older women now usually have lives of their own and no longer spend them in return for keep as unpaid handmaidens in relatives' families.

A baby sitter may be a college or high school girl or boy earning spending money, a mature woman, or a young mother interested in taking care of another young child occasionally at the standard rate of pay. The age and experience of the sitter is usually taken into consideration and sometimes there is a sliding scale—so much per hour if light housework is done, such as dishwashing, bedmaking, and preliminary meal preparation, so much for child care and nothing else, so much once the child is asleep.

HOW OLD SHOULD A SITTER BE?   For daytime care of a small child, with the mother within hailing distance, a child of twelve or thirteen, if responsible, may be satisfactory. A tired mother needing a relaxing bath and a nap might employ such a sitter to watch the baby in the playpen, sandbox, or nursery. But she shouldn't go out and leave the two alone, though she might take the older child on a shopping trip to help with the younger one.

For evening care of a child an older person is needed—a boy or girl in the late teens, known to be stable, conscientious, and really fond of children. For overnight, and longer periods, children should be left with an older woman or, if possible—particularly in an isolated country house—with a man and his wife. The mother should always consider that an emergency might occur, with which an immature person might not be able to cope.

Before going out the mother should tell the child a sitter is coming, and if the sitter is someone new she should be introduced into the routine before the mother departs. All instructions—and they should cover any possible emergency—should be carefully written down. If a formula must be prepared it should be written down, too, and the mother should be sure the sitter knows how to prepare it.

Exact instructions concerning meals should be left and a memorandum on what food the sitter may have as an expected snack. The rate of pay should be carefully established before the sitting starts and the sitter paid promptly at the end of the agreed period. Transportation or an escort to her home should be provided for any girl or woman after midnight.

SHOULD THE SITTER ENTERTAIN?   A baby sitter's main interest should be the child or children she has in charge. A teen ager should not be permitted to have the gang in while he or she is baby sitting, nor should a teen-age girl be allowed to have a boy visit her while she is on the job.

Once the child is asleep, the baby sitter can be permitted use of the television or radio or may study or sleep—so long as the baby can be heard easily if he wakes and calls. Young baby sitters who take too many late sitting jobs night after night are dangerous, because they can fall so soundly asleep that virtually nothing will wake them. Their charges, therefore, have no protection during the parents' absence.

Older women often enjoy having a woman friend or a couple come in during a long, late evening, and, if the habits of all concerned are well-known and there will be no contact between the guests and the children, such visiting is permissible if the baby is within hearing at all times. Of course, there should be no drinking permitted at any time.

SHARING SITTERS   If two or more mothers wish to leave their children with one sitter in the home of one of the parents, the amount of pay should be increased in proportion to the added responsibility.

NEIGHBORS SIT FOR EACH OTHER   The hiring of sitters is often quite a financial problem. In many communities families work out a club sitting plan whereby one mother or father will sit certain nights of the week or month for others in the group, who will reciprocate by sitting for them. Careful accounting must be kept so that there is a fair exchange for each family's sitting time.

MOTHER NEEDS A NIGHT OUT TOO It is considered a good idea for couples to have two nights out a week, but one of these nights may be stag for each. On mother's night out father should sit with the baby. One of the satisfactions of modern life is the father's increasing, informed participation in the actual physical care of his children. The children feel closer to their fathers, and the fathers learn that even a tiny baby will respond contentedly to their ministrations, awkward though these may be at first.

CHAPTER FIFTY-ONE

THE RELIGIOUS EDUCATION OF CHILDREN

HOW ABOUT SUNDAY SCHOOL?

Most children benefit from some ethical and religious instruction in groups with other children. From it they get a valuable grounding in the Bible, knowledge of which is so vital for a full understanding of literature, our mores, and our moral precepts. If all the other children in your neighborhood go to Sunday school and your child, because you have no particular religious affiliation or, perhaps, conviction, stays home, you run the risk of letting him become an outsider in the activities of the group. I am thinking not only of the pleasure, inspiration, and spiritual growth children get from the Bible stories as they hear them in Sunday school but of the skills that the child may develop from Sunday school activities, such as singing. It seems to me that young people should not wait for courses in comparative religion in high school or college to find out about these emotional and ethical experiences that influence our thinking and effect our literature, our laws, our whole cultural pattern. Consider, for example, how meaningless would be such titles as "The Voice of the Turtle," "The Grapes of Wrath," such expressions as "Adam's rib," "manna from heaven," "he has a cross to bear," "it was another case of David and Goliath," to someone entirely ignorant of the Bible as the living literature it is.

From a cultural standpoint the entire Bible is helpful to those who hope to understand its profound influence on a large part of the world and on the shaping of history. But also no one can be truly cultured who is ignorant of religious writings other than those of the Bible or uninformed on those customs of peoples which stem from other religious beliefs.

CHAPTER FIFTY-TWO

THE ADULT-CHILD RELATIONSHIP

YOUR MANNERS WITH CHILDREN

Little children—as well as older ones—should always be treated as the individuals they are. A baby in a carriage rightly and usually loudly resents the passing stranger who, placing her face close to his, pokes or tickles him or makes silly, gurgling sounds meant to denote friendliness. If you want to make friends with a baby, be gentle and quiet. Let the baby make the overtures, if any. Don't force yourself upon him or try to take him from the arms of his mother or nurse. Don't make loud noises around him. Never confuse a young child by telling him it's all right to do or have something that his mother has just said he couldn't do or have, even if you are the hostess.

If you are entertaining a mother with a young child, don't disturb the child's ordinary routine any more than absolutely necessary. Don't insist the child is old enough to come to the dinner table if the mother, very rightly, wishes to feed it earlier and without the confusion of strange faces and the expectation of grown-up manners.

A pleasant, adaptable child at home can be turned into a little nuisance while visiting by too much attention on the part of other people, who, after overtaxing and overentertaining him, are then horrified if he ends the day in tears or a tantrum.

A very young child accompanied by an adult on a visit should not be ignored, of course. In fact, if you ignore him, he will soon show you how much he dislikes being overlooked. But he should be treated with dignity and respect—even if he's a babe in arms. He can't possibly understand your standard of behavior, so don't become irritated at his occasional and necessary interruptions of your conversation with his mother.

It is grossly impolite to speak in a foreign language or use obscure phraseology in front of a child with the purpose of excluding him from the conversation. He is usually quite conscious of what you are doing and will respond by making an issue of the matter immediately. If you speak in a perfectly simple and normal way, even of subjects beyond his comprehension, he is usually satisfied, so long as you take his presence into consideration from time to time by directing your conversation to things at his level. To expect a little child to sit at the dinner table with the only attention paid him of a correctional nature, is to expect entirely too much.

YOUR TONE OF VOICE

There is nothing so catching as the sharp manner. Have you noticed that children whose parents speak to them in a petulant, annoyed tone of voice speak to others in the same way? Conversely, if a child, right from the beginning, is spoken to with the same politeness and consideration one would give an adult, even when he is a tiny baby and can understand only the tone, not the words, he is usually a gently spoken child. Waspish mothers make waspish children who grow into waspish parents.

Take time and effort, if possible, before any necessary admonition of a child to control your irritation with irrelevant things or toward other people. The smallest child is quick to resent anger unjustly taken out on him for trivial transgressions. To vent one's irritation on the handiest person, especially on a child who does need correction, is human enough. But, if it happens, your relationship with your child will be better if you can apologize. No child thinks his parents are infallible creatures. Children know that parents are often wrong, sometimes make mistakes. It improves our stature as parents if we can say, even to the youngest child, "Johnny, I'm sorry I was cross, just now. You know how it is when people get too tired. They sometimes get cross without much reason." This isn't spoiling Johnny. This is treating him like a real human being and teaching him that the quickest way to dispel another's anger is to admit you're wrong—sometimes even when you aren't completely convinced that you really are.

CONVERSATION WITH CHILDREN

The only way to teach children how to converse is to start very early indeed to include them in your conversation. If they have only a few words of their own, use those words with them, including them in sentences. If the baby says "Hot!" when he sees the fire, say to him, "Yes, the fire is hot. See, Mother puts wood on the fire so it will burn. Baby mustn't touch the fire, because it is hot. Fire would hurt the baby." Shortly, baby gets the idea, and he also adds words to his vocabulary, especially if you never laugh at his attempts to do so or repeat his baby talk in his presence, no matter how enchanting it is. He is trying to talk as you do and to do the things you do. He doesn't want to remain a baby forever. Laugh with him, never at him, and encourage him in every little step toward maturity, so long as he makes it himself.

This maturity is a delicate matter. Grown-ups so often make the mistake of refusing to consider a child's chronological age and the fact that maturity usually comes very unevenly. A big child of six may be able to go to the store but may not be able to sit through the long family dinner without being excused from time to time. A very bright child may well be emotionally younger than his actual age in some things. Take these things into consideration and never expect a child to measure up equally well to all standards accepted for his age group. If he is above his age group in certain of his abilities, do not expect him to be so in all of them, nor in his emotional needs.

A child from whom too much is expected, either emotionally or intellectually, grows to feel unable to do anything well enough to please his parents. In self-defense he sometimes refuses to make more than the barest effort to get by academically or socially. Such a child needs encouragement, never ridicule or increased severity.

TEACHING CHILDREN TO BEHAVE

Most children eventually conform to the behavior standards their parents lay out for them, provided those standards are reasonable and attainable. The best way to understand this is to attend P.T.A. meetings and to talk over your children's behavior with other parents. Too often, if we don't do something like this, we get the fixed notion that only our children act like hellions. Actually, the whole business of growing up is a matter of fitting one's real desires and energies—sometimes painfully—into a socially acceptable pattern. All children must go through it and with some it is harder than others—mostly because of the way their parents go about the necessary saddle-breaking.

In social behavior it is much more comfortable to conform than to be in a constant state of rebellion. Children can be made to understand that, and they usually accept the logic of it.

WHY WE MUST HAVE RULES   Family life must have rules—although occasionally they should be relaxed for good cause, just as rules outside the family are sometimes relaxed, within reason. Parents must know that children need and want direction. They don't want wishy-washy parents, sometimes easy and sometimes—and most inconveniently—rigidly strict. A little child will say with pride, "I am not *allowed* to visit after school without permission from my mother." The child who is permitted to do anything he pleases is not secure. He is rudderless and shows it by his behavior.

BEDTIME

Every pre-school and school child should have a fixed bedtime, for which he should be pleasantly but firmly prepared. Give children plenty of advance warning of bedtime—or mealtime. Children's play is their "work," from which they can't be suddenly separated without warning. They have little sense of time, even after they can tell time. It is better to say, "You have just time to put your blocks away—see, Mother will help—before bathtime," than to say, arbitrarily, "In twenty minutes, have these blocks put away and be ready for your bath!"

You may be relieved that the end of the day has come and the children will be soon in bed. But if you show it you are in for trouble—dawdling trouble and "drink-of-water" trouble. Children hate to give up, even when they are dog-tired. They are afraid they'll miss something and that all fun really begins when they are out of the way. So they refuse to get out of the way, using all kinds of legitimate and illegitimate pretexts to keep you with them or to rejoin the adult world.

If bedtime trouble regularly crops up in your household, examine your manner with your children at the end of the day, see if it is polite and un-hurried. Be sure you make them feel you still have adequate time for them —again within reason. Keep in mind the bedtime deadline—and have *them* keep it in mind—but be relaxed about it. When the deadline comes, see that they are in bed and arrange your household affairs so that you do have time to hear prayers, tell a bedtime story, or sing a lullaby. One little boy I know learned to relax at bedtime when his mother and he told little jokes together —had what they called a "laugh" time—just before he went to sleep.

When, occasionally, you can't keep this bedtime date with your children, realize their disappointment, substitute a little treat of some kind to make up for your necessary dereliction.

THE USE OF THREATS   Never make a threat to a child which you don't intend to or can't keep if infraction does occur. It is cruel and stupid to say, "If you do that, Mother won't love you." Or, "If you get out of that bed once more, Mother will go out and never come back." Quite intelligent parents often resort to such threats in desperation, so increasing the anxiety and unmanage-ability of their children. Parents' love must be inviolable. They cannot always love the *behavior* of their children, and they have every right to take prompt steps to correct it, but they must never withdraw love itself as a means of punishment. To damage a child's love-security is to open the way to his be-coming a neurotic.

It is certainly better to use the pleasure-principle than the punishment-principle when dealing with a child. How much more sensible—and effective —to say to a child who keeps jumping out of bed, "Now settle down, darling, and get your sleep. Tomorrow, if the weather is nice, we'll go on a picnic," than to threaten, "If you don't go to sleep immediately, I won't take you on that picnic tomorrow even if it is a nice day." Did *you* ever try to go to sleep promptly, on order?

Where threats are necessary, express them quietly, if possible. "If you do spend all your allowance today, Esther, remember, you will have to wait until next Saturday before you get any more money. And I know you want to buy a new pencil." Be reasonable and mean what you say.

INTERFERENCE

Don't let friends or other members of the family undermine your discipline. One parent should not knowingly countermand the order of another. Many a quick-witted child manages to play one parent against the other very nicely, to the detriment of his own character development. If any change in orders must take place, let the parents be in polite agreement, "Joe, I know you asked Bobby to help you clean the cellar, but you and he didn't know I planned to take him to get his hair cut this afternoon and it is the only chance I'll have all week." Not, "I don't care *what* your father says, you're coming with me to get your hair cut!" Family politeness, alone, should prohibit such conflicts, but unfortunately it often doesn't, to the confusion of the child and the irritation of the parents.

IS IT A CHILD'S WORLD?

Some modern parents have the mistaken idea that adults no longer count. Parents, too, actually do have their rights and should assert them. No child should be permitted to make the adults around him miserable or to deprive them of all peace, quiet, and privacy. There are—and should be—limits to all adults' patience with children. A child who has discovered that he can ride roughshod over the adults in his family is far from contented with his tyrannical role. Consideration of others comes slowly to the young and must certainly be regularly imposed within the child's ability to understand. And that understanding can be absorbed very early, indeed, if the handling of the child is relaxed and loving. One of my boys at twenty months learned to "put it back" and "pick it up" with obvious satisfaction in response to gentle requests. And, on his own, he threw his apple cores into a scrap basket instead of on the floor.

Habits are fixed through doing the same thing over and over again. If you pick up after your children—scolding as you do so—and expect them to become neat as a result, you are making a sad mistake. A child must go back and do the routine things over and over before they become habits. He needs to be reminded—patiently and firmly reminded—to do the things expected of him. But don't nag. Use charts, stars, rewards of various kinds, praise when he remembers, pleasant reminders when he forgets. Don't get his back up. You didn't learn to wash your teeth, comb your hair, scrub your nails, tie your shoelaces, and wash your face automatically, merely being asked to do so once or twice.

WE SHOOT TOO HIGH

If our children were always spotlessly clean, never made any noise, were always pleasant when spoken to, jumped up at every request, and never talked back, there would be something very much the matter with them.

They aren't born that way, and it is a very long time before they come to believe there is some virtue in what we ask of them.

Healthy children must get dirty. It is part of the business of playing, and the dirtier they get the better they like it. When a child is afraid to get dirty, to put his hands in mud pies, to yell and run with the other children, he's not normal. Adult standards have been imposed upon him to too great effect and to the detriment of his whole life.

There are times when it is better if a child manages to keep reasonably clean—if he's in his Sunday best, for example—but if he does, by accident of course, walk into puddles or slide down a cellar door the world is not going to collapse.

Children all come to the stage when, because of a growing consciousness of the other sex, they want to wash, to keep their hair combed, and to clean their nails. In fact, they want to do all these and other more startling things to a degree that may even alarm you. They begin to memorize etiquette books and to criticize their parents' appearance, behavior, and belongings to an embarrassing degree. But it's all part of their growing up, which, like everything else connected with them, we shouldn't take in too hard and fast a way.

THE TREATMENT OF SERVANTS BY CHILDREN

Children usually reflect our own attitude toward our employees, but there are imperious children who attempt to "get away with" things with servants which would never be permitted by their parents. Servants rightly resent the high-handed treatment they get from some children and should be given full permission to cope with it firmly, short of physical punishment. The chauffeur should know he may say authoritatively to the son of the house, "Johnny, you may not remove tools from the car's tool chest. If we had a breakdown on the road and the tools weren't available, your father would hold me responsible." The cook should be able to keep her kitchen as inviolate as her usually sensitive nature desires. She can't be expected—unless she is unusually agreeable—to keep an eye on the baby as she prepares dinner. She won't be happy, either, if children pour into her kitchen and congregate there while she's in control, or if they are permitted free access to her supplies. She is responsible for the meals and for the condition of her bailiwick. She must be given full—though reasonable—authority within it.

Children who rebel at parental authority sometimes try to take out their anger on servants. It is too much to expect a calm, poised reaction from a maid or houseworker who has just been kicked or reviled by a small child. Children must be made to understand at the earliest possible age that they may not vent their anger or annoyance on those not in a position to fight back, except perhaps at the cost of their jobs. Parents must prevent such occurrences by working out their children's behavior problems themselves, if necessary with professional help.

CHAPTER FIFTY-THREE

ADOPTING A CHILD

Not so long ago adoptions were not announced, because our attitude toward adoption was concerned less with the child itself than with the possible circumstances of its birth. Not with the wonderful fact that a couple wanted a child so much, but rather with speculation as to why they couldn't or wouldn't have one of their own. The very fact of his adoption was often kept from the child until maturity when, presumably, he could stand the shock of such a disclosure.

Today there are more people willing to be adoptive parents than there are babies to be adopted. Sometimes couples wait for years for a child. Often one adopted child in a family is followed by two or three more adopted ones all carefully chosen by trained, licensed agencies to suit the child to the physical and mental qualities of the adoptive parents. There is nothing hush-hush about adoptions now, and children are usually told as early as possible that they were "chosen." As someone said to a friend of mine who had just adopted an infant girl, "I have never seen a more beautiful baby. It is wonderful to be able to *choose* your child, not just wait to see what God will send you." The new mother replied, "Yes, that is true, but you know we feel that God did send her to us nevertheless."

While modern adoptions under proper auspices are proudly proclaimed by new parents, there are still certain discretions necessary on the part of friends of such a family. The parents themselves probably know nothing of the actual parents of their child. For the protection of all, this information is locked in the agency file. Nor does the mother relinquishing her child know, usually, who its new parents will be. She knows, however, that it is being placed in a home where it is wanted, where its financial and emotional security has been assured, as far as possible, by social workers investigating all aspects of the adoption.

For this reason, when a new baby arrives via the adoption route we do not exclaim "What a darling! Where did you get her? Why in the world did her parents ever want to give *her* up?" Of course, the adoptive parents are prepared to deal with such thoughtlessness by either polite evasion or as much frankness as they wish. Sometimes they offer the information that the child came from some well-known adoption center.

Later, when the child grows older, outsiders should never assume that in the parents' opinion the time has yet arrived to tell the child of its adoption. This is a matter for the parents to decide and for them to handle. For this reason discussions with our own small children of another's adoption should not be gone into unnecessarily. Children must accept their contemporaries as children like themselves not as set apart by some circumstances of birth.

Well-advised parents do make public from the start the fact of adoption. Usually, because of possible disappointment, they do not announce before the fact that they are seeking to adopt a child, but once the adoption is under way they may send out announcements, either before the child actually comes to their home or after its arrival. Individual notes may be sent to close friends and relatives, of course, or engraved cards, if they wish to send them, may read in a variety of ways.

A plain card engraved in black could read:

> Mr. and Mrs. Robert Shore Lewis
> announce that
> Miss Betsy Anne Lawson
> has been adopted as their daughter
> and will hereafter be known as
> Miss Betsy Anne Lewis

This form indicates that the child, usually not an infant, may be an orphaned relative or one whose parenthood is publicly known and whose name-change by means of the adoption needs to be announced.

Another might read:

> Dr. and Mrs. Arthur George Adamson
> take pleasure in announcing that
> Bruce McKay Adamson
> born on the sixth of June, 1952
> has been adopted as their son.

> Eighteen Fox Lane
> Red Hook
> New York

The birth date, of course, is always the actual one of the child, not the date on which he was adopted.

Or:

Mr. and Mrs. James Stern Harris
have the pleasure of announcing the adoption of
Miss Donna Phillipe Harris
born February 28th, 1952

CHAPTER FIFTY-FOUR

TRAVELING WITH CHILDREN

If your children are very young, don't travel with them at all if you can possibly help it. Or, if travel is necessary, try to keep to the usual meal and rest schedule and watch for signs of overstimulation and fatigue. Travel, even with older children, is likely to be tiring for all concerned. What seems like ornery behavior in the small travelers is probably exhaustion. But whatever causes it, it is hard to endure. Hard for the parents, but even harder for those with whom the whole irritated group may come in contact.

I once saw all the passengers in a sleeper to Chicago come pale and cross into the diner in the morning because a tiny, teething baby in an upper berth with her exhausted mother had cried violently all night. I have seen roadside restaurants thrown into an uproar because of small, car-weary youngsters whose parents could not keep them under control any longer. The inevitable spanking, of course, effected nothing but the mollification of the proprietor.

If travel with young children is absolutely unavoidable, travel if you can by car rather than in a public vehicle. If some public transportation system must be used, spend extra, if at all possible, to insure maximum privacy and comfort—a compartment or a roomette on a train, a cabin to yourselves in a boat, or, whenever feasible, plane transportation. Babies take well to the air, and the mother has the expert assistance of stewards and stewardesses during the flight. Air travel shortens the journey. Flight seems to act as a soporific to little children and interests the older ones to such a degree that their behavior is usually exemplary during the trip.

START EARLY Never, if it is humanly possible, start a trip with children in the middle of the afternoon or at the end of their day. Even for grownups, traveling early and quitting early makes for less fatigue. In traveling by car or by bus don't push on at nightfall to get to an objective the same night, if it is possible to find a resting place at the usual time for bedding-down the children. The extra expense will be amply repaid next morning when you all start out early again, refreshed and cheerful.

TRAVEL SICKNESS Keep the traveling children on ultra-simple meals, away from candy and soda pop. Travel in as relaxed a manner as possible, taking time for orderly departures. Tenseness and hurry on the part of parents are communicated to children, who often react with travel sickness. But some children, under the best of circumstances, throw up even during the course of simple travel. Small, leisurely meals and a minimum of liquids, with rest afterwards, may help.

The airplane technique of having a waterproof paper bag or other disposal paper container handy in the event of air sickness works well when parents are traveling with children. Often the knowledge that something of the kind is instantly available and there need be no hurried flight to window or lavatory, steadies a child. Needless to say, warning a child not to be sick or scolding him afterwards, no matter how dire the result, is useless and unkind.

SUPPLIES

In traveling with children do not overburden yourself with clothes, toys, special foods, a medicine cabinet, fancy equipment. If you have a baby's bottle to consider, you can buy a bottle warmer that is attached to the lighter socket of your car or you can take along an electric bottle warmer that plugs into any light socket. Actually, bottles can be left behind and with them the washing and sterilizing problem. There are plastic, disposable bottles, a little more expensive it is true, but worth the difference in convenience. There are also disposable diapers in every drugstore en route, but you should carry with you the lightest-weight cotton ones, with a detergent for washing them if you need to use them. They dry in an hour or so—but not, please, over your hostess's guest room chair back.

A playpen can double as a crib even for a child as old as three or four, if you are going some place where a crib may not be available. In most inns and hotels cribs are obtainable, but in some of the smaller places there is one crib per floor, or even one per hostelry, so it is well to be prepared for such emergencies. Often a twin bed can be pushed against a wall and so protected with chairs that it serves as a crib. But when in doubt, it is safer to bed a child on a pile of blankets on the floor than to put him in some precarious makeshift.

TRAVEL CLOTHES Travel clothes for children should be of the simplest materials—seersucker, denim, nylon in the summer. If you are traveling by car, let the soiled clothes accumulate for a day or two, then stop off at a self-service laundry, wash the clothes, have them put through a drier, or hang them to dry on wooden hangers or a portable clothes line in the car as you go on your way. In winter, knit clothes for the little ones, with nylon or other water-

534

resistant (not waterproof) underpants for protection, stand up best and are healthful for most babies. Nylon underthings, including nighties and pajamas, are a good investment, for they dry instanter and cut down on packables.

Each child should be allowed one favorite toy of reasonable size, one book. Inexpensive toys and books can be added en route, as boredom threatens, and discarded as they become burdensome.

OTHERS HAVE RIGHTS

It may be rank necessity that forces you to travel on public conveyances with your children, but others have paid for the right, too, with the expectation of comfortable transportation. If the trip on a train is long and there is no sleeping accommodation, possibly it will be wiser to break the journey early so the children may bathe and sleep before they become unbearably cross. It is very hard to discipline children under the circumstances and in the presence of annoyed strangers. If you are occupying a section on a train you may ask the steward to make it up, or make up the lower only, when it is time for rest. But do this, of course, only if you are willing to keep it this way during the remainder of your trip. Sometimes on a long train ride this is the only way to handle a baby in the crawling stage if you have no drawing room or compartment.

DO NOT DESCEND ON FRIENDS

It is difficult for any parent to believe his children are not as attractive to others as they are to himself. The grim truth is that others, even relatives, are usually unwilling to accept the inevitable little lapses with good will. Besides, even people who really love children often don't wish to be bothered with other people's, especially without notice.

Never, if you would be considerate, visit even a close friend with your child or children without asking if it will be convenient. This rule should hold even for an hour's visit and even when there are other children in the household with whom your own are friends. Your friend's children may have plans of their own and resent being saddled with another child even briefly. Or they may have just been put to nap only to shoot out of bed again at the excuse of a visitor's presence, to the ill-concealed irritation of the mother.

Never, of course, arrive with your brood unasked and unannounced for an overnight stay with anyone, even relatives. Always remember that all visitors make work and inconvenience for a household, children most of all.

CHAPTER FIFTY-FIVE

THE TEEN AGER

Strictness, in itself, is not the perfect answer to children's social problems. Any smart child can circumvent an overly strict parent who thinks in terms of the discipline he or she received as a child, rather than of the effectiveness of it. Along with the firm rules about home-coming and frequent reporting of activities must go an understanding heart and a real friendliness with the child. The teen stage is a difficult time—when one is not quite on one's own, not altogether sure one wants to be on one's own, yet resentful of too much parental pressure and old-fogyness.

TEEN DRINKING

There should be no place for alcohol in the lives of children. A girl or boy of eighteen may possibly be permitted a cocktail or an occasional glass of wine with his or her parents to celebrate some event, but regular social drinking at this age should not be encouraged. A teen-age boy or girl younger than eighteen might be allowed a glass of champagne at a wedding or on New Year's Eve, but only with his or her parents. They should not be allowed to mix or pass drinks.

Children usually look with great superiority on any observed inebriateness of their elders. It might, however, be too much to ask a lively young son to abstain from alcohol until he reached his majority or until he entered college if an example of insobriety has been set by his parents. Yet when we think of the foolish things adults do when intoxicated, despite all their knowledge of the world, we shudder at the too-young adding alcohol to their difficulties.

We hope that our children will not grow into immoderate drinkers as adults, but lectures on the evils of alcohol will accomplish very little. If they have seen alcohol used at home as a pleasant, controlled adjunct to living and never abused, they are likely to follow the same behavior pattern if they are well-adjusted young people.

On the other hand, I have seen overindulgence among boys and girls whose parents have been overstrict concerning drinking. These parents have made such an issue of adolescent experiments with alcohol that their objections have had a too dramatic effect. And sometimes an unhappy young son may use alcohol as a means of compelling attention from a stern, withdrawing father.

The best attitude, I think, is for parents to realize that in most communities a certain amount of drinking goes on among boys and girls in their late teens and early twenties. If they set agreed-upon limits for these young people, instead of prohibiting what they cannot really control, they will be helping their children to responsible maturity—the kind of maturity which considers too much drinking unattractive and socially unacceptable but not a heinous sin. If children can discuss the problem of drinking with their parents quietly and without recrimination on their parents' part, alcohol need be no more dangerous than many other temptations the flesh is heir to— especially in the early years.

SMOKING

Smoking is another habit which to most children, even those who come from non-smoking families, represents the wonderful state of being "grown-up." Most boys and many girls, too, experiment with at least substitute tobacco (brown paper, corn silk, etc.) at the age of twelve or thirteen. Nothing much can be done about that, either, except to get them to smoke the odiferous things outdoors and to be careful about the matches. But this unpredictable activity is followed sooner or later by experiments with real tobacco. The first signs of the ersatz should be treated in a relaxed manner and with some such words as these: "I see you've been smoking corn silk. It doesn't taste very good, as I remember." (Surprise on the child's part.) "When you feel you must try your first real cigarette, tell me and I'll let you do it here at home. No, I wouldn't like you to smoke regularly yet, for a great many reasons you're hearing in school. I would like you to wait until you're eighteen or maybe even until you're twenty-one. And, of course, I wouldn't be displeased if, once you tried it, you decide not to be a smoker at all. Lots of people don't smoke and manage to get along very nicely. But if you do smoke, I hope you'll be moderate about it so that smoking will never be a serious problem with you."

When it comes to important habits that can interfere with growth or sleep or nerves, children, even older teen agers, do *not* have to do what most of the others in the group do. If one mother lets her silly Sue smoke at age fifteen and some misguided father thinks the way to cure Bill of his interest in alcohol is to get him sick-drunk at seventeen, all children in the group don't have to follow the same foolhardy pattern. Children who love their parents and vice versa are guided on conduct by parental judgments, if these judgments are given reasonably and in a kindly fashion and if they see daily examples of maturity in the behavior of their own parents.

MAKE-UP AND PERMANENTS

It is always advisable to let a child be a child and to encourage the enjoyment of being whatever wonderful age he is. The happy little girl, under no parental pressure to grow up and so be, supposedly, "less difficult," is usually willing enough to be her age. At ten she isn't agitating for a permanent wave and at thirteen she doesn't try to make herself up like a movie star, except perhaps in play.

Even the straightest, stringiest hair can be styled for a child in an attractive manner without a permanent. Party occasions may call for curlers or the iron, but permanent waves are inappropriate until the middle or late teens, as is dark nail polish, very obvious lipstick, powder base, rouge, and all but a dusting of powder.

Most adolescent girls are unimpressed with their mothers' logical reasons as to why heavy make-up is inadvisable for them. They are even unimpressed with the quite obvious argument that, if at fourteen they get themselves up to look twenty, when they *are* twenty no one will believe it. Usually the group is a fairly good criterion, in this case, of what represents the compromises of most of the mothers—a natural pink lipstick at thirteen or fourteen for parties, a little darker one at fifteen, and from sixteen on lipstick as they wish, a little powder and dark polish if all the others wear it. But cheeks should be free of pancake make-up and spots of rouge. Rouge can so easily make even a charming young girl look *déclassée*. Eyebrow pencils, mascara, and eye shadow should be among the interdicted beauty aids for teen agers.

ABOUT CHAPERONES

Chaperones still have their place, especially in the lives of teen agers. Where they are necessary and advisable, they should be chosen for their complete acceptability to the most conservative critics. An eighteen-year-old is not acceptably chaperoned by a twenty-year-old divorcée, for example.

When we insist on chaperones for our children, it is to guard them from possible physical harm in the streets at night, from their own possible foolishness, and from destructive gossip.

Just how much chaperoning is necessary for a teen ager depends on the community and the customs of the child's group. This does not mean that if some parents are dangerously careless, all parents should follow along in their footsteps. But a golden mean can be achieved. Too much chaperonage where other children have relative freedom can set a child off too much from her group.

The old and often forbidding line of chaperones at children's parties has disappeared. It is enough for children, once they are beyond babyhood, to be escorted to such affairs and fetched afterward. If mother or nurse does stay she remains very much in the background. The official chaperone in this case is the mother of the child who is giving the party, and her presence is, of course, imperative at all times at very youthful parties. She must be in the immediate background at older ones, as well. No child should be permitted to attend a party where no adults are present, at least to receive guests with the young host or hostess, be in the background, then see them safely away.

In many communities, and especially in large cities where many children must necessarily achieve independence early, boys and girls in their middle teens are allowed to go unchaperoned to lunch, the movies, and theater matinees. Their places of entertainment and their choice of shows should be approved by their parents. They should not be permitted to go to the so-called "bistros," restaurants that are essentially night clubs, to wrestling or boxing exhibitions, to offensive reviews. Later, in the late teens, they may go occasionally to a night club, preferably with their parents, but if they are alone, their behavior should be extra-circumspect.

CAN THE GROUP CHAPERON ITSELF? Many parents feel safe in permitting their teen-age children to go places at night with a group of other boys and girls. This is fallacious reasoning, for the group, once out of sight of parents, may break up into twosomes immediately, with the rules of behavior determined by the boldest. This independent course should be permitted only if the group is going to a specific, approved place and will return at an exact, agreed-upon time. Its whereabouts should be known by the parents at all times, and no unaccountable junketing around the countryside in some boy's car should be allowed. Remember, adolescents want rules and need them. They do not respect the too "easy" parent, or the one who is in bed and asleep when they arrive home.

TEEN DATES

When does dating begin? Earlier and earlier, it seems. It is often difficult these days to distinguish a thirteen-year-old girl from her seventeen-year-old sister if a misguided or overpressured mother permits the little one to dress and wear make-up as her sister does. Physically, each generation's girls are bigger, and this physical bigness often deceives parents into believing that emotional development necessarily follows size.

Boy-and-girl dating may begin at about fourteen on a limited basis—early movies, dates at home of course, various sports, days at the beach, bicycle trips that bring the two home before dark, etc. Steady dating should be firmly discouraged throughout the early teens, because tastes are formed through a variety of contacts.

Every mother of a popular young daughter knows that there are periods when one boy seems to be more in evidence than others. When this becomes quite obvious the family often undertakes to reduce him in status in various ways. Such passing attachments always do seem more of a menace than they usually are and should be accepted with a certain amount of humor untinged with ridicule. Puppy love is serious to the lovers, if a little ludicrous to parents, brothers, and sisters, but it should be respected, for it has its painful aspects. Very few daughters really wish to settle their affections for life on a teen-age boy when it comes right down to it, though the fantasy of undying devotion is very evident for a time.

HOW DOES A BOY ASK FOR A DATE?   At what age a boy dates depends very much on the boy himself. And again physical size bears no relation to emotional readiness. Anywhere from fourteen on a boy may be ready to leave the teasing group of boys and go on his first date. His family should be well prepared for the metamorphosis that will occur.

The first sign, of course, is cleanliness. He will suddenly begin bathing without reminders, lengthily combing his hair before setting out for school instead of merely running the comb—or more likely, his fingers—through it. Suddenly his shoes will be shined to a glassy polish, and he will stop biting his fingernails. He will require two or three times his usual number of clean shirts, and he will take an unusual interest in ties, socks, and handkerchiefs, hitherto items of no interest at all. He will also begin to agitate about his inadequate allowance and start wondering out loud how he can augment it by a little manual labor. He constantly asks if anyone notices how deep his voice is getting.

It is usually Mother who sees the signs first. She knows instinctively that her son is about to take his first steps away from her apron strings. Most of what she can do for him she has already done. Soon he will probably turn more and more to his father for counsel, or to some father substitute.

Boys usually don't need advice on how to ask a girl for a date. They bungle through somehow in the early years of dating, eventually acquiring a certain polished technique only experience can bring. Parents can help by showing that they expect their children to date whenever they are ready. They should never force the issue or make the choices for the children.

Boys usually begin by going to games and school dances stag. They yearn from the sidelines, while pretending a vast disinterest in the equally cohesive girls. After a certain amount of this mothers often suggest, "Joe, why don't you take Mary to the game this afternoon?" This is usually met with a derisive snort, but soon, sure enough, Mary and Joe are eating popcorn together in the bleachers. As a result of the motherly approval he needed, Joe has probably blurted, "You want to go to the game tomorrow, Mary?" And Mary has said "Sure." From then on making dates is easy enough.

DATES AND MONEY   Dating, for boys, does bring with it increased financial responsibilities. While a certain amount of Dutch treating goes on, especially in group entertainment, a boy usually does pay for the entertainment of his special date. If his allowance is not adequate for his participation in the social activities of his high school group and if his parents cannot comfortably increase it, then after-school jobs must provide the difference. And boys should learn early to be unembarrassedly frank with girls about what entertainment they can afford to offer. Pretending to have more money than one actually has is an acutely uncomfortable business, and usually no one is deceived by the pretension.

A boy might say, "Jane, I can take you either to dinner or the movies. Which shall it be?" Jane will probably answer, "I'll ask mother if I may ask you here to dinner. Then we can go to the movies afterward." And, of course, it's perfectly proper for parents to furnish theater, concert, or opera tickets and permit their daughters to ask boys to escort them or for a father or mother to go along occasionally, say to the circus or to a country fair and to pay for everything for both young people.

A realistic attitude toward money is important to teen agers. It should never be a dominant factor in their relationships. If a girl comes from a moneyed family she adjusts her tastes in entertainment to the young men with whom she goes out and does not selfishly expect them to impoverish themselves in order to be with her. The boy who must make the best of the spending money available to him is likely to turn out much better than the boy with limitless funds who is permitted to run to his parents for all kinds of extras as well.

REFUSING A DATE It is always a woman's prerogative to refuse an invitation from a man. Suppose there is a country club dance. Mary, like every other girl in her group, is dying to go and waiting impatiently for the telephone to ring. The wrong boy calls up. Must she accept, or, having refused, not go to the dance at all if she later receives the invitation she is waiting for? No, she leaves the way open. She says, "Thank you very much John, but I'm not quite sure I'll be free that evening. I hope you'll ask me again sometime." Then if she is invited by the boy she hopes will ask her, she may attend without offending the first boy. Or, if she is not invited by someone else, it is possible the first boy will try again a day or so before the party. She should remember it is never necessary for a lady to make detailed explanations as to why she cannot accept an invitation.

SUBSCRIPTION DANCES, SCHOOL DANCES, AND PROMS

At subscription dances or dances given by a sorority or by a girl's school the girls pay for their escorts' tickets and their own. They may freely ask any boy or boys of their choice to attend with them. The boys furnish transportation and corsages (See Section on "The Masculine Graces") as well as any entertainment, such as midnight scrambled eggs and coffee, on the way home.

At a boy's school or at a fraternity dance the boys, of course, supply the tickets as well as brief transportation to and from the dance (See "Dances at a Distance").

Often dance programs are used at such affairs, with host or hostess making out the program in advance with dancing partners for his or her guest. The first dance and the last, at least, are reserved for the boy or girl who has issued the invitation. The floor committee sees to it, in non-card dances, that all girls are kept dancing. Boys on the stag line may cut in without introduction, but once a girl has been cut in upon she should not permit another partner to interrupt the dance.

DANCES AT A DISTANCE   When a dance is some distance from a girl's home, requiring a train or bus trip, she pays her own fare to the point where she is met by her escort. If overnight provision is made for her it is preferably in a private home or, if in a hotel, with other girls going to the dance and under acceptable chaperonage. All bills for overnight or week-end accommodations are paid by the girl herself, never by her escort.

CHAPTER FIFTY-SIX

DIVORCE AND SEPARATION

DIVORCE

With one divorce now to approximately every four marriages, this social upheaval touches the lives of every one of us in some way. Sometimes, though our own families are happy and intact, we find our children in a school group where most of the children come from broken homes. Our own children may become affected by the insecurity of so many of their associates. A sudden divorce may disturb long-standing business relations or remove from the neighborhood part or all of a family that had been friendly and congenial.

Divorce should never be entered into in the midst of battle but should follow, if all efforts of settlement of differences fail, only after as lengthy a separation as possible. It is not only poor taste but a foolhardy procedure to air one's domestic troubles in public. Even the poorest marriages usually have some roots, and sometimes after a quiet separation it is possible for two people to correct the causes of their difficulty and give those roots a new chance to grow into a sound marriage.

Even separation is, however, a drastic step, which may so wound one of the partners that he may not be able to come to a reconciliation, perhaps because of injured pride. So, especially where there are children to consider, one or both of the partners should seek outside, objective help before deciding to part. The causes for separation and divorce are so twisted and complex, so involved with emotions rather than reason, that it takes a wise counselor to bring the problems into proper focus. Where are such wise counselors to be found?

Some progressive churches have marriage counselors, who meet with young people before marriage and help prepare them for the union they contemplate. These advisers, usually psychiatrically trained, are also available for consultation by married couples who are having domestic difficulties.

As it is important that those contemplating divorce seek objective help, they should not take their troubles to their friends who, however well-meaning, often find themselves taking sides. Usually a lawyer should be the last resort, because he is geared for the one kind of action he understands—legal action of one kind or the other. (It does happen, however, that a wise, understanding lawyer who sees some possibility of adjustment will refuse to take a case and suggest psychiatric aid.) A priest, minister, or rabbi may be the right sympathetic counselor, and they are all likely to be necessarily conservative in their suggestions.

Psychiatric or psychoanalytic aid, especially where one or both partners may have a history of previous divorce, may be the most complete answer and, contrary to popular belief, troubled people seeking such assistance are rarely "advised" to divorce. Their consultations or analytic sessions help them make their own decisions and they are cautioned from the beginning against taking any decisive step until their problems can be brought to light and understood. For it is a sad fact that millions of us, divorced or thinking of divorce, could never be happy in any marriage, no matter how perfect the other partner, because of our own inability to lead relaxed and happy lives. Marriage itself is not at fault. But in our increasingly complex world the individuals who enter into marriage need to be more and more adult. People who are anxious, insecure, tense, and frightened find no magic security in the responsibilities of marriage and are inclined to retreat at the first obstacle.

While many communities have no resident psychiatrist or psychoanalyst, many do have psychiatrically trained social workers whose assistance is available either free or for a modest sum. All big cities have practicing psychiatrists and psychoanalysts whose qualifications should be checked on by your family physician and who should be members of a recognized group —such as the American Psychiatric Association or American Psychoanalytic Association.

Throughout the country in the larger cities there are important clinics where patients may live in and receive counsel or analysis at whatever fee they are able to pay, or they may be out-patients, going to the clinic for private or group consultation daily or several times a week.

Information on recognized psychiatrists and psychoanalysts may be had, free, from the National Association for Mental Health, 1790 Broadway, New York City, from the American Psychiatric Association, 1760 Avenue of the Americas, New York City, and from the American Psychoanalytic Association, Menninger Clinic, Topeka, Kansas.

People in difficulty with their marriages do not necessarily require a lengthy psychoanalysis. They may be able to adjust their difficulties after a certain number of consultations with a psychiatrist.

SEPARATION

Trial separation, that is, temporary separation by simple agreement, should never be openly announced even to one's friends. News of it is bound to seep out eventually if it is prolonged but direct questions concerning it should be delicately parried by both parties, because of the possibility of a reconciliation. If the fact of a trial separation has been covered up as well as possible, then it is relatively simple for two people who have had time to consider the gravity of their step to come together again. If there has been a public airing of their problems, reconciliation is usually impossible.

When, even after a trial separation, in which the husband usually has removed himself from the home by his wife's request, it seems unlikely that any coming together again is possible, no step toward divorce should be taken until a legal separation or at least a separation agreement drawn by a lawyer is entered into. A separation agreement still permits the fact of the separation to be relatively unknown if the couple finds a way to keep up the fiction of an intact marriage—by having one or the other remove to another city, for example—as it is merely a formal instrument signed by both parties. It does not go through court channels except in the event of a lawsuit based on its violation or a separation or divorce suit when it may be used as the basis of settlement. In a regular judicial or court separation, both parties go into court, where certain requirements as to the husband's financial contribution and his provision for the children are agreed upon or, in the event of disagreement, settled by the court and entered into the record.

Especially if children are concerned, it is wise and advisable for one or the other type of separation to be entered into, whether or not divorce is actually contemplated, as it settles without haste and by considered agreement important matters of support, division of property, and custody. In the event that the separation has been brought about by the insistence of one partner that he wishes to remarry immediately, it is good sense for the other to insist on separation for at least one year before divorce proceedings may be started. The partner trying to jump from the frying pan into the fire will, nine times out of ten, be grateful for this cooling hiatus, whether or not it results in the patching up of his existing marriage. New marriages hastily entered into after old ones have been dissolved usually end in the same disaster.

If either judicial separation or separation-by-agreement occurs, no public announcement need be made through advertisements in the press, such as "My wife having left me, I am no longer responsible for, etc." This is never *legally* necessary. While he is still her husband, a man is financially responsible for his wife's debts for "necessaries," those incurred by her during the marriage, no matter how much he may protest to the contrary. They may have only their own "gentleman's agreement" concerning the handling of charge accounts and the incurring of obligations.

Only the vulgar announce their separations by way of newspaper inter-views, often taking the opportunity to announce their "engagements" to others at the same time. Requests by newspapers for comment on possible separation should be politely denied and any printed rumors pointedly ignored. Many and many a couple which has adhered to this course of behavior has been able to come together and live a long and happy married life even if they did encounter a few rough spots in the road.

When a husband moves out or a wife gathers up the children and returns to her mother, the partner who receives their joint mail punctiliously for-wards it to the other but does not give a change-of-address for the other to the postman. Phone calls are parried with, "Mr. Green is away just now, but I can take the message and have him call you." Or his temporary number may be given, without explanation, if the matter seems urgent.

Where legal separation actually takes place, the couple is *still married* though no longer living together. Therefore, the wife is still Mrs. William Green, not Mrs. Robertson Green, the name she may assume if she does divorce her husband—a combination of her maiden name and her married name. She wears her wedding ring, especially if she has children.

It is the wife who still replies to formal invitations, whether or not it is she who has left home. She refuses any to which the couple has been jointly invited. She has her own quiet social life, as does her husband, but she should conduct herself always as a married woman should, carefully giving the impression that the marriage is intact and that for some reason that is none of the public's business the couple does not attend social functions together at the moment. Or she may invent a believable fiction. Polite people never press for such information, anyway.

If divorce becomes inevitable, the fact that it is impending should never be publicly announced. A divorce is never a divorce until it becomes final, and even if the unhappy procedure has been entered upon reconciliation is still possible. But even when any idea of reconciliation is firmly over, it is always poor taste for people to announce in a jubilant fashion that they are getting divorced. If they have no sensibilities themselves, they should con-sider the example they are setting for the young in treating divorce so lightly.

When people are so prominent that their divorce proceedings become news—if they haven't been sensible enough to insist on proceedings behind closed doors—then they should make a discreet announcement to the press. (See "Special Press Problems.")

CHANGE OF NAME AND ADDRESS

Only when a divorce is final does a woman change her name from "Mrs. William Green" to "Mrs. Robertson Green." She signs her checks and her letters "Mary Robertson Green," but she never, I hope, becomes that poor nonentity "Mrs. Mary Green."

If a woman has children she usually continues to wear her wedding ring, though she may either put away her engagement ring or have its setting redesigned.

OUR ATTITUDE TOWARD DIVORCE AND THE DIVORCÉE

Anyone who has read what I have written about divorce knows I believe it can never be cause for rejoicing. It is only the shallow and silly who ever return from the divorce courts in a carnival frame of mind, desirous of public celebration. Whatever our inner relief may be that an impossible situation has been faced and legally, at least, rectified, it is normal and decent to keep our feelings and our experience to ourselves as much as possible. And even close friends should be careful not to assume that a divorce is accepted by the divorcé or divorcée as an unmitigated boon. Actually it is like a painful operation, the necessity for which cannot occasion any joy.

Any remarks directed toward the newly divorced should be tactful indeed. Friends should not attempt to extract information concerning the proceedings from one obviously unwilling to discuss the matter. And even when a divorced person seems to feel the necessity to discuss the case with sympathetic listeners it is their cue to make only the most non-committal remarks in return. Such emotional outbursts are often greatly regretted later and the one who gave the confidences frequently feels a certain resentment against those who avidly received them.

7

YOUR PUBLIC LIFE

Dining in Restaurants   549

Cards and Calls   557

Hospitals and Doctors   577

Speaking Before an Audience   581

Simple Parliamentary Procedure   588

Your Appearance at Public Functions   590

Your Press Relations   598

You and Celebrities   602

YOUR PUBLIC LIFE

At some time or other there is an occasion when we must rise to our feet and express ourselves before some sort of group. This public performance may be in the form of an interview we must give or a talk before our local branch of the Audubon Society or a speech on a local radio station, or even an appearance before a large television audience. Whatever the locale, the occasion, or the subject matter, it is good to feel at ease and able to cope with the situation—and upsetting to feel nervous and inadequate.

If we belong to organizations and wish to have our opinions carry weight, we must learn to express ourselves well publicly. If we aspire to office in such organizations, we need to learn through frequent practice to verbalize well. The quiet member, talented though he may be, is rarely thrust forward into leadership. Part of belonging is active participation in the groups that interest us. It is possible to learn how to participate with poise and assurance.

Part of our public life is, of course, concerned with what others see when we venture forth from the social security of our homes. Can we pay a call with grace and terminate it within the accepted time without being brusque? Can we go into restaurants, theaters, and other public places so that we fit in in a well-mannered, unobtrusive way? If the circumstances of our lives are such that we are more or less public figures, can we treat the press and the public courteously, without arrogance—and also have a real sense of noblesse oblige?

If we are able to do all of these things gracefully we can indeed feel that we can take our proper place in the active life of the community.

CHAPTER FIFTY-SEVEN

DINING IN RESTAURANTS

A man entering a restaurant removes his hat and, if accompanying a woman, excuses himself while he checks it, his coat, and any packages or umbrellas they may have been carrying, first guiding the woman out of the line of traffic. If there is a headwaiter who comes forward to seat them, then the man steps back and lets the woman go first. Otherwise, the man goes first, finds a table, pulls out a chair, and seats the woman, preferably to his right. The choice of the woman's seat, either by the waiter or her escort, depends on the view she will get. She should be able, if possible, to look out into the main part of the restaurant or be by a window with a good view, but she should not be placed where passing traffic may strike her chair. If the table is poorly situated, she should not be facing the rear wall or a swinging door. If the two are to be seated together on a banquette, the table is pulled out at one end usually, so the woman may slide in and seat herself on the man's right, but if she can't seat herself in that position without disturbing others around her or causing her escort to seat himself awkwardly she should sit, quickly, in the nearest available seat.

If there is only one wall seat, the woman takes it and the man, of course, sits in the aisle seat. When there is a group of four the women take both wall seats and the men seat themselves opposite them.

If a younger couple is dining with a much older one, the older couple is offered the wall seats and the younger couple sits together on the aisle so that the younger man is opposite the older woman. Where two women are seated together opposite two men, they sit opposite their own escorts—husbands or not.

Where two young couples seat themselves, the women take chairs opposite each other. If one man is the host, he tries to seat himself so the woman to be honored is at his right even if it is his wife—this may be her birthday or their anniversary. No great point, however, need be made over the seating.

Where one woman is accompanied by two men, she seats herself between them, unless there is a divan. In that case she sits on the divan with the man she knows less well. If a woman is doing the seating of other women, she indicates the wall seats for others and takes the aisle seat herself.

Where two women are shown to a booth, the hostess indicates the seat with the better view for the guest. If it is a "Dutch treat" lunch, any much younger woman steps back to let the older take the preferred seat in the booth or on the divan. Otherwise, the one who reaches the table first offers the better seat to the other, unless in a crowded restaurant it seems expedient for her to seat herself as quickly as possible. But she should then offer to place the other's bag and gloves on the seat beside her.

ORDERING

When previously arranged luncheons or dinners are given in restaurants or hotel dining rooms, the order is often given in advance by the host or hostess and no menu is handed to the guests by the waiter. Guests accept what is put before them, and, even if they don't care for the host's or hostess's choice in some dish or other, they make at least a pretense of eating it.

Otherwise, when two or more people are lunching or dining together, one, whether he or she is actually the host or hostess and will pay the bill, takes the initiative and does the ordering after a little consultation, unless the group is awkwardly large in which case the waiter will take the order from each one. Where a woman is accompanied by a man, even at a business luncheon, it is always assumed that the man is the host and he is expected to do the ordering after the woman has had a few minutes to look over the menu presented to her by the waiter. He says, "What do you think you'd like to have?" She chooses, preferably, the table d'hôte—the meal in which everything is included in the price of the entrée—and says what she will have, beginning with the first course if there is no extra charge for it. If she orders à la carte—where each item on the menu has its own price— she names only the entrée, the main course, and lets her host suggest a first course to her, as he should. When the woman, out of respect to her host's pocketbook, has not selected a first course even though he has invited her to have one, the man should not order one for himself without first asking her again, "Are you sure you won't join me? I'm going to have blue points." She may then take it for granted that he can well afford the gesture, or in the case of a business luncheon has the time, and she may say, "I believe I'll have something after all," and quickly chooses something that appeals to her.

Where a woman accompanied by a man is asked directly by the waiter what she will have, she looks at the proffered card and then tells her host what she wishes to eat. She may, of course, ask the waiter a direct question if she wishes, such as, "Are the snails prepared with much garlic?" Then, if the answer is satisfactory, she turns to her host and says, "Good, then I'll have snails," but she does not give her order directly to the waiter.

It is sometimes difficult for a woman guest to concentrate on the menu if she is immediately offered suggestions from her host. While the host should have his guest well in mind, he should give her a little opportunity to choose something by herself before he makes any suggestions. If she seems to hesitate, let him say, for example, "I understand they make a specialty of steak here. Would you like a filet mignon?" Or, "How about the salmon? Would you like to try it, too, or does something else appeal to you more?"

As a guest, in ordering table d'hôte avoid ordering the most expensive entrée unless you are certain the cost of the meal is of no consideration at all to the person entertaining you. But don't choose the least expensive things either, lest your host suspect you think he can't afford to entertain you well. Unless, of course, the least expensive thing on the menu, tripe perhaps—happens to be the one thing you really prefer above anything else there. Then you might say, "I'll have tripe. I do like it if it's done nicely, and I haven't had it in quite some time."

OMITTING COURSES It often happens that women prefer to eat less than do men and, on a table d'hôte luncheon or dinner, really wish to omit certain courses. There is no reason why they shouldn't say so and equally no reason why a man should not accept the course even if his guest does not. Certainly no guest should be urged to eat a course he or she really does not want, even to keep the other company.

DRINKS

There is equally no obligation for all in a party to take cocktails or wine just because some do, even if it is only a party of two and the man wishes a cocktail and the woman does not. In this case, whoever wishes the drink should have it without urging the other to join him or her.

ORDERING WINE Where a restaurant meal has been ordered in advance, the wine, if any, is indicated in the order with the entrée, whether meat or fish, determining the choice. A white wine is now considered suitable throughout a meal, even a meal with red meat, though traditionally it is served with fish and poultry while a red wine is reserved for meats and game. One wine is considered enough except at banquets or gourmet dinners, where two or even three wines may be used if the host knows what he's about.

Where a restaurant meal has not been ordered in advance, the host or hostess asks for the wine card—or for the sommelier, or wine steward, if the restaurant boasts one (he's the man with the chain and keys). If the party is given by a woman and there are men present, it is usual for her, even if she is expert herself, to ask one of them to select the wine for her. A man may do this gracefully even if he knows little about the subject, merely by saying to the waiter or wine steward, "What do you suggest?" If some of the guests have chosen poultry or fish, the wine steward will usually indicate a choice of white, dry, still wines. It is not at all axiomatic that any imported wine is better than a good domestic one. On the contrary, some domestic wines are far better than some of the cheap, imported ones, and it is a good thing to familiarize oneself with the various offerings, or if unsure, to ask the opinion of the steward or of others at the table who may be informed on the subject.

Various chicken dishes or kidneys are often prepared with red wine, such as burgundy, and if such a dish has been ordered by anyone present it is well to ask if red wine has been used in its preparation. If so, a red wine can quite suitably be ordered if the other orders at the table are for meat.

Champagne can quite properly be ordered in place of cocktails and can be served throughout a dinner and even throughout the evening instead of being reserved just for dessert—although such a champagne should be dry rather than sweet. The sweet wines, both white and red—port (of course, there is also a dry port), madeira, angelica, sweet chablis and tokay—are dessert wines and should not be served before luncheon or dinner or during them. A dry sherry (amontillado), served cold, may substitute for cocktails and be drunk during a meal, while a sweet sherry at room temperature, like port, is reserved for dessert or may be taken with a biscuit or a bit of simple cake in the afternoon in place of tea or cocktails.

IF YOU DON'T WISH WINE   If, as a guest in a restaurant, or in someone's home, you don't wish to be served the wine, you may check the pouring of it by lightly touching the rim of your glass with your fingertips, without turning, as the waiter or butler leans over you, but you may never place your glass upside down to indicate refusal. You may permit the server to pour a little, then raise your hand, even if you don't intend to taste the wine. This is a better procedure at a small table where a host might notice your empty glass and think you had been neglected.

If you do not take wine, the server, or your hostess, may properly ask you if you'd wish something else—scotch or rye with soda (or with plain water, if you prefer), white wine with seltzer (a Spritzer), or even milk unless it's a very formal meal. It is perhaps a little masculine for a woman to refuse wine and specify a highball, as formerly it was only the men who were asked to state such an alternative if they did not wish wine.

PRESENTATION OF DISHES

At better class restaurants the food is served from individual serving dishes onto the plate of each diner and each main dish before it is cut into is presented to the host or hostess for approval. Such a dish should really be inspected by a careful host. Is the steak medium-rare, as ordered, or perhaps overdone? Has an error been made in the vegetable order? Is the guest picking at the shrimp cocktail he ordered? Seafood must be absolutely fresh to be safe.

Too much fussiness about the food in a restaurant, too much of the pose of gourmet is boring, but a nice attention to the wants of guests is as important in a restaurant where one is playing host as it is at home. A host or hostess should never assume, even in the best restaurant, that his guests are being well cared for—he must be alert concerning the service and food.

COMPLAINTS

Any complaints should be made quietly but firmly to the waiter at your table or to the section headwaiter if there is one—and by the host. When necessary, they are made to the headwaiter, whose business it is to see that things go smoothly at each table. Hot food should be really hot, cold food cold. It is better to send food back to the kitchen—without fuss—than to expect a guest to eat something not up to standard just because you may feel too embarrassed to complain. At the same time, ostentatious complaints about every little thing impress no one, least of all your guests. But if you keep in mind what each guest wanted, you can make little changes or corrections where they are necessary, just as smoothly as you would at home. Any good restaurant appreciates a customer who understands the niceties of dining—and exacts good service. I suspect they secretly despise the man, especially, who will accept any sloppy sort of service and poor seating as good enough because he is intimidated by the atmosphere of expensive chic in which he finds himself.

BUFFET SERVICE

In some restaurants, especially Swedish ones, and at some private restaurant parties the food is served buffet style. If there are small tables at which to be seated, a man locates one, seats his lady, and goes to the buffet to select an assortment of foods for her. He then returns with food for them both, picks up napkins and silver, if necessary, and sees that they both have whatever beverage is being offered. If there are no waiters to do so, he later clears the table of soiled dishes—or takes the lady's dish if they have eaten standing—excuses himself, and locates the dessert. If she has not been left with a group and therefore will have to wait alone at a table, a woman may wish to go along to the buffet table—unless it is too crowded—to make her selections herself. In that case the man goes first, hands her a plate, and indicates to the waiters, if there are any, what she would like to have. Otherwise, he serves her himself, and at a smörgåsbord she may serve herself with perhaps occasional suggestions from him. He hovers in her vicinity, of course, to see if he may assist her in any way, even though he may be filling his own plate at the same time so as not to leave her too long alone.

When she has an escort a lady does not wait at a buffet table to pick up her own wine or other beverage. That is always the man's responsibility, especially as there is always the danger that someone may knock into the drink-bearer and spill the contents of the glasses. It is always proper for a man in a group lunching or dining buffet, in which there may be unaccompanied women, to ask, "May I get you a drink?" if any of them have not been served by someone else. The sight of women pressing through a crowd of a buffet-bar is not attractive.

PRESENTATION OF THE CHECK

When the meal is finished the host catches the waiter's eye and says, "The check, please." If he can't catch his eye and the table is in a hurry, he waits until the waiter is somewhere within hearing and then calls out in an ordinary tone of voice, "Waiter!" Just that. In the case of a waitress he says, "Waitress!," not "Miss!" He does not whistle, tap his glass, or say "Psst" or "Hello!" in the European fashion, although, and especially in a European-style restaurant, he is justified in tapping his glass with a piece of tableware if his table seems to have been forgotten by both the server and the headwaiter and it is imperative that his group move on without further delay. He may not, naturally, rise and fetch the inattentive servitor (though preparing to leave will surely bring him).

When the check comes it is presented on a small plate, face down. The host turns it over, without disclosing its figures to his guests, and looks at it sufficiently long to see if there are errors but never so long and methodically as to make him seem niggardly. It is wise for a host to know approximately what a restaurant's ordinary prices are before going to it. Once there, he should not have to worry about the bill, for if he has judgment, he will not attempt to entertain in a place he can't easily afford.

If there is something obviously wrong with the bill, the host asks quietly for the headwaiter, explains his puzzlement, and accepts the correction or explanation without unnecessary comment. A host should, of course, never embarrass his guests by making a scene over a bill, or even discuss his dilemma with them. And they, at bill-paying time, should ignore the transaction.

If an adjustment is not to his liking, he still accepts it with good grace and privately decides to boycott that restaurant in the future. But he does not make his guests feel that the evening or luncheon has been spoiled because of such an incident, any more than he would make too much of a point of some mishap in service at home in the presence of guests.

TIPPING IN RESTAURANTS

If a man frequents a certain restaurant, it is not necessary for him to tip the headwaiter on each occasion, unless he has had special consideration—worked out the menu in advance with the headwaiter, had his table changed, or ordered some spectacular dish such as crepes suzette, the completion of which has been presided over by this factotum. The tip is given on the way out. When the headwaiter is also an owner of the place he receives no tip but is thanked on the way out if he shows out his guests.

If one is well known in a restaurant, he may tip the headwaiter—in a popular spot often enough to make himself remembered—as he leaves, as insurance against getting poor tables in the future. Such a tip is quietly slipped into the waiting palm in an unobvious manner, but if the room headwaiter is not at his post he is not sought out by the patron. The tendered tip in an expensive place is usually five dollars. In a less elaborate establishment it is certainly never silver—always at least a dollar. A woman who entertains frequently in favorite restaurants uses the same tipping scale but tips a little less frequently, perhaps on the theory that between times she is often accompanied by tipping escorts.

The wine steward, if his services have been enlisted, receives 10 per cent of the bill in round figures. Where drinks begun at the bar have been brought with the bar bill to the table later, the bartender receives his 10 per cent.

In restaurants that employ headwaiters for sections—men who do no more than take the order and pass it on to table waiters for execution—no tip is expected by the section headwaiter, unless, of course, special service has been requested in which he has taken some active part. In that case his tip is not less than a dollar bill and may be two dollars if the party comprises more than two people.

A waiter receives 15 per cent to 20 per cent (depending on the place) in round figures (don't leave pennies on the plate unless they add up to an even amount). If the bill has been very small, then he should receive a minimum of ten cents per person; in night clubs, twenty-five cents per person, minimum.

A cigarette girl usually arranges her change to indicate what she'd like to get, but ten or fifteen cents surcharge on a pack of cigarettes is enough and no one need feel like Shylock for picking up the additional change from a dollar bill.

The bus boy is not tipped. In a nightclub or expensive restaurant the attendants in the men's and women's lounges usually put decoy coins on a plate to indicate what they expect in the way of a tip, as does the hat-check girl. Unless some service has been asked, the tip need not be, for instance, a quarter, but can well be ten cents.

Whether or not we like the tipping system, we must consider that the wages of such employees are predicated on their receiving tips, that the tips are part of their salary and part of what we pay for the over-all service. To ignore someone usually tipped, unless he has been blatantly forgetful or rude, is to be unfair. Again, if the cost of going into such places must be minutely considered, we don't belong there at all.

Doormen who perform a service—secure a taxi, summon or bring your parked car—usually receive a quarter. At an inexpensive place, if just a taxi has been summoned in good weather and the job has entailed no more than his blowing his whistle, a dime is sufficient.

PUBLIC DINNERS

TIPPING AT PUBLIC DINNERS   At public dinners there is sometimes (and this is an excellent idea) a small card on each table which reads, "Gratuities have been taken care of by the Dinner Committee." This relieves the guests at each table of any obligation concerning the waiters If there is no such

notice, the waiters, immediately after the service of dessert and coffee and
before the speaking begins, come to the host or hostess of each table and
place a silver salver before him or her, often with the murmured explanation that something is expected for the table's waiters. Often a "host" or
"hostess" at a table may merely have organized the table, each guest having
bought his own ticket. Unless all at the table are personally invited guests,
host or hostess makes no attempt to tip for the whole table and after placing
a dollar (per service for which he or she feels responsible) on the tray,
directs the waiter to the gentlemen at the table, each of whom should leave
(at an eight dollar to ten dollar per plate dinner) a dollar for himself and
one for the lady he escorts. Women should not be approached for tips if
there are gentlemen at the table.

GUESTS OF HONOR AT PUBLIC DINNERS At official and other public dinners
there is usually a private reception for the guests of honor and the officers of
the organization sponsoring the affair. Admission to the reception is usually by
card, and a ticket to the dinner does not entitle a guest to attend the reception unless he has been invited to do so.

At the reception there may be a receiving line if many are expected, or
at a small gathering the guests of honor may stand around informally chat-
ting with guests who are presented by organization officials or members of
the dinner committee.

The dinner guests are usually standing behind their chairs before those
to be seated on the dais make their entrance. As the guests of honor enter,
the assembly remains standing until those on the dais have been seated. On
the introduction of a very important speaker, such as the President of the
United States, a major government official, royalty, or a very distinguished
woman, the assembly rises, sits again until the speech is over, then rises
once more in final tribute. If such a distinguished guest must leave immediately after his speech and before another has begun, the guests all rise
until he has left the dais.

DRESS AT PUBLIC DINNERS It is quite common for the men to appear in dinner
jackets and lately, alas, even in dark suits, unless they are seated on the
dais, which still calls for white tie and tails. Invitations to such public dinners now often read "White or Black Tie," for without that choice being
offered, many would refuse to come.

Properly, women wear full evening dress and long evening gloves to a
formal dinner (removing the gloves before eating, of course), but here
again one more often sees dinner dresses, especially at public dinners,
rather than full décolletage.

LEAVING RESTAURANTS

If a table has had both host and hostess, the hostess rises, once the bill
has been paid, to indicate the party is ready to move on. Where there is
only a host, he rises first, after making some such appropriate remark as,

"We'd better get started, don't you think?" If he is a gentleman escorting a lady to dinner or a night club and the next stop is home, she must be the one to terminate the evening, although he can say, "Perhaps you'd like to go on somewhere else?" She should take the hint and say, "Oh no, it really is late. Will you take me home, now?" Under no circumstances may she say to her escort, unasked, "Let's get out of here and go to such and such a place," as he would, politely speaking, be required to accept her suggestion. Very young and thoughtless girls sometimes do such things with no thought of a man's working day or of his pocketbook, demanding to be taken from one night spot to the other, mainly, I suspect, for the sole purpose of being seen there.

In walking out of a restaurant, the man, on rising, is seen by the headwaiter, who then properly steps forward and makes a path for the lady or ladies in the group to file out after him. If there is no headwaiter, the man goes first, making a path and opening any doors. Once in the lobby, or wherever the checkroom is, he again places his companion out of the traffic, picks up his hat and coat, and holds the door for her to go into the street. If it is late at night or the street is dark, the man may well go out the main door first, with permission, to hold an umbrella or offer his arm the minute she makes her exit. It always looks sad to see women in evening dresses blowing out through a revolving door into a windy street while their escorts lag a matter of seconds or even minutes behind—even when there is a doorman, supposedly, immediately available.

CHAPTER FIFTY-EIGHT

CARDS AND CALLS

CALLING CARDS

While the full ritual of the calling card is these days known by few, and practiced less and less, it is helpful to be familiar with it. Formal calls are sometimes still expected in older and very conservative circles and always in diplomatic and military ones. Instruction in the proper leaving of cards is given in our military academies as part of a young officer's necessary training. The simplest-living family of a small midwestern town may, by reason of the voters' action, be thrown into the formality of the nation's capital. Or we may go abroad and find ourselves in circles where knowledge of such etiquette is expected of us.

WHEN CARDS ARE LEFT   There are definite rules for card leaving. Whether or not you cleave to them depends very much upon the formality or lack of it among your own friends and acquaintances. Military or diplomatic etiquette aside, the leaving of a card upon a hostess who has entertained you for the first time greatly depends on what is usual in the circle in which she and you move. She might vastly prefer a little thank-you note to having your calling card handed to her by her maid or butler and followed by you in person if she is "at home." In busy cities the party call is almost extinct, especially among men and career women who, excused by business activities, presumably may find it much more practical and just as gracious to thank their hostesses by means of flowers accompanied by their cards, by a phone call, or by note.

THE SIZE AND STYLE OF CARDS   Social cards should always be engraved, although business ones may be printed. But even in business an executive who tenders a properly engraved card gives an impression of stability in regard to his job that the man or woman with a printed card does not.

Both business and social cards must follow certain standards of size and style if they are to be in good taste. A salesman once sent me in a card reading, "Mrs. Patrick's little boy Harry," and I have seen a doll-sized card used by a girl publicist which certainly failed to fix her name on my mind. As in all phases of social behavior, avoid the freakish if you want to be comfortable.

Visiting cards may be engraved on parchmentlike paper, whose virtue is that it's so thin it permits the carrying of more cards in your card case or wallet. Card styles change in minor details from decade to decade, and at present even a young girl does not use a plate-marked card and a man never does. A plain white card is supplied for engraving by all good stationers and the major jewelers, and may be in a variety of sizes and in several qualities—all of them standard. A man's card differs from a woman's in width but may be the same length as hers. Among the standard sizes permissible for women's cards are those 3¼" x 2¼", 2¹³⁄₁₆" x 2", with the length of the name determining the size selected. The men's narrower cards, designed to fit standard card cases or wallet sections, may be any of the lengths used for women's cards but are rarely more than 1½" wide. A 2¹³⁄₁₆" x 1½" is usual for a man's card.

A child's card should be small but follows his elders' in style. Although to some it may seem affected, there are calling cards available for children, literally from birth through college, with the size of the child determining the size of the card.

A charming manner of announcing the birth of a baby is to attach a tiny, engraved card, bearing the baby's name, to the father and mother's card, or to a card especially engraved for the purpose. Sometimes the baby's card is pink or blue bordered and attached with pink or blue ribbon. More often it cleaves to the formality of its parents' card and is the same as theirs in all but size and is attached with white ribbon. A girl of two or three may

Amy Bettauer

LITTLE GIRL'S CARD

Henry Gray Walter III

LITTLE BOY'S CARD

Olga Ann Borden

March 21st, 1951

Mr. and Mrs. John Borden, III

BIRTH ANNOUNCEMENT combining baby's card with parents' card. Ribbon in pink, blue, or white.

have a card, size 2⅛″ x 1⅜″, engraved in black and usually reading "Susan Priddy" rather than "Miss Susan Priddy" before the age of fourteen (although the "Miss" is used on mail to her). When she's over sixteen she is "Miss" on cards and uses the same size her mother uses. She never uses a nickname.

Boys' cards are 2½″ x 1 9/16″ for tiny children, 2 9/16″ x 1¼″ for those eight to ten or twelve years old, and 2¾″ x 1⅜″ for prep schoolers with "Master" omitted. Boys in their teens use the full-sized cards that men use. Those away at school may list addresses in the lower right-hand corner, as may girls, but this is not done when the children are living at home. A boy may, if he wishes, use "Mr." on his cards when he comes of age, but many do not until they have finished college. The omission of the "Mr." on a man's social card indicates a very young man still under his parents' aegis. In addressing a letter or gift to a young man under age, use "Master" up to age twelve only. In his teens and until he is twenty-one he is just "John Jones" on his cards and on mail addressed to him.

Small children use their cards to enclose with gifts and flowers but leave them only when paying calls with their parents. They may use them, as their mothers do, for issuing invitations, however, writing on their address and phone number and the date of the party.

ADDRESSES ON CARDS It is correct, if you wish, to have your *street address* only engraved in small letters without abbreviations in the lower right-hand corner of your card. But, perhaps because of the this-century insecurity of our living arrangements, only about fifty per cent of engraved cards carry this information. People write on, where desired, an address or phone number. A business card may considerately carry the telephone number, but a personal one does not. Cards for use in the country frequently are addressless, although the addition of the address in simplest form (if one is well known to the post office) i.e., Darien, Connecticut, is helpful, because such cards are often given to city friends, traveling companions, and acquaintances so that the address may be recorded. A telephone number is occasionally included on country cards, just as it is frequently put on country stationery and correspondence cards for the convenience of one's friends.

ENGRAVING Script used to be the most popular, and is therefore considered by some the most correct, style of engraving for a visiting card.

Mr. and Mrs. William Malcolm Pksra

TYPO ROMAN SCRIPT

It is less of a favorite today but still much used by both men and women. More modern and perhaps better suited to younger people and for business cards are the modified English period types—shaded Roman, Norman, and St. James. Illustrated cards in this section are Typo Roman. Any simple type face is correct, but don't seize on the highly stylized types used in advertising copy. And do avoid the quaint or ornate. Be guided by a top-quality stationer's advice. Never have your cards engraved in other than black ink, and do not have them plate-marked.

A MAN'S SOCIAL CARD

A bachelor who does not have his own apartment or who does not live at home with his parents, but who belongs to a club, uses the club address on the left-hand corner of his card, whether or not he has quarters there. If he lives in a residence hotel in permanent style, he may prefer to list that address. But any bachelor's status and living arrangements may

Mr. Gery Addison Harder, Jr.

The Yale Club

A BACHELOR'S SOCIAL CARD showing club address

Mr. James John Sweeney

A MAN'S SOCIAL CARD

change, and a club address is, therefore, more likely to be of continuing usefulness on his card. After he marries, the formerly footloose one has a choice of listing his home address or not, but he usually reserves it for the card carrying his wife's name, too. If he commutes to the city where his club is situated, he may find it useful to give out a club address where he may receive mail and messages, English style. However, there is some slight danger here that a club address on a married man's card might be construed to mean that he is separated from his wife. He avoids that by not using the card socially, or at least not without explanation. Or he can get around it by writing in his home address for those to whom he wishes it known.

"JUNIOR AND SECOND" The use of "junior" on a social card does not, as with the initials "M.D.," preclude the necessity for "Mr." before the name. A man is "Mr. Karl Austerlitz, junior," or, where the name is a long one, "Jr." The first letter of abbreviations of titles is capitalized in forms of address and on cards, but non-capitalized when the title is spelled out in full. On his card a man is "junior" only while his father is alive and, of course, only if he bears the identical name. If he bears his grandfather's name, which differs from his father's name, he is "junior" during his grandfather's lifetime. If grandfather, son, and grandson all have the same name, the father is, of course, "junior" and the grandson is "third." When the grandfather dies the father becomes "Mr. Karl Austerlitz" and the grandson becomes

"Karl Austerlitz, junior" (using "Mr." after he comes of age). The use of "second" indicates that the bearer of the name is a cousin or nephew of the original holder of it. It is sometimes used when a child has been named for a famous personage who has gone or may go down in history, and there may or may not be any actual relationship. A Roosevelt baby four generations hence might well use the "second" throughout his lifetime if he is christened "Franklin D.," even if he is very remotely related to F.D.R. It is possible he may grow up to be a distinguished personage himself and that the press will wish to refer to him in such a distinctive way. The use of the "second" will help future historians, too, if he does make a mark for himself that would put him within the orbit of the great men of the country.

A son of "Karl Austerlitz, second" (or II or 2nd) would have to be Karl Austerlitz, "third," but if there is already a "Karl Austerlitz, third" it is courtesy and common sense to break up the sequence and create a new name for the child by adding a middle name of his own. He then needs no suffix.

MEN'S TITLES ON CARDS Clergymen, doctors of medicine (or allied sciences such as psychology, dentistry, veterinary medicine), judges, senators, mayors, military or naval officers, governors, professors who make teaching their profession and are holders of university professorships—all use their titles on their social cards. It is Doctor Phelps Harvard, Captain Joseph Wiley Coates, The Very Reverend Herman Hoffman (Dean of a cathedral), The Right Reverend Clair Croix (Bishop), The Venerable Percy Prime (Archbishop), The Reverend Canon Guy Waters, The Reverend Geoffrey Gates, Brother Francis (of a Catholic or Episcopal order), The Reverend Stephen O'Mara (Catholic priest), The Reverend Selig Wise (for a rabbi), Right Reverend (or Very Reverend) Monsignor John P. Bowdin (for a Catholic prelate). All of these titles may be abbreviated, if necessary, to prevent crowding the card.

The governor of a state is simply "The Governor of Connecticut" on his card. More sensible but presumably less "correct" is the use of his name, prefaced by "Mr."—not "The Hon." which is never correct on an American card—with "Governor of Connecticut" in smaller type beneath it. A mayor's card follows the same form.

The letters of degrees, no matter how important, are not used on social cards. The holder of an LL.D. has the privilege of calling himself "The Rev. Dr. Charles Percival" on his card (spelling it all out if there's room). But the holders of all honorary degrees show better taste in omitting "Dr." on their cards, although they may use the title otherwise socially except in social signatures or on engraved announcements or invitations whose form should follow that of the social card.

HUSBAND AND WIFE CARDS

A joint card used by a husband and wife often carries their home address and is necessarily large enough to accommodate their names on one line. Convenient sizes are 3¼" x 2¼" and 3½" x 2½" depending on the length

---

Mr. and Mrs. John Murton

3 Wilder Terrace

---

of the combined names. Because of the necessity of combining much in a small space, titles permissible to use are abbreviated if necessary—"Dr. and Mrs. Grant Simpson"—to avoid crowding the line. It is considered better form for a military or naval officer and his wife to use separate cards for post calls. When an officer has retired from active service he usually does not use a joint card, because the word "Retired" must appear in the left-hand corner of his card. A joint card is possible however. It reads:

Admiral Lande Crouse, Retired
Mrs. Crouse

A man never leaves a joint card. If his wife doesn't accompany him on a call he must leave his own card only and may not include one of hers. The woman is properly responsible for the family's social obligations and must make her own calls.

The joint card is used to accompany wedding presents. On formal visits the wife may *leave* such a card upon her departure when not accompanied by her husband but should not *present* it when calling without him. It is included in flowers for a funeral, to a debutante or to anyone to whom the couple may wish to send flowers. It is now used sometimes for informal invitations and in reply to them, as is the joint informal. Joint cards may announce a new address or tell friends you are leaving town for a while if both husband and wife are on equal footing with the people to whom the card is sent. In this case the initials P.P.C. (*pour prendre congé*) are written in the lower left-hand corner. They mean "to take leave." Any thank-you notes must be sent separately, however, as the P.P.C. cards don't in any way fulfill the function of thanks for various kindnesses or entertainment.

A WOMAN'S SOCIAL CARD

A wife's card should match her husband's usual use of his signature. If he calls himself "J. Frederic Parks" her card must read "Mrs. J Frederic

Parks," not "Mrs. Jeremiah F. Parks" or even "Mrs. Jeremiah Frederic Parks" unless he prefers to use his name in full on his own cards. If a man has been blessed with a string of names, he'd better drop a few rather than confound the world with a line of initials no one remembers anyhow.

Mrs. William Malcolm Parks

A MARRIED WOMAN'S SOCIAL CARD

If your name is Mary Carolyn Green and you are known to your friends as Carolyn, don't call yourself "Miss M. Carolyn Green" on your cards—a definitely masculine procedure. Either omit the Mary or leave your name in full, even if it may puzzle a few people. But I prefer shearing names of parts that are superfluous.

Miss Hope Harding

A SINGLE WOMAN'S SOCIAL CARD

A widow shows respect for her husband by keeping his name on her cards and by using it *socially* in every way. She is Mrs. George Grayson, not Mrs. Alice Grayson, no matter how long she survives her husband. On legal documents, checks, and in business matters she may be Alice Grayson (but not *Mrs.* Alice). If it is necessary to show the prefix, she signs "Mrs. George Grayson" in parentheses under her signature. If she has a son who was named for his father she does face some dilemma when he reaches the "Mr." age and lives with her or in the same community. The son always ceases to be "Jr." on the death of his father, unless his father was so dis-

tinguished a person as to remain even after his death a public figure—
John D. Rockefeller, for example. In such a case the son is virtually forced
to remain "Jr." and his mother has no problem about the continued and
proper use of her husband's name. Where the "Jr." has been dropped and
some confusion might arise, the mother may add "Sr." to her name to
distinguish herself from present or future daughter-in-law.

I did know a wonderful old girl who had buried her husband some thirty
years or so previously and who, had she lived in the days when divorce was
respectable when necessary, would certainly have shed him. She refused to
be tagged with his name by the time she reached her belligerent seventies
and became to all comers, "Mrs. Rebecca Brown." She couldn't become
plain "Mrs. Brown," as befitted her dowager station, because her name was
too common a one and the city in which she lived, too large. You do find
matriarchs becoming simply "Mrs. Redding" when they like to feel they are
the acknowledged feminine head of the family. The post office and business
houses might prefer a little closer identification, however. I always feel such
simplification of a name indicates great age, and what woman wants to
classify herself that way these days?

A woman who is divorced does not use her given name on her card unless
she reverts to the original "Miss" before it and takes back her maiden name.
This is often done by young women who have had no children by the
marriage and who intend to follow professional or business careers. But
a divorcée does not become "Mrs. *Gertrude* Glen" or keep her husband's
name, which would surely lead to confusion. Instead, if she wishes to retain
the Mrs. (and she should *socially* if she has children), she prefixes her
married name with her own surname, if the combination is at all possible.
Sometimes such a coupling turns up a name so resoundingly long and
fancy as to be ludicrous—"Mrs. Butterworth Chomleley-Brownell," for example. Where her own maiden name doesn't team well with her ex-hus-
band's, a divorcée is perfectly free to choose some other preferably family
name to go with it—her maternal grandmother's, for example.

If she is going to have or continue a career, it is simpler for her to use
two names, her own maiden name so that she will be "Miss" in business,
and "Mrs.," socially, especially if she has children. Otherwise, if she uses
"Mrs." in business it is almost impossible for her to avoid people's use of
her given name with it socially *and* in business. She becomes "Mrs. *Gertrude*
Glen" no matter how hard she may try to be "Mrs. *Wentworth* Glen," at
least socially. And in business most people, seeing her signature, will assume
she is "Miss" anyway, so she has still another name foisted upon her—
"*Miss* Gertrude Glen."

Where a divorcée's children are by another marriage than that from
which she has just emerged, she may choose for convenience's sake to return
to the name her children bear. But no divorcée with children, no matter
how identified she is with her career, should call herself "Miss" socially.
Doing so has the effect of making her children seem illegitimate and

startles conservative people into hurriedly prefixing "Mrs." to her maiden name, the only one they happen to know.

A woman who divorces her husband and continues to call herself by a variation of his name—"Mrs. Atterbury Groves"—in business will soon be ticketed "Mrs. *Sally* Groves" because she must sign her mail "Sally Groves" and few will pay any attention to the "(Mrs. Atterbury Groves)" beneath the signature. The use of "Mrs. Atterbury Groves" on her business card necessitates further confusion as many business associates will not recognize the name.

Should she remarry, she will more or less be forced to continue to use her former husband's name in business if she's achieved any prominence at all, because her name will have become her trademark. This may lead to annoyance on the part of her new husband—quite understandably—that she should be "Mrs. Groves" in business and "Mrs. Lawrence" at home. It makes her seem a bigamist. But if she makes still another upheaval in her identity and now tries to call herself "Mrs. James Lawrence" in her office, there is always the probability of her being called "Mrs. Sally Lawrence" anyhow, a social anathema (and it sounds as if she were divorced from poor Lawrence too). There is also the possibility that if she and her husband have conflicting careers her husband might be held, by some, to be responsible for any business acts of hers that ran counter to his professional interests. That's been known to happen, too. For that reason, I believe any businesswoman is better off using her maiden name in her career, keeping it separate and distinct from her married name. I'm a Lucy Stoner up to the social point.

There are widows or divorcées in the business and professional world who are known as "Sally Groves," "Mary Blossom," etc. and who seem to have no objection to being addressed as *"Mrs. Sally Groves"* and *"Mrs. Mary Blossom"*—in fact, by furnishing no other name on their cards or under their signatures, they give their public no choice but to use a form of address incorrect and certainly awkward for social purposes. (It makes a woman seem so unattached.)

A widow whose husband died twenty years ago is probably loath to use his name in business, and, of course, she can't use the device of the divorcée and combine her own maiden name with his. Many women give up the struggle and accept the title of "Miss," because that's what most people properly assume they should be called when they use their given names without indicating a prefix parenthetically. If a woman started her career with her married name, I guess she's stuck with it, come what may, if she becomes successful. "Mrs. Sally" she is, and, as few people ever know what her proper title should be, she remains that not only in business but, for the most part, socially whether she likes it or not. I know I'd prefer to be referred to as "Sally Groves" like a shop or a ship, with no prefix at all if people didn't know what to call me, than to be that sad little nonentity *"Mrs. Sally."* And I'd take a strong stand with my business cards and inscribe myself as "*Miss* Sally Groves," hoping my friends would realize that in my social life with my family I wished to be called "Mrs. James Groves" in deference to my husband.

WOMEN'S TITLES ON CARDS

A woman doctor who practices her profession has a choice, as does any other professional woman, of using her maiden or her married name while following her career. If she chooses the latter, "Dr. Mary Pike" (her husband's name), she cannot be "Dr. James Pike" as that would confer an honorary doctorate on her husband—so "Dr. Mary" she must be. Like any professional woman she may hide her calling under cloak of her husband's name, socially. She may be Mrs. James Pike on her social card, if she prefers, even if she has a practice.

If she uses her husband's name professionally and he is not a doctor himself, it would seem a little belittling for her to use, with him, a joint card, for it would have to read "Mr. James Pike and Dr. Mary Pike." If he *is* a doctor, their joint card should read "Dr. James and Dr. Mary Pike." A woman physician's card for social purposes should read "Doctor Mary Pike," as whenever possible the title should be spelled out in full—that is, when the length of the name permits. Her business card may read "Mary Pike, M.D."

ADVERTISING THE SPINSTER

Spinsters have gone out of style. You seldom see two maiden sisters with a joint card reading "The Misses Roades," or the eldest daughter bearing a card reading "Miss Bowles." Women today, even if they are elderly and unclaimed by any male, want more identity for themselves than that.

IS A GIRL EVER JR.?

You hear it and you see it in print, but a girl should never be referred to as "Greta McCarthy, Junior" even if her mother is a very well-known "Greta McCarthy" whose name frequently figures in the social, business, or theatrical news and who, for professional reasons, may also be known as "Miss." It's too bad the parents didn't think to give the poor girl her own identifying name at birth to avert such confusion, but, as it is, the daughter may have her cards read "Miss Greta McCarthy, second" or, if she prefers, "younger" but she can't use the masculine "junior." If I were she, I'd invent or exhume a middle name and call myself "Miss Greta *Ann* McCarthy." She certainly needs to do something to keep her mother from receiving her mail, her flowers, her invitations. Even if her mother carefully uses her husband's name socially, it is unavoidable that a certain amount of her mail arrive addressed to her professional name, since many people never know her other one although they do know her home address.

WHEN YOU MAY SEND YOUR CARD

Your calling card may go without you any place you might, and in other and less hectic times did, go yourself. Our communities have broadened so much geographically that the average socially popular woman, bearing the responsibility of her family's social obligations, could well spend a highly disproportionate amount of time in the mere traveling from her home to the home of friends or acquaintances on whom she should call. So today she more often phones, wires, or preferably sends her card with a necessarily brief message written on the face. "With deepest sympathy" (to someone bereaved). "It was a wonderful party!" (though I prefer a little thank-you note, on an "informal"). "Much happiness to you both" (to a girl newly engaged).

Your card is a great convenience for gift or flower sending, and no message need be written on it. Where you have charge accounts at a florist's, you may find it very convenient to supply him with some of your cards in their accompanying small envelopes. Remember that your card is a highly personal thing, sometimes an "open sesame," so give it this way only to the most meticulous tradesman who can be depended upon to guard it from misuse. If you are sending the box and write a very personal message on your card, enclose it in its own sealed envelope, if you have one with you, or in one of the tradesman's envelopes. Be sure he places the card directly on the flowers and doesn't attach it in some manner outside, where it is easily lost in the unwrapping. If you plan to deliver the box yourself, have him lay the card in its unsealed envelope among the flowers.

Often you see cards with lines through all or part of the name. If you are an intimate "first name" friend and go to a shop yourself to choose flowers or some other gift, you may wish to draw a fine pen line through your name, write a message on the face of the card, and sign it "Betty" or "Joe," as the case may be. I have often seen just the last name and the title "Mr.," "Captain," or "Miss" lightly crossed out, with just the first name remaining. Obviously a married woman or a man with a nickname must cross out all of the name and write "Marie" or "Pete." There is no rule that says this must be done, but when a message is included and friends are intimate it often is. Do not, of course, ask your florist to do this for you. Such pen scratchings should always indicate you chose the flowers or merchandise in person. If you phone in your order to a florist's where you have no personal cards, the florist may write your name and message on a plain white card for you, signing it in any way you wish. The dictated message in this instance should never be embarrassingly intimate, and it goes in an unsealed envelope. If you write such a casual message yourself, you may choose to send it in an envelope whose flap is tucked in rather than sealed.

USING YOUR CARD FOR INVITATIONS

Your calling card is an ever-ready messenger for the issuing of invitations. If you have small neat handwriting, so much the better, for you can restrict your messages to the lower left corner. For example, you may note—Dinner, Tuesday, January 12th at 7:30. Black tie. If you write R.S.V.P. (please reply), the answer must come back to you in written form, preferably written in the third person if the recipient knows his etiquette. However, it is quite customary to answer such semiformal invitations by mailing your own card with a brief message of regret or acceptance—"Looking forward to Tuesday!" or "Sorry we can't come Tuesday." But if you want a speedy answer, so you can reshuffle your guest list if necessary, you just write your telephone number on the card and your intended guest will certainly get the idea. For further information on using the calling card as an invitation, see the Correspondence Section.

HOW SHALL YOU MAIL THEM?   The post office will loathe you—and probably send you a notice indicating disapproval—if you make a regular practice of sending large numbers of your cards through the mail in the small envelopes supplied with them. Such envelopes require hand stamping and thus slow down the post office's work. It is preferable to enclose such cards in a normal-sized envelope.

WHEN NO R.S.V.P. IS REQUIRED

Here again be guided by the usual practice among your friends. Any large reception, tea—especially a debutante tea—or garden party, for which formal invitations have been issued, does not require a reply unless the R.S.V.P. is included. But if you can't go, it is entirely correct (and in diplomatic and military circles, expected) to send your card and cards of the members of your family through the mail, so that they arrive the morning of the affair. They should be sent to the hostess. In the case of the debutante tea, the cards go only to the debutante's mother or sponsor, whoever has issued the invitations. Write nothing on the cards. Send one of your own, if you are a woman, one of your husband's (or a joint card for you both), and one for everyone in your household likely to have called with you.

THE P.P.C.

The P.P.C. or "Good-by!" card is usually mailed to friends and acquaintances to indicate you're leaving, but it may be left, as any card is left, at the door whether or not the hostess is at home—and if you do leave it, it is not necessary to ask for your hostess. In strict military etiquette such cards are left rather than mailed. The initials, in capital letters, are written in ink in the lower left-hand corner of your card without further elaboration.

It is assumed that most of your friends know you are leaving and where you are going. If you are moving from a neighborhood, you may later mail your cards with your new address.

HOW MANY CARDS ARE LEFT AT ONE CALL?

When your hostess is at home, you send up your own card, via the servant who has opened the door, together with that of anyone actually with you (or you may use a joint card if your husband is with you). After you have been received you leave cards from other members of your family on the card tray, which should be in the hall—or in any convenient spot on the way out. You leave one card of your own for each lady in the household—but not more than three of any one card. You leave one of your husband's cards and one of any sons who are of age for each lady and gentleman of the household, including any house guests. You leave your card for women only, but you may leave a joint card for husband and wife.

Properly you call upon gentlemen only when you are actually accompanied by your husband or a close male relative living with you. All this is important to remember, or refer to, if you move in military or diplomatic circles. If you lead an average life in a community only mildly interested in these stiffly social matters you can forget it all and use your card in all sorts of secondary ways, instead.

TO INSURE YOUR CARD'S DELIVERY   If there seems to be some doubt about your card reaching the right person, pencil the name on the top—"For Miss Mary Carson" or "For Mrs. Worthing Frost." This is a necessary precaution if you are calling on one of several daughters or are leaving your card at a hotel desk or with an apartment house doorman.

WHEN NOT TO USE YOUR CARD

Don't enclose your card with Christmas greeting cards except under business or professional circumstances.

MEN'S BUSINESS CARDS

A man's business card differs from his social card in omitting the "Mr." before his name. It is larger than his social card and for an executive always engraved or printed in black conservative type faces, not script. Salesmen's cards used for advertising purposes may be printed or engraved in colors, but that of the company's top executives should not be.

A business card is approximately 3½" x 2" and is engraved, preferably, or printed on fine quality parchment or good white pasteboard. The thinner parchment, of course, permits a larger quantity to be carried at one time, which is an advantage to a business person.

Stephen Saunders

Sales Manager
Gordon Sales, Inc.
San Francisco, California

John F. Hasty

Williams, Inc.   Fifth Avenue and 51st Street
Tel. Plaza 5-3599   New York

A company president's card reads:

Loring K. Peters

President
Peters Engineering, Inc.
Portland, Oregon

Possible variations: the address may be given if the firm is located in a large city; the telephone may be listed in right-hand corner; the title may be omitted if the man is known as founder and president of his company.

A representative of the same firm without a major title (vice-president, treasurer, secretary) has his card with the company name appearing first:

Peters Engineering, Inc.

George R. Duffy
Traffic Department
Portland, Oregon

While on social cards initials are avoided, they are common on business cards. In the cards shown, the names could read "L. K. Peters" or "G. R. Duffy." The firm's name always appears exactly as it is registered, although elsewhere on the card everything is spelled out as on a social card. Telephone numbers, where shown, have the exchange written out, followed by the numerals.

WOMEN'S BUSINESS CARDS

A woman's business card is exactly like that of the men in her firm with the exception that she should be designated as "Miss" or "Mrs."

Miss Lois Severy

President
Publicity Advisers, Inc.
Empire State Building
New York 1, N.Y.   Longacre 3-4098

SOCIAL CARDS VS. BUSINESS CARDS

A man's wallet should contain both business and social cards, for his business card may never double for social purposes. Of course, for an executive or a professional man, business and social activities often overlap, but they should never do so obviously. A businessman sending flowers to a customer or client who is in the hospital is making a social gesture (even if he has to do so for business reasons) and should enclose his social card. If his connection with the customer is so remote that the latter would not be able to identify his name without that of his firm, he should not be intruding in an essentially personal situation. If a customer is opening up a new place of business, flowers may go from one firm to the other, accompanied by the business card of an executive or representative of the company.

IF YOU HAVE NO CARDS

Engraved calling cards are a pleasant social convenience, but perfectly nice people have been known to get along successfully without them. It's preferable to do that rather than use printed cards, which are quite taboo. If you are asked for a card, don't fumble for a non-existent one. Merely say, "Please say Miss Addington is calling." If you have no personal card to enclose with a gift, most shops will supply a plain white one in a matching envelope. Write a little message in longhand and seal it. You won't need a card if you are going to present the gift yourself, unless you're going to a party where it would be helpful to have your gift identified by card. When you call on a friend or neighbor and don't wish to trust a servant's or a member of the family's memory, or if the person on whom you are calling is not at home, ask for a memorandum pad, write a little greeting—"So sorry not to find you here, was in the neighborhood and hoped to find you home"—and hand it, folded, over for later delivery. Above all, don't use prepared thank-you cards or greeting cards for these purposes.

MAKING AND RECEIVING CALLS

In Victorian days and up until the First World War the making of calls was a highly stylized business. The duty fell on the women of the household, who left their husbands' cards with their own. However on certain occasions, such as calls of condolence, of congratulation, or calls on the sick, men often made their appearance and left their cards in person, too, as they still properly may.

Today with increased apartment living, virtually servantless households, and fewer women who live a purely social life, formal calls involving the leaving of cards on various members of the household and their house guests are growing fewer and fewer. In some quiet communities and in some wealthy and conservative older circles in New York formal calls are still expected and do take place. But few and far between are the hostesses who by engraving a day of the week on the lower left of their cards let it be known they are "at home" to callers on a certain day. One very celebrated hostess I know finally gave up keeping a silver salver in the entry hall of her town house, not only because it received few cards but because it was regularly stolen by delivery boys.

A personal call, however, is still necessary to make new neighbors feel at home in your country or suburban community. This custom is not followed in cities, and in some places in the country it is a neglected courtesy. Strictly speaking, you should call, formally, when you hear of any event that requires sympathy, welcoming, or special rejoicing—the illness of a friend, an engagement, the return of a newly married couple from their wedding trip, the arrival of new neighbors, the birth of a baby. But you can make other arrangements in regard to all of these things, too, without making a personal appearance or even owning a visiting card and still not be considered socially a pariah.

In these days it is almost impossible to arrange to have a servant on more or less constant duty at the door during accepted calling hours. In most households where there are servants one must fulfill the duties of several, and the old formalities are dying out for lack of the necessary setting for them. A lady lacking a butler, not to mention a footman, and with one or perhaps two maids busy with—or resting from—the housework might feel rather silly opening the door herself to visitors who had no intention of coming face to face with her and had planned only to leave cards. In this case she is obliged to receive them, and they must go in for the prescribed twenty minutes. So today, calls are preferably "by appointment."

All over the country it is becoming the accepted thing to phone first before paying a call, because call-making—when it does take place—quite sensibly is taking on more meaning.

It is a considerate thing to phone any newcomer on whom you plan to call to ask when it will be convenient for her to see you. If she is in the middle of unpacking her goods and chattels and without the leisure or peace of mind to receive you, she will appreciate your not dropping in until she is settled. Even then she might well appreciate a forewarning of your visit. You can do this on very short order the day you wish to call. Don't plan to run into any such household in the morning, as used to be the eleven o'clock custom. Choose the afternoon between three and five or, if it's an informal home and an informal neighborhood, in the early evening after dinner, first making sure you are welcome. If you are a woman, you don't call on a man who has moved into your country neighborhood, but, of course, some male member of the family may call or you may go with your husband or any adult male relative living with you. Also you may phone or write to invite such a man to call on you.

THE CALL ITSELF Ask for your hostess at the door during the accepted calling hours that I have mentioned. If the servant says she is not at home, it may mean, merely, that she is not receiving any visitors, a necessary social device not intended to offend. Just leave your card, but don't bend over a corner as used to be done to indicate the caller appeared in person and didn't just send his card by a messenger, chauffeur, or coachman. If no card tray is offered you by the servant at the door, simply announce your name and in leaving place your card on any convenient table.

If your hostess is able to see you, do not remove your coat or gloves. Leave within twenty minutes. Do not expect refreshments on a formal call, although if you pay your party call on one of the old guard on her official "at home" day, you may be offered them.

A man making a formal call removes his overcoat or topcoat and leaves it with his hat, gloves, and stick, if he carries one, in the hall. No visitor trails rubbers, umbrella, or galoshes into a drawing room, needless to say.

CONVERSATION DURING CALLS No one expects you to discuss any very vital topics while making a social call. The hostess will know why you are there. Light conversation about the party you attended, the attractiveness of the people you met, something amusing that has happened, even that conversation piece, the weather, will do. Don't prolong your farewell. At the end of twenty minutes, or at most a half hour, thank your hostess again and leave promptly.

FLOWERS FROM CALLERS Sometimes it is pleasant to take flowers to your hostess if you make no special point about it. Leave them in the hall for the servant to arrange and take in after you've left, or have them arrive with your card after you leave.

The cost of flowers should always be in keeping with your income if money is any consideration, and even when it is not, pretentious bouquets should never be sent where your hostess's quarters may be too small to accommodate them. Two or three gardenias arranged for use in a flat container, or a small fragrant bunch of lilies of the valley or violets may be much more welcome than two dozen towering gladioli. Many florists will send flowers already arranged in containers—a godsend to people who live permanently or temporarily in small quarters.

THE ELIGIBLE MAN

Living under the same apartment roof in a big city with neighbors does not sanction a social call unless some introduction has taken place. You might receive a visiting card from a friend with the notation, "John Oakes, my ex-classmate, has moved to your building. Do look him up!" Even this doesn't suggest you and your husband call on him unannounced—a procedure very unpopular among bachelors in or out of cities. If you are a single woman you might arrange to include such a man when you are having a cocktail party or tea, mailing your card to him or sending it by the hall man or your own servant in a sealed envelope. It might read, on the face of the card, "Cocktails at five, Thurs., Dec. 5th, Apt. 601." It is to be assumed that your friend has told him about you. However, if you feel he may be puzzled to receive an informal invitation this way and might not immediately recognize your name, phone him or drop him a note reading something like this:

Dear Mr. Oakes,

Our friend in common, Gordon Ward, tells us you are now a neighbor in the building. Some friends whom I feel you might enjoy meeting are coming to tea next Sunday.

Will you join us around four-thirty in apartment 601?

Sincerely (or, less formally,
Cordially, which is now
an accepted closing, so-
cially and in business)

If you include Mr. Oakes, whom you have never entertained before, on your invitation list for a formal affair, remember that he may not immediately recall his friend Ward's promise to make him known to you so you might ask him to call. It is better to invite him to the small gathering first. If you do include him on a party list for which you are issuing formal third-person invitations (which are sent increasingly rarely except for weddings, receptions, debuts, balls), send your card, on which you might write "at Gordon Ward's suggestion," or phone him first. You might say something like this, "Mr. Oakes, this is Jessie Gray, Gordon Ward's friend. I believe he told you I live in this building too. I just wanted to tell you you'll receive an invitation to dinner shortly. I do hope you'll come."

Do not by any chance ask the gentleman to call on you, unless friends will be present, if you are a woman living alone and are of marriageable age (and when does that cease to be?). The more eligible he is, the more it must seem that the courtesy you are extending him in asking him to call comes at another's request. Never be too obvious in your bachelor-gathering. If he does not accept your invitation, it would be very pleasant of him to send flowers with a note on his card to the effect that he hopes you'll think of him again. From there on it should be his move. He may ask to call on you. If he doesn't, better look elsewhere for bachelors to enliven your parties.

THE BACHELOR HOST AND CALLS

A man living alone who entertains at home, even if he's of high military or diplomatic station, does not receive party calls, phone calls, or even notes or cards of thanks from the ladies who were present. It is the man who must always thank the ladies who have been his guests, although any departing guest says a few graceful words of thanks on leaving. The only exception is when some woman receives with him as hostess pro tem—his mother, sister, or other female relative—and then it is she who should receive the party thanks.

CALLS OF CONDOLENCE

You leave your card at the door and do not ask to be received when making a call of condolence, unless you are very intimate with the family. On such a call, where you do not feel you can offer to do more, say to whoever opens the door, "Will you kindly tell [naming the member of the family you know or saying 'the family'] that I called to offer my sympathy?" Such calls are not returned. They should be made within a month after the funeral, but most considerate people make them as soon as the death is known. The call of condolence is about the only call that still seems almost obligatory in all circles where it is at all possible for friends to offer their sympathy this way in person.

CALLING ON A PUBLIC OFFICIAL

Anyone has the right to request to see the President of the United States, the governor of one's state, the mayor of one's city, or anyone else holding public office. Such a request must be motivated by something more than a desire to shake his hand, as all these executives run on split-second timing of their engagements.

Requests to see the President are made to his aide but may be made to the aide through anyone close to the President in an official or unofficial capacity through whom you have a personal approach. A relatively small number of those seeking an audience can receive it, so be sure before making such a request that it *is* only the President who can be of help in the matter. And, if possible, put your request in writing so it can be attended to without a personal audience. Of the thousands and thousands of letters the President receives every year, none goes entirely unnoticed. All those actually requiring a reply receive it. Some come to the President's personal attention and receive an answer from him or from a secretary. Some are referred to other departments of the government for follow-up. Threatening and abusive letters go to the FBI.

CHAPTER FIFTY-NINE

HOSPITALS AND DOCTORS

HOSPITAL VISITS

Most hospitals have strict visiting rules. There are certain hours during which private patients may have callers and usually more limited ones for ward or semiprivate patients. Unless there is some valid reason for doing so, never ask for any extension of official hours.

Unless you are a close friend or relative who can really help in the nursing of the patient and are needed, don't stay more than a few minutes on any visit. If the patient is well on the road to recuperation, you may, with permission of the nurse in charge, stay perhaps as much as the full visiting time in the afternoon or evening if there are no other visitors. It is unfair to the patient and to the nurses to cram a sickroom full of visitors. In fact, many hospitals limit the number of visitors a patient may have at one time, and some have enforced quiet periods for patients, especially maternity patients, every afternoon during which not even telephone calls may be received.

VISITING THE NEW MOTHER   A baby is always a matter for rejoicing, and a hospital call on a new mother is the kind people like to make. But childbirth is tiring and the mother needs plenty of rest, and this may be the only time for months that she may really be able to get it. So, if you call upon her, be brief. A note or a little gift for her or for the baby may be better than a phone call, if she has a phone, and better than a personal visit. Just talking on the phone when your whole body is weary can be fatiguing to the point of tears—especially when well-wishers call in great numbers or stay on the phone too long.

ABOUT FLOWERS   Before sending flowers to a person who may be literally blanketed with them it is well to phone a relative to see if more flowers will be welcome. Sometimes, depending on the cause for hospitalization, delicacies are preferred, but be sure the patient is not on some sort of diet that would prohibit fruit, candy, or your best homemade cake or cookies. There is hardly a diet, however, that rules out ice cream, and, as hospital ice cream is often dull, a really good ice cream brought in from outside is usually a treat.

Very often to women patients a pretty bed jacket or nightgown, a bottle of eau de cologne, or an armful of pocket-size books that are easy to hold are sometimes more welcome than more flowers. If you do send flowers, it is sometimes better to send them during the latter part of the patient's stay, for in the first days of an illness so many bouquets arrive. And if you do send them, provide, if possible, a container for them, because most hospitals have too few vases and those available are usually inadequate in the making of an attractive arrangement. The best thing, perhaps, is to send a flowering plant that needs little care from overworked nurses, or one of those permanent arrangements of flowers that do not have to be taken apart each day.

IF YOU ARE THE PATIENT When you go into a hospital you are not entering a luxury hotel, no matter what superior accommodations you are able to pay for. Only a few years ago I was in a hospital at the same time a distant relative of mine arrived there for a sojourn with her own table linen, silver, china, personal maid, and all kinds of special equipment to make her feel at home. Even her food was sent in. But I doubt whether, today, even hospitals badly needing endowments would permit such special privilege. In fact, there isn't room in hospitals today for any but the very ill. Stays are often limited for certain things, such as childbirth, tonsillectomies, or appendectomies, unless, of course, some complication occurs.

We are so short of hospitals that it isn't even possible today to name one's accommodations if you are an emergency patient. You may land in a semiprivate room or even a ward, may have to have floor nursing. This means great curtailment of your notions of service. You may not summon the floor nurses as you would a private nurse, and you must consider at all times that you do not occupy the quarters by yourself—the other patient or patients must be considered. Actually, once you get used to the lack of privacy, a pleasant roommate may speed your recovery, although an inconsiderate one can certainly slow it up.

HOW TO SHARE A HOSPITAL ROOM

In wards your conduct is pretty strictly regulated by the ever-present nurse, but if you are behind the heavy door of a semiprivate room, you may be quite a menace to the recovery of your roommate—sometimes without fully realizing your thoughtlessness. Some hospitals, rightly I think, prohibit the installation of telephones in semiprivate rooms or, if they do allow them, limit the hours they may be used to regular visiting hours. The constant ringing of the phone, from early morning until late at night, and protracted, sometimes alarmingly clinical conversations are a painful nuisance to the other person sharing the room. One smoker can make a non-smoker miserable by filling the sickroom with cigarette, cigar, or pipe smoke. The unremitting noise of one patient's radio can distress the other. Guests who overstay, who are too numerous or too loud in their conversation make it impossible for other patients to have the necessary rest. If you ever find yourself on the receiving end of a hospital nuisance, don't suffer in silence. Explain the situation to the floor nurse or to the house doctor who visits you or to your attending physician, and steps will be taken, one way or the other, to correct the trouble. Your peace of mind is important in your doctor's regimen for you.

YOU AND YOUR NURSES

Patients often make the mistake of asking a nurse all sorts of questions about their own condition, which nurses are, ethically speaking, not permitted to answer. If you want to know the result of your operation or the state of your temperature, ask your doctor, not your nurse.

Your nurse's attitude toward you should be strictly objective, so don't try to make her your confidante, as you may regret it very much after you leave. On the other hand, don't treat her like a servant—she is a professionally trained person working under the direction of your doctor. She is there to fill your requests, if advisable, but not to take your orders. If you don't like your nurse—and some few, perhaps because of overwork or limited social outlet (nursing is one of the lonely professions), are crotchety—ask your doctor to try to replace her with someone less irritating.

If you have a private nurse for a week or more, you pay her bill weekly—and promptly. Don't ask her to run errands for you on her hours off.

When she leaves you, you may show your appreciation by giving candy, flowers, or handkerchiefs, cigarettes and books. But don't feel obligated to give beyond your means, especially if the hospital cost has been hard for the budget to bear. And to the very occasional surly or sadistic nurse, if it has been your lot to get one, give nothing.

If you have just had a baby and the baby has been kept in the hospital nursery, it is thoughtful for you to remember at least the head nurse there. If you have been a ward or semiprivate patient, it is not necessary to give anything—in fact, it is never *necessary*.

VISITING YOUR DOCTOR

If you live in a small community and your doctor has his office in his home, there are various courtesies that should be considered. Even a general practitioner has office hours, and these should be respected. Don't drop in on him before or after these hours just because you are passing his house and think it might be a good time for him to look at Danny's tonsils. If an emergency arises, phone his office, not his home, if your town has an answering service that takes doctors' calls. It is not fair to ask the doctor's wife to take his messages or chase him up at other patients' homes, if by phoning the office, day or night, you can reach him through the service he maintains.

When you do go to your doctor's office, remember that he has little free time for unnecessary conversation, even if he is a personal friend. If he makes a call at your home, don't expect him to give a once-over to all the members of the family without billing you for this additional attention. Offer him, if you wish, a soft drink, coffee, or tea. The conscientious doctor takes nothing stronger on calls because the odor of alcohol on his breath might cause the next patient to doubt his competency, especially in an emergency. Think twice before you call him at night or in very bad weather. Often phone advice will tide you through and save the doctor's energy. Many mothers of young babies pay a doctor a flat fee for one year's care of the child, and this service includes telephone consultation as often as necessary. But calls should, even then, be made during office hours, if possible. A list of questions, prepared beforehand, saves the doctor's time as well as your own.

PROFESSIONAL ETHICS It is incredible the questions patients ask their doctors concerning the troubles of other people. They want to know why Mrs. Kelly is in the waiting room, if her husband is still drinking, if her daughter is going to have a baby. Your doctor has taken an oath not to reveal such professional secrets. Don't ask him such questions, and don't be annoyed when he side-steps all personal questions about his treatment of other patients or concerning his relations with them. Do not pass on to others the names of patients waiting to see a doctor—especially an obstetrician or a psychiatrist. People may or may not wish their visits to such specialists known by the general public.

MEDICAL EXAMINATIONS You would think that no man or woman would turn up for a prearranged doctor's appointment without having bathed and dressed in clean clothing. But the reports I have received from nurses and doctors prove otherwise. Evidently, even a Park Avenue practice doesn't protect a doctor from unfastidiousness.

PERSONAL RELATIONSHIPS It is only human to believe that your doctor, because of his intimate relation with you, has a very special personal interest in your welfare, which he may indeed have. But his interest is basically professional and if he is to serve you best, it should be kept on that basis. Doctors rarely treat their own families because they are likely to lose their objectivity when prescribing for people with whom they have too close a relationship.

The young doctor or the pretty nurse is often embarrassed by the reaction some patients have to the necessarily close physical association. A doctor is often deluged by gifts, many of them silly and useless, from what he terms G.P.s—grateful patients. Be grateful and appreciative of your doctor's care, but never expect more than professional consideration from him and be on guard lest your own warm feelings for him, engendered by the flattering, personal attention he must give your every complaint, embarrass him in any way. The best thing you can do to show your appreciation is to pay your bills promptly, be on time for appointments, and take no more of his time than is actually necessary. Any gifts should be simple and impersonal.

Be chary of suggesting any social invitations, unless he indicates a desire for them. A doctor should never be put in the position of either having to see his patients socially or lose them. Again, objectivity between patient and doctor makes for the best professional relations.

Doctors have little enough uninterrupted social life as it is, without having to discuss symptoms with friends, or even perfect strangers, when they do go to a dinner party. If you meet a doctor socially, never ask his professional advice unless you're willing to go to his office for it. It is true that many doctors like to talk "shop" in their free time, but usually not with laymen unless the latter are particularly well informed on scientific matters. Never use a social contact with any professional person to ask advice for which you would be charged if you applied for it under the usual circumstances.

CHAPTER SIXTY

SPEAKING BEFORE AN AUDIENCE

Like death and taxes, some form of public speaking comes at one time or another to all of us. We may only find ourselves on our feet at the Parent-Teacher meeting or at our club, but for the uninitiated, the shy, the unsure even this mild public appearance is agony in anticipation and often in actuality.

Extemporaneous speaking is an art fostered by plentiful practice. It is said that George Bernard Shaw, struck dumb when he first tried to speak in public, joined the contentious Fabian Society in England, and on any and all occasions rose to his feet until glibness became through constant practice part and parcel of his personality. Many a seemingly extemporaneous speech has been carefully memorized and lengthily extolled beforehand so that it comes forth smoothly—but not so smoothly as to seem well-prepared.

It is cheering to know from the testimony of experts that people do not wish us to be completely perfect in our delivery. Many excellent public speakers deliberately stumble or stutter occasionally to make their perform-ance seem more humanly fallible. The man who speaks with too much as-surance in his own performance sometimes finds his audience somewhat hostile. Perhaps this is because each person in the audience at some time mentally puts himself in the place of the speaker and suffers what he be-lieves to be his diffidence or embarrassment, his strangeness in these sur-roundings or circumstances. For this reason the speaker starting his talk with too much self-assurance or brashness often finds his audience is not with him at all.

INTRODUCING YOUR SPEECH   It takes an audience a few minutes to get used to you, so when you get on your feet you do not immediately proceed to the matter at hand. People are adjusting to your appearance, the tone of your voice, your bearing, and in my opinion they don't actually hear your opening words. I think it is this, rather than the routine dullness of most speech openings, that focuses the audience's attention so slowly on what you are saying. For the first few minutes the practiced speaker, therefore, fills in time with his "Thank you" to the chairman introducing him, calling him or her by name—"Thank you, Mrs. Wirk." Then come his formal salutations, "Mr. President, honored guests [if there are any], ladies and gentlemen." Some speakers, at this point, drag in some pointless joke or anecdote to tide them through what I think of as the inspection period, but as the preoccupied audience rarely gets the point of it and just laughs automatically, it seems better technique to begin with a little appropriate preamble that leads logically to the heart of what you have to say. One way of doing this is to prepare in advance an outline of what you plan to discuss. It is perfectly sound technique to state categorically what you have been asked to speak about and to indicate what you hope to prove or what points you wish to develop, but not at such length as to dull people's anticipation of your talk.

CLICHÉS   The speech that is studded with clichés, especially those old saws of public speaking, "I come before you today," "Unaccustomed as I am to public speaking," "I point with pride," "We view with alarm," ". . . and in conclusion let me say," etc., is dreary. More is expected of us since the development of radio and television than the old-fashioned arm-waving oratorical approach. The more natural your speaking voice, the simpler your language and presentation, the more believable you will be.

USING THE VOICE CORRECTLY   If a microphone is placed before you, it is well if you have noted how the person who introduced you used it. Properly, microphones are tested beforehand for volume and the speaker is told just how to speak into the one presented to him. Because of the wide use of the public address system and of radio microphones, the well-versed public speaker knows he must avoid the shouting that he used to do from the old lecture platform when he wanted to emphasize a point. He knows, too, that he must stand quietly and talk at all times directly into the microphone. Turning his head from side to side to take in the full sweep of the audience often partially blots out what he is trying to say. If he raises his voice perceptibly for emphasis, he must step back a little from the microphone to avoid blasting his hearer's eardrums. But often greater emphasis is made, when a mike is in use, by the lowering of the voice, even to a whisper. This technique, occasionally and artfully used, causes the audience to hang literally on each softly spoken word.

COUGHING DURING A SPEECH   If a speaker must cough or sneeze or blow his nose during the course of a speech, he need not be embarrassed but may think of it as a useful, human diversion that brings a perhaps needed little break in the flow of his speech. He of course turns his head away, especially from a microphone, and excuses himself in the case of a cough or sneeze but not if he blows his nose or takes a sip of water. Some accomplished speakers use the drinking of water as a way of heightening suspense before making some dramatic charge or assertion. "And now I am going to tell you something that will shake every one of you, that will bring tears to the eyes of every man and woman in this hall——" (drink of water).

READING A SPEECH No speech should ever be read if you want your audience to listen to what you have to say. It is sometimes quite satisfactory to have before you a written speech the gist of which, at least, and phrases from it, have been committed to memory. But to read it verbatim, unless you are in a radio studio and the reading of a script is required, is to lose your audience at the start. Even if you read well, the audience will be bored and restless if it sees you in the act. Using an outline or notes on small cards held in the palm of the hand is much better and makes for a more believable, more personal presentation of your ideas. Many good speakers use the written speech before them as a reminder or a guide, especially when discussing scientific or political matters or in presenting professional papers, but they make it a point to look up frequently, to develop little techniques that make them at least seem to be extemporizing.

DIRECTING YOUR TALK Some speakers find it disconcerting to talk generally to an audience, so, before they rise, they select one face, sometimes one they know, and direct the entire discourse to it. This device may be effective for the speaker but works better, I think, if he chooses several faces in opposite parts of the hall and directs his words sometimes this way, sometimes that, to lend a little variation.

THE USE OF JOKES, ILLUSTRATIONS, AND ANECDOTES Jokes and anecdotes, if at all appropriate, do have a function in that they loosen up an audience—and the speaker too—especially at the difficult beginning of a speech. But they are better omitted if a speaker tells a story badly and self-consciously. And if they have nothing whatsoever to do with the case, they are certainly better omitted. Otherwise members of the audience may be so puzzled by the introduction of the stories that they will spend the rest of the time trying to determine the connection and so not hear, as consciously as they should, whatever else you have to say. It is good, in making a speech, to remember that many, many people are not ear-minded, that is, they don't easily digest what they get through the ears alone. For this reason points need to be made more than once, propositions put in several ways. Wherever possible, illustrate what you are saying visually in some way, with charts, graphs, slides, motion pictures, or some form of illustration in which you take part—sketches, exhibits, instruction in techniques. The action involved breaks up a too smooth presentation and makes the audience feel more at ease—and you will, too. A spotlight pointer where slides or movies are used is the most effective way of calling attention to certain details.

CLOSING A SPEECH   Many a speech loses its effectiveness if the closing is too greatly drawn out or if, on the other hand, it is too abruptly terminated. Give some indication that you have said about all you are going to say on the subject a few minutes before sitting down. Many graceful speakers say something like this, "You have been kind enough to give me this amount of time, and, while I could develop this subject to a much greater extent, we are all anxious to hear what the next speaker has to say, etc." Then comes some brief summing-up point or points and a final statement of conclusion, but never say, without preamble, "I guess that's all," or "That's all I have to say." A speech should end on a point the hearer will take away with him, if possible, or on an anecdote that sums up in capsule form part, at least, of what the speaker was trying to say.

MAKING YOUR DEPARTURE   Often a principal speaker will end his speech and almost without pause make his getaway from the speakers' table. He may have to make a train or fulfill another engagement, and, if so, the chairman should, if possible, prepare the audience for such a sudden departure when he thanks the speaker. The chairman in thanking him should repeat the speaker's name for late-comers or those who may not have caught it correctly before. "Thank you, Mr. Graham Saunders" is better than "Thank you, Mr. Saunders." Otherwise, it is courteous for the speaker to hear out his successors, if any, with at least a show of interest and to linger after the speeches to receive the felicitations or answer the questions of those assembled whenever this seems advisable.

DRESS OF THE SPEAKER

A MAN'S DRESS   A man making an evening speech inquires beforehand what those at the speakers' table will wear—business suits, tuxedos, or full dress. It frequently happens that people at the speakers' table wear full dress and the others at the dinner come in dinner jackets. At public dinners it is never incorrect for the speaker, the chairman, and those at the speakers' table to wear full evening dress, even if the body of the assemblage comes informally attired. For the same reason, a lecturer, a conductor, or any personage making a public appearance in the evening wears formal clothes if there is any possibility of some of his hearers doing likewise. He should set the highest sartorial standard for the occasion so as not to embarrass any who come formally attired to do him proper honor.

A WOMAN SPEAKER'S DRESS   A woman speaking in the evening wears a long or short dinner dress or a formal evening gown, depending on the occasion and on what the majority of women present will be wearing. If she is to open the opera season with an appeal for subscriptions she wears formal evening dress and her finest jewels. If she is to get up in the high school auditorium to explain the functioning of the Girl Scouts she dresses in street clothes and usually wears a hat.

Clothes so vivid or spectacular that they distract the hearers' attention from what you are saying are certainly a mistake. At the same time you should look your best, being sure that your clothes are not so new and high style that you are at all conscious of them. Overdressing is more likely to be criticized than underdressing for the occasion. For most speaking occasions, when in doubt, wear a good, tailored, but not sport, suit. Many younger women speak without a hat, or, if they wear a hat, they are careful to choose one that does not in any way shield the face. Shoes should be suitable to the costume, of course, but should not have spike heels if the talk is to take any length of time.

YOUR RADIO APPEARANCE

Many citizens of distinction—and many of no particular distinction—find themselves for one reason or other in a broadcasting studio and confronted with a microphone. Mike fright, like stage fright, is very common, even in professionals, and results in stuttering, stammering, or a positive inability to say anything at all.

The psychological reasons for mike fright are probably very complex. They may have to do with the idea that we are such poor creatures that no one would be interested in what we have to say—about the Boy Scout Drive or whatever. Perhaps the situation is painfully reminiscent of our school recitations. Whatever the cause, there are a few physical and mental tricks I find do help overcome mike fright. Here they are:

Before your turn at the microphone, keep your mind on the individuals before you and off the nebulous millions supposedly listening in. You are going to talk to these few flesh and blood people, who, your reason tells you, are quite ordinary and harmless.

Just as you are about to speak into the microphone, take a deep breath so your first words will not be tight and breathless. Keep your hands and body relaxed and limp. Keep your eyes on one person to whom you are talking, not on the microphone.

Smile as you speak and your words will come more easily. It is hard to be tense if you are smiling. Your outwardly easy manner helps reassure those with you so that they expect you to acquit yourself well, and you do.

Hold your head still about one foot from the microphone, and speak directly into the microphone, trying to attain your usual conversational tone of voice.

If you are taking part in an interview, be sure to let the other person finish his question or answer completely. Overlapping voices in radio create a meaningless jumble for the listener.

Have handy a glass of water, a piece of paper, and a pencil (for doodling if you're a doodler). Sometimes fear that your mouth will become dry and no water be available to you is enough to make you nervous. Have the water on hand before you start. And take a sip or two if you wish while you are on the air. Little breaks in your talk are natural and human. They make what you are saying more attractive to the listener.

If you must read a script and you lose your place, don't be afraid to say to the person opposite you, "Now where was I? Oh, yes, I was saying, etc." Remember that in ordinary conversation people lose momentary track of what they were saying, too. A too smooth delivery on radio is uninteresting. The ideal is to try to make everything seem unrehearsed and spontaneous.

THE DO'S AND DON'TS OF RADIO APPEARANCES Speak in a natural tone of voice.

Don't shout into the microphone or lower your voice—unless for the latter you move closer to the microphone at the same time. Sometimes it is more effective to lower the voice in making a point than to raise it, but it takes some practice to know how to do this on radio effectively.

Don't wear jewelry that rattles or fabrics that rustle.

Don't tap your feet or drum your fingers.

If you must cough, sneeze, or blow your nose, turn aside from the mike and don't apologize.

Get to the studio a half hour before your broadcast, if possible.

Go through a rehearsal, if requested, with the same care you will accord your actual broadcast.

If you read from a script, remove clips or staples beforehand, and as each page is completed, drop it gently to the floor. Rustling and turning of pages is clearly audible to the audience.

Watch the studio warning lights. When the light is green, it is all right to talk to others in the studio—you are off the air. But keep alert. When the light changes to red you are on the air, and then you speak on cue only.

If others precede you at the mike, take your place, when your turn comes, very carefully. Don't touch the mike at any time, and if you must seat yourself before it during the broadcast, do so without scraping the chair or jarring the table.

If you have never been on a radio program before, do not hesitate to ask a few questions of someone in the studio before you go on. If you are to follow the engineer's instructions, ask to have the hand signals demonstrated to you. But briefly, here are a few signals with which you are most likely to be concerned: If the engineer, announcer, or interviewer places his hand palm up horizontally and makes a lifting motion, this means "keep your voice up." If he turns his palm down with a patting motion, this means "lower your voice." If he raises five, three, two, or one finger, this means you must finish what you are saying in that number of minutes. If he makes a circle with his index finger and thumb, this means you are doing fine. If he lays his finger on his nose, that means you are finishing right on time. If he "cuts his throat" with his hand, this means the program has been cut off the air. Watch the light at this point—the program may resume and words not meant for broadcast go out over the air.

At the end of the program—if you have stayed until the end—it is courteous to thank your interviewer (if you've been interviewed) for asking you, and to thank the announcer and the engineer as well if they have not already gone on to other things. However, schedules in radio are on a split-second basis, so don't detain artists or staff unnecessarily.

In most radio studios there are "No Smoking" signs, but if others in the studio are smoking nevertheless, before or while the program is on the air, you may do so too if you really believe it will help maintain your poise.

But never do what some misguided amateurs do—take a few cocktails before going on the air in the expectancy that that will help.

YOUR APPEARANCE ON TELEVISION

The continuing development and changes in television make it difficult to give very much in the way of advice to those likely to appear on television programs.

For studio shows there are always detailed rehearsals under powerful lights. Scripts are rarely obviously read, although if necessary the text, or notes from the text, may be in large type somewhere out of the camera range. More often what is to be said is memorized or presented ad lib. For rehearsals it is often advisable to wear dark glasses or at least reading glasses, if one has them, to protect the eyes from the glare of the lights. Glasses are removed, whenever possible, when the show goes on.

For black-and-white television, light clothes, preferably patterned, are preferred. Shiny jewelry or trimmings should be avoided as they catch the light and divert televiewers from the subject. Sometimes jewelry, such as a pearl necklace, which seems necessary to the costume may be worn if its shine has been reduced temporarily with a film of soap or other substance applied by the make-up department.

Everyone receives special make-up for studio television appearances, and at large public dinners and other events to be televised public figures try to meet some of the make-up man's specifications whenever possible. Men should be newly and closely shaven. If their beards are very dark, pancake make-up, not too obvious to nearby guests, can help improve the speakers' appearance on the television screen.

The make-up department indicates, when there is advance preparation, what color lipstick is most suitable for a woman—green, purple, or brown. When no instructions are given, women expecting to be televised should wear very dark pancake make-up and very dark—almost brown—lipstick.

Like modern public speaking, appearance before the television cameras requires a minimum of gestures and facial contortions. The speaker should play to the camera, turning his head as directed when one camera takes over from a different angle than the other or others.

CHAPTER SIXTY-ONE

SIMPLE PARLIAMENTARY PROCEDURE

At one time or another most of us witness or take part in some meeting that is conducted by the ancient and formal form of English parliamentary procedure. The American method is slightly different from the original English one. This highly stylized form is used for the conduct of various clubs, societies, and church bodies as well as in ordinary business. Anyone asked to serve on a board of directors or who is elected to club or other office needs to know in greater detail than I shall set forth now the exact functioning of parliamentary procedure. Standard work on the subject is Robert's *Rules of Order,* obtainable in any library, but actual attendance at meetings can be, perhaps, more helpful to the prospective board member or chairman than study of this legal reference work.

The chairman of a meeting, sometimes in religious or debating assemblages called the moderator, must keep it in order and conduct its business. All members of the assembly are subject to the rulings from the chair. The chairman may not, himself, take part in debate unless he temporarily relinquishes the chair in order to do so.

Meetings conducted by means of parliamentary procedure may not open until a quorum is present, that is, a sufficient number of voting members to pass a resolution put to vote—a two-thirds majority or, in some cases, a simple majority. When a sufficient number is assembled, the meeting is called to order by the chairman, who then directs the secretary to read the minutes of the last meeting. The minutes are then approved or amended, and the chairman proceeds, according to the order of business furnished him by the secretary, asking first for various committee reports. These are followed by discussion, if any, with each member who wishes to take the floor attracting the chairman's attention, usually by rising, and saying, "Mr. Chairman" or "Madam Chairman," sometimes "Mr. President" or "Madam President" (even in the case of an unmarried woman). After he is recognized by the chair—and only one person at a time may have the floor—he states his name and his business connection, if any, unless he is well known to the group. In small meetings the members often do not rise, especially if they are sitting around a small table in a board room, but no matter how well the members are known to each other they are, correctly, formal in reference to one another. "I am informed by Mr. Burns, etc.," instead of "Joe tells me, etc." The chairman, who may have known you all your life, will still recognize you by saying, "Yes, Mrs. Carlson," when you take the floor, not "Yes, Mae," although he may sometimes just bow, if everyone knows you. Sometimes he will clarify your appearance at the meeting by explaining before you begin to speak, "Mrs. Carlson is here in behalf of the League of Women Voters."

Sometimes very acrimonious charges are made in board and other meetings, and keeping matters on a formal level in proper parliamentary style helps to foster the necessary objectivity, especially between chairman and assemblage.

Often brief informal discussion on the main question before the meeting—which must not go into debate—takes place after introduction of the topic by the chairman. "Gentlemen, we have met this morning, as you know, to take up the matter of increasing the tax rate. Before we make a motion, I would like Mr. Flannigan, here, to outline the method he's worked out for collecting the higher tax on a quarterly basis, assuming we pass a motion to increase taxes." During informal discussion, questions may be put by members of the body if the chairman so permits. One asks, "Mr. Chairman, I would like to ask a question." Then, if permitted, he may put it direct to the speaker, not wait to have it rephrased by the chair as in formal debate.

When, after informal discussion and formal debate, if it takes place, a question is ready to be moved upon, a member rises and says, for example, "I make a motion that dogs not be permitted on the public beach." The chairman usually asks that someone second it, and when the motion is seconded by someone saying, "I second the motion" (he does not need to obtain the floor or in small assemblies even rise), the chairman restates it. If no one seconds the motion—something that sometimes happens when it seems obvious the feeling is generally in favor of it—the chair may go on to further business, though any member may make a point of order that the motion has not been seconded and the chair must go back and complete the seconding of the motion.

Votes are taken when it seems clear that the whole assembly is not in agreement on some matter brought before it. The chair asks for a show of hands or says, "All in favor say 'aye,' opposed 'no,'" or sometimes ask proponents to rise and be counted.

TAKING LEAVE

Anyone taking part in a board or other meeting, not there just as a spectator, may not leave the meeting permanently unless excused by the chair. If he has explained to the chairman before the start of the meeting that at some point he must leave, he may make his departure after catching the chair's eye at an opportune time and bowing. Sometimes in the case of an important member the chair makes some explanation, "Mr. Pryn has another meeting, gentlemen, and has asked to be excused at this time." The departing member then leaves without farewells, merely nodding to various members and the chair as he leaves. If in the middle of a meeting he is called to the phone, he may leave quietly without the chair's permission, unless a vote is about to be taken and he is necessary for a quorum.

All members, unless specifically excused, must remain in place until the end of the meeting. When all business has been settled and all reports are in the chairman may say, "Is there anything more to come before the meeting?" If he receives no reply, he says after a suitable pause, "The meeting is adjourned." It is then proper to take farewell of one's fellow board members or others in the meeting in a pleasant manner, even after heated and perhaps unpleasant discussion.

CHAPTER SIXTY-TWO

YOUR APPEARANCE AT PUBLIC FUNCTIONS

DRESSING FOR THE OPERA

As with many other social customs there has been an increasing trend toward less formality at the opera. It was once unthinkable for a man or woman sitting in a box or in the orchestra to appear in anything but full evening dress. Today, except on opening night—or in New York on fashionable Monday night—full dress is the exception rather than the rule. Dinner jackets and even dark blue or Oxford gray suits are seen in the orchestra, and dinner jackets are worn in the boxes. Women in the orchestra wear dinner suits, dinner dresses, or simple dark street dresses as they might wear to a concert. Women in boxes, accompanied by dinner-jacketed men, wear dinner dresses rather than full décolletage. Women alone in the orchestra dress inconspicuously, often in a "little black dress" with or without hat.

In the balconies dark suits are worn by the men and dark dresses or suits by the women. As in the theater, the balcony is a "don't dress" section, unless a couple is going on to some other function where evening dress is expected. A couple in evening dress but sitting in the balcony might seem to be slumming, though it is true that those who know music and the dance prefer the vantage point of the first balcony to the more fashionable orchestra.

SEATING IN OPERA BOXES

Promptness at the opera is only decent courtesy to the performers and to the rest of the audience. Conservative hostesses arrive at their boxes at least fifteen minutes before curtain time and seat themselves in the first row in the seat farthest from the stage (in a centrally located box the hostess is at the right). As guests arrive older women guests are seated with the hostess in the front row, the younger women sit in the second row with the older men, and the young men sit in the last row with the host.

Between the acts box holders and guests may repair for refreshments, now generally offered in most opera houses, and for the fascinating promenade on the stairs, hallways, and lobby. If the hostess or any older women wish to remain in the box during intermission, some male guest (or guests) stays with them. Any woman guest wishing to visit friends during intermission excuses herself to her hostess and visits, briefly, accompanied by some male guest in the box. All should return to the box as soon as the "curtain rising" signal is given. Those who must leave before the end of an act excuse themselves before the act begins and slip out from a rear seat as quickly as possible.

APPLAUSE AT THE OPERA AND AT CONCERTS

It is proper at the opera to applaud after arias—the "claque" usually indicates when—and of course at each curtain. Entrances should not be applauded—but sometimes are by the over-enthusiastic who thus break the spell of the introductory measures.

At concerts applause is held, even after a solo, until the conductor, by turning on the podium toward the audience, indicates that the selection is over. Even at the end of a program the enchantment should never be broken by applause until the conductor has turned for his bow to the audience. His each appearance from the wings is applauded, however, but the house becomes quiet the minute he turns to face the orchestra.

BEHAVIOR AT THE THEATER

It is not fashionable to be late for the theater at any time. On important opening nights, with everyone vying to be later than the next celebrity so as to steal the spotlight, such showing-off often delays the curtain interminable minutes, thus penalizing those courteous enough to be prompt and modest in their behavior. Anyone late for the first act should be considerate enough to stand at the back of the theater until the act is over, even if an usher is permitted to seat late-comers. An exception might be the holder of an aisle seat who could slip into it with the minimum of disturbance to others.

SEATING   The host (or hostess in a party of women) produces the tickets at the door and stands back to let guests file in. Guests then wait until the host or hostess may precede them with the usher to their seats. The hostess in a mixed group places a man first in a line of seats so a woman guest need not sit next to a stranger. She also places a man, usually the host, on the aisle. If two women must sit together in such an arrangement, one is the hostess.

The host sees to it that each guest has a program, and he also offers to secure cold drinks during the intermission.

Men and women may file out together during intermission to smoke in the lobby, or the women may stay together in their seats while the men go out after asking to be excused. No one woman is left alone, however, except in the case of a couple, and then the man may ask to be excused briefly after seeing that his companion is comfortable.

TALKING Talking during the progress of a play, concert, or opera, is very bad manners and usually brings down well-deserved shushing from neighboring seats.

EATING Candy or other things should not be noisily passed or eaten during a performance. Even the rattle of candy papers can disturb others, and the bending forward of heads over a candy box can obscure the view of those behind. Candy may be passed during intermissions.

ATTENDING AUCTIONS

Any auction at all is fun so far as I'm concerned. An *aficionado* begins to appreciate the very special show the auctioneer puts on and to understand his rage, real or simulated, at the interruptions from, and the mistakes of, tyro bidders. For there are definite rules of behavior and of bidding at auctions.

The uninitiated often comes away from any auction laden with white elephants, for which he has paid a price out of proportion to that the articles would have brought when new or in good guaranteed condition in an antique shop. In his excitement, and from his tenth-row perch on a precarious folding chair, he does not notice the virtually unrepairable filigree on the Victorian what-is-it nor the crack in the milk glass compote which renders it valueless as a collector's piece. Most auctions hold exhibition days prior to the actual auction day, and careful inspection of merchandise before the excitement of competitive bidding begins can save money and disillusionment.

INSPECT BEFORE YOU BUY In most auctions where many items are to be put up each is ticketed with an identifying number and these numbers with descriptions are sometimes listed in a catalogue. Note the numbers of things which interest you and their condition. If possible, make up your mind beforehand on where you are going to put this particular piece in your probably overcrowded home, and then be sure that you have an approximate idea of what such things have been bringing at other auctions or in shops. One way to be knowledgeable of current values is to attend a few auctions without your wallet, just to get an idea of the market.

ORDER OF SALE If you cannot stay all day at a sale, you can often find out in advance, especially if the articles are numbered, which will be offered in the morning, which in the afternoon, although you are always taking a chance that the sale will move along faster than the auctioneer expects. Sales are usually geared so the less valuable things are offered during the time the crowd is still congregating. But in these early hours of the sale prices are usually relatively high, because the amateur auction-goers are there with money to spend and feel they must start spending it right away. By late afternoon, if they stick, they usually have qualms of conscience and pains in the pocketbook, leaving the fields to fresher aspirants and to the dealers. The bargains are usually found in the last hour of the sale, because people have become conservative and tired and the dealers have bought what they came after. The auctioneer is hoarse and wants to get home and is inclined to cut short the bidding.

ASKING FOR SPECIFIC ITEMS   If you wish to have something that's taken your fancy put up for sale at a time before you must leave, you may discuss the possibility with the management, preferably before the selling starts. If your choice is a major item in the sale, it is unlikely that the auctioneer will oblige you, but he may be willing to tell you at about what price he thinks it will go and you can leave your bid with him or with one of his assistants in the hope of success.

THE AUCTION STARTS   Arrive at an auction a good half hour before the sale in order to get a seat that will provide you with a clear view of the articles offered. Even if you have attended the exhibition-before-sale, you may not remember everything that interested you or, even if you have made notes, things may move too quickly. Items tucked away on shelves may look more attractive—or less—under the lights.

CAREFUL WITH YOUR HANDS AND GREETINGS   Women especially create havoc at auctions by waving to their friends and nodding to acquaintances. "If you have the urge to wave your hands, ladies," I heard one New England auctioneer say bitterly, "*sit* on them. Otherwise I'll think you're upping the bid."

BID EVEN AMOUNTS   When items in an auction are expected to bring less than a dollar they are usually bulked together with other low-value things and offered as a miscellaneous lot. The auctioneer usually tries to start the bidding at a dollar, but if it is apparent that he will be unsuccessful you may call out any figure you wish, so long as it is a multiple of five. If you feel brave, you can even begin at five cents, but don't bid an odd amount such as thirteen cents, which would be unacceptable.

CONFUSION IN BIDDING   Sometimes two bidders will name the same bid at the same moment, making it impossible for the auctioneer to accept one or the other. He seizes on the amount only as a springboard to the next increase, which should come from one of the two competitors. "M. K. and Griffin both offer eighteen dollars," he will announce from his stand. "M. K., will you make it twenty?"

If you have made a bid and hear the auctioneer calling it, yet are unsure if it is your bid he's accepted, get his eye and point questioningly to yourself. If it's your bid, he'll tell you so and you will then not be in the possible position of raising your own bid, a raise you can't refute once you've made it at least without causing any comment.

A beginner can be very embarrassed by not knowing the procedure on group or pair sales. Again, listen carefully, and be sure you know whether a pair of lamps—or a group of assorted after-dinner cups and saucers—is being offered with the price to be established for one applicable to the others and the successful bidder getting first choice of the others, or whether, in bidding on one, you must take the mate or each object in the group at the price of one. Inattention here may mean you have involved yourself in the purchase of ten porcelain cups at five dollars each rather than the whole ten at five dollars for the lot, which is what you thought you were bidding.

MUST THE AUCTIONEER ACCEPT YOUR BID? Suppose the crowd at the auction is small and obviously intent on buying one sort of thing, say, odd lots of kitchen and household equipment, and uninterested in some valuable offering such as a grand piano also in the sale. Must the auctioneer sell the piano even if he gets only picayune bids? If the auction is "unrestricted" he must sell everything, no matter how low the final bids. But usually he is allowed to use his discretion and to refuse to sell something very greatly below its expected auction price. Instead he may withdraw it from the sale.

DO YOU GIVE YOUR NAME? When you have made one purchase and you are asked for a deposit or the full amount, you are also asked your name. It is not necessary to give your real name. You may say, "Mrs. R. K." or "California" or anything that comes to your mind, if for some reason you do not wish your own name announced so publicly, because as you make other later bids, your name is called out in connection with your bid.

The auctioneer will shout, "What am I bid on this superlative stoneware platter? Do I hear ten dollars?" He hasn't heard ten dollars, but he's hopeful that someone who doesn't know this device to trap a generous bid will *think* he has and scramble to up the price to eleven. Let us assume that you would like to start the bidding at five dollars. You gesture to him, palm down with a cutting gesture to the side, and he knows you want to halve his suggested price. He will then call out, "Mrs. R. K. bids five dollars" or "I have a bid of five dollars, do I hear ten?" He may again hear nothing at all despite a great show of excitement and shouting. Be careful at this point not to outbid yourself and so pay more than necessary.

The auctioneer, when he calls out the opening bid, is sometimes bidding for a dealer who has commissioned him to buy this piece at a certain price, if possible. Then he may open the bidding by calling, "I *have* ten dollars— do I hear fifteen?" If you wish to increase the bid to such an extent, you may nod if you can catch his eye in time—or that of one of the helpers—or raise your hand quickly. Bids on valuable glass and china and on furniture, pictures, rugs, and other things expected to sell at fairly substantial prices usually rise, at first, in five, ten, twenty-five dollar, or even much higher units. As the bidding draws to a close, increases are less—one of fifty cents or a dollar may turn the trick, although a fifty-cent bid on something that's reached eighty dollars may call down the auctioneer's wrath upon you (which needn't trouble you at all). If you want to increase a bid by one dollar, hold your closed fist aloft with one finger lifted—the sign for a one-dollar bid. Two dollars, two fingers, etc.

DEALERS AS YOUR COMPETITORS   You can easily identify dealers at auctions. They know what's there in advance, and they bid professionally with a nod of the head, hand signals, or other methods of their own devising—such as lifting the hat or pulling the ear lobe. They are quiet and seemingly uninterested, and it is quite obvious that they are known to the auction personnel, who watch their reactions as each thing is put up. Auctioneers often refer to them in their spiel. "A fine piece, isn't it, Mr. Prentice?"—Or more likely "Mr. P," as dealers like to be as inconspicuous and dead-pan as possible. Beware the price when the dealers withdraw from the bidding, for they are probably doing so because they can't compete with some moneyed collector who must have a sought-after piece at any price and does not need to consider shop overhead and resale value.

IMPERFECT MERCHANDISE   A conscientious auctioneer will frankly state the condition of the items he is auctioning. He may say, "This Aubusson carpet is slightly worn in the center but can be repaired" or "This daisy and button spoon holder has a small chip on the under side of the base which doesn't affect its appearance, but I want you to know you are buying it 'as is.' " If he doesn't describe the article properly as to condition or if he makes a flat statement that something is in perfect condition, and you find, on delivery to you in the auction room, that the article is broken, you need not accept it. The auctioneer may either put it back in the sale to be sold "as is," or he may withdraw it from sale entirely.

CHECKING FOR AUTHENTICITY   Listen carefully to the auctioneer's descriptions. You may become so excited about the possibility of acquiring something that you will not notice that he said, "*supposed* to be a Chippendale original," and you will buy a chair at a fantastic price only to find when you get it home that it is one of the myriad reproductions of the master craftsman's work, although it may be quite a good, sound chair at that. Or the auctioneer may carry on an engaging repartee with one of his assistants, "This *is* cranberry glass, the real thing, don't you think, Bill?" Bill may mutter that he "doesn't know a thing about it but it's a pretty pitcher all right," but the impression may remain in your mind and in other minds, too, that the auctioneer has authenticated the piece on which you are bidding, when as a matter of cold fact he hasn't at all.

MORE CAREFUL INSPECTION   If the bidding is running close on some large piece and you are doubtful whether it is worth an increased bid from you, you are privileged to go up and inspect it more closely, as dealers often do, so long as you don't interrupt the auctioneer. If he feels you are seriously interested, however, he will often pause until you have had a chance to make up your mind, especially if you make it a practice not to leave your seat for this purpose except under exceptional circumstances. If there is a pause in the auctioneer's chant, you might call out, "May I see that more closely?" Or if one of the porters is carrying, say, a set of dishes through the audience, you may summon him to you by calling, not gesturing, as any gesture may be interpreted as an increase in bid.

BUYING ANTIQUES The buying of antiques, if it is informed and intelligent, is an investment. The wise buyer should think in terms of resale value, even if he plans to use the piece in his own home. Homes are smaller and smaller, and people as they grow older these days tend to move to more manageable quarters. Often such lovingly collected things must be sold. So it is sensible to consider that possibility when you buy at an auction. Get things in good or really restorable condition (no cracked or chipped china or glass, though, with certain rare exceptions), and pay no more than you would be willing to pay for the equivalent in a modest antique shop. Antiques as sold in high-price city shops are not good criteria in judging market value, although almost any good antique will increase in value over the years. New furniture, glass, and china become merely secondhand if you wish to sell them.

PAYING BY CHECK If you establish your identity with those in charge before an auction begins, you can usually pay by check at the end of the sale for all the things you buy. Otherwise, the minute your bid is accepted you will probably be expected to make at least a deposit in cash on the article, in proportion to its selling price, and you may on small items be asked to pay up immediately in full. Hold on to each receipt. Where no deposit is requested, as sometimes happens as country auctions or where you are known, the bookkeeper makes up your statement as the sale proceeds.

On furniture and bulky things and on merchandise on which you have merely paid a deposit you are expected to wait until the end of the selling day (or until a luncheon recess) before demanding your bill and merchandise. This is because the porters are occupied in moving the various objects to and from the auction platform.

DELIVERY OF MERCHANDISE Large items are removed from the auction room, home, or gallery, if possible, the day of sale with the cost of removal borne by the buyer. Often the auctioneering organization will arrange crating and shipping for you, where necessary, or arrange to have some local carter pick up your purchase or purchases for delivery to you. Large auction rooms sometimes permit you to leave things you have bought for a day or two, but at country auctions things must be cleared out, usually, by the end of each day, especially on a one-day sale.

Be careful of what you sign in this final transaction. The auctioneer's responsibility for the merchandise ceases the minute you have paid over your money, even though he may do you the courtesy of letting you store it a day or so. The express or moving company may give you a contract that doesn't adequately protect your shipment in the event of damage or loss. It may provide for the settlement of any claim on a *per pound* basis. Be sure you don't run the risk of losing your prize through carelessness in delivery. Insist on knowing any additional shipping rates that offer more complete and fair coverage of what you have bought. Or take out an additional floater policy to cover the load in case of fire, theft, or damage.

QUIET, PLEASE   Many people at auctions earn their livings through them, one way or the other. They don't want to be distracted from what they are doing by unnecessary comings and goings, loud conversation, or other interruptions. The auctioneer is, of course, under a certain strain trying to hear and sift all the bids. So be as quiet as possible and never lean over to speak to an active bidder or you may spoil his chance of getting the bid. Never make audibly derisive remarks about the things up for auction or you may be neatly and clearly reprimanded by the irritated auctioneer. I once heard a Yankee auctioneer, who overheard a woman snorting about some soaring knickknack that she "had one just like that at home," say cuttingly, "Madam, you have my *sympathy*."

THE COUNTRY AUCTION

DIFFERENT AUCTIONS, DIFFERENT ATMOSPHERES   Most informal is the country auction which takes place in an auction barn, at a farm or country place, or on a church grounds. Lunch is usually served by the Ladies' Aid or by a local caterer, and the whole affair is somewhat in the nature of an outing. The country auctioneer, usually native to the terrain, is well worth his hire for the show he puts on and his usually shrewd knowledge of what he is selling. Close attention to his sales talk can give you an insight on what things have become collectors' items, what criteria to use in buying furniture, glass, or china. He shows you the pontil marks, scrapes off a bit of varnish to verify his suspicion that a chest is pumpkin pine, throws in a little history, rings a goblet to prove its soundness and quality, and in general conducts himself with an open charm often missing in the smooth, abrupt, matter-of-fact auctioneers found on any side street of the cities.

The country auction, especially if it's held out-of-doors, is loud and boisterous, often intimate. A woman, who missed out in getting the miscellaneous lot, including the wash boiler, she wanted, can and does make a side deal with the buyer—who didn't want the wash boiler but did want the ten yards of good clothesline. In big cities, except where the auction rooms are open to the street, bidding is mostly by signal and the auctioneer is relatively subdued. Business is conducted in an impersonal manner, usually for cash.

CHAPTER SIXTY-THREE

YOUR PRESS RELATIONS

THE GOSSIP COLUMNIST AND THE SOCIETY WRITER

Celebrities and notorious characters, scandal and helpful publicity, all go into the potpourri of the gossip column. Next to the doings of one of society's most conservative older hostesses is the latest witticism of an underworld character, with the writer, or so one assumes by his easy reference, on intimate terms with both. He may well be, or at least his sources are more or less reliable. The dowager may be annoyed to find her dinner-table conversation quoted in a chitchat column read avidly by several million people. She may look suspiciously at her new butler, but she'd be more right in suspecting some ambitious young career person in her circle who gets around and who is regularly called upon by the best-known columnists to furnish material for their columns. This opportunist is flattered by the attention given his more or less accurate reportage and his compensation is an occasional reciprocal item plugging something that interests him.

Is it possible for a well-known individual to keep out of gossip columns? Probably not, for even if his behavior is exemplary, his conversation dull and quoteless, his appearance unspectacular, his name or connections will still be grist for the mill. He will find restaurants quietly pointing out his presence to interested reporters, and columnists will be noting the girls he escorts. Short of never going out of his own door, he will have to endure it, for there is a free press in this country. If the reportage becomes really damaging he always has recourse to the libel laws.

The average individual patronizing newsworthy restaurants, first-night performances, charity benefits, and other places where society and gossip columnists gather will not find himself in print unless he or she makes news in some way. The playboy who stood on his head at the opera certainly did not expect his performance to go unremarked. The debutante who, perhaps in sheer desperation because she has not been photographed quite as much as her sister debs that season, enters a night club with a gazelle on a leash, can be virtually sure to make at least a line of print somewhere. The dowager who chats unrestrainedly with the nice man whose face looks familiar but whose name she didn't catch should not be irritated to find some of her more choice observations quoted.

WHAT ABOUT PICTURES?

Most people in public life learn to be gracious about posing for news pictures. There is a nice balance between self-important reticence and pleasant willingness, if asked, but the individual who virtually thrusts himself before every camera makes himself as ridiculous as the one who goes to fantastic lengths to avoid it. Sometimes by being a super-shy subject a celebrity puts a virtual premium on his pictures and is thus pursued twice as much as the agreeable newsworthy sitter.

Reasonable requests for photographs that do not violate good taste or infringe too much on privacy are usually granted if the purpose of the picture is carefully explained. Releases permitting the use of photographs should not be signed without being read. Publications using news photographs for which no release was signed do so with the understanding that they were taken with the subject's consent and knowledge. If you pose willingly and then, not liking the result in the paper or magazine, threaten suit, you have no case. Even if the shot of you has been "stolen," you probably have no case either unless you can prove beyond a doubt that the picture has in some way injured your reputation, caused you anguish, or interfered with your ability to work. Few such suits are ever brought. No suit followed even in the celebrated case of the great financier who allowed himself to be photographed with a midget on his knee under the misapprehension that it was a child.

ENDORSEMENTS

Socially prominent people or those well-known in arts, sports, or business are often asked to give their endorsements to various commercial products. Large sums are frequently paid to the sponsors of the products and often a fee goes to the person proposing or arranging the tie-up.

Many of the most conservative people in the country have given endorsements strictly on a business basis and with no pretense that the money received is to be given to a "favorite charity." If a society woman is asked by a cigarette company to pose in front of the fireplace in her country home smoking its brand of cigarette in return for several thousand dollars, she can be sure she is giving value for the money she receives.

While it is now acceptable for prominent people to give their endorsements to various products for a fee or in some cases for the reciprocal publicity, the boundaries of good taste should never be overstepped. It is assumed, and it should be true, that the copy accompanying the photograph or drawing of the individual and its use in the layout has been approved by him or her. It would be poor taste, of course, to allow this copy to be too explicit about one's possessions. You could permit yourself to be called "wealthy" or "socially prominent," but not "the heiress to $20,000,000." Your parents or grandparents might be mentioned, if their names are what make you socially prominent, but preferably not without their knowledge and consent if they are living. The use of their names in an advertisement, even just to identify you, constitutes an oblique endorsement of the product to which exception might well be taken.

WHAT TO INDORSE Foods, liquors, cosmetics, cigarettes, furnishings, cars, radios, musical instruments, various means of transportation are among the things it is socially permissible to endorse. Anything too intimate and personal —depilatories, mouth washes, tooth pastes, foundation garments, underwear, stockings, patent medicines—is, obviously, unsuited to social endorsement.

It is important, not only to know what the copy is and how it is to be used in connection with an approved photograph, but also to approve, in writing, the final proof of the advertisement before it begins to run in the chosen publications. The schedule of publications chosen should also be approved. Blanket permission to run an endorsement indefinitely in the same or different advertisements and in direct mail advertising should not be given. Approval of each separate advertisement or variation of it should be insisted upon. Any major additions to the original, approved schedule for the advertisement should be okayed, too, and, if a fee is involved, the fee should be increased proportionally. Otherwise it is possible for an advertiser to base his advertising campaign for years to come on the same personality without additional payment, should the firm so desire. Therefore, all permissions should be specific and with necessary limitations on the use of the endorsement.

BE FAIR AND HONEST Advertisers expect endorsers to use or accept for use the products they publicly endorse. An individual who regularly smokes one kind of cigarette and then appears in an endorsement with a statement that he smokes another kind *exclusively*, may cause an investigation by the Federal Trade Commission, which is greatly concerned with fair advertising practices. If you endorse products, use them, or at least possess them for possible use. And do not endorse a product that competes with another you have formerly endorsed. Always tell querying advertisers what you have already endorsed or what you are considering endorsing.

YOU AND THE LAW

We are protected by law from true invasion of our privacy, and we need never answer any question put to us by the press if for some reason we do not wish to. Courtesy to the press and consideration of the reporters' orders from their editors to "get the news" should temper possible irritation with individual insistence. It is often better to give what news there is to give, in a dignified manner, than to deny an interview, for reporters then must get the information from others or write speculative stories stating that you "refused to comment" or you "refused to confirm or deny."

Do not talk freely to newspaper people over the phone or in a personal interview and then ask them not to print what you have told them—or worse, later try to deny that you said what you did say. Never ask a reporter to submit what he has written about you before publication, especially if you have sought the interview. The possible exception is when the material is of a technical nature, possibly scientific, in which case a reporter unfamiliar with the subject may ask to have his article checked by the interviewee before publication. Otherwise, a publication is responsible for damaging misquotation. Most reporters are careful to quote correctly.

SPECIAL PRESS PROBLEMS

When there is occasion for news of your activities to reach the press it is well, if possible, to have the main facts in writing for distribution to inquiring reporters. In the case, for example, of prominent people seeking a divorce, a fact already widely known to their friends, insistent queries from the press are referred to the wife, who may avoid discussion of the painful subject by issuing a brief written statement to reporters, to the effect that she and her husband have separated and that she is or is not seeking a divorce and if so, where and when. This information, terse and direct, in writing, tends to discourage the gossipy kind of news coverage that is so unpleasant to sensitive people.

It is inevitable, if people are prominent, that such news concerning them will reach the press eventually. It is preferable to have it brief and controlled. Certainly no one of taste discusses intimate difficulties with the press. Discreet public behavior should be part of the effort to avoid blatant publication of marital or other family troubles. If unpleasant news does get out, it may be countered by a short statement, preferably from a family representative. A social secretary might hand reporters a typewritten statement like this, in the case of separation and impending divorce:

Mrs. Emmett Coles Freylingheusen regrets to announce that she is leaving on Thursday for her home in Palm Beach, to institute divorce proceedings against Mr. Freylingheusen. A separation agreement has been reached.

The principals need not see the press themselves but should refer to the statement as embodying all they can say at the moment. It is gratifying that the public forgets very quickly.

In the event of news interest in a possible romance between a prominent man and woman who is not in the public eye, the man should not permit himself to be trapped into making any announcement of marriage plans, or, on the other hand, a denial of them, as either of these two announcements places a woman in an awkward position—as if she were of too little social consequence to reply for herself. A gentleman approached by the press concerning his interest in a lady he has been seen escorting must be very careful, if his interest is quite platonic, not to give the impression in his reply to queries that this would be the last woman on earth to appeal to him. No woman is ever flattered by outraged denial of any interest in her. The proper way to handle such a query has not only to do with the words spoken but the way they are spoken and the manner of the speaker. A reporter, convinced by the frank manner of a man he's been asked to interview concerning a rumored marriage, is likely to skip the whole thing if the denial has been a simple, "Yes, I know Miss Jones. She's a charming girl but I am only one of her many escorts. It would be a good story if there were something to say but there really isn't."

If there really is a romance, with marriage plans about to be announced and the press so avid for the news that is seems impossible to hold it up for formal announcement to the papers from the girl's family, then the prospective bridegroom, if queried, may say, "Yes, I know Miss Jones. But any plans we may have will be announced by her family [or by her]." Sometimes in such cases a joint press conference is granted, with the girl protected by her fiancé or his press representatives from too personal questions.

CHAPTER SIXTY-FOUR

YOU AND CELEBRITIES

HOW NOT TO TREAT A CELEBRITY

Fame sits uncomfortably on many celebrities. It is safer to assume that they do not wish to appear unduly conspicuous than to behave as if they desired public attention. Perhaps it depends very much on the kind of activity that has brought fame. A movie star or actor who can go with impunity into a restaurant or other public place and have people pay little or no attention to him is undoubtedly not buoyed up by the well-bred lack of stir he creates. On the other hand, an Einstein or a Heifetz hopes to live a normal life among others, without being forever pointed out and approached by autograph hunters. And certainly not even the most publicity-loving movie star can enjoy having the clothes torn literally off his back. Physical discomfort—even danger—and continual lack of privacy are a high price to pay for so ephemeral a thing as fame in the entertainment field.

ASKING FOR AUTOGRAPHS

The autograph of a really famous person, even if he is still alive, has a financial value—it can be bought and sold like a commodity. The more autographs such a person gives, the lower the market value of the autograph. You may desire an autograph for a serious collection of your own or for one you may be starting for a child, but you may be quickly rebuffed if the object of your interest is someone who rarely, if ever, gives an autograph because he knows that those that exist are bought and sold. Why should he stop and hand you, a stranger, the equivalent of a few dollars? On the other hand, even such hardened cynics as George Bernard Shaw in the matter of autographs have been known to respond to a really sincere appeal from someone who seems moved by admiration rather than the profit motive in making such a request. Remember, autographs given freely to all and sundry have no value either historically or monetarily (if that interests you). The rare ones are the good ones, if the person who gives them is of the stuff that makes for more than transitory fame.

If you are really interested in the subject, study it and be an intelligent collector—not just a grabber of meaningless signatures in an autograph book. I'd rather encourage a child to ask grown-up friends to save important signatures for him from their own mail or collect them for him as a result of their connections, than have him turn into a little autograph-pest with no ability to discriminate between the worth-while and the meretricious. To ask a really important person to sign an autograph book full of the names of nobodies is to insult him, no matter how graciously he may rise to the occasion in his acceptance of the request—or more probably, in his refusal.

ENTERTAINING THE CELEBRITY

If you had a banker in to dinner, you'd hardly ask him to set up a cashier's desk and put on a little demonstration after dinner of how the bank handles money. Why, then, ask a famous singer who innocently enough has accepted your invitation to dinner, to literally sing for his supper? Would you ask a famous designer to run you up a dress? I can cite an actual case of a high-priced hat designer, though, who, having been invited to dinner—and a none-too-good home-cooked meal it was, she says—was presented a lapful of the hostess's old hats immediately after dinner, with the request she retrim them, then and there.

Be very diffident indeed about requesting any of these professional people to render their services to you without pay. They need recreation, too. As a matter of fact, whether they are guests in your home or not, never ask authors to read your manuscript, playwrights to go over your play, singers to appraise your voice unless they maintain such advisory service on a professional basis—in which case they should be approached in their offices, not in your own home.

Don't invite celebrities to your home and then surround them with numerous uncongenial people whom you wish to impress by the fact that you have snared a literary or other lion. Treat a celebrity as you would any other honored guest. Provide him with good talk, good food, decent privacy. Don't expect him to repay your hospitality with a free performance of his specialty.

LO, THE POOR AUTHOR

The general public is under the misapprehension that authors get limitless numbers of free copies of their books to dispense to friends and acquaintances. Many think the most flattering thing you can say to an author is, "Will you be sure to give me an autographed copy the minute the book comes out?"

Actually, in standard contracts, an author receives six free copies of his book as *part of his remuneration*. If he wants to sell them, that's between him and the Bureau of Internal Revenue. But his agent, his mother, his wife, his mother-in-law, and his closest friends all expect one of these precious copies. And he needs one or two for his reference library. He is acutely embarrassed by requests for copies of his books, for he can't fill them except by paying his publisher for the books—at a discount, possibly, but nevertheless, it is money out of pocket.

It is, of course, all right to request an author to put you on the mailing list for information concerning the publication of the book. Publishers like to have lists of interested people and sometimes take advance orders by mail for the first edition of a book from those people who have put themselves on record as especially eager concerning it.

It isn't fair, however, to ask an author to get his own or other books from his publisher for you at the trade discount. Such little transactions always mean extra bookkeeping and are a real nuisance to all involved.

8 OFFICIAL ETIQUETTE FOR CIVILIANS

Attending Annapolis Hops   607

Visiting West Point   612

Etiquette for the Bride of the Military Man   616

Ship Launchings and Visiting a Naval Vessel   619

The New Resident in Washington   625

The Flag and Our National Anthem   628

OFFICIAL ETIQUETTE FOR CIVILIANS

The civilian once under the mantle of officialdom, wherever it may be, is subject to the rules governing civilian behavior under official circumstances. The flag, for example, is our official emblem and a designer may not turn it into an evening wrap, however high her motive may be. A father visiting his son at Annapolis is subject to regulations even in respect to his son. He should not, for example, offer him a drink on or off the Reservation.

Transatlantic passengers are civilians subject to the captain, whose law is final aboard his ship. Visitors to military posts and installations, to government buildings and monuments, to national airports, and many other public places are subject to official regulations governing them.

In Washington, especially in time of war or during periods of great defensive preparation, protocol changes very rapidly. Armed with basic information on Washington's social pattern, the newcomer may consult his representatives for recent changes in procedure. Anyone planning to move to the capital and to entertain diplomatic and government representatives virtually requires the services of a social secretary on a regular basis or as needed, depending on the extent to which the new resident hopes to enter into this life so concerned with protocol. But even the casual visitor to Washington often needs to know something of its social requirements.

Each of us, at one time or another, will very likely find himself in a situation that calls for at least a modicum of knowledge of official etiquette. The section following endeavors to give the salient points of official protocol and to reassure the civilian who is frequently appalled and sometimes frightened by the official mind at work.

CHAPTER SIXTY-FIVE

ATTENDING ANNAPOLIS HOPS

A date at Annapolis is a coveted one for any girl and one, I hope, she has at least once in her lifetime if she can possibly arrange it. Annapolis means, of course, the United States Naval Academy at Annapolis, capital of Maryland, the naval equivalent of the Army's West Point. Its four-year course of college study, with accent on things naval, leads to a Bachelor of Science degree.

A man to be admitted to Annapolis (or to West Point) must be an excellent physical and mental specimen. Although most students (called midshipmen) are appointees by Senators, Congressmen, and President and all get college education free, they may come from any family, rich or poor. Even though Uncle Sam gives the midshipman his training, he must fulfill certain rigid standards of intelligence, of moral and physical fitness. While he is at Annapolis he is a poor man, for no matter what his financial background he must live as the other midshipmen live and get along on a small amount of spending money—as little as three dollars a month for a plebe, or fourth year man, and thirteen dollars a month for a first classman (senior). Out of this come all extras—entertaining of "drags" (dates), soft drinks (midshipmen are not to drink), candy, stamps, and sundries. A girl who accepts an invitation to Annapolis for the week end pays for her transportation there and back and for her hotel or other accommodations. However, her escort can quite correctly make her reservations for her, probably at Carvel Hall for the first trip, and later at one of the approved guest houses run, more out of civic duty than for possible revenue, by some of the fine old families of Annapolis. Fifteen dollars is about as much as any girl can possibly use once she is at Annapolis and this will even include modest bus or interurban trolley transportation costs from nearby Washington or Baltimore. Most girls arrive by these public conveyances, because only first classmen ride in cars, except during June Week when the entire "brigade" may ride and first classmen may even drive their own cars.

No Saturday bus arriving in Annapolis before one o'clock may be met, as midshipmen are confined to the reservation in the morning. If you arrive before that time—and, of course, all the arrangements for this big week end have been made weeks, maybe months, in advance—you take a taxi to your hotel or the approved private home where you are to stay. You are careful to eat lunch before the start of your date, not only out of consideration for your midshipman's pocket money (he refers to it as "the monthly insult"), but to save time, every minute of which is carefully accounted for. For example, a fourth year man is allowed no more than sixty minutes to get you home from the hop. Infractions of rules mean demerits for your escort. Unbecoming behavior, or even unthinking behavior on your part, that brings censure on him—unspoken or not—means no future week ends at Annapolis for you.

The Navy is no place for individualism. That goes for the girl who is the guest of the Navy, and that is the way you should think of yourself. You are the guest of the Navy and subject to strict naval etiquette, not just the guest of an individual member of the Navy—for though your man is still in Annapolis, he is nevertheless as much in the Navy as an enlisted man. Your date will probably be a third, second, or first year man, for fourth year men, or plebes, are permitted to "drag" only once during the year previous to the Farewell Ball in June Week.

If you are met—and never be later than one o'clock—you will be starting off right if you have brought a minimum of luggage, preferably one light bag. You will need neither golf sticks nor riding clothes. You don't need a bathing suit. All social activities are within prescribed limits, so don't plan on taking your man for a little run down to Chevy Chase to see Aunt Prue.

Mrs. Grundy may have retired in the big cities, but at Annapolis she is omnipotent. Even at a private house where there may be no one else to do it your escort may not carry your bag to your room. He must leave it in the hall or parlor, and you, if necessary, must carry it the rest of the way. And even if you are engaged, don't try to hold hands with him in public, don't take his arm on limits, or expect him to walk arm-in-arm or with his arms around your waist—"lollygagging" is the Navy term for such relaxed behavior.

It is, literally, a felony for a midshipman to take a drink within seven miles of the Academy Chapel Dome—and he isn't allowed to go beyond that seven-mile limit! So for a girl to take liquor with her, even for her own use in her room, is poor form, to say the least. And it is against the rules for her to take it there if her room is in a hotel. Even beer may not be served to midshipmen in public restaurants in Annapolis, and for their "drags" to take it when they can't is certainly impolite.

On the usual Annapolis week end, never depend on receiving flowers from your escort, though in June Week he probably will be able to manage them for you. Everyone understands the economics of this, and for a moneyed "drag" to bedeck herself in orchids is to proclaim that she has bought them for herself—or accepted them from a non-Annapolis admirer, an unpardonable sin.

The naval reservation is referred to as the "Yard." Within its confines you are subject to strict naval rules. You smoke in "Smoke Hall" (the recreation room in Bancroft Hall) but not on the street (I hope you won't do that anywhere) or on the dance floor. Your midshipman may not chew gum in public, and you should not either while you are with him.

The Navy man has conservatism drilled into him in all things touching on social and naval behavior. If you do anything to make a big splash, by wearing too sophisticated clothes or too conspicuous and expensive jewelry, by drinking, or by any attention-drawing behavior, you embarrass him, to say the least. He will wonder why he ever risked inviting you.

CLOTHES NEEDED

Saturday noon to Sunday afternoon doesn't call for a very extensive wardrobe. If you try to ring in numerous changes, you will be wasting the time and temper of your escort and very probably infuriating the dates of his classmates. Here's the maximum you'll need, in addition to underclothing:

1. Traveling suit or sport dress (you'll arrive in it and wear it Saturday afternoon, for the game or a walk, and leave in it).
2. Comfortable walking shoes—one pair for suit, one pair for dress (high heels would be murder on those cobblestones).
3. Sneakers or rubber-soled saddle oxfords in summer for possible sailing. (Never wear leather-heeled shoes on a sailboat.)
4. Warm, carefully-tailored slacks, socks, and sweaters for sailing. (It gets mighty cold if you have a long beat in.) Shorts, though not prohibited, are frowned upon.
5. A waterproof topcoat because you'll walk, no matter what the weather, even in evening clothes.
6. A becoming but not too spectacular evening dress and accessories for dancing Saturday night.
7. An evening wrap or, in winter, a fur coat or jacket (but the men hate shedable "bunny" fur, especially in angora jackets or sweaters because it comes off on their blues). The right kind of rather dressy raincoat can serve as topcoat, evening wrap, and raincoat. You'll be better off with it than with a perishable evening wrap, because it's better not to ask a midshipman to carry an umbrella.
8. Those zip-up plastic and packable galoshes that can be worn over evening shoes in case of bad weather.
9. A scarf or hood to keep your head dry. Taxis don't drive into the Yard with midshipmen.
10. A daytime dress for church and for Sunday dinner.
11. A hat for church.

THE HOP

The Annapolis Hop (dance) occurs at nine o'clock on most Saturday nights during the Academy year and is always formal. An official hostess presides, one whose husband is on duty at the Academy. At the opening ball in the fall and at the Graduation Hop in June Week either the "First Lady," wife of the superintendent or the wife of the commandant receives. She is assisted by the chairman of the hop committee, who introduces those approaching the receiving line to the hostess, after first being presented to the guests himself by their escorts.

The superintendent or the commandant usually receives with his wife, as do various of the senior officers and their wives. It is, of course, necessary to go down the entire line as soon as you arrive. In greeting, look cordial, smile, and say, "How do you do," taking the proffered hand of hostesses and hosts. Never hold up the receiving line, even if you know a host or hostess well and this is your first encounter since your arrival. Conduct yourself with dignity and nicely adjusted dispatch. Even if you have removed your evening gloves during the dancing, put them back on for the farewells. Remember, a lady does not remove her gloves to shake hands (but see Business Calls at the White House). This is a man's gesture.

It is compulsory to be at a Hop on time and to remain until "The Star-Spangled Banner" is played at midnight. Wandering out of the hall is strictly contrary to regulations.

ENTERTAINMENT OF MIDSHIPMEN

If this is your first invitation from a midshipman, it is usual for him to do whatever modest entertaining is possible for him. On successive trips—assuming you're lucky—you may in all propriety invite him to Sunday dinner at your hotel, usually Carvel Hall, where his check can be put on your bill without embarrassment to him. Taking him to any of the little, inexpensive tearooms in the area changes the situation, unless you can arrange beforehand for payment of your bill so that it won't be handed to him.

THE SOUVENIR HUNTER

All the gilt accessories a naval man wears cost money—cost him money, I should say, if they have to be replaced—as do buttons, buckles, and the gold-thread insignia. One such replacement for a midshipman might mean the loss of his spending money for the month. Asking for a miniature of his ring is actually proposing marriage. The ring in miniature is worn insignia-in as an engagement ring. The insignia is turned out after the marriage has taken place. Collecting fraternity pins may be considered fair sport by some admitted flirts, but the wearing of a Navy ring is a serious matter. Don't put on a midshipman's hat, either, unless, of course, you want him to kiss you. For him to refuse to do so under the circumstances would be for him to be guilty of behavior unbecoming to a Navy man.

ANNAPOLIS SLANG (WITH FULL CREDIT TO THE ACADEMY)

ANCHOR MAN The last man in his class

ARMY BRAT Son or daughter of an army officer

BILGE To be assigned to civilian duty; to flunk

BLACK "N" Mythical award for a major offense

BLIND DRAG A blind date

BOW WOW Battalion Officer of the Watch

BRACE UP To rotate hips, chest out, chin in

BREEZE, SHOOT THE Conversation

BRICK Blind date reputed to have looks, personality, and money and who turns out to have money only; to saddle one with such a date

BUCKET One who doesn't understand academic subjects

BUSH Weekly list of near-casualties in academics

BUZZARD Sleeve insignia of a midshipman petty officer

CHIT Note, statement, or requisition

CHOP Double time

CHOW HOUND Man who takes everything from the serving dish

C.I.S. Chit from best girl saying she married your buddy or any similar chit meaning "I can't come."

CLUTCH To freeze or blank out in a quiz

CUTTHROAT A greasy grind

DAGO Any foreign language taught at the Naval Academy

DEMO A demerit

DOPE Information on any subject

DRAG To escort; young lady escorted

EXTRA DUTY Disciplinary drill

EYES IN THE BOAT Head and eyes to the front

FIN OUT Fingers straightened at the side

FIRST-CLASS ALLEY Between the tables and the bulkhead in the mess

FLYING SQUADRON Those who run all the way back to the Rotunda after the Hop and are late anyway

FRAP Conduct report; put a man on conduct report

FRENCH OUT To take French leave

FRUIT Anything that insults the intelligence; easy

GEDUNK Anything purchased at the midshipmen's soda fountain

GOUGE Right answers

GREASE Influence aptitude for service

GREASY Said of one who butters up

GYRENE A marine

HAPPY HOUR Free study time

HOP Academy formal dance

JIMMYLEGS A yard watchman

JOE Coffee made by the men themselves, not in the galley

JOE GISH Midshipman John Doe

JUICE Electrical engineering

KAYDET A West Point cadet

MIDDY Odious maternal, newspaper, and Hollywood term for midshipman

MISERY HALL The infirmary

MONTHLY INSULT Pay

NAVY JUNIOR Son or daughter of a naval officer

NO-REG Not regulation

NUMBER JUMPER Greasy grind

O.A.O. One and only (sweetheart); one among others

PAP Same as frap; From "Publish and Post" appearing in the *Daily Report*

PLEBE Fourth classman

PODUNK The home town

P-WORK Any quiz covering more than one day's lesson

QUEEN Opposite of a brick; a dream girl

RACK OUT To take a nap

RADIATOR SQUAD Canteen society of non-athletes

RATEY   One assuming the privileges of a senior

RED MIKE   Loves wine and song but is faithful to the O.A.O.

REINA   The U.S.S. *Reina Mercedes,* the station ship

R.H.I.P.   Rank hath its privileges

RIVER   Term examination

ROBBER'S ROW   Maryland Avenue, the shopping center

SACK   Bed; responsibility you'd rather someone else had

SANDBLOWER   Shorty (he walks in a hole)

SAVOIR   Academically on the ball; opposite of bucket

SKINNY   Chemistry and physics

SLASH   To study excessively

SLIP-STICK   Slide rule

SNAKE   Stag

STEAM   Marine engineering

STEERAGE   The canteen

STRIPER   Midshipman officer in the brigade organization

SWABO   Zero

TEA FIGHT   Annapolis tea dance

TREE   Weekly list of those whose marks have been unsatisfactory

UNSAT   Not passing or one who is unsatisfactory

WIFE   Roommate

YARD ENGINE   A girl who lives inside the Yard

YOUNGSTER   Third classman

ZIP   Zero

CHAPTER SIXTY-SIX

VISITING WEST POINT

Many a teen ager dreams of being invited to a West Point Hop but, should the coveted invitation come, a girl hates to ask her escort what's expected of her. She likes to pretend at least that she knows all about the Point, that she has been invited there before, though unable to accept.

The cost of a West Point week end is very modest, even though the girl pays her own way some of the time. She is responsible for getting herself to the Point and back by train, bus, or her own car. Her cadet makes a dormitory room reservation for her, if possible at the U.S. Hotel Thayer, the hotel on the Reservation. The room cost is a dollar seventy-five per night and meals are available at moderate prices. If the Thayer is filled, the cadet arranges to put up his drag at approved quarters in the village, Highland Falls, through the Office of the Cadet Hostess, again at a dollar seventy-five per night, which is paid by the guest, of course.

The week-end guest is not met at the bus or train that took her to the Point but taxies to her designated quarters sometime Saturday morning. West Pointers have classes half a day Saturday but expect their dates to be available by 2 P.M. When there are home football games cadets are free at 1:30 P.M.

As at Annapolis, there are strict rules concerning transportation and other matters. At the Point a cadet may not drive a car but may be driven in his guest's car or in his family's car. So a girl with a car will prove popular with her escort and will not have to pay taxi fares (twenty-five cents, point to point) to the dress parade or chapel (a Sunday morning must for cadets—and the considerate guest goes, too).

A West Pointer is allowed to carry a small amount of money now but not enough to take care of all week-end entertainment. Off the Reservation, especially, the girl pays, quietly of course, although everyone knows the rules in this respect. And, as a West Point cadet is not permitted to drink at all, not even beer, a considerate guest does not drink in his presence and, of course, does not bring liquor of any kind into the Reservation itself, even for personal use.

There is usually a hop or other entertainment on Saturday night at the post, for which cadets make all arrangements. Fairly conservative dance dresses are worn. The girl showing up in attire more suited to burlesque than the starchy Point is unlikely to be asked back.

A cadet is conditioned to walking and expects his girl to be able to get around on her own two feet without wincing. A good pair of walking shoes is essential. A nicely tailored suit or a sweater and skirt is expected for sports or an afternoon walk. Slacks and shorts are never worn.

There is no riding for guests at the Point, but there is swimming in summer and ice skating in winter. A conservative bathing suit for swimming (and non-pretentious skating clothes in winter) is a safe choice. Unless you are a ballerina on skates, don't get yourself up in a fancy skating costume. Wear a sweater and skirt.

For Sunday chapel you will probably wear what you arrived in—a soft suit or dress and coat and of course a hat. If you want to wear flowers at any time, you will probably have to buy them yourself, except at Graduation Hop when the cadet traditionally sends them to his chosen girl.

It is poor taste at any time for a girl to smoke on the street, so don't smoke while walking with your cadet, who is not allowed to smoke on main roads and sidewalks. Don't take his arm or kiss him in public—don't even attempt to hold hands while on the Reservation, except on Flirtation Walk where a little romantic leeway is permitted. And, of course, you wait to be invited there.

At the Hop, guests and cadets all pass down the receiving line before beginning to dance. The line consists of, first, the Hop manager, then an officer's wife and her husband, chosen by the Hop manager to act as hosts for the evening. The cadet gives the name of his guest to the Hop manager as he approaches the line. The Hop manager then introduces the guest and the cadet to the hostess, who in turn presents them to the host.

After a Hop all classes may now escort their guests to their quarters, on or off the Reservation, but may not take more than one hour for the courtesy and may not enter any building after leaving the place of entertainment.

614

Even if you are a cadet's *best* girl, don't ask him for buttons (which are expensive) or for a miniature of his ring (which really is considered an engagement ring).

As West Point is near New York, it is possible for a cadet to get to town for dates. First classmen are allowed two week ends a month away from the Academy, second classmen are given just two a year. But even here, his spending money is very limited, and if you can't entertain him at home you must arrange entertainment for which you can quietly pay in advance.

WEST POINT SLANGUAGE (WITH FULL CREDIT TO THE POINT)

AIR GADGET Air cadet

AREA BIRD A cadet who usually spends his free afternoons serving punishment tours

ARMY BRAT The son or daughter of a regular army officer

B-ACHE v. To explain, make excuses n. Official explanation of delinquency; a complaint

BEAST BARRACKS Elementary training of a new cadet before he joins the corps. Barracks occupied during above period of training

BENO A cancellation, negative report, derived from the official phrase, "There will be no . . ." Often comes in the form of a letter from a femme, i.e., "Sorry can't come."

BENO WAGON Mail truck

B. FOOD Cereal or breakfast food, hot or cold

B.J. Fresh; lacking in respect; "Bold before June."

B.P. Barracks policeman; division janitor

BOARD FIGHT A recitation in which cadets are sent to the blackboard, where they fight their way through a maze of problems

BOLO To fail miserably

BOODLE Cake, candy, ice cream, etc.; all eatables in general, excluding those served in the mess hall

BOODLE FIGHT A gathering of one or more persons at which boodle is consumed

BOODLERS Refreshment room in Grant Hall. Also refers to the boodle dispensing centers at the Cadet Store and the Thayer Hotel

BRACE n. The correct military carriage for a plebe
v. To correct a plebe's posture

BREAK IN, OUT To be admitted to or released from the hospital

BROWNBOY Synonymous with sleep or sack; khaki-sacky

BUCK n. A cadet private
v. To work against, to oppose

BUCK-UP v. To improve upon something

BUGS Oysters, small pieces of vegetable, or other solids found in soup

BUST To revoke the appointment of a cadet commissioned or noncommissioned officer

BUTT Any fractional part of any whole, as in a "butt of a glass of milk"

C-STORE The Cadet Store

CIT A civilian

CITS Civilian clothing

COLD Absolutely, thoroughly, as in a "cold max" (See max.)

COLD JUG One who has an extremely sober air, also, Cold bottle

COM The commandant of Cadets

COME OFF Stop, cease, as in "Come off all th' noise!"

CON Confinement to quarters, as a punishment for breach of discipline

CRAWL To correct a fourth classman; to rebuke

D. Deficient, below average, particularly in academics or appearance. To have any rating below 2.0 on the cadet grading system, where 3.0 is a maximum and 2.0 is a minimum passing grade.

DEMO A demerit

DIV A division of barracks

D.P. Permission for a cadet to dine anywhere on the Post other than the Mess Hall. Dining permit.

DRAG v. To escort visitors, particularly a young lady visitor. To dump water on and otherwise disorder the appearance of a cadet on the occasion of his promotion, birthday, etc. n. Date

DRIVE AROUND, UP, DOWN, ETC. To come or report to a specified place, as in "Drive around to my room at six o'clock"

D.T. To double-time; run

DUCROT The name of any plebe, as "Mister Ducrot!" (Pronounced Doo-crow)

DUMBJOHN See Ducrot. Also Dumbguard, Dumbflicket, Dumcrot, and so on

DULL TOOL One who is exceedingly gross

ELEPHANT One who can't dance

ENGINEER A cadet who is high ranking academically

F.D. Full-dress uniform

FEMME A young lady

FIFTY-FIFTY Uniform composed of gray dress coat and white trousers; also F.D. fifty-fifty

FILE A person (male). A relative rating in academic or military rank

FILEBONER One who incessantly strives to get ahead. An apple-polisher

FIND To discharge a cadet for deficiency in studies or conduct

FLANKER A tall person

FOUNDATION The day on which the list of cadets found deficient in academics is published

FOUNDLING A cadet who has been dismissed

FRIED EGG Insignia of the U.S.M.A. worn on cadet headgear

GOAT A man near the bottom of his class in academics

GRIND n. A joke
v. To laugh, smirk

GROUNDHOG A ground cadet, i.e., not an air gadget

HELL CATS Orderlies; musicians who sound reveille and calls, and the drum and bugle corps for noon meal formations

HIVE v. To understand, to comprehend
n. An intelligent person, or one who learns quickly; an engineer

HOP A dance

I.C.C. "I can't come." See Beno

L.P. Unattractive, undesirable

MAX n. A complete success; a maximum
v. To make a 3.0 in academic recitations; to do a thing perfectly

MUCK n. Muscle, brawn, physical strength
v. To strain at physical work

O.A.O. The one and only. *Her*

-OID Suffix denoting agent or doer, as in sluggoid, hopoid, specoid, etc.

P. A professor, an instructor

PLEBE SKINS First issue gray flannel trousers; gymnasium trousers

PODUNK A cadet's home town; the newspaper thereof

POOP Information in general

POOP-DECK The balconies on cadet headquarters where the O.C. (officer in charge) watches formations. Also the balcony in the Mess Hall where the O.C. eats and from which the orders are published

POOP-SHEET A page of information. Also a booklet of problem solutions

PRO Proficient; above passing in studies, or looks

QUILL SHEET   Company delinquency list, published daily except Sundays

RECOGNIZE   To place a fourth classman on upperclass status

R.H.I.P.   Rank hath its privileges (as well as its responsibilities)

SACK   n. Bed, sleep
v. To sleep (to sack-up)

SLIPSTICK   Slide rule; that instrument from the mechanical world which ultimately becomes an integral part of every cadet

SNAKE   n. An expert stag at the hops
v. To attend a hop, or other social function, for the express purpose of enjoying the company of other cadets' drags

SOIREE   n. A task requiring begrudged effort

v. To inconvenience

SPEC   n. Something memorized. (Pronounced: speck)
v. To memorize verbatim, as in "I speced it cold"

SPOON-UP   To put in order; clean up

SPOONY   Neat in appearance

TARBUCKET   The full-dress hat

TENTH AVENUE   The street (there aren't nine others) running between East and West Academic Buildings. Part of Thayer Road

TROU   Trousers (only women, children, and midshipmen wear pants)

TRUCK DRIVER   Air gadget training to be a bomber pilot

WIFE   A roommate

WILCO   Will comply

YEARLING   A member of the third class

CHAPTER SIXTY-SEVEN

ETIQUETTE FOR THE BRIDE OF THE MILITARY MAN

The bride whose first home is a military post or a navy yard must be well-coached in military etiquette. Here, at least, there may be no cutting of social corners.

If she is the wife of a commissioned officer there is usually a reception given for her by the wives of the other officers. If it is a large one the bride and groom stand in a receiving line with the commanding officer and his wife.

Sometimes a wedding gift is presented on behalf of the post or yard's officers and their wives. The bride acknowledges this at the time of presentation with a brief little speech.

Living at any military or naval post means living in a tight, gossipy little community. Senior wives, so gauged by their husband's rank, take social precedence. Protocol is followed more strictly than it is in Washington, and the post social call follows a pattern that must be committed to memory.

The commanding officer must meet new arrivals at the post, so it is considered proper to consult the adjutant about the most convenient time to arrange calls. In these busy days calls are not made at any certain set interval after arrival. Two cards are left by the officer—one for the commander and one for his wife. The officer's wife leaves her personal card for the commander's wife. A joint card is never used for post calls.

Soon after this visit the newly assigned officer must call upon his immediate superior, following the same procedure with reference to leaving cards. If that officer should be unmarried but has his mother or another close relative acting as his official hostess, cards are left for her just as they would be for a wife.

Thereafter the couple are free to settle in their new quarters before notifying the adjutant that they are ready to receive visitors. When they are reasonably well-settled they give their cards to the adjutant for posting on the bulletin. From then on they will receive formal calls at official calling hours. The wife arranges to be at home at such hours for the following few weeks. She is not expected to serve tea or other refreshment, as the callers usually have other territory to cover during the same period. However, having something ready does help the newcomer through the small formality of receiving, if the visitor has time.

It is wise for the hostess to note on the back of each card in pencil when the call was received, for she must return it promptly, within two weeks if possible.

HOW TO TELL MILITARY RANK

Our armed forces, organized under the Department of Defense, consists of the Army, the Navy, and the Air Force. The Marine Corps is part of the Navy, and in time of war the Coast Guard is under the jurisdiction of the Navy, as well. In time of peace the Coast Guard operates as a service of the Treasury Department.

In all services staff officers, or non-combatant officers, are distinguished from line officers by a device signifying their staff corps. Line officers, generally speaking, are those entitled to command combat forces. There are certain specialists, however, who though technically line officers, do not command combat forces.

In the Army, devices signifying the corps in which men serve—the caduceus of the doctor, the cross of the chaplain, etc.—are worn on the lapel. In the Navy these staff officer devices are worn on the sleeve above the stripes indicating rank.

THE ARMY

Cap device—eagle clutching two arrows
In order of rank the officer personnel of the Army are:
GENERAL—Four silver stars
LIEUTENANT GENERAL—Three silver stars
MAJOR GENERAL—Two silver stars

618

BRIGADIER GENERAL—One silver star
COLONEL—Silver eagle
LIEUTENANT COLONEL—Silver oak leaf
MAJOR—Gold oak leaf
CAPTAIN—Two silver bars
FIRST LIEUTENANT—One silver bar
SECOND LIEUTENANT—One gold bar
CHIEF WARRANT OFFICER—One gold bar, brown enamel top, gold longitudinal center
WARRANT OFFICER, JUNIOR GRADE—Same as above except gold center is latitudinal

THE NAVY

Cap device—crossed anchors, shield and eagle
On blue uniforms rank is indicated by gold stripes on sleeves, on white or dress khaki uniforms rank is indicated on detachable shoulder boards.

In order of rank the officer personnel of the Navy are:

FLEET ADMIRAL—Five silver stars, one 2" stripe and four ½" sleeve stripes with star of line officer
ADMIRAL—Four silver stars, one 2" stripe and three ½" sleeve stripes, with star of line officer, or corps device
VICE-ADMIRAL—Three silver stars, one 2" stripe and two ½" sleeve stripes, star of line officer or corps device
REAR ADMIRAL—Two silver stars, one 2" stripe and one ½" sleeve stripes, star of line officer or corps device
COMMODORE—One silver star, one 2" sleeve stripe, star of line officer or corps device
CAPTAIN—Silver spread eagle, four ½" stripes, star of line officer or corps device
COMMANDER—Silver oak leaf, three ½" stripes, star of line officer or corps device
LIEUTENANT COMMANDER—Gold oak leaf, two ½" stripes with ¼" one between, star of line officer or corps device
LIEUTENANT—Two silver bars, two ½" stripes, star of line officer or corps device
LIEUTENANT, JUNIOR GRADE—One silver bar, one ½" stripe with ¼" one above
ENSIGN—One gold bar, one ½" gold stripe and star of line officer or corps device
CHIEF WARRANT OFFICER—One ½" broken gold stripe and specialty device
WARRANT OFFICER—One ¼" broken gold stripe and specialty device

THE MARINE CORPS

Cap device—eagle, globe, and anchor
The top rank in the Marine Corps is general. He wears the four stars and

shoulder rank of the Army. Other insignia in the Marine Corps are the same as those in the Army, despite the fact that the Marine Corps is an arm of the Navy.

THE AIR FORCE

Cap device—wings flanking U.S.
The top rank in the Air Force is general. All insignia in the Air Force are the same as that in the Army.

THE COAST GUARD

Cap distinguished by single anchor, eagle, and shield
The top rank in the Coast Guard is vice admiral. All insignia are the same as those in the Navy.

THE WOMEN'S SERVICES

Each branch of the service has its women's division. Nurses in the service are commissioned officers ranging from second lieutenant to colonel in the Army and from second lieutenant to captain in the Navy. The other women's corps are the Army's WACS with ranks up to that of colonel, the Navy's WAVES with ranks up to that of captain, the Women Marines with ranks up to that of captain, the Coast Guard's SPARS with ranks up to that of captain, the Air Corps WAFS with ranks up to that of colonel. They all compare with men of the same rank in pay, privileges, and precedence.

ARMY POST CALLS

Visits of courtesy or *Courtesy calls* hours are daily, except on Saturday (when they are excluded), from 7:45 P.M. to 9:00 P.M. On Sunday they are from 4:00 to 6:00 P.M.

CHAPTER SIXTY-EIGHT

SHIP LAUNCHINGS AND VISITING A NAVAL VESSEL

The bottle of wine, traditionally smashed on the hull of a ship about to be launched, symbolizes the actual animal or even human sacrifice that went with this rite all the way back to the launching of the Ark. The wine is usually champagne because of its festive nature and because it bursts more showily and with greater éclat than a still wine. Occasionally water is used for christening a ship, but it is usually some special water brought from the vicinity for which the ship was named and sometimes is mixed with wine, for sailors tend to believe that water alone doesn't make an appropriate baptismal bath.

As in many other fields, women have taken over in the matter of ship launchings, with the first known christening by a woman in this country taking place in Portsmouth, New Hampshire, in 1828. Since then it seems to be mostly women who are honored by being asked to name a ship formally.

The person naming the ship is its sponsor, and she is attended by a maid or maids of honor. They are selected, as she was, by the builder of the ship, who makes all arrangements for transportation and entertainment of the sponsor, maids of honor, and distinguished guests. For the occasion, the guests wear formal daytime dress, not sports apparel. The sponsor receives a corsage from the builder and a commemorating gift, often a piece of jewelry. The dignity of the occasion is comparable with that of a child's christening and has serious significance to the men who will man the ship.

The bottle of champagne—or special water—must be swung against the bow by the sponsor at the indicated time with sufficient force to break it, if possible, the first time. At that moment the sponsor says, "I christen thee ———." The pieces of the bottle are then retrieved and usually presented to the sponsor in a suitable, inscribed box as a memento of the occasion.

When a battleship is christened by the widow or other female relative of some naval officer for which the ship is named, it is usual for the sponsor to present the ship with a memento, such as a photograph, portrait, or dress sword of the man honored by the ceremony. Naval personnel attending the launching wear service dress, blue or white.

VISITING A NAVAL VESSEL

If you are "in the Navy" as wife, mother, or fiancée, you will certainly be well schooled in the many visiting regulations. But the untutored civilian planning to visit one of our ships needs to know the accepted Navy way of doing these things.

EMBARKING When you go aboard a naval vessel at anchor, you embark in a small boat which takes you out to the ship. The trip may be choppy and the seats uncomfortable. Even when the small boat is still fast to the dock it may heave and rock menacingly—from the standpoint of the less sure-footed or the queasy. The idea, therefore, is for the youngest women to go aboard first, taking the seats up forward, leaving seats between them for younger officers or younger men civilians. Older and distinguished visitors are last to embark, take seats in the stern. When the small boat is alongside the ship it is the "brass" and their wives who disembark first—wives first unless there is no one at the foot of the ladder to assist them and the sea is rough, then a younger officer or two may disembark first to help the ladies. Very young women hold back until older women or the wives of dignitaries disembark, then dignitaries and high-ranking officers leave before the younger men and women. It is an honor to be last or among the last into a boat, barge, gig, or any such ship's boats and first or among the first to leave. Children, therefore, should not be allowed in their enthusiasm to clamber up the ladder, perhaps past the captain himself, although in a rough sea a very old person or mother and small baby would probably take precedence even over the President.

GOING ABOARD Making connection between the stern of a small boat and the gangway of a ship is sometimes quite an athletic undertaking even when the weather on shore looks perfectly calm. Adequate underthings are a requisite, also a skirt that allows for a wide step and heels that won't be perilous. A visit to the engine room, when allowed, requires a perpendicular descent on steel ladders with blasts of air coming from beneath, so be forewarned (and take an extra pair of nylons and white gloves). Descents on the ordinary ladders between weather decks are steep, too, and the wind seems to find them even when a ship is tied snugly up to the dock.

MAKING A CALL ABOARD A NAVAL VESSEL Suppose you have been invited aboard the U.S.S. *Monsoon* by an officer you've met. In wartime you need a pass and your host will arrange to furnish it for presentation to the boat officer for a specific day and time. You will, of course, have to fulfill the usual precautionary requirements. Otherwise, calls on ship take place conveniently, as they do on land, during afternoon naval calling hours, between three-thirty or four and six, unless you have been asked to an affair (usually by formal invitation) that takes place at a stated time.

If you are expected aboard by your host at a certain hour, he will probably be on deck to meet you, but, even if you see him standing there as you come over the side, you first greet the officer of the deck stationed on the quarter-deck at the head of the ladder. You recognize him by the telescope he always carries—the officer of the deck glass (O.O.D. glass in seaman's terminology)—and by the gloves he must wear, white with whites, gray with his blue uniform. He is, during his watch, anyhow, in charge of the ship, the captain's surrogate on the quarter-deck. To you he is the official host, of whom you take cognizance the minute you arrive by saying, "How do you do," or "Good afternoon," (shaking hands after his salute, if you wish, if you are a civilian man) and of whom you take polite official leave. Your navy escort, if you have one, the captain excepted, must say to the O.O.D. as he leaves, "I have permission to leave the ship, Sir."

If your naval host has come out with you in the boat, you precede him up the gangway, greet the O.O.D., and step aside to await your host before joining any groups already formed on deck, even when you know members of them, although you may bow in recognition, of course. But you don't rush aboard and take charge of the ship, leaving your confused or angry escort to his own devices while you play the belle. Remember, almost any woman aboard ship looks good to men who have restricted shore leave.

SALUTING THE QUARTER-DECK The quarter-deck is the small raised deck in the stern of the ship where in ancient times sacred images of the altar were kept, later the flags of kings. In deference to tradition, sacred in all the navies of the world, uniformed men, as they reach the upper gangway platform, face aft and salute the quarter-deck after first saluting the flag. Civilian men show correct deference by lifting their hats to the quarter-deck before stepping aboard, although with them the gesture is one of courtesy and not, as with the armed forces, obligatory.

HONORS TO CIVILIANS The President or some other official might receive special honors as he boards—a salute from the guns or the running up of his flag. If so, he remains on the gangway platform with his hat over his heart, in the civilian flag salute until the honors have been completed. He then greets the O.O.D. by shaking hands before accepting the welcome of the captain and other officers.

PROHIBITIONS CONCERNING NAVAL VESSELS

It is not permitted for a civilian to transport liquor to a naval vessel either for his own use there or as a gift to his host. No one, even in peacetime, may take aboard a camera or a pet. No one may go aboard in an intoxicated condition, either, and part of the O.O.D.'s job is to prevent the boarding of such unwelcome guests.

Meals aboard are in the wardroom—enlisted seamen may not entertain aboard—or possibly in the captain's cabin, but the wardroom is run like a men's club with meals billed—even his own—to each officer on a monthly basis. Do not invite yourself to meals aboard under the mistaken assumption that they will be on Uncle Sam. Your entertainment is provided by the members of the mess. If you do eat there, the senior officer of the wardroom and president of the mess is your official host. Excuse yourself to him if you must leave before others.

Two topics are traditionally never mentioned in the wardroom—religion and women, presumably so the men can eat or relax in relative peace as they might in a well-ordered club. If you are taken through or to the wardroom, conduct yourself as you would in a club lounge—observe relative quiet and impeccable deportment. You may smoke there if invited to do so, but you may not smoke on deck or in companionways.

OFFICERS' STATEROOMS

With the exception of the captain, all officers share their rooms with one or more other officers. While a lady making a tour of a ship may be asked to inspect these quarters, she must treat them as the communal rooms they are, even if it's her husband's stateroom that interests her particularly. Doors must be left open—even when wives are inspecting the rooms—and congregating must take place on deck or in the wardroom, not in the individual rooms. Tender moments, if any, aboard a ship are best arranged by your host. He may be "off duty" officially, but he is under constant surveillance while he's on his ship. Don't try to break down his very necessary dignity and decorum.

MARITIME TERMS

The layman often makes mistakes in referring to maritime matters, thereby unintentionally insulting serious followers of the sea. Never, by any chance, refer to a ship or a boat as anything but "she." Only small craft, pulling boats, dories, and small power boats of various kinds are "boats." Anything from a patrol craft up is a "ship." Houseboats get the same terminology as houses—they have a living room and porches, not saloons and decks. They have a kitchen and a bath, not a galley and head.

Aboard a battleship there is no saloon, as on an ocean liner. Instead there is the wardroom for the officers' mess (dining) and recreation, the junior officers' mess, the warrant officers' mess, the chief petty officers' mess, and the enlisted men's mess. The captain's cabin is his mess hall. There are no companionways on a battleship. Instead, the ladders leading from deck to deck are simply ladders. The hurricane deck becomes a weather deck. Topside is any exposed deck, and below deck is any covered deck. Officers have rooms, not staterooms, and enlisted men are quartered in compartments.

NAVAL INVITATIONS AND REPLIES

Our embassies and legations frequently use the French language, the accepted one for social and diplomatic correspondence. As an American naval ship in foreign waters in peacetime is usually there more or less for diplomatic reasons, invitations to the ship, even those sent to fellow Americans in the port, are likely to be in French, as are those from our embassies in non-English speaking countries. Invitations from English-speaking hosts, if written in other than English, must be replied to in the language used.

INVITATION TO VISIT A SHIP

Here is one accepted form of invitation from a ship, in French:

Le Commandant et les officiers
du croiseur *Milwaukee* vous prient
de leur faire l'honneur de diner avec eux le vendredi
8 août à bord croiseur *Milwaukee*

à 18 heures 30.   R.S.V.P.
2 août

(The commander and officers of the *Milwaukee* invite you to dine with them on board on Wednesday, August eighth, at six-thirty. August 2)

The French use, very generally now, the twenty-four-hour method of time telling, especially in writing, to eliminate the phrase "du matin," "de l'après midi," or "du soir."

On formal French invitations the date the invitation is sent is usually indicated at the lower left, continental style, whereas we omit this information. Figures are used, not written out as in formal English invitations.

ACCEPTANCE Monsieur et Madame Paul Cobb ont l'honneur d'accepter l'aimable invitation du Commandant et des officiers du croiseur *Milwaukee* pour diner le mercredi 8 août à 18 heures 30.

(Mr. and Mrs. Paul Cobb have the honor of accepting the kind invitation of the Commander and officers of the cruiser *Milwaukee* for dinner Thursday, August 8th, at six-thirty.)

REGRETS Monsieur et Madame Paul Cobb remercient le Commandant et les officiers du *Milwaukee* de leur gracieuse invitation pour le 8 août, et regrettent vivement de ne pas pouvoir l'accepter parce qu'ils sont déjà engagés.

(Mr. and Mrs. Paul Cobb thank the Commander and officers of the *Milwaukee* for their gracious invitation for the eighth of August and regret they cannot accept because of a previous engagement.)

As in regrets in English, it is not necessary to repeat the time of the invitation you must refuse, merely the date. In all acceptances the time is repeated to show that it has been carefully noted.

OTHER FORMAL INVITATIONS IN FRENCH

Our diplomatic service uses more or less standard forms of invitations in French in non-English-speaking countries. Here is one that might be sent by an ambassador to other diplomats, to distinguished citizens, and important visiting or resident Americans:

(State Department Seal)
L'Ambassadeur des États-Unis d'Amérique
et Madame McInnerney prient
Le Comte et Comtesse de Passy
de leur faire l'honneur de venir passer la soirée
dans les jardins de l'ambassade le vendredi 4 juin à 21 heures.

R.S.V.P.   Smoking

(The American Ambassador and Mrs. Innerney invite you to an evening in the gardens of the Embassy Friday, the 4th of June, at nine o'clock. Black tie.)

ACCEPTANCE Le Comte et la Comtesse de Passy ont l'honneur d'accepter l'aimable invitation de M. L'Ambassadeur des Etats-Unis et Madame McInnerney pour la soirée dans les jardins de L'Ambassade le vendredi 4 juin à 21 heures. (The Count and Countess de Passy have the honor of accepting the kind invitation of the American Ambassador and Mrs. Mc-Innerney for the evening of Friday, June 4th, in the Embassy gardens.)

In French the months of the year are not capitalized, figures and abbreviations are usual on even formal invitations, and accents are never omitted even on capital letters. As in English, follow the exact form and spacing of the engraved or printed invitation when writing your one-page reply in long-hand on your best, preferably white, notepaper. Reply to all official dinner invitations from the diplomatic corps within twenty-four hours by hand—taking your answer yourself to the Embassy, Legation, or Consulate or sending it by messenger.

CHAPTER SIXTY-NINE

THE NEW RESIDENT IN WASHINGTON

Anyone moving to Washington and expecting to be part of the social scene may leave cards at the White House during the official season—October until Lent—upon the President and his wife. A joint card may be left for the President and his wife with an extra card of the husband's for the President.

Callers do not actually see the incumbents except by personal appointment, and such calls are never returned by the White House. But all such cards are kept for possible inclusion of the names on invitation lists for receptions, musicales, etc. For this reason the Washington address of each caller is written on each card, and cards are also left for each relative living with the callers in Washington. The relative's relation to the callers should also be noted, "father of Mrs. Leslie Morse," and, again, the address. Cards are left with the doorman on the Pennsylvania side of the White House or at the sentry box at the gate.

During the social season, in normal times, there are five special receptions at the White House, those for the Diplomatic Corps, the Judiciary, Congress, the Armed Forces (Army, Navy and Air Force) and Departmental.

RECEIVING A WHITE HOUSE INVITATION

An invitation to the White House takes precedence over any other social invitation. It should be answered in person or by messenger within twenty-four hours if one is in Washington, by wire or by special delivery if one is out-of-town. If the recipient is to be away or some personal or business matter prevents his attending, his excuse must be clearly stated:

Mr. and Mrs. Jonathan Streeter
regret that owing to Mr. Streeter's
absence in London
they will be unable to accept
the very kind invitation of
The President and Mrs. Jefferson
to dine
on Monday, the tenth of February

Recent death in the family, illness, absence at a great distance from Washington are all tenable excuses. An invitation from the White House also takes precedence over any other social invitation, even a formal one that has already been accepted. In this latter case a regret to one's hostess reads:

Mr. and Mrs. Jonathan Streeter
regret exceedingly that an invitation to
the White House
prevents their keeping
their engagement to dine
on Monday, the tenth of February

An acceptance to a formal White House invitation follows the usual formal acceptance. Informal invitations, usually sent by the President's secretary or his wife's secretary, are answered in the form in which they are sent —by note, by phone, or by wire, with the acceptance or regret addressed to the secretary. Where husband and wife receive the invitation, the wife replies. A man alone replies in his own name, not through his secretary. The forms are:

Tuesday

Dear Miss Metcalfe,
My husband and I accept with great pleasure the kind invitation of the President and Mrs. Monroe to dine at the White House on Monday, the tenth of February, at eight o'clock.

Sincerely,
Louise Streeter

or

Tuesday

Dear Miss Metcalfe,

Because I am sailing for France on February the ninth, I regret that I shall be unable to accept the President and Mrs. Monroe's kind invitation to dine on February 10th.

Sincerely,
Luis Dávila

BEING RECEIVED AT THE WHITE HOUSE

Reception guests at the White House enter through the East door, sometimes through the diplomatic entrance. The President receives with his wife in the Blue Room. An aide makes the presentations, with gentlemen preceding their ladies down the line where they are greeted first by the President, then by the First Lady. The President is "Mr. President," his wife is "Mrs. Monroe." The guest says merely, "Good evening, Mr. President" and passes on immediately unless the President stops him briefly to say a few words. But the guest does not engage in conversation on the line, no matter how well he may know the President.

Often the President leaves after receiving his guests, but his wife, or a hostess acting for the family, remains. Refreshments are served in the State Dining Room. Dancing is in the East Room.

Not all reception invitations require an answer, but it is courteous to give one anyhow.

If one has dined at the White House, cards must be left within one week upon the President's wife.

BUSINESS CALLS AT THE WHITE HOUSE

MAKE YOUR CALL BRIEF If you are given an appointment in business hours to see the President, present yourself at the White House executive office a few minutes before the stated time. Diplomats and high dignitaries wear striped trousers and top hats or black Homburgs. Ordinary citizens usually wear conservative business suits or in the summer the usual tropicals or seersuckers. A woman wears a simple street dress or suit, a hat and gloves. She removes her right glove when shaking hands with the President. If she is being received as a delegate, say, or as Somebody of the Year, and will be photographed with him, she may wear a small corsage. Whatever your business, you will usually be told the maximum amount of time the President can give you. Keep your call within that limit and leave sooner, if possible.

DON'T FOR CALLS AT THE WHITE HOUSE Don't take a gift to the President without clearing it through his aide or secretary. A small package carried in a handbag or pocket and produced during the call might precipitate an assassination scare as, of course, the President is at all times guarded by Secret Service men, one or more of whom will be present during your interview, unless, perhaps, you are a personal friend.

WARNING BUZZER If you are in the White House hallways at the moment when special buzzers sound, this indicates that the President or members of his family are about to enter or leave the White House. You will be required by your attendant to step out of the hallway and into a closed room until the passage has been effected. This, too, is for the President's and his family's safety.

The White House is the President's home rather than a public building. A gentleman removes his hat the minute he enters the portico. No visitor smokes unless smoking is suggested by the person he has gone to see.

GIFTS TO THE WHITE HOUSE

Don't send a gift to the President without receiving permission from his secretary or aide or from other members of the White House staff. If you are an admirer of the President and decide to send him one of your home-grown geese, he'll never taste it unless it has been ascertained beforehand that the acceptance of such a gift from you is safe. The White House housekeeper is responsible for any gifts of food for the White House and must vouch for the safety of any accepted. Animals, pets of various kinds, and other things the President sometimes accepts must be offered through some accredited organization, individual, or aide before they are shipped or acceptance will be refused, and quite properly.

CHAPTER SEVENTY

THE FLAG AND OUR NATIONAL ANTHEM

DISPLAYING THE FLAG

Many homes and most business houses, fraternal organizations, and all public buildings own and from time to time display the flag. Some in doing so do not realize that there are definite rules concerning the proper display of the flag which protect it from desecration. It can't be used, for example, as a trademark or part of a coat of arms, even in slightly altered form. There are federal statutes to enforce this ruling and others concerning the respectful use and display of the flag.

Here are the major regulations concerning display of the flag:

1. Never fly it upside down except as a distress signal.
2. Don't let it trail on the ground—or even touch it—or in the water.
3. Display the flag only from sunrise to sunset out of doors and lower it promptly if it rains.
4. Hoist the flag briskly but lower it slowly and reverently.
5. City and State flags or those of organizations flown from the same staff as the United States flag should be placed below the flag. No other flag is ever flown above it.
   On boats signal and flag officers' flags are flown from the mast considerably above the national flag flown from the aft deck.
6. When organization or other flags are flown in conjunction with the U.S. flag on adjacent flagstaffs, the U.S. flag is always hoisted first and is last to come down (except in case of rain). Flags flown on adjacent flagpoles should always be placed on the left of the flag itself. No other flag is ever placed to the flag's right (observer's left).
7. When other nations' flags are flown with ours, they should be on separate standards, should be the same size as the U.S. flag and flown at the same height. In times of peace, no nation's flag takes precedence in an arrangement of flags, but it is usual for the U.S. flag flown on U.S. soil, on its ships or bases, to have the central position in such a grouping of flags. In wartime, no immediately adjacent flag is ever flown at the U.S. flag's own right, even in a grouping of allies' flags.
8. A flag flown from a staff fastened to a window sill or balcony or fixed to the front of a building must be flown with the union, or blue field, at the peak of the staff unless the flag is at half-mast. Flags are flown at half-mast only by official state, federal, or city order, never flown in such a manner to indicate personal loss to a family or to a business or other organization. In the last case, the deceased is so honored occasionally but then only by official decree if he has been of civic importance.
9. When a flag is suspended over a sidewalk on a cord from the building to a pole on the sidewalk, the flag is hoisted from the building to the pole, union first (so it may be taken in quickly in a storm).
10. When a flag is displayed without a staff, it should lie flat against an upright support, indoors or out, never draped or festooned. (Use bunting for this purpose.) When it is displayed horizontally or vertically against a wall, the union or field is uppermost, to the flag's own right. When the flag is displayed from a window it is always shown with the union to the left of the observer in the street.
11. A flag displayed over the middle of the street should hang vertically with the union to the north in an east and west street or east in a north and south one.
12. In displaying the flag on a speaker's platform, place it above and

behind the speaker, flat, union to the flag's right, observer's left. If it is flown from a staff on the platform, it should be flown to the speaker's right, in the place of honor. It must never be used to cover a table or desk. Never drape it over the platform.

13. Flags carried in a mourning parade or procession are never put at half-mast but may display a black crepe bow knot with or without two black crepe streamers at the fastening points by order of the President. It may not be used in this way for private funeral processions.

14. When the flag is to be flown at half-mast, it is first hoisted to the peak, then put at half-mast. Before lowering it for the night, hoist it again to the peak.

15. On Memorial Day the flag is flown at half-mast only from sunrise until noon, when it is hoisted to full staff.

16. Don't use the flag to unveil even a patriotic statue or monument, although it is properly used in the attendant ceremonies.

17. The only exception in the draping of the flag occurs when it is used to cover a casket, union at the head and over the deceased's left shoulder. The flag must not touch the ground nor be lowered into the grave. The casket is carried foot first. The flag is used for this honor only for members of the armed services, for cabinet officers of the federal and state governments, and for others of national importance for whom the President decrees official mourning.

18. When a flag becomes torn, tattered, or otherwise unfit for display it is never heedlessly discarded. If it is beyond mending and cleaning it should be destroyed in one piece, privately, by burning. Its fabric may not be reused for some other purpose. An old flag, faded, worn, and torn beyond restitution, deserves and must receive respectful destruction so it will never fall into vicious or thoughtless hands.

19. The flag must never be dipped to any person or thing. Only personal, state, regimental or other flags may be used to render this honor.

20. Never place any object or emblem on or above the U.S. flag with the exception of the American eagle.

21. Never fasten the flag in a way that it can be easily torn.

22. The flag may not be draped on any vehicle. If it is to be displayed on a train, boat, or car it must be firmly fixed to a staff.

23. The flag must not be displayed from a parade float except from a staff.

24. The flag may not be used to cover the ceiling.

25. The flag may not be carried horizontally in a procession, but must be aloft and waving.

26. The flag should never be used as decoration for civilian clothing, pillows, furniture, or athletic uniforms. It may not be printed on paper napkins, tablecloths, or boxes. It is used only on official U.S. stationery, never on personal stationery.

27. No lettering of any kind may be placed on the flag.
28. The pole from which the flag flies must never carry advertising signs or pennants. It may not be used in any form of display advertising, except that placed for the United States Government.
29. A flag displayed in the body of the church is flown from a staff, to the congregation's right as it faces the pulpit. Service, state, or other special flags are flown to the left of the congregation. If the flag is to be displayed from the chancel or the platform it is placed on the clergyman's right, to the congregation's left. Other flags are flown from the clergyman's left.
30. Store the flag in such a way that it will be protected from moths and other damage. Never place it on the floor even for a moment, and never permit anyone to step on it or show it any disrespect, unwitting or not.

THE SINGING OF THE NATIONAL ANTHEM

In times of national emergency very strict attention must be paid to any playing of the National Anthem. During wartime it is usually played before the beginning of such public performances as concerts, plays, sports events. In fact, in time of war it *must* be played at certain designated gatherings. You may have seated yourself at the opera after an impressive entrance, but you must rise promptly when the anthem is played, unless you are exceedingly infirm or very, very old, or else so young that you cannot be expected to understand the significance of rising to your feet at the sound of this music. Even then, quite young children should be taught to stand quietly and respectfully when they hear "The Star-Spangled Banner" and, like the rest of us, they should, as soon as possible, learn the words of at least the first and last stanzas.

The National Anthem is not easy to sing, but most people can transpose the high notes an octave lower, as they go along, into something they can manage. Don't stand mute because you are afraid of those high notes. If you can't transpose, sing everything *but* the high notes and let the sopranos reach for them. It is shameful that so few of us can sing the words accurately, although I can sympathize with anyone's difficulty with the range. The idea behind the mass singing of the Anthem is to stir a feeling of patriotism and unity. Fine voices aren't essential. Enthusiastic, heart-warming, not half-hearted, singing by everybody does proper honor.

When the Anthem strikes up in any public place men, women, and children should stand at complete attention and should sing if they possibly can. If they can't sing they should stand quietly and respectfully without whispering, talking, or fidgeting until the Anthem is finished. Civilian men and boys remove their hats, hold them with the right hand over their hearts. Women stand at attention or place the right hand over the heart. It is usual if more than the first stanza is to be sung for the assemblage to go right into the last stanza, omitting the second and third unless the words appear on printed programs. Memorization of the first and last stanzas should be sufficient.

"THE STAR-SPANGLED BANNER"

O say, can you see, by the dawn's early light,
 What so proudly we hailed at the twilight's last gleaming?
Whose broad stripes and bright stars, through the perilous fight,
 O'er the ramparts we watched were so gallantly streaming?
And the rockets' red glare, the bombs bursting in air,
 Gave proof through the night that our flag was still there.
O say, does that star-spangled banner yet wave
O'er the land of the free and the home of the brave?

LAST STANZA

O thus be it ever, when freemen shall stand
 Between their loved homes and the war's desolation!
Blest with vict'ry and peace, may the heav'n-rescued land
 Praise the Power that hath made and preserved us a nation.
Then conquer we must, when our cause it is just,
 And this be our motto: "In God is our trust."
And the star-spangled banner in triumph shall wave
O'er the land of the free and the home of the brave.

         —Francis Scott Key

Don't chew gum, eat, or smoke during the playing of the anthem in public places. Don't continue making your way to your seats, even if you are in an aisle when the music starts. If any confusion arises anywhere in the assemblage, all those except the individuals immediately involved continue their singing and their attitude of attention as if nothing untoward had occurred. As with many other such ceremonies, the singing of the anthem (which you may not like as music or for what are called, by some, its chauvinistic lyrics) is a mark of respect for one's country and flag. There are other patriotic songs—"America the Beautiful," "Columbia the Gem of the Ocean," "God Bless America," "Yankee Doodle," etc.—but they do not require the respectful response which must be given "The Star-Spangled Banner," designated as our official National Anthem.

The hearing of the National Anthem at home over radio or television does not require the rising of those present if they are gathered informally together in a small group. If a large dance or ball is being given in a private home and the orchestra for some reason opens the entertainment with the Anthem, then, of course, everyone rises.

The Anthem is never played even in private homes merely for entertainment, is never improvised upon for dance purposes.

Every public appearance of the President is preceded by the rendition of the march, "Hail to the Chief," a signal for all to stand at attention. Before the opening of ceremonies at which the President is to speak, "The Star-Spangled Banner" is played. It is played directly after a public toast to the President (on the rare occasions when one is proposed). Usually only the first stanza is played, and singing accompaniment is not expected, although it is not incorrect to sing.

ANTHEMS OF OTHER NATIONS

In America public gatherings often open with the playing of our National Anthem. If another country's representatives are present, as, for example, members of the cavalry teams from various countries in the National Horse Show, or a great pianist from another country at, say, a White House musicale, the visitors' National Anthem is played immediately after ours or at the time of their appearance and before their performance or ceremony begins. Americans give the anthem—and colors, if they are shown or flown —of another country due respect in the presence of their representatives by standing at attention. They may sing the anthem if they wish—many Americans seem to know the "Marseillaise" and "God Save the Queen" (whose music is the same as that of "America")—but they need not actually salute any but their own flag. Abroad they never pledge allegiance to another flag, just as no non-American ever repeats the words of our Pledge.

9 TRAVEL ETIQUETTE AT HOME AND ABROAD

Traveling by Ship, Plane, and Train   637

Tips to the Stay-at-Home   646

How Customs Differ Abroad   647

An Audience with the Pope   656

Motoring Manners   659

TRAVEL SECTION

If you wish to be at ease under any circumstance with any kind of person, by all means travel as much as your time and pocketbook permit. Travel is broadening if you undertake it with an open mind and a receptive heart.

Even though English is now virtually an international language, the knowledge of English alone is limiting to the traveler. Knowing at least a little of the language of the country or countries you are to visit not only is courteous to the people there but adds to your own pleasure and convenience. It is so easy to pick up the basic vocabulary of almost any language these days through the study-methods developed by the Army. You don't even have to be a linguist to become amazingly proficient in a relatively short time. Studying a new language in preparation for a trip can give your travels a breadth and interest they would never have had without this new, exciting stimulus. It helps, along with knowledge of what is expected, to make travel more enjoyable. Perhaps the best advice to the traveler is—

Go to new countries and new places as if you had no set tastes and standards by which you could judge what you are about to see and experience, even what you are about to eat.

Do not seek out your own countrymen in foreign lands, stay away from so-called American restaurants and tourist traps. Do not demand American-style efficiency, sanitation, manners and service.

Accept your surroundings with grace and tact. Relax and learn to enjoy the new and different life without making invidious comparisons. You may be as American as you wish when you get back home.

CHAPTER SEVENTY-ONE

TRAVELING BY SHIP, PLANE, AND TRAIN

BEHAVIOR ABOARD SHIP

A ship may be compared to a country hotel. It is good manners to greet other passengers in a friendly fashion without, however, making presumptuous overtures. You speak to the people next to you in deck chairs, but you do not force conversation upon them. In general, as in a friend's house, the roof is the introduction, but this does not mean you are expected to do more than bow in greeting to fellow passengers as you encounter them during the day. Congenial people usually introduce themselves to one another in short order aboard ship, but it should be kept in mind that shipboard friendships, like shipboard romances, usually end when the boat docks, despite many protestations to the contrary. The passenger who bares his soul to all who will listen to him within the first hour or two of embarkation looks very silly to sophisticated travelers.

SEATING IN THE DINING ROOM   Prior to the ship's departure it is desirable to see the second steward about your table reservations, unless you have made application in advance from the steamship company.

People with small children are expected to take the first sitting, unless the children are to eat with their nurse and the parents eat alone at a later hour. If you are seated at a table with any of the ship's officers, bear in mind that the officer acts as the table's host and passengers await his appearance before ordering. If he is unavoidably detained, he sends a message to that effect. It a lady seated with several gentlemen and perhaps another lady does not wish to come to a meal, it is courteous of her to send word to the table with her steward so the others will not wait.

DRESS ABOARD TRANSATLANTIC SHIPS   Clothing aboard ship is casual during the daytime—the sort of clothes worn at a country club in any good resort. At best they are conservative, with shorts and bathing apparel confined to the swimming and sports area. Slacks on women to whom they are becoming are seen on all decks, to some extent in the dining room for breakfast and, to a lesser extent, at lunch. Men wear coats at all meals, too, on first-class liners. They do not wear sport clothes at night in the public rooms or dining room.

Women may or may not wear hats, as they please, on deck or at daytime meals. In the evening, except in tourist and cabin class, there is some attempt at formality, depending, of course, on the ship on which one travels. On the great transatlantic liners dinner jackets are the general, though not obligatory, rule. It is never bad taste to appear in dinner dress, and on ships where a Captain's or Gala Dinner is given, formality is expected, with men wearing dinner jackets and women appearing, if they wish, in full evening dress. On some ships this special night is made into a fancy dress affair, which permits considerable leeway in costumes. These are usually available from the ship's stores, but if you know a costume affair to be the ship's custom you may take along your own. The costumes that win the prizes, however, are usually the ones that are extemporized out of whatever happens to be on hand in one's baggage. But quite a few diehards attend such evenings in their usual clothes and enjoy themselves nonetheless, with perhaps a paper hat added to give the right festive note.

WHEN ONE DOESN'T DRESS   On the first and last nights out it is customary for passengers to wear their ordinary travel clothes. Presumably the exigencies of packing and unpacking are too great for any degree of formality to be expected on these nights.

BEHAVIOR AT TABLE   Other passengers at your table are treated exactly as if you were with them in your own home. Conversation is expected, gentlemen rise when ladies are seated and wait until ladies' orders are taken before ordering themselves. On ships where wine or cocktails are not included in the meal it is usual for a guest at the table who wishes either or both of these to include the others at the table in an invitation to join him, an invitation which may be refused, of course, with proper courtesy.

When passengers are assigned to various tables in the dining room by the second steward, a table for the captain and other tables for the ship's officers are made up from the passenger list. Distinguished personages, presumably, occupy these coveted seats. It is possible to refuse to sit at the captain's table, or elsewhere in a place of honor, if one has a very good excuse. During the trip it is permissible to shift seats at table in order to join friends only with the consent of the chief steward.

TIPPING ABOARD SHIP   Just before debarking, a passenger tips the following personnel: room steward, table steward, headwaiter, wine steward, if he's been used, and deck and bath stewards. The steward who has taken care of your cabin receives seven-fifty to ten dollars per person as does the table steward and head waiter. Ladies are attended by both steward and stewardess. The tip of seven-fifty to ten dollars is divided between them at the end of the voyage. Deck stewards receive one dollar or more depending on the amount of service they have rendered. Passengers without private bath tip the bath steward one dollar at the end of the voyage, and the "boots" receives one dollar for keeping shoes shined. Cabin boys are usually tipped at the time they perform their small services, if at all. Bar attendants are usually tipped at the time of service if the bill is settled at the time. If the check is signed by a regular frequenter of the smoke room, he might prefer to tip at the end of the voyage. On some ships the card-signing custom prevails, on others payment is required at the time of ordering.

On most ships the chief steward is classed as a ship's officer and, as such, is never tipped.

DRESSING FOR CRUISES Cruises are always less formal than transatlantic crossings. A larger wardrobe of sport clothes—including sun suits, beach robes, and even clothes for active sports (such as riding ashore if time permits)— is usual. Dinner clothes are not essential, but the majority of people wear them. For men a white dinner jacket is customary on tropical cruises, but an ordinary dinner jacket is also acceptable, and by some even preferred.

PLANE TRAVEL

It is vital to determine the amount of weight a plane carries before it takes off. For this reason all luggage and sometimes the passenger, too, is weighed and the amount any one person can take is strictly limited. Each passenger is allowed so many pounds free of charge and sometimes may take additional luggage at a special high freight rate on international or long distance planes. The rate, of course, is high to discourage such excess baggage taken with you.

"Transportation" covers airport to airport, not transportation from terminals to planes. The airlines provide optional limousine service at extra cost to the passenger.

On sleeper trips a passenger is allowed to take with him to his seat a small bag for overnight things, along with his wraps. The rest of his baggage is stowed before the take-off, to be reclaimed with his baggage stub at the terminal.

On international planes meals are served free of charge. On some domestic planes there is now a charge for meals. Airline terminals usually provide some eating facilities. On the huge multi-decked international planes there are bars, but on other planes drinking is either prohibited or discouraged.

On entering a plane, the passenger is greeted by a steward or stewardess. There is sometimes a plaque with the name of this employee, who then is referred to as "Stewardess" or "Miss James," "Steward" or "Mr. Benson." The stewardess is specially trained for her job, may even be a practical nurse. Her job, or the steward's (one or the other serves, usually not both), is to check aboard the passengers, who give their names as they board, to take coats and hang them up before or after the take-off, serve meals, heat baby bottles, attend any airsick passengers, offer reading material and gum (chewing gum helps reduce pressure on eardrums as the plane loses altitude in the landing operation). A stewardess is also there to keep the passengers at ease and should not have her time monopolized by any one passenger (usually male) who wants merely to be entertained. You need never exchange a single word with your seat mate, but conversation is permissible. (See "Speaking to Strangers.")

A passenger selects his own seat as he boards a plane. Seats directly behind the wing are considered choice. Once seated, he fastens his seat belt immediately and waits for the steward or stewardess to take his coat as soon as she is free to do so, if she hasn't taken it at the door. But first she must see that everyone is aboard, in his seat, and with the safety belt properly fastened. The door must be bolted shut and the signal given to the pilot. Passengers do not smoke at the take-off if a sign above the pilot's compartment is lighted in the no-smoking warning. Smoking may be resumed when the light goes off.

All commercial planes are equipped with a lavatory, usually in the rear of the ship. In these are electrical outlets for 110-volt electric razors. In addition the plane will supply its own 24-volt razors for use on a special outlet. In a pocket at the back of each seat, for the passenger facing it, is, among other things, a waterproof paper bag for quick use in case of airsickness. Or a paper container, a "burp cup," is supplied by the hostess, if one rings. She also has all kinds of little remedies for airsickness and keeps on hand a medicine cabinet to cover any emergency. On overseas planes there is a life preserver under each seat, and instruction is usually given at the beginning of the trip by stewardess, steward, co-pilot, or flight officer on its use. Just before landing, passengers must fasten seat belts and keep them fastened until the "fasten seat belt" light goes off and the plane has come to a full stop.

No member of a plane's personnel is ever tipped. One says good-by to the steward or stewardess in attendance at the gangplank when debarking.

TRAIN TRAVEL

BAGGAGE When traveling by train one should take as little baggage as possible, for storage space is limited. The passenger who must have his numerous belongings piled on the platform, where they obstruct passage from car to car, is a nuisance. When much luggage is necessary for a trip part of it should be sent ahead by express or else shipped through in the baggage car on the ticket—150 pounds go free. In the latter case, however, it is important to know that baggage cannot be shipped on the passenger's ticket beyond the point of his descent, and there is often a wait while the freight car is unloaded and baggage sorted out.

In a Pullman large bags are usually placed on the platform by the porter, unless they fit under the seat. They should be locked, of course. A small bag may go to a seat, but not if it is likely to be in the way of a seat mate. At night such a bag should be small enough to fit in the hammock above the berth. In a roomette or compartment all hand baggage is stored by the porter in the allotted space.

SEATING The occupant of a lower berth is entitled to the forward seat of a Pullman section. It is courteous of anyone occupying this preferred place to offer to share it with the passenger riding backwards. If the occupant of the lower is a gentleman he usually cedes the seat during the daytime to a lady if she is the occupant of the less desirable seat. If he wishes, he may even offer to take the upper berth at night, especially if she is elderly, pregnant, or ill, but, of course, having bought the preferred lower he is in no way actually obliged to give it up, especially if the other passenger is reasonably young and healthy. An elderly or infirm man, of course, might also be offered the lower berth. An upper-berth passenger should be sound and spry enough to negotiate the ladder.

OCCUPYING A SECTION Occupants of a section consult each other courteously as to when the berths are to be made up for the night. Usually the porter likes to complete the work of bedmaking by ten or, at the latest, ten-thirty, doing the berths of those who have rung for him first. In order not to impede his work, those who wish to retire late usually go into the observation car until they are ready for bed.

DRESSING AND UNDRESSING Attached to the curtains of each berth are hangers for clothes, and the hammock-rack for hats, shoes, bags, etc., is put in place after the berths are made up. The adept traveler, therefore, dresses and undresses completely in his berth, after preparing for the night in the dressing room. A toilet kit or bag for use in the dressing room is necessary. Women who prefer to cope with their girdles and to put on their dresses or suits after washing and making-up in the morning, make the trek to the dressing room in a dark tailored robe, having neatly combed their hair, if not finally arranged it, before their emergence from the berth. In the dressing room they occupy a minimum of shelf space for their belongings and complete their toilette as speedily as possible, unless most of the other passengers have already dressed.

USE OF THE LADDER Passengers occupying the upper berth must ring for the porter when they need the ladder. They are not permitted to put it in place themselves. Before going to bed the occupant of an upper should wash and be prepared to stay in his berth once he has been assisted into it. If he must descend during the night he rings for the porter—he never attempts to clamber down himself.

THE ROOMETTE AND THE COMPARTMENT The occupant of a roomette can easily operate the berth himself. The bed is made up before the passenger takes possession of the space and is out of sight in the wall. A lever lowers it into place, but, as it occupies the full length of the roomette once it's down, washing and undressing is done before the lever is pulled. Then the curtain is fastened over the door so the passenger in nightclothes will have privacy while he negotiates the bed. Once in, he reaches over and slides and locks the door.

Beds in a compartment are made up by the porter when he is summoned for the purpose.

Occupants of roomettes or compartments may have meals served in privacy if they wish, but occupants of Pullman and parlor car seats should go to the diner or to the observation car for refreshment.

THE DINER A train that has been made up in the station has the diner ready for service if the train is pulling out at meal time. A passenger may go to the diner at any convenient time during the normal service of meals. On going to the diner, he should always take his ticket or his ticket stub with him. He waits at the door until the chief steward, or in some cases, the headwaitress assigns him to a table. A lady alone takes something to read. On a long trip dining car occupants usually greet each other when seated vis-à-vis and may carry on conversation, if they wish. But on a trip requiring but one or perhaps two meals in a diner, table mates rarely speak. (But see "Speaking to Strangers.")

After the meal is over, passengers should not linger in the dining car, even if they are among the last to dine. If other passengers are not waiting to be seated, the dining car crew usually is or at least wishes to clean up.

TIPPING A dining car steward is tipped 15 per cent of the bill, never less than a quarter per person if a meal has been served. An observation car steward who has served drinks is tipped 15 per cent of the total bar bill, not less than a quarter.

TRAIN MANNERS Occupants of private quarters may, of course, play portable radios with the door closed, have gatherings of friends, serve drinks, and smoke. But Pullman and parlor car occupants must maintain quiet, speak in low tones so as not to disturb others, drink and smoke only in areas set aside for the purpose. They keep their belongings in the space they occupy and do not litter the floor with papers or food.

Passengers on long trips who descend at stops to walk on the platform conduct themselves inconspicuously and return at the conductor's first warning.

HOTEL TIPPING

DOORMAN The quality of the hotel, the amount of baggage one has, and the service expected, all have bearing on the size of the tips dispensed in hotels.

The man who opens the door of the cab and sets bags on the curb usually does no more than call a bellhop to take over. If he performs no service, no tip is required. If, on the other hand, he helps unload heavy and extensive baggage or assists anyone into the hotel itself, or at some other time summons a taxi, tipping is expected. For summoning a taxi from the stand in front of the hotel and merely opening its door for a passenger, a doorman usually gets ten cents. If he must fare forth in the rain and find one in the midst of traffic, the tip is gauged by the amount of trouble he has had—

twenty-five cents or fifty cents or, perhaps in a bad storm late at night for guests in evening clothes, as much as a dollar. People who seek shelter under a hotel marquee in the rain and ask the doorman to find them a cab should always tip him anything from ten cents to a quarter, depending on the difficulty he has had in procuring one.

BELLHOP The standard tip for a bellhop carrying up luggage for a newly registered guest or couple is a quarter if he is able to bring all the luggage in one trip. If two or more trips are needed the tip advances on the basis of twenty-five cents for each trip involved. Bellhops who deliver telegrams, a newspaper, or other small things to the room receive a dime. A large bulky package or an armful of clothes from the valet should bring him a quarter tip.

PAGES Page boys usually receive a tip of ten cents to a quarter from the person paged, depending on the hotel. That is, a large hotel with many corridors and anterooms requires more work on the page's part than does a small country hotel with one lobby in which a guest is easily located.

CHAMBERMAID In hotels where one is a transient the tip for the chambermaid is twenty-five cents to fifty cents for an overnight stay, depending on the quality of the hotel. The tip is best left under a pillow on the bed if one leaves before the beds are made up, otherwise it may be left on the bureau or the chambermaid may be sought out in the linen room on the floor.

In a hotel where one is a resident the chambermaid receives a dollar a month per room. Where a guest stays a week or two the chambermaid receives a dollar per week for each bedroom in her charge.

PORTER A hotel porter receives twenty-five cents per trunk carried up to a room. If there is other heavy baggage as well, fifty cents.

If he performs special services, such as making reservations or securing theater tickets, he receives anything from fifty cents to two or three dollars, depending on the difficulty involved.

CHECKROOM ATTENDANT At any checkroom in a hotel specially set up to serve a special affair such as a dance or ball, the attendant receives a quarter per person. At a mere cloakroom outside a hotel restaurant the usual tip is ten cents, despite the quarter "decoys" on the plate.

ELEVATOR STARTER A long-time guest in a hotel usually tips the elevator starter fifty cents or more on leaving if he has been helpful and another quarter or more to elevator men who have served him. A resident in a hotel tips elevator men regularly serving him a dollar a month approximately and remembers the starter, too, at regular intervals.

ROOM WAITERS Room waiters are tipped not less than fifteen cents (for an individual small order such as a pot of tea and toast) or for a dinner order 15 per cent of the bill or not less than twenty-five cents and usually not

more than fifty cents when the bill is for two or more persons. If champagne
has been served there should be an extra tip for the handling and serving
of it. Guests may add a notation at the bottom of the bill concerning the
amount of the tip they wish given the room waiter. Resident guest tip room
waiters for each service, too, but usually see that head room waiters receive a tip about twice a year, the tip depending on the amount of room
service the guest requires—a minimum of five dollars each time and possibly as much as ten.

DINING ROOM WAITERS   The dining room waiter is the man in charge of the
service in the dining room of a hotel. He takes over from the headwaiter or,
in some cases, the hostess, and ushers guests to their seats. Transients tip the
dining room waiter sometimes, especially if they want to be sure of a good
table on their next visit. Such tips are always given after the meal. A dollar
is usual every third or fourth visit. Hotel residents tip the dining room
waiter the same way as transients do, but they give the headwaiter, not
normally tipped in hotels by transients, three to five dollars once a month
depending on the hotel.

VALETS   Hotel valets, usually operating their own shops within a hotel, do not
expect tips, except for rush jobs or those done outside of the usual hours.

TALKING TO STRANGERS WHILE TRAVELING

Americans are gregarious people, and, while our social customs are much
based on those of the English, we never did care for the rule that says one
does not speak to strangers without introduction or permit strangers to open
conversations except for some valid reason—to ask a direction, say.

A teen-age girl traveling alone on a train might reply courteously to a
man in the next seat who tried to open a conversation, "I am sorry, but I am
not allowed to talk to strangers." She is too young to have discretion about
such things, too inexperienced to be able to distinguish between the for-
wardness of a man attracted by her youth and charm and the friendliness of
another person who merely wants someone to talk to on a journey of several
hours. Her answer is the only possible one and the one her mother insists on
for her self-protection. If the stranger persists in his attentions, she should
change her seat or if there are no other seats and he is really offensive, as
sometimes happens, say to the conductor as he comes through, "I wonder
if you will arrange to change my seat." The conductor knows immediately
what the trouble is and acts accordingly. If there is no conductor immediately available, any girl or woman being annoyed is justified in turning to
another passenger, man or boy, and saying quietly, "I wonder if you will
change seats with me." This is easily done and the annoyer properly
chastened—often to a degree that he leaves the car.

A woman of more sophistication is usually able to appraise strangers and
their motives for speaking without introduction. In the subway, on buses, in
shared taxis, where this is necessary, on ferryboats, and on suburban trains,

it is relatively unusual for strangers to try to engage others in conversation, though it does happen, often from the most innocent motives.

I can remember getting on a Fifth Avenue bus at Thirty-fourth Street, having my fare paid by a perfectly strange old gentleman, having a few words with him, and being given his card—all within eight blocks. I had been waiting for a taxi in the rain, then in desperation had boarded a bus without first having the fare in hand. I stood, swaying, trying to reach my change in the depths of my bag, when a gentleman behind me reached forward and put the coin in the meter for me. "Do permit me," he said. I found my fare as I made my way down the aisle and, turning, offered it to him. It so happened that the only seats were two next to each other, so we sat down together. He refused to take the money, but he was such a decorous old gentleman that I could hardly be offended. "I am the Mayor of ——" he said, naming a western town. "Here's my card. Now when you come to our town you just look me up and repay that fare if it bothers you. My wife will be glad to meet you. So remember." I realized that out West his friendly gesture would seem the most natural thing in the world, while here, at first thought, it did seem embarrassing.

On long train, bus, or plane rides it is almost axiomatic that other travelers seated vis-à-vis or alongside a woman will try to open a conversation sooner or later. They should not be rudely snubbed, though if they seem hopelessly unattractive people or obviously impertinent, they are usually shut off by a murmured "Uh-um" in answer to some obvious question such as, "You bound for Chicago?" A book or paper is always a safe refuge, and boorish indeed is the person who persists in trying to maintain a conversation with someone who buries her nose in the printed page or one who answers everything in monosyllables.

In talking with strangers, it is unwise to volunteer information about oneself except in the vaguest manner. One rarely exchanges names or tells one's plans or home address. Conversation, if any, should be kept on impersonal topics—the weather, the scenery, perhaps the daily news. Certainly a woman never accepts the hospitality of a strange man, by allowing him to pay for refreshments or a meal en route or by accepting an invitation to lunch or dine when both reach a common destination. A woman accepting such an invitation, even from a man who has established that they have friends or acquaintances in common and who has carefully identified himself, makes a serious mistake. If the interest is really mutual and she wishes to see him after the trip, she can arrange for him to call when she will be with friends or relatives who can help appraise him. Otherwise, she may find herself in a position with which it is difficult to cope. A man may easily leap to conclusions if his invitation to a woman to whom he has not really been properly introduced is unquestioningly accepted.

It is, of course, dangerous for a woman to accept an invitation even from another woman encountered during travel. Yet, again, there are always exceptions, and one usually learns to recognize motives. I once found it absolutely necessary, because of an undelivered cable, to share a room in a crowded Basle hotel with an English girl whom I had talked to on the train but about whom I knew nothing, except her name. It was that or sit up all night in the lobby—and we both decided to risk being roommates. I put my money under my pillow and said my prayers. She was up before me and off to Italy, but I never forgot her kindness in letting me have part of the room that was really hers—for it was my reservation that had gone wrong.

CHAPTER SEVENTY-TWO

TIPS TO THE STAY-AT-HOME

BIDDING BON VOYAGE

In seeing off friends use good sense in your gift-giving. It is wiser, if you have some particular gift in mind, to present it well in advance so it may be a planned part of the luggage. Things to wear come under this category, of course, for the pair of travel slippers and the traveling iron given as train pulls out or ship embarks may have to be carried as a separate package. Air passengers should receive nothing at point of embarkation that will add to the weight of their baggage.

Bon voyage gifts for a shipboard passenger should be suitable for the quarters he is to occupy. A woman sharing a small cabin with a stranger will not be popular if the space is so crowded with her flowers that the two can't move around. The huge offerings of fruit so often sent usually go to waste or are given away because few passengers can manage to eat more than the elaborate meals offered aboard. And a woman can wear but one corsage at a time. It is wise then, if she is likely to receive many and you still wish to send one, too, to select flowers that can be kept fresh in the ship's refrigerator so that she can wear it after the first-day corsage has faded. Orchids, gardenias, and carnations refrigerate well.

Candy is not the best possible choice for travelers, unless it comes in small containers. Books, magazines, nylons, gloves, handkerchiefs, cosmetics, scarves, cigarettes, underwear, compact kits of various kinds are always welcome. But one of the most welcome gifts is an arrangement with the steamship company to serve a bottle of wine or champagne during the voyage with the compliments of the donor.

GOING ABOARD   In seeing friends off on a ship, check with the steamship company as to permissible visiting hours. After bidding farewell, leave the ship at the warning gong. If you can't see your friends off, you may write them a bon voyage note addressed to the ship in time for it to be aboard to welcome passengers when they receive their mail. Or you may send a telegram addressed to them aboard ship. For example, Mr. and Mrs. Joshua Bodwin, H.M.S. *Queen Elizabeth,* Cunard Line, Pier 90, North River, New York. Sailings, in peace time, are listed in the metropolitan newspapers.

TRAIN AND PLANE FAREWELLS It is less usual to see friends off on planes, as visitors are rarely allowed beyond the gate and farewells are of the briefest sort. Train farewells are equally unsatisfactory, as good-bys are usually said at the gate in large stations. Flowers, gifts, and telegrams, however, may be delivered to trains if you know the seat, car, or compartment numbers and the hour of departure. You address a telegram (even after the train is en route it is possible for a passenger to receive a wire in this country): Miss Jessie De Groot, Aboard the *Linet* leaving Los Angeles at 2 P.M. Tuesday, Seat 43, Car 1166.

CHAPTER SEVENTY-THREE

HOW CUSTOMS DIFFER ABROAD

TAKING BATHS

A hotel room with bath is still unusual in Europe and will not be readily found except in luxury hotels, but washing facilities are provided in each room, though not necessarily running water. It is the European custom to take sponge baths daily, tub baths perhaps not oftener than once a week. The shower is uncommon.

As there may be only one or two bathrooms to a floor in a European hotel, the patron desiring to take a bath goes through a certain ritual. In most cases he rings for the maid and makes an appointment for his bathtime. When the hour arrives the bathroom will be vacant and ready for him and his bath drawn for him at the temperature he requests. In a small Paris hotel he may find a clean linen sheet lining the carefully scrubbed bathtub and a clean bath towel laid out for him, but, as elsewhere on the Continent, he is usually expected to furnish his own soap. There is, in addition, usually an extra charge for a bath, or at least the maid expects an extra *pourboire* (tip) for her trouble. Why can't these Americans get themselves clean in a sponge bath and *bidet* like normal people?

THE W.C.

All over Europe and the British Isles the letters "W.C." are to be found posted in public places, on signs, or on doors. This is the English abbreviation for "water closet," lavatory to us. Often there is just one door marked "W.C.," in which case the lavatory is for the use of both men and women. If there are two doors, there may be the "W.C." sign but on each door will be written the native equivalent of "Men" and "Women" and these foreign words, at least, must be understood by the traveler. As almost no one travels abroad without a pocket dictionary, it is easy enough to determine these words for each country to be visited. In pronouncing the letters "W.C." in France one says "dooble-vay-say," in Germany and Holland "vay-say"; in Latin countries the word is some easily recognized variation of our "lavatory" or "toilet." In Dutch-speaking countries the word is "retirade."

The word "lavatory" in England has come to mean the toilet, itself, and never the washbasin, the bathroom, or restroom as in our inclusive use of the term. A friend of mine who spent much time in England says that the English are shocked, therefore, at such a bald American statement as "I'll just rinse out my stockings in the lavatory." To be really polite, in England you use that euphemism "Where may I wash my hands?" when in search of a bathroom.

THE POURBOIRE

Many an American unused to the French language finds himself muttering "What?" to the mumbled "*Pourboire?*" he gets from the usher in a cinema as he is shown to his seat. A *pourboire* (literally, "for a drink") is a tip. Most European servitors have mastered the English word by now and use it freely, but "*pourboire*" is still the most common word an American will hear, and, unaccustomed as he is to anyone's actually asking for a tip or being obvious about the outstretched palm, he is sometimes deaf to that insistent, soft "*Pourboire?*"

The tipping system, which is expected to make up the difference between base pay, if any, and a living wage, is even more widespread in Europe than it is here. It is a continental custom to tip the theater usher—even the cinema usher. In the British Isles theater ushers are not tipped, but where there is a program, there is a charge for it. The equivalent of twenty cents, usually a coin about the size of our quarter—a shilling, a franc, a lira, half a guilder, etc.—is a generous tip in Europe for anything other than a meal, the tip for which is, roughly, 10 to 15 per cent in round numbers, as it is here— 20 per cent where lavish tipping seems expected. For small services, the equivalent of ten cents or so—a sixpence, in the British Isles, for example— is considered usual.

THE "BOOTS"

A British stand-by is the "boots," who expects to find your shoes outside your hotel door each night for him to clean and put back silently. The "boots" by some other name is sometimes found on the Continent, but it is safer to be sure before putting out your footwear. Usually the cleaning of shoes—men's and women's—is a complimentary service on the part of the hotel, but even if there is some charge on the bill the "boots" receives a tip —about ten cents per night—or if there is no billed charge for the cleaning roughly 10 per cent of the cost of the room, put out for him weekly in the shoes, as the "boots" is a nightworker whose face you may never see.

TRAVEL

One may not even pass through some foreign countries on the train without a visa for each country, although much has been done recently to simplify travel. While you may have had the matter of visas taken care of at home when you purchased your tickets, be sure, if your plans change, that any passage through a country not previously in your itinerary is covered by visas, wherever they are still necessary, as the lack of them may be a serious matter at borders. Visas are not requested when a traveler boards a train but only after he has passed through the territory in question and has been through customs.

In the British Isles train travel has a strict formality, which even visiting Americans are expected to follow. In a big station like Waterloo, after buying your ticket, you line up in the queue at the gate. There is no mass frontal attack on the gates when the train is ready to load, with women and children trampled underfoot, as happens here. The British queue is respected at all bus stops, cinemas, fish markets, and bargain counters. It makes for better tempers and saves time in the end.

Trains in England usually carry two classes of accommodation, first and third. These accommodations, which are divided into compartments, open onto a corridor on longer journeys. On short runs, one car may be first-class, or one car may be divided into first- and second-class and there is no connecting corridor. It is important to locate the accommodations called for on your ticket and then to hold on to the ticket until you are safely through the turnstile at the end of your trip. A British train ticket is only punched by the conductor and is taken up finally at the station at which you detrain.

In Paris one is permitted to board a bus only if he holds in his hand a special "place" ticket for the conductor to see. This he is expected to tear off a pad attached to a tree or post at the bus stop. Passengers are admitted to the crowded busses in numerical order.

In European dining cars meals are served as they are on boats—first, second, third sitting. On boarding a train with dining facilities, one makes a reservation for a sitting with the steward in charge, giving one's name and seat number. The passenger is then assigned to a particular service and listens for the announcement called out for it during the dining hours. In many places on the Continent, as on small railroads here, it is expected that passengers will stop over for meals at the station restaurants provided and that is what the (to us) interminable wait-overs are for—so passengers can alight and eat.

On the Continent the trains are usually divided into first-class, second-class, and third-class, the last frequently equipped with hard wooden benches and replete with large families who do everything but the family wash en route.

EATING CUSTOMS

In Holland, as elsewhere on the Continent, the meat knife is always steel-bladed. A lady's escort in a Dutch restaurant reaches over and, taking her knife, neatly sharpens the blade against his own. It is, by the way, quite incorrect in Europe to use the meat knife on potatoes, which should always be cut with a fork (a steel blade would turn them an unappetizing black). Fish is always eaten with special, non-steel fish knife and fork, so that the fish will not have a metallic taste.

SMOKING AT TABLE   In England at public dinners there is no smoking before the "Queen's Toast," the first toast offered. This is a rule foreigners are certainly expected to know and must observe. In fact, there is much less smoking at meals abroad than there is here, and it is wise, even in a group of young people, to let the hostess make the first move toward offering cigarettes during the course of a meal.

IS THE WOMAN ALWAYS PLACED TO THE RIGHT OF THE MAN?   On the Continent a gentleman is careful to seat a lady on his right. In Victorian and earlier times any lady a man seated on his left was no lady. He so proclaimed the fact to prevent any passing male friend from introducing her to his wife. Among younger people, this convention certainly no longer holds, except in Latin countries, but it is just as well for a lady to sit at a man's right even in a car or taxi. The theater is excepted, if to sit on a man's right would place the woman in an aisle seat. On the street, especially in Latin countries, the lady is always on the man's right whether or not this places her on the curb side temporarily. In olden times, in fact, it was considerably safer, especially in London's narrow, congested streets, with the many dark alleys and people's habit of dumping refuse into the street, for the man to cede the safer curb side to the woman. Generally speaking, we cling to the opposite convention here, because in our early days alleys were not a menace but the flying mud from unpaved streets was.

In the Scandinavian countries the place of honor is always on the left, or heart side, whether a gentleman is walking with a lady or a hostess is seating a guest of honor.

ARE WE BOORISH ABROAD?

It takes a seasoned and sophisticated traveler to so conduct himself in a foreign country that he is barely noticed as a stranger. It does seem ego-centric to insist on doing everything in one's own national way while travel-ing, when minor adjustments would be more courteous. A guest—and even when we are paying our own way we are always guests abroad—should try his best to conform to local customs unless, of course, they offend his own sense of decorum in some major manner.

Americans abroad are often considered patronizing because of their fuller wallets and their sometimes noisy, flamboyant, and exhibitionist behavior. Our wide gestures at self-entertainment offend quiet, sober, and thrifty people, even though they benefit, at the same time, by our munifi-cence. And we are worst when we descend en masse on Europe in the sum-mertime, acting in non-English-speaking countries as if everyone *should* speak English and in English-speaking countries as if their brand of English should conform exactly to our own.

During World War II the Government understood the importance of teaching our military men and women some of the subtleties of proper social behavior in foreign lands. Proper *American* social behavior was not enough. Our soldiers and sailors learned to remove their shoes before enter-ing a Japanese home, or a Mohammedan mosque, or a Buddhist temple. They squatted or sat cross-legged at table and ate out of communal dishes in Mohammedan lands and in various Oriental countries. They tried to remember certain shibboleths and taboos and what English words could not be politely used in English drawing rooms—"bloody," for example. They noted that in England "napkin" or "nappie" often meant diaper; "flannel" meant a washcloth, and "serviette" meant a napkin as it does on the Con-tinent. Our truck became a "lorry" or a "van," and our trolley was a "tram," a closet was a "cupboard," and molasses "treacle." "Tea" could be just that or the equivalent of our Sunday night supper. A shower was a "douche" and a tiny toy, a "dinkie," a boutonniere, a "buttonhole." To charge something was "to put it down," and to do an errand was "to run a message."

Shortly, under military instruction and because it was more convenient, our men and women learned to do in Rome as the Romans. If this works under the stress of war, it will work in peacetime. As much as possible, while still identifying ourselves as Americans, we should behave as those we visit behave, not try to take the freest manners and language of our Main Streets abroad.

AMERICAN WOMAN IN LATIN COUNTRIES

Urban Latins are getting used to us, but to the less sophisticated the be-havior and appearance of American girls and women abroad is an open invitation to unwelcome advances.

I have seen young American girls in Mexico City run in and out of the lobby of the Reforma in the shortest of shorts and bra tops. Had they been able to understand the comments of the guides and the peddlers on the corner, they would have gone to their rooms and stayed there in humiliation. Would these same young women walk in and out of the lobby of the Waldorf-Astoria in such a get-up? And, if not, why should it be considered good enough for a foreign country?

On the Continent and in Latin America there is never the kind of drinking among women that goes on sometimes in the United States. Any woman or group of women entering a bar for the purpose of drinking, especially drinking hard liquor, can expect "incidents." In fact, right in the United States, unescorted women in bars, if indeed they are admitted, can expect trouble and a lone woman drinker in a bar is frankly suspect.

In some Latin countries one or two young, or even not-so-young, women traveling alone must be circumspect to the point of prudery or else develop a keen parrying power. Two college girls on a summer trip to Rome were plagued by a pair of Italian boys who, misunderstanding their free American manners, followed them openly through several streets. Finally the older of the two girls, knowing how quickly the Italian "gentleman" takes offense, turned around and calmly tossed their pursuers a lira. What an insult for Roman Romeos to be taken for mere beggars! They were gone in an instant.

It is better sense for American women to fare forth at night in Latin countries in groups or with male escorts. If they must go alone, they should summon a taxi from a public stand. Latin women are so carefully protected that the woman who goes out alone, especially at night, is fairly sure to be accosted, if only verbally. And even if she knows the language, a woman in a foreign land spoken to impertinently by a passing stranger does just what she does at home—pretends she has heard nothing and goes quickly and quietly on her way.

In America we love the color red, but in Europe and in Latin America it is considered *déclassé*—except when Paris declares it fashionable and when it is used as an accent color in bag or shoes on the young (who pay less attention to the supposed significance of red) or in a peasant costume. Beware of wearing a red boutonniere, again an invitation to unwelcome advances in some countries—Holland, for example.

Anklets, which used to be *déclassé* here but are now quite popularly worn, have a most unpleasant connotation in Europe. American women who ordinarily wear a gold anklet, if only for identification purposes, should remove it before going abroad.

American women, if they are unmarried and definitely not elderly, should not permit their hands to be kissed publicly or, unless they wish to encourage ardent attention, privately either. (See "Hand Kissing.")

In all Latin countries it is mere social technique for men to indulge in the wildest hyperbole, quite publicly, concerning the women they accompany. Such remarks as "You are absolutely magnificent!" or "The angels should have such eyes!" should be taken with a grain of salt and an unstartled "Thank you." In Latin etiquette all social intercourse has a very personal connotation but its very personalness is stylized. Not every man is madly in love, or about-to-be-madly-in-love with every woman to whom he is presented. But the very fact that, for social reasons, it almost seems he is makes for warmth and gaiety in Latin gatherings. Everyone knows it is just a graceful social game with all holds barred, but the atmosphere is certainly more conducive to conversation than that of a restrained English or German group. Perhaps this is because, in Latin etiquette, the extravagant, admiring phrases are directed as frequently to the old as to the young and tempting.

It is our cold, English culture, of course, that makes us, if not suspicious of the stranger, at least most restrained and impersonal in our casual contact with him. The Latins do not place courtesy on two separate levels—the embarrassed, eyes-averted kind for strangers and another warmer kind for friends and acquaintances. The warmth of the Latin is in everything he does and must not be misconstrued. He will speak to an unaccompanied woman with no encouragement whatsoever, whether or not he has performed some routine service for her. His motives are not necessarily ulterior. If they should turn out to be, it is quite easy to rebuff him politely.

The Latin's personal brand of courtesy extends to people who serve him (in shops, particularly) as well as to those he serves. A little polite conversation precedes the purchase of a bunch of bananas in the *mercado*, a little passing of the time of day. Latin purveyors find time to greet the customer, serve her in a leisurely manner, and bid her farewell, to which the customer replies in kind. In even the busiest shop in France each customer greets the sales person with a *"Bonjour, madame"* (or mademoiselle, or monsieur), or the equivalent in other countries, and the sales person returns the greeting before the transaction begins. Americans who cannot give these greetings in the language of the country should remember at least to give them in English, adding the polite "madame" or other title, as is always done in Latin countries. When we omit these little ceremonies we are adjudged boorish.

In all Latin countries funerals are shown great respect. Often the procession is on foot, and if it passes us, we should do whatever others on the sidewalk are doing. Women usually bow the head or, if Catholics, make the sign of the cross and, if possible, wait until the funeral has passed before continuing on their way.

And, of course, women as well as men should be able to recognize the national anthem of any country they are visiting and should rise (men should uncover their heads) with others in public places whenever it is played.

AMERICAN MEN IN LATIN COUNTRIES

Italian and French men often embrace and kiss on both cheeks their male relatives and close men friends on meeting. Spaniards do little of this, and

Latin-American men don't do it at all. A ceremonial kiss, when an honor is bestowed, may be preceded by the usual handclasp in France, Spain, and Italy. The bestower of the honor, some dignitary, places the ribbon or medal on the recipient, clasps his hand briefly, then leans forward and kisses him first on one cheek, then on the other. They then shake hands, and the ceremony is over.

American men must be very chary indeed with their attentions toward unmarried Latin women. Any attention is frequently construed by wary parents as serious *intention*. Chaperones, in most countries, are required for all girls of good family after 6 P.M. and on some occasions even in the daytime, although in the more modern countries groups of boys and girls often go out together, especially if the girls' brothers are in the party. A Latin brother is trained to be even more careful of his sister's honor than is the most fusty chaperone. The "date" as it exists in America is unknown in most Latin countries, where all upper-class girls are protected.

Once you have been presented to a girl under proper auspices, it is correct to ask if you may call. A first call always takes place in the presence of a chaperone or the family and is very formal. Later, without prior arrangement, a young man may present himself at the young lady's grilled window, in those countries where this is the custom (now pretty much confined to small towns—mostly in Spain) and talk to her or serenade her. She is permitted to chat through the grille, unchaperoned, far into the night if she is so disposed, but it is not only futile but dangerous for a suitor to try to get into her apartment.

A popular girl may have more than one suitor beneath her window at a time. It is for them to work out whether they will both stay or whether the one there first will have the evening to himself. About nine o'clock is suitable for calling on a Latin beauty at her window, but if she does not come to the grille within a few minutes it is considered poor taste to stay, as she may be waiting for some more welcome caller.

Some Latin married women are given considerable freedom. They do not herd together as American women do at luncheon and tea spots, but often lunch with men, their husbands, or their husbands' friends—with the husbands' knowledge. It is considered quite correct for a man who has been entertained in someone's home to ask his hostess to luncheon or tea without her husband—especially in France. He may call also upon her at her home in the afternoon hours, so long as their conduct is *sans reproche*. In America, if a business man left his office to call on the wife of a friend at four o'clock, it might not seem exactly cricket to an absent husband when no one else but servants was present, but in France particularly such calls are quite usual.

DANCING ABROAD

The American system of "cutting in" is a hold-over from pioneer days, when at any dance there were never enough women to go around. We try to maintain this situation artificially, in New York especially, by having a large stag line or, at subscription dances, requiring each girl to bring more than one partner. This is supposed to insure that all the girls will be constantly awhirl—but doesn't. Good dancers and popular girls enjoy the cutting in of eager gentlemen, but the shy girl hates the system. Rarely is her partner cut in on, and the boys avoid her for fear of being "stuck." Short of breaking an ankle, her partner must stay with her until he can unload her on some-one else or she has sense enough to plead fatigue and retreat to the ladies' room.

In Europe and Latin America dances are never the social agony they often are for the young here. In the first place, the chaperone system guaran-tees that the girl will have a place to go when the music stops, and her partner is always expected to return her to her chaperone or to the spot where he claimed her, where she was standing or seated with friends. A bow and thanks and her partner is gone. There is no cutting in, so a girl can relax and enjoy her dance with one partner throughout the musical selec-tion and not have to keep a weather eye out for the stag line.

Furthermore, continental style, the young men at a dance do not con-centrate their dancing attention on the eligible girls alone but do consider-able duty dancing with their parents' friends. And because the married women are kept dancing, older men have plenty of opportunity of dancing with their friends' daughters, an expected thing. In this country an older man trying to compete with the stag line is considered a silly old "wolf," and the older woman dancing with a twenty-year-old is either pitiable or suspect.

THE PAID DANCING PARTNER

In many large continental hotels paid dancing partners are frequently on duty at teatime and dinner where there is a dance orchestra. These gentle-men, who do not care for the word "gigolo," usually move discreetly among the tables seeking partners for a small fee.

If a young girl is with her family or a chaperone, such a professional dancer (in France "un danseur," or "un animateur" if he's a social director paid by the management) will quietly request the person in charge (who later pays) for a dance with the girl. If permission is given, and it usually is, the two dance with little or no effort at conversation. In fact, the girl is careful to give no information about herself, and the man is never introduced nor does he ever try to follow up the brief contact socially. His is merely a business deal and the hotel, in permitting him to operate—often as a con-cessionaire—underwrites his acceptability, at least as a public dancing part-ner. For unaccompanied women to employ these dancing parters in public places is correct, but for them to put the arrangement on any kind of personal plane is begging trouble. It is no shame to employ a dancing partner abroad—the most conservative women do it. But everyone knows on what basis such a man is in a woman's company, and it is ridiculous to pretend he is anything but what he is.

The payment for a dancing partner varies but is usually by the dance—approximately the equivalent of forty cents—and he dances with the same partner until he is dismissed. In large resort hotels the "danseur" is on the staff and receives about the same tip as the headwaiter. He is usually not invited to join a party, but if he does sit with an unescorted woman his drinks are put on her check by the waiter and his sitting-out time must be compensated for as well. An evening's dancing at various night spots with a paid companion is contracted for in advance and through the hotel desk. All expenses are paid by the woman quite openly, or, if she prefers, she is rendered an exact accounting of disbursements at the end of the evening and settles promptly.

TAKING PICTURES

Our country is very large and the number of tourists descending upon it yearly and bent on picture-taking is relatively small. Have you ever been stopped on the street and asked to pose—as a local curiosity—for a foreigner's box camera? Probably not, but Americans abroad always think in terms of people-in-their-pictures and are pretty abrupt in their posing orders, at that. Think how it must be on, say, an island like Jamaica for a whole boatload of tourists to descend all at once, all focusing their cameras on the passing citizenry without, usually, even a "by-your-leave."

Strange as it may seem, many people are not pleased at being camera subjects. Unless you have the kind of camera that can take action shots inconspicuously, always ask people to pose (if you must) and with great politeness—in the sign language, if necessary. And where the practice seems acceptable, give tips to your models. In countries where national costumes are worn many working people are plagued to death by camera addicts during the tourist season. It is only fair to offer them some compensation for the time all this posing takes.

CHAPTER SEVENTY-FOUR

AN AUDIENCE WITH THE POPE

Visitors to Rome, Catholics and non-Catholics, usually desire to visit the historic and beautiful Vatican City and have an audience with the Pope, head of the Roman Catholic Church.

The etiquette concerning an audience with the Pope is very rigid. Requests by Americans are cleared through the North American College in Rome and are presented to a papal secretary by means of introductory letters from prominent Catholic laymen or priests. The greatly sought-after audiences cannot be quickly arranged, so letters should be presented as soon as possible on arrival and in person.

Reply to your request will arrive by courier within a few days. The invitation to an audience, if issued, will be in Italian, and, as you have formally requested it in person, you do not need to reply. Needless to say, once an audience has been granted you do not refuse it for any reason save illness. In the case of illness an explanatory note in English should be sent by hand to the papal secretary with whom you have been dealing. He in turn will make necessary explanations to the official in charge of the audience.

If you cannot decipher the details of the audience as they appear on the Italian summons, get assistance from your embassy or from your hotel manager who is probably very familiar with the procedure at the Vatican.

CLOTHES TO WEAR Well in advance of presenting your credentials, check your wardrobe to see if you have the necessary clothes. Military personnel are received in uniform, with the men hatless, the women with hats or caps. Civilian men and women, Catholic and non-Catholic, must comply with Vatican rules concerning dress in order to be received by the Pope.

For a private or semiprivate audience men must wear either a dark blue or Oxford gray suit, but if neither of these is available, then evening clothes are worn for an audience with the Pope. Hats are optional since men do not appear before the Holy Father with anything on the head. No boutonnieres are ever worn, although orders, such as the ribbon of the Chevalier of the Legion of Honor or the sash of some important official order, are encouraged. Jewelry should be as inconspicuous as possible and without colored stones, with the possible exception of amethysts.

The rules of dress for women are very circumscribed. Women must wear black. The neck of the costume must be high, the sleeves to the wrist, and the head must be covered by a black veil or black mantilla. Shoes, gloves, and stockings must be black. Any jewelry must be strictly functional. Wedding and engagement rings are, of course, permitted, but bracelets and decorative pins should be removed, although a pin actually needed to hold together a neckline is allowed but should be preferably of dull gold, pearl, platinum, silver, or jet—not brightly colored stones. A simple strand of pearls is allowable, but earrings are usually removed as too frivolous.

Children may wear white to an audience. A small boy is acceptable in gray with a white shirt, black shoes and socks, black or white gloves, and a black or gray tie, but even in winter a white summer suit for a boy who is not old enough for a tuxedo is quite usual. Girls must cover their heads, too, with white veils or with black veils to match black or white costumes.

For general audiences regular, conservative church-going clothes are quite acceptable with, of course, some kind of suitable headcovering for women. Men may wear conservative business suits, white shirts, solid-color dark ties.

WHAT TO TAKE Catholics usually go to the Vatican with a few rosaries, a sacred statuette, or missal for the papal blessing (as gifts for their family and friends). Protestants who wish to make such gifts to Catholic friends do the same, buying the things to be blessed in the various shops in Rome, which sell religious articles or bringing their friends' own rosaries or other religious possessions with them for the blessing.

THE AUDIENCE There are three classes of papal audience—private, semi-private, and general. The first is reserved for very distinguished persons. The second is limited to a few people at a time who, in the opinion of the secretaries, merit special attention from His Holiness. The third is for the many pilgrims to the Vatican, who from time to time have the privilege of attending services conducted by the Pope in the Eternal City.

In private and semiprivate audiences those who are to receive the papal benediction are instructed to get on both knees just before the entrance of the Pope. As the Pope enters the room he offers a general benediction, then addresses each pilgrim separately, stopping in front of him. The pilgrim receives the benediction with bowed head, makes the appropriate responses in Latin if he's a Catholic, or receives them in respectful silence if he's a non-Catholic. The Pope then extends his hand. The proper procedure is to place your hand under his and kiss the ring, symbol of his churchly office.

If this very special and circumscribed formality conflicts in any way with your own convictions, you do not attempt to modify the procedure to suit yourself. Instead, you forgo asking for an audience.

Those seeking the audience take with them, if they wish, their rosary or rosaries and any religious object they may be able to hold gracefully in the left hands while leaving the right hand free. The benediction is considered to be extended to such objects as a pilgrim brings with him to the audience.

MAKING THE SIGN OF THE CROSS Although the rest of the procedure is rigidly prescribed, no one who does not ordinarily make the sign of the cross in his devotions is expected to do so during an audience with the Pope after his benediction.

LEAVING THE AUDIENCE While the Pope is present those in the room, with the exception of his retinue, remain on their knees. Those who have received the benediction remain on their knees until the Pope has left the room or has signaled that those present may stand. Anyone leaving the papal presence backs away a few steps, then moves to the side before turning around, as with royalty on whom one must never turn the back.

WHEN INTERVIEWS ARE ARRANGED Again as with royalty, one must not open the conversation but must wait for the Pope to speak first. One leaves only after permission to leave has been granted or if the Pope rises to indicate that the interview is at a close.

CHAPTER SEVENTY-FIVE

MOTORING MANNERS

TAKING TAXIS

When you hail a taxi that carries a meter, be sure the driver pushes the flag up to start the meter again. Otherwise, the previous passenger's fare will be added to yours. The minute the cab pulls to a stop the meter should be stopped by the driver's pushing the flag down. The driver is not supposed to let the meter run while he makes change. If you are careful to insist upon this you protect the next passenger. It is against the law for a metered taxi to proceed with the flag down while carrying a passenger, unless the taxi has been engaged for a trip out of town at a flat rate. A passenger may not make such a flat rate with a company driver. Such a driver must phone his company to get permission to leave city limits and get the flat rate. The driver of an independent cab may fix his own flat rates but not within city limits if he has a metered cab. If you ask any driver of a metered taxi to set you a flat rate within the city limits—perhaps late at night when the police may be less alert—you are asking him to break the law, and, if caught, he can lose his license. If the trip takes a metered taxi outside city limits and you have neglected to ask for a flat rate, you can be held responsible for the metered cost of the return trip if the car breaks down.

PROTECTION When you enter a cab, look immediately at the license in the back and be sure the driver's face corresponds with the picture on the license. These pictures are in most cities taken with the driver wearing a cap, not a hat, to make identification easier for the passenger. If you entrust a woman or child to a taxi, make a notation of the driver's license and that of the car. For safety's sake, in the case of a child or sick person, have someone phone you on his arrival. All taxi drivers must be licensed and fingerprinted. To ride in a cab not driven by its proper driver as indicated on the posted license is to risk accident, robbery, attack, and even death.

BEHAVIOR IN TAXIS Many people behave in cabs as if the drivers were wooden Indians. It is quite possible for drivers to hear all conversation in the back of the cab when the window is down, and many cabs have strategically placed rear-view mirrors that permit the driver a full view of the back of the cab. A taxi, therefore, is as public as the library, about as private as the back seat of a bus.

Taximen are a philosophical, often cynical crew. They must drive all day, relatively unprotected from the weather for eight hours—sometimes longer, if they have the stamina to work for overtime pay. To pass the time they often open conversations with passengers—if the passengers don't get the conversational drop on them first. Such conversations should be kept impersonal. Why take violent issue—say on politics—with a taximan whom you will probably never see again. He needs to blow off a little steam from his tiresome spot behind the wheel. Listen and sometimes learn, but never, if you're a woman, permit remarks that seem too personal or prying. It is quite easy to roll up the window separating you from the driver if you don't want to talk or if his remarks get out of hand. The law says, that, with or without conversation, he must deliver you where you want to go within the area in which his cab operates.

LOSING BELONGINGS IN TAXIS   In all big cities drivers must keep a log of each trip they make. You have seen them filling the log out as you enter and leave the cab or sometimes when they must stop for a light. These cards note where the passenger—or passengers—were picked up, the number of passengers, and where they alighted, together with the meter reading for the trip. The cards must be kept over quite a long period of time in case of police checkup. If you leave something in a cab and do not remember what company operated it, it is still possible to trace your property. Notify the police at once and tell them where and at what time you took the cab and how many passengers were in the car. If the article has not been turned in to police headquarters, a fairly quick check on your driver can be made. Most cab drivers are very honest, and there are many regulations they have to observe. They must, for example, check the cab for forgotten articles as you leave, for they can be held responsible if a subsequent passenger appropriates lost property.

Where a taxi driver does turn in something of impressive value left in his cab, it is usual to give a reward of at least 10 per cent of the actual value of the article.

TIPPING IN TAXIS   For rides under fifty cents, never give less than a ten-cent tip. If the meter reads thirty or thirty-five cents, do not expect change from a fifty-cent piece. Drivers work on a base salary plus tips. Every time you undertip or—as some parsimonious people do—fail to tip at all, you cut their salary. For longer rides 15 per cent of the total is fair. As women tend to undertip, don't be surprised if your driver looks less than cordial when you start counting out your money. He expects the worst. If you think of the tip as part of your fare, not as gratuity, it will be easier to endure the usual stony silence when you give even a generous tip.

GOOD MANNERS AND YOUR CAR

Nowhere in the world are there so many privately owned automobiles as there are in America. Or such widely practiced bad car manners.

If you are really observant, you can learn more about a person's poise, considerateness (or lack of it), probity, and judgment by riding with him at the wheel of his car than you can by studying him long hours in his living room. You will see the timid man, or woman, grow bullying and bellicose behind the wheel. You will note the neighbor's fender scraped as your man pulls heedlessly out of the parking spot, the pedestrian narrowly missed and roundly cursed although he has the right of way. You will experience the senseless weaving in and out of traffic with the many near-accidents it causes.

The established rules of driving are for the protection of other drivers and the non-driving public, but they are also related to good manners. If you do scrape someone else's fender in leaving a parking space, you should, as a well-mannered person, leave your car and arrange to make good the damage, even if the law didn't hold you responsible under the circumstances. Most careful people carry liability and property damage even in states where it is not actually required, but most insurance doesn't cover such slight property damage as is occasioned by the scraping of a fender. The owner of the car must pay for that himself. You who inflicted the damage may find your own insurance will cover even such minor damage to some-one else's car, but even if it doesn't, you should make yourself responsible. If no one is in the other car, leave a card or note with your name and address so that matters may be arranged between you. In some states any damage over a certain amount to another car or to your own—even, in the latter case, if you inflicted it yourself—must be reported to police. Else-where, adjustments of this kind are a matter of good manners.

HAND SIGNALS While hand signals are almost everywhere obligatory, there is usually no policeman behind a car to check on whether the driver uses them consistently. Hand signals should be second nature to the good driver, which means he should use them automatically even when they don't seem strictly necessary as, for example, on a country road. It is much too easy if you do a lot of country driving to get out of the habit of using hand signals. Yet forgetfulness of them in even slightly heavy town or city traffic can cause accidents or at least inconvenience to other drivers.

Your state's Department of Motor Vehicles probably issues a pamphlet which shows, usually graphically, all accepted hand signals and all state driving regulations. If you have been driving many years without having had to take additional driving tests, it is possible that you are not properly informed about local and state driving ordinances and that your driving may eventually bring you into conflict with ever-toughening state laws.

THOUGHTLESS ACTS The innocent bystander who is mud-spattered because you didn't avoid or proceed more slowly through the mud puddle in the road doesn't have recourse to law, but he does have his opinion of your manners. The householder who finds his driveway blocked by your car can call the police, but usually he just fumes until you turn up to move your vehicle.

In some places citizens aroused by the noise of your unmuffled muffler can do something about it, but in other communities it's up to you to see that you are not creating a nuisance.

THE GOOD DRIVER   A really good driver has been taught to drive by another really good driver. He learns that he touches the foot brake as little as possible if he would avoid jerks and sudden stops. He lets the engine brake the car. He never grinds his gears or slips backward on a hill before starting up. He sounds his horn only as necessary and never when the traffic is held up and other drivers are stupidly leaning on their horns on the assumption that they will thus speed things along.

No considerate person ever sounds his horn outside another's home in summons if he can possibly leave the wheel or send someone in with a message. And when he takes to the road he has with him any necessary repair tools, so as not to annoy passing motorists by asking to borrow a jack or a wrench in the case of a blowout.

In cold climates the considerate motorist carries in winter a shovel or trowel and some sand in his car and, if possible, a tow line, not only for his own car's probable use but to help others stuck on the road. At all times he carries a flashlight and a first-aid kit (which he knows how to use). If he's really sensible, he has a fire extinguisher—the kind with carbontetrachloride or with CO_2—or at least knows enough to put out an engine fire with sand or earth.

THE WELCOME PASSENGER   A passenger should know, above all else, when to keep quiet. He should not chatter when the car is in heavy traffic, and he should abstain from giving gratuitous advice in times of difficulty. He should sit as still as possible and not distract the driver by reaching into the back of the car, bouncing around on the seat, or opening the door while the car is in motion. Let the passenger keep his hands and belongings well inside the car, too, to avoid confusing drivers behind him.

It is the driver, not the passenger, who must determine whether or not the car radio is to be on or whether or not smoking will disturb him.

No one leaving a car should fail to close all doors carefully.

DOUBLE PARKING   In some towns and cities even momentary double parking, while the boy runs out with your groceries or you call a greeting to a neighbor, may get you a ticket. Elsewhere it's a matter of manners. If no one is trying to pass you, there is nothing against a brief double parking (if it's legal), but keep your motor running so you can make way if you find yourself blocking free passage.

IS THE SLOW DRIVER BEST?   It takes constant exercise of judgment to make the good driver. Sometimes slow driving is the best driving. In other cases a fast clip, evenly sustained, is sometimes required. Never, for example, keep your car in the left-hand lane of a through route, if you do not plan to maintain the maximum speed. By doing so you hold up the drivers behind you, who will be irritated—probably noisily so—by your refusal to let them pass. On a narrow road, especially at night, if you prefer to proceed at a very moderate rate—which is your privilege—and another car is forced to tail you at your speed, although he obviously would like to overtake you, pull up to the side of the road to let him pass, unless you know the road will soon widen enough to let him go by.

YOU AND THE LAW

It is curious how so many otherwise law-abiding people feel they can break traffic laws with impunity. When they are occasionally caught up with for their infractions, they tend to become abusive to the arresting officer, or at least show indignation.

If you are picked up for speeding or some other flouting of the traffic laws, treat the officer, who must caution you, serve you with a ticket, or take you in, as the representative of the public (and of you yourself) that he is, not as an archenemy. Hand him the papers he asks for—your license, the car registration. Answer his questions quietly. You may be quite in the right, but abusive language now will nullify any chance you might have to avoid this mark against your record. Above all, never threaten or try to bribe a traffic officer or state policeman. Trying to do such a thing may land you in even hotter water.

Policemen are human, too. If you have been in the wrong, an immediate admission of the fact instead of an argument may get you off with a warning instead of a ticket.

In case of any serious accident involving your car, do not leave the scene until the police have arrived and taken all information. Do not move anyone with possible back or bone injury until a doctor has arrived.

HITCHHIKERS

In some states it is against the law for people to hitchhike. Everywhere the motorist himself takes a real chance from a liability standpoint when he picks up someone at the side of the road, even if that person is known to him. Every car should carry liability insurance to protect car owners against possible suit by passengers, hitchhikers or not.

Many women, especially in rural areas, make it a rule not to pick up any but children. And it is true that in many communities not served by buses or other public transportation hitchhiking is an accepted thing. It is a good idea, if you permit your children to hitchhike in the neighborhood, to restrict them to cars bearing your own state license plates or, better still, to cars whose owners they actually know. Let them, if possible, phone you when they start out, and from various spots en route if they must hail more than one car.

If you do pick up a hitchhiker who seem to answer specifications as to appearance, find out immediately where he wishes to go. It is not necessary to carry on a conversation with him, except perhaps one that will identify him, more or less, to you. Give no information about yourself. Pay extra strict attention to your driving, for you may have a liability in your car.

SELECTING AN AUTOMOBILE

COLORS IN CARS   Cars are available in all colors of the rainbow if you want to go to the trouble and expense of a special paint job. But for town cars the conservative colors—black, dark blue, maroon, forest green, or gunmetal—look best. Save your yearning for a fire-engine red for the roadster or convertible used in the country—making sure before you invest in it, that fire-engine-red cars are permissible in the state in which it will be registered.

CAN YOU LIVE UP TO YOUR CAR?   It is certainly not unheard of for a man, usually a young one, to invest his all in a car that he can't possibly live up to. A five- or ten-thousand-dollar imported car—even though it cost considerably less secondhand—can bring its owner much embarrassment if he lives in a neighborhood out of tune with such luxuries. If he's not careful, the car, not he, will be the master, dictating where he must go, what he should spend, and how he must dress, even though his income is nowhere in line with what the possession of such a car would indicate.

I once knew a promising young man, whose name was on all the social lists, who, although he had a very modest job, strained every nerve to keep up a front, however false. On his small salary he supported a secondhand Rolls-Royce, an extravagance that forced him to share a little walk-up apartment with two other boys. He missed many a meal and often had to abandon his car to possible street vandals for lack of gas to get it home. Yet he felt he was investing in his future. I often wonder what happened to him.

On the other hand, if you will notice, there are millionaires who do not hesitate to drive around in antique relics. To a certain kind of mind, old things, once good, have a kind of aura of respectability and stability. People with money do not necessarily have expensive cars, and the old snobbishness about the price of a car is gone. Many who could afford super-elegant cars prefer simple small ones in sufficient number to accommodate a busy family that, very probably, chauffeurs itself.

THE STATION WAGON

Station wagons, originally thought of as estate trucks to be used for humble purposes such as hauling the family baggage and groceries, have risen in the social scale to such a degree that they often replace other vehicles entirely and fulfill all the family needs. One need never apologize for meeting even the most distinguished guest in a station wagon. It does, however, seem a little posey for a city family with no country place at all to have a station wagon for city use—although even that is done.

MARKING THE STATION WAGON Many estates have place names instead of street numbers. In that case it is perfectly proper to have the name of the estate and its address, if you wish, on the front doors of the wagon, either on the woodwork, if any, just below the windows or in the panel beneath them. This lettering usually matches or blends with the color trim of the station wagon or is of the colors favored by the estate or farm. Usually the lettering is outlined in gold paint or in black, to make for better visibility. Whatever appears should be in modest-size lettering and kept simple. Use capitals instead of quotes and, preferably, avoid any, probably coy, illustrations. My own station wagon reads, in dark green letters with gold:

DAISYFIELDS

WESTPORT, CONN.

Some marking of a station wagon, if only with the owner's initials (never his name, as this seems commercial), is useful when you direct people to it. In the country many station wagons are used and there are relatively few makes and the colors are limited in those manufactured.

INDEX

Abbot, forms of address, 449
Accent
  foreign, 257
  regional, 484
Acceptance of invitations
  formal, 434
  informal, 435
  in French, 625
  by telegram, 433
  by telephone, 433
  to visit a ship, 624
  wedding, 42, 45
  wedding anniversary, 109
  week-end, 311
  White House, 626
Acceptances, filing of, 28
Accessories, clothing, for men, 152
  with cutaway, 145
  with dinner jacket, 145
  handkerchief, 154
  jewelry, 155
  ties, 152
  with tail coat, 147
Accessories, clothing, for women, 195
Address
  on Christmas-card envelopes, 420
  on social envelopes, 408
  on stationery, 402
  on visiting cards, 560
  use of "Esquire," 462
  wedding announcements and invita-
    tions, 30
Address, forms of
  ambassadors, foreign, 443
  American Ambassador, 441
  American Minister, 441
  British officials, 452–53
  British peerage, 453–59
  Cabinet officers, American, 438–39
  cantor, 448
  chargé d'affaires, American, 442
  Chief Justice of United States, 440
  congressmen, 444
  consul, American, 442
  consul general, American, 442
  Eastern Orthodox clergy, 450–52
  envoys extraordinary, foreign, 443
  governors, 444–45
  judges, American, 442
  Justice of Supreme Court, 440
  mayors, 445
  military, 463
  ministers, foreign, 443
  President of United States, 438
  Protestant clergy, 445–46
  rabbis, 448
  Roman Catholic clergy, 449–50
  vice-consul, American, 442
  Vice-President of United States, 438
Admiral
  forms of address, 463
  insignia, 618
Adoption, 530–31
  announcement of, 531
Adult-child relationship, 524–29
Advertising, endorsements of commercial products, 598
Afternoon tea
  ceremony of serving, 353
  club tea, 227
  debutante, 114
  formal, 279
  informal, 268
  refreshments, 280
  sandwiches and canapés, how to eat,
    239
  tray, *illus.*, 269
  See also Tea
Age, as topic of conversation, 214, 216
Air Force
  military ranks, 619
  women's services, 619

Airsickness, 640
Air travel, 639
  bidding farewell, 647
  tipping, 640
Acknowledgment cards, 135
A la carte ordering, 550
Alcohol. See Drinking
Alexander cocktail, 287
Alfresco meals, 299
Alsatian wine, 288
Ambassador
  American, forms of address, 441
  Army title retained by, 441
  British, forms of address, 461
  foreign, forms of address, 442
  invitations sent by, 624
  lady, form of address, 441
  wives of, form of address, 441
  "Ambassadress," title not used, 441
American chargé d'affaires, forms of
    address, 442
American Minister, forms of address,
    441
Amer Picon, 290
Amontillado wine, 552
Anecdotes, in public speaking, 582
Angelica wine, 289
"Angry" letters, 412
Anklets, wearing of, 652
Annapolis
  etiquette for dances, 607–10
  slang, 611
Anniversaries, wedding, 107–9
  invitations to, 108
Announcements
  adoption, 531
  birth, 558; illus., 559
  of change of name, 256
  death notices, 130
Announcements, engagements, 120
  breaking of, 126
  picture to newspapers, 122
  release date to newspapers, 121
  wording of, with divorced parents,
    123
Announcements, wedding
  addressing envelopes, 30
  after elopement, 92
  coat of arms, 467
  divorcée's remarriage, 40
  engraving of, 29
  mailing of, 30
  military forms for, 43
  naval forms for, 43
  of newsworthy persons, 123

  release date to newspapers, 121
  stationery for, 29
  time for sending, 28
  wording of, 40
Announcing guests
  in ballroom, 281
  at formal luncheon, 277
Anthem, National, 631
  of other nations, 633
Antipasto, 386
Antiques at auctions, 595
Apology
  of late guest, 262
  letters of, 413
  in the street, 189
Apostolic protonotaries, forms of ad-
    dress, 450
Appetizers, 286
Applause, at opera and concerts, 591
Apples, how to eat, 237
Appointments, lateness at, 185
Apricots, how to eat, 237
Aquavit, 290
Archbishop, forms of address, 449, 451
Archdeacon, forms of address, 446
Archimandrite, forms of address, 451
Army etiquette
  calls on military post, 619
  forms of address, 463
  officers' titles in wedding announce-
    ments, 43
  ranks, 617
  service wedding, 54
  West Point Academy rules, 612
  women's services, 619
Artichokes, how to eat, 235
Ascot tie, 145
Ash trays, 317
Asparagus
  how to eat, 235
  how to serve, 265
Assemblyman, forms of address, 444
Assistant secretaries, forms of address,
    439
Associate Justice, forms of address, 440
"At home" cards
  examples, 429
  wedding, 27, 41
Attorney General, forms of address, 439
Auctions, 592–97
  china and glassware at, 336
  country, 597
Author, 603
  letter to, 417
Autographs, 602

Automobile
  choice of, 664
  damage inflicted to others, 661
  etiquette of motoring, 659–64
  hitchhikers, 663
  picnics, 298
  smoking in, 222
  station wagon, 664
Avocados, how to eat, 237

Baby
  choice of name, 499
  clothes, 501
  hospital call for birth of, 576
Baby sitter, 521
Bacardi cocktail, 287
Bachelor
  calling card of, 560; *illus.*, 561
  at dance in Europe, 655
  dinner, 57, 291
  as host and caller, 575
  social problems of, 175
Bacon, how to eat, 235
Badminton, 168
  lady's clothing for, 196
Baked potatoes, how to eat, 239
Baldness, 172
Balls
  at Annapolis, 610
  dancing abroad, 655
  debutante, 113
  formal, 281
  invitations for, 427
  supper at, 282
  at West Point, 612–14
Bananas, how to eat, 237
Bank accounts
  checking, 393–98
  children's, 387
Baptism, 246
  certificate, 111
  See also Christening
Baptists, 247
Bar, at cocktail party, 269
Barbecue dinner, 298
Barbera wine, 288
Bar mitzvah, 248
Baron, forms of address, 458
Baroness, forms of address, 458
Baronet, forms of address, 459
Bathing suit, 197
Bathroom
  care of by week-end guest, 318

gift suggestions for, 314
linens for, 94, 95, 328, 329
Battleship, christening of, 620
  visiting of, 621
Beach
  clubs, 227
  gentleman's behavior at, 168
  how ladies should dress, 197
Beauty care, 200, 493
Bed
  in guest room, 307
  linens for, 94, 328
  in maid's room, 362
  making of, 323; *illus.*, 322
  turning down, 307
Bedroom, cleaning of, 378
Bedtime problems, 526
Bed-wetting, 520
Beer mug, *illus.*, 334
Behavior. *See* Manners; Table manners
Bell, hanging of the, 129
Bellhop, tipping of, 643
Berries, how to eat, 237
Best man, 51
  at bachelor dinner, 57
  at bridal table, 82
  clothes, 60
  in double wedding, 71
  duties of, 52
  gift from groom, 56
  groom's father as, 52
  in Jewish ceremony, *illus.*, 74
  in processional, Christian ceremony,
    illus., 64
  in recessional, Christian ceremony,
    illus., 65
  responsibility for ring, 52, 67, 69
  in wedding ceremony, 67
Beverages
  before dinner, 286
  card table service, 355
  at informal dances, 270
  at informal dinner, 342
  at informal lunch, 267, 340
  See also Wine
Bible, 523
Bibs, 502
Bidding at auctions, 592
Birds, how to eat, 235
Birth announcements, 558; *illus.*, 559
Birthday party, 516
  invitation to, 430
  place cards at, 357
Birthmarks, 203

Bishop, forms of address, 445, 446, 449, 451
Bishop drink, 287
Bitters, 289
Blank checks, 394
"Black tie," 147
Blessing
  papal, 658
  of wedding ring, 75, 76
Blouses, 193
Blowing one's nose, 231
Blue jeans, 198, 503
Bon voyage, bidding, 646
Bookplates, coat of arms on, 466
Books
  asking author for copy, 603
  gift to hostess, 324
"Boots," the, 649
Bouillon, serving of, 230
Bouquet
  debutante's, 114
  sending of, to girl, 184
  See also Bouquet, bride's
Bouquet, bride's, 62
  groom's boutonniere from, 59
  throwing of, 81
Bourbon, 286
Boutonniere
  bridegroom's, 59, 61
  with cutaway, 145
  with dinner jacket, 147
  with tail coat, 148
  for ushers, 53
Bow, use of
  by boy, 515
  by gentleman, 188, 190
  by lady, 188, 218
Bowles (drink), 287
Bow tie, 152
Boxed wedding cakes, 84
Brandy glasses, illus., 334, 335
Bread
  at family dinner, 383
  at formal dinner, 347
  at formal luncheon, 278
  at informal luncheon, 267
  use of, as "pusher," 232
Bread-and-butter letters, 411
Breakfast, 336–38
  cups and saucers for, 351
  family conversation at, 490
  house guest's attire at, 319
  in servantless home, 378
  table setting, illus., 338

tray service, 355, illus., 337
  wedding, 84
Bridal gown, 57
  use of family gown, 58
Bride
  bouquet of, 62
  ceremony procedure, 67
  choice of bridesmaids, 50
  clergyman's daughter, 90
  corsage for, 62
  dancing at reception, 81
  dinner with attendants, 57
  divorced parents, daughter of, 85
  dress of. See Bride's dress
  in double wedding, 71
  elopement, 92
  gift from groom, 56
  gifts to attendants, 56
  "giving away" by mother, 69
  "giving away" by divorced father, 85
  "giving away" of mature, 69
  in Jewish ceremony, 74; illus., 74
  jewelry for, 58
  of military man, 54, 616
  orange blossoms for, 58
  in processional, Christian ceremony, illus., 64
  in recessional, Christian ceremony, illus., 65
  in receiving line at reception, 78, 80; illus., 79
  in service wedding, 54, 65
  showers for, 100–2
  superstitions, 59
  table at reception, 82; illus., 82
  thank-you letters, 104
  the thirty-ish, 72
  throwing of bouquet, 81
  trousseau of, 93–100
  wedding gifts for, 102
  wedding pictures of, 50
Bridegroom
  bachelor's dinner, 57
  choice of best man and ushers, 51
  clothes of. See Bridegroom's clothes
  dancing at reception, 81
  in double wedding, 71
  elopement, 92
  expenses for wedding, 62
  gift from bride, 56
  gifts to ushers and best man, 56
  honeymoon expenses, 105
  in Jewish ceremony, illus., 74
  kissing the bride, 68
  officer groom, 54

previous marriage of, 50
in receiving line at reception, 78;
    illus., 79
in processional, Christian ceremony,
    64
in recessional, Christian ceremony,
    65; *illus.*, 65
service wedding, 54, 65
shower for, 101
ties and gloves to ushers, 52
wedding gifts for, 103
wedding picture of, 122
wedding ring, 119
Bridegroom's clothes
    for civil marriage, 92
    for formal wedding, 59
    for home wedding, 88
    for informal wedding, 59
Bridegroom's parents
    clergyman father, 91
    dress of, 61
    father as best man, 52
    invitation lists, 27
    in Jewish ceremony, *illus.*, 74
    parents' table at reception, 83; *illus.*,
        83
    in receiving line, 78, 79; *illus.*, 79
    wedding gift from, 98
    wedding given by, invitation, 34
Bridesmaids, 50
    bouquets for, 62
    in double wedding, *illus.*, 70
    dresses at wedding, 60
    gifts from bride, 56
    meeting at bride's home, 56
    in processional, Christian ceremony,
        64; *illus.*, 64
    in receiving line at reception, 78;
        illus., 79
    in recessional, Christian ceremony,
        illus., 65
Bride's dress
    for formal wedding, 58
    for home wedding, 88
    for informal wedding, 57, 58
    for civil marriage, 92
    for rectory wedding, 89
Bride's parents
    clergyman father, 90
    divorced, 85
    father's clothing, 61
    "giving away" by mother, 69
    invitation lists, 27
    in Jewish ceremony, *illus.*, 74
    mother's clothing, 61

mother's entrance into church, 54
post-wedding calls, 106
in processional, 63; *illus.*, 64
in receiving line at reception, 78;
    illus., 79
silver as wedding gift from, 98
table at reception, 83; *illus.*, 83
wedding expenses of, 62
wedding invitations, wording of, 32
Bridge game, 295
    behavior at, 296
Bridge table service. *See* Card table
    service
Brigadier general, insignia of, 618
British Ambassador, forms of address,
    461
British forms of address, 437
British peerage, forms of address, 453–
    60
Brother (religious title), forms of ad-
    dress, 450
Budgeting, 387–98
    boy dating girl, 539
    in buying for household, 364
    charge accounts, 390
    checking accounts, 393
    children's bank accounts, 388, 506
    credit rating, 392
    deficit financing, 390
    girls sharing apartment, 210
    installment buying, 390
    wedding, 118
Buffet parties
    ball, 282
    christening party, 112
    dinner, 381; *illus.*, 382
    luncheon, 338
    in maidless home, 380
    at restaurants, 553
    supper, card table, 355
    table setting for, 349, 355; *illus.*, 350
    wedding reception, 84
Burgundy wine, 288, 290
Burial service, 129
Busboy, tipping of, 555
Business cards, 558
    gentleman's, 570, 571
    lady's, 572
Business etiquette, 176–83
    calls at White House, 627
    Christmas cards, 419
    entertaining, 492, 550; by business-
        woman, 208, in the home, 492
    greeting callers, 177
    letter of resignation, 183

Business etiquette—(*Cont'd*)
  men's clothes, 141
  precedence in, 178
  secretary, relationship with, 178, 179, 180
  smoking, 178
  social relations with employees, 182
  on the telephone, 181
Business letters
  of complaint, 423
  lady's, 421; signing of, 406
  stationery for, 404, 405, 406; *illus.*, 407
  travel reservations, 424
Business suit, 141–44; *illus.*, 144
Businesswoman, 205–8
  calling card, 563, 564
  entertaining by, 208
  executive, 207–8
  smoking, 207
  stationery, *illus.*, 404
Butler
  announcing guests in ballroom, 281
  chief-of-staff, 370
  clothes, 371
  demitasse, serving of, 354
  duties, 372
  how to address, 316
  as major-domo at formal dinner, 271
  making invitations by telephone, 433
  service at formal dinner, 274
Buttered rum, 287
Butter plates, 331, 332
  for formal luncheon, 346; *illus.*, 345
  for informal dinner, 342
  for informal luncheon, 338
  knife placement on, *illus.*, 339
Buying at auctions, 592

Cabinet officers, forms of address, 438, 439
Cadet, 463
  West Point Hop, 612–14
Cake
  christening, 112
  how to eat, 236
  wedding, 84
Calling cards, 557–72
  children's, 558; *illus.*, 559
  for condolence notes, 136
  etiquette at military posts, 617
  with flowers for funerals, 132
  gentleman's, 560, 561, 570, 571

invitations on, 430, 569
joint cards, 563
lady's card, 563, 564
lady's titles on, 567
leaving of, at White House, 625, 627
leaving of, after ball, 282
as pew cards, 38
replies to invitations, 435
titles, use of, 569
uses of, 566
with wedding gifts, 103
Calls, 572–76
  aboard naval vessels, 621
  bachelor, 575
  businessman etiquette, 177
  of condolence, 575
  by eligible man, 574
  funeral, 132
  in hospitals, 576
  in Latin countries, 654
  at military posts, 617
  party, 558
  post-wedding, 106
  receiving personal, in office, 207
  at White House, 575, 627
Camomile tea, 385
Canapés, how to eat, 239
Canceling invitations
  formal, 434
  wedding, 44
Candlesticks
  at formal dinner, 347
  at formal tea table, 280
  at informal dinner, 340
Candy on formally set table, 354
Canon (religious title), forms of address, 446
Canopy
  in church weddings, 49
  in Jewish wedding ceremony, 75
Cantor, forms of address, 448
Captain
  forms of address, 463
  insignia, 618
Card, informal, 432
Card games
  bridge, 295
  after-dinner entertainment, 293
  for money, 297
  poker, 297
Cardinal, forms of address, 449
Cards. *See* Calling cards; Menu cards; Place cards
Card table service
  for buffet dinner, 381

setting of, 355
at wedding reception, 83
Career woman. *See* Businesswoman
Carving meat or fish
handling of garnishes, 356
at informal dinner, 265, 344
Catering service
at ball, 281
at formal dinner, 271
Catholic Church. *See* Roman Catholic
Church
Celebrities, 602–4
letters to, 416
Celery, how to eat, 236
Centerpiece. *See* Table decorations
Chablis wine, 289
Chairman, procedures at meeting, 587
Chamberlain, papal, forms of address,
450
Chambermaid
duties of, 376
hotel, tipping, 643
Champagne
at christening, 112
at formal luncheon, 279
glasses, 290; *illus.*, 335
how to serve, 289
with meals at restaurant, 552
semidry, 289
at ship launching, 619
at wedding reception, 84
Champagne cocktails, 289
Chaperone
at dances abroad, 655
for engaged couples, 126
in Latin countries, 654
teen agers, 537
Chaplains, forms of address, 463
Charge accounts, 390
Chargé d'affaires, forms of address, 442
Charity
donations in memoriam, 135
letter asking for contributions, 421
mass debuts for, 113
Chauffeur
clothing, 373
duties of, 373
how to address, 316
Checking accounts, 393
care in handling, 398
Checkroom attendant, tipping, 643
Checks, 395–98
paying by, at auctions, 595
paying by, at restaurants, 554
postdated, 398

printing and dating, 395
signature on, 406
stopping payment on, 397
Chef, 271
Cherries, how to eat, 237
Chesterfield overcoat, 150
Chevalier de la Légion d'honneur, insignia, 160
Chianti wine, 288
Chicken, how to eat, 236
Chief Justice of the United States,
forms of address, 440
Chief warrant officer, insignia, 618
Children, 499–523
adoption, 530
allowance, 505
baby sitting, 521
bank accounts, 387
bedtime problems, 526
birthday parties, 516
calling cards, 558; *illus.*, 559
calling of, by servants, 361
calling parents by first names, 513
conduct rules, 512–13
conversation with, 525
disciplining by house guests, 318
of divorced parents, 543
eating habits, 508
fear of dark, handling of, 519
introductions, 515
invitations, 515
name, choice of, 499
of previous marriage at wedding, 71
referring to grown-ups, 254
relationship with adults, 524–29
relationship with servants, 529
religious education, 523
speaking voice, 485
table manners, 507
traveling, 532–34
See also Children's clothes; Children's parties; Teen ager
Children's clothes, 501–5
baby's christening, 110
at papal audience, 657
at party, 503
tastes in, formed by children, 505
for traveling, 533
Children's parties
chaperones, 537
dressing for, 503
invitation, 430
China, 331
coat of arms on, 466
trousseau basic list, 96–97

Chinese servants, 316
Christening, 109–12
    godparents, 110
    hats worn by women, 205
    refreshments at, 112
    smoking at reception, 221
    toasts, 291
Christening a ship, 619
Christian Science wedding ceremony, 76
Christmas cards, 419
    addressing to English peers, 453
    to Jewish friends, 244
Church cards, 39
Church ceremonies
    christenings, 111
    conduct during, 86
    funerals, 133
    invitations to, 31
    weddings, 63–78
Cigarette case, 156
Cigarette girl, tipping, 555
Cigarettes
    offering of, 185
    placing on table at meals, 283
    See also Smoking
Cigar smoking, 219, 346
Circumcision, 246
Civil marriage, 92
Clams
    how to eat, 241, 242
    use of finger bowls after, 285
Claret wine, 290
Cleaning house
    part-time day workers, 377
    routine in servantless home, 378
Clergyman. See Minister
Clerical dress, 249
Clothes
    for afternoon tea, 269
    for best man, 60
    for bride, 57–59
    for bridegroom, 59–60
    for bridesmaids, 60
    for christening, 110
    for civil marriage, 92
    debutante's, 114
    for the deceased, 129, 159
    at dinner, 196
    for flower girls, 60
    for formal wedding, 57–61
    for funerals, 137
    for home wedding, 88
    for matron of honor, 60
    during mourning, 137

for the opera, 589
for papal audience, 657
at public dinners, 556
for ship launching, 620
speaker's, 583
for television appearance, 586
for ushers at wedding, 60
for weddings, 57–59, 60, 86, 88, 92
for week-end trips, 315
    See also Children's clothes; Gentleman's clothes; Lady's clothes; Servants' clothes; Sports clothes
Clubs, 222–28
    address on bachelor's calling card, 561
    beach, 227
    country, 227
    golf, 161
    guests at, 225, 228
    joining, 223
    letter of objection, 224
    men's, 222–26
    new member, letter proposing, 223–24
    procedures at meetings, 587
    resigning from, 225
    teas at, 227
    tipping in, 223
    women's, 226
Coast Guard, insignia, 619
Coat, lady's, 192
Coat of arms, 464
    on flat silver, 467
    full, masculine, 466; illus., 466
    on wedding announcements, invitations, 29
Cocktail party
    informal, 269
    invitations, 429, 430
    in maidless home, 380
Cocktails
    before dinner, 286
    dry wines, in place of, 289
    glass for, illus., 335
    at restaurant, 551
Coffee
    Continental fashion, serving of, 276
    English fashion, serving of, 276
    formal serving of, 286
    iced, 267
    informal serving of, 263, 264, 266, 353, 384
    testing of, 230
    See also Demitasse
Coffee table, 327

Collectors
  of ancient glass, 333
  of autographs, 602
  of china, 333
College of Arms, 464
Cologne, use by men, 173
Colonel, forms of address, 463
  insignia, 618
Color
  of business suits, 142 ff.
  in living-room decoration, 328
  of stationery, 401
  in ties, 152
  in woman's wardrobe, 191
Columnist, gossip, 597
Coming out. *See* Debutante
Commander
  forms of address, 463
  insignia, 618
Commandeur de la Légion d'honneur, 160
Commercial products, endorsed by society people, 599
Commodore, insignia, 618
Communion, 248
Community clubs, 227
Community relations, 243–49
Commuter trains, 494
Companion, lady's, 374
Company dinner party, 261–68
Compliment, acknowledgment of, in America, 253
Concerts, 590
Condolence
  calls of, 575
  letters of, 136, 410
Conduct. *See* Manners; Table manners
Confection cakes, how to eat, 236
Confirmation Day, 248
Congratulation, letters of, 410
Congregational Church
  baptism, 247
  wedding ceremony, 67
Congressman
  forms of address, 444
  letter to, 417
  protest to, over phone, 419
Conserves, how to serve, 230
Consul, forms of address, 442
Conversation
  after-dinner entertainment, 293
  age as topic of, 214, 216
  on the beach, 168
  on board ship, 637
  during calls, 573

  with children, 525
  children at table, 508, 509
  dangerous topics of, 215
  at formal tea, 280
  greetings, 212
  lady's skill in promoting, 294
  personal questions, 214, 215
  with strangers while traveling, 644
  in the street, 189
  at table, 232
  in taxi, 659
  "turning the table" at formal dinners, 276
  use of foreign words and expressions, 467–84
  at wedding receptions, 79, 87
Cook, 271, 375
  addressing, 316
  relationship with children, 529
Cookbooks, 386
  international cookery, 483
  menus for informal and family dinners, 262
Cooking
  culinary terms, 482
  garnishes, 357
  outdoor, 298
Corn on the cob, how to eat, 236
Coronet (heraldry), 466
Correspondence, 400–86
  addressing foreign diplomats, 443
  apology letters, 413
  Christmas cards, 419
  forms of address, 437–63
  invitations, 425–37; in French, 623
  use of Esquire, 462
  by social secretary, 375
  See also Letter writing
Corsage, 184
  bride's, 62
  mother's, at wedding, 63
Cosmetic defects
  men, 174
  women, 202
Cotillions, 113
Coughing at the table, 231
Countess, forms of address, 456
Country clubs, 227
Country entertaining
  calling for guests, 301
  care of guests, 306
  gifts to hostess, 312
  guest room, 307–9
  guest's "don'ts," 317–20
  host delegate, 300

Country entertaining—(Cont'd)
  house guests, 310
  planning entertainment, 316
  problem guests, 302
  week-end guest, 311
Courtship, 115
  giving and receiving gifts during, 116
  in Latin countries, 654
  proposal, 117
Crabs, how to eat, 241
Credit
  establishing, 392
  poor risks, 392
  rating of family, 391
Crest, 464
  on man's informal, *illus.*, 431
  on wedding announcements and in-
    vitations, 29
Cruises, 639
Crumbs, picking up, 285
Cuff links, 155
Culinary terms, 482
Culture
  American, 251
  knowledge of foreign languages, 467
Cummerbund, 146
Curtains
  in guest room, 308
  in nursery, 339
Curtsy, 515
Customers, how to address, 217
Cutaway, 144–45
  butler's, 371
  worn by groom, 59
"Cutting in" at dances, 654

Daiquiri cocktail, 287
  glass for, *illus.*, 335
Damask tablecloth, 330, 356
Dances and dancing
  Annapolis Hop, 609
  customs abroad, 655
  "cutting in," 654
  debutante, 113, 114, 428
  duty dances, 218
  foreign terms, 482
  formal, at home, 281
  informal, 270
  introductions at, 218
  invitation to formal, at home, 427
  paid dancing partner, 655
  refusing a dance, 219
  supper, 282
  teen agers, 540

wedding reception, 81
West Point Hop, 612
Dates, 209
  Annapolis Hop, 607–10
  asking for, 539
  in Latin countries, 654
  teen agers, 538
  West Point Hop, 612
Daughters of the American Revolution,
  226
Dean, forms of address, 446
"Dear," use of, 437
Death notices, 130; *See also* Funerals
Debuts, 113–15
  evening, 114
  invitations, 428
  mass debut, 113
  tea, 114
Decanting wine, 290
Decorations, wearing of, 160, 161
Deficit financing, 390
Delmonico glass, *illus.*, 335
Demitasse, service of, 354
  at formal dinner, 348
  at informal dinner, 344
Derby hat, 151
Dessert
  guests only for, 387
  at informal luncheon, 268, 339
  maidless dinner, 384
  setting, *illus.*, 352
  silver for, at formal dinner, 384; *illus.*,
    343
  spoon, uses of, 99
  wines with, 289, 552
Diet, 497
Dietary laws, 244
Dinner
  aboard naval vessels, 622
  bachelor, 57
  cocktails before, 286
  conversation at, 232
  debut party, 113
  dressing for, 196
  with employer or secretary, 179
  entertainment after, 293–97
  gentleman's clothing for, 149
  lady's clothes for, 196, 201, 205
  last-minute business invitation to, 492
  naval invitation, 623
  outdoor, 299
  public, 555
  in restaurants, 549–57
  semiformal, 262
  table manners, 228–42

use of word, 351
week-end parties, 315
See also Dinner, formal; Dinner, informal
Dinner, formal, 271–76
    butler's service, 372
    china for, 331
    coffee, 286
    damask cloth, 356
    demitasse, serving of, 353, 354
    guests at, 283–86
    invitation to, 426
    keeping engagement for, 303
    menu, 263
    seating, 272; *illus.*, 272
    smoking at, 283, 650
    table linen, 330
    table setting, 346
    toasts, 291
    wines, 288
Dinner, informal, 261–63
    buffet, 381; *illus.*, 382
    card table service, 355
    china for, 332
    invitation to, 431, 433
    place settings, *illus.*, 341
    table linen, 331
    table setting, 340
    toasts, 292
    wines, 288
    with one maid, 264
    without maid, 381, 385
Dinner jacket
    appropriate use of, 159
    at opera, 589
    on transatlantic liners, 638
Dinner suits, 196, 589
Diplomatic officials
    formal invitations in French, 624
    forms of address, 441–42
Directors, board of, meeting procedures, 587
Dishes
    tipping of, 230
    washing properly, 321
Divorce, 541–42
    announcing engagement before decree, 126
    in Eastern Orthodox Church, 77
    in Jewish religion, 73
    press interference in, 600
    remarriage for Protestants, 49
    "waiting period" for remarriage, 49
Divorcée, 545
    bride, "giving away" of, 69

calling cards, 565
children of, at second marriage, 71
wedding invitation of, 35
wedding announcement of, 40
Divorced parents
    and wedding announcements, 123
    at wedding ceremonies, 85
    wording of wedding invitation, 32
Doctor
    in Army, forms of address, 463
    relationship to patient, 579
    use of title socially, 253
    woman, use of title on cards, 567
Doilies, 330, 331
Domestic prelates, forms of address, 450
Doorman, tipping, 642
Double parking, 662
Double-ring ceremony, 69
Double wedding
    formal ceremony, 71
    invitations, 33
    processional, Christian ceremony, *illus.*, 70
    recessional, Christian ceremony, *illus.*, 70
Dowager, title, 459
Draperies, 308
Dress. *See* Clothes
Drinking, 286–93
    by ladies, abroad, 652
    mixing of, at cocktail parties, 269
    Navy rules, 607
    problem drinkers, 305
    problem with servant, 360
    restaurant dining, 551
    at table, 229
    teen ager, 535
    toasts, 291
    West Point rules on, 613
    wines, 287
Driving. *See* Motoring manners
Dry wines, 288
Dubonnet, 289
Duchess, forms of address, 453
Duck hunting, 169, 197
Duke, forms of address, 453
Duty dances, 218

Earl, forms of address, 455
Earthenware, 331
Eastern Orthodox Church
    baptism, 247
    hierarchy, forms of address, 450
    wedding ceremony, 76

Eating
  children's habits, 507
  overweight and underweight, problems, 496
  when to begin, at table, 229
  by women, in office, 207
  See also Table manners
Education
  family budgeting for, 388
  importance of foreign languages, 468
  religious, 523
  social behavior of children, 511–13
  and speech, 485
Elective clubs, 226
Elevator
  hat problems in, 186
  smoking in, 221
Elevator men, tipping, 643
Elopement, 91
  gifts, 92
Emergency instructions to house guests, 310
Employer-employee relationship
  in business, 177, 178–81, 182
  in home, 358–70
Employment agencies, 358, 361
Endorsements of commercial products by society people, 599
Engagements, 117–27
  announcement of, 120
  behavior during, 126
  breaking of, 118, 126
  conference with father, 117
  length of, 118
  ring, 118, 119
  toasts, 291
English customs
  evening meal, 351
  toasts, 292
  train travel, 649
English forms of address, 437
English language
  foreign words in, 257
  incorrect use of words and phrases, 478–82
  literary quotations, 474–78
  regional accents, 484
Engraving
  calling cards, 558, 560
  change-of-name cards, 256
  Christmas cards, 420
  formal invitations, 425
  stationery, 402
  wedding announcements and invitations, 29

Ensign, 618
Entertaining, 260–82
  abroad, 654
  after dinner, 293
  Annapolis Hop, 610
  business, in home, 492
  by woman executive, 208
  celebrities, 602
  cocktail parties, 269
  dance, formal, 281
  dancing at home, 270
  debut parties, 113–14
  dinner party, formal, 271–81
  dinner party, informal, 261–70
  formal, 271–86
  guest's behavior, at formal, 283–86
  by girls sharing apartment, 209
  house guests, 316
  indoors, 293–97
  informal, 261–70
  lunch, formal, 277
  lunch, informal, 267
  in maidless home, 379
  one-maid dinner, informal, 264
  out of doors, 298, 299
  picnics, 298
  at restaurants, 549
  by single woman, 300
  social secretary's role in, 375
  tea, formal, 279
  tea, informal, 268
  thank-you notes, 411
  week-end, 311
  at West Point, 613
Envelopes
  addressing social, 408
  lined, 402
  for wedding announcements and invitations, 29, 30
Envoy extraordinary, forms of address, 443, 462
Episcopal Church. *See* Protestant Churches
"Esquire," use of, 462
European customs
  dancing, 655
  differences in, 647
  hand kissing, 186
  paid dancing partner, 655
  traveling, 649
Evening clothes, gentleman's, 145–50
  house suit, 149
  when not to wear, 159
Evening clothes, lady's, 195–96

at opera, 589
on transatlantic liner, 638
Evening debut, 114
Excess hair, removal of, 202
Expenses
of bridegroom, 62–63
of bride's parents, 62
in dating, 539
for debut, 113
funeral, 128
of girls sharing home, 210
Eyebrows, care of, 172
Eye shadow, use of, 202

Family
adoptive, 530
adult-child relationship, 524–29
behavior at country and beach clubs, 227
budgeting, 387–98
children, 499–523
credit rating, 391
daughter's suitor, meeting, 115
divorce, 541
heraldry, 464
income, 390
in-law problem, 497
marriage, manners in, 489–99
religious education, 523
rules for children, 526
of suitor, meeting, during courtship, 116
teen ager, 535–41
wedding announcements and invitations, 30
See also Marriage
Fashion, 190
Father (religious title), use of, 447, 452
Fees
christening, 111
civil marriage, 93
funeral, 134
wedding, 62, 63
Felt hats, 193
Fiancé. See Engagement
Finger bowl, 285
at formal dinner, 276, 349; illus., 352
Fire, emergency instructions, 310
First lieutenant, insignia, 618
First-name calling, 213
children by nurse, 361
in office, 179
parents by children, 513
proper use of, 190

Fish
at formal dinner, 275
garnishes for, boiled, 357
how to eat, 236
serving of, 265
Fishing, 169
Flag, displaying, 628
Flannels, white, inappropriate use of, 160
Flat silver. See Silver
Fleet admiral, insignia, 618
Floors, cleaning of, 379
Flower girl
dress, 60
in Jewish ceremony, illus., 74
in processional, Christian ceremony, illus., 64
in receiving line at reception, 78
in recessional, Christian ceremony, illus., 65
Flowers
acknowledging of, after funerals, 135
card accompanying gift of, 565
church decoration, for weddings, 49
debutante's, 115
at formal ball, 281
at formal dinner table, 278
at formal luncheon table, 278
at funerals, 131
for hostess, 314, 574
sent to hospital, 577
for wedding, 49, 61, 62
when to send, 183
See also Banquet; Bouquet, bride's; Corsage
Flower teas, 385
Food
"foreign matter" in, 231
garnishing, 356
how to eat special, 235
packaging of, for picnics, 299
"spoiled," 231
stirring of, 230
when too hot, 231
Footman, 370
livery, 371
duties of, 271, 274, 275
Foreign accent, 257
Foreign decorations, wearing of, 161
Foreign representatives, forms of address, 442
wives of, forms of address, 443
Foreign words and phrases, 470–74
anglicized, 257
French, 470–72

Foreign words and phrases—(Cont'd)
  Latin, 472–73
  use of, in conversation, 468
Fork
  Continental use of, 252
  at formal dinner, 348; *illus.*, 347, 348
  at formal luncheon, 346; *illus.*, 345
  at informal dinner, 342
  placement of used, 284
  table setting, 252
  use of, 229
Formal dinner. *See* Dinner, formal
Formal luncheon. *See* Luncheon, formal
Formal tea. *See* Afternoon tea
Formal wedding. *See* Wedding, formal
Four-in-hand tie, 152
Frappé drinks, glass for, *illus.*, 334
French language, 468
  formal invitations by diplomatic corps, 624
  list of words and phrases, 470–72
  menu, words used in, 483
  naval invitations, 623
  toasts, 292
French Legion of Honor, 160
Friends
  double wedding of, 34, 71
  making, abroad, 652
  making, in new community, 572
  visiting unexpectedly with children, 534
  wedding at home of, invitation to, 37
Friends, Society of, marriage ceremony, 77
Frock coat, 149
Frogs' legs, how to eat, 235
Fruit, how to eat, 237, 238
Fruit cakes
  as boxed wedding cake, 84
  how to eat, 236
Fruit juice, 286; glass, *illus.*, 334
Funerals, 127–38
  acknowledgments, 135
  arranging of, 128
  attending, 131
  calls, 132
  expenses, 128
  at funeral homes, 130, 135
  hanging the bell, 129
  interment, 134
  in Latin countries, 653
  mass cards, 132
  smoking at, 221
Fur coat, 192

Furniture
  for guest room, 306
  interior decoration, 326
  for servants' quarters, 362, 363

Gambling, 297
Games
  after-dinner entertainment, 294
  card, 295
  rules in sports and, 168
  See also Sports
Gardener, 317
Garnishes, 356
General (military title)
  forms of address, 463
  insignia, 617, 618
Gentleman
  acting as host to lady, 300, 301
  in business world, 176
  decorations, wearing of, 160
  first-name calling, 213
  hat problems of, 186
  heavy smokers, 220
  introductions, 218
  in public conveyances, 187
  rules of conduct, 190
  sending flowers, 183
  social graces of, 183–90
  social stationery of, 405; *illus.*, 404
  street manners of, 188
  use of word, 254
  well-groomed, 171–76
Gentleman's clothes, 140–61
  aboard ship, 637
  bathing suit, 168
  for business call at White House, 627
  business suit, 141–44
  cutaway, 144
  dinner jacket, 145
  evening clothes, appropriate wearing of, 159
  evening house suit, 149
  lounge suit, 150
  at opera, 589
  overcoats, 150
  for papal audience, 657
  at public dinners, 556
  raincoat, 157
  smoking jacket, 149
  as speaker, 583
  suits, 141–44
  tail coat, 147
  use of color in, 153

for week-end trips, 315
See also Accessories; Sports clothes
German language, 468
    familiar words and phrases, 474
"Ghosts," game, 294
Gifts
    card accompanying, 566
    to children, 312
    christening, 110
    during courtship, 116
    before engagement, 116
    godparents' to baby, 110
    to hostess, suggestions for, 312
    to nurses, on leaving hospital, 578
    to President of United States, 628
    refusal of, 116
    for the sick, 577
    thank-you notes for, 412
Gifts, wedding, 102–4
    for anniversaries, 107
    to best man, 56
    bride and groom to each other, 56
    to bride's attendants, 56
    from bride's parents, 62
    display of, 103
    for elopers, 92
    from groom's parents, 98
    honeymoon as, 105
    from military post, 616
    obligations to send, 102
    to officiating official in civil marriage,
        93
    returning of, when wedding is can-
        celed, 44
    for second marriage, 92
    sent after wedding, 102, 103
    shower gifts, 100
    silver from parents, 98
    suggestions for inexpensive, 102
    thank-you letters for, 104
    to ushers, 56
    ushers' to bride, 55
Gin cocktails, 287
"Giving away" bride
    by divorced father, 85
    mature bride, 69
    by mother, 69
Glassware, 332
    basic list of, 96
    collecting antique, 333
    at formal dinner, 349; *illus.*, 347
    glass china, 331
    how to hold glass at table, 233
    at informal dinner, 344
    for serving wine, 290

    stemmed, 233
    types of, *illus.*, 334, 335
    washing, 321, 332
Glög, 287
Gloves
    gentleman's, with formal dress, 148
    handshake, 186, 217
    lady's, with evening dress, 196
Godparents
    choice of, 110
    for christening ceremony, 111
    for circumcision ceremony, 246
    responsibilities of, 110
Golf
    men's clothes, 162
    rules on course, 161
    women's clothes, 197
Gossip columnist, 598
Governess, how to address, 317
Government officials
    American, forms of address, 438–45
    British, forms of address, 460
Governor, forms of address, 444
Grace
    saying at table, 233
    examples, 234
Graduation Hop, 610
Graduation party, 270
Grand Croix de la Légion d'honneur,
        160
Grapefruit, how to eat, 237
Grapes, how to eat, 237
Grave marking, 134
Gravy, 265
Greek language
    familiar words and phrases, 474
    knowledge of, 468
Green tea, 385
Greeting
    callers, 216
    forms of, 212
    guests, 277
    "how do you do," 254
    among men in Latin countries, 653
    servants, 315
    in the street, 186
Groom. *See* Bridegroom
Grooming
    gentleman's, 171–74
    lady's, 200–3
Group sales, at auction, 593
Guest
    announcing of, at ball, 281
    behavior at formal meals, 283–86
    bringing to friend's home, 302

Guest—(*Cont'd*)
  at clubs, 225
  at cocktail party, 270
  for dessert course, 387
  at dinner party, 261, 272
  doing the dishes, 321
  at family clubs, 228
  gifts of, to hostess, suggestions, 312
  greeting of, 272, 277
  house, 300–24
  how to take leave, 307
  at informal dance, 270
  introducing servants to, 362
  late arrivals at dinner, 262
  at opera, 590
  problem drinkers, 305
  selection of, 260, 293
  at ship christening, 620
  uninvited, 303
  at wedding, 53, 86
  week-end, 311
  at White House, 627
  on yacht, 167
Guest of honor
  at ball, 282
  dinner for, 427
  at formal dinner, seating, 273, *illus.*, 272
  at informal dinner, 262
  at public dinner, 556
Guest house, 309
Guest room
  in city apartment, 324
  in country home, 306
Guns, 169

Hair, care of
  gentleman's, 172, 173
  lady's, 200, 202
Handkerchiefs, 154
Hand kissing, 186, 652
Handshake, 185, 217
Hand signals, 661
Handwriting
  envelopes of wedding announcements
    and invitations, 31
  formal invitations, 425, 426
  letters that must be handwritten, 410
  personal letters, 405
Hanging the bell, 129
Hat, gentleman's
  with cutaway, 145
  in elevator, 186
  formal, 149
  hunting, 151
  keeping on while talking to lady, 190
  tipping, for greeting in street, 186, 217
Hat, lady's, 192
  fur, 193
  at opera, 589
  when to remove, 205
"Head usher," 54
Headwaiter, tipping, 554
Health, and eating habits, 496
Heiress, coat of arms of, 465
Heraldic devices, 464–67
  married woman's use of, 466
  on stationery, 401
  on wedding announcements, 29
Herald's College (London), 464
Herb teas, 385
Highball glass, *illus.*, 335
Hitchhiking, 663
Hock glasses, 349; *illus.*, 335
Holy Days, religious, 245
Home christening, 111
Home wedding, 88–89
  invitation to, 36
Honeymoon, 105–6
Honorable (title), when to use, 438, 442, 444
Honourable (British title), correct use of, 456, 457, 459
Hop
  Annapolis, 607–10
  West Point, 612–14
Hors d'oeuvres, 386
Horse shows, 151
Hospital
  children in, 518
  flowers, sending to, 577
  gifts to nurses, 579
  sharing room at, 578
  visits to, 577
Host
  behavior of, toward house guests, 304
  carving and serving the meat, 265
  at formal dance, 282
  at formal dinner, 272
  greeting guests, 300
  at informal dance, 270
  at public dinner, 556
  in restaurant, dining, 550
Hostess
  businesswoman, paying restaurant
    bill, 208
  celebrities as guests, 602

at club teas, 227
at cocktail parties, 269
at formal dance, 281
at formal dinner, 272
at formal luncheon, 277
at formal tea, 280
gifts to, suggestions, 312, 313
help from guest, 320
leaving restaurant, 556
promoting conversation, 294
at public dinner, 556
in restaurant, dining, 550
self-invited guest, 302, 303
at semiformal dinner, 262
serving at one-maid dinner, 266
"turning the table," 276
Hotel
bath customs in Europe, 647
the "boots," 649
employer and secretary at, 180
paid dancing partner, 655
reservations, business, 180
reservations, husband and wife, 424
tipping, 642
House of Commons, members of, forms
of address, 460
House dress, 201
House guest
behavior of, 304, 315
bringing to another's party, 303
in city apartment, 324
"don'ts," 317–19
dressing for breakfast, 319
duties in city, 324
helping hostess, 320
washing dishes, 321
Household management, 326–98
budget problems, 390–98
butler, duties of, 372
chambermaid, duties of, 376
chauffeur, duties of, 373
china, 331
cleaning routine, 378
companion, duties of, 374
cook, duties of, 375
employer-servant relationship, 358
furnishings, 326–36
by girls sharing apartment, 211
housekeeper, duties of, 374
kitchen maid, duties of, 375
lady's maid, duties of, 376
last-minute dinner invitations, 492
linens, 328
menu suggestions, 385
part-time help, 361, 377
professional help, 317
servantless household, 377
service problems, 351–57
social secretary, duties of, 374
staff duties, 370
table setting, 336–51
valet, 373
See also Servants
Housekeeper
duties of, 374
how to address, 316
lady acting as, 364
social secretary acting as, 375
Houseman
duties of, 370
how to address, 316
House-sharing, 211
Houseworker, general. See Maid
"How do you do," answers to, 254
Hunting
gentleman's clothes for, 150
lady's clothes for, 199
rules of, 169
Husband
agreeable kind, 490
checking account, joint, 389
help of, in household, 491
last-minute dinner invitations, 492
separation, 544
and understanding wife, 489
See also Marriage
Husband and wife cards, 561

Iced tea
glass, illus., 334
serving of, 352
spoons, 352
Illegible signatures, 408
Income, 390
"Informal" card, 431
for replies to invitations, 435
Initials
on bed and bathroom linens, 328
on leather articles, 155
on men's handkerchiefs, 155
on stationery, 401; illus., 403
on station wagon, 665
on tablecloths, 328
on wedding rings, 119
See also Monograms
Inks, 402
Insignia of decorations, wearing of, 160
Installment buying, 390

Insurance
  on automobile, 661
  against servants' injuries on job, 367
Interfaith understanding, 243–49
Interior decoration
  draperies and curtains, 308
  living room, 326
  nursery, 329
Interment, 134
Interviews
  with press, 600
  with prospective servants, 359
Introductions, 217
  of ambassador, 441
  at ball, 282
  on board ship, 637
  children's, 515
  formal, 438
  at formal dinner, 272
  of government officials, 438–45
  of guests, 300
  husband's title in, 253
  in Latin countries, 654
  letters of, 414
  of new servant to household, 361
  of servants and guests, 362
  of President of United States, 438
  of Vice-President of United States, 438
  at wedding reception, 87
  of woman executive at meeting, 178
Invitations, 425–34
  by boys and girls, 515
  to christening, 109
  to English peers, 453
  last-minute, by husband, 492
  naval, 623
  to papal audience, 657
  by strangers on train, 645
  use of "Esquire" in England, 462
  on visiting cards, 430
  wedding anniversaries, 107
  for week-end visit, 311
  to White House, 625
  to woman Senator, 444
  See also Invitations, formal; Invitations, informal; Invitations, wedding
Invitations, formal, 425
  acceptance of, 434
  "at home," 429
  to dance, 427
  to debutante dance, 428
  to dinner, 426

  in diplomatic circle, 623
  in French, 624
  handwritten, 410
  to luncheon, 277
  postponement of party, 434
  regrets, 436
  by telegram, 433
  to visit ship, 623
  wedding, 31–36
Invitations, informal, 430
  acceptance of, 435
  on calling cards, 567
  to dinner party, 261
  handwritten, 410
  on husband and wife cards, 562
  on informal card, 431
  regrets, 437
  by telegram, 433
  by telephone, 433
  wedding, 41
Invitations, wedding, 27–48
  addressing of envelopes, 30
  church cards for, 39
  to church ceremony and reception, 37
  to clergyman's, 91
  coat of arms on, 467
  to double wedding, 33
  engraving of, 29
  expenses for, 62
  to home wedding, 36
  lists, 27
  mailing of, 30
  military forms for, 43
  to those in mourning, 42
  naval forms for, 43
  and pew cards, 38
  recalling of, 44
  and reception invitation, 40
  replying to, 45
  separated parents, issuing joint, 85
  time to send, 28
  and train cards, 38
  wording of, 31–36, 41

Jellies, how to eat, 230
Jewelry
  for bride, 58
  for burials, 129
  gentleman's, 145, 155, 156
  instead of engagement ring, 119
  permitted at papal audience, 657
Jewish religion, 243–49
  burial customs, 129
  circumcision, 246

Conservative congregation, wedding, 75
dietary laws, 244
flowers at funerals, 131
forms of address in, 448
funeral service, 133, 134
grace, saying of, 234
Holy Days, 246
Orthodox congregation, wedding, 73; *illus.*, 73
Reform congregation, wedding, 73
time of wedding, 28
Jodhpurs, 151, 198
Joint checking accounts, 389
Jokes, in public speeches, 582
Judge, forms of address, 442
Julep, 287
"Junior"
in children's names, 500
loss of appellation at father's death, 562
not used by girls, 565
use of, on cards, 561, 567

King, forms of address, 452
Kissing
the bride, 68
in greetings among men, 653
hand, 186, 652
in public, 189
Kitchen equipment, bride's basic list, 95
Kitchen maid, 376
Knife
butter, placement of, *illus.*, 339
at formal dinner, 348; *illus.*, 347, 348
at informal dinner, 342
placement of used, 284
in table setting, 252
use of, American fashion, 229
use of, Continental fashion, 252
Knight, forms of address, 459
Kosher home, 244
Kumquats, how to eat, 237

Lady (British title), 454, 455, 456, 460
"Lady," use of word, 216, 254
Lady's clothes, 190–200
aboard ship, 637
for Annapolis Hop, 609
basic wardrobe, 191
for business call at White House, 627
coat, 192
dinner dresses, 196

evening, 195
fur coat, 192
hats, 192
house dresses, 201
at opera, 589
at public dinners, 556
speaker's dress, 584
suits, 193
underwear, 194
for week-end trips, 315
for West Point week end, 613
Lady's maid, 376
Language
knowledge of foreign, 467
newcomer's difficulties with, 257
proper use, in business letters, 421
regional accents, 484
Lateness
at appointment, 185
at dinner parties, 262
Latin countries, difference of customs, 651–53
Latin language, 468
words and phrases, 472–73
Laundry, 378
checking of, 329
Layette, 502
Legal separation, 544
Legal signature, 406
Legion of Honor, insignia, 160
Lent
dietary laws, 244
weddings usually not performed during, 28
Letter writing
of apology, 413
bread-and-butter, 411
business letters, 421
to celebrities, 416
for charity contributions, 421–22
of complaint, 413
of condolence, 136
forms of address, 257
handwritten, 410
inks used, 402
of introduction, 415
ladies' business letters, 421
love letters, 414
personal, writing in office, 207
to President of United States, 416, 438
of proposal and seconding to clubs, 223
to public officials, 417
punctuation in, 422

Letter writing—(*Cont'd*)
  of reference for servants, 368
  of resignation, in business, 183
  of resignation from club, 225
  sequence of pages, 408
  signature, 407
  social letter, 410
  thank-you notes, 411–12
  to Vice-President of United States, 438
Liability insurance
  on automobile, 661
  on servants, 367
Liebfraumilch, 288
Lieutenants, insignia, 617–18
Linens
  bathroom, 328
  bride's trousseau, 93–95
  damask tablecloth, 356
  marking for laundry, 328
  nursery, 329
  table, 329
Line officers, 617
Lipstick, 201
  for teen agers, 537
Liqueurs, 291
  glass for, *illus.*, 335
Livery, 371
Living room
  cleaning routine, 378
  furniture, 327
Lobster
  finger bowls for, 285
  how to eat, 241; *illus.*, 240
Lohengrin, Wedding March, 49
Lord (British title), 454, 455, 458
Lounge suit, 150
Love letters, 414
Love-making, 189
Lozenge (heraldry), 465
  use of, 466; *illus.*, 466
Luggage
  for air travel, 639
  for train travel, 640
Lunch
  conversation at the table, 232
  employer with secretary, 179, 181
  outdoors, 299
  at restaurants, 549–57
  table manners at, 228–42
  table wines for, 288
  white wine for, 288
Lunch, formal, 277
  butler's attire, 371
  demitasse, serving, 353, 354

  guest at, 283
  invitation to, 429
  smoking at, 283
  table setting for, 344
Lunch, informal, 267
  buffet style, 338
  card table service, 355
  dessert silver, placement of, *illus.*, 339
  invitation to, 430
  table setting for, 338

"Madam," use of word, 216, 217
Madeira wine, 289
  decanting, 290
Maid
  chambermaid, 376
  full-time, 364
  general houseworker, 364
  hotel, tipping, 643
  how to address, 316
  lady's, 376
  and table service, 264, 265, 267
"Maiden dinner," 57
Maiden name, on calling cards, 563
Maid of honor, for ship christening, 620
Maid of honor, for wedding, 50
  bouquet for, 62
  at bride's table, 82
  at double wedding, 71
  dress of, 60
  gift from bride, 56
  in Jewish ceremony, *illus.*, 74
  procedure during Christian ceremony, 67
  in processional, Christian ceremony, *illus.*, 64
  in receiving line at reception, 78; *illus.*, 79
  recessional, Christian ceremony, *illus.*, 65
  shower for bride, 100
Maid's room, furnishings, 362
Major, insignia, 618
Major-domo, 271
Make-up, 201
  for teen ager, 536
  for television appearances, 586
Malaga wine, 289
Malocclusion, 203
Mangoes, how to eat, 237
Manhattan cocktail, 287
Manners
  abroad, 651

adults with children, 524
in badminton, 164
on board ship, 637
and bridge playing, 296
children's, 511, 513, 517
in clubs, 227
differences between America and Europe, 252–54
duty dances, 218
during engagement, 126
gentleman's, in Latin countries, 653
of girls sharing apartment, 210–11
on golf course, 162
in hospitals, 578
of house guest, 315–24
while hunting, 168
interfaith courtesy, 247
lady's, in business world, 205
lady's, in Latin countries, 651
in marriage, 489
motoring, 659
and National Anthem, 632
office etiquette, 206–7
in public conveyances, 187
in restaurants, 549–57
while skiing, 170
smoking, 219–22
social pleasantries, 212–19
on street, 188
on tennis court, 164
traveling, 642, 644, 651
of week-end guests, 315, 317–19
See also Table manners
Mantling (heraldry), 464
Marchioness, forms of address, 453, 455
Marine Corps, United States
insignia, 618
women's services, 619
Maritime terms, 623
Marquess, forms of address, 453, 455
Marriage, 489–99
agreeable husband, 490
agreeable wife, 493
annoying habits, 494
divorce, 541
home, establishment of, by young couple, 120
in-law problem, 497
publicity problems for announcement of, 601
special adjustments in, 494
wife's beauty care, 493
See also Wedding
Marriage announcements. See Announcements, wedding

Marriage license, 62
Marriages, mixed. See Mixed marriages
Married woman
career and job, 206
heraldic devices of, 466
Martini cocktail, 286
Mascara, use of, 202
Mass cards, 132, 135
Mass debut, 113
Matron of honor, 50
bouquet for, 62
at bride's table, 82
in double wedding, 71
dress of, 60
gift from bride, 56
in Jewish ceremony, illus., 74
procedure during Christian ceremony, 67
in processional, Christian ceremony, illus., 64
in receiving line at reception, 78; illus., 79
in recessional, Christian ceremony, illus., 65
shower for bride, 100
Mats, place. See Place mats
Mayor
forms of address, 445
letters to, 418
Meals. See Breakfast; Lunch; Dinner; Supper
Meat, serving of, 265
Medal of Honor, ribbon, 161
Meetings, procedures at, 587
Men. See Gentleman; Bachelor
Men's clubs, 222–26
See also Clubs
Menu
for breakfast, 336
choosing from, at restaurant, 550
for formal dinner, 273
for formal luncheon, 277, 279
French cuisine, 483
garnishes, 357
for informal dinner, 262
for informal lunch, 267, 338, 340
for outdoor luncheon, 299
for picnic supper, 298
suggestions for maidless dinners, 385
for wedding breakfast, 84
Menu cards
coat of arms on, 466
for formal dinner, 273
"Messrs.," use of, 409
Methodist Church, baptism, 247

Microphone, use of, 581
Middle name, 501
Midshipman, 607
Military etiquette. *See* Army etiquette; Navy etiquette
Mink coat, 192
Minister, government
    American, forms of address, 441
    British, forms of address, 462
    foreign, forms of address, 442
    lady, forms of address, 442
Minister (religious)
    christening, officiating at, 111
    forms of address, 447, 450
    funerals, officiating at, 129, 134
    wedding of, 90–91
    weddings, officiating at, 48, 63, 72, 89
Minister plenipotentiary, forms of address, 443, 462
Minorities, respect for, 243
"Miss," use of
    on calling cards, 563, 566
    in invitations, 428
    in speaking, 216, 217
Mixed drinks, 287
Mixed marriages, 72
    dispensation for, 49
    Jews and non-Jews, 76
    Mormons, 78
Moderator, procedures at meetings, 587
Moles, 174, 203
Monogram
    on informals, *illus.*, 432
    on men's handkerchiefs, 155
    on napkin, 278, *illus.*, 278
    on place cards, 273
    on silver, 100
    on trousseau linen, 94
    See also Initials
"Monsignor," use of, 450
Monuments for dead, 134
Mormon marriage ceremony, 77
Morning coat. *See* Cutaway
Moselle wine, 288
Moslems
    circumcision, 246
    dietary laws, 245
Mother, debutante's, 114
    See also Bride's parents; Bridegroom's parents; Family
Mother-in-law problems, 497
Motoring manners, 659–64
    double parking, 662
    driving rules, 661

    hitchhikers, 663
    passengers' behavior, 662
    in taxis, 659
    traffic laws, 663
Motto, heraldic, 466
Mourning, 136–38
    death in family before wedding, 47
    traditional idea of, 137
    wedding invitations to persons in mourning, 42
Movies
    teen agers, 538
    when to remove hat, 205
"Mr.," use of, 560, 566
"Mrs.," use of, 563
Muscatel wine, 289
Music
    cost of, for wedding, 62
    for evening entertainment, 295
    terms of, 482
    at wedding, church, 49
    at wedding reception, 81
Mussels, how to eat, 241
"My dear," use of, 437

Nail polish, 202
    for teen ager, 537
Nails
    biting, 495
    care of, 172
Name
    announcements of change of, 256
    boy's names for girls and vice versa, 501
    calling by, in public places, 189
    on calling cards, 562
    change of, after divorce, 544
    change of, by newcomers, 255
    choice of, 499
    christening of Catholic children, 247
    first-name calling, 213
    forgetting, 213
Napkins, 230
    on breakfast tray, *illus.*, 337
    card table service, 355
    folding of, *illus.*, 278
    for formal luncheon, 278, 344; *illus.*, 345
    for informal dinner, 340; *illus.*, 341
    placement at informal meals, *illus.*, 339
    proper use of, 252
National Anthem, 653

Naval etiquette
  Annapolis regulations, 608
  forms of address, 463
  invitations, 623
  at Navy post, 616
  rank, insignia, 618
  ship launching, 619
  visiting battleship, 620
  women's services, 619
Neighbors
  baby sitting for, 522
  calling on, 572
  community relations, 243
  letter of complaint to, 413
  newlyweds, 106
Newcomers to United States, 250–58
  changing name, 255
  differences in manners, 252–54
Newspapers. *See* Press relations
New York City
  private debuts, 113
  single woman starting life in, 212
  time of weddings, 28
Night club, tipping in, 555
Nose
  blowing at table, 231
  plastic surgery, 203
Notes to servants, 365
Nurse
  in home, how to address, 317
  in hospital, 579
  in military service, 619
Nursery linens, 329

Obituary notice, 130
Office etiquette, 176–83, 205–7
  businesswoman, 205, 207
  employer-secretary relationship, 178
  personal visits, 182
  smoking, 178, 207, 221
  social relationship between employer and employee, 182
Official dinner, 556
Officier de la Légion d'honneur, insignia, 160
Old-fashioneds, 286
  glass for, *illus.*, 334
Olives, how to eat, 236
Opera, behavior at, 590, 591
Opera hat, 149
Oranges, how to eat, 238
Orange blossoms, 58
Order of sale, at auction, 592
Orders, ribbons, 657

Organ music
  for funerals, 135
  for weddings, 50, 62
Orvieto wine, 288
Outdoor entertaining, 298–99
Outdoor wedding, 88
Overalls, 503
Overcoats, 150
Overnight guest. *See* House guest
Overweight problems, 496
Oysters
  fork for, 252, 346, 348; *illus.*, 345, 347
  how to eat, 242
  served in living room, 386

Page boy, hotel, tipping, 643
Page boy, in wedding
  clothes for, 60
  in Jewish ceremony, *illus.*, 74
  in processional, Christian ceremony, *illus.*, 64
  in recessional, Christian ceremony, *illus.*, 65
Paid dancing partner, 655
Pallbearers, 133
Papal audience etiquette, 656–58
  blessing, 658
Papal chamberlain, forms of address, 450
Paper napkins, 230
Parents. *See* Bride's parents; Bridegroom's parents; Family
Parfait glass, *illus.*, 335
Parliament, members of, forms of address, 460
Parliamentary procedures, 588
Parties. *See* Children's parties; Entertainment
Part-time worker, 361, 367, 377
Party call, 558
Patient
  in hospital, 577
  relationship to doctor, 579
Patriarch, forms of address, 451
Peaches, how to eat, 238
Pears, how to eat, 237
Peerage, English, forms of address, 453–60
Permanents, 535
Persimmons, how to eat, 238
"Personal," use of, on envelope, 409
Personal calls, 572

Personal questions, dealing with, 214, 215
Personal stationery
  business, 405; *illus.*, 404
  gentleman's, *illus.*, 407
  lady's, *illus.*, 403
  paper, 401
Pew cards, 38
Phone. *See* Telephone
Photographs
  endorsements of commerical products, 598
  of engaged girl to newspapers, 122
  taking of, abroad, 656
  wedding, 50, 62, 122
Pickles, how to eat, 238
Picnics, 298
  how to package food for, 299
Picture. *See* Photograph
Pillow, 324
Pilsener glass, *illus.*, 334
Pineapple, how to eat, 238
"Pink" coat, 150
Pinot blanc wine, 288
Pipe smoking, 220, 346
Place cards
  coat of arms on, 466
  at formal dinner, 273
  at formal luncheon, 277
  need for, 357
Place mats, 329
  at breakfast, 337
  at informal luncheon, 338
  at formal luncheon, 278
Place plate, 264, 275, 346; *illus.*, 347
Place settings
  for buffet dinner, 382
  for formal dinner, 346; *illus.*, 347, 348
  for formal luncheon, *illus.*, 345
  for informal dinner, 340; *illus.*, 341
  for informal luncheon, *illus.*, 339
  place cards at, 357
  See also Napkins; Silver
Plane travel, 639
Plastic surgery, 203
Plebe, 607
Plums, how to eat, 237
Poker game, 297
Polo shirt, 503
Pope
  audience with, 656–58
  forms of address, 449
Porcelain, 331
Porter, hotel, tipping, 643

Portion
  second helping, 283
  token, 284
Port wine, 289
  decanting, 290
  glass, *illus.*, 335
Postponing
  invitations, 434
  weddings, 44
Posture
  sitting, 203
  at table, 233
Post-wedding calls, 106
Potatoes
  French menu terms for, 482
  how to eat, 238
Pourboire, 648
Powder, cosmetic, 202
  for teen ager, 537
P.P.C., 567
Precedence
  in leaving a room, 178
  in table service, 229
Presbyterian Church
  baptism, 247
  wedding ceremony, 67
Pre-school children
  bedtime problems of, 526
  clothes for, 503
Preserved fruit, how to eat, 238
Presidential citation, ribbon, 161
President of United States
  being received by, 627
  business calls, 627
  forms of address, 438
  gift to, 628
  leaving cards for, 625
  letter to, 416, 418
  request to make call on, 576
Press relations, 597–602
  announcing so-called engagements, 126
  death notices, 130
  distribution of pictures to papers, 122
  engagement and wedding announcements, 121
  engagement news, releasing, 120
  legal protection for privacy invasion, 600
  pictures, use of, 599
  separation announcements, 544
Priest, forms of address, 450, 452
Prime Minister, forms of address, 461
Prince, forms of address, 453
Print dress, 196

Printed Christmas cards, 420
Printed stationery, 402
Privy councillor, forms of address, 461
Processional, 64
  for Christian wedding, *illus.*, 65
  for double wedding, 71; *illus.*, 70
  for Jewish wedding, *illus.*, 74
  Lohengrin, Wedding March, 50
  maid and matron of honor in, 57
  ushers in, 54
Professional woman, 206
  calling cards for, 563, 564, 565
  stationery for, *illus.*, 404
Proms, 540
Proposal, marriage, 117, 610
Protestant churches, 243–49
  ceremonies, 246
  christenings, 111
  church marriage of divorced persons, 49
  clerical dress, 249
  clergy, forms of address for, 445
  communion, 248
  time of wedding ceremony, 28
  wedding ceremony, 67; *illus.*, 66
Protonotary, Apostolic, forms of address, 450
Public conveyance, conduct in, 187
Public dinner, 555
  guest of honor at, 556
  smoking at, in England, 650
  speaker at, 584
  tipping at, 555
  toasts at, 292
Publicity
  endorsements of commercial products, 598
  See also Press relations
Public official
  calls on, 575
  letter to, 417
Public speaking, 581–87
  man's clothes for, 158, 583
  on the radio, 585
  reading a speech, 583
  on television, 587
  woman's clothes for, 584
Pumps, when to wear, 158
Punch, 270, 287
  glass, *illus.*, 334
Punctuation in letters, 422

Quaker marriage ceremony, 77
Quarter (heraldry), 466

Queen, forms of address, 452
Quotations from English literature, 475–78

Rabbi
  forms of address, 448
  in wedding ceremony, 73; *illus.*, 74
Races, yachting, 166
Radio appearances, 584
Radishes, how to eat, 238
Raincoat, 157
Ranks, military, 617
Rear admiral, insignia, 618
Receiving blanket, 502
Receiving line
  at Annapolis Hop, 610
  at ball at home, 281
  conversation at, 79
  at debutante tea, 114
  at evening debut, 114
  at wedding reception, 78–82; *illus.*, 79
  at West Point Hop, 613
Reception, wedding, 78–88
  answering invitation to, 45
  best man's role at, 53
  bridal cake, 82
  bride's table at, *illus.*, 82
  in church vestibule, 78
  for clergyman's wedding, 91
  dancing at, 81
  display of wedding gifts at, 103
  divorced parents at, 85
  given by divorced father, 85
  guests' conduct at, 87
  at home wedding, 88
  invitation to, 27, 37, 39, 40
  music at, 81
  parents' table at, *illus.*, 83
  receiving line at, 78–81; *illus.*, 79
  for rectory wedding, 90
  ushers' duties at, 55
Receptions
  christenings, 112
  debutante, 113, 114
  invitation to debutante, 428
  hat etiquette at, 205
  for newlyweds at military post, 616
  at public dinners, 556
  at White House, 625, 627
  See also Receptions, wedding
Recessional
  at double wedding, 71; *illus.*, 70
  at Jewish wedding ceremony, *illus.*, 74

Recessional—(*Cont'd*)
    maid of honor in, 51
    order of, in Christian ceremony, 65;
        illus., 65
    ushers in, 54
Recipe file, 386
Rectory wedding, 89–90
Reducing diets, 497
Red wine, 288
    glasses for, *illus.*, 335
    sweet, 289
    when to serve, 551
References, for servants, 361, 368, 370
Refreshments
    at christening reception, 112
    at formal tea, 280
    at informal tea, 268
    at wedding reception, 83
Refugees, problems of, 250
Regrets, sending
    for invitations, 436
    for naval invitations, 624
    for wedding invitations, 28, 45
    for White House invitations, 626
Reisling wine, 288
Religious Holy Days, 245
Reminder cards after telephone invita-
    tions, 433
Reply to invitations. *See* Acceptances;
    Regrets
Representatives, United States, forms of
    address, 444
Reservations, hotel, 180, 424
Resignation, letter of
    in business, 183
    from club, 225
Restaurant dining, 549–57
    buffet service, 553
    drinks, 551
    ordering, 550
    paying the bill, 554
    table service, 552
    tipping, 554
Return address, 30
Reverend, correct use of, 446, 450
Rhine wine, 288
    glasses for, 349; *illus.*, 335
Ribbons, drawing of, at church wed-
    ding, 54
Riding clothes
    gentleman's, 150, 151
    at horse shows, 151
    lady's, 198
Right Honourable, correct use of, 455,
    456, 461

Right Reverend, correct use of, 446,
    449, 450, 451
Ring
    cadet's, 614
    gentleman's, 156
    midshipman's, 610
    See also Ring, engagement; Ring,
        wedding
Ring, engagement, 118
    family heirloom, 119
    returning of, if engagement is broken,
        119
Ring, wedding, 67
    blessing of, 67, 75, 76
    double-ring ceremony, 69
    engraving on, 119
    groom's expenses for, 62
    man's, 69, 119, 156
    relationship to engagement ring, 118
    ring bearer, 61
Roast, 275
Roman Catholic Church, 243–49
    banns, for marriage, 49
    ceremonies, 246
    christenings, 111
    clerical dress, 249
    funeral services, 133, 134
    grace, saying of, 235
    hierarchy, forms of address, 449–52
    mass cards, 132
    meatless Friday, 244
    papal audience etiquette, 656
    weddings, 28, 67, 72
Rouge, use of, 202
Royal family, British, forms of address,
    452
R.S.V.P., use of, 567
    on formal invitations, 426–29
    on informal invitations, 430
    on wedding invitations, 36
Rum cocktails, 287

Sabbath, 249
Sack suit, 141, 143
    butler's, 371
Sailing. *See* Yachting
Salad
    for formal dinner, 276
    how to eat, 239
    for informal dinner, placement of,
        illus., 343
    for informal lunch, 339
Sale, order of, at auction, 592

Salespeople, how to address customers, 217

Salts and peppers
  at formal dinner, 349
  at informal dinner, 343
  use of, 239

Salutations, in letters, 258

Sandwiches, how to eat, 239

Sauces, 230, 265

Sauterne wine, 289

Scallops, how to eat, 242

School children
  bedtime problems of, 526
  clothes for, 503
  table manners of, 509

School dance, 540

Scotch, 286

Scuppernong white wine, 288

Sea, travel by, 637–39

Seafood, how to eat, 241

Seating
  at church wedding, 55
  at formal meals, 272–73; *illus.*, 272
  in opera boxes, 590
  in restaurants, 549
  at semiformal dinner, 262
  in ship's dining room, 637
  at theater, 591
  in train, 641

"Second," use of on cards, 561

Second helpings, 263, 283

Seconding letters for club membership, 223

Second lieutenant, insignia, 618

Second marriage
  bridegroom's, 50
  children at, 71
  wedding gifts for, 92

Secretary, business, 206
  driving with employer, 179
  how to announce callers, 216
  how to answer telephone, 182
  procedures at meetings, 587
  relationship to executive, 178
  traveling with employer, 180

Secretary, social
  duties of, 374
  how to address, 317
  making invitations by telephone, 433
  public, 375
  reply to invitation sent to, 427

Self-invited guest, 302

Semiformal dinner. *See* Dinner, informal

Semillion wine, 288

Senator
  forms of address, 444
  letter to, 418

Separation, 543–45
  announcing, 543
  trial separation, 543
  wedding procedure with separated parents, 85

Servants, 358–77
  couple, 370
  discussing, 367, 369
  drinking problem, 360
  general houseworker, 364
  greeting by guests at table, 284
  hiring of, 358
  and house guests, 318
  how to address, 316
  interviewing, 359
  introducing to guests, 362
  kind criticism of, 365
  part-time worker, 361, 367, 377
  quarters, furnishings of, 362–63
  references, 368–70
  relationship with children, 529
  relationship with employer, 358–70
  smoking, 360
  time off, 366
  use of telephone, 366
  wages, 358–59
  workman's compensation, 367
  See also Servants' clothing

Servants' clothing
  butler, 371
  chambermaid, 376
  chauffeur, 373
  cook, 375
  kitchen maid, 376
  lady's maid, 376
  valet, 373

Service plate. *See* Place plate

Service wedding, 54, 65

Serving procedures
  for buffet dinner, 381
  butler, duties of, 372
  finger bowls, use of, 285
  for formal dinner, 274, 347
  guest's behavior during, 283–86
  hostess serving, 266
  for informal lunch, 267
  for maidless dinner, 383
  for one-maid dinner, 265
  precedence, 229
  at restaurant, 552
  special problems of, 351–57

694

Serving procedures—(Cont'd)
  tray, use of, 354
  valet, duties of, 373
  wine, 291
Sexton's fee, 135
Shaking hands, 185, 217
Shaving, 172
Sherbet, 275
Sherry, 289, 552
  before dinner, 286
  at formal luncheon, 279
  glasses for, *illus.*, 335
Shield (heraldry), 464
Ship launching, 619
Shirt
  baby's, 502
  gentleman's, with cutaway, 145; with dinner jacket, 147; with tail coat, 148
  lady's riding, 198
  monograms on, 155
Shoes
  baby's, 502
  gentleman's, 158
  lady's, 193
Shooting
  gentleman's clothes for, 169
  lady's clothes for, 199
  rules of, 168
Shorts, 162, 163
Shot glass, *illus.*, 335
Shower, bridal, 100–2
  gift suggestions for, 101
  groom included, 101
  guest's duties at, 102
Shrimps
  how to eat, 242
  served in living room, 386
Shyness, 520
Signature
  on Christmas cards, 420
  illegible, 408
  incorrect, on checks, 397
  lady's, 407
Silver, flat
  at breakfast table, 337
  bride's trousseau, 98–100
  buffet table arrangement, 351
  card table service, 355
  choice of style, 98
  coat of arms on, 467
  dessert, informal placement, *illus.*, 339
  for formal dinner, 346; *illus.*, 347, 348

  for formal luncheon, 346; *illus.*, 345
  for informal dinner, 340, 341
  for informal luncheon, 338
  initials on, 100
  monograms on, 99–100
  placement of used, 284; *illus.*, 284
  table settings in Europe, 252
  for tea service, 98
  wedding present from parents, 98
Single woman, 209–12
  calling cards for, 564
  choosing roommate, 210
  entertaining, 300
  gentleman as host for, 301
  joining groups in big cities, 211
"Sir," use of, 459
Sister (religious title), form of address, 450
Sisters' double wedding, 71
  wording of invitations, 34
Sitting, 203
  at introductions, 218
Skating
  gentleman's clothes for, 170
  lady's clothes for, 197
Skiing
  gentleman's clothes for, 170
  lady's clothes for, 170
Slacks, wearing of, 141, 162
Slang
  at Annapolis, 611
  use of, 213
  at West Point, 614
Smoking, 219–22
  aboard naval vessels, 622
  in bed, 495
  cigar, 219
  "don'ts" of, 221
  European customs, at table, 650
  by lady, in office, 207
  lady's permission to, 190
  not at formal dinner table, 347
  offering cigarettes, 185
  in the office, 178
  pipe, 220
  servants, 360
  at table, 283, 317, 344, 346, 349
  teen ager, 536
  on yachts, 167
Smoking jacket, 149
Smörgåsbord, 350
Snails, how to eat, 242
Social calls, 572–76
Social cards. *See* Calling cards
Social letters, 408, 410, 414

Social life
    bachelor's problems, 175
    children's behavior, 511
    employer and employee, 182
    general rules for, 212–19
    influenced by culture, 467
    in Latin countries, 651–55
    during mourning, 138
    during separation, 544
    single woman's problems, 209
    social secretary, 375
Social secretary. See Secretary, social
Social stationery. See Stationery
Society of Friends, marriage ceremony,
    77
Society people, giving endorsements to
    commercial products, 598
Society writer, 597
Socks, 147, 157
Sofa, 204, 327
Sorority dance, 540
Soup
    at formal dinner, 275
    at informal dinner, illus., 341
    at lunch, 267
    at maidless dinner, 383
    served in cup, 230
Spaghetti, how to eat, 242
Spanish language, 468, 474
Sparkling wine, 291
Spars, 619
Spats, wearing of, 145
Speaker of House of Representatives,
    forms of address, 440
Speaking, 485
    See also Public speaking
Spiced wine, 287
Spilling
    food, 285
    wine, 291
Sponsor
    of debutante's party, 114
    at ship launching, 620
Spoon
    for coffee, 351
    for formal dinner, 348; illus., 347
    for iced tea, 352
    for informal dinner, 342
    teaspoon, 351
Sports, 161–71
    customs, dress, taboos, 168
    fishing, 169
    golf, 161
    hunting, 168
    skating, 170

skiing, 170
    swimming, 167, 168
    tennis, 163–66
    yachting, 166–67
Sports clothes
    beach wear, 168, 197
    for cruises, 639
    gentleman's, 141, 162–70
    for golf, 162, 197
    for hunting and shooting, 169, 199
    lady's, 196–200
    for riding, 150, 198
    for shooting, 169, 199
    shorts, 163
    for skating, 171, 197
    for skiing, 170, 197
    for tennis, 163, 196
    week-end wardrobe, 315
    for yachting, 167, 198
Staff officers, 617
"Star-Spangled Banner," 631
Stationery, 401–6
    business, 406
    gentlemen's, 404, 405
    invitations, 425
    lady's, 401; illus., 403, 406
    lined envelopes, 402
    printed, 402
    for replies to condolence letters, 136
    stickers for, 405
    for wedding announcements and in-
        vitations, 29
Station wagon, 664
Stem whisky sour glass, illus., 335
Steward, tipping, 638
Stewardess, air, 639
Stewed fruit, how to eat, 238
Stickers for stationery, 405
Stingers, 287
Street manners, 188
    greeting a lady, 186
    smoking, 222
Subscription dance, 540, 655
Suit, gentleman's, 141–44
    business, 141
    evening house suit, 149
Suit, lady's, 193
    dinner, 196
Sunday school, 523
Superstitions, of brides, 59
Supper
    dance, 218, 282
    meaning of word, 351
    picnic, 298

Surname
  change of, 255
  names to agree with, 500
  use of, addressing servants, 361
Sweet wines, 289, 552
Swimming, 168
  lady's bathing suit, 197
  from yachts, 167
Swizzles, 287
Swords, arch of, 54
Sylvaner wine, 288

Table decorations
  for breakfast, 336
  for formal dinner, 347
  for formal luncheon, 278, 344
  for informal dinner, 340
  for informal luncheon, 338
Table d'hôte, 550
Table linens, 330
  damask cloth, 356
  for formal luncheon, 344
  for informal dinner, 263, 331
  for informal luncheon, 338
  trousseau basic list, 95
Table manners, 228–42, 283–86
  aboard ship, 638
  of children, 507, 512
  Continental vs. American, 252
  coughing, 231
  eating, when to begin, 229
  eating difficult foods, 235–38
  European customs, 650
  placement of used silver, 284, *illus.*, 284
  saying grace, 233
  smoking at, 283
Table setting, 336–51
  for breakfast, 336, *illus.*, 337
  for buffet, 349, *illus.*, 350
  for buffet dinner, 381, *illus.*, 382
  candy at, 354
  card table service, 355
  for formal dinner, 346
  for formal luncheon, 344
  for formal tea, 280
  for informal dinner, 263, 340
  for informal luncheon, 338
  silver, European fashion, 252
  for supper, 351
Table wines, 288
  glasses, 290; *illus.*, 335
Tact, in conversation, 214, 215

Tail coat, 147
  bridegroom's, 59
  butler's, 371
  occasions for wearing, 159
  at public dinners, 556
Tangerines, how to eat, 238
Tasting another's food, 232
Taxi
  behavior in, 659
  sharing of, 187
  tipping doorman for, 642
Tea
  how to make, 384
  kinds of, 385
  serving by hostess, 353
  testing of, 230
  tray, 268; *illus.*, 269
  See also Afternoon tea
Teaspoons, 98, 351
Tea wagon, 383
Teen ager, 535–41
  dates, 538
  talking to strangers while traveling, 644
Teeth, care of, 175, 205, 220
Telegram
  breaking social engagements by, 436
  invitation by, 433
  making reservations by, 425
  to public officials, 418
  recalling wedding invitation by, 44
Telephone
  announcing calls, 573
  answering by butler, 372
  breaking social engagements by, 436
  businesswoman answering, 207
  Continental habits, 253
  executive, answering, 181
  invitations by, 433
  servants using, 366
  in shared apartment, 211
  wedding invitations by, 41
Television, 295, 586
Tennis
  behavior on court, 164–66
  gentleman's clothing, 163
  lady's clothing, 196
Tequilla, 290
"Thank you," use of, 253
Thank-you notes
  for entertainment, 411
  for gifts, 104, 412
Theater, behavior at, 591
Thumb-sucking, 520

Ties, 152–54
  with cutaway, 145
  with dinner jacket, 147
  with tail coat, 148
Tipping
  aboard ship, 638
  by businesswoman paying bill, 208
  in clubs, 223
  dining car, 642
  European system, 648
  in hotel, 642
  at public dinners, 555
  in restaurants, 554
  servants, by house guests, 319
  taxi drivers, 660
Titles
  British, 437
  on business cards, 570
  on calling cards, gentleman's, 569
    lady's, 565
  crossing out on visiting cards, 566
  on wedding announcements and in-
    vitations, 43
Toast, serving of, 336, 338
Toasts, 292
  to the bride, 57, 82
Toilet water, for gentleman, 173
Tokay wine, 289
Tom Collins, 287
Toothpick, use of, 252
Tortillas, how to eat, 242
Traffic laws, 663
Train cards, 38
Traminer wine, 288
Transatlantic liners, conduct on, 637–39
Travel, 638–46
  by air, 639
  with children, 532–34
  clothes for, 533
  conduct abroad, 651
  employer and secretary, 180
  engaged couples, 127
  in England, 649
  in Europe, 649
  farewell to friends, 646, 647
  hotel reservations, 180, 424
  letters of introduction, 415
  by sea, 637–39
  talking to strangers, 644
  tipping, 638, 642, 644
  by train, 640
Tray service, 354
  breakfast, 336
  tea tray, 268; *illus.*, 269
Trimming food, 356

Trousseau, household, 93–100
  china, basic list, 96–97
  expenses for, 62
  flat silver, 98–100
  glassware, 96
  kitchen equipment list, 95
Trousseau, personal, 93
  expenses for, 62
Tumbler, water, *illus.*, 334
"Turning the table," 276
Tutor, how to address, 317
Tuxedo, 146, 159
Typing, personal letters, 405

Underwear, lady's, 194
Underweight problems, 496
Uniform
  for chambermaid, 376
  for lady's maid, 376
Uniforms
  for Navy personnel, 618
  for officers at church weddings, 54
United States Naval Academy, 607–10
  slang used at, 611
Ushers
  at ball, 282
  at debutante's party, 114
  at funeral service, 133
  See also Ushers, wedding
Ushers, wedding
  arch of swords, 54
  at bachelor dinner, 57
  choosing of, 51
  clothes of, 60
  cutaway for, 144
  in double wedding, 71; *illus.*, 70
  duties of, 53, 86
  gift from groom, 56
  in Jewish ceremony, 73; *illus.*, 73, 74
  procedure during Christian ceremony,
    illus., 67
  in processional, Christian ceremony,
    illus., 64
  at reception, 55
  in recessional, Christian ceremony,
    illus., 65
  in uniform, 55

Vacuum cleaner, 379
Valet
  home, 373
  hotel, 644
Vegetable juices, 286

698

Vegetables, serving of, 265
Veil, bridal, 57, 67
Venerable (title), use of, 446
Venetian blinds, 308
Vermouth, 289
Very Reverend, use of, 446, 450, 451
Vest, 142, 146, 157
Vicar general, forms of address, 450
Vice-admiral, insignia, 618
Vice-consul, forms of address, 442
Vice-President of United States, forms
    of address, 438
Viscount, forms of address, 456
Viscountess, forms of address, 456, 457
Visiting. See Calls
Visiting cards. See Calling cards
Vocabulary, 468
Vodka, 290
Voice, modulation of, 485
    with children, 525
    in public speaking, 581
Voting, 224, 588

WACS, ranks, 619
WAFS, ranks, 619
Wages, servants, 358
Waistcoats, 143, 145, 148
Waiter
    restaurant service, 550–52
    tipping, 553, 643
"Waiting period" for remarriage of di-
    vorced persons, 49
Walking stick, 60
Warrant officer, insignia, 618
Warts, 203
Washing machine, 378
Washington etiquette, 625–29
    White House reception, 625
Watches, 156
Water goblet, illus., 334
Watermelon, how to eat, 238
Water tumbler, illus., 334
WAVES, 619
W.C., 648
Wedding, 27–104
    arranging of, 48–63
    attendant dropping out of, 68
    best man, 51, 52, 60
    breakfast, 83, 84
    bridesmaids, 50, 60
    cake, 82, 84
    canceling, 44
    children at second marriages, 71
    civil marriage, 92

clergyman's wedding, 90
clothes. See Wedding clothes
death in the family, 47
divorced parents, 85
double wedding, 71
evening, 88
expenses of, 62
flower girl, 60
flowers, for the wedding party, 61
flowers, church decoration, 49
formal. See Wedding, formal
gifts. See Gifts, wedding
given by divorced mother, 85
given by groom's family, 35
guests, conduct of, 86
at home, 88–89
informal. See Wedding, informal
invitations. See Invitations, wedding
maids and matrons of honor, 50, 60
out of doors, 88
page boy, 60
picture, 50
postponing, 44
press problems for announcements of,
    601
recalling of invitations, 119
reception. See Reception, wedding
rectory wedding, 89–90
rice throwing, 59
ring bearer, 61
ring, blessing of, 67, 75, 76
seating of guests in church, 53
separated parents, 85
showers, 100–2
smoking at, 221
superstitions, 59
of thirty-ish bride, 72
time of, 28
transportation to and from church, 56
trousseau, 93–100
ushers, 51, 53, 60
Wedding, formal
    arranging, 48–49
    bride's clothes for, 57–58
    church decorations for, 49
    church music for, 49–50
    groom's clothes for, 59–60
    guests, proper dress for, 61
    photographs, 50
    reception for, 78–82
    wedding party, clothes for, 60–61
    See also Wedding
Wedding, informal
    arranging, 48–49
    bridal party, clothes for, 60–61

bride's clothes for, 57–58
church decorations for, 49
groom's clothes for, 59
guests, proper dress for, 61
reception for, 83
in rectory, 89
See also Wedding
Wedding anniversaries, 107–9
Wedding ceremony, 63–78
Christian Science, 76
church arrangements, 48, 49
double-ring ceremony, 69
double wedding procedure, 71; *illus.*, 70
Eastern Orthodox Church, 76
"giving away" the bride, 69
Jewish, 73–76
kissing the bride, 68
Mormon, 77
music, 49
processional, 64
Quaker, 77
recessional, 65
rehearsal, 63
Roman Catholic, 72
Wedding clothes
according to hour, 59
best man, 60
bride, 57–58, 88
bridesmaids, 60
bride's mother, 61
bridegroom, 59, 144
bridegroom's mother, 61
for formal wedding, 57–60
guests, 61
hats worn by women, 25
maid of honor, 60
ushers, 60
Wedding trip. *See* Honeymoon
Week end
at Annapolis, 607–10
bread-and-butter letters, 411
gift suggestions for hostess, 312
at West Point, 612
Week-end entertaining, 311
West Point Hop, 612–14
Whisky sours, 287
glasses for, *illus.*, 335
White House
business calls at, 627
invitation to, 625
letter to, 416
reception at, 627
"White tie." *See* Tail coat

White wine, 551
dry, 288
glasses for, *illus.*, 334, 335
sweet, 289
Widow
calling cards for, 562, 564
children at second marriage, 71
"giving away" at marriage, 69
invitation to marriage, wording of, 35
Wife
agreeable, 493
calling card for, 562
checking account of, 389
husband's last-minute invitations, 492
meeting commuting husband, 494
separation, 544
See also Marriage
Wine, blessing of the, 75
Wines, 287–91
decanting of, 290
dry red, 288
dry white, 288
at formal lunch, 279
at informal dinner, 344
informal lunch, 267
ordering at restaurant, 551
in place of cocktails, 289
sweet, 289
table, 288
Wine steward, 551
Wire. *See* Telegram
"Woman," use of word, 216. *See also* Lady
Woman, single. *See* Single Woman
Women
in business world, 205–8
calling cards for, 562
conduct with stranger on train, 645
cosmetic defects, 202
crest, use of, 466; *illus.*, 466
decorations, wearing, 160, 161
first-name calling, 213
grooming, 200–3
heavy smoker, 220
honor guest at formal dinner, *illus.*, 272
introductions, 218
legal signature, 406
make-up, 201
precedence over men, 178
senator, form of address, 444
sitting posture, 203
social stationery, 401–5
when to remove hat, 205
Women's clubs, 226–27

Women's military services, 619
Workman's compensation for servants, 367
Writing. *See* Letters

Yachting, 166–67
   gentleman's clothes for, 167
   lady's clothes for, 198
   smoking, 222